AFRICAN-AMERICAN
SPORTS GREATS

R

AFRICAN-AMERICAN SPORTS GREATS ———————

A Biographical Dictionary

Edited by
David L. Porter

GREENWOOD PRESS
Westport, Connecticut • London

Library of Congress Cataloging-in-Publication Data

African-American sports greats : a biographical dictionary / edited by
    David L. Porter.
        p.   cm.
    Includes bibliographical references and index.
    ISBN 0–313–28987–5 (alk. paper)
    1. Afro-American athletes—Biography—Dictionaries.   I. Porter,
    David L.
    GV697.A1F37   1995
    796'.092'2—dc20
    [B]   95–7189

British Library Cataloguing in Publication Data is available.

Library of Congress Catalog Card Number: 95–7189
ISBN: 0–313–28987–5

First published in 1995

Greenwood Press, 88 Post Road West, Westport, CT 06881
An imprint of Greenwood Publishing Group, Inc.

Printed in the United States of America

The paper used in this book complies with the
Permanent Paper Standard issued by the National
Information Standards Organization (Z39.48–1984).

10   9   8   7   6   5   4   3   2   1

Copyright Acknowledgments

The editor and publisher gratefully acknowledge permission for use of the following material:

Cover photos:
Photo of Joe Louis courtesy of *The Sporting News*. Photo of Jackie Robinson courtesy of the
National Baseball Library & Archive, Cooperstown, N.Y. Photo of Jackie Joyner-Kersee courtesy
of *The Sporting News*. Photo of Magic Johnson courtesy of Malcolm Emmons/*The Sporting News*.
Photo of Michael Jordan courtesy of Don McAdam/*The Sporting News*. Photo of Jerry Rice
courtesy of Greg Trott/*The Sporting News*.

Every reasonable effort has been made to trace the owners of copyright materials in this book,
but in some instances this has proven impossible. The editor and publisher will be glad to receive
information leading to more complete acknowledgments in subsequent printings of the book and
in the meantime extend their apologies for any omissions.

Contents

Preface

African Americans have played a very significant role in the saga of American sports. In *A Hard Road to Glory*, Arthur Ashe, Jr., ably traced the historic struggles faced by African-American athletes in boxing, baseball, football, track and field, basketball, and other sports.[1] Biographies[2] and autobiographies[3] have detailed the accomplishments, achievements, and personal struggles of African-American sports greats.

During the last decade, several sports historians have compiled collective biographies including African-American sports greats. In 1984 Bill Mallon and Ian Buchanan collaborated on *Quest for Gold*, which contains brief biographies of numerous Olympic medal winners including African Americans.[4] This editor's six-volume *Biographical Dictionary of American Sports* series, published between 1987 and 1995, contains some profiles of African-American sports greats.[5] In 1994 James A. Riley authored a biographical encyclopedia covering over 4,000 Negro League baseball players.[6]

However, no comprehensive, multisport biographical encyclopedia has yet appeared concentrating exclusively on the accomplishments, achievements, and personal struggles of African-American luminaries. This book profiles 166 African-American greats representing 11 different sports. Around two thirds of the African-American greats were connected with baseball (40), football (43), or basketball (30). The remaining athletes engaged in track and field (27), boxing (16), auto racing (2), golf (2), horse racing (2), tennis (2), bicycling (1), and figure skating (1). Some sports, most notably bowling, ice hockey, soccer, swimming, and wrestling, are not represented because they have not produced African-American greats. African-American athletes achieving stardom in more than one sport are classified under the sport for which they won greatest fame.[7] Most biographical subjects excelled as athletes, but some made their primary impact as managers, coaches, club officials, or league administrators. The profiles, which appear alphabetically and usually range from 700 to 1,200 words, mostly feature African-American athletes impacting the sports scene since World War II.

Selection of the biographical entries proved challenging. Before making final choices, the editor thoroughly researched several books on African-American athletes.[8] The criteria for selectees resembled that used in my *Biographical Dictionary of American Sports* series. Nearly all either were born in or spent their childhood years in the United States. They compiled exceptional career athletic accomplishments and profoundly affected the development of at least one major sport, often overcoming formidable barriers. Superior statistical sports achievements and major athletic honors and awards filled their careers. Many earned sports hall of fame recognition, being ranked among the great performers. Some shone in Olympic competition, winning Gold, Silver, and/or Bronze Medals. Several set records and/or won major races, tournaments, or championships. Many served as excellent role models for American youth, although a few unfortunately have not demonstrated exemplary behavior outside of sports.

Forty-two contributors, mostly members of the North American Society for Sport History (NASSH), the Society for American Baseball Research (SABR), the Professional Football Researchers Association (PFRA), and/or the Popular Culture Association (PCA), wrote biographical entries. A majority of contributors teach at colleges, universities, and public or private schools, while others are freelance writers, library or government employees, businessmen, or medical doctors. Contributors are listed after each essay and cited alphabetically with occupational affiliation following the index.

Profiles blend both personal background information and athletic career achievements through May 1995. Contributors trace each subject's personal, family, and educational backgrounds, indicating the enormous personal struggles and obstacles many overcame to excel in their sport. Entries also describe each subject's athletic career, including his or her entrance into sport, major accomplishments, records set, awards and honors, and overall impact. For team sports participants, profiles identify position played, teams affiliated with, All-Star Game appearances and selections, and postseason playoff performances. Biographies of managers or coaches indicate their teams and the premium players they guided, major statistical achievements, career win-loss records, and philosophy, strategy, and innovations. Profiles of club executives and league officials describe their various positions held, notable accomplishments, and sports impact. Brief bibliographies list pertinent books, articles, and other sources about each biographical subject. Whenever an essay cites a subject covered elsewhere in the book, the person's name is printed in boldface type.

Several additional features are included. The introduction briefly traces the historic struggle of African-American athletes in professional and Olympic sports. The entries profile many contemporary African-American sports stars, including Charles Barkley, Barry Bonds, Ken Griffey, Jr., Tony Gwynn, Rickey

Henderson, Bo Jackson, Michael Jordan, Jackie Joyner-Kersee, Carl Lewis, Warren Moon, Shaquille O'Neal, Kirby Puckett, David Robinson, Barry Sanders, Emmitt Smith, and Frank Thomas. Quotations by or about the sports greats embellish their life stories. Photos of a number of African-American sports greats also are featured. Appendixes provide an alphabetical listing of biographical entries and entries by particular sport.

The editor deeply appreciates the enormous time, energy, and effort expended by the contributors in gathering biographical information and preparing profiles of the African-American sports greats. Barbara Rader, Karen Davis, and Susan Badger of Greenwood Publishing Group initiated the book project and furnished both adept guidance and numerous valuable suggestions, facilitating the planning and writing of this volume. William Penn College librarians—notably Julie Hansen, Lauran Lofgren, Jim Knutson, and Jim Hollis—provided invaluable assistance. The National Baseball Hall of Fame, the Naismith Memorial Basketball Hall of Fame, *The Sporting News*, Keeneland Library, and the Nevada Historical Society granted me permission to use selected photographs.

My wife Marilyn again demonstrated considerable patience, understanding, and support throughout the project.

NOTES

1. Arthur R. Ashe, Jr., *A Hard Road to Glory: A History of the African-American Athlete*, 3 vols. (New York: Amistad Press, 1988).

2. Sample biographies of African-American sports greats include: William J. Baker, *Jesse Owens: An American Life* (New York: Free Press, 1986); William Brashler, *Josh Gibson: A Life in the Negro Leagues* (New York: Harper & Row, 1978); John M. Carroll, *Fritz Pollard: Pioneer in Racial Advancement* (Urbana: University of Illinois Press, 1992); Finis Farr, *Black Champion: The Life and Times of Jack Johnson* (New York: Charles Scribner's Sons, 1964); Thomas Hauser, *Muhammad Ali: His Life and Times* (New York: Simon & Schuster, 1991); Mark Ribowsky, *Don't Look Back: Satchel Paige in the Shadows of Baseball* (New York: Simon & Schuster, 1994).

3. A few autobiographies of African-American sports greats include: Hank Aaron with Lonnie Wheeler, *I Had a Hammer: The Hank Aaron Story* (New York; HarperCollins, 1991); Muhammad Ali with Richard Durham, *The Greatest: My Own Story* (New York: Random House, 1975); Arthur R. Ashe, Jr., with Arnold Rampersad, *Days of Grace* (New York: Alfred A. Knopf, 1993); Roy Campanella, *It's Good to Be Alive* (Boston, MA: Little, Brown, 1959); Bob Gibson with Phil Pepe, *From Ghetto to Glory: The Story of Bob Gibson* (Englewood Cliffs, NJ: Prentice-Hall, 1968); Bob Gibson with Lonnie Wheeler, *Stranger to the Game: The Autobiography of Bob Gibson* (New York: Viking Press, 1994); Leroy Satchel Paige as told to David Lipman, *Maybe I'll Pitch Forever* (Garden City, NY: Doubleday, 1962); Jackie Robinson as told to Alfred Duckett, *I Never Had It Made* (New York: G. P. Putnam's, 1972); Bill Russell and Taylor Branch, *Second Wind: The Memoirs of an Opinionated Man* (New York: Random House, 1979); Gale Sayers with Al Silverman, *I Am Third* (New York: Viking Press, 1970).

4. Bill Mallon and Ian Buchanan, *Quest for Gold: The Encyclopedia of American Olympians* (New York: Leisure Press, 1984).

5. David L. Porter, ed., *Biographical Dictionary of American Sports*, 6 vols. (Westport, CT: Greenwood Press, 1987–1995).

6. James A. Riley, *The Biographical Encyclopedia of the Negro Baseball Leagues* (New York: Carroll & Graf, 1994).

7. Bo Jackson and Deion Sanders both play major league baseball but earned their greatest recognition in football. Michael Jordan, who performed in minor league baseball, ranks among the greatest all-time basketball players. Bob Hayes and O. J. Simpson achieved track and field and football stardom, the former gaining more recognition in track and field and the latter in football. Jim Brown, an extremely gifted all-around athlete, attracted greatest fame in football.

8. In addition to the above books, the editor examined Ocania Chalk, *Pioneers of Black Sport: The Early Days of the Black Professional Athlete in Baseball, Basketball, Boxing, and Football* (New York: Dodd, Mead, 1975); Edwin B. Henderson, *The Negro in Sports* (Washington, DC: Associated Publishers, 1949); and Edwin B. Henderson, *The Black Athlete: Emergence and Arrival* (Cornwells Heights, PA: Publishers Agency, 1976). Baseball works consulted included Robert W. Peterson, *Only the Ball Was White* (Englewood Cliffs, NJ: Prentice-Hall, 1970); James A. Riley, *All-Time All-Stars of Black Baseball* (Cocoa, FL: TK Publishers, 1983); Phil Dixon and Patrick J. Hannigan, *The Negro Baseball Leagues: A Photographic Essay* (Mattituck, NY: Amereon Limited, 1992); Bruce Chadwick, *When the Game Was Black and White: The Illustrated History of Baseball's Negro Leagues* (New York: Abbeville Press, 1992); John B. Holway, *Voices from the Great Negro Baseball Leagues* (New York: Dodd, Mead, 1975); John B. Holway, *Blackball Stars: Negro League Pioneers* (Westport, CT: Meckler Books, 1988); Joseph Thomas Moore, *Pride Against Prejudice: The Biography of Larry Doby* (Westport, CT: Greenwood Press, 1988); Donn Rogosin, *Invisible Man: Life in Baseball's Negro Leagues* (New York: Atheneum, 1983); Stephen Banker, *Black Diamonds: An Oral History of Negro League Baseball* (Princeton, NJ: Visual Education Corporation, 1978); Mike Shatzkin, ed., *The Ballplayers* (New York: William Morrow, 1990); John Thorn and Pete Palmer, eds., *Total Baseball*, 3rd ed. (New York: Warner Books, 1993); *The Baseball Encyclopedia*, 9th ed. (New York: Macmillan, 1993); Lawrence Ritter, *The 100 Greatest Players of All Time* (New York: Crown Publishers, 1981); and Martin Appel, *Baseball's Best: The Hall of Fame Gallery* (New York: McGraw-Hill, 1980). Football books examined included George Allen with Ben Olan, *Pro Football's 100 Greatest Players* (Indianapolis, IN: Bobbs-Merrill, 1982); David S. Neft et al., eds., *The Football Encyclopedia*, 2nd ed. (New York: St. Martin's Press, 1994); and Beau Riffenburgh, *The Official NFL Encyclopedia*, 4th ed. (New York: New American Library, 1986). Basketball sources reviewed included Robert W. Peterson, *Cages to Jumpshots: Pro Basketball's Early Years* (New York: Oxford University Press, 1990); Zander Hollander and Alex Sachare, eds., *The Official NBA Basketball Encyclopedia* (New York: Villard Books, 1989); and Wayne Patterson and Lisa Fisher, *100 Greatest Basketball Players* (New York: Crescent Books, 1989). Gilbert Odd, *The Encyclopedia of Boxing* (Secaucus, NJ: Chartwell Books, 1989); Reid H. Hanley, *Who's Who in Track and Field* (New Rochelle, NY: Arlington House, 1973); and Peter Allis, *The Who's Who of Golf* (Englewood Cliffs, NJ: Prentice-Hall, 1983), provided invaluable information on African Americans in other sports.

History of African Americans in Professional and Olympic Sports

African Americans have played a significant role in the development of American sports since the early nineteenth century, overcoming numerous obstacles on the path to athletic glory. Prizefighting marked their first significant athletic avenue. Southern planters often matched their strongest slaves in the ring against those of neighboring plantations. Virginia slave **Tom Molyneux** earned his freedom in 1809 by triumphing against a fellow slave. After conquering several New York City boxers, Tom fought in England. In 1810, English champion Tom Cribb defeated him in a controversial bout at Capthorn, Sussex. Molyneux did not remain in good physical shape and easily lost a rematch to Cribb.[1]

After the Civil War, African Americans encountered resistance in organized professional baseball. The National Association of Base Ball Players and the National League (NL) both excluded African Americans. The American Association, another major league, briefly permitted integrated teams in 1884, when Moses Fleetwood Walker and Welday Walker played for Toledo. Cap Anson, Chicago White Stockings player-manager, however, refused to let his NL club play an exhibition game against Toledo until the Walker brothers were removed from the lineup. Toledo did not extend contracts to the Walker brothers for the 1885 season. African Americans still played minor league baseball and performed against white major league teams in exhibition games during the late 1880s, but players, managers, and white spectators often ridiculed them. Both the major and minor leagues banned African Americans from organized baseball during the Jim Crow segregation era from the 1890s to 1945. African-American barnstorming teams, however, competed against all comers across the United States.[2]

Before 1900, other sports gradually involved African Americans. A few Af-

Boldface type denotes subjects covered in this book.

rican Americans attracted fame as thoroughbred racing jockeys. **Isaac Burns Murphy,** the most noted jockey, rode Kentucky Derby winners in 1884, 1890, and 1891; **Willie Simms** and Jimmy Winkfield each saddled two Kentucky Derby victors.[3] Although bicycling organizations discouraged African Americans from participating, **Marshall Taylor** captured three consecutive national sprint championships from 1898 to 1900 and shattered many national and world records.[4]

African Americans enjoyed considerable success in prizefighting, an individual, unregulated, countercultural sport. From 1892 to 1900, George Dixon claimed the featherweight title. Joe Walcott led the welterweight division from 1898 to 1906, while **Joe Gans** held the lightweight crown from 1902 to 1908. **Jack Johnson** defeated Tommy Burns for the heavyweight championship at Sydney, Australia, in 1908. The American media and fight promoters immediately launched a national campaign for a Great White Hope to wrest the heavyweight crown from Johnson. Many whites considered Jack, who exhibited a controversial lifestyle outside the ring, an enormous threat to the Jim Crow segregation system. In 1910 Johnson triumphed over popular white ex-champion James J. Jeffries to retain the heavyweight title. Jack's reign ended five years later, when white boxer Jess Willard upset him at Havana, Cuba.[5]

Few African Americans participated in early twentieth-century professional football. Charles Follis, the sport's first African-American player, performed at running back for the Shelby Athletic Association in Ohio from 1902 to 1906. Other African-American professional football pioneers included Charles "Doc" Baker of the Akron Indians from 1906 to 1908 and Henry McDonald of the Oxford Pros and Rochester Jeffersons from 1911 to 1917. Thirteen African Americans appeared on rosters of American Professional Football Association (APFA) and National Football League (NFL) clubs between 1920 and 1933. Halfback **Fritz Pollard** helped catapult the Akron Pros to a share of the 1920 APFA title and later coached the Milwaukee Badgers. End **Paul Robeson** and tackle Duke Slater also attained NFL stardom during the 1920s. By 1933, however, Joe Lillard and Ray Kemp were the only remaining African-American NFL players. The NFL owners' gentlemen's agreement then excluded African Americans until 1946.[6]

Still banned from organized baseball, African Americans formed separate leagues by the 1920s. The Negro National League (NNL), founded by **Rube Foster,** fielded diamond teams from 1920 through 1948 except for 1932. The Eastern Colored League operated from 1923 to 1928, while the Negro American League lasted from 1937 through 1950. The Negro Leagues produced many legendary players, most notably pitchers **Satchel Paige** and **Smokey Joe Williams;** outfielders **Oscar Charleston** and **Cool Papa Bell;** infielders **Pop Lloyd, Ray Dandridge,** Martin Dihigo, and **Buck Leonard;** and catcher **Josh Gibson.**[7]

Two brilliant all-African-American professional basketball teams also emerged in the 1920s. The New York Rens, organized by **Bob Douglas** in

1923, rivaled the renowned Original Celtics and dominated professional basketball by the early 1930s. The 1933 squad, featuring center Tarzan Cooper, boasted an 88-game winning streak. In 1939 the Rens defeated the Oshkosh All-Stars in the World Basketball Tournament, becoming the first African-American team to capture a professional title in any organized sport. From 1923 to 1949, the Rens compiled 2,318 wins against only 381 losses. The Harlem Globetrotters, an African-American quintet founded in 1927 by Abe Saperstein, likewise accomplished legendary feats. They entertained spectators with amusing antics on an exhausting schedule of one-night performances. The Globetrotters began traveling abroad in 1939 and won the 1940 World Basketball Tournament. Goose Tatum, Marques Haynes, and Meadowlark Lemon especially made basketball fun with their court entertainment.[8]

In the early years of this century, track and field also featured several outstanding African-American performers. In the 100-meter dash, Howard Drew held the world record from 1912 to 1921. During the mid-1920s, William DeHart Hubbard broke the world long jump mark. The following decade, sprinters Eddie Tolan and Ralph Metcalfe shattered world standards in the 100-meter and 200-meter dashes. The 1930s also showcased record breakers Archie Williams in the 400-meter dash and Cornelius Johnson in the high jump. Sprinter **Jesse Owens** reached legendary heights as a track and field hero among both whites and African Americans. As an Ohio State University sophomore in 1935, Owens demolished four world records during the Big Ten Conference track and field meet at Ann Arbor, Michigan. Jesse endured a heavy propaganda barrage by Nazi dictator Adolf Hitler to earn four Gold Medals at the 1936 Berlin, Germany, Summer Olympics.[9]

By the late 1930s, African Americans again made boxing headlines. **Joe Louis** won the heavyweight boxing crown in 1937 and held the title an unprecedented 12 years. In 1938, Louis knocked out Max Schmeling of Germany in the first round at New York. The Nazis heavily propagandized the 1938 Louis-Schmeling fight, broadcast widely across the United States. Louis gained enormous popularity among both whites and African Americans and successfully defended his crown 25 times, a record for any weight division. **Henry Armstrong,** the first prizefighter to hold three world titles simultaneously, captured featherweight, lightweight, and welterweight titles in the late 1930s.[10]

After World War II, organized baseball finally desegregated. In 1945 Brooklyn Dodgers president Branch Rickey signed star infielder **Jackie Robinson** of the Kansas City Monarchs. Robinson overcame blatant discrimination by players, management, and fans alike to win the 1946 International League Most Valuable Player (MVP) award with the Montreal Royals. Jackie joined the Brooklyn Dodgers the following year, earning NL Rookie of the Year honors. His other accolades included capturing the 1949 batting title and being selected in 1950 as the first African American to participate in a major league All-Star Game. Robinson blazed the organized professional sports trail for countless African-American athletes. Brooklyn quickly added catcher **Roy Campanella**, pitcher Don Newcombe, and other African-American stars. The Cleveland Indians integrated the American League (AL) in 1947, when owner Bill Veeck signed outfielder Larry Doby. **Satchel Paige** helped pitch Cleveland to the 1948 AL pennant. For the New York Giants, outfielders **Willie Mays** and Monte Irvin played crucial roles in the miraculous 1951 NL pennant drive.

All major league rosters carried African Americans by 1959. **Hank Aaron,** an outfielder, set the career home run record. Outfielders Mays, **Frank Robinson,** and **Reggie Jackson,** along with infielders **Willie McCovey** and **Ernie Banks,** belted over 500 round-trippers between 1951 and 1987. Valuable clutch hitting also was supplied by outfielder **Dave Winfield** and infielders **Eddie Murray** and **Joe Morgan.** Outfielder **Rickey Henderson** shattered the all-time stolen base record, while outfielder **Lou Brock** established the NL stolen base mark. Several batting titles were won by outfielder **Roberto Clemente,** infielder **Rod Carew,** and outfielder **Tony Gwynn.** Shortstop **Ozzie Smith** dazzled fans with spectacular defensive play. Pitchers **Bob Gibson, Ferguson Jenkins,** and **Juan Marichal** enjoyed several 20-game victory seasons and demonstrated remarkable strikeout artistry. During the 1990s, outfielders **Barry Bonds** and **Ken Griffey, Jr.,** and first baseman **Frank Thomas** emerged as formidable sluggers. Since the 1970s, African Americans also have made significant strides as major league managers and executives. Frank Robinson, Cito Gaston, Dusty Baker, and Don Baylor achieved success as major league managers, while **Bill White** served as first National League president.[11]

Professional football likewise desegregated after World War II. Between 1946 and 1949 the All America Football Conference (AAFC) clubs signed six African Americans, including running back **Marion Motley** and lineman **Bill Willis** of the Cleveland Browns and running back **Joe Perry** of the San Francisco 49ers. The National Football League ban on African Americans ended in 1946, when the Los Angeles Rams signed running back Kenny Washington and end Woody Strode. Seventeen years elapsed, however, before every NFL club integrated. **Jim Brown** of the Cleveland Browns, the best running back in pro football history, led the NFL in rushing for eight seasons between 1957 and 1965, while **Walter Payton** of the Chicago Bears set the NFL career record for rushing yardage. Backs **Eric Dickerson, Tony Dorsett, Franco Harris,** and **O. J. Simpson** also rushed for over 10,000 career yards.

The NFL has produced many other legendary African-American running backs, including **Gale Sayers, Earl Campbell, Barry Sanders,** and **Emmitt Smith.** Wide receiver **Jerry Rice** of the San Francisco 49ers established the NFL career record for most touchdowns, while **Art Monk** became the NFL career reception leader. Offensively, receivers Charlie Joiner, Charley Taylor, **John Mackey,** Kellen Winslow, and Sterling Sharpe and linemen Roosevelt Brown, **Jim Parker,** and **Gene Upshaw** also achieved NFL stardom. Defensively, linemen **Deacon Jones, Joe Greene,** and **Reggie White,** linebackers

Willie Lanier and **Lawrence Taylor,** and backs **Emlen Tunnell, Dick "Night Train" Lane, Herb Adderley, Ken Houston,** and **Ronnie Lott** have ranked among the NFL best. Few African Americans, notably **Warren Moon** and Randall Cunningham, have enjoyed success at quarterback. **Art Shell** and Dennis Green have pioneered as NFL head coaches.[12]

Professional basketball also integrated following World War II. The 1946–1947 National Basketball League (NBL) rosters included African Americans Pop Gates of the Tri Cities Blackhawks and Dolly King of the Rochester Royals. Chuck Cooper of the Boston Celtics, Earl Lloyd of the Syracuse Nationals, and Sweetwater Clifton of the New York Knicks desegregated the National Basketball Association (NBA) in 1950–1951. Since then, the NBA has produced many legendary African-American stars. Center **Bill Russell** led the Boston Celtics to 11 NBA titles, including 8 consecutive, from 1956 to 1969. Center **Wilt Chamberlain** ranks second in NBA career scoring and first in NBA career rebounding, averaging over 30 points and nearly 23 rebounds a game. Guard **Oscar Robertson,** a brilliant playmaker, and forward **Elgin Baylor** consistently placed among the leading NBA scorers in the 1960s.

African Americans comprised nearly 60 percent of NBA rosters by 1970. During the 1970s, forward **Julius Erving** thrilled crowds with his acrobatic dunks, and forward **Elvin Hayes** became third highest scorer in NBA history. Center **Moses Malone,** another prolific scorer, earned three MVP awards between 1979 and 1983. During the 1980s, center **Kareem Abdul-Jabbar** and guard **Magic Johnson** paced the Los Angeles Lakers to five NBA crowns. Abdul-Jabbar, the all-time leading NBA scorer, won a record six MVP awards in 20 NBA seasons, while Johnson paced the NBA in career assists. Guard **Michael Jordan,** arguably the best all-around and most exciting player in NBA history, set a league record with a 32.3 points per game average and led the Chicago Bulls to three consecutive NBA titles from 1991 to 1993. **Len Wilkens, K. C. Jones,** and Al Attles enjoyed considerable success as NBA coaches, while Wayne Embry pioneered as an NBA executive with the Milwaukee Bucks and Cleveland Cavaliers.[13]

African Americans continued to perform well in the ring after World War II. **Sugar Ray Robinson,** the most skillful fighter pound for pound in history, dominated boxing in the 1950s. Robinson held the lightweight title for four years, captured the middleweight crown five different times, and nearly garnered the light heavyweight championship. No other boxer regained a title even four times. The next two decades featured **Muhammad Ali,** born Cassius Clay. Ali, the most popular global American athlete, gained the heavyweight crown in 1964 and then converted to the Muslim faith. In 1967 boxing authorities stripped Ali of his heavyweight belt because he refused to serve in the Vietnam War. Ali regained the heavyweight title by defeating **George Foreman** in 1974 and retained it against **Joe Frazier** in 1975. Leon Spinks upset Ali in 1978, but he soon regained his heavyweight crown. The 1980s marked the **Sugar Ray Leonard** era. Leonard held the world welterweight championship from 1979 to 1982 and added the junior middleweight title in 1981 before retiring in 1982. Sugar Ray launched a sensational comeback in 1987, edging middleweight champion **Marvin Hagler.** He also won the world super-middleweight and light heavyweight belts in 1988, making him the first boxer to garner world crowns in five weight classifications. Leonard's storied bouts placed him among the richest sportsmen in history.[14]

Track and field likewise continued to produce African-American luminaries. **Carl Lewis,** the most dominant modern male trackster, earned eight Gold Medals and one Silver Medal in Summer Olympic competitions between 1984 and 1992. His events included the 100-meter and 200-meter dashes, 4 × 100 relay, and long jump. **Harrison Dillard,** who participated in the 100-meter dash and 110-meter hurdles, overcame adversity to capture four Gold Medals in the 1948 and 1952 Summer Olympic Games. Other outstanding male track and field performers included **Bob Hayes** and Jim Hines in the 100-meter dash, **Tommie Smith** in the 200-meter dash, **Michael Johnson** in the 200-meter and 400-meter dashes, **Lee Evans** and **Butch Reynolds** in the 400-meter dash, **Lee Calhoun** and Rod Milburn in the 110-meter hurdles, **Edwin Moses** and **Kevin Young** in the 400-meter hurdles, **Bob Beamon** and **Mike Powell** in the long jump, and **Rafer Johnson** and **Dan O'Brien** in the decathlon. In women's competition, **Evelyn Ashford Washington** won four Gold Medals and one Silver Medal in the 4 × 100-meter relay and 100-meter dash in the Summer Olympics between 1984 and 1992. **Jackie Joyner-Kersee** and **Florence Griffith Joyner** also garnered five Olympic medals, including three Golds, during the same span. Joyner-Kersee specialized in the hepathlon and long jump, while Griffith Joyner starred in the sprints. **Wilma Rudolph, Wyomia Tyus,** and **Valerie Brisco** each earned four Olympic medals, including three Golds. Rudolph excelled in the 100-meter and 200-meter dashes, Tyus in the 100-meter dash, and Brisco in the 400-meter to 1,500-meter distances.[15]

Tennis, golf, stock car racing, auto racing, and figure skating provided fewer opportunities for African-American athletes. **Arthur Ashe, Jr.,** made the biggest impact in men's tennis, winning the 1968 U.S. Open and 1975 Wimbledon singles championships, playing on 11 U.S. Davis Cup (DC) teams, and captaining the victorious 1980 and 1981 DC squads. **Althea Gibson** captured the 1957 and 1958 U.S. and Wimbledon singles tennis titles, while Zina Garrison-Jackson and Lori McNeil have ranked among the top 10 U.S. women tennis players during the last decade. **Charles Sifford,** the first successful African-American Professional Golfers Association (PGA) Tour golfer, prevailed in the 1967 Hartford Open and 1969 Los Angeles Open. Lee Elder and **Calvin Peete,** who triumphed in 12 PGA tournaments mainly in the 1980s, also pioneered among African-American golfers. **Wendell Scott** drove on the National Association for Stock Car Auto Racing (NASCAR) circuit, while **Willy T. Ribbs** competed in two Indianapolis 500 auto races. In figure skating, **Debi Thomas Vanden Hogen** earned a Bronze Medal at the 1988

Winter Olympic Games.[16]

African Americans have taken the hard road to glory in both individual and team professional and Olympic sports. After overcoming enormous obstacles, they now enjoy full participation in professional sports.

NOTES

1. Elliot Gorn, *The Manly Art: Bare-Knuckle Prize Fighting in America* (Ithaca, NY: Cornell University Press, 1986); Nat Fleischer, *Black Dynamite: The Story of the Negro in the Prize Ring from 1782 to 1938* (New York: *Ring* Magazine, 1947). For general historical background, see Arthur R. Ashe, Jr., *A Hard Road to Glory: A History of the African-American Athlete*, 3 vols. (New York: Amistad Press, 1988).

2. Robert W. Peterson, *Only the Ball Was White* (Englewood Cliffs, NJ: Prentice-Hall, 1970); Arthur R. Ashe, Jr., *A Hard Road to Glory: The African-American Athlete in Baseball* (New York: Amistad Press, 1993).

3. David K. Wiggins, "Isaac Murphy: Black Hero in Nineteenth Century American Sport, 1861–1896," *Canadian Journal of History of Sport and Physical Education* (May 1979), pp. 15–23; Peter Chew, *The Kentucky Derby: The First 100 Years* (Boston: Houghton Mifflin, 1974).

4. Peter Nye, *Hearts of Lions: The History of American Bicycle Racing* (New York: W. W. Norton, 1988); Marshall W. Taylor, *The Fastest Bicycle Rider in the World* (Worcester, MA: Wormley Publishing, 1928).

5. Arthur R. Ashe, Jr., *A Hard Road to Glory: The African-American Athlete in Boxing* (New York: Amistad Press, 1993); Gilbert Odd, *The Encyclopedia of Boxing* (Secaucus, NJ: Chartwell Books, 1989); Finis Farr, *Black Champion: The Life and Times of Jack Johnson* (New York: Charles Scribner's Sons, 1964); Randy Roberts, *Papa Jack: Jack Johnson and the Era of White Hopes* (New York: Free Press, 1983).

6. Arthur R. Ashe, Jr., *A Hard Road to Glory: The African-American Athlete in Football* (New York: Amistad Press, 1993); Ocania Chalk, *Pioneers of Black Sport: The Early Days of the Black Professional Athlete in Baseball, Basketball, Boxing, and Football* (New York: Dodd, Mead, 1975); Edwin B. Henderson, *The Negro in Sports* (Washington, DC: Associated Publishers, 1949); David S. Neft et al., *The Football Encyclopedia*, 2nd ed. (New York: St. Martin's Press, 1994); Beau Riffenburgh, *The Official NFL Encyclopedia*, 4th ed. (New York: New American Library, 1986); John M. Carroll, *Fritz Pollard: Pioneer in Racial Advancement* (Urbana: University of Illinois Press, 1992).

7. Peterson, *Only the Ball Was White*; Donn Rogosin, *Invisible Men: Life in Baseball's Negro Leagues* (New York: Atheneum, 1983); James A. Riley, *The Biographical Encyclopedia of the Negro Baseball Leagues* (New York: Carroll & Graf, 1994); James A. Riley, *All-Time All-Stars of Black Baseball* (Cocoa, FL: TK Publishers, 1983); John B. Holway, *Voices from the Great Negro Baseball Leagues* (New York: Dodd, Mead, 1975); John B. Holway, *Blackball Stars: Negro League Pioneers* (Westport, CT: Meckler Books, 1988); Phil Dixon and Patrick J. Hannigan, *The Negro Baseball Leagues: A Photographic Essay* (Mattituck, NY: Amereon Limited, 1992); Bruce Chadwick, *When the Game Was Black and White: The Illustrated History of Baseball's Negro Leagues* (New York: Abbeville Press, 1992); Ashe, *Baseball*; William Brashler, *Josh Gibson: A Life in the Negro Leagues* (New York: Harper & Row, 1978); Leroy "Satchel" Paige as told to David Lipman, *Maybe I'll Pitch Forever* (Garden City, NY: Doubleday, 1962);

Mark Ribowsky, *Don't Look Back: Satchel Paige in the Shadows of Baseball* (New York: Simon & Schuster, 1994).

8. Arthur R. Ashe, Jr., *A Hard Road to Glory: The African-American Athlete in Basketball* (New York: Amistad Press, 1993); Chalk, *Pioneers of Black Sport;* Robert W. Peterson, *Cages to Jumpshots: Pro Basketball's Early Years* (New York: Oxford University Press, 1990); Glenn Dickey, *The History of Professional Basketball Since 1896* (New York: Stein and Day, 1982). Chuck Menville, *The Harlem Globetrotters* (New York: David McKay, 1978).

9. Arthur R. Ashe, Jr., *A Hard Road to Glory: The African-American Athlete in Track and Field* (New York, Amistad Press, 1993); William J. Baker, *Jesse Owens: An American Life* (New York: Free Press, 1986); Richard D. Mandell, *The Nazi Olympics* (New York: Macmillan, 1971).

10. Ashe, *Boxing;* Chris Mead, *Champion: Joe Louis, Black Hero in White America* (New York: Charles Scribner's Sons, 1985); Gerald Astor, *And a Credit to His Race: The Hard Life and Times of Joseph Louis Barrow* (New York: Saturday Review Press, 1974); Joe Louis with Edna and Art Rust, Jr., *Joe Louis: My Life* (New York: Berkeley Publishing, 1981); Anthony O. Edmonds, *Joe Louis* (Grand Rapids MI: William B. Eerdmans Publishing, 1973).

11. Ashe, *Baseball;* Jules Tygiel, *Baseball's Great Experiment: Jackie Robinson and His Legacy* (New York: Oxford University Press, 1983); Jackie Robinson and Alfred Duckett, *I Never Had It Made* (New York: G. P. Putnam's, 1972); Joseph T. Moore, *Pride Against Prejudice: The Biography of Larry Doby* (Westport, CT: Greenwood Press, 1988). For brief profiles of African-American baseball stars, see Mike Shatzkin, *The Ballplayers* (New York: William Morrow, 1990). Memoirs include Hank Aaron with Lonnie Wheeler, *I Had a Hammer: The Hank Aaron Story* (New York: HarperCollins, 1991); Henry Aaron with Furman Bisher, *Aaron* (New York: Thomas Y. Crowell, 1974); Roy Campanella, *It's Good to Be Alive* (Boston, MA: Little, Brown, 1959); Willie Mays and Charles Einstein, *Willie Mays: My Life in and out of Baseball* (New York: E. P. Dutton, 1972); Bob Gibson with Phil Pepe, *From Ghetto to Glory: The Story of Bob Gibson* (Englewood Cliffs, NJ: Prentice-Hall, 1968); Bob Gibson with Lonnie Wheeler, *Strangers to the Game: The Autobiography of Bob Gibson* (New York: Viking Press, 1994); and Rickey Henderson with John Shea, *Off Base Confessions of a Thief: An Autobiography* (New York: HarperCollins, 1992).

12. Ashe, *Football;* George Allen with Ben Olan, *Pro Football's 100 Greatest Players* (Indianapolis, IN: Bobbs-Merrill, 1982); Neft, *Football Encyclopedia;* Riffenburgh, *NFL Encyclopedia;* Jimmy Brown, *Off My Chest* (New York: Doubleday, 1964); Gale Sayers with Al Silverman, *I Am Third* (New York: Viking Press, 1970).

13. Ashe, *Basketball;* Henderson, *The Black Athlete;* Chalk, *Pioneers of Black Sport;* David S. Neft and Richard M. Cohen, eds., *The Sports Encyclopedia: Pro Basketball,* 5th ed. (New York: St. Martin's Press, 1992); Zander Hollander and Alex Sachare, eds., *The Official NBA Basketball Encyclopedia* (New York: Villard Books, 1989); Wayne Patterson and Lisa Fisher, *100 Greatest Basketball Players* (New York: Crescent Books, 1989); Kareem Abdul-Jabbar and Mignon McCarthy, *Kareem* (New York: Random House, 1990); Wilt Chamberlain, *Wilt* (New York: Macmillan, 1973); Earvin "Magic" Johnson, *Magic: My Life* (New York: Random House, 1992); Bob Greene, *Hang Time: Days, Dreams, and Destinations with Michael Jordan* (Garden City, NY: Doubleday, 1992); Jim Naughton, *Taking to the Air: The Rise of Michael Jordan* (New York: Warner

Books, 1993); Bill Russell and Taylor Branch, *Second Wind: The Memoirs of an Opinionated Man* (New York: Random House, 1979).

14. Ashe, *Boxing*; Jeffrey T. Sammon, *Beyond the Ring: The Role of Boxing in American Society* (Urbana: University of Illinois Press, 1988); Odd, *Encyclopedia of Boxing*; Allan Goldstein, *A Fistful of Sugar* (New York: Coward, McCann and Geoghegan, 1981); Peter Heller, *In This Corner: Forty World Champions Tell Their Stories* (New York: Simon & Schuster, 1973); Muhammad Ali with Richard Durham, *The Greatest: My Own Story* (New York: Random House, 1975); Thomas Hauser, *Muhammad Ali: His Life and Times* (New York: Simon & Schuster, 1991); Sam Toperoff, *Sugar Ray Leonard and Other Noble Warriors* (New York: McGraw-Hill, 1987).

15. Ashe, *Track and Field*; Bill Mallon and Ian Buchanan, *Quest for Glory: The Encyclopedia of American Olympians* (New York: Leisure Press, 1979); Reid M. Hanley, *Who's Who in Track and Field* (New Rochelle, NY: Arlington House, 1973); Carl Lewis with Jeffrey Marx, *Inside Track: My Professional Life in Amateur Track and Field* (New York: Simon & Schuster, 1990); Wilma Rudolph, *Wilma* (New York: New American Library, 1977); Lewis H. Carlson and John J. Fogarty, *Tales of Gold: An Oral History of the Summer Olympic Games Told by America's Gold Medal Winners* (Chicago, IL: Contemporary Books, 1987).

16. Arthur R. Ashe, Jr., and Neil Amdur, *Off the Court* (New York: New American Library, 1981); Arthur R. Ashe, Jr., with Arnold Rampersad, *Days of Grace* (New York: Alfred A. Knopf, 1993); Althea Gibson, *I Always Wanted to Be Somebody* (New York: Harper and Brothers, 1958); Charlie Sifford with Jim Gullo, *Just Let Me Play: The Story of Charlie Sifford, The First PGA Black Golfer* (Latham, NY: British American Publishing, 1992); Peter Allis, *The Who's Who of Golf* (Englewood Cliffs, NJ: Prentice-Hall, 1983); Al Barkow, *The History of the PGA Tour* (New York: Doubleday, 1989).

AFRICAN-AMERICAN
SPORTS GREATS

Biographies

HANK AARON
(February 5, 1934–) ——————————————————— *Baseball*

Hank Aaron, one of the most complete players in baseball history, excelled in every phase of the game. Henry Louis Aaron was born on February 5, 1934, in Mobile, Alabama, to Herbert Aaron, a rivit bucker in a shipyard, and Estelle (Taylor) Aaron. He has three sisters, Sarah, Gloria, and Alfreda, and three brothers, Herbert, Jr., Alfred, and Tommie. Tommie played first base with Hank on the Atlanta Braves National League (NL) club and later managed the top Braves farm team at Richmond, Virginia.

Aaron grew up in the Deep South's segregated society. Hank's adult life and baseball career were influenced significantly by the civil rights movement. Many resented the breaking of the color line in organized baseball. During his chase of Babe Ruth's home run record in 1974, Hank received threats on his life and the lives of his family and was sent thousands of "hate mail" letters.

Aaron attended Central High School and graduated from Josephine Allen Institute in 1951. Hank played end and halfback on the football team, but no African-American school fielded a baseball team then. Florida State University considered Aaron a football scholarship prospect. Baseball, however, represented his true love. Hank first played on a field across from his home that Mobile had developed into the first recreational area for African Americans. Mobile, a hotbed for African-American baseball, developed a large number of major league–caliber African-American players, including **Satchel Paige, Willie McCovey,** and **Billy Williams,** all National Baseball Hall of Fame members.

At age 17, Aaron joined the Mobile Black Bears semi-pro team and played shortstop for $10 a game. The Bears manager arranged an exhibition game with the Indianapolis Clowns of the Negro American League (NAL) to show-case him. Although batting cross-handed, Hank already hit with power and consistency. The Clowns immediately offered Aaron a contract, but Hank knew that his mother would never agree to a baseball career until he finished high school. The next spring, he received a contract in the mail offering him $200 a month and was told to report for spring training in Winston-Salem, North Carolina. The 17-year-old African-American youngster, who had hardly been beyond the Mobile area, regarded the trip as frightening and the envi-ronment as strange and almost quit to return home. Aaron's talent quickly made him a starter and soon a team star. By the end of May, the Clowns sold his contract to the Boston Braves (NL). Aaron reported to Boston's Eau Claire, Wisconsin, farm team. The Braves paid the Clowns $2,500 immediately and promised an additional $7,500 if they kept him in the organization for 30 days. Hank received only a $350 a month contract.

When Aaron joined the minor leagues, a manager changed Hank's cross-handed style. Aaron once experimented with hitting left-handed, but the bat slipped from his hand and broke the nose of a teammate. He gave up the experiment, later regretting it. According to Aaron, his cross-handed experi-ence could have made him a successful switch-hitter.

In 1953, Aaron joined Felix Mantilla and Horace Garner in breaking the Sally League color line with Jacksonville, Florida. The Milwaukee Braves (NL) moved Hank from shortstop to second base because Mantilla was considered the best prospect in their organization. Just as he had done at Eau Claire, Aaron made the All-Star team. He batted .362, knocked in 125 runs, and hit 22 home runs. Aaron's stellar performance landed him at the Braves spring training camp the next spring. During the winter, he played baseball in Puerto Rico and moved to the outfield.

At the beginning of spring training, the *Milwaukee Sentinel* wrote, "Not since Mickey Mantle was moved up to the [New York] Yankees has there been a player with as big a buildup as Aaron, a lithe 19-year-old Negro." Aaron hardly expected to make the Milwaukee NL team since the Braves had four experienced outfielders, including his boyhood idol Bobby Thomson. The Braves had acquired Thomson during the winter to play left field. A contract dispute slowed the fourth outfielder, while Thomson was injured as spring training season ended. So Hank started on opening day.

Aaron made the NL All-Star roster in 1955 in his second major league season, the first of 24 All-Star appearances. He earned the Braves' Most Val-uable Player (MVP) honors after batting .314 and belting 34 home runs. *The Sporting News* named Hank Player of the Year in 1956 and again in 1963. In 1957, Aaron paced the NL in home runs (44) and runs batted in (RBIs) (132) and was named NL MVP. He led Milwaukee to the World Series, where the Braves defeated the New York Yankees in seven games. Hank batted .393 in the World Series with 3 home runs.

Aaron was compared with **Willie Mays** of the New York Giants. Pittsburgh

Pirate manager Bobby Bragan declared, "In my book, he's [Aaron] a better hitter than Willie Mays. He's going to get better, too." Del Crandall, Milwaukee catcher, lauded Aaron's all-around greatness: "There is no question in my mind that he could have stolen sixty to seventy bases a season if that had been his style. There is nothing he couldn't do."

Milwaukee repeated as NL champions in 1958 but lost to the New York Yankees in the World Series. The 1958 campaign marked Aaron's last appearance in the World Series. Hank won the Gold Glove Award in 1958 and on two other occasions. Charlie Grimm, Aaron's Milwaukee manager, liked his all-around greatness: "You can't make a Willie Mays out of him. He's not the spectacular type. Everything he does, he makes look easy."

When the Braves moved to Atlanta, Georgia, in 1966, Aaron already had hit 398 home runs. Since Atlanta had the highest and hottest major league stadium, Hank recognized the home run potential. In his next eight years, he averaged 40 home runs per season. Hank reached 713 round-trippers at the end of the 1973 campaign. On opening day in 1974 against the Cincinnati Reds he tied Babe Ruth's career home run record. Aaron broke Ruth's record against the Los Angeles Dodgers three days later in Atlanta and increased the career record to 755 before retiring.

During his major league career, Aaron established 12 major league records. Besides the career home run mark, Hank played in more games (3,298) and had the most at bats (12,364), most total bases (6,856), most extra base hits (1,477), and most RBIs (3,771). He ranks second in career runs scored (2,174), eighth in doubles, and sixth in putouts and chances by an outfielder. Aaron set more major league career records than any other player. Hank's lifetime batting average stood at .305 with a .555 slugging percentage. Although mostly a major league outfielder, Aaron also played first base, second base, and third base in the majors.

In 1969, Atlanta Braves fans named Hank the Greatest Player Ever. After spending his final two years with the Milwaukee Brewers American League (AL) club in 1975 and 1976, Aaron returned to the Atlanta Braves as corporate vice president in charge of player development and built the farm system into one of the most productive in baseball. In January 1982, Hank was elected into the National Baseball Hall of Fame. He missed unanimous selection by only 9 votes, securing 406 of 415. Willie Mays alone received more votes, while only Ty Cobb gained a higher percentage of tallies. In 1994, *Sports Illustrated* ranked Aaron on fifteenth on its "40 for the Ages List."

Aaron married Barbara Lucas on October 3, 1953, following his baseball season at Jacksonville. Hank also became a close friend of Bill Lucas, Barbara's brother and later the first African American to serve as a major league general manager. Lucas held the position with the Atlanta Braves until an untimely early death. The Aarons had five children, Gail, Hank, Jr., Larry, Dorinda, and Ceci, before their 1971 divorce. Hank married Billye Suber Williams on November 12, 1973.

In December 1989, Aaron was appointed senior vice president and assistant to the president of the Braves. Hank works with President Stan Kasten on many phases of the Braves operations and represents the Braves in community relations. He serves as vice president and member of the board of directors of Turner Broadcasting and vice president for Business Development for the Airport Channel. Aaron also participates on the national board of the National Association for the Advancement of Colored People (NAACP), the national board of Big Brothers/Big Sisters of America, and the Sterling Committee of Morehouse College and remains very active in the Hank Aaron Rookie League Program.

BIBLIOGRAPHY: Henry Aaron and Furman Bisher, *Henry Aaron* (New York, 1974); Hank Aaron with Lonnie Wheeler, *I Had a Hammer: The Hank Aaron Story* (New York, 1991); Atlanta Braves publications and media files, Atlanta, GA; Stanley Baldwin, *Bad Henry* (Radnor, PA, 1974); Robert T. Bowen, interview with Henry Aaron, January 17, 1985; James A. Riley, *The Biographical Encyclopedia of the Negro Baseball Leagues* (New York, 1994); Milton Shapiro, *The Henry Aaron Story* (New York, 1961).

Robert T. Bowen, Jr.

KAREEM ABDUL-JABBAR
(April 16, 1947–   ) ——————————————————————— *Basketball*

Abdul-Jabbar was regarded by many as the greatest basketball player of all time. During his early career, critics and pundits alike wondered if he would ever emulate the exploits of the legendary **Wilt "the Stilt" Chamberlain.** In the 1980s, Abdul-Jabbar surpassed Chamberlain's feats and earned recognition as a truly great player. If it had not been for the rise of **Michael Jordan** and his "three peat" starring role with the Chicago Bulls, Kareem would have remained as the premier basketball player of this century. His longevity, compared with the stunning retirement announcement by Jordan in 1993, may persuade sport historians to reestablish Abdul-Jabbar as the premier player of his generation.

Abdul-Jabbar, born Lewis Ferdinand Alcindor on April 16, 1947, in New York City, was the only child of Cora and Ferdinand Alcindor. At 13 pounds and 22 inches, Lew was a big baby. His parents were both over six feet in height, his father being a New York City Transit Authority police officer. Alcindor's middle-class upbringing came in a section of upper Manhattan. He grew up a Roman Catholic, attending St. Jude's elementary school. Early enthusiasms for swimming, ice skating, and Little League baseball were replaced by a passion for basketball. During elementary school, a combination of his height and precocious basketball skills made Lew a widely recruited prep player. Eventually, Alcindor selected an Irish Christian Brothers institution known as Power Memorial Academy. Under the tutelage of coach Jack Donohue, the six-foot-eight-inch 13-year-old quickly transformed into a high school sensation. During his sophomore year in 1962–1963, Alcindor averaged 19 points. A year later, the point average grew to 26 points per game. As a senior, Lew tallied 33 points per contest. Power Memorial Academy charged to 71 consecutive victories and won its third consecutive New York City Catholic High School championship. Alcindor's career 2,067 points established a New York City high school record.

Despite both the spotlight and high expectations for him at Power Memorial Academy, Alcindor remained happy. Everyone wanted Lew to do well—and he did! After an avalanche of scholarship offers, Alcindor selected John Wooden's University of California at Los Angeles (UCLA). Adjusting to life on a West Coast college campus proved more difficult than the transition from St. Jude's to Power Memorial Academy. Coach Wooden, one of the great motivators of all time, greatly helped him.

After a phenomenally successful freshman year, Alcindor joined the UCLA varsity team for the 1966–1967 season. On December 3, 1966, Lew debuted in a 105–90 defeat of the University of Southern California. Alcindor poured in 56 points for a UCLA single-game record. In the 1967 final National Collegiate Athletic Association (NCAA) tournament game against the University of Dayton, UCLA won its third championship in four years. Although Dayton held Lew to 20 points, his consistent play throughout the season primarily enabled the Bruins to continue their legacy of success. Coach Lou Carnesecca observed at the time, "I think he's unbelievable."

With an IQ of 131, Alcindor majored in history at UCLA. College basketball programs listed him at 7 foot 1⅜ inches and 235 pounds. In a 1966 *New York Times* interview, Alcindor commented on his lack of muscle: "You can only develop your skills according to your physiological make-up. I have to build up my upper torso. I'm too skinny, and more bulk will help my rebounding work on the boards." Lew carried a reputation as a solitary and introspective athlete with ambivalent feelings about the fame and hoopla of championship basketball. He seemed unhappy about the attention given to his height and basketball scoring. The press lauded his prowess as a basketball player, but Lew was more attracted to the political turmoil created by **Muhammad Ali** (particularly his anti–Vietnam War stance) and the religious zeal of Malcolm X.

In a March 1967 *Ebony* interview, Alcindor stated, "We've got to stand by ourselves before we can make it. Nobody is going to help us." Lew showed that his 1967 season performance was no fluke. In 1968 and 1969, the Bruins again won the NCAA championship. Alcindor rounded out a brilliant college career with 2,325 points and averaged 26.4 points per game average. Mere statistics only give a partial picture. Just as **Jack Johnson** totally dominated boxing in the early twentieth century, Lew controlled college basketball from 1967 to 1969 and was named First Team All-American for his three varsity years.

Two professional teams held the draft rights to him. The Milwaukee Bucks

of the National Basketball Association (NBA) and the New York Nets of the
American Basketball Association (ABA) battled one another to secure Alcindor's services. Lew picked Milwaukee and pocketed over $1 million for his
rookie season in 1969–1970. Alcindor, in a major spiritual and intellectual
decision, converted to the Islam faith. This switch represented no sudden,
quixotic decision. His California years had heightened his consciousness regarding a capitalistic culture that offered much materialistically but was
plagued by racism. In avoiding tryouts for the 1968 United States Olympic
basketball team, Alcindor stated, "We have been a racist nation with first class
citizens and my decision not to go to the Olympics is my way of getting the
message across." Some sportswriters saw his change of religion as cosmetic.
Lew changed his name to Kareem Abdul-Jabbar, representing a profound
personal, spiritual renewal for the New Yorker.

During his first season for Milwaukee, Abdul-Jabbar tallied 2,361 points
and made 1,190 rebounds. Kareem won both MVP and top rookie honors and
led Milwaukee to an NBA title. In 1975, the biggest "player swap" deal in
NBA history transferred Abdul-Jabbar to the Los Angeles Lakers (NBA). In-
exorably, he surpassed Chamberlain's records as the NBA all-time leader in
all offensive areas.

Arthur Ashe, Jr., described the 1973–1989 era as the "Kareem Abdul-
Jabbar era." After noting the impact of Kareem as the collegian "sensation,"
Ashe listed Abdul-Jabbar's major accomplishments. He led the Lakers to five
NBA titles before retiring in 1989. Abdul-Jabbar was named NBA MVP 6
times and made the All-NBA First Team on 10 occasions. Kareem's scoring
figures take one's breath away. As Ashe noted: "He remains the NBA all-time
leader in several categories including: most points scored (38,387), most games
played (1,560), most minutes played (57,446), most field goals made (15,837),
and most field goals attempted (28,307)."

During Kareem's final tour of NBA cities with the Lakers, crowds flocked
to see his sky hook and regarded the gangling man as the epitome of a "living
legend." The thick, bushy Afro hairstyle of the late 1960s had given way to
the bald shaven head of an older athlete. The skills and soaring majesty of the
aging Abdul-Jabbar declined, but nobody really wanted to see the end of a
great chapter in professional athletics. Teammate **Magic Johnson** and coach
Pat Riley were moved to tears as they expressed their affection and esteem
for the withdrawn and solitary man.

Peter C. Bjarkman, in his entry in David Porter's *Biographical Dictionary
of American Sports*, describes Abdul-Jabbar's personal problems. There have
been major financial setbacks and, despite four children, an on-again, off-again
marriage. Happily, the 1990s have witnessed a coming of age for the superstar.
Belatedly, Kareem has received some attractive TV commercial sponsorship
deals. It would have been nice if his face had become as well known as that
of Jordan, **Shaq O'Neal,** and **Bo Jackson.** For the African American who
graced an athletic stage on the college and professional levels for more than

a quarter of a century, the hope remains that he will enjoy a well-deserved happy old age. In 1995 the Naismith Memorial Basketball Hall of Fame inducted him.

BIBLIOGRAPHY: Arthur Ashe, Jr., *A Hard Road to Glory: A History of the African-American Athlete Since 1946,* vol. 3 (New York, 1988); Bill Becker, "Alcindor Is Eager to Start Varsity Career," *New York Times,* October 15, 1966; *Current Biography Yearbook* (1967), pp. 3–6; Sam Goldpaper, "Alcindor Clarifies TV Remark, Criticizes Racial Bias in US," *New York Times,* July 23, 1968; David L. Porter, ed., *Biographical Dictionary of American Sports: Basketball and Other Indoor Sports* (Westport, CT, 1989).

Scott A.G.M. Crawford

HERB ADDERLEY
(June 8, 1939–) ————————————————— *Football*

Herb Adderley, one of America's most gifted and versatile football players, enjoyed a highly successful professional career. Adderley's career included performing for Super Bowl championship squads with the Green Bay Packers National Football League (NFL) club in 1966 and 1967 and the Dallas Cowboys (NFL) in 1971. His parents, Charles Adderley and Rene (White) Adderley, christened him Herbert A. Adderley. The Philadelphia native, born on June 8, 1939, amazed coaches, teachers, and fellow students at Northeast High School with his ability to succeed in three different sports. He lettered in football, basketball, and baseball, earning All-City honors in each sport. Herb received many scholarship offers from the nation's leading colleges and universities. People wondered which sport he would concentrate on. His ultimate choices were Michigan State University and football.

With the Spartans from 1957 to 1961, the well-built six-foot, 200-pound offensive back distinguished himself with three football letters. Herb co-captained the 1960 Spartans team and led them in rushing in 1959 and receiving in 1959 and 1960. His abilities impressed college football to such an extent that in 1960 Adderley was chosen to participate in the East-West Shrine game, the Hula Bowl, and Coaches' All-America and College All-Star Games. Altogether, he performed on seven College All-Star teams. Adderley typified the best sort of athlete-scholar role model. The exciting, elusive running back graduated with a B.S. degree in education in 1961. In his senior year, the Michigan State football team ranked fifteenth nationally. Exciting teams like the Spartans boosted college football attendance in the 1960s to 30 million from a ceiling of 20 million in the 1950s. Adderley was selected by Green Bay on the first round of the NFL draft. Herb enjoyed an outstanding career with the Packers from 1961 to 1969 and finished his NFL career with the Dallas Cowboys from 1970 to 1972. Like many great college running backs, his promotion to the professional ranks brought a new assignment. In Adderley's case, he was converted to a defensive back. Herb played on five NFL championship teams (1961–1962, 1965–1967) and two National Football Conference (NFC) title squads (1970–1971). In the early Super Bowl years, his impact verged on the phenomenal. Of the first six Super Bowls, he played in four and performed on the victorious squad in three.

In 1962 and 1965, Adderley led the NFL in touchdowns via interceptions. Herb also paced the NFL with interceptions in 1965 and 1969. He led the Green Bay Packers in kickoff returns from 1961 to 1964 and interceptions from 1963 to 1965. With the Dallas Cowboys, Adderley equaled the club record for most interceptions in a single game with three and starred as a defensive back with six interceptions for 182 yards.

Following his college football success, Adderley gained similar recognition in the NFL. Herb was named an All-NFL defensive back on six occasions, gaining honors in 1962, 1963, and 1965 through 1968. During his NFL career, he displayed remarkable consistency and enjoyed his greatest years from 1963 to 1967. In that period, Adderley was selected for five consecutive Pro Bowls. This professional athlete performed 12 seasons with teams, compiling 127 victories, 46 losses, and five ties. He made 48 career interceptions with an average of 21.8 yards per runback and returned 120 kickoffs for 3,080 yards.

In 1968, the *New York Times* described Super Bowl II between Green Bay and the Oakland Raiders. The Super Bowl game at the Orange Bowl drew a crowd of 75,546 and a television audience of an astonishing 50 million. The prize money amounted to $15,000 for each of the winners and $7,500 for each of the losers. Adderley was lauded as a part of a "magnificent defensive unit." Herb's crowning moment as cornerback came when he intercepted a pass by Daryle Lamonica intended for Fred Biletnikoff. He "streaked 60 yards for a touchdown."

The father of one daughter, Adderley subsequently announced football games for Temple University and the Philadelphia Eagles (NFL) and served as an assistant football coach at Temple University. He also coached with the Philadelphia Bell team of the short-lived World Football League. Herb followed his coaching stints with service as an assistant radio station manager and as an "ideas man" for Schlitz Breweries. In 1980, nearly 20 years after he donned the dark green, gold, and white of the Packers uniform, Adderley was elected to the Pro Football Hall of Fame. Subsequently, he made the AFL-NFL 1960–1984 All-Star Second Team. Herb joined the Hall of Fame with defensive end **Deacon Jones**, defensive tackle Bob Lilly, and center Jim Otto.

In 1959, legendary Vince Lombardi took over the job of head coach for struggling Green Bay and announced, "Let's get one thing straight. I'm in complete command here." Lombardi used Adderley most effectively as a rookie cornerback in 1961. The public saw Lombardi as a strong, controversial coach, but he and Herb worked well together. A year after Lombardi left Green Bay to assume a leadership role with the Washington Redskins, the

Packers in 1970 traded Adderley to Dallas. He finished his playing career in 1972 under coach Tom Landry. Herb played for the two greatest coaches of all time. Adderley starred during a decade of incredible growth in professional football. The AFL was established in 1960 and the Super Bowl in 1967. The eventual merger of the AFL and the NFL took place in 1970. These years saw football become the national game of the United States.

Arthur Ashe, Jr., praised Adderley in his *A Hard Road to Glory* "as the best cornerback the game had seen." Ashe commented that African-American athletes had starred in every Super Bowl and mentioned Adderley's pass interception and score against the Oakland Raiders in Super Bowl II. Ashe perceived Adderley as a sports hero and grouped him with football's great stars.

Legendary coach George Allen rated Herb among the top echelon of professional footballers. Allen's tribute to Adderley, a testament to an intense coach filled with admiration and respect for an outstanding athlete, reads: "Herb Adderley was the ideal back. He would have been an outstanding offensive back, too. He was smart and quick, strong and tough. He had fast feet and good hands. Boy, did he have good hands! It wasn't a gamble when he went for the ball. When he went for it, he caught it. And when he got it, he could really run with it. He also made great runs returning kicks. He was dynamite."

BIBLIOGRAPHY: George Allen with Ben Olan, *Pro Football's 100 Greatest Players* (New York, 1986); Arthur Ashe, Jr., *A Hard Road to Glory: A History of the African-American Athlete Since 1946*, vol. 3 (New York, 1988); Lowell R. Greunke, *Football Rankings* (Jefferson, NC, 1984); John McCallum and Charles H. Pearson, *College Football USA, 1869–1972* (New York, 1972); Robert Mechikoff and Steven Estes, *A History and Philosophy of Sport and Physical Education* (Dubuque, IA, 1993); David S. Neft et al., eds., *The Football Encyclopedia* (New York, 1994); *New York Times*, January 15, 1968; *The NFL's Official Encyclopedic History of Professional Football* (New York, 1977); *Official 1984 National Football League Record and Fact Book* (New York, 1984); David L. Porter, ed., *Biographical Dictionary of American Sports: Football* (Westport, CT, 1987).

Scott A.G.M. Crawford

MUHAMMAD ALI
(January 17, 1942–) ————————————————————— *Boxing*

Muhammad Ali has been described as "the most recognizable human being on earth." During the 1960s and early 1970s especially, Ali's skill as a prizefighter, fame as heavyweight champion, and notoriety as a Black Muslim and opponent of the Vietnam War gave him celebrity status second to none.

Ali was born Cassius Marcellus Clay on January 17, 1942, in Louisville, Kentucky. His father, Marcellus, was employed as a sign painter, while his mother, Odessa (Grady) Clay, worked as a household domestic. His father described Cassius as "a good boy" who didn't give his parents "any trouble." If it had not been for his discovery of boxing at age 12, Clay might well have followed in his father's footsteps as a sign painter. Indeed, Cassius hardly "starred" in high school, graduating three hundred and seventy-sixth in a class of three hundred and ninety-one. But boxing became his passion. Louisville policeman Joe Martin introduced Clay to the sport in October 1954. According to Martin, young Cassius was enraged because his bike had been stolen and wanted to "whup whoever stole it." Martin convinced him that he needed to learn to box before challenging people to fights.

Cassius devoted most of his energy to prizefighting the next five years, appearing in 108 amateur bouts. Clay won six Kentucky Golden Glove championships, two National Amateur Athletic Union (AAU) titles, and two National Golden Glove crowns. He first gained national recognition when he won the Gold Medal in the light heavyweight division during the 1960 Rome, Italy, Summer Olympic Games. In October 1960, Cassius made his professional debut as a heavyweight, taking a six-round decision in Louisville from Tunney Hunsaker. After several victories over less capable opponents, Clay earned a championship bout against the supposedly invincible Sonny Liston. A heavy underdog, Cassius stunned supporters and detractors alike with a sixth-round technical knockout of Liston.

Clay further startled boxing fans shortly after the fight by announcing that he had joined the Black Muslim religion (the Nation of Islam) and changed his name to Muhammad Ali. Many Americans considered the Black Muslims a dangerously violent group. Ali defended his crown nine times in the following two years, but his title was revoked in 1967 when he refused to be conscripted into the military. Muhammad argued that he should not serve because of his Islamic religious faith, but he was sentenced to a five-year prison term. In 1970, the U.S. Supreme Court unanimously reversed Ali's conviction for "draft-dodging," enabling him to resume his boxing career. On October 30, 1974, Ali regained the heavyweight championship by upsetting **George Foreman.** In the next four years, Muhammad defended the title a remarkable 10 times before losing the crown to former Olympic boxer Leon Spinks in February 1978. He regained it in a September 1978 rematch. Ali announced the following year that he was retiring from boxing but tried to launch a comeback in 1980. Muhammad's attempt to reclaim the title for a fourth time ended in a humiliating defeat to **Larry Holmes.** Trevor Berbick defeated Ali in 1981, causing him to retire permanently.

Since 1981, Ali's life has combined sadness and contentment. In 1984, Muhammad was diagnosed as suffering from Parkinson's syndrome, a brain disease that leads to a slowness of movement and speech. Doctors believe that the condition was caused partly by "repeated blows to the head over time." Although the condition has slowed him down, he still maintains a busy schedule. He spends much of his time raising money for the Muhammad Ali Foundation and frequently appears at sports tributes and fund-raisers. His personal life seems more content as well. After three failed marriages, Ali wed Yolanda Williams in 1986. They currently live in Berrien Springs, Michigan, with their first and Ali's ninth child.

Muhammad remains a major figure in the history of prizefighting, partly because of his ring achievements. Ali won 56 fights and lost only 5, taking the heavyweight championship on three different occasions, and earning over $60 million from his bouts. His boxing style, involving dancing, feinting, and weaving almost like a student of ballet, appealed to boxing fans.

Muhammad's personality enhanced his celebrity status. Ali stirred controversy even before his membership in the Black Muslims and confrontations with the military. As Cassius Clay, he violated a sacred American belief about sports figures by lacking humility. Clay bragged, pranced, and even predicted the round in which he would knock out opponents. He wrote an autobiographical "epic poem" entitled "Feats of Clay."

The controversy intensified when Cassius joined the Nation of Islam, changed his name to Muhammad Ali, refused to serve in the military during the Vietnam War, and even showed some sympathy for America's enemy, the Viet Cong. Ali symbolized many of the conflicts and tensions that affected America in the 1960s. Many Vietnam War opponents, for example, saw Muhammad as a hero, while war supporters denounced him as a traitor. Similarly, many young African Americans hailed his commitment to an all–African American religious group, while other people, including most whites, found that commitment threatening.

Above all, Ali realized that prizefighting, like all sports, should be entertaining. With his extraordinary style, both inside and outside the ring, Muhammad was certainly worth watching. In 1987, *The Ring* magazine, the major publication of the boxing world, named Muhammad Ali the greatest heavyweight champion of all time. Arguably, the honor was richly deserved. The U.S. Olympic Hall of Fame inducted Muhammad in 1983, while the International Boxing Hall of Fame enshrined Ali in 1990. In 1994, *Sports Illustrated* ranked him first on its "40 for the Ages List." In April 1995, the Muhammad Ali Museum opened at the Louisville Galleria.

BIBLIOGRAPHY: Muhammad Ali with Richard Durham, *The Greatest: My Own Story* (New York, 1975); Dave Anderson, "On His 50th, Ali Is Still 'The Greatest,' " *New York Times*, January 16, 1992, sec. B, p. 11; Thomas Hauser, *Muhammad Ali: His Life and Times* (New York, 1991); Robert Lipsyte, *Free to Be Muhammad Ali* (New York, 1978); Jeffrey T. Sammons, *Beyond the Ring: The Role of Boxing in American Society* (Urbana, IL, 1988); Rick Telander, "Facing Facts About Ali," *Sports Illustrated* 75 (July 1, 1991), p. 78; Jose Torres, *Sting Like a Bee: The Muhammad Ali Story* (New York, 1971).

Anthony O. Edmonds

MARCUS ALLEN

(March 26, 1960–) ————————————————————————— *Football*

At every level of his athletic career, Marcus Allen has achieved the top rung of success. He has always demonstrated a strong sense of his own strengths without arrogance. After Marcus joined the Los Angeles Raiders National Football League (NFL) club in 1982, veteran team leader **Gene Upshaw** commented, "The reason you never hear a bad word about him is because we all like him—because he's not like some other backs . . . with big heads. He'll never be that way, either, because he's not that kind of kid."

Marcus LeMarr Allen was born on March 26, 1960, in San Diego, California, to Harold "Red" Allen, a general contractor, and Gwen Allen, a registered nurse. Marcus, his three brothers, Harold, Jr., Damon (a Canadian Football League star), and Darius, and a sister, Michelle, were afforded a strong family presence and various opportunities in sports, scouting, music, and church activities. Allen credits his parents for instilling each child with independence and self-worth, "to depend on no one," to be "proud, dignified and confident," and to carry oneself "as a winner."

At San Diego's Lincoln High School, Marcus starred in basketball and football and left the hardcourt for the gridiron when named quarterback in his junior year. Allen excelled as defensive safety and offensive leader. His senior year, one of the best in California Scholastic football history, featured him running for 1,098 yards in 123 carries (8.9-yard average) with 12 touchdowns and passing for 1,434 yards and 9 touchdowns while winning the City Championship. On defense, Allen intercepted 11 passes, returning 4 for touchdowns, and was credited with 311 tackles, 94 unassisted. Marcus received numerous All-America team accolades, garnering the Hearst newspaper's California High School Athlete of the Year honor and the Hertz Number 1 Award as the best California high school athlete. Lincoln retired his football jersey, making him the only player in its history so honored.

Although highly recruited nationwide, Allen quickly chose the University of Southern California (USC) and majored in public administration. Marcus followed in the footsteps of **O. J. Simpson,** his football idol. Allen remarked, "It was always SC. I first started watching them when O. J. played. From that point on, that was the school I wanted to go to." Coach John Robinson recruited Marcus as a defensive back but moved him to running back after one week of practice. Robinson explained, "Since the first time he put on a uniform, it's been obvious that Marcus has three things you need to be a tailback at USC: the personal ambition, the magnetism, and that tailback look in his eye." For his first two years at USC, Allen backed up tailback Charles White, 1979 Heisman Award winner. As a freshman, Marcus totaled 171 yards. After switching to fullback his sophomore year, he blocked ferociously for White while gaining 649 yards and scoring 8 touchdowns. Allen stepped into the

Trojan's tailback spotlight in his junior year and gained 1,563 yards in 10 games, including 3 in excess of 200 yards. He also scored 14 touchdowns, ranking second nationally. With his pass receiving included, Marcus led the nation's backs in total offense with 179.4 yards per game.

Allen's senior year was climaxed with his selection to seven All-America teams, earning College Player of the Year honors from the Maxwell Club, Walter Camp, United Press International (UPI), *The Sporting News,* and *Football News,* and winning the 1981 Heisman Trophy. He rushed for 2,342 yards to break **Tony Dorsett**'s single-season rushing record by 400 yards. Altogether Marcus amassed 4,682 career yards rushing on 893 attempts and 801 yards passing on 86 catches. He established 12 NCAA records and still holds the NCAA record for most career 200-yard games with 11. Allen gained at least 100 yards in 20 of 21 starts at tailback and scored 46 career touchdowns, including 23 as a senior to lead the nation.

NFL scouts questioned Allen's professional prospects based upon his 4.6-second time for the 40-yard dash and believed that USC's skilled offensive line mainly accounted for Marcus's yardage totals. The Los Angeles Raiders chose the six-foot-two-inch, 205-pound Allen as the tenth pick overall and the third running back in the 1982 NFL draft. The decision paid immediate dividends for the Raiders. In the strike-shortened nine-game 1982 season, Marcus led all American Football Conference (AFC) running backs with 38 receptions for 401 yards, paced the AFC with 14 touchdowns, and gained 697 yards on 160 carries. He was named All-Pro and Rookie of the Year and invited to the Pro Bowl.

Allen's second season in 1983, a Raider dream campaign, culminated with their 38–9 Super Bowl XVIII domination of the Washington Redskins. In 1983 Marcus carried the ball 334 times for 1,014 yards and led the AFC backs with 68 receptions for 590 yards, exceeding the 100-yard mark in combined yardage in 10 games. In 3 post-season playoff games, Allen averaged a stunning 8 yards per carry in totaling 466 yards, caught 14 passes for 118 yards, and scored 4 touchdowns. He was awarded the Super Bowl MVP for his 191-yard performance on 20 carries, and jaunted a record 74 yards from scrimmage. Marcus told reporters, "Before the game I actually pictured myself breaking free for a long run but didn't picture myself going in for a touchdown. The reality was better than the dream."

Allen's 11-year tenure with the Raiders from 1982 through 1992 brought unqualified success. He rushed 8,545 yards for twelfth place in NFL history and carried 2,090 times, tenth most in NFL annals. Marcus scored 98 touchdowns, ninth on the NFL career list, made 79 rushing touchdowns, eighth most, and amassed 12,803 all-purpose yards, eleventh all time. His Raider team records included most points in a game; touchdowns in a career, game, and season; rushing attempts for a season; career and season rushing yards; and career rushing touchdowns. As a Raider, Allen set NFL records for most consecutive games with 100 or more yards rushing (11) and the single-season mark for combined yards with 2,314 in 1985. His finest NFL season came in 1985, when he rushed for an NFL-leading 1,759 yards on 380 carries and earned NFL MVP awards from the Professional Football Writers Association, *The Sporting News,* Associated Press (AP), and *Football News.* The UPI's Offensive Player of the Year made his third of five Pro Bowl appearances as a Raider, an honor he achieved in 1982 and 1984 through 1987. From Allen's peers came unqualified praise. Running back **Eric Dickerson** observed, "Nobody cuts back at full speed the way he does. Plus, he'll knock your jock off blocking, and he throws the ball better than half the quarterbacks in the league." Adept at the Raider halfback option pass, Marcus completed 10 of 24 career throws for 267 yards and 4 touchdowns. All-Pro defensive back **Ronnie Lott** noted, "When I prepare for the Raiders, I prepare for Marcus Allen. I know that every, every, every play he can beat you."

Allen's years with the Raiders after 1987 became increasingly unpleasant, marked by an apparent personal feud with owner and managing partner Al Davis. Following his stellar 1985 campaign, Marcus signed a five-year, $3.5 million contract. In 1988, he led the Raiders in rushing for a seventh consecutive time and carried at least 200 times for his sixth straight year. In 1986 and 1987, Allen ranked second in team receiving. The 1987 mid-season arrival of Heisman Trophy winner and two-sport star **Bo Jackson** changed his playing status, as the duo shared team rushing duties. Marcus started five games at fullback, blocking for Jackson. Allen held out in the 1989 pre-season, hoping that Davis would increase his $1.1 million salary to approximate Jackson's $1.356 million for a half season. Davis refused to renegotiate. Marcus rejoined the Raiders for the regular season, but his on-field role diminished appreciably. His offensive statistics dropped markedly from 1989 through 1992. Allen charged the Raiders with a personal vendetta, but Davis denied those allegations.

On June 8, 1993, Marcus signed a free agent contract with the Kansas City Chiefs (NFL), joining recently acquired All-Pro quarterback Joe Montana. They formed an experienced backfield tandem, seeking to prove that their skills had not diminished. Chiefs coach Marty Schottenheimer, who had liked Allen's team commitment when blocking for Jackson in 1987, remarked, "I was sold on him from that minute on. Can you imagine, a great runner like that, going to fullback and not saying one word? He was obviously a guy who would subordinate his personal goals for that of the team." Marcus delivered for the Chiefs. During the 1993 season, the 33-year-old Allen became a starter in the sixth game and led the Chiefs in rushing with 764 yards on 206 tries and in rushing touchdowns with 12. He earned his sixth invitation to the Pro Bowl after a seven-year absence. The Chiefs fell one victory short of the Super Bowl in three postseason games, but Allen carried 53 times for 191 yards and 3 touchdowns. In NFL playoff history, Marcus moved to third in the all-time rankings in rushing yardage, rushing touchdowns, and total touchdowns. He again led the Chiefs in rushing in 1994, gaining 709 yards (3.8 yard average) and scoring 7 touchdowns. In accounting for his playoff success, Allen stated, "Experience plays a big part of it, being in that situation many times and realizing you have to step up to get to the next level. The pace of the games picks up. . . . It's all or nothing. Everyone realizes that. If you don't [win], you go home. And I don't think anyone wants to go home at this point."

Allen's season with the Chiefs dispelled any notion that his career was over. During the 1994 season, he moved past **Earl Campbell** into ninth place on the all-time rushing list. Marcus never lost faith in his own abilities, explaining, "I have a burning desire to be the best. If I don't make it, that's o.k. because I'm reaching for something so astronomically high. If you reach for the moon and miss, you'll still be among the stars." Allen's career provides a beacon of excellence for others to follow.

BIBLIOGRAPHY: Current Biography Yearbook (1986), pp. 3–6; Kansas City Chiefs Media Guide (1993); Los Angeles Times, August 13, 1992; June 9, 1993; September 28, 1993; New York Times, January 23, 1984; January 20, 1994; David L. Porter, ed., Biographical Dictionary of American Sports: Football (Westport, CT, 1987); Ira Simmons, Black Knight: Al Davis and His Raiders (Rocklin, CA, 1990).

David Bernstein

HENRY ARMSTRONG
(December 12, 1912–October 22, 1988) ———————————— *Boxing*

Henry Armstrong remains the only fighter to hold world titles in three different weight classifications simultaneously. Born Henry Jackson, Jr., he was the grandson of a white plantation owner and his slave wife. He was born on December 12, 1912, in Columbus, Mississippi, the eleventh of 15 children. His father, an African-American farmer and butcher, moved his family to St. Louis, Missouri, during World War I. After his half-Cherokee mother died in 1918, Armstrong spent much of his youth being cared for by his grandmother. During the Great Depression, Henry toiled as a railroad worker to support his brothers and sisters. One day at work, the sports section of a discarded newspaper literally floated toward Henry. Armstrong took it as a sign to pursue a career in the ring. "That particular sheet was just twirling in the air," he recalled. "It just fell on the ground in front of me, and the wind just stopped. It was a miracle." Armstrong was fascinated by a story about boxer Kid Chocolate, who was earning $75,000 for a bout with Al Singer. Henry immediately quit his railroad job to take up boxing.

Armstrong fluctuated between amateur and professional boxing in the early 1930s before turning totally to the professional game. Henry adopted the last name Armstrong from an early trainer, who taught him the finer points of the sport. The 5-foot-5½-inch Armstrong, whom the press dubbed "Homicide Hank" because of his explosive knockout power, dominated the lower weight classifications by the mid-1930s. Since purses were usually small, he regularly fought at least 12 times per year from 1933 to 1944. His management, which included entertainer Al Jolson, realized that heavyweight champion **Joe Louis** was the sport's most attractive athlete. Henry needed a publicity gimmick to garner attention. "All the fans were talking about Joe Louis," Armstrong remembered. "They were saving up their money to buy tickets to his fights. That's when we came up with the idea to try to win three different titles."

Henry won his first championship, the world featherweight title, on October 29, 1937, knocking out Petey Sarron in New York City. The bout marked the last time Armstrong fought under the 126-pound limit. Armstrong never defended his title and skipped a full division to challenge world welterweight titleholder Barney Ross, garnering the 147-pound championship with a 15-round decision in Long Island City, New York, on May 31, 1938. Less than three months later, Henry dropped back to the lightweight division and defeated champion Lou Ambers in New York City for his third title. He relinquished the featherweight crown shortly thereafter but held the distinction of being the only fighter to hold three undisputed championships at once. *The Ring* named Armstrong Fighter of the Year for 1938, breaking Joe Louis's grip on the award.

Henry defended his two remaining titles 12 times in 1939. Lou Ambers defeated him on August 22, 1939, in New York City in a rematch for the lightweight crown. In 1940, Armstrong made six successful defenses of his welterweight championship before losing a decision to Fritzie Zivic in a rough contest on October 4 in New York City. Zivic knocked out Henry in a 12-round rematch in New York City on January 17, 1941. Armstrong earned a chance to win an unprecedented fourth title in 1940, but his fight against middleweight champion Ceferino Garcia ended in a controversial draw. "[My bout versus Garcia] was called a draw," lamented Henry. "I beat him easily in this ten-round fight. [In my opinion] I beat him eight out of ten rounds."

The rematch against Zivic marked Armstrong's last world title fight. Nevertheless, he remained active as a professional boxer until losing to journeyman Chester Slider in Oakland, California, in 1945. Henry announced his retirement from the ring and toured China, India, and Egypt, giving boxing exhibitions for Allied troops in 1945. The tour sparked Armstrong's interest in religion. "I went overseas in 1945. I went all through Egypt. I had a very good feeling of Christianity when I got to Egypt where Moses was. I just made a decision that when I got back [to America] I was going to enter the ministry." Henry, who became an ordained Baptist minister in 1951, worked with juvenile delinquents in the Los Angeles, California, area and became director of the Herbert Hoover Boys Club in St. Louis, Missouri, in 1972. He married Willa Mae Shondy in 1934 and had one daughter, Lanetta. Armstrong died in Los Angeles on October 22, 1988.

His final career record included 145 wins (98 by knockout), 20 losses, and nine draws. **Thomas Hearns** and **Ray Leonard,** along with Armstrong, have held multiple titles at one time, but only Henry's titles were undisputed ones.

The others' crowns were only recognized by one of boxing's many sanctioning bodies. In 1990 the International Boxing Hall of Fame enshrined Henry. Boxing historian Bert Sugar described Armstrong's ring achievements as "a benchmark against which all future generations will be measured."
BIBLIOGRAPHY: Sam Andre and Nat Fleischer, *A Pictorial History of Boxing* (New York, 1975); Peter Heller, *In This Corner: Former World Champions Tell Their Stories* (New York, 1973); Bert R. Sugar, ed., *1983 Ring Record Book* (New York, 1983); Bert Randolph Sugar, *The 100 Greatest Boxers of All Time* (New York, 1984).

John Robertson

ARTHUR ASHE, JR.
(July 10, 1943–February 6, 1993) ——————————————— *Tennis*

Tennis player Arthur Ashe, Jr., was an excellent role model for all athletes and especially those in tennis. The courageous, graceful, and sportsmanlike Ashe ranks among the most admired athletes of all time. When his illness due to acquired immunodeficiency syndrome (AIDS) was publicly announced, Ashe became an ambassador for others through his involvement in AIDS awareness and AIDS education.

Arthur Robert Ashe, Jr., was born in Richmond, Virginia, on July 10, 1943, the son of Arthur Robert Ashe, Sr., and Mattie Cordell (Cunningham) Ashe, and had one brother, Johnny. His mother died in March 1950 at age 27. In 1947, Arthur's father was hired as a special policeman by Richmond and assigned to a playground. The Ashe family moved to the middle of the 18-acre Brookfield Playground. Arthur saw Ron Charity, the most accomplished African-American tennis player in Richmond, hitting tennis balls. After Charity finished practicing, he asked Ashe if he would like to learn to play tennis. Arthur replied "Yes, I would." Charity served as Ashe's first teacher, while Dr. R. W. Johnson later gave Arthur tennis instruction.

When Ashe was age 12, he accompanied Charity to enter a U.S. Tennis Association (USTA)–sanctioned tournament at Byrd Park in Richmond. Since the facility was a white park, Ashe was not allowed to enter. At that point, Arthur learned that he must take charge of his life if he wanted to be a tennis player. Ashe acknowledged, "I've learned to be self-reliant. It was kind of forced on me." Ashe won the American Tennis Association (ATA) National Boys 12 Singles title in 1955, the ATA National Boys 16 Singles in 1957, 1958, and 1959, the ATA National Boys 18 Singles in 1960, and the ATA Men's Singles from 1960 to 1963. Ashe entered his first national championship (nonsegregated) in 1959 at age 16 and won the National Interscholastic Singles championship in 1961. He moved from Richmond to St. Louis, Missouri, to continue his high school education and train full-time in tennis with Richard Hudlin.

The University of California at Los Angeles (UCLA) gave Ashe a full schol-

arship to play tennis and study business administration. An All-America selection, Arthur in 1965 won the NCAA Singles title and led the Bruins to the
team championship. After graduating with a B.S. degree in business administration in 1966, he fulfilled a three-year U.S. Army commitment. Renowned
tennis teacher Harry Hopman described Ashe as "the most promising player
in the world." In 1968 Arthur was ranked first in U.S. Men's Tennis and won
10 tournaments, including the U.S. Open Singles and the U.S. National Singles. He also reached the semi-finals at Wimbledon and finals in the U.S.
Open Doubles. With the U.S. Davis Cup team, he took 11 of 12 singles
matches. Ashe was ranked second nationally in 1969, although recording only
2 tournament victories. Arthur reached the semi-finals at Wimbledon and the
U.S. Open. He was listed third in the United States in 1970 with 11 tournament victories, including the Australian Open. In 1971 Ashe rose to second
in the United States, attaining the semi-finals at both the U.S. Open and the
Italian Open and quarterfinals at the French Open. Besides capturing the
French Open Doubles championship, Arthur made the finals in Wimbledon
Doubles.

In 1972 contract pros were not ranked, but Ashe won 3 of 31 tournaments.
Arthur earned the World Championship Tennis (WCT) Winter-Fall Playoff
championship and appeared in the U.S. Open finals. He was rated third in
the United States in 1973 with 2 tournament victories and reached the finals
at the WCT, ATP (Association of Tennis Professionals), and U.S. Pro championships. In 1973 Ashe, who advocated the end of apartheid, became the
first African-American athlete to play in an integrated sporting event in South
Africa. Arthur's listing dropped to fifth in 1974 despite winning the Stockholm,
Sweden, Open, the Bologna, Italy, WCT, and the Barcelona, Spain, WCT and
making the U.S. Pro Indoor finals.

Ashe was ranked first in the United States and world in 1975, winning 9 of
29 tournaments and appearing in 5 finals. Arthur defeated Jimmy Connors
6–1, 6–1, 5–7, 6–4 on July 5, 1975, at Wimbledon, becoming the first African
American to win that crown. Ashe also captured the WCT championship and
made the semi-finals at the Grand Prix Masters and U.S. Pro championships.
Arthur led the men's tour in 1975 earnings with $326,750. The following year,
he was ranked third nationally and won 5 WCT events. Ashe played only 5
tournaments in 1977, taking the Australian Open Doubles championship. The
1978 tour marked his last year of entering many tournaments at 28. Arthur
was rated ninth, being a finalist at the Grand Prix Masters and a semi-finalist
at the Australian Open. In 1979 he played 13 tournaments, appearing in the
finals at the U.S. Pro Indoor and U.S. Indoor tournaments and ranking fifth
nationally. Ashe played on the U.S. Davis Cup team for 10 years, taking 27
of 32 singles matches. The first African American named to the Davis Cup
team, he led the United States to five Davis Cup victories as a player from
1968 to 1970 and captained the squad from 1981 to 1985. Altogether, Arthur
captured 33 career singles titles and reached the finals 32 other times. Ashe

cherished his involvement in Davis Cup. "Although other involvements marked that period of my life," he wrote, "my captaincy was its highlight." In 1985, the International Tennis Hall of Fame inducted Arthur.

Ashe married Jeanne-Marie Moutousammy in February 1977 and had one daughter, Camera. He suffered three heart attacks and underwent two heart bypass operations, a quadruple and a double. Arthur suffered his first heart attack in 1979 while ranked seventh in the world in tennis and retired as an active player in 1980. In 1988, Ashe underwent brain surgery after his right arm became paralyzed. The surgery revealed a parasitic infection that quickly led to a diagnosis of AIDS. Arthur believed he became infected during bypass surgery in 1983 from a blood transfusion. Arthur did not want his illness made public, but *USA Today* kept pursuing the story that he was ill. He became a leading spokesman for education about AIDS with the same courage and grace that had marked his tennis career, creating the Arthur Ashe Foundation for the Defeat of AIDS and the Safe Passage Foundation to deal with problems in inner cities. Ashe died on February 6, 1993, in New York City. In 1988, he published *A Hard Road to Glory*, an authoritative three-volume history of the African-American athlete. *Sports Illustrated* in 1994 ranked Ashe twenty-seventh on its "40 for the Ages List."

BIBLIOGRAPHY: Lawrence K. Altman, "Ashe Was Stricken Suddenly After Years of AIDS," *New York Times*, February 8, 1993, sec. C; Arthur Ashe, Jr., with Neil Amdur, *Off the Court* (New York, 1981); Arthur Ashe, Jr., with Arnold Rampersad, *Days of Grace* (New York, 1993); Ira Berkow, "The Changing Faces of Arthur Ashe," *New York Times*, October 25, 1992, sec. 8, p. 1; Ira Berkow, "Ashe's Legacy Is the Gift for Inspiration," *New York Times*, February 8, 1993, sec. C.

Miriam F. Shelden

EMMETT ASHFORD
(November 23, 1914–March 1, 1980) ————————————— *Baseball*

Emmett Ashford earned recognition as the first African-American umpire in major league baseball history. Emmett Littleton Ashford was born in Los Angeles, California, on November 23, 1914, to Littleton Ashford and Adele (Bain) Ashford. His father, a truck driver, abandoned the family when Emmett was only two or three years old. His mother, a secretary for the *California Eagle*, an African-American weekly newspaper, stressed self-pride, hard work, and education to Emmett and his younger brother. Ashford was influenced by his mother's admonitions not to "do things halfway" and to remember "no matter how full the bottle of milk, there's always room for cream at the top." He recalled, "I just couldn't stand to do things halfway. I always believed: Whatever you do, do it well and do it right—give it the best that you have in you."

As a youngster, Ashford sold newspapers, shined shoes, and worked as a stockboy and cashier at a supermarket. At Jefferson High, Emmett sprinted on the track and field team, edited the school newspaper, belonged to the scholastic honorary society, and served as the first African-American student body president. After graduating from Los Angeles Community College, he took a U.S. government civil service exam in 1936 and became a postal clerk. Emmett, whose love for baseball far exceeded his playing ability, also began umpiring semi-pro and recreation league games.

After serving at the U.S. Navy air base in Corpus Christi, Texas, during World War II, Ashford advanced to an administrative job in the Payroll and Finance Division of the U.S. Post Office and expanded his officiating activities. He worked baseball, basketball, and football at the high school and college level. Emmett, the first African-American basketball referee in the Pacific Coast Conference (PCC), officiated there from 1950 to 1958. He also umpired girl's softball and was assigned to the 1948 National Softball Congress World Tournament. The all-white team from racially segregated Georgia initially protested the presence of an African-American umpire but later, impressed by his performance, insisted that he umpire the plate in the championship game.

After a four-game tryout held in Mexico because of racial attitudes in the United States, Ashford took a leave of absence from the U.S. Post Office in 1951 to pursue his dream of becoming a professional umpire. He signed with the Class C Southwest International League and on July 7 debuted as the first African-American umpire in organized baseball. Emmett moved to the Class C Arizona-Texas League in midseason 1952 and advanced to the Class A Western International League in 1953. The next year he jumped to the Class AAA Pacific Coast League (PCL), the highest minor league classification. Ashford spent 12 years in the PCL, including 3 as umpire-in-chief (1963–1965), and also umpired in Dominican Republic Winter League in 1959 and 1964. Emmett's personality and colorful umpiring style made him the league's most popular umpire, but his race kept him from advancing to the majors. When asked why he persisted umpiring so long without advancement, he replied, "How many men go to their graves without ever doing what's in their hearts?"

Ashford's dream came true after the 1965 season, when he signed with the American League (AL). After 15 years in the minors, Emmett debuted in 1966 as the first African-American umpire in major league history. He umpired the 1967 All-Star Game and 1970 World Series but was forced to retire after the 1970 season because of the AL's mandatory retirement policy at age 55.

Ashford's brief five-year major league career sparked controversy. Some fellow umpires resented Emmett's popularity with fans and the press and, like some players, considered him a "clown" or "showboat" because of his flamboyant umpiring style. Some, mostly African Americans, considered his refined language, elegant clothes (he always wore cuff links, even while umpiring), fondness for the opera and museums, jocularity, and "colorful" antics on the field as currying favor with whites and perpetuating racial stereotypes. Others criticized him as a poor umpire, who reached the majors only because of pressure from civil rights groups.

Such exaggerated criticisms stemmed primarily from the problem of race that affected Ashford throughout his umpiring career. His flamboyant style, a natural expression of his personality, did not affect the accuracy of his calls. "I'm an extrovert, and I couldn't help hamming it up," he explained. Emmett's umpiring skills had diminished when he finally reached the majors at age 51. He sometimes had difficulty calling pitches and seeing outfield hits, but Bill Kinnamon, a crew member with Ashford for two seasons, said "he was a good umpire. If Emmett Ashford had come up ten, fifteen, twenty years earlier, he would have been one hell of an umpire."

Although racial attitudes plagued him throughout his umpiring career and delayed his promotion to the majors, Ashford remained positive about his achievement. "I feel proud having been an umpire in the big leagues not because I was the first black man, but because major league umpires are a very select group of men. But the greatest satisfaction I've gotten is the feeling of accomplishment in doing what I set out to do in the first place when they said it couldn't be done." After retiring, Emmett umpired three summers in the Alaska Summer League, conducted umpiring clinics in Asia and Europe, and served as special assistant to Baseball Commissioner Bowie Kuhn, handling various public relations duties on the West Coast. He died on March 1, 1982, in Marina del Rey, California.

Ashford, married four times, never experienced with his three children the kind of family life he had missed as a child. Umpiring became a way of life for this courageous, dedicated man, whose pioneering achievements opened the door to African-American officials in professional sport.

BIBLIOGRAPHY: Larry R. Gerlach, *The Men in Blue: Conversations with Umpires* (New York, 1980; reprint 1994); *Los Angeles Times*, March 7, 1980; Joe McGuff, "Emmett Ashford: The Majors' Pioneer Black Umpire," *Baseball Digest* 39 (July 1980), pp. 65–66; Alan Margulies, "The Entertainer," *Referee* (September 1992), pp. 44–48; *New York Times*, March 4, 1980; Art Rosenbaum, "Colored Umpire with Color," *Baseball Digest* 21 (December 1965), pp. 57–59; Art Rust, Jr., *"Get That Nigger Off the Field!"* (New York, 1976).

Larry R. Gerlach

ERNIE BANKS

(January 31, 1931–) —————————————————— *Baseball*

"Mr. Cub" to several generations of Chicago Cub fans, Ernie Banks was the team's star player in the 1950s and 1960s. The good-natured, intense infielder arguably remains the most famous player ever to don a Cubs' uniform. That honor has special meaning because the Cubs are the National League's (NL) oldest franchise, dating back to the NL's first season in 1876.

Banks's enthusiasm for the game, as revealed in his favorite expression "Let's play two," remained as legendary as his willingness to talk with the fans and sign autographs. "I really don't mind signing autographs. It's part of my life and it gives me pleasure to make people so happy by doing so little." Ernie enjoys being with people and has a simple philosophy: "The spirit of friendship is the balance of life. You can have all the money, all the cars, all the houses, all the fame, but friendships are the balance of life. The key part of it is family and friends. All my career that's what I worked on, building friendships."

The Cubs did not enjoy much success on the field then, making Banks often all the fans had to cheer about. The Cubs sank to such depths that Ernie played in 2,528 major league games without appearing in a post-season or World Series game. No other major league player has played that long without doing one or the other. Nevertheless, he responded with a career National Baseball Hall of Fame effort, being elected in 1977 on his first time eligible. Twice, Ernie was selected as the NL MVP (1958, 1959).

Banks was not dismayed by failing to appear in post-season competition. "It's just something that was meant to be," Ernie stated. "I'm not a losing person. I just feel there are greater ways of winning . . . winning the respect of your family, your friends, and the writers. Also winning the respect of baseball fans around the country and in other parts of the world. *That* kind of winning has been a real blessing for me and it's been longer lasting."

A boy who came from a family of 12 and picked cotton for $5 a day in his native Texas accomplished all this. Ernest Banks was born in Dallas, Texas, on January 31, 1931, the son of Eddie Banks and Essie Banks. Poverty marked a way of life for the Banks family, although his father often worked seven days a week. Ernie, as the oldest boy, performed housework, kept the kerosene lamps lit, carried in wood for the stoves, and hauled water from the pump in the backyard. His interest in sports came when he entered Booker T. Washington High School in Dallas.

During two summers as a high schooler, Banks played baseball for an African-American touring team, the Detroit Colts. Upon graduation in 1950, Ernie signed with the Kansas City Monarchs of the Negro American League. He endured racial prejudice both then and during his early years with the Cubs. Like slugger **Hank Aaron,** his life was also threatened. Banks refused to bow to such pressure, answering with his playing. To this day, Ernie refuses to criticize. "Any kind of criticism is negative. That's why I don't say anything. Sometimes stress can make you say things that you regret."

A two-year tour in the U.S. Army interrupted his baseball career. Banks returned to the diamond in September 1953, when the Cubs purchased his contract. Ernie's very good rookie year featured a .275 batting average with 19 home runs. His next season propelled him into superstar status. During 1955, Banks set a major league record by hitting 5 grand-slam home runs. Babe Ruth, Lou Gehrig, and others had shared the major league record with 4 grand slams in a season. Ernie batted .313, hit 39 home runs to set a since-broken NL record for shortstops, produced 154 RBIs, and led NL shortstops in fielding.

Outstanding performances by Banks continued for several years. Unfortunately, the Cubs did not capture Ernie's attitude. "I think people like to be motivated, disciplined, and have a good, positive mental attitude. That's all it takes to have a successful professional team." He switched to first base in 1961 and proved an excellent defensive player. In 1969, 38-year-old Banks led the Cubs in a gallant race for the NL pennant, only to finish second. Ernie retired after the 1971 season with 512 career home runs, 1,636 RBIs, and a .274 batting average. He twice led the NL in home runs (1958, 1960) and RBIs (1958, 1959) and holds many club records.

Banks married Eloyce Johnson in 1958 and had three children, twin sons Joey and Jerry and daughter Jan. On August 9, 1977, Ernie was inducted into the National Baseball Hall of Fame. The essence of "Mr. Cub" came out in his acceptance speech: "This is the happiest day of my life. I have read that a man's success depends on the people who believe in him. I owe so much to my parents for all they put up with me; and to my wife and children—you don't know what a baseball wife has to put up with."

Banks later served as a Chicago Cub coach and goodwill ambassador. Ernie moved back to Chicago, Illinois, in 1994 from Los Angeles, California. "I do mostly charity things," he stated. "I work with the school for dyslexic children in Los Angeles. I'm with an organization called The World Children's Baseball Fair. . . . I'm starting my own foundation for senior citizens, Let's Play Two Foundation for Experienced People."

Banks, who coauthored the book *Mr. Cub* in 1977, still follows the wisdom he offered so many: "From what I've seen in both sides of life—the business side and the sports side—it takes a real commitment, a plan and a commitment. It takes early preparation, then you have to do it and then you have to follow through."

Ernie, the eternally sunny, good-natured "Mr. Cub," does not live in the past. "I work very hard to stay current, not to hold on to the past or live in the past." He finds there are always more people to meet, more smiles to give, more goodwill to disperse, and more friendships to develop.

BIBLIOGRAPHY: *Chicago Cubs Vineline* 2 (April 1987), pp. 8–10; 6 (December 1991), pp. 9, 12; 7 (January 1992), p. 21; Eddie Gold and Art Ahrens, *The New Era Cubs 1941–1985* (Chicago, IL, 1985), pp. 76–82; James A. Riley, *The Biographical Encyclopedia of the Negro Baseball Leagues* (New York, 1994).

Duane A. Smith

CHARLES BARKLEY
(February 29, 1963–) ——————————————————————— *Basketball*

Charles Barkley gained fame as a college, professional, and Olympic basketball star. He was born on February 29, 1963, the oldest of three sons of Charcey Mae (Edwards) Barkley Glenn in the small mining town of Leeds, Alabama. His father, Frank, abandoned the family when Charles was only 13 months old. After the death of her second husband, his mother, Charcey Mae, moved in with her mother, Johnnie Mae Edwards. The two women became a dominant force in the young boy's life, giving him a strong work ethic and a firm faith in God. Charles's stepfather, Clee Glenn, and his grandfather, "Little Daddy" Adolphus Edwards, provided the young boy with some guidance in his early years. But Barkley regretted not having a father as a role model.

His mother labored as a domestic, while his grandmother worked in a frozen food plant and as a beautician. Charles was, therefore, often left alone to take care of his two younger brothers in their small apartment in the "projects." Here he learned early the lessons of leadership and responsibility. Charles admits his being tempted as a boy to run with friends but, except for a few minor brushes with the police, stayed out of trouble and avoided drugs.

Barkley attended integrated schools in Leeds but did not take his schooling seriously. Charles also regretted that he did not stay in college and earn his degree and "wished someone had set higher academic standards" for him when he was in school.

A somewhat small and sickly child, Barkley struggled to become a basketball star. Charles did not make his high school varsity squad until his junior year. Strenuous jumping exercises and work on fundamentals enabled him finally to make the team, making him realize that he could get to college through his basketball skills. Barkley later said, "Without basketball, I'd probably have ended up in jail." In his senior year in high school, he attracted attention in a Christmas tournament game by scoring 25 points and making 20 rebounds. Although Barkley was still regarded as lazy and overweight, major basketball schools now recruited him. After some hesitation, he chose to attend Auburn University and began a checkered three-year career. Charles disliked practices and drills, openly feuded with his coach, whom he said did not respect his student athletes, and threatened to transfer to another school after his sophomore year. Weighing as much as 280 pounds, he also gained a reputation as a voracious eater and earned such derogatory nicknames as the "Round Mound of Rebound" and "Boy Gorge." An indifferent student, Barkley claimed the athletic department discouraged him from concentrating on his studies. Charles was academically ineligible to play after his third year. He left Auburn in 1984 with 1,183 points and 806 rebounds in three seasons, scoring 25 points and 17 rebounds against the University of Kentucky as a freshman, leading the Southeastern Conference (SEC) in rebounding all three seasons, converting 63.6 percent of his shots, and being selected UPI and SEC Player of the Year in 1983–1984. Barkley also recorded a 25-point, 11-rebound performance in a 1982 Sports Festival game. But, to his disappointment, coach Bobby Knight did not select Charles for the 1984 U.S. Olympic team.

Professional scouts, however, already knew Barkley well, as he became the fifth overall selection in the first round of the 1984 National Basketball Association (NBA) draft. The Philadelphia 76ers (NBA) signed Charles to a contract after difficult salary negotiations. He joined a team still dominated by **Julius "Doc" Erving** and center **Moses Malone.** Malone helped the young star adjust to the rigors of professional play. Barkley soon became a dominating power forward with his bulk, strength, quick first step, and phenomenal vertical leap. With his weight under control, Charles recorded a remarkably low body fat rating. However, he still resisted the weight training and body strengthening popular with contemporaries. Barkley also gained recognition for his stellar all-around play and credited playing guard in high school for teaching him to dribble, pass, and lead the fast break. Charles admitted that he had to learn as a professional to shoot from the outside. With relatively small hands, he scored many of his points from inside on layups or on explosive two-handed dunks.

Since the 1985–1986 season, Barkley has averaged better than 20 points per game (28.8 points in 1987–1988) in the NBA. Although standing a fraction under six foot five inches tall, Charles still ranked first in 1986–1987 and second in 1988–1989 in rebounding. Selected for the All-Rookie team in 1985, he was named to the All-NBA Second Team in 1986, 1987, 1992, 1994, and 1995 and to the All-NBA First Team from 1988 through 1991, and in 1993. Barkley played in nine All-Star Games by 1995, being named the game's MVP in 1991 and selected Shick Pivotal Player of the Year from 1986 to 1988. In 1993 Charles achieved a personal goal when he was chosen the NBA's MVP after averaging 25.6 points, 12.2 rebounds, and a credible 5.1 assists per game.

Barkley played from 1987 to 1992 with a weak Philadelphia team, being often injured and worn down by the rigors of the long NBA season. By 1993, Charles had emerged with his friend Chicago Bulls star **Michael Jordan** as one of the two most outstanding NBA players. Barkley claimed he was the best! In June 1992, he finally got his wish and was traded to the contending Phoenix Suns (NBA). In the 1992–1993 season, he helped Phoenix gain the final round of the playoffs before losing in six close games to the "3-Peat" Chicago Bulls. In the summer of 1992, Charles made the U.S. Olympic "Dream Team" and helped it win the Gold Medal at the Barcelona, Spain, Olympic Games.

Throughout his career, Barkley has attracted attention with his "trash-talking," physically intimidating play, and fights with the Detroit Pistons' Bill Lambier and other players. Charles also has experienced constant conflicts with officials and fans. Despite signing an eight-year, $13 million contract in 1986, he carried on a public feud with 76er owner Harold Katz and accused him of failing to develop a contending team. Barkley has also had problems with an agent, whom he claimed did not invest his money properly. At various times Charles has been charged with carrying an unregistered gun and assaulting fans, but he has been found innocent of all charges. Upon reaching the pinnacle of fame, he has also received many lucrative advertising contracts and appeared regularly in magazines, billboards, and television all over the world.

Barkley does not hesitate to speak out on issues of the day, being convinced that America (especially Philadelphia) still suffers from racism. He and his white wife, Maureen, a legal secretary and model whom he married February 9, 1989, have been subjected to racial slurs from time to time. But Charles says, "Racism is the racist's problem, not ours" and that "sports is the one area of society that brings the races together without a hint of racism." Barkley also admires such outstanding white players as the Boston Celtics' Kevin McHale and his ex-76er teammate Bobby Jones. Ultimately, he adds, "People should be judged by their actions, their words, and what they stand for, not for something over which they had absolutely no control—their race."

At times, Barkley seems to speak out to attract attention. But there is a ring of truth to his pleas that young people should remain in school and reject the use of drugs. Charles also criticizes those who try to make him a role model. He says, "It's asinine to make someone a role model simply because of what they've accomplished as an athlete or entertainer. Parents should be the child's primary role model," a responsibility Barkley takes seriously for his one young daughter, Christiana. Charles also tries to put sports in perspective when he says, "There are a lot more important things in life than winning the NBA title."

Life in Phoenix has brought mixed blessings to Barkley. There have been new commercial opportunities and the adulation of a new set of fans. After playing a major role in the Dream Team's Olympic victory, Charles helped the Phoenix Suns make the final round of the NBA playoffs and was finally chosen the NBA's MVP. But his move west has also brought at least a temporary estrangement from his wife and daughter. Barkley also realized that his body would not let him continue to play much longer. But Charles has remained very much himself and stated, "Until I die, I'm going to do whatever it takes for me to stay who I am—not who anyone else wants me to be."

BIBLIOGRAPHY: Charles Barkley and Roy S. Johnson, *Outrageous* (New York, 1992); "Chuck," *Esquire* 119 (May 1993), pp. 90–93; Jeff Coplon, "Headstrong," *New York Times*, March 17, 1991, sec. 6; Zander Hollander and Alex Sachare, eds., *The Official NBA Basketball Encyclopedia* (New York, 1989); Jack McCallum, "Now Barkley Owns the Ball," *Sports Illustrated* 68 (January 11, 1988), pp. 36–39; Rick Reilly, "Hot Head," *Sports Illustrated* 76 (November 9, 1992), pp. 66–70; A. Richman, "Call Him 'Round Mound' at Your Peril," *People Weekly* 27 (April 27, 1987), pp. 77–83; V. E. Smith and A. Press, "Who Are You Calling Hero?," *Newsweek* 121 (May 24, 1993), pp. 64–65; *The Sporting News* (June 7, 1993), p. 46.

Daniel R. Gilbert

ELGIN BAYLOR
(September 16, 1934–   ) ——————————————— *Basketball*

Douglas Noverr and Lawrence Ziewacz, in *The Games They Played: Sports in American History, 1865–1980,* described Elgin Baylor as "the prototype of many other black ballplayers entering the leagues in the fifties and sixties." Although lacking early experience as a basketball player, Elgin averaged 24.9

points per game by the 1958–1959 season. Elgin Baylor was born in Washington, D.C., on September 16, 1934, the third son of John Baylor and Uzzel Baylor. As a young child, the unfortunate doctrine of a "public separateness" for African Americans prevented Baylor from having access to public playgrounds. Consequently, Elgin did not play basketball until age 14. Despite his lack of playing experience, he made the All-City Washington, D.C., squad with the Phelps Vocational High School basketball team. Eventually Baylor entered Springarn High School, recording his best single-game performance with 68 points. Elgin's athleticism allowed him to become a positive symbol of racial integration and ethnic pride. Due to his prowess on the basketball court, he was the first African American ever named to the metropolitan area All-Star team.

Academic shortcomings nearly denied Baylor a college career, but Elgin eventually found a new home in isolated Idaho. The College of Idaho gave him an athletic scholarship, as the six-foot-five-inch 225-pounder performed on both the football field and the basketball court. The elegant Baylor became identified with a new type of athlete, dispelling the notion of the big, tall awkward, primarily physical player. Elgin moved like boxer **Muhammad Ali.** The fluency and fluidity of his ball control and shot taking fascinated sportswriters and basketball fans alike.

Baylor's road through college was fraught with pitfalls and setbacks. **Arthur Ashe, Jr.,** in his *A Hard Road to Glory*, records a telephone conversation with Elgin in August 1985. Baylor recalled having indifferent coaches, who were neither devious nor deceitful. "While colleges did not explore black high schools . . . [they] didn't know anything about us. I went to the College of Idaho for the first year on a football scholarship." When the basketball program at Idaho was mothballed, Elgin relocated to Seattle University. NCAA transfer and eligibility requirements forced Baylor to "sit out" a year before being able to play. During the 1956–1957 season, Elgin emerged as Seattle's impact player and finished as the nation's number-one rebounder and third best scorer. Seattle completed the season with an impressive 22–3 record, as Baylor enjoyed his selection for the All-West Coast All-Star team. A year later, Elgin maintained his sporting momentum with 31.5 points per game and gathered 590 rebounds. In the 1958 NCAA finals, the University of Kentucky defeated Seattle, 84–72. Baylor's 25 game points, however, gave the highly favored Wildcats a lot to think about!

Baylor's collegiate record marked him as a player with tremendous potential for the NBA. In 1958, Elgin was voted to *The Sporting News* All-America First Team and named the NCAA University Division MVP. His career points reached 2,500.

Despite a year of collegiate eligibility remaining, Baylor joined the Minneapolis Lakers (NBA) club. Elgin's arrival brought renewed life for a team in the doldrums. Minneapolis owner Bob Short knew that the franchise salvation lay in the capable hands of Baylor. If Elgin had declined, the Lakers would "have gone out of business" and "the club would have gone bankrupt."

Baylor's NBA career demonstrated remarkable consistency. During the 1958–1959 season, Elgin played 2,855 minutes, made 1,050 rebounds and 287 assists, and scored 1,742 points for a 24.9 points per game average. Eleven years later with the Los Angeles Lakers in 1969–1970, he logged 2,213 minutes, had 559 rebounds and 292 assists, and tallied 1,298 points for a 24.0 points per game average. Baylor's performance did not drop off until his last two seasons in 1970–1971 and 1971–1972. The 1959 NBA Rookie of the Year made the All-NBA First Team every year from 1959 to 1969.

Baylor's NBA All-Star Game record illustrated his rare ability to produce and be effective among elite performers. Elgin's low score of 15 points in the 1964 game was more than offset by his 24-, 25-, and 32-point performances in the 1959, 1960, and 1962 games. Besides being the NBA All-Star's Co-MVP in 1959, he held the career All-Star record for most free throws made (78) and shared the career mark for most free throws attempted (98). Baylor also shared the single-game record for most free throws made with 12 in 1962.

Arthur Ashe, Jr., wrote that Baylor, despite being an instinctively gifted player, spent "thousands of hours" as a teenager honing his skills. Elgin's magnetism as a player played a key role in solidifying the membership of the NBA Players Association, who rebelled in 1964 over an unsatisfactory pension plan. The association, led by Baylor and Jerry West, threatened to strike prior to the All-Star Game, but the owners eventually capitulated. Elgin remained a popular captain of the Lakers but played on only one (1971–1972) championship team. During his career, the Lakers lost to the Boston Celtics six times in the NBA playoffs.

In the 1970s, Baylor briefly coached the New Orleans Jazz (NBA). Elgin's experiences with the Jazz made him uncomfortable, as he coached in the face of statements like "We're not going to make this an all-nigger team." Not surprisingly, "Black players couldn't wait to be traded." His four-year coaching record produced 86 wins and 135 losses for a .389 percentage.

By the end of the 1960s, NBA rosters contained 58 percent African Americans. Baylor dominated during an era that saw the college game move from being "a regional delight" without "major national appeal" in the late 1950s to "a hugely popular high drama . . . in living color" with John Wooden's reign at UCLA.

With **Wilt Chamberlain** and Nate Thurmond, Baylor ranked among the first African-American basketball players to earn more than $100,000 a year. Not until 1968, however, did Elgin earn a superstar's salary.

Baylor was elected to the Naismith Memorial Basketball Hall of Fame in 1976. Following his coaching stint with the Jazz, Elgin served as executive vice president and general manager of the Los Angeles Clippers. Critics ranking the three greatest basketball players of all time have reached a consensus, rating **Michael Jordan** tops, **Julius Erving** second, and the elegant Baylor third. Elgin was chosen to the NBA 35th Anniversary All-Time Team in 1980. Frank Deford, in a 1966 *Sports Illustrated* article, affectionately portrayed this

basketball legend as epitomizing "all smoothness, all power. He is one of a kind; were Elgin Baylor an animal, he would be a satin tiger."
BIBLIOGRAPHY: Arthur Ashe, Jr., *A Hard Road to Glory: A History of the African-American Athlete Since 1946*, vol. 3 (New York, 1988); Frank Deford, "A Tiger Who Can Beat Anything," *Sports Illustrated* 25 (October 24, 1966), pp. 40–48; Buddy Martin, "The Final Four and the National Media" in *Rocky Mountain Basketball—Naismith to Nineteen-Ninety* (Denver, CO, 1989); Douglas A. Noverr and Lawrence E. Ziewacz, *The Games They Played: Sports in American History, 1865–1980* (Chicago, IL, 1988); David L. Porter, ed., *Biographical Dictionary of American Sports: Basketball and Other Indoor Sports* (Westport, CT, 1989); Matthew Siegel, assorted materials and press releases, Naismith Memorial Basketball Hall of Fame, Springfield, MA, January 1994.

Scott A.G.M. Crawford

BOB BEAMON
(August 6, 1946–   ) ————————————————— *Track and Field*

In the 1968 Summer Olympic Games at Mexico City, Mexico, Bob Beamon long jumped into athletic immortality with a leap of 29 feet 2½ inches. Bob surpassed the existing world record by nearly 2 feet and remained the global standard bearer for almost 24 years. Robert Beamon was born on August 6, 1946, in Jamaica, New York. Bob's natural father died before his birth, while his mother died of tuberculosis when he was 11 months old. According to Beamon, his mother was so ill that she "hardly ever came near me, and when she did, she covered her face with a handkerchief." Bob was brought up by his stepfather, James Beamon, a "hard-drinking" construction worker, and by his grandmother, Minnie Beamon, the "only person" whom he believed "really cared about him" as a child. Beamon, known as a "troublemaker" throughout elementary and junior high school for fighting, shoplifting, and drug dealing, recalled that people "predicted I would be in prison by the time I was fourteen."

Beamon did not go to prison by age 14 but rather to Public School 622, one of New York City's reform schools for juvenile delinquents. Bob continued to misbehave at the reform school until a teacher used physical force to make him remove a baseball cap in class. "That was the best thing anyone could've done for me," confessed Beamon, because "it really straightened me out." Success in basketball and track and field dramatically changed his life. Bob, who stood 6 feet at age 15, outrebounded and outscored other youngsters his size and age because of his great leaping ability. A year later, he long jumped 24 feet to win the local Junior Olympic title. Beamon wanted to leave the reform school after two years and asked Larry Ellis, the dean of boys and track and field coach at Jamaica High School, if he could transfer there to "better himself." Ellis approved Bob's transfer because he could not "turn his back on him."

At Jamaica High School, Beamon developed into a good basketball player and a track and field superstar. Bob earned a varsity basketball position in 1964 and quickly won acclaim for his rebounding and shot-blocking skills. "Beamon," observed one reporter, "was above the basket as often as he was under it." In 1965, Bob averaged 15 points and 11 rebounds a game and scored over 20 points in an All-Star Game. Between 1964 and 1965, Beamon improved his national ranking in the long jump from tenth to second and his ranking in the triple jump from sixteenth to first. In 1965, he long jumped 25 feet 3½ inches, just 1¼ inches behind the national high school record set that year by Californian John Johnson. On June 12, 1965, Bob exceeded Johnson's standard by 1 inch. An aiding tailwind, however, disqualified the performance from record status. His triple jump of 50 feet 3¾ inches still marked a national high school record. After Beamon finished fourth in the long jump at the Amateur Athletic Union (AAU) championships, Ralph Boston, the national champion, predicted that Bob would "put the world record out of sight" one day.

Beamon, who graduated from Jamaica High School in 1965, earned an athletic scholarship to North Carolina Agricultural and Technical University, a predominantly African-American institution at Greensboro. Despite achieving personal bests of 25 feet 7 inches in the long jump, 55 feet 8 inches in the triple jump, and 9.5 seconds in the 100-yard dash there, Bob transferred to Texas Western University at El Paso in 1967. Wayne Vandenburg had assembled an outstanding cohort of track and field talent there. That year, Beamon captured the AAU indoor championship and established an American record of 26 feet 11½ inches in the long jump. Bob's third place in the 1967 AAU outdoor championships previewed his Silver Medal–winning performance in the long jump at the Pan-American Games. Beamon set indoor world records of 27 feet 1 inch and 27 feet 2¾ inches in winning the 1968 National Association of Intercollegiate Athletics (NAIA) title and 1968 NCAA championship, respectively. At the 1968 NCAA championship, he also won the triple jump title. Asked his secret of success by a *Time* reporter, Bob replied, "There's nothing to it, really. I just jump."

For Beamon, the rest of 1968 was marred by controversy. In April, Bob and seven other Texas Western athletes boycotted a track and field meet against Brigham Young University (BYU) in Provo, Utah, to protest Mormon views "that blacks are inferior to whites and are disciples of the devil." Beamon lost his scholarship because Vandenburg ruled that the boycott participants "voluntarily removed themselves from the team." Although "sympathetic" to a movement among African-American athletes to boycott the 1968 Summer Olympic Games at Mexico City to protest American racism, Bob declined to join because "I had worked very hard for many, many years" to be an Olympian. At the Olympic Games, his years of hard work came together in one remarkable long jump of 29 feet 2½ inches. Upon learning what he had done, Beamon fell to his knees, holding his face in his hands, mumbling, "It's not possible. I can't believe it. Tell me I am not dreaming." Experts

debated the effect of Mexico City's elevation of 7,575 feet on Bob's performance, but U.S. Olympic official Dan Ferris, who had attended every Olympic
Games since 1912, praised it as "the greatest single achievement I've ever
seen."

Beamon, who suffered a hip injury after the 1968 Summer Olympic Games,
never repeated his Olympic feat. His best performance came in the 1969 AAU
championship with a winning long jump of 26 feet 11 inches. Track and field
meet directors, nevertheless, wanted the Olympic champion to appear at their
competitions, even if only to jog around the track and wave at the crowd. Bob
received bitter criticism from the press for "going around the track circuit,
not jumping, just making appearances." In 1972, he retired from track and
field after failing to qualify for the U.S. Olympic Trials. That year Beamon
graduated from Adelphi College in Garden City, New York, earning bachelor
degrees in sociology and physical education. In 1973, Bob toured with the
Professional International Track Association (PITA) and tried out unsuccess-
fully for the San Diego Conquistadors of the American Basketball Association
(ABA). Beamon earned a master's degree in psychology at San Diego State
University and operated a center for ghetto youth. Since 1982, Bob has worked
in the Sports Development Office of the Metro-Dade County Parks and Recreation Department in Miami, Florida. At the 1991 World Championships at
Tokyo, Japan, **Michael Powell** surpassed Beamon's world record with a long
jump of 29 feet 4½ inches. Bob was enshrined in the National Track and
Field Hall of Fame in 1977 and the U.S. Olympic Hall of Fame in 1983.

BIBLIOGRAPHY: Arthur Ashe, Jr., *A Hard Road to Glory: A History of the African-
American Athlete Since 1946*, vol. 3 (New York, 1988); Ira Berkow, "Beamon's Moment
Suspended in Time," *New York Times Biographical Service* 15 (March 1984), pp. 289–
290; Mark Heisler, "Captured by One Moment in Time," *Los Angeles Times*, July 25,
1984, pt. 8, pp. 24, 30; Kenny Moore, "Giants on the Earth," *Sports Illustrated* 66
(June 29, 1987), pp. 48–50; Kenny Moore, "Great Leap Forward," *Sports Illustrated*
75 (September 9, 1991), pp 14–19; Coles Phinizy, "The Unbelievable Moment," *Sports
Illustrated* 29 (December 23, 1968), pp. 53–56; David L. Porter, ed., *Biographical
Dictionary of American Sports: Outdoor Sports* (Westport, CT, 1989); Dick Schaap, *The
Perfect Jump* (New York, 1976); Red Smith, "To Reach the Unreachable Star," *New
York Times*, December 24, 1971, p. 56.

Adam R. Hornbuckle

COOL PAPA BELL
(May 17, 1903–March 7, 1991) ⎯⎯⎯⎯⎯⎯⎯⎯⎯⎯⎯⎯ *Baseball*

James Thomas Bell, nicknamed "Cool Papa" and the fastest baseball player
ever, thrilled audiences with his legendary speed on the base paths of the
Negro League baseball diamond. Cool Papa was born on May 17, 1903, in
Starkville, Mississippi, the grandson of an Oklahoma Indian and son of a
farmer. His mother, Bell later remembered, "always told me that it didn't

make any difference about the color of my skin, or how much money I had. The only thing that counted was to be an honest, clean-living man who cared about other people." Cool Papa played baseball in the fields and sandlots of the area. In 1920, James moved to St. Louis to finish high school and worked in a packing plant. He also began to play organized baseball with the Compton Hill Cubs.

Soon Bell attracted the attention of a scout from the St. Louis Stars, who offered him a contract paying $90 per month. Cool Papa joined the Stars as a left-handed pitcher and brought with him a wide variety of throwing styles and pitches, including the knuckleball, screwball, and curveball. He earned his unique nickname by playing with great poise and keeping his "cool" while performing under pressure in tight ball games. His pitching career was short-lived, however, as an arm injury forced him to move to the outfield in 1924.

Bell was widely known for his base-running abilities. Numerous stories circulated about his legendary speed. Some said Cool Papa could hit a baseball up the middle of the diamond and be called out when the same ball hit him as he was sliding into second base. **Satchel Paige** claimed "he could turn out the light and jump into bed before the room got dark." These colorful embellishments are obvious exaggerations, but other accounts are more accurate. Bell allegedly could circle the bases in an amazing 12 seconds, enabling him to get many extra base hits. Cool Papa could steal two bases on one pitch and once scored from first base on a bunt in a game against major league All-Stars. Oftentimes, a routine infield grounder bouncing only twice would give him enough time to reach first base safely. "If he bunts and it bounces twice, put it in your pocket," said one competitor who had difficulty throwing Bell out. In a game against Kansas City, Cool Papa hit two-hoppers to shortstop **Jackie Robinson**'s right and reached safely. Shortstop was not Robinson's best position. Robinson later became the first modern Negro League ballplayer to play in the major leagues. As an outfielder, Bell used his speed to play a shallow center field and routinely ran down long fly balls with dramatic catches.

Bell played on three of the greatest teams in the history of African-American baseball, including the St. Louis Stars (1930–1931), Pittsburgh Crawfords (1935–1936), and Homestead Grays (1943–1945). A switch-hitter, James demonstrated good bat control and compiled high averages. In fact, Cool Papa retired after 25 years with a lifetime .341 batting average against fellow Negro Leaguers and an amazing .391 mark in exhibition games against major leaguers. In an 85-game season in 1926, he managed a .362 batting average, hit 15 home runs, and stole 23 bases in what may have been his best season. James once stole 175 bases in 200 games. Bell regularly was selected to the East-West All-Star Game from 1933 through 1944. His "team player" attitude made him a favorite with the fans. In addition to appearing in the Negro Leagues, Cool Papa spent a year playing in Santo Domingo with fellow Negro Leaguer Satchel Paige and four years of Summer League ball in Mexico. Bell said "The people [in Santo Domingo] told us if we didn't win the title, we would be executed. Some of our boys got so nervous, they couldn't play. But we won." He also performed 21 Winter League seasons in Cuba, Mexico, and California. Everywhere Bell played, he starred.

In 1947, Cool Papa joined the Detroit Senators as a player-manager. From 1948 to 1950, he served as a player-manager for the Kansas City Stars, a farm club of the Kansas City Monarchs. In 1951, Bell accepted an offer to become a scout for the St. Louis Browns American League (AL) club. He completed his baseball career in 1954 and worked as a custodian and night security officer at the St. Louis City Hall until 1970. In 1974, Bell was inducted into the National Baseball Hall of Fame, where he ranks among the best baseball players ever to play the game. Cool Papa died March 7, 1991, in St. Louis, Missouri.

BIBLIOGRAPHY: *The Afro-American*, 1935–1948; James Bankes, *The Pittsburgh Crawfords* (Dubuque, IA, 1991); *The Baseball Encyclopedia*, 9th ed. (New York, 1993); *The Chicago Defender*, 1923–1931, 1948; John Holway, *Voices from the Great Black Baseball Leagues* (New York, 1975); Robert W. Peterson, *Only the Ball Was White* (Englewood Cliffs, NJ, 1970); *The Pittsburgh Courier*, 1932–1946; James A. Riley, *The All-Time All-Stars of Black Baseball* (Cocoa, FL, 1983); James A. Riley, *The Biographical Encyclopedia of the Negro Baseball Leagues* (New York, 1994); James A. Riley, interviews with former Negro League players, James A. Riley collection, Cocoa, FL; Mike Shatzkin, ed., *The Ballplayers* (New York, 1990), pp. 63–64.

James A. Riley

BARRY BONDS
(July 24, 1964–) _____ *Baseball*

Barry Bonds seemed destined from birth for a major league baseball career as the son of former major league player Bobby Bonds and his wife, Pat Bonds, and the godson of Hall of Fame outfielder **Willie Mays.** Barry Lamar Bonds was born on July 24, 1964, in Riverside, California, and grew up in the comfortable San Francisco suburb of San Carlos. Barry graduated from Serra High School, where he played football, basketball, and baseball. Bonds attended Arizona State University. He played outfield and hit .347 with 45 home runs, 175 RBIs, and 57 stolen bases during a three-year baseball career there. At Arizona State, Barry was named to the All-Pac-10 Conference baseball team for three consecutive years and to *The Sporting News* College Baseball All-America Team in 1985. In June 1985, the Pittsburgh Pirates National League (NL) club signed Barry as their first-round selection in the free agent draft and sixth player taken overall.

After only 115 minor league games, Bonds debuted with Pittsburgh on May 30, 1986. At that time, the Pirates ranked among the worst baseball clubs. The arrival of Bonds and the addition of other talented players, including Andy Van Slyke, Bobby Bonilla, and Doug Drabek, laid the foundation for a baseball renaissance in Pittsburgh. Between 1990 and 1992, the Pirates won three consecutive NL East Division championships.

As left fielder for the Pirates, the six-foot-one-inch, 190-pound, left-handed Bonds led all first-year NL players in home runs (16), RBIs (48), stolen bases (36), and walks (49). Pirate manager Jim Leyland brought Barry along slowly. Bonds blossomed in 1990 when Leyland moved him from leadoff to the fifth spot in the batting order. During 1990, Barry hit .301 with 104 runs scored, 33 home runs, 114 RBIs, and 52 stolen bases. He led the NL in slugging percentage (.565) and was named NL Player of the Month for July, making his first All-Star appearance.

At the end of the 1990 season, numerous awards came. Bonds was selected the NL Most Valuable Player (MVP), while *The Sporting News* named him Major League Player of the Year. *The Sporting News* also designated him its NL Player of the Year in 1991 and 1992. Barry also won the first of four consecutive Rawlings Gold Gloves for his outfield performance. During the 1990 season, he became the first Pirate to ever hit at least 30 home runs and steal 30 or more bases in the same season and only the second major league player to hit at least 30 home runs and steal 50 or more bases in the same season.

His superb play continued for the Pirates during the 1991 and 1992 seasons. In 1991, Bonds drove in 116 runs and finished second in the NL MVP balloting. In 1992, Barry won his second NL MVP award while hitting .311 with 34 home runs and 103 RBIs. He led the NL in runs scored (109), slugging percentage (.624), walks (127), intentional walks (32), and home run ratio (1 every 13.9 at bats).

Despite his spectacular regular-season performances, Bonds performed badly in post-season play. In three NL Championship Series appearances (1990, 1991, 1992), Barry hit a miserable .191 (13 for 68) with only one home run and three RBIs. His failure to produce virtually destroyed the Pirates' chances of advancing to the World Series. Nevertheless, teammate Andy Van Slyke called Bonds "the greatest player I ever played with or will ever play with."

At the end of the 1992 season, Bonds became a free agent. On December 8, 1992, the San Francisco Giants (NL) signed Barry for $43.75 million over six years. The size of his contract startled fans. Few imagined anyone being paid such a princely sum to play a game. Bonds considered baseball pure and simple entertainment and deemed himself entitled to compensation equal to that of any star entertainer. In regard to his salary, Bonds said, "I'm worth it."

Bond's contract also illustrated that underfunded major league baseball teams playing in small markets, such as the Pirates, could not compete successfully for first-rate talent. Pittsburgh desperately wanted to retain Barry but could not match San Francisco's offer without risking bankruptcy. Not all the Pirate players, however, were unhappy to see Bonds leave. His arrogance, moodiness, and selfishness prompted one anonymous teammate to say, "I'd rather lose without Barry Bonds than win with him."

Others have criticized Barry's surliness and rudeness, citing his less-than-cordial relations with the media. At times, Bonds seems intent on aggravating the situation with the media. "I thrive off you guys [the media] because I love to make you come back to my locker begging." Perhaps his father, Bobby, summed it up best when he affirmed, "Barry just wants to play baseball. He's not pushing ballots for popularity."

Unquestionably, Bonds can play baseball. Barry sparked San Francisco in 1993 to 103 victories, the most for a Giant team since 1962. Although San Francisco finished one game behind the Atlanta Braves in the NL West, he enjoyed his best year. Barry led the NL with 46 home runs, 123 RBIs, and a .667 slugging percentage, hitting .336 with 181 hits and 129 runs scored. These all marked career highs. For his efforts, Barry won his third NL MVP award, joining Stan Musial, **Roy Campanella,** Mike Schmidt, Jimmie Foxx, Joe DiMaggio, Yogi Berra, and Mickey Mantle as the only other three-time MVP holders. No player has won four MVP awards, but Bonds aspires to that goal. The Associated Press (AP) voted Barry the 1993 Player of the Year, making him the first player to win that award in consecutive seasons.

In the strike-shortened 1994 campaign, Bonds led the NL in walks (74), ranked third in runs scored (89), home runs (37), and slugging percentage (.647), finished fifth in total bases (253) and on-base percentage (.426), and placed sixth in stolen bases (29). He placed fourth in the 1994 MVP balloting and won a fifth consecutive Gold Glove Award. During nine seasons through 1994, Barry has batted .285 with 1,287 hits, 276 doubles, 259 home runs, 760 RBIs, a .537 slugging percentage, and 309 stolen bases. In 1995, Bonds was selected to play in the All-Star Game.

Bonds is separated from his wife Sun, a native of Sweden. Barry has two children, Nikolai and Shikari, and resides in Murietta, California.

BIBLIOGRAPHY: *The Baseball Encyclopedia*, 9th ed. (New York, 1993), p. 681; Richard Hoffer, "The Importance of Being Barry," *Sports Illustrated* 78 (May 24, 1993), pp. 13–21; Walter Leavy, "Barry Bonds: Baseball's $60 Million Man," *Ebony* 48 (September 1993), pp. 118–122; *Pittsburgh Pirates 1991 Record and Information Guide*, pp. 29–31; "Playboy Interview," *Playboy* 40 (July 1993), pp. 59–72, 148; "The Rising Stock of Bonds," *Newsweek* 122 (May 31, 1993), p. 90; *San Francisco Giants 1993 Record and Information Guide*, pp. 52–53; Bruce Schoenfeld, "Unfinished Business," *Sport* 85 (April 1994), pp. 81–84.

Frank W. Thackeray

RALPH BOSTON
(May 9, 1939–   ) —————————————————————— *Track and Field*

Ralph Boston dominated long jump competition in the 1960s. Ralph Harold Boston was born on May 9, 1939, in Laurel, Mississippi, the tenth child of a poor family. His mother, Eulalia, who claimed that Ralph "was always the quiet fellow," worked as a housemaid. Boston, an all-around track and field performer at Laurel High School, won eight events at one high school track and field meet. Ralph long jumped 20 feet 10 inches as a 15-year-old and improved his personal distance by nearly a foot a year. He admired world record holder **Jesse Owens,** who had "showed Hitler and everybody else that we Negroes were as good as the next fellow."

In 1962, Ralph graduated from Tennessee State University, a school better known for its female track and field athletes, with a bachelor's degree in biochemistry. The versatile 6-foot-1½-inch 166-pounder with slim legs earned six first places in one quadrangular college meet and five blue ribbons at the National Association of Intercollegiate Athletics (NAIA) championships in June 1961. His performances included a 9.7-second 100-yard dash, 6-foot-9-inch high jump, 13.7-second 120-yard high hurdle, 13-foot-6-inch pole vault, 200-foot javelin throw, and 125-foot discus throw.

The long jump marked Boston's specialty. After finishing third at the 1959 NCAA meet, Ralph captured the crown in 1960. The Amateur Athletic Union (AAU) meet saw him finish fourth in 1959 and an uncharacteristic sixth the next year. The 1959 Pan-American Games Trials marked the turning point of Boston's career. Although leaping a personal best 25 feet 3 inches, Ralph barely missed the American team. "It was," he recalled, "one of my biggest disappointments." He started training seriously for the first time. At the 1960 Olympic Trials, Boston won the long jump and made the U.S. Olympic team. At Walnut, California, on August 12, Ralph jumped 26 feet 11¼ inches to break Jesse Owens's 25-year-old world record by 3 inches.

The world mark made Boston a favorite for the title at the 1960 Rome, Italy, Summer Olympics. Ralph leaped over 26 feet in his first two jumps but landed short of Owens's record. Before his third jump, a friend placed a piece of paper in the pit at an even 27 feet and urged Boston to stretch his leap over that distance. Ralph jumped 26 feet 7¾ inches, edging U.S. teammate Irvin "Bo" Roberson for the Gold Medal and breaking Owens's Olympic record. He held mixed feelings about breaking Jesse's record. "After all you've done for Negroes," Boston had told Owens the night before, "it just wouldn't be right."

In 1961, Boston won his first U.S. AAU long jump title. At the California Relays at Modesto on May 27, 1961, Ralph became the first long jumper to surpass the 27-foot barrier. His jump covered 27 feet ½ inch. Two months later, he won the USA-USSR Dual Meet with a leap of 27 feet 1½ inches in Moscow, Russia.

Upon arriving in Houston, Texas, to compete in the "Meet of Champions" in June 1961, Boston discovered that the crowd would be segregated. The NAACP persuaded Ralph and 19 other African-American athletes to withdraw from the meet. "I still feel that I did the right thing in withdrawing," he declared.

Boston, rated by *Track and Field News* as the world's best long jumper from 1960 through 1967, captured the AAU title every year from 1961 through

1966. Ralph excelled at other events, placing fourth in the high jump at the 1963 Pan-American Games and sixth in the triple jump at the 1963 AAU meet. He finished 1961 undefeated in the high hurdles and won that event at the 1965 AAU indoor meet.

Boston and Igor Ter-Ovanesyan of the Soviet Union, who also set several world standards, battled for long jump supremacy by 1964. Ralph was favored to retain his long jump crown at 1964 Tokyo, Japan, Summer Olympics and set two more world long jump records earlier that year, leaping 27 feet 4½ inches in winning the Olympic Trials. He actually jumped 27 feet 10¼ inches, but that mark was disallowed because of an excessive following wind. At the 1964 Summer Olympics, however, Lynn Davies of Great Britain upset both Boston and Ter-Ovanesyan for the Gold Medal. Ralph earned the Silver Medal, while Ter-Ovanesyan placed third.

Boston set his last world record in 1965 with a 27-foot-4¾-inch leap at the California Relays in Modesto. Until suffering a knee injury in 1967, Ralph had won 128 of 140 long jump competitions and set six world standards. Nine of his 12 losses had been by 3½ inches or less. **Bob Beamon** defeated Boston at the 1968 Olympic Trials and stunned the world with a 29-foot-2½-inch jump at the 1968 Mexico City, Mexico, Summer Olympic Games, shattering the previous world record by almost 2 feet. Beamon still thought Boston could win the Gold Medal, but Boston replied, "No, no. It's over for me. I can't jump that far." Ralph finished third, ending his Olympic career with a complete set of medals.

Boston retired from competition in 1969 and joined a national television network as track and field analyst. In 1972, Ralph's attempt to make a fourth U.S. Olympic team failed. Boston, who works as a research biochemist and administrator at Tennessee State University, was elected to the National Track and Field Hall of Fame in 1974 and the U.S. Olympic Hall of Fame in 1985.
BIBLIOGRAPHY: Fred Katz, "Record Breaker," *Sport* 33 (February 1962), pp. 38–39; *The Lincoln Library of Sports Champions*, vol. 2 (Columbus, OH, 1975), pp. 108–112; Bill Mallon and Ian Buchanan, *Quest for Gold: The Encyclopedia of American Olympians* (New York, 1983); James A. Page, *Black Olympian Medalists* (Englewood, CO, 1991); David Wallechinsky, *The Complete Book of the Olympics*, 3rd ed. (London, England, 1991).

Bill Mallon and David L. Porter

VALERIE BRISCO
(July 6, 1960–) ————————————————— *Track and Field*

In the 1984 Summer Olympic Games at Los Angeles, California, Valerie Brisco became the first athlete, male or female, to capture Gold Medals in both the 200 and 400 meters in the same Olympic Games. Valerie Ann Brisco, the sixth of 10 children of Arguster Brisco and Guitherea Brisco, was born on

July 6, 1960, in Greenwood, Mississippi. The Briscos moved to Los Angeles, California, when Valerie was five years old. Valerie realized she possessed extraordinary running ability when she outran "the fastest girl on the track team" during a physical education class at Locke High School in the Watts section of Los Angeles. After that performance, she recalled, "The track coach automatically put me on the team." Brisco's older brother, Robert, who starred in athletics at Locke High School and encouraged her to develop her athletic gift, died from gunfire while running on the Locke track in 1974. Valerie often looked back to that tragic event for motivation, drawing strength "from her deep well of feeling for him."

At Locke High School, Brisco developed into the nation's leading prep sprinter. As a senior in 1978, Valerie clocked 10.5 seconds for 100 yards, 11.57 seconds for 100 meters, and 23.77 seconds for 200 meters. Each clocking ranked as the nation's fastest time that year. Her 53.70-second clocking for 400 meters ranked as the nation's second fastest time. Brisco, who graduated from Locke High School in 1978, acknowledged that she "wasn't interested in going to college" until Robert Kersee, the track and field coach at California State University at Northridge, offered her a scholarship. In 1979, her times dropped in the 200 meters to 23.16 seconds and in the 400 meters to 52.08 seconds. The same year, Valerie also captured the 200-meter title in the Association of Intercollegiate Athletics for Women (AIAW) championship, placed second in the Amateur Athletic Union (AAU) championship, and fourth in the Pan-American Games. At the Pan-American Games, she also garnered a Gold Medal on the triumphant 4 × 100-meter relay team. *Track and Field News* described Brisco, who ranked tenth in the world in the 200 meters in 1979, as "new blood seeping into the event."

Valerie's world-class success ended almost as quickly as it began. After an injury-plagued 1980 season, she married Alvin Hooks in 1981, a former California State track and football standout who played wide receiver for the Philadelphia Eagles National Football League (NFL) club. Brisco briefly competed in 1981 for Long Beach City College but then retired from track and field and moved to Philadelphia, Pennsylvania. In 1982, Valerie gave birth to a son, Alvin, Jr. By 1983, however, she wanted to return to athletic competition. Valerie admitted, "I'd go crazy if I had to stay home as a housewife." Brisco embarked on "stringent dieting and a daily routine that involved running in place in the bathroom, with the shower steaming," to shed 40 extra pounds that she had gained during her pregnancy. The Hooks had returned to Los Angeles, where Alvin had joined the Los Angeles Express of the newly formed United States Football League (USFL). The Express soon released Alvin because of a serious knee injury sustained while playing for the Eagles. Unable to play football, Alvin became Valerie's manager and told her to "do what you have to do" to be a world-class runner once again.

Brisco also found support and guidance from Robert Kersee, who now coached track and field at the University of California at Los Angeles (UCLA) and at his World Class Track Club. By following Kersee's prescription of "Spartan training and selective competition," she peaked for the 1984 Los Angeles Summer Olympic Games. A week before the Olympic Trials, Valerie captured the 400-meter crown in the Track Athletic Congress (TAC) championships and clocked 49.83 seconds to become the first American woman under 50 seconds. At the Olympic Trials, Brisco won the 200 meters and finished second to Chandra Cheeseborough in the 400 meters. Cheeseborough reclaimed the American 400-meter record in 49.28 seconds. Valerie, unchallenged in the Olympic Games, captured both the 200 and 400 meters in American and Olympic standards of 21.81 seconds and 48.83 seconds, respectively. She also garnered a third Gold Medal in the 4 × 400-meter relay, in which the United States established American and Olympic records of 3 minutes 18.29 seconds. Brisco became the first woman to win three Gold Medals in track and field since **Wilma Rudolph** in 1960. She wept upon watching a video of her Olympic performance, telling herself, "I really won. This is what I really did."

Despite her Olympic achievement, *Track and Field News* ranked Brisco fourth in the world in both the 200 and 400 meters. Ranked ahead of her were three East German athletes who did not compete in the 1984 Summer Olympic Games and supported the boycott led by the Soviet Union. "Had the East Germans been in the Olympics," she confessed, "the results might have been different." Valerie, however, defeated her German rivals in 1985 and also established indoor world records of 52.99 seconds for 400 meters and 1 minute 02.3 seconds for 500 meters. In 1986, she concentrated on the 100 meters and clocked 10.99 seconds, then the third fastest American time. Brisco competed on U.S. 4 × 400-meter relay teams, capturing the Gold Medal in the 1987 Pan-American Games at Indianapolis, Indiana, and a Bronze Medal in the 1987 World Championships at Rome, Italy. In a display of unparalleled generosity at the Pan-American Games, Valerie gave her Gold Medal to a deaf youngster with whom she had posed for a photograph after the race. "It's not that the medal didn't mean anything to me," she said. "I am sure it meant more to him." Valerie, who had divorced her husband in 1987, placed fourth in the 400 meters and earned a Silver Medal in the 4 × 400-meter relay in the 1988 Summer Olympic Games at Seoul, South Korea. Her 48.5-second relay leg contributed to an American 4 × 400-meter record of 3 minutes 15.51 seconds.

BIBLIOGRAPHY: Peter Alfano, "3 Golds Change Little in Brisco-Hooks' Life," *New York Times Biographical Service* 16 (January 1985), pp. 102–103; Tony Castro, "After the Glitter, Some Gold," *Sports Illustrated* 62 (June 3, 1985), pp. 44–50; Aldore Collier, "Valerie Brisco-Hooks: Olympic Medal Winner," *Ebony* 40 (November 1984), pp. 172–174; Michael D. Davis, *Black American Women in Olympic Track and Field: A Complete Illustrated Reference* (Jefferson, NC, 1992); Michelle Kort, "Catch a Rising Star," *Women's Sports & Fitness* 6 (November 1984), pp. 46–48; Michelle Kort, "The Gift of Power," *Women's Sports & Fitness* 9 (November 1987), pp. 40–43; David L. Porter, ed., *Biographical Dictionary of American Sports: Outdoor Sports* (Westport, CT, 1988); David Wallechinsky, *The Complete Book of the Olympic Games*, 2nd rev. ed. (New York, 1988).

Adam R. Hornbuckle

LOU BROCK
(June 18, 1939–) ——————————————————————————— *Baseball*

Lou Brock ranks among the greatest base stealers in baseball history. Louis Clark Brock was born in El Dorado, Arkansas, on June 18, 1939, the seventh of nine children of Maud Brock and Paralee Brock. After separating from Maud, Paralee Brock moved her family to Colliston, Louisiana, and did farm work and cleaning. The Brock children attended an all-African-American grade school in Mer Rouge, Louisiana. Lou recalled, "As a kid they bused us for miles way out of town, past a dozen white schools, to the black school."

A junior high teacher caught Brock throwing spitballs and assigned him to research baseball stars **Jackie Robinson,** Stan Musial, Don Newcombe, and Joe DiMaggio. Lou discovered their baseball success meant salaries he never dreamed possible. Little did he know that 12 years later he would succeed National Baseball Hall of Famer Musial in the St. Louis Cardinals' (NL) outfield.

At Union High School in Mer Rouge, Brock poured his energy into basketball and baseball. For three winters, Lou played guard and forward on the Union basketball team. He performed in the outfield and pitched for four years on the baseball squad, batting .536 his senior year. Lou applied for scholarships at southern colleges but discovered that integrated schools offered few scholarships for African Americans and African-American colleges possessed little scholarship money at all. Southern University, an all-African-American college in Baton Rouge, Louisiana, offered Brock a work-study job as janitor and groundskeeper for the fall semester in 1958. With determination and constant study, Lou earned a scholarship his sophomore year. He batted over .500 as a sophomore, earning All-Southwestern Athletic Conference (SAC) honors. Southern won the National Association of Intercollegiate Athletics (NAIA) championship Brock's junior year. Lou, who played in the Pan-American Games in Chicago, Illinois, in 1959, married Katie Hay in December 1960. They had two children, Wanda and Louis, Jr.

The Chicago Cubs National League (NL) club gave Brock a $30,000 signing bonus in 1961 and assigned the outfielder to St. Cloud, Minnesota, where he won the Northern League batting title with a .361 average, led the league with 117 runs scored, 181 hits, and 33 doubles, and also swiped 38 bases. Lou also played 4 games for the Chicago Cubs in 1961 and started at right field in 1962, batting .263 in 123 games. The next season, Brock batted .258 with just 37 RBIs. By mid-June 1964, he had driven in only 14 runs and led NL outfielders with 14 errors. Chicago dealt Lou to St. Louis (NL) on June 15, 1964, for Ernie Broglio, a popular hurler who had won 21 and 18 games for the Cardinals. Broglio triumphed in just 7 more major league games.

Cardinal manager Johnny Keane planted Brock permanently in left field. Lou thought that "power-hitting was where the money was" but began realizing that he would not make it as a power-hitter. But he hit the ball hard and ran very well. After arriving at Busch Stadium in St. Louis, Brock exploded the rest of the season by batting .348 and stealing 33 bases. Lou ignited the Cardinals to their first NL pennant since 1946. He batted .300 in the 1964 World Series, helping St. Louis defeat the New York Yankees in seven games.

From 1964 to 1974, Brock pounded out more than 180 hits each season, scored over 100 runs seven times, and batted over .300 eight times. His batting average fell below .285 only three times from 1964 to 1979. Despite batting at the top of the order throughout his career, Lou drove in 900 runs. For 12 consecutive seasons, he stole more than 50 bases. Brock's base-path exploits forced hurlers to change the way they pitched and infielders to alter their positions when he was on base. Opponents expected Lou to run with two outs in the eighth inning and the scored tied as much as in the first inning. He usually started with a short leadoff to lull the pitcher into a false sense of security. Then Lou tried to get a walking start. "The mind game, that was the beauty of it," recalled Brock. With head down, he zoomed to the next base and used a hard, pop-up slide. Lou considered reading pitchers the crucial element to successful base theft. "I had a decided advantage over the pitcher," he said, "because I can change my stealing technique, but a pitcher's motion is mechanical and set." Fans poured into Busch Stadium to watch Brock work his magic on the bases. Red Schoendienst, his manager for 12 seasons, commented, "Lou Brock is just the most exciting player in baseball."

Four other periods highlight Brock's illustrious career. In 1967, Lou slammed a career-high 21 home runs and batted .414 in the World Series to help the Cardinals defeat the Boston Red Sox in 7 games. He set a World Series record with 7 stolen bases. Second, in 1968, Brock led the NL with 46 doubles and 14 triples. Lou batted .464 in the World Series against the Detroit Tigers and again stole 7 bases. The Cardinals, however, succumbed to the Tigers in 7 games. Next, in 1974, he pilfered 40 bases in the first third of the Redbird schedule when the idea emerged that he might break Maury Wills's all-time record of 104. The 35-year-old Brock had registered 66 thefts by August 1, making Wills's record look secure. The final 56 Cardinal games, however, saw Lou steal an incredible 52 bases to finish with 118 thefts, still the NL record. Finally, in 1977, he surpassed Ty Cobb's major league record 892 career steals. Brock's batting average, though, dipped to .272, his lowest mark in 14 years. In 1978, Lou plummeted to a career-low .221 batting average. Sportswriters and fans began sounding the death knell on his career. Just 100 hits shy of the coveted 3,000 plateau, Brock returned in 1979. Now

40 years old, Lou compiled a .304 batting average, swiped his last 21 bases, and was named *The Sporting News* Comeback Player of the Year.

Brock's major league career included 2,616 games, 3,023 hits, 486 doubles, 141 triples, 149 home runs, and 1,610 runs scored. Lou stole 938 bases, the NL record. He played in 2,507 games in the outfield, fifth highest in major league history. The National Baseball Hall of Fame enshrined Brock in 1985, his first year of eligibility.

Lou did not want money or fame to be the goal of his life. In 1965, he started raising money for the Tandy Boys Club of St. Louis, later renamed the Lou Brock Boys Club. Lou chaired fund drives for various charitable organizations in St. Louis. The St. Louis Sports Collectors have held an annual show since 1979 to raise funds for the Lou Brock Scholarship Fund, which provides four-year college scholarships for St. Louis–area students. In 1975, St. Louis fans voted Lou the "Most Memorable Personality." Brock's numerous civic honors include the St. Louis Award for Distinguished Service to the Community, St. Louis Jaycees' Man of the Year Award, the B'nai B'rith Brotherhood Award, and the Roberto Clemente Award for service. Lou, who lives in St. Louis, works in retail and wholesale soft goods through his Broc-World Products International and remains one of the most beloved personalities in the Gateway City. In October 1994, he rejoined the St. Louis Cardinals as a coach.

BIBLIOGRAPHY: Lou Brock and Franz Schulze, *Stealing Is My Game* (Englewood Cliffs, NJ, 1976); Bob Broeg, *Redbirds: A Century of Cardinal Baseball* (St. Louis, MO, 1981); David Craft and Tom Owens, *Redbirds Revisited* (Chicago, IL, 1990); Bob Fortus, "Success Story: Lou Brock's Climb to the Hall of Fame," *Baseball Digest* 44 (November 1985), pp. 39–44; Bill Gutman, *Carew, Garvey, Munson, Brock* (New York, 1978).

Frank J. Olmsted

JIM BROWN
(February 17, 1936–   ) _____ *Football*

In the three decades since Jim Brown retired from pro football to pursue a movie career, others have surpassed most of his rushing records. Many had considered Brown's records unbreakable at one time. A longer season and rule changes that opened up defenses have helped younger runners produce numbers comparable to Jim's marks. Nevertheless, most people who saw Brown in action still regard him the greatest running back in football history. James Nathaniel Brown was born on St. Simons Island, Georgia, on February 17, 1936, the son of Swinton Brown and Theresa Brown. His gambler father soon deserted the family. When Jim was only two years old, his mother moved north to find work. Young Jim was brought up by his grandmother and aunt until he was eight years old. When his mother found a dependable position as a domestic in Manhasset, New York, she sent for him.

At Manhasset High School, Brown proved popular and a class leader. Jim's athletic skills made him a local celebrity. He starred in every sport he tried, winning 13 varsity letters. Brown averaged 18 points a game in basketball and set the Long Island scoring record, later broken by Art Heyman. The New York Yankees American League (AL) club offered Jim a minor league baseball contract. But football remained his first love, as he averaged 14.9 yards per carry and received 45 scholarship offers. Syracuse University, however, did not make Brown an offer. Several Syracuse alumni in Manhasset wanted to see Jim in the football uniform of the Orangemen. Without his knowledge, they raised the money for his first year in school. Brown entered Syracuse in 1953 under the impression that he had received a scholarship from the school. Jim was housed away from the other players, and the coaches treated him as a "walk-on," causing him to become confused. Additionally, as the only African American on the team, he found himself lumped in his teammates' minds with an African-American player of a few years before who had earned a reputation for selfish play. Brown contemplated quitting school but was dissuaded by one of the men who had arranged for him to go to Syracuse. Eventually, Jim surmounted his problems and performed well enough on the freshman football team to receive a complete scholarship from Syracuse as a sophomore. He only learned the details of his "Manhasset scholarship" after he graduated.

Brown continued to excel in several sports at Syracuse. Jim averaged 13.1 points per game in basketball and placed fifth in the national decathlon championship in track and field. He was named All-America in lacrosse and later was elected to the National Lacrosse Hall of Fame. Football, however, put Brown in the national spotlight. As a senior in 1956, Jim scored 43 points against Colgate University to set a collegiate record that stood for 35 years. He finished the Orangemen's eight-game regular season with 106 points and was named a unanimous All-America. Syracuse was chosen to play powerful Texas Christian University in the Cotton Bowl. Although the Texans won, Jim rushed for 132 yards and scored 21 points.

The Cleveland Browns National Football League (NFL) club drafted Brown in the first round in 1957, when the quarterback they preferred was selected by another team. After playing in the College All-Star Game, Jim joined the Browns and was immediately installed as the starting fullback. He led the NFL in rushing as a rookie with 942 yards. One game saw him set a new single-game mark of 237 yards. Brown's performance helped Cleveland win the Eastern Division championship. In 1958, Jim set an NFL rushing record with 1,527 yards in a 12-game season.

At six foot two inches and 232 pounds, Brown combined the power and determination of a great fullback with the speed and elusiveness of a breakaway halfback. No runner, before or since, has so perfectly combined all these qualities. Coach George Allen recalled, "He was a very big, very fast guy who combined size and speed, strength and speed, power and elusiveness better than any other runner pro football has ever had." Jim led the NFL in rushing in each of his first five seasons, surpassing 1,200 yards every year after his rookie outing. His streak finally ended with 996 yards in 1962, when an injured wrist made it impossible for him to use his famous stiff-arm. Although his personal honors piled up, Brown's team was unable to climb back to the top. Jim disliked playing in Cleveland Coach Paul Brown's restrictive system, which he felt kept him from using all his talents. In 1963, Coach Brown was replaced by Blanton Collier. Collier introduced an elective blocking system that let the runner decide which hole to run to and which way to cut. Brown responded with 1,863 yards, making him the first NFL player to rush over a mile in a season. After coming close in their first season under Collier, Cleveland won the NFL championship in 1964 with a 27–0 victory over the Baltimore Colts. The Browns repeated their Eastern Division title in 1965 but lost to the Green Bay Packers in the championship game.

Brown was featured in the movie *Rio Conchos* in 1964. A commitment to make the movie *The Dirty Dozen* kept Jim from reporting to the Browns in 1966 and forced his retirement. His films during the following years included *Ice Station Zebra, 100 Rifles, Tick ... Tick ... Tick, The Split,* and *Three the Hard Way.* Additionally, Brown promoted African-American economic causes, participated in prison reform, and counseled Los Angeles street gang members. Known for his straight-from-the-shoulder, often blunt way of talking, Jim has authored two autobiographies.

When Brown retired from football, he held NFL rushing records for career, season, and game yardage and the career mark for touchdowns. Jim's career rushing totals included 2,359 attempts for 12,312 yards for a 5.2-yard average (still the record for any runner with 750 or more attempts) and 106 touchdowns. His 126 career touchdown record was finally broken by **Jerry Rice** of the San Francisco 49ers in 1994. Brown led the NFL in rushing in eight of his nine seasons, in touchdowns three times, and in scoring once. An extremely durable player, Jim never missed a game because of injury despite being the target of every opposition defense. George Allen recalled, "He was very difficult to stop, especially when he got up a head of steam. He was so big and strong, had such powerful legs and good balance that he broke more tackles than any player who ever played." He was selected to nine straight Pro Bowls, twice was named Player of the Game, and made First-Team, All-NFL selection every season except 1962. United Press International (UPI) chose him Player of the Year in 1958, 1963, and 1965. In 1971, he was elected to the Pro Football Hall of Fame.

BIBLIOGRAPHY: George Allen with Ben Olan, *Pro Football's 100 Greatest Players* (Indianapolis, IN, 1982); Jim Brown with Myron Cope, *Off My Chest* (New York, 1964); Jim Brown with Steve Delsohn, *Out of Bounds* (New York, 1989); Jack Clary, *Pro Football's Great Moments* (New York, 1981); *The Official National Football League 1994 Record and Fact Book* (New York, 1994); David L. Porter, ed., *Biographical Dictionary of American Sports: Football* (New York, 1987); Beau Riffenburgh, *The Official NFL Encyclopedia,* 4th ed. (New York, 1986).

Robert N. "Bob" Carroll

LEE CALHOUN
(February 23, 1933–June 21, 1989) ————————————— *Track and Field*

Lee Calhoun became the first Olympian to win successive victories in the 110-meter hurdles. In the 1956 Melbourne, Australia, Summer Olympic Games, Lee ran a personal best of 13.5 seconds. Four years later at the Rome, Italy, Summer Olympic Games, he lowered that mark to 13.4 seconds. In 1956, Calhoun triumphed in the indoor 110-meter hurdles at the AAU and captured the 110-meter hurdles outdoor at the National Association of Inter-collegiate Athletics (NAIA), NCAA, and Amateur Athletic Union (AAU) meets. Lee repeated these victories the following year. After losing his amateur standing in 1958, he was reinstated in 1959 and won his third 110-meter hurdles title at the AAU outdoor championship and the Gold Medal at the Pan-American Games.

Lee Quency Calhoun was born on February 23, 1933, and grew up on a farm about eight miles from Laurel, Mississippi, the hometown of Metropolitan Opera star Leontyne Price and fellow Olympic Gold Medalist **Ralph Boston**. Lee's father had 14 children with his first two wives, but Lee was the only child of wife number three.

When Calhoun was nine years old, his parents moved north to Gary, Indiana. Athletics did not enter Lee's life until eleventh grade, when Bo Mallard, the track and field coach at Roosevelt High School, "persuaded" him to become a high jumper. As Calhoun recalled, "Most of the coaches in those days stood around the hallways or by the gym door, slapping the side of their legs with a paddle, which we called 'the persuader.' Bo called me over and said, 'We need a high-jumper this year.' I told him that I'd give it some thought. He kept tapping his leg with that paddle, and it didn't take me long to make up my mind because I knew that if I didn't go out for the team, my next two years in physical education were going to be real physical. After all, I figured there couldn't be much more to high jumping than seven steps and a leap."

During his senior year, Calhoun began to run the hurdles with lackluster results. At the 1951 State championship, Lee hit the first five hurdles and finished fifth. He, nevertheless, attracted the attention of Dr. Leroy Walker, who offered him a track and field scholarship to North Carolina Central University. In 1976, Walker, later president of the United States Olympic Committee, coached the U.S. Olympic track and field team and designated Calhoun as his assistant.

After spending two years at North Carolina Central and participating on two conference championship track and field squads, Calhoun was drafted into the U.S. Army in 1953. Lee served in Korea and coached the 8th Army Track Team to a victory over the Japanese National Team at the same site as the eventual 1964 Tokyo, Japan, Summer Olympic Games.

Lee returned to North Carolina Central University in 1955 and that winter dominated the indoor circuit, setting world bests in the 60-yard, 70-yard, and 80-yard hurdles. Calhoun's fast start made him unbeatable in the short, indoor distances, as he eventually set world records in the 45-yard, 50-yard, 60-yard, and 70-yard hurdles. In the spring of 1956, Lee also greatly improved his 110-meter times and ran a dead heat against Jack Davis in the Olympic Trials. Since the 1956 Melbourne, Australia, Summer Olympic Games were held in November and December and because he already had missed two years of school while in the service, he initially expressed a reluctance about participating. As no Olympian ever had represented North Carolina Central before, the president of the school insisted that Calhoun travel to the Melbourne Games.

In 1958, Dan Ferris of the AAU informed Lee that he would be banned for life from amateur competition if he married on the television program "Bride and Groom." The contestants were chosen on the basis of their love stories. The story of Lee's fiancée had been selected, but Ferris insisted Calhoun could not go on television and accept any gifts. When NBC threatened to sue and certain Olympic fund-raisers intervened, Ferris lifted the ban after one year. Two decades later, Lee met Ferris and introduced his wife. "Oh, by the way, Dan," he said, "I want you to meet my wife. We're still together, although twenty years ago you suspended me for marrying her."

In 1960, Calhoun set a world record of 13.2 seconds in a pre-Olympic meet in Bern, Switzerland, and then edged teammate Willie May by .01 of a second at the Rome, Italy, Summer Olympic Games. Lee eventually lost his world records but did not believe his successors were necessarily better hurdlers. Lee stressed, "The hurdling form today is not as good as in my day. We didn't hit hurdles. The hurdles are lighter today, the tracks are faster, and the athletes are bigger and stronger. They just run through the hurdles as if they are not even there. They don't care if they knock all ten of them down. When we used to hit one of those iron monsters, we were stopped in our tracks."

After graduating from North Carolina Central University, Calhoun coached track and field at Grambling College. Lee became an assistant coach at Yale University in 1970 and head coach in 1975. After a disagreement with the athletic director, he left Yale in 1980 to take a similar position at Western Illinois University. Calhoun was elected a charter member of the National Track and Field Hall of Fame in 1974 and the U.S. Olympic Hall of Fame in 1991. On June 21, 1989, 56-year-old Calhoun died in Erie, Pennsylvania, of complications resulting from a stroke.

BIBLIOGRAPHY: Lewis H. Carlson and John J. Fogarty, *Tales of Gold: An Oral History of the Summer Olympic Games Told by America's Gold Medal Winners* (Chicago, IL, 1987); Bill Mallon and Ian Buchanan, *Quest for Gold: The Encyclopedia of Amer-*

ican Olympians (New York, 1984); David L. Porter, ed., *Biographical Dictionary of American Sports: Outdoor Sports* (Westport, CT, 1988).

Lewis H. Carlson

ROY CAMPANELLA
(November 19, 1921–June 26, 1993) ————————————— *Baseball*

In 1947, **Jackie Robinson** broke the unwritten color barrier that had separated African-American from white players since the late nineteenth century. Roy Campanella followed right behind Robinson in showing how talented African-American baseball players were. He was born on November 19, 1921, in Philadelphia, Pennsylvania, of an African-American mother, Ida (Mercer), Campanella, and a Sicilian father, John Campanella, who sold vegetables for a living. Roy lived in Nicetown, a working-class neighborhood, and attended Gillespie Junior High School. He started his professional career by playing for the Bacharach Giants on weekends in New York, New Jersey, Connecticut, and Pennsylvania. A solidly built young man behind the plate, Campanella then played for the Baltimore Elite Giants in the Negro National League and performed in the Mexican and Winter Leagues. Roy quickly established his reputation as that of a workhorse behind the plate, catching four games in a single day. He likewise ignored the nagging injuries often associated with catching. "You didn't get hurt in the Negro Leagues," Campanella later explained. "You played no matter what happened to you because if you didn't play, you didn't get paid." Roy attracted a big following among both African American and whites. His high-pitched, enthusiastic voice often brought smiles and laughter to his teammates' faces.

At five foot nine inches and 205 pounds, the right-handed Campanella proved a solid, immovable presence behind home plate. In 1937 at age 15, Roy caught for the Baltimore Elite Giants on weekends to spell veteran backstop Biz Mackey. He soon challenged legendary **Josh Gibson** as the premier African-American catcher, appearing in the 1941, 1944, and 1945 Black All-Star Games.

Campanella's break came when he caught in a five-game exhibition series against a team of white players, managed by Charlie Dressen. Dressen, the right arm of Dodger manager Leo Durocher, recommended Roy to president Branch Rickey of the Brooklyn Dodgers National League (NL) club in October 1945. The Dodgers sent Campanella to their farm club in Nashua, New Hampshire, where he roomed with outstanding fireballer Don Newcombe. Roy hit .290 and led the New England League in catching, being voted the Most Valuable Player (MVP) award.

In 1947, Campanella played for the Dodgers' top farm club at Montreal, Canada, earning the International League's MVP honors. Buffalo manager Paul Richards called Roy the best catcher in either the major or minor leagues.

Although Campanella was ready for the majors, Rickey asked him to play for St. Paul, Minnesota, of the American Association and break the color barrier there. Roy enjoyed a great beginning there and was recalled to Brooklyn, where he starred behind the plate for the next nine seasons.

Campanella uniform #39 proved a mainstay of those great Brooklyn teams from 1948 through 1957 and, along with Robinson, Pee Wee Reese, Duke Snider, and Carl Erskine, a subject of Roger Kahn's 1972 classic book *The Boys of Summer*. The Dodgers opposed the New York Yankees in the 1949, 1952, 1953, 1955, and 1956 World Series and lost all of these post-season contests except 1955, when they defeated the Bronx Bombers in seven games. Campanella made many great contributions to these Dodgers teams and won the MVP award three times, including 1951, 1953, and 1955. Roy's best season came in 1953, when he hit .312 and scored 103 runs. His 142 RBIs and 41 home runs set records for his position that season. He actually belted 42 round-trippers that year, with 1 coming as a pinch hitter.

After earning his third MVP, Campanella said, "When you win the first award, you're happy. When you win the second, you're very happy. But when you win the third, you're overwhelmed." The wear and tear behind the plate caused Roy to suffer many serious and nagging injuries with the Dodgers. A 1954 spring training injury, a chipped bone in the heel of his left hand that damaged a nerve, affected his hitting. Off-season surgery helped the following year, but the problem returned in 1956.

After the 1957 season, the Dodgers moved the club to Los Angeles. Between seasons, Campanella operated a liquor store in Harlem. Roy was driving to his Long Island home on a cold night in January, when his station wagon skidded on the icy roads, slammed into a telephone pole, and overturned. The accident broke his neck and left him dangling upside down in the vehicle, fearing that at any moment his life would be extinguished in a fiery explosion. The extraordinary neck muscles that Campanella had developed as a professional athlete probably saved his life. The accident left Roy paralyzed and confined to a wheelchair for the rest of his life. His career statistics included a .276 career batting average in 1,215 games with 242 homers, 856 RBIs, and 627 runs scored. Ty Cobb, one of the five original inductees into the National Baseball Hall of Fame and a man not known for praise, claimed, "Campanella will be remembered longer than any catcher in baseball history."

Dodger owner Walter O'Malley staged an exhibition game for Roy on May 7, 1959. Over 93,000 fans attended the benefit, with thousands being turned away. Dodger captain and good friend Pee Wee Reese wheeled Campanella onto the field in front of his adoring fans. From his wheelchair, Roy said, "I thank God that I'm living to be here. I thank . . . every one of you from the bottom of my heart. It's something I'll never forget!"

Despite his tragedy, Campanella remained active in the sport he gave so much to as a player with his own radio show and youth speeches and served as a goodwill ambassador and friend to fans all over the nation. Roy proved to be as heroic in tragedy as he was in glory, dedicating his life to community service projects. Had it not been for his accident, he just might have become the first African-American manager in baseball history.

Campanella lived in Hartsdale, New York, with his second wife, Roxie Doles, whom he married in 1964, and adopted her two children. Roy was survived by his five children, Roy, Jr., Tony, John, Joanie, and Ruth. His first wife, Ruthie Willis, died in 1960.

Campanella in 1959 wrote *It's Good to Be Alive*, later made into a movie starring Paul Winfield. In 1969, Roy was inducted into the National Baseball Hall of Fame. He once said, "You have to have a lot of the little boy in you to be a good ball player." Campanella died of a heart attack on June 26, 1993, at his home in Woodland Hills, a suburb of Los Angeles, at age 71.

BIBLIOGRAPHY: Bill Borst, *A Fan's Memoir: The Brooklyn Dodgers, 1953–1957* (St. Louis, MO, 1983); Bob Broeg, "Campanella Never Lost Enthusiasm for Baseball," *St. Louis Post-Dispatch*, June 28, 1993, p. 7C; Roy Campanella, *It's Good to Be Alive* (New York, 1959); Harvey Frommer, *Rickey and Robinson: The Men Who Broke Baseball's Color Barrier* (New York, 1982); Roger Kahn, *The Boys of Summer* (New York, 1972); David L. Porter, ed, *Biographical Dictionary of American Sports: Baseball* (Westport, CT, 1987); Lowell Reidenbaugh, *Cooperstown: Where Baseball's Legends Live Forever* (St. Louis, MO, 1983); James A. Riley, *The Biographical Encyclopedia of the Negro Baseball Leagues* (New York, 1994); Gene Schoor, *Roy Campanella: Man of Courage* (New York, 1959); Mike Shatzkin, ed., *The Ballplayers* (New York, 1990); Robert McG. Thomas, obituary, *New York Times*, June 28, 1993, p. B12.

William A. Borst

EARL CAMPBELL
(March 29, 1955–) ——————————————————————— *Football*

Earl Christian Campbell, "the Tyler Rose," overcame rural poverty to become one of the most powerful running backs in professional football history. Earl was born on March 29, 1955, in a small, dilapidated farmhouse six miles north of Tyler, Texas, the sixth of 11 children. His parents, Burk C. Campbell and Ann (Collins) Campbell, struggled to provide for the family. Besides growing vegetables and roses on their 14-acre plot, "B.C." worked at odd jobs and "Mama" cleaned houses for wealthy white families. The family endured even harder times after B.C. died in 1966. Earl was nicknamed "Bad Earl" for delinquent behavior, but the influence of his stern, deeply religious mother prevented serious problems with the law. She insisted that he attend church every Sunday, and he sang for four years in the choir at Hopewell Baptist Church. Earl's attitude and life improved during high school, thanks partly to football.

During his senior year at Tyler High School, Campbell was moved from football middle linebacker to the offense because of a shortage of running backs. He initially resisted the change, recalling, "I didn't want to be a running back. I cried like a baby, but I guess that turned out to be a good decision." Earl made High School All-America, rushing for 2,036 yards and scoring 28 touchdowns in leading 15–0 Tyler to the 1973 State 4A championship. He received a football scholarship to the University of Texas and became the first four-year All-Southwest Conference (SWC) selectee. The powerful 5-foot-11-inch, 225-pound Campbell played fullback for the first three seasons but shifted to tailback his senior year when new head coach Fred Akers changed the offense from the wishbone to the "Veer" and "I" formations. Earl again initially disliked a change that turned out for the best. Utilizing his speed and quickness, he led the nation in 1977 in rushing (1,744 yards) and scoring (114 points on 19 touchdowns) and was named All-America and Heisman Trophy winner as college football's Player of the Year.

The first player chosen in the 1978 National Football League (NFL) draft, Campbell signed a five-year, $1.4 million contract with the Houston Oilers of the American Football Conference (AFC). Coach O. A. "Bum" Phillips installed the "I" formation to take advantage of Earl's rare combination of speed and power. The first rookie since **Jim Brown** in 1957 to lead the NFL in rushing, Campbell gained more than half of the Oilers' rushing yards and set eight team rushing records. His 1,450 yards in 302 attempts comprised the most yardage ever gained by a rookie. Named the NFL's Rookie of the Year and MVP, the All-Pro led the Oilers to the AFC playoffs. Houston lost the AFC championship game to the Pittsburgh Steelers, eventual winners of Super Bowl XIII. The next season, rival defenses keyed on Earl but could not stop him. He set an NFL record by gaining more than 100 yards in seven straight games, led the NFL in rushing attempts (368) and yards (1,697), and repeated as All-Pro and MVP. The Oilers again lost the AFC title game to the Steelers, victors in Super Bowl XIV. Houston lost in the first round of the 1980 playoffs, but Campbell enjoyed his finest season. Named All-Pro and MVP for the third consecutive year, Earl gained over 200 yards in four games, topped 100 yards 11 times, and led the NFL in all four rushing categories with 373 attempts, 1,934 yards, 5.2 yards average per carry, and 13 touchdowns.

Despite leading the AFC in carries (361) for the third straight year and rushing (1,376) for the fourth consecutive season, Campbell saw his productivity decline in 1981. New head coach Ed Biles diversified the offense by switching from the "I" to the "pro-set." Earl continued to lead the Oilers in rushing attempts and yards gained in 1982 (146—538) and 1983 (322—1,301), but the physical pounding began to wear him down. He also became frustrated with the coaching strategy, the team's lack of success, and growing public criticism of his performance. Houston traded Campbell in October 1984 to the New Orleans Saints (NFL) of the National Football Conference (NFC), where he was reunited with head coach Bum Phillips. Relegated to a backup role, Campbell retired after the 1985 season.

A three-time All-Pro (1978–1980) who played in the Pro Bowl six consecutive years (1978–1983) as an AFC All-Star, Campbell ranks among the most productive runners in NFL history. A workhorse, Earl carried the ball at least 302 times and gained at least 1,301 yards five of his first six years and fell below those marks only in the strike-shortened 1982 season. Although his eight seasons are far fewer than most career rushing leaders, he ranks ninth in carries (2,187) and tenth in yardage (9,407) and tied for eleventh in touchdowns (74) through 1994. His 1,934 yards gained and 19 touchdowns scored in 1980 remain the third and fourth best single-season marks, respectively. Campbell, a one-dimensional back who caught only 121 passes for 806 yards and no touchdowns in eight seasons, possessed a running style that actually shortened his career. A powerful, punishing runner, Earl used the strength in his massive shoulders and thighs to gain most of his yardage after initial contact. Consequently, he received unusually heavy punishment from the gang-tackling required to bring him down.

Despite fame and fortune, Campbell maintained the virtues of integrity, hard work, and humility taught by his mother. After signing with the Oilers, Earl built his mother a new house next to the shack in which he grew up. His numerous civic and charitable activities in Houston included the Earl Campbell Crusade for Kids, devoted to helping underprivileged children. Campbell finished his education at Texas, receiving a bachelor's degree in speech communication in 1980. The same year, Earl married Reuna Smith, his girlfriend since junior high. He teaches his son, Earl Christian II, the virtues of quiet confidence and modesty. Although declaring, "I've always been the guy who said . . . 'I'll get it done,' " he also proudly says he "never once spiked a football."

After retiring, Campbell moved to Austin, Texas, and owns a sausage and meat company and a small cattle ranch there. Earl was elected to the National Football Foundation (NFF) College Football Hall of Fame in 1990, the Pro Football Hall of Fame in 1991, and the National High School Sports Hall of Fame in 1994.

BIBLIOGRAPHY: Sam Blair, *Earl Campbell: The Driving Force* (Waco, TX, 1980); *Current Biography Yearbook* (1983), pp. 45–48; Melissa Ludtke Lincoln, "The Real Earl Campbell Stands Up," *Sport* 69 (September 1979), pp. 20–27; John McClain, "Earl Campbell: Deep in His Heart a Texan," *Football Digest* 14 (November 1984), pp. 20–26; David S. Neft et al., eds., *The Sports Encyclopedia: Pro Football* (New York, 1994); Bruce Newman, "The Roots of Greatness," *Sports Illustrated* 51 (September 3, 1979), pp. 94–98ff; Ron Reid, "This Oiler's a Gusher of a Rusher," *Sports Illustrated* 49 (September 18, 1978), pp. 24–25; Ron Reid, "Oilers Hit a Gusher," *Sports Illustrated* 49 (December 4, 1978), pp. 20–23; *The Sporting News*, January 1, 1983; November 21, 1983; October 22, 1984; December 10, 1984; December 17, 1984; *USA Today*, July 8, 1994.

Larry R. Gerlach

ROD CAREW
(October 1, 1945–   ) ————————————————————— *Baseball*

Rod Carew, who won seven American League (AL) batting championships and made over 3,000 hits, was elected to the National Baseball Hall of Fame in 1991. Rodney Cline "Rod" Carew was born October 1, 1945, on a train carrying his mother from Gatun to Gamboa in Panama. He was named for Dr. Rodney Cline, who delivered him. A nurse, Margaret Allen, who assisted at his birth, became his godmother. The son of Eric Carew, a construction and tugboat worker, and Olga Carew, Rod has one brother and three sisters. He recalled, "We were poor, really poor. I almost never had shoes or clothes good enough to go to church or Sunday School like other kids. But no matter what, my mother always saw that I had baseball shoes and a glove. She knew how much the game meant to me."

Carew coped with both childhood illness and poverty. At age 11, Rod was hospitalized for six months with rheumatic fever. He could not play Little League baseball until he was nearly 12. Carew then progressed as a hitter because of the instruction of his uncle, Joe French, who was in charge of physical education programs in the Canal Zone. Rod's baseball skills developed so rapidly that before reaching age 14 he played with 17-year-olds. In 1962, his godmother suggested that life for the Carews might be easier in New York City and arranged for them to go there. Rod's father told his wife to move with the children, promising to join them when he could. He never did join them, however.

The Carews settled in Washington Heights, near the old Polo Grounds. Rod entered George Washington High School and worked hard in school because his native language was Spanish. Classes were taught in English, which he spoke very little. He disliked his neighborhood with its dope pushers, hoodlums, and little room to play. Carew worked in a grocery store and played sandlot baseball on weekends with the Cavaliers, a racially integrated team of promising young players.

Herb Stein, the father of one of his Cavalier teammates and observer for the Minnesota Twins, urged the Twins to give Carew a tryout. The Twins signed Rod in 1964 for a $5,000 bonus and assigned him to Melbourne, Florida, of the Cocoa Rookie League as a second baseman. He hit .325 and led the Cocoa Rookie League in triples. The next year, Carew moved up to Orlando, Florida, of the Florida State League, as the first African-American player there and batted .303. In 1966, Rod was promoted to Wilson, North Carolina, of the Carolina League. Although hitting only .242, he made great progress there because of the coaching of Vern Morgan. In 1967, Carew skipped two levels of organized baseball to join the Minnesota Twins (AL).

By this time, the six-foot, 182-pound Carew, who batted left and threw right, had become an outstanding hitter and won the AL Rookie of the Year award with a .292 batting average. Rod remained with the Twins through the 1978 season, playing mostly at second base until moving to first base in 1976. He showed his versatility by appearing in a few games as a shortstop, third baseman, and outfielder. Altogether, Carew won seven AL batting championships (1969, 1972–1975 1977–1978). Rod probably would have won another crown in 1970 with his .366 mark, but he did not have enough plate appearances. He was sidelined because of surgery on a torn cartilage, caused by a base runner crashing into him while he was pivoting at second base on a double play. Carew excelled all around, not just as a great hitter. A skilled base runner, Rod tied major league records in 1969 by stealing home seven times and three bases in one inning. Gene Mauch, his manager, remarked, "He's got everything—intelligence, strength, confidence, speed afoot, and hand-eye coordination. Many ballplayers are pleasant to manage, but managing Rodney is a privilege."

During his years with the Twins, Carew married Marilyn Levy, a white Jewish girl from North Minneapolis, Minnesota. They are parents of three daughters, Charryse, Stephanie, and Michelle. The interracial marriage triggered much hate mail, but Rod, a loner and devoted family man, kept to himself, refused to be caught in controversy, and avoided publicity. When Dave Anderson interviewed him upon his being named the AL's Most Valuable Player (MVP), Carew responded, "All this publicity has been great for me, but it's not going to make me different. . . . I'll always look back to what I had as a kid. I know where I came from."

In February 1979, the Twins traded Carew to the California Angels (AL). Rod, who played first base there, was happy to leave the Twins. In his autobiography, he wrote, "I could no longer work for a man like Calvin Griffith. Calvin is a hard-hearted guy who has not admitted to himself that times do actually change." With the Angels, Carew reached 3,000 hits on August 4, 1985, against his old team and collected 53 more during his playing career. The Angels released Rod following that season, but no offer came to manage or coach. He combined with Ira Berkow to write *Carew* (1979), collaborated with Frank Pace and Armin Ketelyon on *Rod Carew's Art and Science of Hitting* (1986), and opened a successful camp to instruct young boys in batting. In 1992, the Angels hired him as a hitting instructor.

For his seven batting titles, 3,053 hits, and lifetime .318 batting average, Carew was elected to the National Baseball Hall of Fame in 1991. Rod's honors included winning the AL MVP award (1977) and being chosen for the AL All-Star teams from 1967 to 1979 and 1982 to 1984. He could not participate in 1970, 1979, and 1982 because of injuries. In 2,469 career major league games, Carew smacked 445 doubles, 112 triples, and 92 home runs. Rod hit at least .300 for 15 consecutive seasons from 1969 to 1983 and led the AL in hits three times. He never appeared in a World Series but played in the 1969, 1970, 1979, and 1982 AL Championship Series.

Carew made a significant impact on baseball because of his batting technique and character. Rod's knowledge of the strike zone, intelligence at the plate, bat control, contact hitting, and spray hitting rather than swinging for home runs influenced later players to adopt his style and become batting leaders. Great hitters, including Wade Boggs and George Brett, followed Carew's technique. Umpire Ron Luciano, who considered Rod one of his favorite players, wrote, "He'll have a three-ball, two-strike count on him and foul off six consecutive pitches. Then he'll finally let one go. Well, if he swung at six and didn't swing at that one, it's got to be ball four. The great hitters get treated that way because they know the strike zone. . . . If Rod Carew asked me to check the ball, I didn't even glance at it. The ball was gone. If Rodney didn't like it, I didn't like it. That's one of the reasons he was such a good hitter."

Carew's strength of character serves as a model to young players. Rod overcame the obstacles of poverty, illness, an indifferent father, a tough neighborhood, a second language, and prejudice to become one of baseball's greatest hitters. Carew's devotion to his family, visits to patients in hospitals, fundraising for various charities, and model behavior off the field make him a role model for boys. Young people in Panama consider Rod a national hero. He was awarded Panama's Medal of Honor and also received the Roberto Clemente Award for Community Service. In his quiet, modest way, Carew has inspired many people, not just baseball players.

BIBLIOGRAPHY: Dave Anderson, "The Frustration of Baseball's Greatest Hitter," *Sport* 65 (October 1977), pp. 34–35, 37–38, 40–41; Larry Batson, *An Interview with Rod Carew* (Mankato, MN, 1977); Rod Carew with Ira Berkow, *Carew* (New York, 1979); Rod Carew with Frank Pace and Armin Ketelyon, *Rod Carew's Art and Science of Hitting* (New York, 1986); *Current Biography Yearbook* (1978), pp. 63–66; Ron Luciano and David Fisher, *The Umpire Strikes Back* (New York, 1982); David L. Porter, ed., *Biographical Dictionary of American Sports: Baseball* (Westport, CT, 1987); *The Sporting News Baseball Register* (1986).

Ralph S. Graber

WILT CHAMBERLAIN
(August 21, 1936–   ) ———————————————————— *Basketball*

No athlete has ever dominated a sport or made a greater impact on a sport than Wilt Chamberlain in basketball. Wilton Norman Chamberlain was born on August 21, 1936, in Philadelphia, Pennsylvania, the son of William and Olivia Chamberlain, and had eight siblings. His father, a custodian, also worked as a neighborhood handyman, while his mother did laundry and cleaned houses. An all-around athlete whose coordination was not diminished by rapid growth, Wilt was heralded as the nation's top high school basketball player. In three years at Overbrook High School, he scored 2,252 points, including 90 in one game, and led the team to a 58–3 record and two City championships. The Philadelphia Warriors of the National Basketball Association (NBA) claimed future territorial draft rights to Chamberlain, while the University of Kansas won an intense recruiting battle for his collegiate services.

Chamberlain revolutionized college basketball. Wilt scored 52 points in his varsity debut in 1956 and was named All-American after leading Kansas to a 24–3 record and the NCAA finals. The Jayhawks fell to the top-ranked University of North Carolina, 54–53, in triple overtime in the championship game, but Chamberlain was named the tournament Most Valuable Player (MVP). Drastic steps were taken to combat Wilt's awesome talent. Opponents double-teamed and even triple-teamed him on defense and held the ball on offense. Rules makers widened the lane from 8 feet to 12 feet, instituted offensive goaltending, banned inbounding the ball from behind the offensive backboard, and forbade the shooter from crossing the free throw line until the ball hit the basket. Chamberlain dunked free throws. Although again named All-America his junior year, Wilt was frustrated by the stalling tactics and collapsing defenses and skipped his senior year to play for the Harlem Globetrotters.

Chamberlain signed in 1959 with the Philadelphia Warriors for an unprecedented $65,000 and immediately dominated the NBA. Wilt set eight NBA single-season records, including most points (2,707) and points per game average (37.6) and most rebounds (1,941) and rebounds average per game (27.0). He averaged 46 minutes played per 48-minute game without ever fouling out. Chamberlain was selected both All-NBA and an All-Star, earning both MVP and Rookie of the Year honors. Wilt announced after the season, however, that he was leaving the NBA because "I got pushed and shoved even more than I had in college, and the officials let the other guys get away with it." He joined the Harlem Globetrotters on their summer European tour but then reconsidered and signed a three-year contract with the Warriors.

Chamberlain dominated the NBA for 14 seasons with the Philadelphia Warriors (1959–1961), Golden State Warriors (1962–1965), Philadelphia 76ers (1965–1968), and Los Angeles Lakers (1968–1973). A four-time MVP (1960, 1966–1968), Wilt made the All-NBA First Team seven times (1960–1962, 1964, 1966–1968) and Second Team three times (1963, 1965, 1972). An All-Star every year except 1970, Chamberlain appeared in 13 All-Star Games. Wilt set numerous career and single-game All-Star records, including 42 points in 1962, and was named MVP in 1960. In 1973 he joined the San Diego Conquistadors of the American Basketball Association (ABA) as player-coach, but the Lakers obtained a court order preventing him from playing in his "option year." The Conquistadors finished with a mediocre 38–47 record. Chamberlain, an indifferent coach, retired after the season, holding or sharing 43 NBA playing records. Nicknamed "the Babe Ruth of pro basketball," Wilt still dominates the NBA record book to an amazing degree.

Both very big and very quick, the seven-foot-one-inch, 275-pound Chamberlain proved a remarkably versatile and consistent performer. The phenomenal scorer's fallaway jump shots and fingertip rolls were unstoppable. The first player to tally 30,000 career points (31,419), Wilt holds the NBA record for career game scoring average (30.1). He led the NBA in scoring seven consecutive years (1960–1966) and field goal percentage nine times (1961, 1963, 1965–1970, 1972–1973). His astounding offensive performance in 1961–1962 included setting NBA records for total points (4,029) and per game average (50.4) and scoring 100 points against the New York Knickerbockers on March 2, 1962, in Hershey, Pennsylvania. Chamberlain's scoring totals would have been much higher had not the career 54 percent free throw shooter often been deliberately fouled while attempting field goals. Since Wilt relied on power moves instead of hook shots like other centers, critics like Rick Barry declared, "Don't call him a shooter, call him a scorer."

Sensitive to criticisms of being a selfish player, Chamberlain eventually passed up numerous scoring opportunities to demonstrate his playmaking and defensive abilities. Wilt led the NBA in assists (702) in 1967–1968 and made the All-Defensive team in 1972 and 1973. He remains the only player to lead the NBA in assists, field goal percentage, and rebounding in a single season, accomplishing the feat in 1960–1961. Chamberlain also set records for endurance and dependability, leading the NBA in most minutes played eight times. Wilt set NBA career records for average minutes per game (45.8) and most complete games played (79) and season marks for most minutes played (3,086), average minutes per game (48.5), and most consecutive complete games (47). The greatest board man in NBA history, he led the NBA in rebounds 11 seasons (1960–1963, 1966–1968, 1971–1973) and set career records for total caroms (23,924) and average per game (22.9). In 1960–1961, Chamberlain set a single-game mark with an amazing 55 boards. Despite the physical play of centers, Wilt played 1,045 games in 14 seasons without ever fouling out. Bob Cousy of the Boston Celtics observed, "He played every minute of every game, scored more points and grabbed more rebounds than any player ever. I don't know what more anyone could have wanted of him."

Despite his achievements, Chamberlain remained misunderstood and maligned. Frequent clashes with coaches and teammates and demands for preferential treatment caused others to consider Wilt egotistical and selfish, but he agreeably changed his style of play to conform to coaching strategy and team needs. Since Chamberlain won NBA championships only with the 76ers in 1967 and Lakers in 1972, he was not considered a team player and was regarded as second best to **Bill Russell** of the perennial champion Boston Celtics. Although Boston was a much better team, Wilt consistently bested Russell in head-to-head competition. In 142 games, Chamberlain averaged 28.78 points to Russell's 14.5 and outscored the Boston center 131 times and outrebounded him 95 times. In separate games, Wilt scored 62 points and pulled down 55 rebounds against Russell. **Kareem Abdul-Jabbar** later surpassed several of Wilt's career scoring marks, but he was not nearly as aggressive, fast, or powerful or as good a rebounder and defender.

Chamberlain's achievements came not simply from his prodigious height, as suggested by the nickname "Wilt the Stilt," but rather from his extraordinary athletic ability. Wilt, possessing a rare combination of strength, speed, and agility, ran the 440- and 880-yard dashes in high school and won the City championships in the shotput and high jump as a senior. He lettered in track and field three years at Kansas and captured the Big Eight Conference high jump crown each year, setting a school record of 6 feet 7 inches. Chamberlain also put the shot 56 feet, surpassed 50 feet in the triple jump, and clocked 10.0 seconds in the 100-yard dash, 20.9 seconds in the 220-yard dash, and 48.9 seconds in the 440-yard dash. During and after his basketball career, Wilt received several offers to become a professional boxer and a tight end in professional football. He rejected such offers and frequent invitations from ABA and NBA teams to return to basketball, concentrating instead on playing racquetball, volleyball, and polo. Chamberlain helped found the International Volleyball Association and sponsored several volleyball and track teams in southern California. Wilt immodestly but honestly said: "I could star in any sport."

The egotistical, extroverted, and opinionated Chamberlain has appeared in numerous commercials and several movies, including *Conan the Destroyer* (1984). The life bachelor designed an oversized house in the hills of Bel Air, California, and has received public criticism for his views and boasts about sexuality. Wilt, who preferred the nickname "The Big Dipper" and perceptively dismissed his detractors by saying, "Nobody roots for Goliath," was elected to the Naismith Memorial Basketball Hall of Fame in 1978 and named to the NBA's 35th Anniversary All-Time Team in 1980. Jerry West, another Hall of Fame basketball player and later general manager of the Los Angeles Lakers, summarized Chamberlain's place in NBA history by saying, "When I think of pro basketball, I think of Wilt Chamberlain. He just stood out."

BIBLIOGRAPHY: Wilt Chamberlain, "Why I Am Quitting College," *Look* 22 (June 10, 1958), pp. 91–94ff; Wilt Chamberlain as told to Tim Cohane, "Pro Basketball Has Ganged Up on Me," *Look* 24 (March 1, 1960), pp. 51–55ff; Wilt Chamberlain, *A View from Above* (New York, 1991); Wilt Chamberlain and David Shaw, *Just Like Any Other 7-Foot Black Millionaire Who Lives Next Door* (New York, 1973); *Current Biography Yearbook* (1960), pp. 85–86; Glenn Dickey, *The History of Professional Basketball* (New York, 1982); John Garrity, "Wilt Chamberlain," *Sports Illustrated* 75 (December 9, 1991), pp. 22–25; Bill Libby, *Goliath: The Wilt Chamberlain Story* (New York, 1977); *The Sporting News*, April 16, 1984, May 28, 1984; *The Sporting News Official NBA Guide* (1993–1994); A. S. Young, "The Track Team that Wilt Built," *Ebony* 37 (October 1982), pp. 68–72.

Larry R. Gerlach

OSCAR CHARLESTON
(October 12, 1896–October 5, 1954) ——————————————— *Baseball*

Oscar Charleston was named in 1976 to the National Baseball Hall of Fame, the second Negro League African American selected following **Josh Gibson.** Charleston was often compared to contemporary Ty Cobb for his baseball skills and competitive nature. Some baseball writers stated that Oscar was not the "black Ty Cobb," but rather, Cobb was the "white Oscar Charleston."

Oscar McKinley Charleston was born on October 12, 1896, in Indianapolis, Indiana, to Tom Charleston, a construction worker, and Mary (Thomas) Charleston. The seventh of 11 children including eight boys, Charleston served as a local batboy. He followed the lead of an older brother, enlisting in the U.S. Army at age 15. While stationed in the Philippines with the Black 24th Infantry, Oscar honed his athletic skills in track and field and baseball and became the only African-American player in the 1914 Manila Baseball League. His army discharge came in 1915, when he was earning $50 per month. Charleston joined his hometown Indianapolis ABCs, sponsored by the American Brewing Company and directed by Negro League pioneer C. I. Taylor. In 1915, Oscar married Helen Grubbs from Indianapolis, but they soon divorced.

After spending three years with the ABCs, Charleston joined the Chicago American Giants under Negro National League (NNL) entrepreneur **Rube Foster.** In 1921, Oscar moved to the St. Louis Giants and gained superstar status, reportedly batting .434 in a 60-game season. His offensive production included 14 doubles and a league-leading 11 triples, 15 home runs, and 34 stolen bases. The barrel-chested, 5-foot-11-inch, 185-pound Charleston, who batted and threw left-handed, played a shallow center field and counted on his great speed to reach any balls hit over his head. "**Willie Mays** was a good outfielder, as was DiMaggio, but this Charleston had . . . something special about him," insisted Kansas City Monarch star Newt Allen.

Peers generally perceived Charleston as a quiet man off the field, but he displayed a fiery competitive temper during games. Oscar fought umpires, opponents, and fans, contesting calls, sliding hard into bases, and battling spectators for balls hit into the stands. Although box score statistics for the Negro Leagues remain fragmentary, Charleston compiled a career batting average around .350 in the Negro Leagues from 1919 to 1937, .365 in Cuban Winter League ball from 1919 to 1929, and .318 versus white major leaguers in 53 exhibition games from 1915 to 1936. National Baseball Hall of Fame hurler Dizzy Dean noted that "Charleston could hit that ball a mile. He didn't have a weakness."

Charleston began the 1922 season in St. Louis and then returned at mid-year to Indianapolis. Oscar made $325 per month, $125 above any other teammate and among the highest salaries in "blackball." In 1924, he jumped to the Harrisburg, Pennsylvania, Giants of the Eastern Colored League (ECL) as player-manager for 4 years, batting .391 in 1924, .418 in 1925 with a league-leading 15 doubles and 16 home runs, and .335 in 1927 with 18 doubles and 12 home runs. At Harrisburg, Charleston married Jane Blaylock, daughter of a Methodist bishop. The couple had no children and divorced after about 20 years. Oscar hit .360 in 1928 and .339 in 1929 for the Philadelphia Hilldales.

The economic depression of the 1930s made the financial life of blackball teams especially precarious. Poorly written contracts were ignored by both players and teams alike. Independent individual clubs raided Negro League ranks because they preferred to barnstorm, a more lucrative opportunity than league play. Cumberland "Cum" Posey, owner of Pittsburgh's Homestead Grays, signed Charleston and other top players from failing franchises for the 1930 season. Oscar, slowed in his outfield play because of added weight, moved to first base. His bat speed, however, remained as quick as ever. For the 1930 and 1931 seasons, Charleston hit a combined .371. Posey and his successor, Gus Greenlee, who bought out Posey in 1932 to stock up his Pittsburgh Crawfords, accumulated the best blackball team in history. The Crawfords included future National Baseball Hall of Famers **Satchel Paige**, Josh Gibson, **James "Cool Papa" Bell**, William "Judy" Johnson, and Charleston, team player-manager from 1932 to 1937. "Craws" teammate Ted Page remembered Charleston's "vicious eyes. Cold steel-grey eyes, like a cat." Oscar batted .376 in 1933, .333 in 1934, and .288 in 1935 while entering the twilight of his career.

The Dominican Republic Summer League enticed many of the Crawford stars in 1937 to move south, causing the Pittsburgh club to collapse. Charleston moved to the Toledo Crawfords in 1939, but that franchise folded in midseason. The manager–first baseman joined the Philadelphia Stars for five seasons. During World War II, Oscar worked at the Philadelphia Quartermaster depot. In 1945, he managed the Brooklyn Brown Dodgers, Brooklyn Dodger executive Branch Rickey's cover team set up to scout **Jackie Robinson** and other blackball players. As the Negro Leagues faded, Charleston's managerial career ended with the Philadelphia Stars in 1946 and Indianapolis Clowns in 1947 and 1948. In 1949, Oscar retired and worked in the baggage department of the Pennsylvania Railway Station in Philadelphia. He died on October 5, 1954, in Philadelphia following a heart attack and stroke. Charleston's election in 1976 to the National Baseball Hall of Fame brought recognition to his career and supported sportswriter Grantland Rice's earlier observation, "It's impossible for anyone to be a better ball player than Oscar Charleston."

BIBLIOGRAPHY: Martin Appel and Burt Goldblatt, *Baseball's Best: The Hall of Fame Gallery* (New York, 1977); *Black Sports* 7 (July 1977); *Dictionary of American Negro Biography* (New York, 1982); John B. Holway, *Blackball Stars: Negro League Pioneers*

(Westport, CT, 1988); *Pittsburgh Courier*, October 16, 1954; James A. Riley, *The Biographical Encyclopedia of the Negro Baseball Leagues* (New York, 1994).

David Bernstein

ROBERTO CLEMENTE
(August 18, 1934–December 31, 1972) ——————————— *Baseball*

After the Pittsburgh Pirates defeated the Baltimore Orioles in the seven-game 1971 World Series, baseball writer Roger Angell described "the shared experience, already permanently fixed in memory, of Roberto Clemente playing a kind of baseball that none of us had ever seen before—throwing and running and hitting at something close to the level of absolute perfection, playing to win but also playing the game almost as if it were a form of punishment for everyone else on the field."

The fierce pride that drove Clemente throughout his career ultimately produced an impressive list of accomplishments. Roberto, the eleventh player in major league history to record 3,000 hits, hit .317 in 18 major league seasons. Besides winning National League (NL) batting titles in 1961, 1964, 1965, and 1967, he was named the NL's MVP in 1966. Clemente hit safely in all of his 14 World Series games and received the Babe Ruth Award for his memorable achievements in the 1971 World Series.

Perhaps even more impressive were Roberto's defensive skills. Many authorities regard Clemente as the best defensive right fielder of all time, a reflection of his 12 consecutive Gold Glove Awards. Several opposing players hit what looked like clean singles to right field, only to be thrown out at first base by the strongest, most accurate arm in baseball. He led NL outfielders in assists four times, although entire teams refused to take any chances on the base paths against him. His great range and acrobatic agility made difficult catches look routine, while ordinary fly balls were caught with his distinctive "basket catch."

Although Clemente consistently turned in spectacular performances, national recognition came only toward the end of his career. For most of his career, Roberto fought for recognition and respect. He became, according to African-American Hall of Famer Monte Irvin, "the Latin Jackie Robinson."

Roberto Walker Clemente was born on August 18, 1934, the youngest of seven children of Melchor Clemente, a sugar mill worker and cutter, and Luisa Clemente, in Carolina, Puerto Rico. As a youth, Clemente eagerly took up his native island's favorite sport of baseball. Although not especially large at 5 feet 11 inches and 185 pounds, Roberto showed such prowess by age 14 that he played in exhibition games against major league and the Negro League players. As a player for the Santurce Crabbers in a Winter League at age 18, he caught the eye of Brooklyn Dodger (NL) scouts. Brooklyn subsequently signed him to a $10,000 bonus contract.

Clemente spent the 1954 season with the Dodgers' Montreal, Canada, farm team. The Dodgers, fearing that other teams would notice his talent, did not play him regularly. Roberto frequently was benched if he played well. Even if Clemente had enjoyed full command of English, the Montreal Royals probably would not have bothered to explain to him what they were doing. Roberto, thus, was especially confused and frustrated.

The Pittsburgh Pirates (NL) detected the flashes of brilliance that the Dodgers tried to hide and drafted Clemente after the 1954 season. Roberto joined the Pirates for the 1955 season as one of several young players, including shortstop Dick Groat, pitchers Vernon Law and Bob Friend, second baseman Bill Mazeroski, and center fielder Bill Virdon. The group spent the next few years gaining experience leading to a World Championship in 1960.

Of these players, only Clemente had to adjust to a new culture. As Roberto saw it, the culture often was too unwilling to adjust to him. He often played in pain, as bone chips, stomach pains, migraines, and most seriously, a back injury from a 1955 auto accident kept him from performing at his best. Clemente's wife, Vera Cristina Zabala, whom he married on November 14, 1964, recalled "many a night when he could not sleep because of the pain." Instead of getting respect for playing as much as he did, Roberto was labeled a "malingerer" and a "lazy Latin."

Such labels infuriated Clemente. Roberto probably grew angriest in 1960 when, after hitting .314 and helping the Pirates win the World Series title, he finished only eighth in the Most Valuable Player (MVP) balloting. "I was bitter," Clemente admitted later. "I am still bitter. I am a team player . . . but I feel I should get the credit I deserve." Roberto's anger fueled an even more spectacular year in 1961, when he hit .351. His best all-around season probably came in 1966. Manager Harry Walker asked him to try to hit for more power. Despite playing in cavernous Forbes Field, Clemente belted 29 homers while batting .317, driving in 119 runs, scoring 105 times, and patrolling right field with his usual brilliance. The baseball world took notice, as Roberto won his MVP award.

Clemente's great seasons continued, with the respect coming more rapidly. His interviewers now believed his explanation for the basket catch. Roberto did not pattern his basket catch after **Willie Mays** but had caught the ball that way all his life because he could watch it all the way into his glove. He no longer had to defend his unorthodox hitting style. Clemente often hit off his front foot and supplied most of his power to the opposite field, but the results spoke eloquently. Pirate broadcasters called him matter-of-factly "The Great One." And Roberto became the unofficial spokesman for a generation of Latin American players. Pirate catcher Manny Sanguillen acknowledged, "He was everything to the Latin ballplayers."

Clemente remained a leader and symbol especially in his native Puerto Rico, where he planned to build a "Sports City" to help underprivileged children. His three sons were born in Puerto Rico, as he continued to live there in the off-season. The plane that carried Roberto to his death on New Year's Eve in 1972 took off from a Puerto Rican airfield on a mercy mission to earthquake victims in Nicaragua.

After his death, the National Baseball Hall of Fame waived its five-year waiting period and inducted Clemente in 1973. Contributions from thousands of people, especially from Pittsburgh, helped to complete the "Sports City." Several major leaguers, including Oakland A's outfielder Ruben Sierra, who wears number 21 in Roberto's honor, participated in baseball programs there. Pittsburgh celebrated his sixtieth birthday in 1994 by dedicating a statue of him at Three Rivers Stadium during the All-Star Game weekend. In 1994, *Sports Illustrated* ranked Clemente twenty-fifth on its "40 for the Ages List."

In the final game of the 1971 World Series, Clemente's home run helped lead the Pirates to a 2–1 victory and a World Championship. Before the game, Roberto told Roger Angell, "I want everybody in the world to know that this is the way I play all the time. All season, every season. I gave everything I had to this game." More than 20 years after his death, his fire still burns in those whose lives he inspires.

BIBLIOGRAPHY: Roger Angell, *The Summer Game* (New York, 1972); Myron Cope, "Aches and Pains and Three Batting Titles," in *Sports Illustrated Baseball* (Birmingham, AL, 1993); Bill Littlefield, *Champions: Stories of Ten Remarkable Athletes* (Boston, 1993); Phil Musick, *Reflections on Roberto* (Pittsburgh, PA, 1994); Jim O'Brien, *Remember Roberto: Clemente Recalled by Teammates, Family, Friends and Fans* (Pittsburgh, PA, 1994); David L. Porter, ed., *Biographical Dictionary of American Sports: Baseball* (Westport, CT, 1987); *Roberto Clemente: A Video Tribute* (Major League Baseball Productions, 1993); Rob Ruck, "Remembering Roberto Clemente," *Pittsburgh* (December 1992), pp. 36–42; Kal Wagenheim, *Clemente* (New York, 1973).

Luther W. Spoehr

RAY DANDRIDGE, SR.

(August 31, 1913–February 12, 1994) ———————————————— *Baseball*

In 1950, Ray Dandridge, Sr., the first African American named Most Valuable Player (MVP) of the recently integrated American Association (AA), led the Minneapolis Millers to the regular-season league title. Minneapolis was a farm team of the National League (NL) New York Giants club. Ray paced the AA in at bats (627) and hits (195) while recording a .311 batting average, 106 runs scored, 11 home runs, and 80 RBIs. He also topped AA third basemen with a .978 fielding average.

After spending 16 seasons as an All-Star infielder in the Negro National League (NNL), Mexican League (ML), and Latin Winter Leagues, Dandridge batted .362 as a 37-year-old AA rookie in 1949. Ray played with the Millers through 1952, leading AA third sackers in assists (282), double plays (36), and fielding average (.975) his final season in Minneapolis.

Nicknamed "Hooks," Raymond Emmett Dandridge, Sr., was born in Richmond, Virginia, on August 31, 1913, the son of Archie Dandridge and Alberta (Thompson) Dandridge. Dandridge attended segregated George Mason School and demonstrated superior athletic ability at an early age. At age 10, Ray followed his mother and sisters to Buffalo, New York. He attended integrated classes there, participating in several sports. His basketball career was quickly squelched, however, when the coach cut him from the team for being too rough. Better suited for football, Dandridge started as a back and continued to play after leaving school. Upon suffering a knee injury, Ray followed his father's advice and abandoned the sport. His mother had convinced him earlier to quit boxing. Dandridge then concentrated on baseball.

Upon turning 18, Ray returned to Richmond, Virginia, to live with his father and became a long ball–hitting semi-pro outfielder. A strong 1933 spring exhibition performance against the Detroit Stars (NNL) launched his professional baseball career.

Dandridge held misgivings about joining the Detroit Stars. "I didn't want to go nowhere," Ray recalled. "I didn't even know where Detroit was." His father and Detroit manager James "Candy" Taylor, however, entertained other ideas. Archie, a disabled textile worker, had played baseball locally and recognized the opportunity being offered his son. Taylor, a former outstanding third baseman, also admired Dandridge's talent. With his father's encouragement, Ray reluctantly joined the Stars. Taylor gave Archie $25 and Ray a verbal contract of $60 a month.

Taylor quickly recognized that Dandridge would not be an NNL power-hitter. He gave the rookie a heavier bat, tutoring him both in bat control and placing the ball. Ray soon developed into a consistent right-handed line drive hitter and excellent hit and run player.

In 1934, Dandridge began a 50-year residency in Newark, New Jersey. Ray joined the Newark Dodgers (later renamed Eagles) NNL entry, being named an All-Star third baseman by 1935. Newark manager Dick Lundy helped Dandridge polish his defensive skills. Ray remained with the Newark Eagles through 1938 and fell in love with local resident Florence Cooper. The couple married on October 2, 1938, and had a daughter, Delores, and two sons, Raymond, Jr., and Lawrence.

In 1940 spendthrift Jorge Pasquel offered Dandridge $350 a month to play in Mexico. Newark had paid Ray only $200 a month. By the summer's end, he had negotiated himself an annual Mexican League salary of $10,000. Ray commented, "Everything was alright. Well, what can I say? I made more money in Mexico than I made most anywhere."

From 1940 through 1943, Dandridge starred for the Veracruz Mexican League team. Ray helped Veracruz to pennants in 1940 and 1941 and led the ML with 131 hits and 70 RBIs in 1943. Upon returning to Newark in 1944, he paced the NNL in at bats (189), runs scored (38), hits (70), and total bases (98) while batting .370. In 1945, Dandridge set an ML record by hitting in 29 consecutive games. Two years later, Ray established an ML mark for assists by a shortstop with 473. He also led the ML in hits with 169 in 1947 and 130 in 1948 and in batting in 1948 with .369. His eight ML campaigns produced 943 hits and a .347 batting average in 644 games.

Dandridge usually played year-round and hit .282 in 11 Cuban Winter League seasons, attaining a .319 high in the 1938–1939 campaign. Ray's 11 stolen bases topped the Cuban loop in 1937–1938. In 1939 and 1940, he also played on championship clubs in Venezuela.

The bowlegged five-foot-seven-inch, 175-pound Dandridge's unique physique and amazing fielding skills earned him the nicknames "Squatty" and "Dandy." National Baseball Hall of Famer Monte Irvin recalled, "I've seen all the great third basemen. But I've never seen anyone who could make the plays any better than Dandridge." Los Angeles Dodger (NL) skipper Tom Lasorda, who saw Ray play in Cuba, continued, "He's the best third baseman I ever saw in my life." Teammate Leon Day concurred, "Without a doubt, Ray was the best third baseman ever, and I've seen a lot of them, from Judy Johnson to Brooks Robinson. He had the best hands; he was like a cat out there. Plus, he was a good hitter, a line-drive hitter."

Dandridge hit an amazing .485 with 16 hits in 33 at bats in NNL and ML All-Star competition. Five of Ray's seven starting All-Star assignments came in Mexico. He played for various All-Star aggregations, most notably **Satchel Paige**'s touring All-Stars of the 1930s. In 1950, Ray was the AA's All-Star third baseman.

Dandridge regretted never playing in the major leagues. After his four-year tenure with Minneapolis, Ray spent 1953 in the Pacific Coast League (PCL). His baseball career ended in 1955, when he hit .360 for Bismarck, North Dakota, of the Manitoba-Dakota League and led the circuit with 118 hits. In five years of organized baseball from 1949 to 1953, Dandridge batted .313 with 725 hits in 588 games. After being barred for so many years from organized baseball due to race, Ray ultimately lost the opportunity to play in the major leagues because of his age.

Subsequently, Dandridge tended bar and worked as director in the Newark recreation department. In 1980, the city honored Ray for his work with youngsters. Five years later a Newark baseball park was renamed after him. Dandridge retired in 1984 to Palm Bay, Florida.

Willie Mays, his Minneapolis teammate, forged a National Baseball Hall of Fame career with the New York Giants (NL) and San Francisco Giants (NL). Dandridge joined Mays in the National Baseball Hall of Fame in 1987 and was inducted into the Mexican Baseball Hall of Fame in 1989. Former Brooklyn Dodger star **Roy Campanella,** who preceded Ray into both Halls of Fame, commented, "He deserves it. I never saw anyone better as a fielder or a runner, and he hit well over .300."

Dandridge hit .320 in 23 years of professional baseball. Only five other African Americans have made the Mexican Baseball Hall of Fame. Ray, one of the last Negro Leaguers named to the National Baseball Hall of Fame, died of cancer on February 12, 1994, in Palm City, Florida. He was survived by his second wife, Heneritta, and three children.

BIBLIOGRAPHY: *The Baseball Encyclopedia,* 9th ed. (New York, 1993); Pedro Treto Cisneros, *Enciclopedia del beisbol Mexicano* (Mexico, 1992); John B. Holway, *Blackball Stars* (Westport, CT, 1988); Fred P. Hutchinson, *Who's Who in the American Association* (Minneapolis, MN, 1950); Robert W. Peterson, *Only the Ball Was White* (Englewood Cliffs, NJ, 1970); David L. Porter, ed., *Biographical Dictionary of American Sports: Baseball* (Westport, CT, 1987); James A. Riley, *The All-Time All-Stars of Black Baseball* (Cocoa, FL, 1983); James A. Riley, *Dandy, Day and the Devil* (Cocoa, FL, 1987); James A. Riley, *The Biographical Encyclopedia of the Negro Baseball Leagues* (New York, 1994); Mike Shatzkin, ed., *The Ballplayers* (New York, 1990); Society for American Baseball Research, *Minor League Baseball Stars: Volume II* (Cooperstown, NY, 1985).

Merl F. Kleinknecht

ERNIE DAVIS
(December 14, 1939–May 18, 1963) ———————————————— *Football*

Ernie Davis, nicknamed "The Elmira Express," broke 10 of **Jim Brown**'s football records at Syracuse University as a varsity halfback from 1959 to 1961. The six-foot-two-inch, 210-pound Davis was born on December 14, 1939, in New Salem, Pennsylvania, the only child of Mrs. Arthur Radford. Ernie's father died while he was just an infant. Davis grew up with his grandmother in Uniontown, Pennsylvania, until age 11, when he joined his mother in Elmira, New York. Although involved in organized sports since age 6, Davis really bloomed with his move to New York State. As Ernie acknowledged, "I liked Elmira, especially the way it had sports programs organized for kids."

Davis, the greatest athlete in the history of his high school, the Elmira Free Academy, earned 11 varsity letters in basketball, baseball, and football. Besides attaining schoolboy All-America status in basketball and football in junior and senior years, Ernie also played first base well in baseball. Coach Bill Wipfler remembered he had a "great glove, lots of power," but "never mastered hitting a curveball." Despite his tremendous athletic achievement, Davis remained a quiet, shy youngster. Ernie dressed neatly in crewneck sweaters and handed in homework before away games. Always popular with schoolmates, he was chosen senior prom king for his likeable personality and sports skill.

Thirty colleges and universities, including Navy and Notre Dame, recruited Davis before he chose Syracuse University on his mentor Jim Brown's advice. At Syracuse, the speedy Ernie clocked 10.1 seconds in the 100-yard dash. He also played varsity basketball and football, participating in 31 gridiron contests for the Orangemen. The versatile Davis ran from a winged-T unbalanced line formation, specializing in game-breaking off tackle and end run plays. Ernie also proved a punishing blocker, reliable option passer, dangerous defensive back, and dependable placekicker and punt returner. In 1961, Syracuse coach

Ben Schwartzwalder remarked, "Ernie does everything well. He blocks well, runs beautifully and is an outstanding pass receiver. He throws well and is good on defense. . . . I would rate him the number 1 back in the nation."

With the undefeated, untied 1959 national championship Orangemen, Davis performed superbly in Syracuse's 23–14 victory over the University of Texas Longhorns in the 1960 Cotton Bowl. Although a hamstring pull made his status doubtful, Ernie scored 16 of his team's 21 points. In the first quarter, he tallied on an 87-yard touchdown pass from Ger Schwedes. In the second quarter, Davis powered over on a fourth-down play from the Texas one-yard line. Ernie also added two 2-point conversions on pass receptions. This bruising contest was marred by charges of racial slurs by Longhorn players, but the gentlemanly Syracuse back avoided discussing such allegations.

Davis reprised his Cotton Bowl performance in the December 1960 Liberty Bowl between Syracuse and the University of Miami in a frigid Philadelphia Stadium. In the first half, the Hurricanes jumped off to a 14–0 lead, and Ernie gained only 38 yards on 10 carries. In the second half, Davis almost single-handedly led a Syracuse comeback by rushing for an additional 102 yards and scoring a 1-yard touchdown. Miami often triple-teamed Ernie, allowing Syracuse quarterback Dave Sarette to pass more freely. Late in the game, Davis made a key defensive contribution by intercepting Miami quarterback George Mira's long pass near the Syracuse goal line. Coach Schwartzwalder considered this game Ernie's crowning glory. "We goofed around in the first half . . . and Miami, a good team, leaped into a 14–0 lead. Then Ernie took over. He carried three of every four times, taking tacklers with him, and gained 140 yards as we finally won 15–14. Ten guys stood around and watched him, but he gave them all the credit."

At Syracuse, Davis set new career standards for rushing yards (2,836), total yards gained (3,414), scoring (220 points), and touchdowns (35). Ernie broke 10 of Jim Brown's records, although he always tried to avoid comparisons with the star Browns' fullback. "I wish they'd stop calling me another Jimmy Brown. I just want to be Ernie Davis." His many awards included being Most Valuable Back in the 1960 Cotton Bowl, *Sport* Magazine 1961 Player of the Year, Walter Camp Trophy winner in 1961, and 1960 and 1961 consensus All-America. Davis in 1961 became the first African American to win the Heisman Trophy, receiving 179 first-place votes for an 824-point total. Another African American, halfback Bob Ferguson of Ohio State University, finished second with 771.

With such glittering credentials, Davis was courted by the Calgary Stampeders Canadian Football League (CFL) club. Buffalo Bills American Football League (AFL) squad, and Washington Redskins National Football League (NFL) team. Washington chose him as the first player selected in the NFL 1961 draft. Ernie was soon dealt to the Cleveland Browns (NFL) for halfback Bobby Mitchell, who became the first African-American Washington player. Cleveland signed Davis to a three-year, $80,000 contract. Ernie exuded happiness: "I love to play football. And I can't think of anything better than getting paid for it."

Yet Davis tragically never played a down for the Browns. When working out for the College All-Star Game against the Green Bay Packers in July 1962, Ernie experienced infected wisdom teeth, trench mouth, and general fatigue. Doctors initially diagnosed his condition as mononucleosis, but in October they discovered he had acute monocytic leukemia, a fatal condition. Ironically, Davis felt fine: "I was never in pain and I never felt sick. That was the hardest part." Ernie continued to lead a largely normal life, working out with the Browns, sitting on the Browns' bench during home games, studying the Browns' playbook, and even golfing and bowling. Some debated whether or not he could play in late-season games, coach Paul Brown quickly quashed that notion because the running back's illness was much too serious. To his credit, Browns' owner Art Modell never gave a thought to invalidating the Davis contract and developed a special bond with Ernie.

On May 16, 1963, Davis visited Modell in his office before checking himself into Cleveland's Lakeside Hospital because of swollen glands. Ernie thanked Modell for all he had done, chatted briefly, and left. Two days later, Davis died. His body lay in state at Neighborhood House, a community gym in Elmira where Ernie had first excelled as a schoolboy athlete. Flags throughout the city flew at half mast. His personal physician, Dr. Austin Weisberger, provided the perfect epitaph for this unusual man: "He was a real gentleman in all senses of the word. He had great courage and dignity."

BIBLIOGRAPHY: Paul Brown with Jack Clary, *PB: The Paul Brown Story* (New York, 1979); "End of the Dream," *Time* 81 (May 24, 1963), p. 61; "Ernie Davis, Everybody's All American," *Ebony* 17 (December 1961), pp. 73–79; Ernie Davis and Bob August, "I'm Not Unlucky," *Saturday Evening Post* 236 (March 30, 1963), pp. 60–62; *New York Times,* 1958–1963; "Pro Patient," *Newsweek* 60 (October 22, 1962), p. 76; Syracuse University, Sports Information Office files, Syracuse, NY; Alfred Wright, "Ernie Davis, a Man of Courage," *Sports Illustrated* 18 (May 27, 1963), p. 25.

John H. Ziegler

ANDRE DAWSON
(July 10, 1954–) —————————————————————— *Baseball*

Andre Dawson arrived in the major leagues in 1976 with the Montreal Expos National League (NL) club. For the next 20 years, this quiet performer provided leadership both off and on the field as an All-Star and a popular player. Life, however, was not as easy as it sounded for Dawson. Andre learned to play with pain throughout his career, with both his knees being operated on several times. In May 1989, he experienced arthroscopic surgery on his right knee that had landed him on the 21-day disabled list. "I like to think I play the game aggressively," Dawson observed. "I'm too much of a competitor to succumb to something like this. I've always been one to work hard. When I decide to retire or leave the game, it won't be because of my knees." Andre returned that season to hit 21 home runs and drive in 77 runs in 118 games.

Self-discipline and determination remained Dawson's trademarks. "One thing I've learned in this game is to be level-headed," Andre disclosed. Nicknamed the "Hawk" for his defensive abilities from 1987 to 1992 with the Chicago Cubs (NL), he stated, "Take the good with the good and the bad with the bad. I don't think I ever got emotional out there whether I'm performing well or going through a tough time."

Dawson performed especially well in 1987, when he was voted the NL Most Valuable Player (MVP). "Only a blessed few," Andre noted, "make it to the big leagues. If you can get there and stay there for more than ten years, then you have to be doing something right. I don't take what I've been blessed with for granted." The 1987 statistics only began to tell the story, as he led the NL with 49 home runs and 137 RBIs while hitting .287. Dawson also won his seventh Gold Glove Award for his fielding and fourth Silver Slugger Award while playing in his fourth All-Star Game.

Dawson enjoyed an "awesome" season, setting several club records and emerging as a Cub fan favorite. Andre seized the fans' attention and "held it hostage from April through early October." Upon reviewing his season, he revealed, "I've always been so demanding on myself. I'm never content with what I do. I've had a few good years, but I've always felt I could do a little better . . . and sometimes a lot better." The quiet player experienced as much happiness as he had enjoyed in years. South Miami, Florida, renamed a street Andre Dawson Drive.

Dawson had always wanted to play baseball, filling vocational interest forms in junior high with "professional baseball player." His counselors and teachers told him to "get serious," but Andre replied, "Baseball was the only thing I wanted to do." His mother, Mattie, supported her son's dream while bringing up eight children and working two jobs in Miami.

The Miami native, who was born on July 10, 1954, has lived there throughout his life. After graduating from Southwest Miami Senior High School in 1972, Dawson attended Florida A&M for three years and played on its baseball team. The Montreal Expos (NL) signed Andre for a $1,500 bonus after selecting him in the eleventh round in 1975.

Dawson quickly worked his way through the Montreal farm system with his hitting, defense, and speed. His great season at Denver, Colorado, of the American Association in 1976 featured a .350 batting average with 20 home runs in 74 games and landed him in Montreal for 24 games at the end of the season. Andre remained with the Expos until after the 1986 season when he signed as a free agent with the Chicago Cubs. His life took on new meaning when he married Vanessa Turner in December 1978. They have two children.

Dawson became a great friend of outfielder Tim Raines, who joined the Expos in 1981. When Tim tragically developed a drug habit, Andre helped him through the crisis. Raines praised Dawson, "When I had my problem back in '82, he was the one I looked to for encouragement and guidance. After the incident, I sort of hung in his back pocket, so to speak. He is the one I just try to pattern myself after. . . . We're like brothers, close friends, and he's like a father figure." Dawson and Raines played together through the 1986 season. Eventually both performed in Chicago, but Tim played with the White Sox (AL).

The "Hawk" left the Cubs in 1993 to join the Boston Red Sox (AL). The pain-filled 1993 season resulted in Dawson's eighth knee operation, but he managed to hit his 400th career home run. In October 1994, the Red Sox released him. Through the strike-shortened 1994 season, Dawson had batted .280 with 2,700 hits, 428 home runs, and 1,540 RBIs. In April 1995, the Florida Marlins (NL) signed him.

As Andre approached the end of his major league career, he began preparing for life after baseball. "When I walk away from this game, I won't do any second-guessing at all. . . . I'll know when it's time to call it quits. And I won't miss the game. I'll miss the people. But there's life after the game. As funny as it may sound, I don't really look forward to it, but yet I do. It will give me a chance to see my kids grow up."

BIBLIOGRAPHY: *Chicago Cubs Vineline,* October 2, 1987, pp. 8–10; June 4, 1989, p. 29; August 5, 1990, p. 9; April 6, 1991, p. 10; July 7, 1992, p. 10; David L. Porter, ed., *Biographical Dictionary of American Sports: Baseball* (Westport, CT, 1987).

Duane A. Smith

GAIL DEVERS
(November 19, 1966–) ————————————————— *Track and Field*

Gail Devers, who overcame Graves' disease in the early 1990s, ranks as history's fastest combination sprinter-hurdler. Yolanda Gail Devers was born on November 19, 1966, in Seattle, Washington, the second of two children of Larry Devers and Alabe Devers. Gail grew up in San Diego, California, where her father serves as associate minister of the Mount Erie Baptist Church and her mother worked as an elementary school teacher's aide. Although Gail and her brother, Parenthesis, were encouraged to read rather than watch television, they often watched "I Love Lucy." Since Gail insisted upon meeting Lucille Ball, she and her father once drove to Hollywood, California, to meet the television star. "After we got to Hollywood," Larry recalled, "we couldn't actually get to Lucille's house, so I pointed out a bent old woman on the street and said, 'There, that's her.' " Gail insisted that the woman was not Lucy, but her father replied, "Yes, that's her. See what makeup does." "No! No!" she exclaimed, with tears rolling down her face. Her father then admitted that he was kidding. Larry used the trip as a way to teach Gail the difference between "illusion and reality and the importance of living your own life."

Devers at age 15 began track and field as a middle-distance runner at National City's Sweetwater High School, south of San Diego. After clocking 2 minutes 11.07 seconds in the 800 meters as a sophomore, Gail "discovered success" when she "moved down to the sprints" during her junior year. She won both the 100 meters and 100-meter hurdles and placed second in the long jump at the 1984 California State High School championships as a senior. The same year, Devers also finished second in the 100 meters at the TAC Junior championship and third in the 100 meters at the Pan-American Junior Games. Now outgoing Gail remembers being "really shy" as a high school performer and says that her "father used to have to stand on the field until I got ready to go out to the track, and then when I got back he had to be right there where I left him. I was there all by myself and I didn't know anyone." Gail, who entered the University of California at Los Angeles (UCLA) in 1984, became the first female athlete from Sweetwater High School to earn an athletic scholarship from a major university.

After not having a coach at Sweetwater High School, Devers learned from one of the nation's finest at UCLA. Robert Kersee, who became the head women's track and field coach in 1984, kept extreme confidence in Gail. He predicted she would "break the U.S. record in the 100-meter hurdles, make the 1988 Olympic team, and be ready for gold in 1992." Devers thought Kersee "was crazy," but "regardless of whether his predictions were going to come true or whether he was just trying to motivate me, I liked them." By 1987, Gail had achieved world-class times of 10.98 seconds in the 100 meters and 22.71 seconds in the 200 meters. That year, she also captured the 100 meters in the U.S. Olympic Festival and the Pan-American Games. In 1988, Devers established American records of 12.71 seconds and 12.61 seconds in the 100-meter hurdles and captured the 100 meters in the NCAA championships. Gail finished third in the NCAA 100-meter hurdles. After the NCAA championship, she married former UCLA miler Ron Roberts. As Gail Devers-Roberts, she placed second in the 100-meter hurdles at the 1988 U.S. Olympic Trials. The 1988 Summer Olympic Games at Seoul, South Korea, however, witnessed Devers finish last in the semi-finals of the 100-meter hurdles. Her performance of 13.51 seconds marked her slowest time since high school.

Friends blamed Gail's poor Olympic performance on her recent marriage, but she suspected that something was wrong with her physically. Devers recalls that "one week I was there and the next week I was at rock bottom." After the 1988 Olympic Games, Gail experienced unexplained migraine headaches, insomnia, fainting spells, muscle injuries, and fluctuations in body weight of more than 30 pounds. Upon the advice of a physical therapist, her thyroid was examined in 1988. Doctors, however, diagnosed it normal. By September 1990, physicians recognized that she was suffering from advanced Graves' disease, a hyperthyroid condition. Radiation treatments caused hair loss and her feet to swell and bleed. Two days before doctors planned to amputate Devers's feet, her condition began to improve. Physicians stopped the radiation treatments. "I believe by April if we can get this under control," an optimistic Kersee told Gail in November 1990, "I can get you on the World Championships team."

Under Kersee's guidance, Devers resumed track and field practice by walking around the UCLA track in March 1991. Gail competed in her first 100-meter hurdle race in Modesto, California, in May. Devers captured the hurdles in the TAC championships and qualified for the World Championships at Tokyo, Japan. In reference to her bout with Graves' disease, Gail told reporters that she "must be President Bush's long-lost granddaughter," as Bush and his wife Barbara also suffered from the same hyperthyroid condition. At the World Championships, Devers finished second to Russia's Lyudmila Narozhilenko in the 100-meter hurdles. "Six months ago I had no idea I would be here," declared Gail. "It was just a matter of believing in myself." Two weeks later in Berlin, Germany, she established an American record of 12.48 seconds in the 100-meter hurdles. In late 1991, she and her husband divorced.

At the 1992 Olympic Trials, Devers garnered the 100-meter hurdles and placed second in the 100-meter dash. Gail captured the 100 meters at the 1992 Summer Olympic Games in Barcelona, Spain, accomplishing a personal best time of 10.82 seconds. The race marked history's closest Olympic 100-meter final, as the first five runners finished within .06 of a second. Devers ran like she "didn't have another chance to win a Gold Medal." Tragedy befell Gail in the 100-meter hurdles, however, as she struck the final hurdle and stumbled over the finish line in fifth place. In 1993, Devers captured the 60-meter dash indoors in both the USA Track and Field (USATF) championships and World Championships. Gail established American records of 6.99 seconds and 6.65 seconds in the two races. At the 1993 World Championships in Stuttgart, Germany, she prevailed in the 100 meters and the 100-meter hurdles. No female performer had accomplished the rare double since Fannie Blankers-Koen at the 1948 London, England, Summer Olympic Games. Devers and Jamaican Merlene Ottey recorded the same 100-meter time of 10.82 seconds, but the photofinish showed Gail winning by inches. Her winning time in the 100-meter hurdles of 12.46 seconds marked an American record. In yet another photofinish race, Devers anchored the U.S. 4 × 100-meter relay in a Silver Medal performance behind Russia with an American record of 41.49 seconds. Gail, recognized by *Track and Field News* as its 1993 U.S. Female Athlete of the Year, still watches "I Love Lucy" reruns and hopes to open a child day care center. In June 1994, she won the 100 meters outdoors at the USATF Championships in Knoxville, Tennessee. Devers won the 100-meter hurdles in 12.77 seconds at the USATF Outdoor Championships at Sacramento, California, in June 1995, but did not compete in the 100-meter dash.

BIBLIOGRAPHY: Barbara Bigelow, ed., *Contemporary Black Biography*, vol. 7 (Detroit, MI, 1994), pp. 54–57; James Dunaway, Sieg Lindstrom, and Dave Johnson, "Gail Devers," *USATF Bio Data Sheet* (1993); "Gail Devers," in *Games of the XXV Olympiad, Barcelona, Spain, NBC Sports Research Information* (New York, 1992); Dave Johnson,

"A Truly Amazing Comeback," *Track and Field News* 44 (December 1991), p. 11; Ruth Laney, "Devers Won Wrong Race," *Track and Field News* 45 (October 1992), p. 53; Ruth Laney, "Controversy Dogs Devers," *Track and Field News* 46 (November 1993), p. 49; Sieg Lindstrom, "A Long Medical Chart," *Track and Field News* 44 (August 1991), p. 24; Sieg Lindstrom, "America's Best," *Track and Field News* 47 (February 1994), pp. 10–11, 14, 17; Kenny Moore, "Gail Force," *Sports Illustrated* 78 (May 10, 1993), pp. 41–43; David L. Porter, ed., *Biographical Dictionary of American Sports: 1992–1995 Supplement for Baseball, Football, Basketball, and Other Sports* (Westport, CT, 1995).

                                                                        Adam R. Hornbuckle

ERIC DICKERSON
(September 2, 1960–   ) ——————————————————————— *Football*

Eric Dickerson ranks among the leading rushers in professional football history. Eric Demetric Dickerson was born on September 2, 1960, in Sealy, Texas, a town with a population of 4,418. Although his parents were Robert Johnson and Helen Johnson, Eric grew up with his great-uncle, Kary Dickerson, and great-aunt, Viola Dickerson, who legally adopted him.

At Sealy High School, Dickerson displayed the versatility frequently associated with stellar running backs **Gale Sayers, Walter Payton, Jim Brown,** and **O. J. Simpson.** Great running backs like Dickerson feature speed. Eric, a champion athlete in football and track and field, won the State 100-yard title in a blistering 9.4 seconds. In his senior year, he rush for 2,653 yards and carried Sealy to the State AAA football championship. In this championship game, Dickerson rushed for 311 yards and four touchdowns. *Parade* named Eric the premier high school running back of 1978.

As a highly recruited athlete, Dickerson received many offers to play collegiate football. Eric stayed in the Lone Star State, entering Southern Methodist University (SMU) in Dallas in the fall of 1979. The Mustangs enjoyed a reputation for football excellence. In selecting the Southwest Conference (SWC), he performed in intense rivalries.

During his first freshman SMU outing, Dickerson rushed for 123 yards and scored three touchdowns against Rice University, the "Harvard of the South." Injuries slowed Eric, as he finished the 1979 season with a moderate 477 yards on 115 carries. In 1980, he rushed for more than 100 yards in five games. His 1,038 total rushing yards for the whole season included a final game performance of 110 yards versus Brigham Young University (BYU) in the Holiday Bowl.

Dickerson's junior year proved exceptional, as he earned SWC Player of the Year honors. Eric's 1,428 rushing yards marked the second best in SMU history, while his 19 touchdowns established a Mustang record. Violations of NCAA rules and regulations, however, excluded SMU from any bowl game.

In his final year, Dickerson became the nation's third best college running back with 147 rushing yards per game and participated in both the Cotton Bowl and Hula Bowl. Eric's 124 rushing yards played a pivotal role in SMU's 7–3 Cotton Bowl victory over the University of Pittsburgh. His 4,450 career rushing yards on 790 attempts (5.6-yard average) shattered **Earl Campbell's** SWC record for both yards and attempts. He scored 48 touchdowns for 288 points, sharing first place with Doak Walker. Dickerson's pace and powerful, direct running style enabled him to score with short and long runs. During his senior year, Eric scored on runs of 80, 80, 79, 70, 63, and 62 yards. His high school track star sprinting ability gave him the necessary pace to penetrate secondary lines of defense. The six-foot-three-inch 218-pounder enjoyed 27 career 100-yard-plus games.

In the 1983 National Football League (NFL) draft, Dickerson was selected second and joined the Los Angeles Rams with a triumphant rookie year. Eric set a National Football Conference (NFC) rookie record with 1,808 yards in 390 attempts for 18 touchdowns. His 1,808 yards that year marked the sixth highest NFL season total at that time. Eric won every NFL Rookie of the Year award, being voted Player of the Year by *Sports Illustrated* and selected for the Pro Bowl.

The following year featured Dickerson at the pinnacle of success. Eric's 2,105 rushing yards surpassed Simpson's record 2,003 yards, established 11 years previously. He recorded 12 games with over 100 yards, breaking another record held by Simpson and Earl Campbell. Dickerson was named NFC Player of the Year by United Press International (UPI), *Football News, USA Today,* the Kansas City Committee of 101, and the Washington, D.C., Atlanta, and Columbus Touchdown Clubs. The NFL picked him as Most Valuable Player (MVP), while he went to his second Pro Bowl.

In 1985, Dickerson rushed for 1,234 yards and 12 touchdowns. The following year, Eric led the NFL in rushing with 1,821 yards and garnered a third Pro Bowl start. He finished runner-up to **Lawrence Taylor** of the New York Giants as MVP by the Associated Press (AP) and *USA Today.*

On October 31, 1987, Los Angeles traded Dickerson to the Indianapolis Colts (NFL). Eric started the final 8 games of the season for Indianapolis, ranking second in NFL rushing and earning a fourth Pro Bowl start. On December 20 against the San Diego Chargers, he passed Brown's legendary record of 8,000 rushing yards in 80 games. Dickerson reached the 8,000-yard barrier in only 74 games.

In 1988, Dickerson captured his fourth NFL rushing title (388 carries, 1,659 yards, and 14 touchdowns) and earned a fifth Pro Bowl selection. Eric, the next year, became the only back in NFL history to achieve 7 consecutive 1,000-yard rushing seasons and garnered 314 carries, 1,311 yards, and 7 touchdowns. He suffered a recurring hamstring injury and missed the first game of his professional career in early November against the Miami Dolphins.

The 1990 season saw Dickerson start 8 out of the final 11 games, but injuries sidelined him the first 5 games. Nevertheless, Eric in 1990 passed Simpson

(11,236) and John Riggins (11,352) in career rushing yards. Although having only three 100-plus games, he reached 61 for his career and moved into second place all-time behind Payton's 77.

Disputes with Colts management led to Dickerson's trade to the Atlanta Falcons (NFL) in 1992. He and flamboyant Falcons head coach Jerry Glanville clashed, causing Dickerson to retire in 1993. During his NFL career, he rushed 2,996 times for 13,259 yards (4.4 yard average) and 90 touchdowns and caught 281 passes for 2,137 yards (7.6 yard average) and 6 touchdowns. Injuries hampered Eric's athletic performance, but he no longer possessed the desire and intensity to continue as a professional football player. In view of the bruising nature of Dickerson's playing position, Eric had survived a decade of NFL collision and contact! Sociologists Stanley Eitzen and George Sage point out that "the median life of a professional football player's career is 3.4 years."

Dickerson remains single, lives in Malibu, California, and is very committed in the Los Angeles area with youth. Los Angeles had experienced the shattering riots in the summer of 1992. Eric set up a pioneering program called "Dickerson's Raiders" to provide social, cultural, and athletic activities for preteens.

BIBLIOGRAPHY: D. Stanley Eitzen and George H. Sage, *Sociology of American Sport*, 5th ed. (Dubuque, IA, 1993); *Indianapolis Colts Media Guide* (1991); David L. Porter, ed., *Biographical Dictionary of American Sports: Football* (Westport, CT, 1987); *The Sporting News Pro Football Register* (1994).

Scott A.G.M. Crawford

HARRISON DILLARD
(July 8, 1923–) ———————————————————————— *Track and Field*

Harrison "Bones" Dillard remains perhaps as well known for a race he never ran as for his four Olympic Gold Medals, 14 Amateur Athletic Union (AAU) titles, and six NCAA championships. In 1948, Dillard ranked indisputably as the world's greatest hurdler, having won 82 consecutive races and setting a world record of 13.6 in the 110-meter hurdles. A bad qualifying race in the Olympic Trials, however, eliminated any chance for Harrison to run his specialty at the London, England, Summer Olympics. Instead, in a major upset, he won the 100-meter dash. Four years later, Dillard captured the hurdles at the Helsinki, Finland, Summer Olympics and thus became the only Olympic athlete to win a Gold Medal in these two very dissimilar races. He also ran on the winning 4 × 100-meter relay teams in both the 1948 and 1952 Olympics.

William Harrison Dillard was born on July 8, 1923, in Cleveland, Ohio. When his father William lost his small ice and coal business during the Depression, his mother Terah started working as a maid. Harrison, who always liked to run and jump, recalls that his first hurdles were seats taken out of abandoned cars. Dillard was nicknamed "Bones" because he was such a small, frail youngster, weighing only 49 pounds as a 10-year-old. Harrison's adult height of 5 foot 10 inches was also short for a world-class hurdler, but his great speed and jumping ability compensated for any physical shortcomings.

Dillard, like so many youngsters of his generation, was tremendously inspired by the magnificent feats of **Jesse Owens,** who also grew up in Cleveland, Ohio: "I first saw Jesse Owens when he came back to Cleveland for a parade following his Berlin victories. I remember exactly what he was wearing. He had on a navy blue suit with a pinstripe, a white shirt, and a dark tie. When his car passed us, Jesse looked down, winked, and said, "How are you doing?" Of course, we thought this was the greatest thing in the world. Our idol had actually spoken to us. Back then we had three idols: Jesse, **Joe Louis,** and **Henry Armstrong.** At that time, black history wasn't taught, so we naturally took our heroes from sports."

Dillard, like Owens, attended Cleveland's East Technical High School, where he won the State championship in the high and low hurdles his senior year. Harrison planned to follow Jesse to Ohio State University but considered 140 miles too far from home. He instead attended Baldwin-Wallace College, only 14 miles away. Dillard was drafted in 1943 into the U.S. Army and fought in three World War II campaigns in Italy with the all-African-American 92nd Infantry Division. After seeing Harrison compete in an All-Army track meet, General George Patton labeled him "the best damn athlete I've ever seen."

In 1946, Dillard returned to Baldwin-Wallace and set his first world record in the outdoor 220-yard low hurdles. The following year, Harrison established a world mark of 13.6 seconds in the 120-yard hurdles. Following a third-place finish in the 1948 Olympic Trials, he was certainly not favored to win the 100 meters at the London Summer Games. But Dillard made a great start and narrowly edged teammate Barney Ewell in Olympic-equaling time of 10.3 seconds. In 1952, Harrison won the 120-meter hurdles at both the AAU National championship and Olympic Trials before breaking the Olympic record at the Helsinki Summer Games. In 1956, the 33-year-old tried to qualify for his third Olympic team but finished sixth at the Trials and permanently retired.

Although mild mannered and always the gentleman, Dillard, nevertheless, remained a fierce competitor: "I was extremely competitive. As a youngster, growing up scrawny and skinny, I was naturally picked on by the other kids, so I had to prove myself by fighting back. Later, I accepted my losses gracefully, but I certainly did like to win, and after a defeat, I couldn't wait for my next chance. I always appeared calm. As a matter of fact, before the 100-meter finals in 1948, I fell asleep in the locker room. Other guys would get very nervous. Mel Patton, for example, would actually throw up. Barney Ewell would get very jittery. Nobody could talk to him. He'd snap your head off if you said anything. My nature was totally different. But I still planned on winning."

After finishing his bachelor's degree in business in 1949, Dillard briefly worked in Baldwin-Wallace's admission office. Harrison spent 10 years in public relations for Bill Veeck, the colorful owner of the Cleveland Indians American League (AL) baseball team. He then became chief of the Business Department of the Cleveland School Board, working there for over 20 years.

Dillard introduced two hurdling techniques, which are common today. Harrison was the first hurdler to start with his head looking down at the ground rather than straight ahead and employed an extremely high action with the trail knee going over the hurdle. This forced the lead leg down a little more rapidly and helped get the trail leg more quickly on the ground.

Dillard won the prestigious 1953 Sullivan Award, given annually to the nation's outstanding amateur athlete. The 1974 charter member of the National Track and Field Hall of Fame and U.S. Olympic Hall of Fame member participates in civic and educational affairs. In 1984, Harrison received an honorary doctorate from his alma mater, Baldwin-Wallace.

BIBLIOGRAPHY: Lewis H. Carlson and John J. Fogarty, *Tales of Gold: An Oral History of the Summer Olympic Games Told by America's Gold Medal Winners* (Chicago, IL, 1987); Bill Mallon and Ian Buchanan, *Quest for Gold: The Encyclopedia of American Olympians* (New York, 1984); David L. Porter, ed., *Biographical Dictionary of American Sports: Outdoor Sports* (Westport, CT, 1988).

Lewis H. Carlson

TONY DORSETT
(April 7, 1954–) ————————————————————————— *Football*

Tony Dorsett, a brilliant 5-foot-11-inch, 190-pound halfback, played football from 1973 to 1976 for the University of Pittsburgh and compiled a career 6,082 yards rushing. Tony's rushing yardage still tops the NCAA Division I-A career statistical charts. Besides being the first college player to amass over 1,000 yards rushing for four seasons, he remains the only gridder boasting three seasons of rushing over 1,500 yards. Dorsett, chosen by the Dallas Cowboys in the first round of the 1977 National Football League (NFL) player draft as the second player selected, ranks third on the NFL's all-time rushing list with a career 12,739 yards between 1977 and 1988. Tony was elected in 1994 to the National Football Foundation College Football Hall of Fame and to the Pro Football Hall of Fame the first year of his eligibility.

Anthony Drew Dorsett, the son of Wes Dorsett, a steelworker, and Myrtle Dorsett, was born in Rochester, Pennsylvania, on April 7, 1954. Tony grew up in Aliquippa, Pennsylvania, and attended high school in nearby Hopewell. He starred in football, basketball, and track and field, compiling 1,034 yards and 1,283 yards rushing during his final two high school gridiron campaigns. Dorsett, a 1972 High School All-State and All-American football halfback, received over 200 college scholarship offers. The 160-pound freshman opted for the University of Pittsburgh because of its proximity to his home and of Panther coach Johnny Majors's strong conviction to build a national championship football squad. The Panthers posted a miserable 1–10 record the year before Tony arrived and had failed to produce a winning season in nine years. In 1973, however, Dorsett helped lift the Panthers to a 6–5–1 finish. Arizona State University defeated Pittsburgh in the 1974 Fiesta Bowl. Tony set two NCAA freshman records, gaining 265 yards against Northwestern University and compiling 1,586 yards rushing for the season. The Associated Press (AP) named him All-America First Team halfback, the first freshman so honored since Doc Blanchard of Army in 1944.

Coach Majors exhibited a veer offense that utilized Dorsett's blazing speed and surprising inside power, guiding Pittsburgh to 7–4 and 8–4 finishes the next two seasons. Tony scurried for 303 yards from scrimmage in 1975 against the University of Notre Dame, the most ever by an individual against the Irish, and sparked the Panthers to an easy 38–19 triumph over the University of Kansas in the Sun Bowl. "It's a terrific feeling to be able to do some of the things that I can do," Dorsett said. "I'm just blessed with some God-given talent and I'm very fortunate to have this. I'm just hoping that I can stay healthy and keep it moving." Tony, a speech-communications major, was nicknamed "Hawk" and "T.D.," the latter for his initials and his unequaled ability to cross the last white line.

In 1976, Pittsburgh finished a perfect 12–0 before humbling the University of Georgia, 27–3, in the Sugar Bowl and was unanimously chosen as national champion. Dorsett, a unanimous All-America, set 15 NCAA game, season, or career records, garnering the 1976 Heisman Trophy, Maxwell Award, and the *Football News* award as the Outstanding Player of the Year. Army coach Homer Smith maintained, "I have not seen a running back like Tony Dorsett since **O. J. Simpson.**" Coach Joe Paterno of Penn State echoed Smith's sentiments. "Dorsett is the greatest player we have ever played against," he stated, "and that includes **Jimmy Brown** of Syracuse, **Archie Griffin** of Ohio State, George Webster and Bubba Smith of Michigan State, and Greg Pruitt of Oklahoma."

Dorsett posted a triple crown in 1976, leading the nation in scoring with 134 points, in rushing with 1,948 yards from scrimmage, and in all-purpose yards running with 2,021. "There'll never be another running back in college football like him!" exclaimed Pittsburgh's All-America middle guard Al Romano. "He amazes us every week. I hate to practice against him. It's like trying to catch a fly." Tony acknowledged, "You've got to give the public some of your time." Dorsett participated in a seven-city NCAA tour promoting college football and appeared on NCAA-sponsored television spots to help fight drug abuse. His jersey, number 33, was retired by the University of Pittsburgh before his graduation in June 1977.

Dorsett, chosen 1977 NFL Rookie of the Year by the AP and *The Sporting*

News, performed most of his first season with Dallas behind Preston Pearson. Nevertheless, Tony led the Cowboys in rushing with 1,007 yards from scrimmage. He capped an excellent initial campaign by scoring a touchdown in Super Bowl XII to help Dallas wallop the Denver Broncos, 27–10. During the 1978 season, Dorsett sparked the Cowboys to Super Bowl XIII. Dallas lost to the Pittsburgh Steelers in a 35–31 nail-biter. Dallas coach Tom Landry exclaimed, "Tony is our catalyst; he is the one who makes us go on offense." Although the Cowboys failed to reach the Super Bowl again before Dorsett retired, Dallas played in National Football Conference (NFC) title games in 1980, 1981, and 1982, losing to the Philadelphia Eagles, San Francisco 49ers, and Washington Redskins.

Tony, an All-Pro in 1981, set the NFL's all-time record for the longest run from scrimmage with a 99 yarder against the Minnesota Vikings in 1983. Only 10 Cowboys were on the playing field due to a substitution error. He played in NFL Pro Bowls following the 1978 and 1981–1983 seasons. Dallas' general manager Tex Schramm lauded him, "He has super quickness, super vision. He knows just when to cut." Dorsett was traded in 1988 to the Denver Broncos (NFL), with whom he played his final season. Besides his humongous 12,000-plus career rushing yards for 77 touchdowns, Tony caught 398 passes for 3,554 yards and 13 touchdowns and finished with 546 career points. In 1994, the Pro Football Hall of Fame enshrined him, and the Dallas Cowboys inducted him into their Ring of Honor.

BIBLIOGRAPHY: Dean Billick, Sports Information director, University of Pittsburgh, "Dorsett Wows 'Em" (Pittsburgh, PA, 1975); John T. Brady, *The Heisman, a Symbol of Excellence* (New York, 1984); Myron Cope, "My, How He Does Run On," *Sports Illustrated* 45 (November 8, 1976), pp. 20–23; Mark Engel, "Pitt's Amazing T.D.," *Football News* (November 9, 1976), pp. 1, 17; Jim Haughton, "Dorsett Is Dynamite," *Football News* (November 11, 1975); Dave Newhouse, *Heisman: After the Glory* (St. Louis, MO, 1985); Tim Panaccio, *Beast of the East* (West Point, NY, 1982); Pittsburgh vs. Navy Football Program, October 25, 1975, pp. 13, 21; David L. Porter, ed., *Biographical Dictionary of American Sports: Football* (Westport, CT, 1987); Beau Riffenburgh, *The Official NFL Encyclopedia*, 4th ed. (New York, 1986); *The Sporting News Football Register* (1989); Sugar Bowl Football Program, Pittsburgh vs. Georgia, New Orleans, LA, January 1, 1977.

James D. Whalen

BOB DOUGLAS
(November 4, 1882–July 16, 1979) ——————————————— *Basketball*

Bob Douglas, the "father of black basketball," owned and managed the New York Renaissance basketball team from 1923 through 1949. Robert L. Douglas was born on November 4, 1882, in St. Kitts, British West Indies, the son of Robert Gould Douglas. His family immigrated to the United States in 1886 and eventually settled in New York City. After World War I, Bob and several friends formed the Spartan Field Club. The club offered the African-American youth of New York City amateur competition in basketball, cricket, soccer, and track and field. Douglas especially liked basketball, as his club sponsored a heavyweight team of the older, more mature boys and a lightweight aggregate for the younger ones. Bob considered his Spartan Braves "very successful" and joined them occasionally as a player on the court.

In the fall of 1923, Douglas formed the New York Renaissance professional basketball team. The team name came from the Renaissance Ballroom, where the team practiced and played. Players and fans soon shortened the name to the "Rens." In their first game on November 3, 1923, the Rens defeated the Collegiate Five, a white team, 28–22. During the 1923–1924 season, the Rens won 15 contests and lost only 8 games.

The Rens comprised the first full-salaried professional African-American basketball team. Douglas, the initial owner to require his players to sign contracts, resembled many of his fellow West Indian immigrants in maintaining a professional businesslike attitude. Former player John Isaacs recalled, "Bob had us sign contracts, but his handshake was his word." Without a high school or college education, Douglas achieved notoriety in both the basketball and business worlds through hard work and perseverance.

Within a couple of years, the Rens played a 150-game schedule. During the 1930s, they became a barnstorming team. The Rens, traveling four months out of the year in their customized bus, played one-night stands and seven to eight games each week. Douglas booked games with various teams, including colleges, YMCAs, amateur clubs, and other professional teams. The Rens played both African-American and white teams in the Northeast and Midwest but only African-American teams in the South. Nonetheless, the players faced racism and discrimination wherever they traveled, as many hotels and restaurants refused to accept them. The team usually stayed in one location and traveled up to 300 miles each day to the game sights. After the game, the Rens traveled back to their temporary home base. When accommodations could not be found, especially in the South, they were forced to eat brown-bag meals and sleep on their bus. In the South, the team occasionally found a hot meal and comfortable bed with a local African-American family.

The Rens featured outstanding fast breaks with quick, lightning-fast passes among players and quick moves toward the basket. To avoid slipping and falling on the ballroom floors, they adapted their play and became a passing team. This trait quickly became a "Ren" trademark.

During the 1930s, the Renaissance ranked as the nation's top professional basketball team. They won 88 consecutive games during the 1932–1933 season, finishing with a 127–7 record. The Rens also consistently defeated the Original Celtics, the top white team at that time. For 14 consecutive seasons in the 1920s and 1930s, they won 100 or more games. Their popularity transcended the color line, as up to 15,000 African-American and white fans paid to watch them play during the depression years. According to Douglas, "I paid all the living expenses of the members of the team while they were on the road. Guys like Fats Jenkins and Tarzan Cooper were getting $250 a month, plus expenses, plus $3 a day for meals—which was big money at that time."

By defeating the white Oshkosh All-Stars, 34–25, Douglas's Rens won the first World Professional Basketball championship in March 1939 at Chicago, Illinois. Due to gas rationing, Bob dramatically decreased the number of games the Rens played during World War II. In lieu of traveling, the Rens limited their games to New York City and the metropolitan area. Following the war, the Rens resumed a regular barnstorming schedule. After 22 years of coaching, however, Douglas became strictly a manager and turned over his coaching duties to the team captain.

In 1948, the Rens moved to Dayton, Ohio, and became the first African-American team to join the National Basketball League. The Rens replaced the Detroit Vagabonds and assumed their losing record. The 1948–1949 season marked the last campaign for the Rens, who compiled a 16–43 record. Half brother James Douglas remembered, "With the formation of the NBA, the Rens could find no other teams of their caliber to play." Consequently, the Rens disbanded.

In their 26-year existence, the Rens recorded 2,318 wins and only 381 losses. In 1971, Douglas was the first African American to be elected as a contributor to the Naismith Memorial Basketball Hall of Fame. The Robert L. Douglas Basketball League, a New York summer pro league, is named for him. Bob managed the Renaissance Ballroom in Harlem from the mid-1930s until 1973 and served as the first president of the New York Pioneer Athletic Club. Douglas died on July 16, 1979, in New York City at age 96. He married Cora Dismond, who died in 1992, and was survived by a half brother, James, who resides in Mount Vernon, New York.

BIBLIOGRAPHY: Arthur Ashe, Jr., *A Hard Road to Glory: A History of the African-American Athlete, 1919–1945,* vol. 2 (New York, 1988); Ocania Chalk, *Pioneers of Black Sport* (New York, 1975); Glenn Dickey, *The History of Professional Basketball Since 1896* (New York, 1982); Robert L. Douglas file, Naismith Memorial Basketball Hall of Fame, Springfield, MA; Ronald L. Mendell, *Who's Who in Basketball* (New Rochelle, NY, 1973); *New York Times,* July 17, 1979; David L. Porter, ed., *Biographical Dictionary of American Sports: Basketball and Other Indoor Sports* (Westport, CT, 1989); Art Rust and Edna Rust, *Art Rust's Illustrated History of the Black Athlete* (Garden City, NY, 1985).

Susan J. Rayl

CLYDE DREXLER
(June 22, 1962–   ) ———————————————————— *Basketball*

Clyde Drexler ranked among the dominant National Basketball Association (NBA) players during the 1980s and 1990s, as the NBA's popularity exploded across the nation and throughout the world. Clyde Drexler was born on June 22, 1962, in New Orleans, Louisiana. His mother, Eunice Drexler Scott, brought up Clyde and his four siblings by herself and always stressed to her children that education should be their first priority. When Drexler was only four, his family moved to Houston, Texas. As he grew older, Clyde began to play Little League baseball and basketball. Although enjoying sports and the thrill of competition, he also spent much time on schoolwork.

Drexler, like most playground youths who play basketball, became fascinated with the dunk shot. Clyde's first dunk came on a playground behind a nearby junior high school. The 15-year-old, six-foot-one-inch Drexler soared over two opponents to the hoop. Drexler's dunk proved even more remarkable because the basket was a foot higher than regulation.

Due to the time involved in playing on the school basketball team, Clyde initially declined to try out for the squad. He feared that it would cut into his time for schoolwork. In his junior year, the Sterling High School basketball coach finally persuaded Drexler and his mother that he should play. Clyde's hard work and dedication led to his steady improvement as a basketball player. He played nearly every position as a two-year starter at Sterling High School. As a senior, he was named the team's MVP and made the All-Houston Independent School District team.

Drexler, although not yet a complete basketball player, was recruited by only three major colleges and chose to attend the nearby University of Houston as a teammate of Hakeem Olajuwan. The Cougars, coached by Guy Lewis, soon ranked among the nation's dominant college teams and were nicknamed "Phi Slamma Jama" for their above-the-rim acrobatics. Clyde developed into one of the nation's best two-way guards with his leaping ability and sleek moves to the basket, bringing him notoriety as "The Glide." "He was a super defensive player," coach Lewis recalled. "He had great quickness, good hands, and great anticipation."

Drexler, the core of Houston's transition game, excelled more as a scorer than pure shooter. Clyde scored and rebounded in double figures in 45 games during his college career, becoming the first Houston player to score more than 1,000 points, grab over 900 rebounds, and collect 300 assists in a career. Houston made two consecutive trips to the Final Four, appearing in the 1983 Championship game. Clyde was named the Southwest Conference Player of the Year as a junior.

Drexler skipped his senior season and turned professional. The Portland Trail Blazers selected him in the first round of the 1983 NBA draft. Clyde needed some time to get accustomed to the more physical, faster-paced professional game. He averaged only 7.7 points per game in his rookie season as one of only two Trail Blazers to appear in all 82 games. The next season, Portland moved Drexler into the starting lineup. Clyde responded with a 17.2-point scoring average and finished second on the team in assists.

Drexler's offensive responsibilities steadily increased with each successive season, as he developed into one of the NBA's top shooting guards. With his six-foot-seven-inch frame and quickness, he defeated teams in several different ways. "If you step back and take a look at Clyde, you'll see that nobody but

Michael Jordan can do the things Clyde can do," Portland coach Rick Adelman later commented. "Very few players can get easy baskets for your team the way Clyde can." In 1985–1986, Drexler scored 18.5 points per game and appeared in his first All-Star Game, tallying 10 points in 15 minutes of action. Clyde averaged 27.0 points a game in 1987–1988 and attained a career-high 27.2-point scoring average in 1988–1989.

Although Drexler ranked among the premier NBA players, the Trail Blazers still encountered trouble advancing beyond the first round of the playoffs. Prior to the 1989–1990 season, Portland obtained power forward Buck Williams from the New Jersey Nets in a trade. The acquisition helped solidify the team. Although relying less on Clyde for scoring, the Trail Blazers won 20 more games than the previous year and reached the NBA finals before falling to the Detroit Pistons.

The following season, 63–19 Portland posted the best NBA record. Drexler sacrificed his scoring for the good of the team, with his game average falling to 21.5 points. Portland, however, unexpectedly lost to the Los Angeles Lakers in the Western Conference finals. Portland returned to the NBA finals the next year, losing to the Chicago Bulls, four games to two. Clyde enjoyed an outstanding season and averaged 25.0 points per game, being named to the All-NBA First Team. He also started for the West All-Stars, garnering 22 points, nine rebounds, and six assists. The year culminated with his selection to the U.S. Olympic "Dream Team," winners of the Gold Medal at the 1992 Barcelona, Spain, Summer Games.

Injuries and age have begun to take their toll on Drexler. Clyde's scoring average and games played have declined due to knee and hamstring injuries. His career NBA scoring average, nevertheless, remains over 20 points a game, as he led Portland in career points scored and steals. Size, quickness, and agility have enabled Drexler to play effectively at both the small forward and shooting guard positions throughout his career. Clyde has appeared in eight All-Star games, making the All-NBA Second Team twice, First Team once, and Third Team twice. In February 1995, the Trail Blazers traded him to the Houston Rockets (NBA). He helped Houston defeat the San Antonio Spurs in the 1995 Western Conference finals and sweep the Orlando Magic in the 1995 NBA finals, providing both scoring and rebounding.

Drexler also excels off the court. Besides spending time with his wife, Gaynell, and his children, Austin and Elise, Clyde participates in many community activities during the off-season. He has served as the honorary spokesman for the Blazer Avia Scholastic Improvement Concepts program, designed to encourage academic achievement. Drexler has also sponsored a summer inner-city youth basketball camp in Houston. During previous summers, Clyde worked in a bank and has gained valuable experience in handling his investments.

BIBLIOGRAPHY: *Great Athletes—The Twentieth Century,* vol. 5 (Pasadena, CA, 1989); Billy Packer and Roland Lazenby, *College Basketball's 25 Greatest Teams* (St. Louis, MO, 1989); *Portland Trail Blazers Media Guide* (1994–1995); *The Sporting News Official NBA Guide* (1994–1995); *The Sporting News Official NBA Register* (1994–1995).

Curtice R. Mang

CHARLEY DUMAS
(February 12, 1937–) ————————————————— *Track and Field*

On June 29, 1956, Charley Dumas became the first athlete to clear 7 feet in the high jump, soaring over 7 feet ½ inch. Charles Everett Dumas, one of five children of Monroe Dumas and Nancy Dumas, was born February 12, 1937, in Tulsa, Oklahoma. At age four, Dumas moved with his family to Los Angeles, California. Charley decided to specialize in the high jump in the eighth grade, after he recorded "the best performance in the high jump in his physical education class." As a freshman at Centennial High School in Los Angeles, he shared second in the high jump in the City championship and placed fourth in the California State championships. During his senior year in 1955, Dumas won the State championship and set a national high school high jump record of 6 feet 9⅜ inches. The Amateur Athletic Union (AAU) National championships saw him share first place with defending national high jump champion Ernie Shelton. Since Charley had graduated from Centennial High School shortly before the championship meet, his performance of 6 feet 10¼ inches was not considered a national high school record.

In the fall of 1955, Dumas entered Compton Junior College near Los Angeles. In 1956, the 19-year-old, 6-foot-2-inch Compton freshman enjoyed an undefeated season and captured the high jump in the AAU championships, Olympic Trials, and Summer Olympic Games at Melbourne, Australia. After qualifying for the Olympic team at 6 feet 9½ inches with Vern Wilson and Phil Reavis, he asked high jump official Dave Schwartz to raise the high jump bar to 7 feet. Wilson, however, told Charley to jump higher than even 7 feet because "a dozen guys will do it next week, once the mental barrier is gone. Put it a half-inch over." With the bar set at 7 feet ⅝ inches, Dumas missed his first attempt and then cleared it easily on his second try. "I wasn't even thinking about seven feet!" exclaimed Dumas afterwards. "I was thinking only of making the [Olympic] team." *New York Times* sportswriter Allison Danzig described Charley's performance, which drew a standing ovation from the Los Angeles Coliseum crowd of over 34,000, as "a moment comparable to, if not as dramatic as, the moment the four minute mile barrier was broken."

At the 1956 Summer Olympic Games in Melbourne, Australia, Dumas met his greatest challenge from Australia's Charles "Chilla" Porter. The 20-year-old Australian, inspired by the support of his countrymen, led the competition with fewer misses at 6 feet 10¾ inches, more than 2 inches higher than his previous best performance. According to track and field historian Roberto Quercetani, Charley "appeared to have [had] no nerves" throughout the competition, "gathered himself together and clinched the gold medal by going over 6 feet, 11½ inches on his third attempt." Dumas, whose winning height marked an Olympic record by 3 inches, acknowledged that "winning the gold medal was very satisfying, but to be the first man to jump seven feet . . . was the magic moment."

For the rest of the 1950s, Dumas dominated the high jump. In 1957, Charley remained undefeated and won the AAU title at 6 feet 10¼ inches. Dumas, who had entered the University of Southern California (USC), garnered second in the high jump at the NCAA championships and the AAU title in 1958. In that year, he also clocked 14.1 seconds in the 120-yard high hurdles. After earning a fifth AAU title in 1959, Charley captured the high jump in the Pan-American Games in a meet record of 6 feet 10½ inches. He topped 7 feet ¼ inch in 1960, but a leg injury limited him to sixth place in the Rome, Italy, Summer Olympic Games. After the 1960 Summer Olympic Games, Dumas retired from competition. Charley reemerged with a performance of 7 feet ¼ inch in 1964 but then slipped back into retirement. Dumas, who "hardly ever jumped in practice," pioneered the use of stretching exercises in preparation for the high jump. According to USC track and field coach Jess Mortensen, "Charley's body is as loose as a sack of ashes."

After graduating with a bachelor's degree from USC in 1959, Dumas pursued a teaching and counseling career in the Los Angeles public school system. He also earned a Master of Arts degree from the University of California at Los Angeles (UCLA). Dumas, who weighs 178 pounds, the same as he did as a competitor, has considered "competing in masters meets" but fears that "I'd push it too hard and pull a muscle. If I got in shape, I think I could jump 6–6." After Cuba's Javier Sotomayor high jumped 8 feet in 1989, Charley remarked, "It's a tremendous achievement. When I think of how long I trained, how hard I worked to [get] that seven-foot jump, well, it's hard to imagine someone going a foot higher than I did." Dumas, who lives in Inglewood, California, with his wife Gloria and two children, was inducted into the National Track and Field Hall of Fame in 1990.

BIBLIOGRAPHY: Earl Gustkey, "Dumas Holds Memories of 7-Foot Leap," *Los Angeles Times,* May 8, 1977; Earl Gustkey, "7–0: When Charlie Dumas Jumped, the Barrier Fell," *Los Angeles Times,* June 29, 1986; Earl Gustkey, "Dumas' Reaction to 8-Foot Leap: What Took So Long?" *Los Angeles Times,* August 1, 1989; "Hall of Fame's 'Class of 1990,'" *Athletics Congress USA Record* 11 (Summer 1990), p. 2; Frank G. Menke, ed., *The Encyclopedia of Sports,* 4th rev. ed. (New York, 1969); Cordner Nelson, *Track's Greatest Champions* (Los Altos, CA, 1986); David L. Porter, ed., *Biographical Dictionary of American Sports: Outdoor Sports* (Westport, CT, 1988); Roberto L. Quercetani, *A World History of Track and Field Athletics* (London, England, 1964).

                                                        Adam R. Hornbuckle

JULIUS ERVING
(February 22, 1950–) _____ Basketball

Julius Erving, known more popularly as "Dr. J.," gained fame as a professional basketball player in the 1970s and 1980s. Julius Winfield Erving II was born on February 22, 1950, in Hempstead, New York, the son of Callie (Erving) Lindsey. Erving began playing basketball on the playgrounds of New York

City and at Roosevelt High School. Julius led the University of Massachusetts in scoring in 46 of his 52 varsity games in 1970 and 1971. A six-foot-six-inch, 200-pound forward, he set career records of 1,049 rebounds and 1,370 points during his two college seasons. As a sophomore at Massachusetts, Erving ranked as the nation's second leading rebounder and averaged 20 rebounds per game and 26 points per contest. In his junior year, he finished third in rebounding and averaged 19 rebounds and 27 points per game. Erving by-passed his senior year at Massachusetts to turn professional. Julius left Massachusetts early to help pay his mother's medical bills. He signed a four-year contract with the Virginia Squires of the American Basketball Association (ABA) for $500,000. In his first season in 1971–1972, Erving was named ABA Rookie of the Year. Julius averaged 27 points and 16 rebounds per contest that year.

Erving's nickname, "Dr. J.," came from high school teammate Leon Saunders, according to his Roosevelt High School coach. Julius referred to Saunders as "The Professor," while Saunders called him "The Doctor." During Erving's first ABA season, Roland "Fatty" Taylor added the initial and Julius became the infamous "Dr. J."

Erving led the Virginia Squires to the ABA playoffs in 1972–1973, his second season, averaging 32 points and 22 rebounds per game. Julius also made the All-ABA First Team four consecutive years from 1972–1973 through 1975–1976. For five consecutive seasons, he made the ABA All-Star team. After his first season with the Squires, Erving attempted to sign with the Atlanta Hawks (NBA). The courts, however, ordered Julius to return to the Squires. Virginia traded him in 1973 to the New York Nets (ABA), where he spent the next three years. Erving, the ABA Most Valuable Player (MVP) in 1974 and 1976, led the Nets to the 1976 ABA championship. During the 6-game final series with the Denver Nuggets, he remarkably averaged 38 points per game. Julius played in 455 regular-season games during his five-year ABA career, averaging 29 points per game with 11,662 total points and 12 rebounds per contest with 4,924 altogether.

In 1976, the Nets and three other ABA teams were absorbed into the National Basketball Association (NBA), and Erving was traded to the Philadelphia 76ers. Over the next 11 seasons with the 76ers, he averaged 22 points per game. Julius, the 1981 NBA MVP, led his 76er team to the 1983 NBA title. In defeating the Los Angeles Lakers, Erving made a windmill reverse layup that **Magic Johnson** called the best shot he had ever seen. Johnson recalled that "hang time seemed like eight seconds." Julius made the NBA All-Star team from 1977 through 1987. During his NBA career, Erving played in 977 regular-season games and averaged 22 points per game with 18,364 points and 7 rebounds per game with 5,601 altogether. Julius ranked as the NBA's third highest center scorer behind **Kareem Abdul-Jabbar** and **Wilt Chamberlain.** During his entire career, Erving played in 1,432 games, tallied 34,606 points, averaged 24 points per game, grabbed 12,136 rebounds, and averaged 8.5 rebounds per game.

Dr. J. possessed several admirable physical and social qualities. Former Nets assistant coach Rod Thorn acknowledged, "Of all the great players, Julius understood the team thing best. Julius was sensitive to every guy on the team. We had a lot of young, unstable guys on that Nets team, but as long as Julius was there, they stayed in line. He looked out for them. They respected him." To Erving, his family and team came first. Julius took time to help out troubled players and brought rookies home for Christmas. "In the ABA, it was one for all and all for one," he recalled. "Those were special days."

Many people considered Erving the **Michael Jordan** of his era, bridging earlier players like **Elgin Baylor** and Connie Hawkins with later performers like Jordan. Julius recalls initially dunking basketballs while in elementary school. "My first dunk was at the Prospect Elementary School, where they had 8-foot baskets and 13-foot ceilings," he remembered. "By the time I was in ninth grade, I was dunking the regular baskets." Many of his dunks began with just one step from the foul line and ended with a different creative movement each time. **Arthur Ashe, Jr.,** described Erving as "perhaps the most physically gifted and acrobatic performer yet seen." Julius displayed grace, awe-inspiring creativity, and self-assuredness, seemingly defying the laws of gravity with his slam dunks.

Erving retired from professional basketball in 1987, having served as a positive role model for youth and helped change the negative perception of African Americans in pro basketball. Although wearing a bushy Afro hairstyle, a goatee, and platform shoes, Julius forced people to look beyond outward appearances through his class-act behavior and eloquent speaking ability. Erving's influence led Temple University to confer a Doctor of Arts degree upon him in 1983. In 1984, he received the Father Flanagan Award for his work with young people.

In his first year of eligibility, Erving was inducted into the Naismith Memorial Basketball Hall of Fame in May 1993. Six months later, Julius signed a multiyear deal with NBC-Sports as a studio analyst for the NBA "Showtime." Erving hopes to keep the history of the sport and legacy of former players alive through his commentating. In 1994, *Sports Illustrated* ranked him fortieth on its "40 for the Ages List." As of spring 1994, Julius still played pickup games in Philadelphia and dunked the ball. He and his wife Turquoise have four children.

BIBLIOGRAPHY: Arthur Ashe, Jr., *A Hard Road to Glory: A History of the African-American Athlete Since 1946*, vol. 3 (New York, 1988); Julius Erving file, Naismith Memorial Basketball Hall of Fame, Springfield, MA; Nelson George, *Elevating the Game: Black Men and Basketball* (New York, 1992); Ronald L. Mendell, *Who's Who in Basketball* (New Rochelle, NY, 1973); *New York Times*, November 11, 1992, p. B13; February 9, 1993, p. B9; February 10, 1993, p. 12; May 11, 1993, p. B12; David L.

Porter, ed., *Biographical Dictionary of American Sports: Basketball and Other Indoor Sports* (Westport, CT, 1989).

Susan J. Rayl

LEE EVANS
(February 27, 1947–) ————————————————— *Track and Field*

Lee Evans, premier distance sprinter, won two Gold Medals at the 1968 Mexico City, Mexico, Summer Olympic Games and set or helped set world records in both events. His time in the 400 meters stood as the world record for 20 years. Lee was born on February 25, 1947, in Madera, California, the fourth oldest of seven children. His father, Dayton Evans, Sr., worked as a brick and mortar carrier in the construction business, while his mother, Pearlie Mae Evans, cared for the seven children. The Evans moved to Fresno, California, and then to San Jose, California, in 1962. While living in Fresno, Lee worked with his mother, brothers, and sisters picking cotton in the San Joaquin Valley because his father's employment was seasonal. Evans, who remembers the field boss cheating in weighing their cotton pickings, said of the injustice, "I was scared they'd send the whole family away, so I didn't say anything. I've always been ashamed of that." Lee began running competitively at age 11. At Overfelt High School in San Jose under coach Stan Dowell, he developed into a powerful sprinter pushing world-class times. In 1966, Evans finished undefeated and won his first of four consecutive Amateur Athletic Union (AAU) 440-yard run titles. At San Jose State University under coach Bud Winter, Lee captured the 1968 NCAA championship in the 400 meters with a 45.0-seconds time and competed on the NCAA title team. In 1967, he won the 400-meters event at the Pan-American Games in 44.9 seconds and participated on the Gold Medal 1,600-meter relay team.

Although not a graceful, fluid sprinter, Evans made up for his awkward, elbow flailing and hip movement style with his muscular physique and power running. At the U.S. Olympic Trials in 1968, Lee won the 400-meters with a world record time of 44.0 seconds. At the Mexico City, Mexico, Summer Olympic Games, he blazed to a 43.86 seconds Olympic and world record in the 400 meters and ran the anchor leg of the 1,600-meter relay team that set a world and Olympic record at 2 minutes 56.1 seconds. His Olympic 400-meter mark was not broken until **Quincy Watts** of the United States clocked 43.50 seconds in the 1992 Barcelona, Spain, Summer Olympics. Evans's world record stood until American runner **Butch Reynolds** clocked 43.29 at a Zurich, Switzerland, meet.

At the Mexico City Summer Olympics in 1968, Evans joined in the African-American athletes' protest against racism and discrimination in the United States. On the victory stand, he and American runners Larry James and Ron

Freeman wore Black Panther–style berets and black socks and raised their arms and fists in a black power gesture during the medal presentation. They did not visibly protest during the playing of the National Anthem, as sprinters **Tommie Smith** and John Carlos had done. The pair was ousted from the 1968 Olympics. Evans was criticized and shunned for his downplayed militancy by John Carlos and Harry Edwards, who had earlier tried to organize an African-American athlete boycott of the 1968 Olympic Games. Smith, a close friend and fellow athlete at San Jose State, supported Lee. According to one writer, Evans was "wounded and confused" by the criticism directed toward him and "lived faster than he ran after the '68 Games, spending much of his time in the streets."

Evans graduated from San Jose State with a bachelor's degree in sociology in January 1970. For a brief period of time, Lee taught physical education and helped coach the track team there and worked as a home school counselor for Silver Creek High School in San Jose. He quit these jobs, however, and drifted for awhile. The drowning death of his younger brother, Dayton, Jr., with whom Lee had been living, stunned and depressed him. His marriage, which produced a son, Keith, in 1967, ended in divorce in 1971. To find a purpose and a goal, Evans returned to running. Lee successfully battled the AAU and the International Olympic Committee (IOC) and gained reinstatement for the 1972 Munich, Germany Summer Olympics. He failed to make the U.S. Olympic team however, in the 400 meters, the event he had dominated, but made the 1,600-meter relay team. A medal ceremony controversy involving two of the relay team's runners however, caused them to be banned, scratching the American relay team from the event. In 1972, Evans reclaimed the AAU championship in the 400-meter championship after John Smith, a runner Lee had befriended, had taken the title from him in 1970 and 1971. Of Evans, John Smith said, "He built my confidence, taught me how to run past people. . . . I admire Lee enough to bow down to him."

In 1973, Evans led money winners at $13,900 as a professional on the International Track Association circuit and operated an antiques shop in San Francisco for nine months before going out of business. In 1975, Lee traveled to West Africa as a Fulbright scholar and then became the physical fitness counselor and coach of the Nigerian National Team. After his period of residence and work in Nigeria, he moved to Dohay, Qatar. Evans recently has become a coach for the Saudi Arabian Olympic team, preparing his runners for the 1996 Games in Atlanta, Georgia.

As a power runner, the 5-foot-11-inch Evans brought excitement and a higher level of competition to the middle-distance and longer-dash events from the mid-1960s to the early 1970s. Fellow competitors recognized and admired Lee for his hard work, demanding conditioning, mental toughness, desire, and fiercely competitive spirit. His classic duels against Tommie Smith, Martin McGrady, Curtis Mills, and Larry James marked the great speed confrontations of track and field. Evans was elected to the National Track and Field Hall of

Fame in 1983 and the U.S. Olympic Hall of Fame in 1989. His 20-year standing record in the 400 meters earned him the title of "Giant on the Earth" by *Sports Illustrated* writer Kenny Moore. As Evans proudly remarked, "I always ran with the competition." As a coach in Africa and the Middle East, Lee has become an international figure in a sport to complement the world-class speed he demonstrated as an 18-year-old in San Jose, California.

BIBLIOGRAPHY: Arthur R. Ashe, Jr., *A Hard Road to Glory: A History of the African-American Athlete Since 1946*, vol. 3 (New York, 1988); Iris Cloyd, ed., *Who's Who Among Black Americans*, 6th ed. (Detroit, MI, 1990/1991), p. 395; Jerry Kirshenbaum, "Generating Eclectic Power," *Sports Illustrated* 40 (February 18, 1974), pp. 32–33, 35–36, 41–42; Bill Mallon and Ian Buchanan, *Quest for Gold: The Encyclopedia of American Olympians* (New York, 1984); Kenny Moore, "Giants on the Earth," *Sports Illustrated* 66 (June 29, 1987), pp. 48–50; "The Olympic Boycott Jolt," *Life* 64 (March 15, 1968), pp. 20–29; Pat Putnam, "The Brief, Violent World of the 600," *Sports Illustrated* 32 (February 9, 1970), pp. 54–56; Pat Putnam, "No! Not John Smith!" *Sports Illustrated* 33 (July 6, 1970), pp. 11–13; Joseph M. Sheehan, "2 Black Power Advocates Ousted from Olympics," *New York Times*, October 19, 1968; Mel Watman, *Encyclopedia of Track and Field Athletics* (New York and London, England, 1981).

Douglas A. Noverr

PATRICK EWING
(August 5, 1962–) —————————————————— *Basketball*

Patrick Ewing won acclaim as a tenacious defensive basketball player. Patrick Aloysius Ewing was born on August 5, 1962, in Kingston, Jamaica, the son of Carl Ewing and Dorothy Ewing. Patrick came to the United States at age 11 with his six sisters and one brother, the fifth of eight siblings. His father labored as a mechanic, while his mother worked in the kitchen of Massachusetts General Hospital and had arrived before the rest of her family. Ewing attended the academically demanding Rindge and Latin High School in Cambridge, Massachusetts, where the withdrawn student slowly acclimated to a different culture and did not test well. Patrick, the only high school player invited to compete for the 1980 U.S. Olympic basketball team, did not make it. His basketball prowess attracted many college coaches, including Georgetown University's **John Thompson.** Thompson faced media criticism in spring 1981 for agreeing to the special academic provisions suggested by Ewing's high school coach, Mike Jarvis, to his prospective college. These provisions included daily tutoring and proofreading of Patrick's assignments, untimed testing, and permission to audiotape lectures.

Jarvis testified to Ewing's attentiveness and intensity: "Patrick tried to listen to every word you said, not only with his ears, but with his eyes. It was the same thing as when he played basketball. If he got knocked down, if he messed up, he didn't quit. He came right back at you. He was totally committed."

Ewing already attracted notoriety before entering college. Georgetown admitted Patrick on a scholarship, despite his low SAT scores, through its Community Scholars program. The program, started in the late 1960s as a method to bring in minority students from the local community, has subsequently expanded nationwide. Although Ewing appeared to be another marginal student admitted largely because of his basketball skills, the intellectually alert student proved a wise investment that many other top-ranked schools also sought to make. Coach Thompson underscored his reasons for signing Patrick, "I did not recruit him for what he can do for society. I did it for basketball, and he's a great player. . . . [But] Patrick Ewing, because of who he is, can influence others."

The seven-foot, 240-pound center competed fiercely with an often scowling face. Ewing's aggressiveness led him to retaliate against opponents with his elbows or fists. Patrick's demeanor on the court contrasted with his shy temperament off it and gave rise to his nickname "The Boy Bull." Coach Thompson also nicknamed him "The Warrior." Opponents charged Ewing with being overly aggressive on the court, but coach Thompson countered, "Pat is not a dirty player. . . . In our society people are afraid of any tall, black man who plays tough. . . . If you talked one-on-one with him, you'd find him a gentle, nice, polite kid."

Ewing wore a T-shirt under his basketball jersey and, like coach Thompson, received racist insults, which only made him play harder. In his freshman 1981–1982 season, a phoned death threat was made against Patrick. During the 1982–1983 season on the road, Ewing faced cruel, inaccurate signs and banners claiming that he could not read. Patrick read the signs but rose above the insults. Fellow player Billy Martin, a sophomore forward, claimed, "If we're playing away, it seems Pat is always the villain. . . . It has to do with the image Pat has projected of himself as an aggressive person. . . . The signs and the jeers don't bother Pat. They only make him play harder." Georgetown reached the NCAA Final Four for the first time, losing a 63–62 heartbreaker to the University of North Carolina.

In his junior year, Ewing performed at his collegiate best in 37 games. Patrick played 1,179 minutes, shot 65.8 percent from the field and 65.6 percent from the line, and recorded 371 rebounds, 608 points, and a 16.4-points-per-game average in leading the Hoyas to their first NCAA championship. The Hoyas again made it to the Final Four during Ewing's senior year, although Villanova defeated them for the title. During his Georgetown career, Patrick played in 143 games with 1,382 field goal attempts, 857 field goals made (62.0 percent), 740 free throws attempted, 470 free throws made (63.5 percent), 1,316 rebounds, 2,184 points, and a 15.3-points-per-game average. He acted graciously in defeat, which did not occur often as a Hoya. Patrick had developed an intimidating, defensive play, a jump shot, and a jump hook and objected to being virtually the only Hoya asked for his autograph. Although not unfriendly, Ewing preferred to shake fans' hands instead.

The triumphs of the four-time All-America and dominant player culminated with a Bachelor of Fine Arts degree in 1985. Ewing resisted the temptation to turn professional early, fulfilling the pledge he had made to his mother, who died in 1984, to graduate. Patrick stated, "I guess it was just the way my mother and father raised me. . . . They said an education is something you have forever, you know, that can't be taken away. And I always believed that. It was important for my parents that I get my degree and it's important to me."

Ewing had rounded out his academic interests with a summer job on Capitol Hill, interning for U.S. Senator Bob Dole of Kansas. His future wife, Rita Williams, a Howard University student, worked for Bill Bradley, the U.S. senator from New Jersey and former basketball superstar with the New York Knicks. Throughout his four years at Georgetown, Patrick had helped to increase awareness of both the school and its athletic program. More minority students, including athletes, applied, and fund-raising also increased.

Ewing was chosen first in the 1985 National Basketball Association (NBA) lottery draft, landing with the New York Knicks. Patrick enjoyed somewhat less success with the low-ranked Knicks than the Hoyas. During his first season, Ewing scored 998 points and averaged 20.4 points per game. The Knicks still finished last in the Atlantic Division of the Eastern Conference in Patrick's first and second seasons, as he could not singly reverse the team's slumping fortunes. And yet he tried his best, maintaining, "I don't like losing, and I don't want to get used to it."

Ewing's statistics through the 1994–1995 season for nine years with the Knicks include 759 games played, 52 shooting percentage, 7,873 rebounds, 1,643 assists, 842 steals, 17,977 points, and a 23.7 lifetime points-per-game average. In December 1993, Patrick surpassed **Walt Frazier** as the Knicks' all-time leading scorer. During the 1994–1995 season, his career scoring reached the 17,000 mark. Ewing joined several stars featured on the "Dream Team," the triumphant 1992 U.S. Olympic basketball contingent, which for the first time comprised professional players.

In 1984, his son, Patrick, Jr., was born to Sharon Stanford, his high school sweetheart. They never married. Georgetown, which shielded its players from publicity, did not release information about Ewing's son until a year after his birth. Patrick signed his son's birth certificate, visited him often, and contributed toward his support. Patrick and his wife, Rita, who became a law student at Georgetown, live in Potomac, Maryland.

Ewing's awards and accomplishments include being member of the Gold Medal U.S. Olympic basketball teams in 1984 and 1992; being named to *The Sporting News* All-America Second Team in 1983–1984; playing on the NCAA Division I championship team in 1984; and being chosen to *The Sporting News* All-America First Team in 1985. His other honors included NCAA Most Outstanding Player in 1984; *The Sporting News* College Player of the Year in 1985; NBA Rookie of the Year in 1986; NBA All-Rookie team in 1986; All-NBA Defensive Second Team in 1988, 1989, and 1992; All-NBA First

Team in 1990; All-NBA Second Team in 1988, 1989, and 1991–1993, and an All-Star Game selection in 1986 and 1988 through 1995.

At festivities for Patrick Ewing Day in Cambridge, Massachusetts, on October 12, 1984, to mark his triumphs at Georgetown and in the 1984 Olympics, Mike Jarvis, Pat's high school coach, rhapsodized: "Patrick had something God gave all of us—potential. First, he discovered it, then he developed it. . . . He learned to listen. Once you told him the answer, he never forgot. Not one day of practice did he miss, not even a study hall."

BIBLIOGRAPHY: *Current Biography Yearbook* (1989), pp. 576–580; John Kavanagh, *Sports Great Patrick Ewing* (Hillside, NJ, 1992); Matthew Newman, *Patrick Ewing* (Mankato, MN, 1986); *New York Times*, December 15, 1993, pp. B13–14; December 16, 1993, p. B21; January 18, 1994, p. B16; David L. Porter, ed., *Biographical Dictionary of American Sports: Basketball and Other Indoor Sports* (Westport, CT, 1989); Leonard Shapiro, *Big Man on Campus: John Thompson and the Georgetown Hoyas* (New York, 1991); *Washington Post*, March 30, 1985; May 16, 1985; May 20, 1985; *Who's Who Among Black Americans* (Detroit, MI, 1994), p. 458; *Who's Who in America*, 47th ed. (1992–1993), p. 1023.

Frederick J. Augustyn, Jr.

CURT FLOOD
(January 18, 1938–) ———————————————————— *Baseball*

Curt Flood teamed with great-hitting outfielders like Stan Musial, **Lou Brock,** Roger Maris, and Vada Pinson during his 12 years with the St. Louis Cardinals National League (NL) club. None, however, matched Flood's defensive mastery. Curtis Charles Flood, the youngest of six children, was born on January 18, 1938, to Herman Flood and Laura Flood in Houston, Texas. When Curt was 2 years old, his family moved to an African-American ghetto in Oakland, California, where his parents worked in low-paying hospital jobs.

Two men profoundly impacted Flood's career. The first, Jim Chambers, taught him art at Herbert Hoover Junior High School. Curt enjoyed painting and sketching, exciting Chambers about his talent. Flood recalled that Chambers taught him "art not as technique alone but as one of the great resources of the human spirit." Sports provided African-American youngsters one of few hopes of leaving the ghetto. Curt excelled in baseball at McClymonds and Oakland Technical High School and credited George Powles, his Little League and high school baseball coach, for his development. Powles, a white, coached many young, mostly African-American athletes, who later played professional baseball, football, or basketball. His pupils included **Frank Robinson,** Pinson, **Joe Morgan,** Billy Martin, and **Bill Russell.** Powles enabled Flood to look at white people as persons of goodwill and worth, instead of through the stereotype of patronizing, condescending do-gooders, or just plain bigots.

The five-foot-nine-inch, 165-pound outfielder signed with the Cincinnati Reds (NL) club after high school graduation in 1956. Flood hit 29 home runs, drove in 128 runs, and batted .340 with High Point-Thomasville, North Carolina, in the Carolina League in 1956. Curt followed with a .299 batting average at Savannah, Georgia, of the South Atlantic League in 1957 but endured constant racial slurs from fans and rejection by most teammates. The Reds briefly recalled him both seasons. Cincinnati already had outfielders Robinson, Gus Bell, Wally Post, and Jerry Lynch with Pinson on the way and consequently traded Flood to the St. Louis Cardinals (NL) for journeyman hurler Willard Schmidt and two minor league pitchers. Cardinal manager Fred Hutchinson made Curt his center fielder for the 1958 campaign. The right-handed Flood quickly established himself as one of the best NL defensive outfielders, making only four errors in his first three seasons with St. Louis and committing only 28 misplays in 1,759 major league games. Curt won seven consecutive Gold Gloves in center field, beginning in 1963. In 1968, *Sports Illustrated* called him "baseball's best center fielder."

Flood also batted well. His batting average exceeded .300 six times from 1961 to 1969 and reached a career-high .335 in 1967. Curt led the NL with 211 hits in 1964 and scored a career-best 112 runs in 1963. With Flood in center field, St. Louis won three NL pennants. Although batting only .221 in three World Series, Curt fielded flawlessly. The Cardinals defeated the New York Yankees in seven games in the 1964 World Series, triumphed over the Boston Red Sox in seven games in 1967, and fell one game short against the Detroit Tigers in 1968.

Flood remembered the 1967 and 1968 Cardinals with particular fondness. Curt and catcher Tim McCarver co-captained the Redbirds. In his autobiography, *The Way It Is*, Flood wrote that the "Cardinals of 1967 and 1968 must have been the most remarkable team in the history of baseball." The outstanding Cardinals dominated the rest of the league, but Curt remained proudest that "the men of that team were as close to being free of racist poison as a diverse group of twentieth-century Americans could possibly be."

Flood publicly grumbled about the injustice of the reserve clause and also protested the 162-game schedule and doubleheaders. Curt refused a 1969 contract for $77,500, holding out for $90,000. On October 7, 1969, he and McCarver were traded to the Philadelphia Phillies (NL) for slugger Dick Allen. Flood refused the trade despite receiving a $100,000 contract offer. Marvin Miller, executive director of the Major League Baseball Players Association (MLBPA), asked Curt to consider the financial ramifications and warned that the action would cost him any chance of coaching or managing in the major leagues. Miller promised Flood full support, however, if he challenged the reserve clause. The MLBPA board voted 25–0 to back Curt's challenge of the reserve clause and retained the counsel of former U.S. Supreme Court justice Arthur Goldberg to defend him. On June 18, 1972, he lost his suit, *Flood v. Kuhn*, in the U.S. Supreme Court by a 5–3 vote. This case, however, prompted the owners in December 1972 to agree to arbitration and free agency, effectively ending the reserve clause. Curt never gained monetarily from his suit but paved a brighter financial road for subsequent players.

The Washington Senators American League (AL) club acquired Flood's contract in November 1971, but Curt batted only .200 and retired after 13 games. During his major league career, he made 1,861 hits, batted .293, scored 851 runs, hit 85 home runs, and recorded 636 RBIs.

Flood married Beverly Collins in February 1959 and has four children. After their first divorce, they married and divorced again. Curt's *The Way It Is* (1971) chronicled his baseball career. Flood spoke candidly of racism at every level of baseball, the sexual promiscuity of baseball players, the tensions between owners and players, and especially the difficulty of finding an identity and maintaining relationships as an athlete. Curt broadcast for the Oakland Athletics (AL) in 1978.

After leaving baseball, Flood returned to his love for art. Curt became a painter on Minorca, one of the Balearic Islands in the Mediterranean Sea. In 1987, he was named president of The Baseball Network, an organization founded to promote minority hiring in baseball, and received the first Jackie Robinson Award from the National Association for the Advancement of Colored People (NAACP). Flood also was named president of the short-lived Senior Professional Baseball Association in 1989 and served on a committee planning the 10-team United League, the first challenge to major league baseball since the Federal League folded in 1915. The Los Angeles area resident owns a public relations firm, continues to do paintings commercially, and plays in Equitable Old Timers games.

BIBLIOGRAPHY: David Craft and Tom Owens, *Redbirds Revisited* (Chicago, IL, 1990); Curt Flood with Richard Carter, *The Way It Is* (New York, 1971); David L. Porter, ed., *Biographical Dictionary of American Sports: Baseball* (Westport, CT, 1987); Ray Robinson, ed., *Baseball Stars of 1966* (New York, 1966).

Frank J. Olmsted

GEORGE FOREMAN

(January 22, 1948 [or January 10, 1949]–) ———————— *Boxing*

George Foreman ranks among the hardest-hitting fighters to hold the world heavyweight championship. The son of J. D. Foreman, a railroad worker, and Nancy (Nelson) Foreman, George was born on either January 22, 1948, or January 10, 1949, in Marshall, Texas. Most record books list the 1948 birthdate, but Foreman claims the 1949 date is accurate. The latter date has gained popular acceptance since George began his comeback. He shunned school and was considered a wayward youth. "I had no role models as a youngster," Foreman recalled. His life turned around, however, when he enrolled in a Job Corps program and was introduced to amateur boxing. George used an awkward, but powerful, left jab to weaken his opponents. Foreman's lethal punches earned him a spot on the U.S. Olympic boxing squad in 1968. At the Mexico City, Mexico, Summer Olympic Games, he captured the Gold Medal in the heavyweight division by stopping Iones Chepulis of the Soviet Union in the second round of the final.

Foreman began his professional boxing career by knocking out Don Waldhelm, a former Golden Gloves champion, in three rounds in New York City on June 23, 1969. The vanquished Waldhelm later recalled, "Getting hit by George was like going to the dentist and getting a shot of novocaine. I remember my lips being very numb." In his first year as a professional, Foreman scored 13 straight victories. These triumphs included 11 knockouts. George in 1970 knocked out 11 of 12 opponents, among them rugged Canadian champion George Chuvalo and highly regarded Boone Kirkman. By December 1970, Foreman was ranked second by *The Ring* among heavyweight contenders. George married Adrienne Calhoun in 1970 and had one daughter, Michi, before their divorce.

Twelve more victories in 1971 and 1972 propelled Foreman into a world title bout with reigning champion **Joe Frazier** on January 22, 1973, in Kingston, Jamaica. George, considered a 3–1 underdog, surprised boxing authorities by having little trouble knocking out Frazier. He decked the champion six times in less than two rounds to capture the title but later confessed to being unusually nervous before the Frazier fight. "[It was] the most scared I've ever been in my life," Foreman disclosed. "I had made a habit of staring everybody down; I was scared that I had to stare him [Frazier] down. But I didn't want Joe to look down because if he had looked to the floor, he would have seen my knees shaking."

His first two title defenses proved relatively easy. Jose "King" Roman failed to last one round with Foreman in Tokyo, Japan, on September 1, 1973, while Ken Norton was knocked out in two rounds in Caracas, Venezuela, on March 26, 1974. George was upset, however, in his third title defense, when **Muhammad Ali** used a daring strategy to knock out Foreman in eight rounds in Kinshasa, Zaire, on October 30, 1974. The 32-year-old Ali covered up on the ropes for the first seven rounds and allowed George to exhaust himself by throwing heavy punches, most of which were blocked. With Foreman's energy spent, Ali seized the offense near the end of round eight and finished him with a solid right-hand blow. George claimed that he was a victim of food poisoning and a quick count, but later admitted, "I know how I lost. Muhammad Ali hit me with a right hand. I didn't say it back then. I had never lost a boxing match. It was pride. I couldn't accept anyone beating me."

In 1975, Foreman began a comeback in hopes of earning a rematch with Ali. His second win over Frazier in Uniondale, New York, on June 15, 1976, and a thrilling, knockdown-filled victory over Ron Lyle in Las Vegas, Nevada, on January 24, 1976, lifted George into title contention. Foreman's chance of redemption against Ali was sidetracked, however, when he unexpectedly lost a 12-round decision to light-hitting Jimmy Young in San Juan, Puerto Rico, on March 17, 1977. After the fight, George became delirious in his dressing room. Trainer Gil Clancy blamed Foreman's peculiar behavior on heat prostration, but George maintains he encountered a religious experience. This episode prompted him to quit boxing and become a preacher.

Foreman disappeared from the boxing scene for nearly a full decade. During that time, he founded the George Foreman Youth and Community Center in Houston, Texas. When this project faced financial problems during the mid-1980s, Foreman decided to reenter boxing partly to finance the youth center. An easy win over journeyman Steve Zouski on March 9, 1987, in Sacramento, California, marked the beginning of George's ring comeback. Several impressive knockouts against opponents of dubious quality and a widespread base of fan popularity made the rotund Foreman a logical contender for the world heavyweight title once again. George's sensational knockout of former contender Gerry Cooney on January 15, 1990, in Atlantic City, New Jersey, ensured him a bout with champion Evander Holyfield for the title in 1991.

Foreman soon became the darling of the media. His friendly manner and likeable wit, two traits that he did not display while champion, made him a natural on the television talk show circuit. "Life begins at forty," George told America as he sought to become the oldest contender for the world heavyweight crown.

On April 19, 1991, in Atlantic City, New Jersey, Foreman and Holyfield met in a memorable 12-round contest for the world championship. George put on a gritty performance and threatened Holyfield's title several times, but Evander won a clear unanimous decision to retain his crown. Nevertheless, Foreman retained his immense popularity and continued his comeback. On June 7, 1993, in Las Vegas, Nevada, Foreman lost a one-sided decision to Tommy Morrison in a fight indicating his age. After the bout, George announced his retirement from the ring.

In November 1994, Foreman startled the boxing world by regaining the heavyweight title. George knocked out defending champion Michael Moorer with a left jab and thunderous right-hand blow at two minutes three seconds of the tenth round to win the World Boxing Association and International Boxing Federation heavyweight crowns. At age 45 years 9 months, he became the oldest boxer to contend for and capture a heavyweight title. Jersey Joe Walcott, the oldest previous champion, had taken the crown at age 37 in July 1951. In April 1995, Foreman defeated Axel Schulz of Germany in a controversial 12-round majority decision.

Foreman's illustrious career covered 78 professional fights, with only four losses. Sixty-eight of his victories produced knockouts. Although his boxing skills could never be compared with Ali's, he demonstrated devastating power that earned him a place among the most feared hitters in boxing history. In 1995, his autobiography, *By George*, was published.

BIBLIOGRAPHY: Sam Andre and Nat Fleischer, *A Pictorial History of Boxing* (New York, 1975); Dan Daniel, "Foreman's Victory Opens Up New Vistas in Heavyweight Ranks," *The Ring* 52 (April 1973), pp. 10–32; Dan Daniel, "Foreman May Challenge Dempsey's Power But Not Charisma," *The Ring* 53 (July 1974), pp. 6–40; Steve Farhood, "George Foreman Is Born Again," *KO Magazine* (February 1989), pp. 32–58; George Foreman, *By George* (New York, 1995); Nat Loubet, "Ali Outfought, Outlasted, and Outwitted Foreman in a Classic Upset," *The Ring* 53 (January 1975), pp. 6–32; Pat Putnam, "No Joke," *Sports Illustrated* 74 (April 29, 1991), pp. 22–27; Jeff Ryan, "KO Interview: George Foreman," *KO Magazine* (June 1988), pp. 42–53; Jeffrey T. Sammons, *Beyond the Ring: The Role of Boxing in American Society* (Urbana, IL, 1988); Bert R. Sugar, ed., *The Ring 1983 Record Book* (New York, 1983).

John Robertson

RUBE FOSTER
(September 17, 1879–December 9, 1930) ———————————— *Baseball*

Rube Foster, considered the father of the Negro Leagues, organized the Negro National League (NNL) in the early 1920s and developed it into a first-class enterprise. The NNL showcased African-American athletes, who were not allowed to play in the major leagues due to racial segregation. Andrew "Rube" Foster was born to Andrew Foster, a minister, and Sarah Foster in Calvert, Texas, on September 17, 1879. Foster began his baseball career upon finishing eighth grade, joining the Waco Yellow Jackets as a pitcher. In 1902, he won 51 games and recorded one victory over great pitcher "Rube" Waddell. The feat earned him the nickname "Rube," which followed him the rest of his life. The same year, Foster joined the Chicago Union Giants. Rube's first appearance at the plate as a pinch hitter proved unsuccessful, but his prowess on the mound more than made up for it. Foster won every game that he pitched except one with Chicago during a three-month period. Rube then hurled for a white semi-pro squad in Michigan temporarily before returning to the African-American baseball teams the next season.

The six-foot-four-inch Foster, an imposing pitcher, possessed an excellent screwball, sharp mind, and wide variety of pitches. "I have smiled often with the bases full with two strikes and three balls on the batter. This seems to unnerve them," Rube acknowledged. He continued to accumulate victories, joining the Cuban X-Giants in 1903 and recording 54 wins against only one loss during the regular season. Foster garnered 4 more victories in post-season playoffs against the Philadelphia Giants. The following year, Rube switched to the Philadelphia Giants and pitched them to 2 victories in a three-game series against his former teammates. He subsequently continued to post impressive numbers while leading the Giants to successful seasons and championships.

In 1907, Foster was appointed player-manager of the Leland Giants after a salary dispute with the Philadelphia club. Rube's reputation as a fair, but demanding, manager enabled him to enjoy substantial success. Fellow Negro Leaguer "**Cool Papa**" **Bell** remembered Foster as "a strict disciplinarian. There was no question he was the boss. You did it his way or you didn't play for him." After sustaining a broken leg during a midsummer 1909 game, Rube missed the championship playoffs and saw his team lose the series. He split with owner Frank Leland and assembled his own team with talent recruited from both of his former ball clubs. Foster's 1910 team compiled an unbeliev-able 128–6 record.

The following season, Foster formed a partnership with John Schorling, a white business owner and son-in-law of Chicago White Sox owner Charles Comiskey. Together, they assembled a team to play at the old White Sox park and split the proceeds 50–50. The extremely popular team, renamed the Chi-cago American Giants, dominated the Negro League until Rube's exit from baseball. Foster gradually played less and, by 1917, rarely performed except to serve as an occasional gate attraction. Rube's managerial success enabled him to build upon his recognition as a dominant African-American pitcher in the deadball era. The American Giants reflected his own philosophy and per-sonality, combining speed and aggressive base-running with sound pitching and fielding. Foster's players mastered both the bunt-and-run and hit-and-run. Most runners were given the freedom to run at will and often stretched singles into extra base hits. Runners frequently advanced two bases instead of one. "Rube knew the value of speed and he knew the value of being able to fit into a directed play," recalled David Malarcher. The American Giants dom-inated African-American baseball, winning every championship but one from 1910 through 1922.

After having difficulty scheduling games for his team with an East Coast promoter, Foster organized the NNL, the first African-American baseball league. Rube served as NNL president and treasurer and developed it into a first-class enterprise. Although drawing no salary, Foster kept 5 percent of the gate receipts and distributed them as he saw fit. As the NNL grew in popu-larity, his influence and power increased in baseball circles. By 1925, however, Rube's autocratic management style began to alienate and offend others in baseball. Foster resigned, despite having received a full vote of confidence from other league owners. By that time, the stress had taken its toll. In 1926, Rube experienced a nervous breakdown and was hospitalized in a mental institution. He died on December 9, 1930, in Kankakee, Illinois, while still institutionalized there. Foster is credited with developing the Negro Baseball Leagues, laying the foundation for African-American athletes to one day be afforded equality and acceptance into modern major league baseball. In 1981, Rube was inducted into the National Baseball Hall of Fame in appreciation and recognition of his many baseball achievements.

BIBLIOGRAPHY: *The Chicago Defender*, 1910–1930; John Holway, *Rube Foster the Father of Black Baseball* (Washington, DC, 1981); Robert W. Peterson, *Only the Ball Was White* (Englewood Cliffs, NJ, 1970); James A. Riley, *The All-Time All-Stars of Black Baseball* (Cocoa, FL, 1983); James A. Riley, *The Biographical Encyclopedia of the Negro Baseball Leagues* (New York, 1994); James A. Riley, interviews with former Negro League players, James A. Riley collection, Cocoa, FL; Mike Shatzkin, ed., *The*

Ballplayers (New York, 1990); Charles E. Whitehead, *A Man and His Diamonds* (New York, 1980).

James A. Riley

JOE FRAZIER
(January 12, 1944–) ——————————————————————— *Boxing*

Joe Frazier, nicknamed "Joltin' Joe," held the heavyweight boxing title. Joe was born in Beaufort, South Carolina, one of 13 children of Rubin Frazier, a farmer, and Dolly Frazier. He grew up on a farm of "hogs, chickens, and vegetables" and received all of 15 cents a crate for picking vegetables. Joe helped his one-armed father build their house, early developing solid work habits. "Work keeps me ticking," he declared. Frazier moved to Philadelphia, Pennsylvania, in 1962 and worked in a kosher meat packing establishment. Upon visiting a local gymnasium, Joe was told that his 5-foot-11½-inch, 200- to 220-pound frame was too small for a heavyweight. He met Philadelphian Yancy "Yank" Durham, who recognized his potential and especially his strong legs. "I can make you champion of the world," Durham told Frazier after only a few months. Joe quickly learned to train hard. Durham guided him through 38 victories in 40 amateur bouts, the climax being an Olympic Gold Medal at the 1964 Tokyo, Japan, Summer Olympic Games.

After turning professional a year later, Frazier defeated Woody Goss in a one-round knockout. His career spanned 16 years, ending with the Jumbo Cummings bout in 1981. Joe absorbed Durham's rigid training routine, building on his natural ability. During training for matches, he performed road work six times a day and pursued a monkish seclusion. Frazier gave a realistic account of his boxing profession: "I like it, fighting. There's a man out there trying to take what you got. You're supposed to destroy him. He's trying to do the same to you. Why should you have pity for him?" In the last few days before a fight, Joe read the Bible.

Frazier steadily ascended the heavyweight ladder, aided by his powerful legs and lethal punch. **Muhammad Ali** had relinquished his heavyweight title in 1967, refusing military induction into the Vietnam War. Joe's five-round knockout of Jimmy Ellis on February 16, 1970, earned him the universally recognized heavyweight championship. During the next year, the nation anticipated a Frazier-Ali bout. "Ten years me and Yank been workin' toward this guy. Ten years, what can I say?" A pronounced feud developed between Muhammad and Joe, with the former claiming the fight would be "no contest." Frazier retorted, "He said the fight would be no contest. But he said it outside the ring. The arm is still mightier than the mouth." Joe described Ali as "an evil guy and a phony."

Ali could not tolerate another African American as dominant in the boxing world. The Frazier-Ali classic match was held on March 8, 1971, in New York

City. Muhammad, master of the art of intimidation, entered the ring and immediately told Frazier, "Ah'm gonna whip your assssss!" Joe, however, countered effectively. In the greatest fight of his career, Frazier decisively outpointed Ali in 15 rounds. Joe floored his opponent in the very last minutes, breaking Ali's jaw. The bout marked Frazier's crowning achievement. "Life's beautiful, baby," he declared.

Joe's success continued the next two years. He fought exhibitions with Cleveland Williams and James Helwig during 1971 and scored knockouts the following year over Terry Daniels and Tom Stander. Frazier stayed active, commenting, "I like a challenge."

In January 1972 at Kingston, Jamaica, **George Foreman,** 1968 Olympic heavyweight Gold Medalist and four years younger than Frazier, shocked the boxing world by knocking out the heavyweight champion in just 2 rounds. George slammed Joe to the canvas an astonishing six times. Films indicate that Frazier was simply overwhelmed. He lost an exhibition to Muhammad Ali in 12 rounds in 1974 and suffered a 14-round technical knockout (TKO) against Ali for the heavyweight title in Manila, Philippines, on October 1, 1975. Surprisingly, the two exchanged cordial words after the fight, with Ali telling Joe's son that his father was "a good man."

Joe's wife, Florence (Smith) Frazier, and their five children sustained him in his sad years. Frazier's active career ended on June 28, 1976, in a useless rematch against George Foreman, who already had lost his title in a knockout by Ali. Joe suffered a five-round TKO, being knocked down twice in the last round. The fight was halted at the request of his corner. Frazier, nine pounds overweight, constantly fought on the defensive. Foreman commented, "I was surprised. I was under the impression Frazier could fight only one way, movin' right at you."

Shortly after the fight, Joe announced his retirement. Frazier acknowledged, "It's time for me to put it on the wall." He still remained surprisingly optimistic about his career, admitting, "The whole doggone game was a highlight, a lot of fun, and if I had the chance to do it again, it still would be a lot of fun."

Joe devoted considerable time to his motorcycles and music. He thought motorcycles "make you feel so powerful." Music occupied second place to boxing in his estimation. He formed an ensemble group, the "Knockouts," which performed rock, Gospel, and other music in nightspots and recorded for Capitol Records. Frazier's singing voice came very close to professional quality, but unfortunately his group did not succeed to the degree desired. Nevertheless, Joe's devotion to music remained steadfast.

Frazier's boxing record shows 32 wins (27 by knockout), four losses, and one draw. He was inducted into *The Ring*'s Boxing Hall of Fame in 1980 and the International Boxing Hall of Fame in 1990. Joe always valued work as the key to success, stating, "I live on a challenge basis, life is a challenge." No one could have expressed it better.

BIBLIOGRAPHY: Dave Anderson, "Beaufort, S.C. Loves Frazier," *New York Times,* April 10, 1971; Gerald Astor, "Joe Frazier: The Six-State Champ," *Look* 33 (June 24, 1969), pp. 89, 91; Ira Berkow, "Spirits of the Time: A Fighting Family Gets Together," *New York Times,* October 29, 1983; Robert H. Boyle, "Smokin' Joe Burns Out," *Sports Illustrated* 44 (June 28, 1976), pp. 68–71; Bruce Jay Friedman, "Will Joe Frazier Be the Next Champ?" *Saturday Evening Post* 240 (September 23, 1967), pp. 97–101; Herbert G. Goldman, ed., *The Ring 1986–1987 Record Book and Boxing Encyclopedia* (New York, 1987); Glen McCurdy, "The Solid Soul of Smokin' Joe," *Chicago Tribune Magazine,* April 25, 1971; David L. Porter, ed., *Biographical Dictionary of American Sports: Basketball and Other Indoor Sports* (Westport CT, 1989); Bert Randolph Sugar, ed., *The Great Fights* (New York, 1981).

William J. Miller

WALT FRAZIER
(March 29, 1945–) ——————————————————————— *Basketball*

Walt Frazier, who helped guide the New York Knicks to two National Basketball Association (NBA) championships, ranked among the most outstanding guards in NBA history. Walter Frazier, Jr., born March 29, 1945, in Atlanta, Georgia, was the first of nine children of Walter Frazier, Sr., and Eula Frazier. His father worked on an automobile production line. Frazier frequently took care of his younger siblings in the family's ghetto home. "I learned a lot about babies and changing diapers," commented Walt. As an adult, he became something of a loner to compensate for a lack of privacy as a child. Frazier began playing sports early in life, competing as a nine-year-old with taller and older boys. Walt refined his defense and playmaking skills to compete. "The ball didn't bounce very straight on the dirt court," he wrote in his book *Walt Frazier: One Magic Season and a Basketball Life,* "so you had to be a good dribbler to keep it going."

At David T. Howard High School, a segregated school in Atlanta, Frazier excelled at football, basketball, and baseball under coach George Coffey. Walt impressed college scouts as a football quarterback and was offered scholarships at the University of Kansas and Indiana University. Neither school, however, promised he would play quarterback in college. Since African-American quarterbacks in professional football were virtually unheard of, Frazier opted to play basketball at Southern Illinois University in Carbondale, Illinois.

In his first season of eligibility as a sophomore, Frazier earned Little All-America basketball honors and averaged nearly 25 points per game. Walt, however, remained less comfortable in class than on the court. After some disagreements with coach Jack Hartman, he decided to quit Southern Illinois at the end of the school year and stopped attending classes. Frazier's mother prodded him to return to Southern Illinois in 1965, but Walt had lost his eligibility for the season because of his failing grades. "It was the making of me as a person," he recalled. "During the year I sat out, no one from the basketball program helped me out. No one enrolled me. I had to take tough subjects . . . and no 'garbage' classes to balance them." Frazier attained a 3.8 grade-point average his first quarter back and finally realized that he belonged with all the other students.

Although Frazier could not play in games, Hartman allowed him to practice with the team. Walt spent the time only playing defense. "After about two weeks," Frazier noted, "I finally understood that I wasn't going to distinguish myself that season by shooting and scoring." Walt dedicated himself to being the best defensive player he could be, a move subsequently paying dividends in the pros. With Southern Illinois and the Knicks, he realized "the only way to make my mark was to show I could do it defensively."

Frazier earned enough credits to return to the basketball team for the 1966–1967 season. Walt led the Salukis to United Press International's (UPI's) number-one ranking among small college teams and to the National Invitational Tournament (NIT) title. He averaged 18.2 points per game while being named team Most Valuable Player (MVP), NIT MVP, a Little All-America selection, and All-America Second Team by *The Sporting News*.

The New York Knicks made Frazier their first pick of the 1967 NBA draft. Walt left Southern Illinois and signed a three-year, $100,000 contract. He started slowly his rookie year but excelled his second year under coach Red Holtzman. During his second season, Frazier averaged 17.5 points per game and ranked third in the NBA with 7.9 assists per game. Walt also made the NBA's All-Defensive First Team, the first of seven consecutive years. Walt provided the defensive leadership on the 1969–1970 NBA championship team, which gave up only 105 points per game. The Knicks defeated the Los Angeles Lakers in the seven-game NBA finals.

Frazier became an offensive force for New York during 1970–1971, when star center Willis Reed developed tendonitis. The Knicks lost in the NBA playoff semi-finals that season, as Walt finished with a 24.2 points per game average. During the 1971–1972 season, he led the Knicks in every offensive category except rebounding and was named to the NBA's All-Defensive team for the fourth consecutive year. In 1972–1973, Frazier again helped lead the Knicks to the NBA title. New York bested Los Angeles four games to one in the NBA finals.

The Knicks traded Walt to the Cleveland Cavaliers in October 1977, but he played only one full season there. A foot injury forced him to retire 12 games into the 1978–1979 season. Frazier finished his career with 15,571 points in 822 games for an 18.9 points per game average and 5,040 assists. Walt held Knicks career records for most games (759), points (14,617), assists (4,791), total minutes played (28,995), most field goals made (5,736), and free throws attempted (4,017). He was almost as well known for his unrestrained lifestyle, earning his nickname "Clyde" for his 1930-ish attire. Frazier wore a full-length mink coat and wide-brimmed hats and drove a burgundy Rolls Royce. Walt's mutton chop sideburns and his smothering defense were both trademarks. In 1987, the Naismith Memorial Basketball Hall of Fame enshrined him. He married his wife, Marsha, in 1965 and had one son, Walter III, before their 1967 divorce. He is president of Walt Frazier Enterprises, co-owns a hairstyling salon in New York City, and has authored three books.

BIBLIOGRAPHY: Contemporary Authors, vol. 103 (1982), pp. 148–149; Current Biography Yearbook (1973), pp. 141–143; Walt Frazier, Walt Frazier: One Magic Season and a Basketball Life (New York, 1988); Walt Frazier and Ira Berkow, Rockin' Steady: A Guide to Basketball and Mr. Cool (Englewood Cliffs, NJ, 1974); Walt Frazier and Joe Jares, Clyde: The Walt Frazier Story (New York, 1970); New York Times, December 11, 1978.

Brian L. Laughlin

CLARENCE GAINES
(May 21, 1923–) ———————————————————— Basketball

Clarence "Big House" Gaines, one of the most successful college basketball coaches of all time, led Winston Salem State University to the 1967 NCAA College Division championship. The title marked the first by a predominantly African-American school. He was elected in 1983 to the Naismith Memorial Basketball Hall of Fame, the first member coach to have spent an entire career at an African-American college.

Gaines was born and grew up in Paducah, Kentucky, where he starred as a high school football player. After graduating in 1941, Clarence attended Morgan State University in Maryland and twice earned All-America honors as a football tackle. His six-foot-three-inch, 300-pound frame earned him the nickname "Big House." Gaines also played basketball, mainly to keep in shape during the off-season. Clarence earned a bachelor's degree from Morgan State in 1946 and his master's degree in physical education the following year from Columbia University. He disclosed, "I never thought anything about coaching." He majored instead in chemistry, hoping to become a dentist.

Gaines, however, became a coach when offered a job teaching and coaching at Winston-Salem Teachers College (now Winston-Salem State University). By his second year there, Clarence coached football, basketball, boxing, and tennis and taught math and physical education. In addition, he served as interim athletic director. After the 1950 football season, Gaines decided to coach only basketball because it was easier to field competitive teams. "Being a teacher's college, it was tough getting boys here," Clarence remarked. "It was easier getting seven or eight than 40 or 50 [for football]." His quintets compiled an 828–447 win-loss record over 47 years and set several marks, including seventeen 20-win seasons. Seven of those 20 victory campaigns came in succession from 1961 to 1967. After years of attracting outstanding African-American players, however, Gaines encountered a tougher time recruiting in the late 1960s. Racial bars at larger universities began to fall, while a small recruiting budget depleted the talent Clarence had to choose from.

Gaines's greatest seasons came from 1964–1965 to 1966–1967 with star guard Earl "the Pearl" Monroe, who led Winston-Salem to 25–8, 21–5, and 31–1 records. The 1967 squad captured the NCAA College Division title, the first NCAA crown won by a predominantly African-American school. Clarence was named College Division Coach of the Year, while Monroe earned consensus College Division All-America and 1967 Player of the Year honors.

Gaines pushed his players both on and off the court, refusing to give athletes special treatment. Monroe recalled a time when Clarence asked him why he was attending school. "I told him I was down here to play ball," replied Earl. Gaines responded, "If you're just down here to play basketball, you might as well go back to Philadelphia right now—you're here to learn." Monroe and many other Winston-Salem players made the Dean's List. Gaines has graduated numerous players, many of whom became politicians, businessmen, doctors, and lawyers. Clarence, always busy off the basketball court, served as athletic director at Winston-Salem and held various offices with the Central Intercollegiate Athletic Association (CIAA), NCAA, National Association of College Basketball Coaches, National Association of Collegiate Athletic Directors, and United States Olympic Committee. Gaines also participated in American Heart Association, Winston-Salem Urban League, and Winston-Salem Boys Club activities.

In 47 years of coaching from 1947 to 1993, Gaines won 828 basketball games and ranks second only to legendary Kentucky coach Adolph Rupp in career victories. His honors have included induction into the Naismith Memorial Basketball Hall of Fame in 1983, Morgan State Hall of Fame, National Association of Intercollegiate Athletics (NAIA) Hall of Fame, Helms Athletic Foundation Hall of Fame, CIAA Hall of Fame, and North Carolina Sports Hall of Fame. Gaines, who now serves as director of the Winston-Salem Foundation, married Clara Lucille Berry and has two children, Clarence, Jr., and Lisa.

BIBLIOGRAPHY: Charlotte *Observer*, February 24, 1993; July 1, 1993; Neil D. Isaacs, *All the Moves: A History of College Basketball* (Philadelphia, PA, 1975); *New York Times*, December 6, 1983; *Who's Who Among Black Americans* (Lake Forest, IL, 1985).

Brian L. Laughlin

JAKE GAITHER
(April 11, 1903–February 18, 1994) ————————————— *Football*

Jake Gaither compiled the highest winning percentage (.844) among college coaches with 200 or more victories. Alonzo Smith "Jake" Gaither was born in Dayton, Tennessee, on April 11, 1903. Gaither guided Florida A&M University's gridders from 1945 to 1969 to 203 wins, 36 losses, and four ties. The Rattlers won six national African-American college championships and 22 Southern Intercollegiate Athletic Conference (SIAC) titles. When Florida

A&M defeated Southern University, 10–7, in 1969 for Gaither's two hundredth victory, only legendary coaches Amos Alonzo Stagg, Pop Warner, and Jess Neely already had surpassed that milestone. Jake guided the Rattlers to three undefeated seasons and 12 one-loss campaigns, producing 36 All-Americas.

Gaither grew up in Memphis, Tennessee, where his father, J. D., served as a Zion AME minister. His father wanted him to become a minister. Jake, one of five children, aspired to be a lawyer instead and worked industriously as a youth digging ditches, shining shoes, being a bellhop, and mining coal. After graduating from high school, he enrolled at Knoxville College in Tennessee and starred in football, basketball, and track and field there. Gaither was named an All-SIAC end in football before graduating from Knoxville College with a Bachelor of Science degree in 1927, the same year his father died. Jake, pressed to help immediately with family finances, taught and coached football in high school and eventually coached football at Henderson, North Carolina, Institute. Coaching and teaching became his real vocations, although he exhibited qualities of a lawyer and preacher. "Where else do they make men quicker than on the football field?" Gaither maintained. "Football is the greatest classroom there is."

Jake, always seeking to better himself, served as head football coach at St. Paul Polytechnical Institute at Lawrenceville, Virginia, and earned a master's degree in physical education and health in 1937 at Ohio State University. He assisted Florida A&M head football coach William Bell, a Buckeye graduate, helping the Rattlers achieve two consecutive undefeated seasons. In 1942, Gaither overcame two brain tumors, temporary blindness, and a broken leg. He moved up to head football coach at Florida A&M in 1945, serving also as classroom instructor and basketball and track and field head coach. Jake married Sadie Robinson, his former Knoxville College classmate who taught English at Florida A&M and whose hard-nosed approach to grading kept the Rattlers on their toes.

Gaither, a devout Christian, did not tolerate swearing. "Your game here isn't worth a dime," Jake vowed, "if it doesn't make better men of you. Your momma's gonna die, poppa's gonna die, your best friends may let you down, sometimes you're going to lose your job and not meet your responsibilities financially. You must learn to face these reversals, get up off the floor, and come back fighting." He insisted that his players graduate. Many became high school teachers and coaches, sending their best players to Jake. Former Ohio State University coach Woody Hayes once observed, "He [Gaither] could sell himself to youngsters. He didn't just regard them as a number on a jersey; he made the best men out of them, and those players respected him." Jake guided three-time All-America center Curtis Miranda and 41 other future pro footballers, including wide receiver **Bob Hayes** (Dallas Cowboys), halfback Willie Galimore (Chicago Bears), cornerback Ken Riley (Cincinnati Bengals), defensive back Major Hazelton (Chicago Bears), and tight end Hewritt Dixon

(Denver Broncos). He also shaped the lives of tennis champion **Althea Gibson** and John D. Glover, the FBI's first African-American inspector. Gaither authored *The Split Line T Offense of Florida A&M University* (1963), detailing his revolutionary offense, one of the most imitated in the nation.

Sports Illustrated writer John Underwood in 1969 declared, "The most famous black coach in America is Jake Gaither. His teams always win, and 39 graduates have been on pro rosters. Players hang on his words, administrators seek him out, alumni worship at his feet. Other coaches, white and black, flock to hear him speak at clinics." Jake maintained, "The coaching profession is right up there with ministers for the concern and influence they have on others. When you get discipline, you get rapport, and you get them both when you're honest, when you're concerned, when you care. They know that long after they've graduated, I'll be writing letters for them, helping them get jobs, trying to improve their situations. They *know* I care." Gaither retired from football coaching in 1969 but continued as athletic director and professor of physical education until mandatory retirement at age 70 in 1973. He arranged the 1970 Florida A&M–University of Tampa football game, the first interracial college football game in Florida. "They talk about what I have given football," Jake remarked at retirement. "No, it's just the opposite; it's what football has given to me. I can never repay the game for the fine things that football has been to me."

Gaither in 1975 became the first person to win the Triple Crown of football awards, garnering the Amos Alonzo Stagg Award presented by the American Football Coaches Association (AFCA), the Walter Camp Foundation Award for contribution and humanitarianism, and election to the National Football Foundation College Football Hall of Fame. He also belongs to the Tennessee Sports Hall of Fame and in 1976 was inducted into the National Association of College Directors of Athletics and the Black Athletes Halls of Fame. The AFCA elected him a permanent member of its board of trustees. Gaither, the first African-American to serve on the Orange Bowl Committee and lifetime member of the board of trustees of the Fellowship of Christian Athletes, was named to the Helms Athletic Foundation College Football Hall of Fame and selected the 1962 College Division Coach of the Year. A Tallahassee city park and its only city-operated golf course, along with the Florida A&M Cougars' gym, were named in honor of Gaither, who died at age 90 in Tallahassee, Florida, after several years of failing health.

BIBLIOGRAPHY: Norris Anderson, "Confidentially," *Football News* (November 11, 1986); Alvin Hollins, Florida A&M Sports Information director, letter to James D. Whalen, October 1993; Michael Hurd, *Black College Football, 1892–1992* (Virginia Beach, VA, 1993); *The Lincoln Library of Sports Champions*, vol. 5 (Columbus, OH, 1974); *NCAA Football Guide* (1938–1970); *Spalding Football Guide* (1938–1970); John Underwood, "The Desperate Coach: Concessions and Lies," *Sports Illustrated* 31 (September 8, 1969), pp. 28–32, 37–40.

James D. Whalen

JOE GANS
(November 25, 1874–August 10, 1910) _____ *Boxing*

Boxing historians rank Joe Gans among the most talented fighters to hold the world lightweight title. Gans, whose actual name was Joseph Gaines, was born on November 25, 1874, in Baltimore, Maryland, perhaps the son of Joseph Butts, an African-American baseball star. At age four, Joe was adopted by Maria Gant and her fishmarket clerk husband. His earliest prizefighting experiences came in "battle royales," brutal competitions in which several fighters brawled in the same ring. The last boxer standing was declared the winner. By 1891, Gans began his career as a legitimate professional boxer. Historians have experienced difficulty in compiling Joe's early ring record, but he scored at least 12 knockout victories as a lightweight between 1891 and 1894 in the Baltimore area.

With an unusual mixture of speed, agility, power, and ring savvy, Gans remained undefeated in 1895 and through summer 1896. Joe lost a well-fought bout to Dal Hawkins, a left-hook specialist, on October 6, 1896, in New York City. Gans, a student of boxing, observed the effects that his punches had on an opponent. "If you happen to hit a man in a certain place that hurts," Joe told referee George Blake, "that's the place to hit him again. You only have to hit him half as hard there as any other place to finish him." Gans rebounded from the defeat to Hawkins, losing only 1 of his next 26 bouts.

By 1900, the 25-year-old's skillful ring style had earned him the nickname "the old master." Joe's first opportunity to win a world championship ended in failure when defending lightweight champion Frank Erne stopped him in 12 rounds in New York City on March 23, 1900. Two of his most famous victories came later that year in New York City, where he avenged his setback to Hawkins by knocking him out in 2 rounds on May 25 and again in 3 rounds on August 31. In both fights Hawkins's potent left hook hurt Gans early, but Joe rallied for dramatic victories. On December 13, 1900, featherweight champion Terry McGovern knocked him out in a blatantly fixed 2-round contest in Chicago, Illinois. Historians believe that Gans's manager, Al Herford, persuaded him to purposely lose the fight to allow his gambler friends to make a fortune on the long odds.

Joe's long winning streak in 1901 and 1902 allowed him to rise above the controversy surrounding his loss to McGovern. On May 12, 1902, he earned a second opportunity to win the lightweight title from Erne. This time, Gans scored a surprising first-round knockout in Fort Erie, Ontario. Joe had remembered a flaw in Erne's fighting style from their previous meeting and exploited it with a single right hand to win the title. He made nine successful defenses of his crown before relinquishing it in 1904. Gans fought just two bouts in 1905, having contracted tuberculosis, but resumed a solid fight schedule in 1906. On September 3, Joe regained the world title in one of boxing's most famous fights by defeating Battling Nelson in 42 rounds in Goldfield, Nevada. Nelson, a rugged competitor lacking Gans's boxing technique, repeatedly fouled Gans throughout the fight because the latter possessed the superior skill. A flagrant foul in round 42 prompted referee George Siler to award the championship to Gans. Joe, despite weakening health, made four successful title defenses through May 1908. Nelson, however, won a rematch in Colma, California, on July 4, 1908, by stopping Gans in the seventeenth round and triumphed again in 21 rounds on September 9, 1908, at Colma, marking Joe's last important fight.

Gans, seriously ill by 1909, made one final ring appearance in March before quitting boxing. He died on August 10, 1910, in Baltimore, survived by his second wife, Margaret. Joe had two children, James and Julia, from an earlier marriage to Madge Gans, a Chicago actress. Although earning a huge sum close to $50,000 in his career, Gans died in poverty due to sizable gambling losses. In 156 professional fights, he won 131 (85 by knockout), lost 9 bouts, and drew 16 times.

As the first African-American lightweight titlist, Joe inspired an entire generation of boxers denied an opportunity to compete for world championship recognition because of their race. Boxing historians usually rank Gans, Roberto Duran, and Benny Leonard as the greatest champions the lightweight division has ever produced. The International Boxing Hall of Fame enshrined him in 1990.

BIBLIOGRAPHY: Sam Andre and Nat Fleischer, A Pictorial History of Boxing (New York, 1975); Daniel M. Daniel, "Gans at His Peak," The Ring 26 (April 1947), pp. 30–35; Herbert G. Goldman, ed., The Ring 1986–87 Record Book (New York, 1987); Bert Randolph Sugar, The 100 Greatest Boxers of All Time (New York, 1984).

John Robertson

GEORGE GERVIN
(April 27, 1952–   ) ———————————————————— *Basketball*

George Gervin, one of the most prolific scorers in National Basketball Association (NBA) history, overcame the dire poverty of the inner-city slum to become a professional basketball star. Gervin's mother brought up six children alone after his father left home in 1954. George soon began playing basketball to keep out of trouble in the ghetto. Gervin attracted the attention of his junior varsity coach, Willie Merriweather, at Detroit's Martin Luther King High School. After almost being cut from the basketball team as a five-foot-six-inch sophomore, he practiced every chance he could get on local courts and at a nearby high school gym. A janitor there allowed him to shoot after he swept the gymnasium floor. By his senior year, Gervin had grown to six foot six inches and was named to the All-State team. His improved play earned him a basketball scholarship to play for Jerry Tarkanian at California State University at Long Beach.

Gervin struggled to fit in at the California school and left after one semester, enrolling in 1970 at Eastern Michigan University. As a sophomore, George scored 29 points per game and led the Eagles through an 18-game winning streak into the NCAA small college tournament. Despite his impressive numbers, his basketball career nearly ended at Eastern Michigan. During a semifinal game with Roanoke College in the NCAA small college tournament, Gervin fouled Roanoke player Jay Piccolla with an elbow and was ejected from the game. Before leaving the floor, George punched Piccolla in the face. The incident led to his suspension from the team and the resignation of coach Jim Dutcher. Gervin was expelled from school, reportedly over low scores on his entrance exam taken a year earlier. George had also been asked to try out for the 1972 U.S. Olympic basketball team, but the invitation was withdrawn after this episode.

In 1972, the six-foot-seven-inch, 185-pound, 19-year-old Gervin began playing semi-professional basketball in Pontiac, Michigan, with the Pontiac Chaparalls for $500 a month. After seven months, Johnny "Red" Kerr, a former NBA star and scout for the new American Basketball Association (ABA), spotted George and convinced the ABA's Virginia Squires to sign him. The Squires gave Gervin a contract worth about $100,000 a year. George roomed with one of his idols, **Julius Erving.** In only 30 games with Virginia, he averaged 14.1 points per game and was named to the ABA All-Rookie team. Virginia teammate Fatty Taylor permanently nicknamed Gervin "Iceman" because he was "just so cool."

Gervin quickly became a scoring star. Although the Squires' fortunes dwindled, fans continued to pack houses to see George play. Virginia traded him in January 1974 to the San Antonio Spurs, where he helped the ABA franchise make the jump to the NBA and became the city's biggest sports legend. Angelo Drossos, the former San Antonio owner who acquired Gervin, stated, "George Gervin was to San Antonio what Babe Ruth was to New York."

In 1976, the ABA merged with the NBA. Gervin's game continued to improve in the NBA, as he won four scoring titles in his first five years. The most exciting scoring crown came in 1977–1978. Gervin and former ABA star David Thompson of the Denver Nuggets battled for the scoring championship. The race came down to the last day of the season, when Thompson scored 73 points and Gervin tallied 63 points. George eked out the scoring title, averaging 27.21 points per game to Thompson's 27.15. The 1978–1979 season marked his career best. He led the NBA in scoring for the third time, compiling a 33.1 point per game average and scoring 55 points in a single game. Gervin, an All-NBA First Team selection, was named Most Valuable Player (MVP) of the All-Star Game with 34 points and 10 rebounds. San Antonio traded him to the Chicago Bulls in October 1985. George retired from the

NBA in 1986 but played in Italy in 1986–1987 and with the Quad City Thunder of the Continental Basketball Association in 1989–1990.

Gervin, one of the greatest scoring stars in NBA history, won four scoring titles in 10 NBA seasons. Only **Wilt Chamberlain** and **Michael Jordan** captured more scoring titles. George ended his NBA career with 26,595 points and averaged 25.1 points per game in his combined ABA-NBA career. He holds the NBA record for most points scored in a single quarter—tallying 33 against the New Orleans Jazz in April 1978. His NBA career scoring average of 26.2 points in 791 games ranks eighth best. Altogether, he made five All-NBA First Teams, two All-NBA Second Teams, and two All-ABA Second Teams.

BIBLIOGRAPHY: Zander Hollander, ed., *The Pro Basketball Encyclopedia* (Los Angeles, CA, 1977); Curry Kirkpatrick, "The Iceman Cometh and Scoreth," *Sports Illustrated* 48 (March 6, 1978), pp. 12–15; David S. Neft and Richard M. Cohen, eds., *The Sports Encyclopedia: Pro Basketball 1891–1993* (New York, 1994); *New York Times*, December 24, 1984; Richard O'Connor, "The Lonest Star in Texas," *Sports Illustrated* 72 (March 3, 1981), pp. 56–60; Terry Pluto, *Loose Balls: The Short, Wild Life of the American Basketball Association* (New York, 1990).

Brian L. Laughlin

ALTHEA GIBSON
(August 25, 1927–) _____ *Tennis*

Althea Gibson overcame enormous odds and racism as the first African-American national and international tennis champion. After reigning as queen of women's tennis, Gibson turned her talent and energies to professional golf. Althea was born on August 25, 1927, in Silver, South Carolina, the eldest child of Daniel Gibson and Annie Gibson. Althea's first three years were spent on a cotton farm, where her parents sharecropped a five-acre plot of land. In 1930, she was sent to New York City to live with her aunt, Sally Washington. Her father followed a few months later and found a job, while her mother joined them shortly afterwards. The Gibsons continued to live with Sally until they could afford their own apartment.

Gibson grew up in a rough neighborhood of Harlem. When she was age nine, her parents moved into an apartment of their own. Althea lived two years in Philadelphia, Pennsylvania, with another aunt. By now, she had three sisters, Millie, Annie, and Lillian, and a brother, Daniel. Gibson "didn't like people telling her what to do" and got into trouble. Althea missed more days of school than she attended. The more disobedient she became, the more her father whipped her.

Gibson's father taught her to box so she could protect herself on the streets. Althea's fighting skill reflected her athletic ability and competitiveness on the Harlem playgrounds. In 1941, she played paddle tennis at a supervised "play street." Musician Buddy Walker, the block play leader and Harlem's Society Orchestra director, spotted her athletic talent. He thought Gibson could play regular tennis and talked to her about it, buying two used rackets and taking her to a park to hit tennis balls. Juan Serrell, a member of the Cosmopolitan Club, New York's most prestigious African-American tennis club, noticed Althea and took her to the club. Gibson played sets with Fred Johnson, club pro, and then began taking regular lessons from him in 1941. Cosmopolitan club members bought her a membership, always looking for ways to promote participation of African Americans in tennis.

On the court, Althea accepted the discipline, etiquette, and rules. Off the court, however, she remained rather wild. Gibson dropped out of high school and left home for a while, living in a children's shelter. She reluctantly returned home, being unwilling to accept the restrictions at the shelter.

In 1942, Althea entered and won her first tournament, sponsored by the all African-American American Tennis Association (ATA). Upon becoming more involved in tennis, Gibson found her personal life more orderly. She lived in an apartment provided by the Welfare Department and received welfare support. The welfare support ended on Althea's eighteenth birthday, forcing her to get a job and her own apartment.

Gibson met boxer **Sugar Ray Robinson** and his wife. She adored Sugar Ray and followed his advice to make the most of her athletic talents. Althea moved in 1946 to Wilmington, North Carolina, to live at the home of Dr. Hubert A. Eaton, practice tennis, and finish three years of high school.

In 1947, Gibson won the first of 10 straight ATA National Championships. Two years later, she competed against white players for the first time and enrolled at Florida A&M University in Tallahassee, Florida. Althea in 1950 entered her first outdoor U.S. Lawn Tennis Association (USLTA) tournament and played in the U.S. National Tennis Championships at Forest Hills, New York. In 1951, she performed in the All-England Tennis Championships at Wimbledon for the first time.

Gibson graduated from Florida A&M in 1953 and moved to Jefferson City, Missouri, where she taught physical education at Lincoln University and continued playing tennis. Althea began working with tennis coach Sydney Llewellyn in 1954 and traveled throughout Southeast Asia on a U.S. State Department–sponsored goodwill tennis tour in 1955 and 1956.

In 1956, Althea became the first African-American to win a grand-slam tennis title by capturing the French Open. The same year, she toured in the Australian tennis tournament circuit. At Wimbledon, Gibson defeated Darlene Hard, 6–3, 6–2, in 49 minutes for the 1957 crown and successfully defended the championship in 1958. In 1957 and 1958, Althea won consecutive USLTA National Championship titles at Forest Hills, New York. After her second victory there, Gibson retired from tournament tennis. Althea also took several doubles championships, including the Wimbledon women's doubles in 1957 and 1958 and the USLTA mixed doubles in 1957. After winning at Forest

Hills in 1958, she took a year's leave of absence to promote her autobiography and her singing career.

In 1959, Gibson released a record album, *Althea Gibson Sings*, and appeared in a film, *The Horse Soldiers*. Althea returned to amateur tennis competition long enough to win the 1959 Pan-American women's championship in Chicago. Her tour with the Harlem Globetrotters began on December 28, 1959, as she played exhibition tennis with Karol Fageros. Abe Saperstein defrayed expenses to have Gibson play against Fageros in a preliminary match to the basketball show. Gibson earned nearly $100,000, while Fageros received $30,000. The *New York Times* reported, "It has been known for months that Miss Gibson . . . planned to enter the pro ranks."

Gibson launched her professional golf career in 1964, when she joined the Ladies Professional Golf Association (LPGA). Althea married Will Darben in 1965, but they divorced 10 years later. In 1971, she retired from professional golf and taught tennis professionally. The same year, she was elected to the International Tennis Hall of Fame. Four years later, Gibson joined the East Orange, New Jersey, Department of Recreation as manager. The International Women's Sports Hall of Fame inducted her in 1980.

BIBLIOGRAPHY: "Althea Gibson Signs Pro Contract for Nearly $100,000," *New York Times*, October 20, 1959; Tom Biracree, *Althea Gibson* (New York, 1989); Karima A. Haynes, "Boxing, Track and New Frontiers," *Ebony* 47 (August 1992), p. 78; "Miss Gibson to Go on Tour as a Pro," *New York Times*, October 17, 1959, p. 20; "Women's Hall of Fame," *Ebony* 47 (August 1992), p. 82.

Miriam F. Shelden

BOB GIBSON
(November 9, 1935–   ) _____ *Baseball*

Jesse Haines and Bob Gibson remain the only National Baseball Hall of Fame pitchers who spent their entire major league careers in St. Louis Cardinals National League (NL) club uniforms. Robert Gibson was born on November 9, 1935, in Omaha, Nebraska, the seventh child of Pack Gibson and Victoria Gibson, and grew up there. His father, a millworker, died three months before Bob's birth. Bob's mother worked in a laundry. The Gibsons lived in a four-room ramshackled frame house and later moved to a segregated government housing project. Bob, a sickly child, suffered from asthma, pneumonia, rickets, hay fever, and a rheumatic heart.

Gibson also grew up painfully aware of how difficult it was for African-Americans to succeed no matter how talented they were. His eldest brother, Josh, powerfully influenced him, instilling morals and values, coaching him in sports, and encouraging him to climb to new heights. Bob starred in basketball his junior and senior years and played baseball his senior year at Omaha Technical High School. The Kansas City Monarchs of the Negro American

League (NAL) tried to sign Gibson in 1952, but he declined. Upon Bob's high school graduation in 1953, the St. Louis Cardinals (NL) offered him a minor league contract. Gibson, however, opted for a basketball scholarship to Creighton University in Omaha and became the first African-American athlete to play varsity basketball and baseball there.

In 1957, Bob signed a contract for $3,000 with a $1,000 bonus with the St. Louis Cardinals to join their Omaha, Nebraska, Triple A farm club, and another for $4,000 to play basketball with the Harlem Globetrotters after the baseball season. From 1957 to 1960, the six-foot-one-inch, 193-pound right-hander worked his way through the Redbird farm system at Columbus, Georgia, with the South Atlantic League, at Omaha with the American Association, and at Rochester, New York, with the International League. Gibson spent considerable time with the St. Louis Cardinals in 1959 and 1960 but did not pitch well until Johnny Keane, his Omaha manager, replaced Solly Hemus midway through 1961. Bob lauded Keane as "an excellent teacher with a world of patience and understanding, and always a word of encouragement for a young ballplayer." He finished 1961 with 13 wins and 12 defeats and struck out 166 batters.

From 1962 to 1972, Gibson ranked among the most dominating major league baseball hurlers. Bob pitched more than 275 innings seven times, attaining a career-high 314 in 1969. He recorded 20 or more victories five times and 19 triumphs twice. In nine campaigns, Gibson struck out more than 200 batters. On July 15, 1967, a line drive by Roberto Clemente of the Pittsburgh Pirates broke Bob's right leg. By September, however, Gibson returned to win 3 more games. In 1968, "Gibby" enjoyed one of the greatest seasons ever by a major league pitcher. Using his blazing fastball, a curveball, and a slider, Bob won 22 of 31 decisions, tossed 305 innings, and struck out a league-leading 268 batters. Gibson also pitched 13 shutouts, the second highest total in major league history, and recorded a brilliant 1.12 ERA, the major league record for a pitcher hurling 300 or more innings. From June 2 to August 19, 1968, Bob won 15 consecutive decisions. During a 92-inning stretch in June and July, he allowed only 2 runs. One of those runs came on a wild pitch. On August 14, 1971, Gibson hurled an 11–0 no-hitter against the Pittsburgh Pirates.

The fierce competitor honed every aspect of his game. Many sportswriters and players rate Gibson, who won nine Gold Gloves, and Jim Kaat as the best fielding pitchers in major league history. Bob's bat frequently kept him in the game. Gibson belted 24 career home runs, batted .303 in 1970, and occasionally pinch-hit. In 1974, "Hoot," a nickname given by his Omaha teammates, became the first major league pitcher since Walter Johnson in the 1920s to record 3,000 strikeouts. Gibson was named to nine NL All-Star teams and pitched in six All-Star Games without a decision. Bob captured the NL Cy Young Award in 1968 and 1970 and was voted NL Most Valuable Player (MVP) in 1968.

In World Series competition, Gibson pitched superbly. The Cardinals played a seven-game World Series in defeating the New York Yankees in 1964 and the Boston Red Sox in 1967 and bowing to the Detroit Tigers in 1968. Bob won seven games and lost two decisions with a 1.89 ERA in World Series play. He established World Series records with eight consecutive complete games, seven straight victories, 17 strikeouts in a game against Detroit on October 2, 1968, and most strikeouts (10.2) per 9 innings. Gibby struck out 92 batters in 81 World Series innings and also slugged home runs in the 1967 and 1968 World Series.

A torn thigh muscle in 1971, torn cartilage in 1973, and arthritis slowed Gibson in his later years. Bob retired in September 1975 after 528 games with 251 wins, 174 losses, 56 shutouts, 3,117 strikeouts, and a sparkling 2.91 ERA. An overwhelming selection to the National Baseball Hall of Fame in 1981, he served as pitching coach for the New York Mets (NL) in 1981 and for the Atlanta Braves (NL) from 1982 to 1984. Bob has worked as a radio sports commentator for the St. Louis Cardinals, owned interest in a radio station, chaired the board of a bank, and operated a restaurant. In October 1994, the St. Louis Cardinals hired him as bullpen coach and assistant to manager Joe Torre.

Gibson married his high school girlfriend, Charline Johnson, in April 1957 and has two daughters, Renee and Annette. In 1968, Bob published his autobiography, *From Ghetto to Glory: The Story of Bob Gibson*. His memoirs, *Stranger to the Game: The Autobiography of Bob Gibson*, were published in September 1994. He continues to pitch in old-timers' games to help distressed retired ballplayers and their families.

BIBLIOGRAPHY: Bob Gibson with Phil Pepe, *From Ghetto to Glory: The Story of Bob Gibson* (New York, 1968); Bob Gibson with Lonnie Wheeler, *Stranger to the Game: The Autobiography of Bob Gibson* (New York, 1994); Charline Gibson and Michael Rich, *A Wife's Guide to Baseball* (New York, 1970); David Halberstam, *October 1964* (New York, 1994); David Halberstam, "This Magic Moment," *Parade Magazine* (July, 24, 1994), pp. 4–6; Jerry Lovelace and Marty Hendin, *St. Louis Cardinals 1974 Official Guide and Record Book for Press, Radio and TV* (St. Louis, MO, 1974); Lowell Reidenbaugh, *Baseball's Hall of Fame: Cooperstown, Where the Legends Live Forever*, rev. ed. (New York, 1993); Steve Rushin, "The Season of High Heart: Gibson and McClain," *Sports Illustrated* special classic ed. (June 19, 1993), pp. 30–37.

Frank J. Olmsted

JOSH GIBSON
(December 21, 1911–January 20, 1947) ⸻⸻⸻⸻⸻ *Baseball*

Josh Gibson, the recognized home run king of the Negro Baseball Leagues, lived a triumphant, yet tragic life. His life marked the triumph of a talented, dedicated, and determined athlete reaching the allowed pinnacle of his profession, but also the tragedy of an ill, depressed, and disillusioned young man dying prematurely.

On September 27, 1930, the rookie catcher for the Homestead Grays drove a home run 460 feet into the left-field bleachers at Yankee Stadium in New York. The round-tripper, the longest ball ever hit in the Bronx ball yard, came in a Championship Series with the New York Lincoln Giants. Gibson hit Lincoln pitching at a .368 clip and added two more round-trippers, helping the Grays claim supremacy over African-American baseball in the East, six games to four.

Joshua Gibson was born in Buena Vista, Georgia, on December 21, 1911, and endured conditions comparable to slavery under the southern Jim Crow laws. Ten years later, his father, Mark Gibson, gave up the hopelessness of sharecropping and moved north to work in the Pittsburgh, Pennsylvania, steel-mills. He settled on the city's northside and sent for his wife, Nancy (Wood-lock) Gibson, and their children, Josh, Jerry, and Annie.

In Pittsburgh, Gibson completed the ninth grade at Allegheny Pre-Vocational School. The natural athlete won several track and field ribbons as a youngster, but baseball became his first love. As a teenager, even-tempered, likable, and industrious Josh held numerous jobs to help contribute to the family's livelihood. Gibson also fell in love with 17-year-old Helen Mason. When she became pregnant, the couple married and lived with her parents. Helen tragically died in August 1930 after giving birth to twins, Joshua, Jr., and Helen. Since Josh's budding baseball career kept him away with both summer and winter play, the children were brought up by their grandparents, James and Margaret Mason.

By 1931, Gibson had achieved stardom. An adept batting eye, excellent bat control, and tremendous power made the right-handed swinger a respected, feared batsman. **Satchel Paige** once said of Josh, "You look for his weakness and while you lookin' for it he liable to hit forty-five home runs."

In 1932, Gibson began a five-year stint with the Pittsburgh Crawfords. With Josh behind the plate, the Crawfords captured the 1933 and 1935 Negro National League (NNL) pennants. Through dedicated practice and personal observation of fellow receivers, he developed into a smooth, reliable catcher with a strong, accurate arm. Gibson's skills and the blind prejudice faced by even the era's greatest African-American players caused Washington Senator star pitcher Walter Johnson to remark, "There is a catcher any big league club would like to buy. . . . He can do anything. He hits the ball a mile. And he catches so easy he might as well be in a rocking chair. Throws like a rifle. Bill Dickey isn't as good a catcher. Too bad this [Josh] Gibson is a colored fellow."

Gibson also developed negotiating skills to accompany his talent and near-mythical reputation, becoming the second-highest paid African-American star. In the NNL, Josh's monthly salary steadily rose from $250 to $1,500. During the late 1930s, he used offers to play in South America and Mexico as leverage to increase his salary with the Grays.

Gibson returned to the Grays in 1937 but played part of the summer in the Dominican Republic. Dominican dictator Rafael Trujillo, challenged by political opponents, lured several Negro League stars south to win a politically crucial baseball tournament. Gibson, Paige, **"Cool Papa" Bell,** Sam Bankhead, and other players performed for Trujillo's Stars. Josh led all tournament batsmen with a .453 average and collected $2,200 for playing 13 games. Upon returning stateside, the players were banned from the Negro Leagues. The players instead barnstormed across the nation in their Dominican uniforms, winning the prestigious *Denver Post* Tournament.

The African-American press constantly protested injustices suffered by African Americans during the depression and World War II. Baseball, with its unwritten race ban, remained particularly vulnerable. Ches Washington of *The Pittsburgh Courier* urged the Pittsburgh Pirates National League (NL) club in the summer of 1938 to sign African-American stars Gibson, Bell, Paige, and Ray Brown. Washington's wire went unanswered.

In 1940, Gibson signed contracts with both the Grays and Veracruz of the Mexican League (ML). The Grays won a court decision against Josh, but the catcher remained in Mexico through 1941. He returned to the Grays in 1942 with all forgiven. In Mexico, Gibson developed a taste for beer, triggering a downward spiral that saw Josh suffer deteriorating physical, mental, and emotional health. On New Year's Day in 1943, he lapsed into a coma from a nervous breakdown and spent 10 days hospitalized. Gibson faced intermittent hospital and sanitarium stays the rest of his life.

Josh, normally easygoing and fun loving, became involved in a stormy, stifling relationship with an older woman and a heated affair with an overseas soldier's wife during World War II. The younger woman appeared to be involved with drugs, arousing suspicion that Gibson joined her in the habit.

Physical problems, including damaged knees from the constant summers and winters of squatting behind the plate, caused Josh to be classified 4F by his draft board. Headaches and dizziness also persisted, while his weight ballooned to 230 pounds on his six-foot-two-inch frame. Occasional disorientation, incoherence, and conversations with imagined companions also plagued him.

Nevertheless, Gibson never lost his ability to hit and allegedly belted the longest homers ever hit in Pittsburgh's Forbes Field, Washington's Griffith Stadium, New York's Yankee Stadium, and countless other ballparks. He claimed home run titles in the Puerto Rican Winter League (PRWL) with 6 in 1940 and 13 in 1942 and the ML with 33 in 1941. His NNL home run titles included 6 in 1944 and 8 in 1945. Josh also led the PRWL in batting with .479 in 1942, a standing league record, and the NNL with .393 in 1945. His two ML seasons produced a .393 batting average with 46 home runs in 116 games. The latest Negro League data indicate Josh batted .362 from 1930 through 1946.

In 1947, Gibson's health quickly declined, as his weight dropped to a frail 180 pounds. After a weekend of intense headaches, Josh died barely 35 years old at his mother's Pittsburgh home on January 20, 1947.

Gibson's parents, especially his mother, were particularly pleased with and enjoyed their son's success on the diamond. His brother, Jerry, pitched semi-pro baseball and hurled a no-hitter witnessed by Josh on June 17, 1939. His son, Josh, Jr., joined the Homestead Grays in 1949 and briefly appeared in organized baseball with Youngstown, Ohio, of the Middle Atlantic League in 1948 and Farnham, Canada, of the Provincial League in 1951.

Gibson's brief life saw him become a baseball legend. He hit .483 in nine East-West (Negro Leagues) All-Star Games and performed on the Gray's 1937, 1938, 1939, 1942, 1943, 1944, and 1945 NNL championship squads, helping his 1943 and 1944 clubs earn Black World Series triumphs. His Veracruz teams captured the 1940 and 1941 ML pennants. In 1941, Josh won the Puerto Rican Winter League MVP award. In 1972, Gibson was elected to both the National Baseball Hall of Fame and the Mexican Baseball Hall of Fame.

BIBLIOGRAPHY: *The Baseball Encyclopedia*, 9th ed. (New York, 1993); William Brashler, *Josh Gibson* (New York, 1978); *Enciclopedia del beisbol Mexicano* (Mexico, 1992); John Holway, *Josh and Satch* (Westport, CT, 1991); Merl F. Kleinknecht files, Galion, OH; Robert W. Peterson, *Only the Ball Was White* (Englewood Cliffs, NJ, 1970); David L. Porter, ed., *Biographical Dictionary of American Sports: Baseball* (Westport, CT, 1987); James A. Riley, *The All-Time All-Stars of Black Baseball* (Cocoa Beach, FL, 1983); James A. Riley, *The Biographical Encyclopedia of the Negro Baseball Leagues* (New York, 1994); Mike Shatzkin, ed., *The Ballplayers* (New York, 1990); *The Sporting News Official Baseball Guide* (1952).

Merl F. Kleinknecht

JOE GREENE
(September 24, 1946–) —————————————————— *Football*

When the Pittsburgh Steelers National Football League (NFL) club played the Houston Oilers at Houston in late 1972, they desperately needed a win to keep their playoff hopes alive. On both offense and defense, however, Pittsburgh was crippled by injuries. Fortunately, defensive tackle "Mean Joe" Greene, sacked Houston quarterbacks five times and recovered a fumble. The Steelers won, 9–3, starting a decade of triumphs. Ahead lay the "Immaculate Reception" victory over the Oakland Raiders, eight consecutive playoff seasons, and four Super Bowl triumphs in six years.

Greene provided the cornerstone of the Steelers' dynasty in the 1970s. In 1969, new Steelers coach Chuck Noll selected the six-foot-four-inch, 260-pound defensive tackle as his first player. The Steelers won only one game in 1969, but Joe was named United Press International's (UPI) Rookie of the Year and played in the Pro Bowl. A few scouts initially had questioned his competitiveness, but sportswriter Roy Blount, Jr., soon pronounced Greene "too strong to be overpowered, too elusive to be hobbled, and too smart to be fooled."

Blount's description of Joe's football talents also applied to his life and career, as he has consistently overwhelmed the doubters. Born into a poor Tem-

ple, Texas, family, on September 24, 1946, Charles Edward Greene was reared
by his mother. For Dunbar High School, he played middle linebacker in
football. At North Texas State University, he majored in physical education
and acquired the nickname "Mean Joe." The nickname complemented his
team's sobriquet the "Mean Green." In 1968 the player described by his coach
as "a fort on foot" was named Missouri Valley Conference's Athlete of the
Year, a consensus football All-America, and the nation's top defensive lineman.

   The Steelers, with their lackluster history, hardly guaranteed Greene a rosy
professional future. But the lineman, who once expressed his frustration with
being held by grabbing the football from the center and throwing it into the
stands, learned to play under control. Talented young players soon looked to
Joe for leadership. The Steelers drafted Jack Ham, Jack Lambert, Mel Blount,
and other standouts to play behind defensive linemen Greene, L. C. Greenwood, and Dwight White, enabling the "Steel Curtain" to shut down opposing
offenses for most of the 1970s.

   On a team of stars, Greene still excelled. Greenwood summarized Joe's
importance: "There's a whole lot of things we can do on the line because he's
Joe Greene. There are certain plays the offense just won't run because that's
his spot. And he comes off the ball so quick. Normally you react off the snap
or the man in front of you, but I don't even watch the ball. I react off Joe."

   In 1972, Greene won the George Halas Award as the NFL's Most Valuable
Defensive Player, the UPI's award as Defensive Player of the Year, and the
Associated Press's award as Lineman of the Year. Two years later, Joe pioneered the technique of lining up on an angle between the center and guard
and proved virtually unstoppable in playoff games against the Oakland Raiders
and Minnesota Vikings. He was named the Most Valuable Defensive Player
by the AP, *Pro Football Weekly*, and Professional Football Writers Association.
In Pittsburgh's first Super Bowl win, a 16–6 victory over Minnesota in January
1975, the "Steel Curtain" held the Vikings to 17 yards rushing. Joe also made
an interception and a fumble recovery.

   Injuries hampered Greene in the 1975 season, but he still contributed to
the Steelers' 21–17 triumph over the Dallas Cowboys in the 1976 Super Bowl.
Joe stayed healthier in 1976 and, with the retirement of Andy Russell, was
named Pittsburgh's defensive captain. In 1977, he made the AP's All-NFL
team and UPI's All–American Football Conference (AFC) team, although not
making the Pro Bowl. For the second straight year, the Steelers missed making
the Super Bowl. The team rededicated itself in 1978. Greene recovered five
fumbles and finished second on the Steelers in sacks, helping Pittsburgh win
the 1979 Super Bowl 35–31, over Dallas. Although slowed by neck and arm
injuries, Joe remained a major force during the 1979 season. The Steelers
captured their fourth Super Bowl title in January 1980 by defeating the Los
Angeles Rams, 31–19.

   By the time injuries finally forced Greene's retirement after the 1981 season, he had established a formidable reputation as a player and leader. The

10-time All-Pro was named to the Pro Football Hall of Fame in 1987, unanimously selected to the NFL's Team of the Decade for the 1970s, and made the All-Time NFL team in 1994. "Intensity is a Pittsburgh tradition," he once told an interviewer. Joe personified that tradition, helping to make winning a part of it.

Although receiving a Clio Award for a Coca-Cola commercial in 1980, Greene has not made show business a career since his retirement. Joe has served as an assistant football coach with the Steelers and Miami Dolphins (NFL). He and his wife Agnes live in Duncansville, Texas, and have three children.

BIBLIOGRAPHY: Roy Blount, Jr., *About Three Bricks Shy of a Load: A Highly Irregular Lowdown on the Year the Pittsburgh Steelers Were Super But Missed the Bowl* (Boston, MA, 1974); Roy Blount, Jr., "He Does What He Wants Out There," *Sports Illustrated* 43 (September 22, 1975), pp. 96–104; Pat Livingston, *The Pittsburgh Steelers: A Pictorial History* (Virginia Beach, VA, 1980); *Pittsburgh Steelers Media Guide* (1981); David L. Porter, ed., *Biographical Dictionary of American Sports: Football* (Westport, CT, 1987); Diane K. Shah, "The Greene Machine," *Newsweek* 95 (January 21, 1980), pp. 60–61.

Luther W. Spoehr

HAL GREER
(June 26, 1936–) ————————————————————— *Basketball*

Hal Greer, one of the greatest guards in National Basketball Association (NBA) history, was selected seven times to the All-NBA Second Team and played in 10 All-Star Games during his 15-year career. Born in Huntington, West Virginia, Harold Everett "Hal" Greer was the youngest of nine children of railroad engineer William Greer. Greer starred in basketball at Huntington's Douglas High School, leading his team to the Negro State Championship. After Hal graduated from high school, his stepmother and coach Cam Henderson convinced him to attend Marshall University. No African American previously had played for a major college basketball team in West Virginia.

Under coaches Henderson and Jules Rivlin, Greer blossomed in three seasons at Marshall from 1955–1956 to 1957–1958. Hal's scoring average per game climbed from 15.5 points as a sophomore to 18.9 points as a junior. Marshall made its only NCAA tournament appearance with Greer in 1956, losing to Moorhead State University, 107–92. The sophomore Hal scored 12 points. As a senior, he enjoyed his best season with 23.6 points and 11.7 rebounds per game and converting 54.6 percent of his field goals. Greer also averaged 83.3 percent from the free throw line, where he became known for jump shooting his foul shots. Marshall compiled a combined 50–21 win-loss record over those three years, with Hal being named All-America as a senior.

Marshall coach Jules Rivlin recommended Greer to Syracuse Nationals

NBA coach Paul Seymour, whom he had coached at the University of Toledo. Seymour selected Hal in the second round of the 1958 NBA draft. Greer's transition to the NBA did not always progress smoothly. Coach Seymour's gradual use of Hal left him wondering why he remained on the bench so much. Late in the 1958–1959 season, however, Greer displayed his talents to the entire NBA. In a game against the Boston Celtics on February 14, 1959, Hal scored 39 points in the first half and 45 points altogether. He started for Syracuse by the end of his rookie season and was considered among the NBA's premier guards by his fourth campaign. The Syracuse franchise moved to Philadelphia as the Warriors following the 1962–1963 season.

Greer's greatest season came in 1966–1967, when he helped the Philadelphia Warriors break the Boston Celtics' long string of NBA titles. The 1967 Warriors team, which included Greer, **Wilt Chamberlain,** Billy Cunningham, Larry Costello, Chet Walker, and Luke Jackson, ranks among the greatest squads in NBA history.

Although an intense defensive player, Greer became known primarily as a shooter. Hal claimed that money motivated him. "The scorers get the money," he remarked. Greer made a quick transition to scoring in the NBA, leading Syracuse and Philadelphia in scoring for five consecutive seasons from 1961–1962 to 1965–1966 and averaging more than 20 points per game from 1963–1964 through 1969–1970. Many NBA coaches believed Hal possessed the "finest middle-distance shot in the game." Besides leading his team in scoring, he compiled a 45 percent field goal average and an 80 percent free throw average. Greer's speed and talent made him a versatile player, as he made 5,665 rebounds and 4,540 assists during his career.

Greer was named to the All-NBA Second Team seven consecutive times from 1963 through 1969 and played in 10 consecutive All-Star Games from 1961 to 1970. As Most Valuable Player (MVP) of the 1968 All-Star contest, Hal scored 21 points in 17 minutes and made all eight shots from the field. He tallied 19 of his points in one quarter to set an All-Star Game record.

Greer's career marks of 1,122 NBA games played, 39,788 minutes, 8,504 field goals made, and 21,586 points remain club records, surpassing even Chamberlain and **Julius Erving.** Philadelphia retired Hal's uniform, number 15. He was elected to the Naismith Memorial Basketball Hall of Fame in 1981, and "Hal Greer Boulevard" in Huntington, West Virginia, was named for him. After retiring from pro basketball in 1973, Greer sold real estate and became basketball coach at Germantown Academy in 1978. In 1980, Hal became coach and general manager of the Philadelphia Kings of the Continental Basketball Association and general manager of the King Arena in Philadelphia, Pennsylvania. He now operates his own network marketing business.

BIBLIOGRAPHY: Edwin B. Henderson, *The Black Athlete* (New York, 1970); Zander Hollander, ed., *The Modern Encyclopedia of Basketball* (Garden City, NY, 1979); Ronald L. Mendell, *Who's Who in Basketball* (New Rochelle, NY, 1973); *NCAA Basketball's Finest: All-Time Great Collegiate Players and Coaches* (Overland Park, KS, 1993); *Of-*

ficial NCAA Final Four Record and Fact Book (Overland Park, KS, 1994); *Philadelphia Enquirer*, February 21, 1981; April 7, 1989.

Brian L. Laughlin

KEN GRIFFEY, JR.
(November 21, 1969–) ———————————————————— *Baseball*

On August 29, 1990, Ken Griffey, Sr., joined his son, Ken, Jr., on the American League (AL) Seattle Mariners club as the first father-son combination to play on the same major league baseball team. Ken, Sr., at age 40, already had enjoyed a long, successful baseball career with the Cincinnati Reds National League (NL), New York Yankees (AL), and Atlanta Braves (NL) clubs, while Ken, Jr., nicknamed "The Kid," had played two seasons with the Mariners. In their 15 games together, Ken, Sr., batted .400 with three home runs and 16 RBIs. Ken, Jr., hit .312 with three home runs and 11 RBIs. On September 14, the two Griffeys belted back-to-back home runs off California Angels pitcher Kirk McCaskill.

Ken, Jr., describes those home runs as his most memorable experience while playing with his dad. "He was batting just before me," Ken, Jr., recalls of his dad's solo shot, "and . . . I shook his hand as he crossed the plate. He grinned. 'That's how you do it, son!' he said. I started to laugh and stepped up to the plate. The count got to 3–0, and [manager] Jim LeFebvre gave me the green light to swing at the next pitch. I hit it solid and knew it was going out. I looked over at Dad and he couldn't believe it. I circled the bases, then trotted into the dugout and hugged him."

George Kenneth Griffey, Jr., was born on November 21, 1969, in Donora, Pennsylvania, the birthplace of both Ken, Sr., and St. Louis Cardinals great Stan Musial. Although Ken, Jr., was born into a baseball family and grew up in major league ballparks, neither his father nor his mother, Alberta "Birdie," pressured him to enter professional baseball. "Dad never pushed me into anything," Ken, Jr., claims. "He just told me to do whatever I wanted—football, basketball, baseball. He was just a dad." Ken, Sr., agrees, "I never had any idea this [major league stardom] would happen—I never pushed him." Younger brother Craig forsook the diamond for the gridiron in high school and played football for Ohio State University but was eventually drafted by the Seattle Mariners.

Ken, Jr., a six-foot-three-inch, 195-pound all-around athlete, starred in both football and baseball at Cincinnati's Moeller High. During his senior year, Griffey, who throws and bats left-handed, batted .478 with seven home runs in 28 games. He was selected first out of 1,263 draftees by the Mariners in 1987 and received a $175,000 signing bonus. Ken, Jr., shot through the minor leagues like a meteor. After 53 games with Bellingham, Washington, of the Northwest League in 1987, Griffey began 1988 in long-season Class A with

San Bernardino, California, of the California League and finished the campaign in Class AA with Vermont of the Eastern League. His outstanding 1989 spring training performance sidetracked the Mariners' plan to send him to Class AAA Calgary, Canada, of the Pacific Coast League. He batted .359, setting Mariner club spring training records with 33 hits and 21 RBIs. Ken, Jr.'s, defensive play demonstrated such maturity that manager Jim LeFebvre made him the Mariners' starting center fielder. He doubled in his initial major league at bat and slammed a home run on his first swing in the Kingdome, the Mariners' home stadium.

For a 19-year-old with no experience at Class AAA, Griffey enjoyed an amazing rookie major league season. He batted over .300 with 13 home runs before the All-Star break. A second-half injury to his left hand, however, limited him to just 127 games overall. Ken, Jr., finished with a .264 batting average and 16 homers. Speed and athletic ability compensated for his lack of defensive experience. Griffey completed the 1989 season with 12 assists and six double plays, the latter topping all AL outfielders. Ken, Jr., finished third in AL Rookie of the Year balloting behind Baltimore Orioles closer Gregg Olson and Kansas City Royals pitcher Tom Gordon.

Ken, Jr., has not batted below .300 since 1989 and has improved every season, hitting 22 homers in both 1990 and 1991 and 27 in 1992. His 45 round-trippers in 1993 ranked season in the AL. During an eight-game stretch from July 20 to July 28, 1993, Griffey tied the major league record for most home runs in consecutive games. After he belted the first 4 homers, people began to catch the excitement. His mother drove to Cleveland, Ohio, from the family home in Cincinnati, Ohio, and asked her son what the record was. "I told her eight," recalled Ken, Jr., "and she said, 'It doesn't look good for you.' " But he eventually tied both Dale Long of the 1956 Pittsburgh Pirates and Don Mattingly of the 1987 New York Yankees, who had hit round-trippers in eight straight games.

On a September 14, 1993, game against the California Angels, Ken, Jr., drove in his 100th and 101st runs of the season to join National Baseball Hall of Famers Joe DiMaggio, Ted Williams, Ty Cobb, and Mel Ott as the only players with three consecutive 100-RBI seasons before reaching their 24th birthdays. Griffey began the 1994 season with a home run–hitting binge. By June 1, he had broken Mickey Mantle's record for most home runs in April and May. By June 24, his 32 homers in 77 games had surpassed the 28 round-trippers in 1961 and the 26 by Babe Ruth in 1927. On July 11, 1994, Ken, Jr., sent 7 long balls out of Pittsburgh's Three Rivers Stadium to win the pre–All-Star Game home run contest. Toronto Blue Jays pitcher David Cone observed, "I watched that, and I don't even know why we pitchers are even here." In the strike-shortened 1994 season, Griffey led the AL with 40 home runs, ranked third in runs scored (94) and slugging percentage (.674), and finished among the top 10 in hits (140), RBIs (90), and batting average (.323). Ken, who won five consecutive Gold Glove Awards from 1990 to 1994, placed second to **Frank Thomas** of the Chicago White Sox in the 1994 MVP balloting.

Through 1994, Griffey has accumulated 972 hits, 194 doubles, and 172 home runs, has scored 518 runs, and has batted in 543 runs. His career batting average (.306), on-base percentage (.379), and slugging average (.541) have risen steadily. He has been selected to the AL All-Star team every year from 1990 to 1995, being named MVP in 1992 and receiving the most fan votes in 1994. Ken, Jr., often compared to his idol **Willie Mays,** excites fans by fielding every hit to center field. He dives for sinking liners and leaps for fly balls over the wall. Griffey broke his left wrist smashing headfirst into the padded wall in right center at the Kingdome in May 1995, robbing Kevin Bass of the Baltimore Orioles of an extra base hit.

The crowd pleaser probably drew at least 48,000 extra fans during his 1993 home run streak. Fans and baseball personnel consistently rate Griffey as the player they would most like to watch take batting practice or build a team around. Detroit Tigers manager Sparky Anderson affirms, "He and **[Barry] Bonds** are the best players in baseball." He is one of very few ballplayers, including Babe Ruth and **Reggie Jackson,** to have had a candy bar named for him.

With enthusiastic fan support and a multiyear contract, Ken, Jr., enjoys playing in Seattle. His manager, Lou Piniella, former Cincinnati Reds skipper, maintains a friendship with the family. Ken, Jr. is still just a kid having fun at the ballpark, enjoying wearing his cap backward, listening to music on his headphones, and playing Nintendo by the hour. This may change some since he and his wife Melissa had their first child, a son, Trey, in January 1994.

BIBLIOGRAPHY: Sam Blair, "Ken Griffey Jr.: A Chip Off the Old Block," *Boys' Life* 82 (April 1992), pp. 34–37, 74; Jack Friedman and Nick Gallo, "Proving that the Son Also Rises, Rookie Star Ken Griffey Jr. Breaks Through the Clouds in Seattle," *People Weekly* 32 (July 17, 1989), pp. 77–78; Tim Kurkjian, "Junior's Hot July," *Sports Illustrated* 79 (August 9, 1993), p. 60; Malcolm Moran, "At 19, Griffey Jr. Strides into Senior Role," *New York Times Biographical Service* 20 (May 1989), pp. 500–501; Ken Rosenthal, "He's Only 23," *Baseball America* 13 (July 12–23, 1993), p. 3; Bob Sherwin, "No Field Can Contain Him," *Baseball Weekly* 3 (August 4–10, 1993), p. 35; Claire Smith, "Hey Junior!" *Sport* 82 (March 1991), pp. 38–45; E. M. Swift, "Bringing Up Junior," *Sports Illustrated* 72 (May 7, 1990), pp. 38–42; John Thorn and Pete Palmer, eds., *Total Baseball,* 3rd ed. (New York, 1993).

Gaymon L. Bennett

ARCHIE GRIFFIN
(August 21, 1954–   ) ————————————————— *Football*

Archie Griffin remains the only collegiate football player selected as the Heisman Award winner for two consecutive years, accomplishing the feat in 1974 and 1975. Griffin, a standout running back for Ohio State University in the early 1970s, also garnered the United Press International (UPI) Player of the Year Award, the Walter Camp Football Foundation Award, *The Sporting News* Award as Player of the Year, and the Maxwell Award. Twice, Archie was named the Big Ten Conference (BTC) Player of the Year. One of the most celebrated persons in college football, he was also the first college athlete named as *The Sporting News* Man of the Year.

Archie Mason Griffin was born on August 21, 1954, in Columbus, Ohio, and grew up in a family of seven brothers and one sister. His father, James Griffin, Sr., often worked three jobs to support the large family. Archie came from a family of athletes. All seven Griffin brothers excelled in football at the collegiate level. Three, including Archie, eventually played in the National Football League (NFL). As a child, however, Archie did not exhibit superior athletic skills because he was overweight. His family nicknamed him "Butterball." But, as Griffin matured, his weight turned to strength. Archie carried 185 pounds on his five-foot-eight-inch frame throughout his collegiate and professional career.

After enjoying outstanding seasons at Eastmoor High School in Columbus, Griffin enrolled at Ohio State University and produced spectacular results. Archie led Ohio State to three consecutive Rose Bowl appearances in 1972, 1973, and 1974 against the University of Southern California (USC). His high school coach recalled, "In three years at Eastmoor, I never had to urge Archie to go all out. Such inner drive! He ran every play in practice like he runs in games. And he studies just like he practices football." Ohio State won 32 games, losing only 4 (including two Rose Bowl defeats by USC), and tying 1 game in Griffin's four years. Archie rushed 5,265 yards for the Buckeyes and graduated from Ohio State in less than the normal four years.

Ohio State marked an outstanding choice for Griffin. Buckeye coach Woody Hayes insisted on a running-based attack, throwing the football only when absolutely necessary. Archie, a quick, agile, and powerful back, set individual game, season, and career rushing records for Ohio State. Archie revealed himself a team-oriented person when a loss to the University of Michigan prevented Ohio State from winning the mythical national championship. He declared that he "would still rather have a national championship than the Heisman." Since he carried the ball so often, usually taking a significant pounding in the Saturday games, Archie frequently missed practice for the next opponent until the middle of the week.

Griffin teamed effectively with Pete Johnson, a large bruising fullback, during Archie's final years at Ohio State. Archie set up many scores with impressive runs and blocked well for Johnson, who specialized in touchdown efforts near the goal line.

Griffin and Johnson both played in the NFL with the Cincinnati Bengals. Pete enjoyed a successful, if not spectacular, NFL career, while Archie could not equal his collegiate excellence at the professional ranks. The latter's size prevented him from dominating the NFL like the larger, equally fast players. Nonetheless, he gained 2,808 yards in the NFL and averaged 4.1 yards per carry. Griffin lasted eight years with Cincinnati at running back and wide receiver. Most running backs last no longer than four years.

Upon retiring from the NFL, Griffin returned to Columbus. After spending a very brief time with the Jacksonville Bulls of the short-lived United States Football League (USFL), Archie came back to Columbus. He worked in human resources at the Ohio State University before joining two of his brothers in opening an athletic shoe store chain. The business, however, ended in bankruptcy. Griffin eventually served in public relations and fund-raising for the Ohio State University Athletic Office. New Ohio State athletic director Andrew Geiger immediately promoted Griffin in 1994 to senior associate athletic director and gave him full responsibility for the football program and 15 other sports. The Columbus resident participates in local civic and community groups. In 1976 he married college classmate Loretta Laffitte of Cleveland, Ohio. They have one son, Anthony, and one daughter, Andrea.

BIBLIOGRAPHY: Edward F. Dolan, Jr., and Richard Lyttle, *Archie Griffin* (Garden City, NY, 1977); Archie Griffin and Dave Diles, *Archie: The Archie Griffin Story* (Garden City, NY, 1977); Ohio State University Sports Information Office, assorted clippings, Columbus, OH.

Harry A. Jebsen, Jr.

FLORENCE GRIFFITH JOYNER
(December 21, 1959–   ) ———————————————— *Track and Field*

In 1988, Florence Griffith Joyner became history's fastest female sprinter, setting exceptional world records in both the 100 and 200 meters. Delorez Florence Griffith, the seventh of 11 children of Robert Griffith and Florence Griffith, was born on December 21, 1959, in Los Angeles, California. Her father, an electronics technician, divorced her mother, a seamstress, when Florence was four years old. She moved with her mother to the Jordan Downs housing project in the Watts section of Los Angeles. Griffith, nicknamed "Dee Dee" to distinguish her from her mother, enjoyed a "happy childhood" despite her family's poverty. She recalled that her family always had food on the table, but some days "we had oatmeal for breakfast, lunch and dinner." "We didn't know how poor we were," recalls Florence. "We were rich as a family."

Griffith, who discovered her running ability "chasing jack rabbits" at her father's home in the Mohave Desert, began competing at age 7 in track and field meets organized by the Sugar Ray Robinson Youth Foundation. She remembered "always winning" the 50- and 70-meter dashes throughout elementary and junior high school. Florence, at age 14, won "an all-expenses paid trip" to a San Francisco meet for her victorious performance at the annual Jesse Owens National Youth Games. Griffith repeated her feat the following year and was congratulated by **Jesse Owens** personally. Since Florence had won the previous year, she was ineligible for the trip to the regional meet in Texas. Owens broke the news to Griffith, who "started crying" and saying, "I don't like that man, I don't like that man." Later Florence learned that the man was indeed the legendary Owens, who had won four track and field Gold Medals in the 1936 Summer Olympic Games at Berlin, Germany. As a senior at David Jordan High School in 1978, she established school records of 10.86 seconds for 100 yards and 24.4 seconds for 220 yards.

After graduating from Jordan High School, Griffith entered California State University at Northridge. Although injured throughout 1979, Florence still finished eighth in the 100 meters and fourth in the 200 meters in the 1980 Olympic Trials. In 1981, Robert Kersee, her California State coach, became an assistant track and field coach at the University of California at Los Angeles (UCLA). She knew that Kersee "was the best coach" for her and followed him to UCLA. Griffith reluctantly transferred to UCLA, however, possessing a 3.25 grade-point average in a business major unoffered by UCLA. "I chose athletics over academics," confessed Florence, who majored in psychology at UCLA. In 1981, she placed fourth in the 100 meters at the Track Athletic Congress (TAC) and second in the 200 meters at both the Association of Intercollegiate Athletics for Women (AIAW) and TAC championships. Griffith also participated on the U.S. 4 × 100-meter relay team, establishing an American record of 42.82 seconds at the World Cup. The next year, Florence captured the NCAA 200-meter title and contributed to American record 4 × 100-meter relay performances of 42.47 and 42.29 seconds. Although Jamaican Merlene Ottey of the University of Nebraska defeated her in the 200 meters at the 1983 NCAA championships, she captured the NCAA 400-meter title in 50.96 seconds. Griffith's third-place finish in the 200 meters at the 1983 TAC championship prefaced her fourth-place results in the 200 meters in the inaugural World Championship at Helsinki, Finland. In 1984, she finished second to **Valerie Brisco,** another Kersee protégé, in the 200 meters in both the Olympic Trials and the Summer Olympic Games at Los Angeles, California.

In the two years following the 1984 Olympic Games, Florence suffered injuries and lost interest in competition. Griffith began working as a customer service representative at a bank during the day and as a hairstylist at night. Her time in the 200 meters slowed by more than a second in 1986, as she gained weight working two sedentary jobs. According to Kersee, Florence was "so wide that he could not tell whether she 'coming or going.'" Under Kersee's guidance, however, Griffith reemerged in 1987 and captured second place in the 200 meters at both TAC and the World Championships in Rome, Italy. Of her comeback, she told Phil Hersh of the *Chicago Tribune* that "it was time to run better or move on." In October 1987, Florence married Al Joyner, the 1984 Gold Medalist in the triple jump and brother of **Jackie Joyner-Kersee,** world champion and world record holder in the heptathlon.

Griffith Joyner's second-place finish in the 200 meters in the 1987 World Championships motivated her to improve her speed in 1988. She remarked in a 1988 *Ms* interview that "when you've been second-best for so long you can either accept it, or try to become the best." Besides her track workouts, Florence lifted weights four times a week and ran 3.7 miles daily. In the preliminary heats of the 100 meters at the 1988 Olympic Trials, Griffith Joyner clocked 10.60 seconds to break **Evelyn Ashford Washington**'s world record by .16 seconds. Unfortunately, officials did not consider her performance a world record because it was wind-aided. With the wind gauge indicating no aiding tailwind in the 100-meter quarterfinals, she recorded an astonishing time of 10.49 seconds for a legitimate world record. After the race, Florence commented that "I felt I could do 10.59, but 10.49? No way." Griffith Joyner, who captured her semi-final in 10.70 seconds and the final in 10.61 seconds, recorded history's four fastest times for women in the 100 meters at the Olympic Trials. She also won the 200 meters in an American record of 21.77 seconds. Florence accented her record-setting performances by wearing brightly colored "bikini briefs and one-legged leotards because most of the uniforms she had to wear were uncomfortable."

Griffith Joyner outclassed her competition in the 1988 Summer Olympic Games at Seoul, South Korea. After establishing an Olympic record of 10.88 seconds in the opening heats of the 100 meters, she lowered it to 10.62 seconds in the quarter-finals and won the Gold Medal in a wind-aided time of 10.54 seconds. In the 200 meters, Florence lowered the American standard to 21.76 seconds in the quarter-finals, established a world record of 21.65 seconds in the semi-finals, and won the Gold Medal in a remarkable world record of 21.34 seconds. After the 200-meters final, Griffith Joyner acknowledged that she had "worked three or four times harder than ever before" for this moment. Florence garnered another Gold Medal in the 4 × 100-meter relay and a Silver Medal in the 4 × 100-meter relay, anchoring the U.S. quartet to history's second fastest time of 3 minutes 15.51 seconds. In December 1988, Griffith Joyner received the Sullivan Award as the nation's most outstanding amateur athlete. Florence's commitments to sponsors and opportunities to write, design and model clothes, and act left little time for her to train and compete and led to her retirement from track and field in March 1989. She bore her first child, Mary Ruth, in November 1990. Since July 1993, Griffith Joyner has served with Tom McMillen, former basketball player and congressman, as a co-chairperson of the President's Council on Physical Fitness and Sports.

BIBLIOGRAPHY: Current Biography Yearbook (1988), pp. 219–223; "Flojo Announces Retirement," *Track and Field News* 42 (April 1989), p. 58; Jon Hendershott, "Griffith Moving to Center Stage," *Track and Field News* 40 (December 1987), pp. 26–27; Sieg Lindstrom, "Flo: All Dressed Up, 100 Meters to Go," *Track and Field News* 41 (September 1988), p. 27; Sieg Lindstrom, "Nobody But Flo," *Track and Field News* 42 (February 1989), pp. 8–9; David L. Porter, ed., *Biographical Dictionary of American Sports: 1989–1992 Supplement for Baseball, Football, and Other Sports* (Westport, CT, 1992); David Wallechinsky, *The Complete Book of the Olympics*, rev. ed. (New York, 1988); Lena Williams, "Still Racing Around, But for the Long Haul," *New York Times*, July 21, 1993, pp. C1–C4; Howard Willman, "What's Griffith's Best Race?" *Track and Field News* 37 (December 1984), p. 26.

Adam R. Hornbuckle

TONY GWYNN
(May 9, 1960–) ————————————————————— *Baseball*

On June 8, 1981, Tony Gwynn was selected in the third round of the free agent draft by the San Diego Padres National League (NL) baseball team. The same day, Gwynn was chosen in the tenth round of the National Basketball Association (NBA) draft by the San Diego (now Los Angeles) Clippers basketball team, the first player to be selected by two professional sports teams from the same city.

Later the same afternoon, Tony received a call informing him that he had been drafted by the San Diego Sockers pro soccer team. Although Gwynn was prepared to believe almost anything, he soon realized that the call was a gag perpetrated by a former college baseball coach. That Tony, a multisport high school and college athlete, might have been drafted in a sport that he had not played extensively, however, is not farfetched.

Anthony Keith Gwynn was born on May 9, 1960, in Los Angeles, California, the second of three sons of Charles A. Gwynn and Vandella (Douglas) Gwynn, and grew up in nearby Long Beach with two very athletic brothers. Tony fondly recalls how he, Charles, Jr., and Chris would cut up socks, "put rubber bands around them and call them baseballs, even though they were the size of golf balls. The pitcher would only be 15 feet away," he chuckles. "I figure if you could hit one of those things, you could hit a baseball."

The sock drill paid dividends. Charles, an elementary school teacher, was drafted by the Cleveland Indians American League (AL) club out of high school in 1976. Charles played baseball for California State University, Los Angeles, but was not redrafted. Chris performed for San Diego State University and was selected number one by the Los Angeles Dodgers (NL) in 1985.

Tony starred in baseball and basketball at Long Beach Poly High School, where he batted .563 his senior year to lead the California Interscholastic Federation. Despite his baseball heroics, Gwynn was bypassed in the 1977 draft and attended San Diego State University on a basketball scholarship. Tony still holds the all-time San Diego State basketball assist record. After a coach requested him to turn out for baseball his sophomore year, he hit .301, .423, and .416 in three seasons for the Aztecs. Tony attracted the attention of the hometown Padres, who chose the 5-feet-11-inch, 210-pound outfielder early in the draft.

Gwynn, who bats and throws left-handed, led Class A Walla Walla, Washington, of the Northwest League with a .331 batting average in 42 games and finished the 1981 season with Class AA Amarillo, Texas, of the Texas League. Tony, desiring the success he had enjoyed at San Diego State, visited an Amarillo sporting goods store and bought two 32-inch, 31-ounce bats similar to one he had used in college. "I went 4 for 4, hit a home run, two doubles, and a single," he recalls. "The next day I went 3 for 4. The small bat stuck." Most major leaguers, however, prefer 33- or 34-inch bats.

In 1982, Gwynn hit .328 against Class AAA pitching in 93 games at Hawaii of the Pacific Coast League (PCL). San Diego promoted Tony on July 19, and he finished the 1982 season with a .289 batting average. After spending the first 17 games of the 1983 season at Class AAA Las Vegas, Nevada, of the PCL, he completed the campaign with the Padres and batted .309 in 86 games.

Gwynn led the NL in both batting average (.351) and hits (213) in 1984, his first full major league season. Tony again paced the NL in hits (218) and runs scored (107) in 1986. His .370 batting average led both major leagues in 1987, while his 218 hits topped the NL. A .313 batting average the next season enabled Gwynn to repeat as NL champion, while Tony paced the NL again in both batting average (.336) and hits (203) in 1989. The likable, easygoing Gwynn believes that unexpected conflicts with a few Padres teammates hampered his performance in 1990, but Tony still batted .309 and tallied 177 hits. He was headed toward a fifth batting championship in 1993 until an injury cut his season short. Gwynn finished second with a .358 batting average, 12 points behind the Colorado Rockies' Andres Galarraga. From July 1, 1993, to July 1, 1994, Tony batted .400. In 1994, he led the NL in batting with a .394 mark, the highest in that league since Bill Terry in 1930. Gwynn also ranked first in hits (165) and on-base percentage (.454) and fourth in doubles (35).

Since 1983, Gwynn's season average has never fallen below the .300 mark. Tony has compiled a .333 career batting average with 351 doubles, 79 triples, and 78 home runs through 1994. In 6,609 at bats, he remarkably has struck out only 329 times. Padres hitting coach Merv Rettenmund claims Gwynn doesn't strike out or walk often because Tony is not restricted by the strike zone. "I've seen him hit balls off the ground and balls eye-high. I've seen him hit balls way off the plate inside and outside," Rettenmund recalls. With above-average speed, Gwynn has stolen 268 bases.

Unfortunately, Gwynn has enjoyed little post-season play. In the 1984 NL Championship Series, Tony batted .368 and made key hits in the final two games to help the Padres defeat the Chicago Cubs, three games to two. He hit .263 against the Detroit Tigers, but the Padres lost the World Series, four games to one.

Gwynn received Gold Glove defensive honors 5 times between 1986 and 1991 and has made the NL All-Star team 11 times in the past 12 years. Tony played all 10 innings of the 1994 All-Star Game, making two hits and scoring two runs, including the winning run in the bottom of the tenth inning. He and longtime St. Louis Cardinals shortstop **Ozzie Smith** savored the NL's first victory after six defeats. "We've been talking about it all day, Ozzie and I," Tony said. "We've about the only ones who remember when we were winning."

Gwynn, admired for his work ethic, has combined video technology with hours of extra drill to transform his natural batting talent into consistent efficiency at the plate and his average fielding ability into Gold Glove quality. Tony shares the secrets to his success at the San Diego School of Baseball, which he partly owns, and in a book entitled *Tony Gwynn's Total Baseball Player.*

Gwynn, the veteran member of the 1994 Padres, is three years older than his general manager, Randy Smith. His 1994 teammates combined had made only 1,793 major league hits, 246 fewer than his franchise-record 2,039. Tony considered leaving the ill-run Padres, but his father's death in November 1993 encouraged him to recommit himself to the team. "Everything I've done in a baseball uniform has come in a Padres uniform," he reflects. "I'm proud of that." As one of the game's most complete players, Gwynn will help rebuild a young, improving team. Tony continues to play near his home in Poway, California, where he resides with his wife Alicea and their two children, Anthony II and Anisha.

BIBLIOGRAPHY: *The Baseball Encyclopedia,* 9th ed. (New York, 1993); Jerry Crasnick, "Gwynn Offers Talent, Perspective," *Baseball America* 14 (August 7, 1994), p. 8; Ron Fimrite, "Small Stick, Tall Stats," *Sports Illustrated* 64 (April 14, 1986), pp. 50–52; Bill Gutman, *Baseball's Hot New Stars* (New York, 1988); Tony Gwynn, *Tony Gwynn's Total Baseball Player* (New York, 1992); Danny Knobler, "Pssst . . . Heard About Tony Gwynn?" *Newsweek* 80 (August 1989), pp. 22–28; Tim Kurkjian, "Beginning Again," *Sports Illustrated* 74 (March 11, 1991), pp. 44–47; Ivan Maisel, "He's a Hefty Problem for Pitchers," *Sports Illustrated* 60 (May 14, 1984), pp. 70–71; Malcolm Moran, "Gwynn Finds Camera Doesn't Lie," *New York Times Biographical Service* 15 (May 1984), p. 660; *San Diego Padres Media Guide* (1991); Samantha Stevenson, "Tony Gwynn: A Portrait of the Scientist in the Batter's Box," *New York Times Biographical Service* 22 (June 1991), pp. 616–617; John Thorn and Pete Palmer, eds., *Total Baseball,* 3rd ed. (New York, 1993).

                                                              Gaymon L. Bennett

MARVIN HAGLER
(May 23, 1954–) ————————————————————————— *Boxing*

Marvin Hagler, one of the most dominant boxers of the early 1980s, ranks among the best world middleweight champions. The oldest of seven children of Robert Hagler and Ida Mae Hagler, Marvin was born on May 23, 1954, in Newark, New Jersey. After race riots inflamed Newark in 1967, his mother moved her family to Brockton, Massachusetts. Shortly after arriving in Brockton, Marvin entered a local gym operated by Pat and Goody Petronelli and aspired to become a boxer. "I had a dream I was going to become champion," he recalled. Although a natural left-hander, Hagler had mastered the ability to lead with either hand. Marvin's natural power often proved too much for his amateur opponents. He scored 57 wins, including capturing the 1973 Amateur Athletic Union (AAU) middleweight title. Hagler turned professional under the management of the Petronelli brothers and fought many of his early pro bouts in Philadelphia, Pennsylvania, a city known for producing rugged fighters.

With a shaved head and beautifully sculpted physique, Hagler often frightened his ring foes with his menacing appearance. Marvin's plentiful skills propelled him to victory in his first 26 professional fights. A draw with 1972 Olympic champion Sugar Ray Seales ended the impressive streak. He lost 2 bouts in 1976 to rival Philadelphia middleweights Bobby Watts and Willie Monroe but later avenged both defeats and the Seales draw with easy victories. Hagler did not lose another fight until 1987.

Marvin's first chance to win the coveted world middleweight title came on November 30, 1979, in Las Vegas, Nevada. Defending champion Vito Antuofermo battled him in a memorable 15-round draw, thus retaining his title. On September 27, 1980, Hagler traveled to London, England, to meet new champion Alan Minter, who had defeated Antuofermo earlier that year. Marvin furiously battered the British champion and won the world middleweight championship with a third-round technical knockout. Enraged British fans pelted the ring with missiles, forcing Hagler and his handlers to seek refuge in the dressing room. His title belts were presented there.

From 1981 through 1986, Hagler defended his undisputed middleweight championship 12 times and won most of the bouts in one-sided affairs. Marvin's unsuccessful challengers included Antuofermo, Tony Sibson, Fulgencio Obelmejias (twice), Mustafa Hamsho (twice), William "Caveman" Lee, **Thomas Hearns**, Wilford Scypion, John Mugabi, and Roberto Duran. Argentina's Juan Roldan alone scored a knockdown against Hagler, favorably compared with past middleweight champions Marcel Cerdan, Harry Greb, Stanley Ketchel, and Carlos Monzon.

In late 1986, the World Boxing Association (WBA) withdrew its recognition of Hagler as world middleweight champion largely for political reasons. The World Boxing Council (WBC), however, still recognized Marvin as champion. In a shocking upset in Las Vegas on April 6, 1985, former welterweight and junior middleweight champion **Sugar Ray Leonard** emerged from a three-year retirement and scored a 12-round split decision over Hagler to win the WBC middleweight title. Leonard cleverly fought a tactical bout featuring ring movement and counterpunching while avoiding dangerous exchanges with Marvin. The split decision prompted heated debate among fans, but every major boxing publication agreed with the decision rendered by the judges. The proud, often vain Hagler, who had his name legally changed to Marvelous Marvin Hagler in 1982, refused to accept the loss to Leonard. "I feel in my heart that I'm still the champion," he told the media after the fight. "I really hate the fact that they took it away from me and gave it to Sugar Ray Leonard, of all people. It really leaves a bad taste in my mouth." Hagler never boxed again, moving to Italy where he performed in several action movies. Leonard remarked, "Being the champion meant everything to Marvin. When he lost his title to me, he lost his identity. He didn't know how to handle [the defeat], so he retired."

Hagler's career record included 62 victories (52 by knockout), three losses, and two draws. Marvin married Joann Dixon in 1980 and has five children, Gentry, James, Celeste, Marvin, Jr., and Charelle. Marvin was voted *The Ring*'s Fighter of the Year in both 1983 and 1985. In 1993, the International Boxing Hall of Fame inducted him.

BIBLIOGRAPHY: Nigel Collins, "Sugar Ray . . . Still in Style," *The Ring* 66 (August 1987), pp. 28–32; Steve Farhood, "So Sweet! So Marvelous!" *KO Magazine* (September 1985), pp. 36–49; Clive Gammon, "Blood, Sweat and Beers," *Sports Illustrated* 53 (October 6, 1980), pp. 26–29; Pat Putnam, "Marvin's Mystery Guest," *Sports Illustrated* 54 (January 26, 1981), pp. 50–55; Pat Putnam, "One Goring, One Boring," *Sports Illustrated* 55 (October 12, 1981), pp. 29–31; Bert Randolph Sugar, *The 100 Greatest Boxers of All Time* (New York, 1984).

John Robertson

FRANCO HARRIS
(March 7, 1950–) ————————————————— *Football*

It was a "desperation pass," thrown in a truly desperate situation. When the play began on that December day in 1972, the clock at windswept Three Rivers Stadium showed 22 seconds remaining. The Pittsburgh Steelers National Football League (NFL) club, trailing the Oakland Raiders, 7–6, faced a fourth down and 10 yards to go, with 60 yards of frozen turf and a stubborn Raiders' defense between them and the Oakland goal line. Steelers' quarterback Terry Bradshaw scrambled away from the onrushing linemen and threw the ball a long distance toward running back Frenchy Fuqua. The football and the Raiders' strong safety, Jack Tatum, arrived at the same time. The ball bounced off one or both of them and caromed away.

Steelers' running back Franco Harris was moving downfield, looking for someone to block and hoping to help. Suddenly, there was the ball. On the dead run, Harris reached out and caught it inches from the ground, cut to the sideline, and raced into the end zone. For an instant, the capacity crowd sat in stunned silence. Then pandemonium broke loose. The Pittsburgh Steelers, who needed a miracle, had gotten one. The NFL's perennial losers had won their first playoff game ever. NFL coach George Allen lauded Franco, "He has been a great pass catcher, a great blocker, and a great runner; and he has the knack of making the big play."

The play, soon dubbed irreverantly "The Immaculate Reception," became a legend and signaled that a great player and great team were coming of age. Both already had played well before their miracle. During the 1972 regular season, Harris had helped the Steelers to their first divisional championship and had become only the fifth NFL rookie to rush for over 1,000 yards in a season. Although the Steelers fell to the undefeated Miami Dolphins, 21–17, in their next game, the future was clearly theirs.

All this had seemed unlikely just a short time before. Pittsburgh fans annually had sighed their sad "SOS" slogan for "Same Old Steelers" as the team stumbled through one dreary season after another. Blessed as usual with a high draft pick in 1972, the Steelers made Harris, a Penn State University star, the first running back selected. Many fans grumbled that this was just one more mistake, claiming that the Steelers should have taken Franco's more highly regarded teammate Lydell Mitchell. Harris, said the rumors, was temperamental and perhaps lacked enough competitive instincts for the NFL.

Harris, however, knew about hard work. One of nine children of Cad Harris, an African American who served for 20 years in the U.S. Army, and Gina (Parenti) Harris, a native of Italy, Franco was born on March 7, 1950, in Fort Dix, New Jersey, and had worked as a shoeshine boy and grocery bagger. But always there had been time for sports. He was selected a high school All-America in football and starred in baseball and basketball at Rancocas Valley Regional High School in Mt. Holly, New Jersey. Harris teamed with Mitchell at Penn State, gaining 2,002 yards in 380 carries and helping the Nittany Lions to victories over the University of Missouri in the 1970 Orange Bowl and the University of Texas in the 1972 Cotton Bowl.

At six foot two inches and 225 pounds, Harris possessed big-enough size to bowl over would-be tacklers. Franco's balance, quickness, and explosive acceleration made him hard to catch, as a Cleveland Brown discovered while chasing him on a 75-yard touchdown run during that 1972 rookie season. Still the doubters continued to whisper, especially when he failed to gain 1,000 yards in 1973. But in 1974 Harris began to silence all critics. Franco passed the 1,000-yard mark in rushing and led the Steelers into Super Bowl IX against the Minnesota Vikings and their "Purple People Eaters" defense. Bradshaw handed the ball 34 times to Harris, who gained a Super Bowl–record 158 yards to help the Steelers win, 16–6.

The good times promised by "The Immaculate Reception" had become glorious reality. The Steelers the next year won Super Bowl X, defeating the Dallas Cowboys, 21–17. After barely falling short in 1977 and 1978, the same cast, led by coach Chuck Noll, returned to win Super Bowl XIII over the Dallas Cowboys and Super Bowl XIV over the Los Angeles Rams. Harris, Bradshaw, wide receivers Lynn Swann and John Stallworth, and the "Steel Curtain" defense, including linemen **Joe Greene** and L. C. Greenwood, linebackers Jack Ham and Jack Lambert, and cornerback Mel Blount, all future Pro Football Hall of Famers, won four Super Bowls in six years for an unprecedented achievement.

The durable, determined Harris helped lead the way, missing only 9 games because of injury in his first 12 NFL seasons. During his NFL career, Franco gained the most rushing yardage in 13 of his 19 post-season games. Altogether, he gained 12,120 yards (fourth all-time) on 2,949 carries (second all-time), scored 100 touchdowns, and caught 307 passes for 2,287 yards, being selected for the Pro Bowl every year between 1972 and 1980. George Allen attributed the running back's success to being "a strong, determined, hard working player" parlaying "consistency."

After spending the 1984 season with the Seattle Seahawks (NFL), Harris retired and returned to Pittsburgh as a respected and prominent community citizen. In 1977, Pittsburgh's Dapper Dan Club had named Franco the city's Sportsman of the Year. He had been active in charity work for organizations battling multiple sclerosis, cystic fibrosis, and other diseases. He and his wife, Dana (Dokmanovich) Harris, and their son, Dok, settled happily into Pittsburgh's North Side. The Pro Football Hall of Fame inducted Harris in 1990.

Harris pursued business with the same spirit and determination that he used to play football, although the training proved more mental than physical. "I can't learn enough now," Franco states. "I wish I had known reading and gathering information was so much fun." His enterprises include the Super Bakery, which starts, in *Sports Illustrated*'s words, "not with profits but with customers' needs." He tried out one new product, a low-fat Super Donut, on Dok. It met not only Dok's taste requirements but also the U.S. Department of Agriculture's standards for child-nutrition programs. Harris also partly owns trading-card and comic book companies and a professional cycling team. "They say if you love what you do, you never have to work a day in your life," Franco states. "Today my passion is business." He continues to head downfield, looking for ways to help.

BIBLIOGRAPHY: Roy Blount, Jr., *About Three Bricks Shy of a Load: A Highly Irregular Lowdown on the Year the Pittsburgh Steelers Were Super But Missed the Bowl* (Boston, MA, 1974); Roy Blount, Jr., "The Ascent of an Enigma," *Sports Illustrated* 57 (August 23, 1982), pp. 72–86; Rick Lipsey, "Franco's Serious Sinker," *Sports Illustrated* 79 (November 29, 1993); Pat Livingston, *The Pittsburgh Steelers: A Pictorial History* (Virginia Beach, VA, 1980); David L. Porter, ed., *Biographical Dictionary of American Sports: Football* (Westport, CT, 1987); *Pittsburgh Steelers Media Guides* (1981–1984).

Luther W. Spoehr

BOB HAYES

(December 20, 1942–   ) —————————— *Track and Field and Football*

Bob Hayes, then "the world's fastest human," won the 100-meter dash in the 1964 Summer Olympic Games at Tokyo, Japan, and achieved legendary success as a pass receiver with the Dallas Cowboys National Football League (NFL) club. Robert Lee Hayes was born on December 20, 1942, in the Jacksonville, Florida, ghetto known as "Hell's Hole." Bob was the youngest of three children of John Hayes, the owner of a shoeshine parlor, and Mary Hayes, a maid. After his parents separated, he and his siblings lived with their mother and visited their father regularly. Although the Hayes family was poor, Mary received financial assistance from her brother. There was always enough money to keep Bob and his siblings fed and clothed. Once old enough to work, Hayes made "twenty to thirty dollars a day" shining shoes for his father. Bob worked at the shoeshine parlor until 1960.

Hayes became one of Jacksonville's most outstanding high school athletes, demonstrating astonishing running speed as a youngster and easily outrunning boys his age and older. Bob impressed the football coaches at Matthew W. Gilbert Junior-Senior High School with his speed and open field running agility in physical education classes but did not play on the football team until his junior year in 1958. He carried the ball only nine times that year for a team brimming with talent. Hayes dominated track and field, winning the 100- and 220-yard dashes, high jump, and long jump and anchoring the triumphant 4 × 110-yard and 4 × 220-yard relay teams in the 1959 Duval County track and field championships for African-American high schools. His winning time of 9.6 seconds in the 100-yard dash eclipsed the State record, but the Florida High School Activities Association, an all-white organization, did not recognize it. In football that fall, Bob scored 57 points, rushed for 525 yards, caught four passes for 68 yards, and returned nine kickoffs for 270 yards and nine punts for 115 yards. He also led the basketball team in rebounding and baseball team in stolen bases and clocked 9.7 seconds for the 100-yard dash.

Hayes graduated from Matthew Gilbert High School in 1960 and entered Florida A&M University, an African-American institution in Tallahassee. Although a football scholarship financed his college education, Bob gained national notoriety as a sprinter on the track and field team. In 1961, he equaled the world record of 9.3 seconds for the 100-yard dash at the National Association of Intercollegiate Athletics (NAIA) championships. Hayes shared the world record less than three weeks, because Frank Budd of Villanova University clocked 9.2 seconds at the Amateur Athletic Union (AAU) championships. Bob also established a national freshman record of 20.1 seconds for 220 yards on a straight course in 1961. He ran the 100-yard dash in 9.2 seconds in 1962, but his share of the world record was denied because the starter's pistol was not the regulation .32 caliber. The same year, Hayes also won the first of three consecutive AAU titles in the 100-yard/meter dash. At the 1963 AAU championship, Bob became sole owner of the world record in the 100-yard dash with a 9.1-seconds performance in the semi-finals. Bert Nelson of *Track and Field News* described Hayes as "the most untouchable sprinter at 100 meters or less." Bob captured the Gold Medal in the 100 meters in the 1964 Olympic Games at Tokyo, Japan, equaling the world record of 10.0 seconds. In the 400-meter relay, he electrified the crowd with an 8.8-second anchor leg to secure the Gold Medal for the United States and establish a world record of 39.0 seconds.

After the 1964 Olympics, Hayes completed his final year of college football at Florida A&M. Bob concluded his college career with a spectacular performance in the Orange Blossom Classic at Miami's Orange Bowl, converting a 50-yard reception into a touchdown and twice dashing to two-point conversions in Florida A&M's 42–15 win over Grambling College. After the North-

South All-Star Game, the Dallas Cowboys (NFL) signed the Olympic sprint champion to a two-year contract. Although historically track men had failed to succeed in professional football, Tex Schramm, the general manager of the Cowboys, insisted that Hayes possessed the "natural moves and instincts of a football player." Game-breaking touchdown receptions, including a 45-yarder against the New York Giants in 1965, characterized the style of play Bob brought to the NFL. His speed revolutionized the game, as coaches abandoned the traditional man-to-man defense and developed the more effective zone defense. In his 1965 rookie year, Hayes caught 46 passes for 1,003 yards and scored 12 touchdowns. The Cowboys registered their then-best season record of seven wins and seven losses. Bob later established club records of 64 receptions for 1,232 yards in 1966 and 20.8 yards per punt return in 1968. During Hayes's career with Dallas through 1974, the Cowboys won five NFL titles and the 1972 Super Bowl against the Miami Dolphins. Bob appeared in four Pro Bowls from 1965 to 1968, competed in the Professional International Track Association in 1973, and spent his final NFL season with the San Francisco 49ers in 1975.

After retiring from professional football in 1975, Hayes held several jobs. Police arrested Bob in a sting operation in 1979. He pleaded guilty to charges of delivering cocaine and methaqualone to undercover narcotics agents. On the witness stand, Hayes admitted his guilt. "People see me as Bob Hayes, dope dealer," Bob lamented, "not Bob Hayes, the citizen. It hurts." Although sentenced to five years in prison, he was paroled after 10 months. Hayes revealed in his 1990 autobiography, *Run, Bullet, Run,* that his abuse of drugs and alcohol began early in his career with the Cowboys. Bob, who was inducted into the National Track and Field Hall of Fame in 1976, resides in Dallas with his wife Altamease and daughter Adrienne.

BIBLIOGRAPHY: *Current Biography Yearbook* (1966), pp. 161–163; Mal Florence, "And Then There Was Bob Hayes," *Los Angeles Times,* July 25, 1984, sec. 8, pp. 16, 23; Bob Hayes with Robert Pack, *Run, Bullet, Run: The Rise, Fall, and Recovery of Bob Hayes* (New York, 1990); David Lipman and Ed Winks, *The Speed King: Bob Hayes of the Dallas Cowboys* (New York, 1971); Bill Mallon and Ian Buchanan, *Quest for Gold: The Encyclopedia of American Olympians* (New York, 1984); David L. Porter, ed., *Biographical Dictionary of American Sports: Outdoor Sports* (Westport, CT, 1989); Roberto L. Quercetani, *A World History of Track and Field Athletics* (London, England, 1964); David Wallechinsky, *The Complete Book of the Olympic Games,* rev. ed. (New York, 1988).

Adam R. Hornbuckle

ELVIN HAYES
(November 7, 1945–) ———————————————————— *Basketball*

Elvin Hayes ranks among the most prolific scorers in professional basketball history. Elvin Ernest Hayes was born on November 7, 1945, in Rayville, Louisiana, and graduated from Eula Britton High School, where he enjoyed a sensational basketball career and averaged 35 points a game. His leadership abilities and extraordinary scoring skills enabled the Eula Britton High School basketball team to achieve an amazing 54 consecutive victories. Elvin made All-Conference for two years and All-America one year, being named MVP in his high school conference. His nickname, "The Big E," stemmed from his dominating six-foot-nine-inch, 235-pound frame. "The Big E," an aggressive, take-charge player, starred as an offensive rebounder.

After graduation from high school, Hayes considered numerous college basketball scholarship offers and eventually picked the University of Houston. Elvin broke racial barriers at that institution, joining teammate Don Chaney as the first African-American Cougar athletes. At Houston, he scored 527 points and averaged 25.1 points a game his freshman year in 1964–1965. A year later, Hayes tallied 789 points and averaged 27.2 points a game. His junior year saw these figures improve to 881 points and 28.4 points per game. Elvin climaxed his career by playing 1,270 minutes as a senior, grabbing 624 rebounds, tallying 1,214 points, and scoring 36.8 points per game. After averaging 35 points a game as a high school senior, he topped that figure as a senior with the Cougars! Hayes made *The Sporting News* All-America First Team in 1967 and 1968 after being selected on their Second Team in 1966 and was chosen *The Sporting News* College Player of the Year in 1968.

Unquestionably, the high point in Elvin's collegiate career came with a Cougar victory over the UCLA Bruins on January 20, 1968. The Lew Alcindor– (later **Kareem Abdul-Jabbar**) led team came to the Houston Astrodome with 47 consecutive victories. The titanic struggle between the Cougars and the Bruins set a (since surpassed) attendance record of 52,693. The *New York Times* captured the contest within the game, featuring Alcindor against Hayes. "Hayes, Houston's All-American, tossed in 39 points and help put the defensive clamp on Lew Alcindor." Houston coach Guy Lewis buoyantly stated, "Isn't that Hayes great? Almost every game he plays is great." In the nationally televised game, Elvin played magnificently. He finished with 17 field goals in 25 attempts, grabbed 15 rebounds, and blocked four shots, although playing the last 12 minutes with four fouls. In both 1967 and 1968, however, the Bruins eliminated the Cougars from the NCAA championships. In the 1968 NCAA tournament, Hayes made 70 field goals in five tournament games. Bill Bradley held the previous mark of 65 with the Princeton University Tigers in 1965.

The San Diego Rockets National Basketball Association (NBA) club drafted Hayes for the 1968–1969 season, in which he scored 28 points, averaged 28.4 points a game, and made the All-NBA Rookie team. The Rockets relocated to Houston in 1971 and traded Elvin to the Baltimore Bullets the following year. The Bullets moved to Washington, D.C., in 1973 and retained Hayes with the organization. Elvin rounded out his NBA career from 1981 to 1984 with the Houston Rockets. He held the single-season record for most minutes played by a rookie with 3,695 in 1968–1969. His many honors included being named to the All-NBA First Team in 1975, 1977, and 1979 and being featured on the All-NBA Second Team in 1973, 1974, and 1976. Hayes led the NBA with

16.9 rebounds per game in 1969–1970 and 18.1 rebounds in 1973–1974. From the 1973–1974 through 1982–1983 seasons, Elvin tallied over 1,000 points every year. In his superb basketball career, he played 50,000 minutes with 16,279 rebounds, 2,398 assists, 27,313 points, and a 21.0 point per game average. His 1,598 points and 19.7-point average led the Washington Bullets to the 1978 NBA title over the Seattle SuperSonics.

Basketball salaries in the mid-1990s seem astronomical, but Hayes's salary package remained relatively modest: "Five years beginning 1972–73 for a total of $1,010,000, payable at 100,000 a year and deferred compensation of 100,000 a year from October, 1977 through October, 1981. There was a 10,000 bonus at signing." Elvin exclaimed, "No athlete is worth the money he is getting, including me." In 1968, he did not try out for the U.S. Olympic basketball team. Hayes joined several African-American basketball players, including **Bob Lanier,** Wes Unseld, Mike Warren, Lucius Allen, and Lew Alcindor, in favor of an Olympic boycott.

Elvin resided in his college and professional NBA home of Houston and participated in numerous business ventures. A May 1979 *Sports Illustrated* cover captured Hayes at the height of his NBA prowess. In his Bullets uniform, Elvin crashed the boards more like a bruising boxer than a tall basketball player. The tireless athlete found basketball an avocation and told **Arthur Ashe, Jr.** of playing three or four games daily as a teenager. He needed no modern facility, content to use "a raggedy old wooden blackboard nailed to an old light pole." Hayes was inducted into the Naismith Memorial Basketball Hall of Fame in 1989. *The Modern Encyclopedia of Basketball* contains a superb photograph of Hayes and Alcindor stretching for a high ball in their celebrated 1968 encounter at the Astrodome. The referee is caught on camera at far right, with his mouth open and head craning upwards looking at the battling airborne giants.

BIBLIOGRAPHY: Arthur Ashe, Jr., *A Hard Road to Glory: A History of the African-American Athlete Since 1946*, vol. 3 (New York, 1988); Zander Hollander, ed., *The Modern Encyclopedia of Basketball* (New York, 1973); "Houston Breaks 47-Game Streak of UCLA, 71–69," *New York Times*, January 21, 1968; David L. Porter, ed., *Biographical Dictionary of American Sports: Basketball and Other Indoor Sports* (Westport, CT, 1989); Matthew Siegel, biographical material and press guides, Naismith Memorial Basketball Hall of Fame, Springfield, MA, January 1994; Gordon S. White, "UCLA Wins by 78–55," *New York Times*, March 24, 1968.

Scott A.G.M. Crawford

THOMAS HEARNS
(October 18, 1958–) _____ *Boxing*

Thomas Hearns, an outstanding fighter of the 1980s, won world titles in five different weight classifications. Hearns was born on October 18, 1958, in Memphis, Tennessee. His mother, Lois Hearns, a single parent, moved her family to Detroit, Michigan, when Thomas was very young. Thomas pursued boxing after watching a documentary about legendary heavyweight champion **Muhammad Ali.** His first boxing lessons came at age 10 at a gym sponsored by a Detroit Baptist Church. After the gym closed, he began training at the Kronk Gym under Emanuel Steward. "All I ever thought about," Hearns recalled, "was being a boxer [and] winning a title. I never stopped dreaming." Thomas used his long 78-inch reach and extreme 73-inch height to dominate his 147-pound welterweight competition, winning 147 of 155 amateur bouts. Just 11 of his victories were knockouts, as he relied on boxing skill rather than punching power.

Hearns captured the National Amateur Athletic Union (AAU) and Golden Gloves titles in 1977 and turned professional later that same year, defeating Jerome Hill in his debut at Detroit on November 25, 1977. His style changed radically from his amateur days, as he utilized his physical attributes to generate knockout power. Knockout victories over worthy contenders Clyde Gray, Harold Weston, and Bruce Curry in 1979 propelled Hearns into world title contention and earned him the nickname "Hit Man" from his rabid Detroit fans. "I don't really like it," said Hearns of the "Hit Man" label. "I'm used to it now, but I prefer 'Motor City Cobra.'" After boasting a perfect 28–0 record with 26 knockouts, Thomas fought World Boxing Association (WBA) welterweight champion Pipino Cuevas on August 2, 1980, in Detroit. Most experts anticipated the bout would be evenly contested. Hearns, however, experienced little trouble flooring the rugged Mexican with a second-round knockout to claim the title.

Hearns made three successful defenses of his title before meeting **Sugar Ray Leonard,** the World Boxing Council (WBC) welterweight titlist, in a much-publicized championship unification bout. His management resented the media attention that the charismatic Leonard generated and saw the fight as a chance for Thomas to emerge as the world's premier welterweight. "I have nothing against Ray Leonard," he noted in a prefight interview. "I still think he's a nice fellow. He just happens to have something I want. If I beat him, I will get the recognition. I need the recognition. I've always wanted to be the best." The first Leonard-Hearns fight took place at Las Vegas, Nevada, on September 16, 1981, and fulfilled expectations. After Leonard clearly hurt Hearns with a tremendous body blow in round 6, Thomas reverted to his safety-first amateur style and led on points after 12 rounds. Leonard, however, scored a knockdown in round 13 and was battering Hearns in round 14 when referee Davey Pearl awarded Leonard the victory by TKO.

The loss to Leonard hurt Thomas's confidence, as he rarely engaged in bold exchanges again. Nevertheless, he defeated Wilfred Benitez in New Orleans, Louisiana, in 1982 to win the WBC superwelterweight (154-pound) title and crushed his WBA counterpart, Roberto Duran, with a second-round knockout in a 1984 unification bout. In another highly publicized bout, Hearns fought undisputed world middleweight champion **Marvin Hagler** for the latter's title in 1985. *KO Magazine* described the contest as "eight minutes of war." Marvin stopped Thomas in the third round of the thrilling fight, which ranked among the best of the decade. Despite the bitter defeat, Hearns triumphed over England's Dennis Andries and Argentina's Juan Roldan in 1987 to capture the WBC light heavyweight and middleweight crowns. Iran Barkley then stunned boxing observers by knocking out Hearns in 1988 to take the middleweight title. Thomas, however, earned a niche in boxing history later that year by winning his fifth title, the World Boxing Organization (WBO) supermiddle-weight championship, with a hotly disputed decision win over James Kinchen.

Nearly eight years after their first bout, Leonard and Hearns met in a re-match in June 1989. The fight ended in a draw, even though Thomas scored the fight's only two knockdowns. His skills began to decline by 1990, although he successfully defended his title in a lackluster bout with Michael Olajide. Hearns's highly successful relationship with manager-trainer Emanuel Stew-ard also ended amid charges of mismanagement. In his last significant victory, Thomas captured the WBA light heavyweight title with a decision over Virgil Hill in June 1991. He later lost the title to Barkley, the only boxer ever to defeat Hearns twice. Through May 1995, Hearns has a 54–4 record and 43 knockouts.

Hearns earned *The Ring*'s Fighter of the Year award in 1980 and 1984 and, along with Leonard and Hagler, helped popularize the lighter weight classi-fications. Multimillion-dollar purses, once only received by heavyweight box-ers, became commonplace for welterweights and middleweights during Thomas's most dominant years. The never-married Hearns still boxes in the 1990s, although not creating the excitement he once did.

BIBLIOGRAPHY: Steve Farhood, "So Sweet! So Marvelous!" *KO Magazine* (Septem-ber 1985), pp. 36–49; Herbert G. Goldman, ed., *The Ring 1986–87 Record Book* (New York, 1987); Randy Gordon, "Pulling No Punches: An Interview with Thomas Hearns," *The Ring* 59 (October 1980), pp. 37–39; Peter King, ed., "Closeup on Thomas Hearns," *KO Magazine* (December 1983), p. 35; Pat Putnam, "A Detroit Tiger for Sure," *Sports Illustrated* 53 (August 11, 1980), pp. 46–48; Pat Putnam, "Clearing the Way for the Big Payday," *Sports Illustrated* 55 (July 6, 1981), pp. 20–23; Pat Putnam, "Sugar Should Frost Him," *Sports Illustrated* 55 (September 14, 1981), pp. 32–49; Pat Putnam, "On Top of the World," *Sports Illustrated* 55 (September 28, 1981), pp. 18–33.

John Robertson

RICKEY HENDERSON
(December 25, 1958–) ——————————————————— *Baseball*

A baseball leadoff hitter not only bats first but sparks the offense and makes his teammates improve. During the 1980s, no leadoff batter performed better than Rickey Henderson. Many authorities agree with former New York Yan-kee general manager Clyde King who insists, "He's the greatest leadoff hitter in the game, and of all time. I don't know of one in the past who could do all the things he does as well as he does." A few leadoff batters have hit for higher batting average or supplied greater power. Bobby Bonds, for example, combined speed and home run punch. None of the best-known leadoff hitters, however, walked more frequently, achieved a higher on-base percentage, stole more bases, or scored more runs per season.

Rickey Henley Henderson was born on December 25, 1958, in Chicago, Illinois, the fourth of seven children of nurse Bobby Henderson. His father, John, left home when Rickey was only two months old, and Bobby moved the family to Oakland, California. Henderson began playing baseball at Bushrod Park, where **Frank Robinson** and Billy Martin once performed, and competed on youth teams with future major leaguers Dave Stewart and Lloyd Moseby.

Rickey also participated in basketball and football, making All-America at running back for Oakland Tech High School. Many schools, including the Universities of Arizona and Southern California, recruited him. At his mother's urging, however, he signed with the hometown baseball Athletics. The Oakland American League (AL) club selected Henderson in the fourth round of the 1976 draft. The muscular 5-foot-10-inch 190-pounder possesses the build of a football player and claims that the start he gets when stealing bases is a running back's crossover step. It's "my cut and acceleration in football," Rickey acknowledges. "My jump's a football jump."

For the Athletics' rookie league farm team in Boise, Idaho, the right-hand-hitting southpaw batted .319 and stole 29 bases. With Modesto, California, in the Class A California League in 1977, Henderson batted .345, drew 104 walks, and stole a league-record 95 bases. Manager Tom Trebelhorn showed the Modesto team films of great base stealers. "The man who had the impact on me," affirms Rickey, "was Ty Cobb. He went into those bases hard every time." Upon breaking Cobb's AL record in 1990, he presented that base to Trebelhorn.

At Class AA Jersey City, New Jersey, in 1978, Henderson batted .310 and led the Eastern League with 81 stolen bases. Rickey continued to impress the Athletics at Class AAA Ogden, Utah, of the Pacific Coast League in 1979, batting .309 and stealing 44 bases before being promoted to the parent club on June 23. At Ogden, he perfected his trademark headfirst slide.

In his first full major league season in 1980, Henderson surpassed Cobb's 65-year-old AL single-season stolen base record of 96 with a league-best 100 thefts. In the strike-shortened 1981 season, Rickey garnered his first Gold Glove Award for defensive excellence and finished second in the AL Most Valuable Player (MVP) voting. He shattered **Lou Brock**'s major league single-season record of 118 on August 27, 1982, completing the season with a record 130 steals.

After the 1984 season, the Athletics traded their flashy, outspoken left fielder to the New York Yankees (AL) in a two-for-five swap. Henderson batted .314, belted 24 home runs, and stole an AL-best 80 bases, becoming the first AL player to hit at least 20 homers and steal at least 50 bases in the same season. Rickey also led the AL in runs scored with 146, the highest tally in either league since Ted Williams recorded 150 in 1949.

Henderson again paced the AL in 1986 with 87 stolen bases and 130 runs, the best single-season combination of power and speed in major league baseball history. In 1988, Rickey led the AL in stolen bases, breaking the Yankee team career record of 248. The Yankees, unwilling to renegotiate his contract and afraid of losing him to free agency, returned him to Oakland on June 20, 1989.

Henderson sparked the Athletics to the AL 1989 West Division championship. Rickey reached base at least once in 80 of his 85 games with Oakland in 1989, stealing 52 bases and leading the majors with 77 steals. Henderson also topped the AL in walks (126) and runs scored (113). In the AL 1989 Championship Series, Rickey garnered MVP honors by leading both teams in almost every offensive category. The Athletics defeated the Toronto Blue Jays, 4 games to 1. In the 1989 World Series, Oakland swept the San Francisco Giants. His 11 steals in both series established a post-season record.

In 1990, Henderson batted .325; led the AL in steals (65), runs scored (119), and on-base percentage (.439); and won the AL MVP award. Oakland again won the AL pennant, eliminating the Boston Red Sox in four straight games. However, the Cincinnati Reds swept the Athletics in the World Series. On May 29, 1990, Rickey topped Cobb's AL career-record 891 stolen bases. He spent that summer chasing Brock's all-time record of 938 steals but did not break it until May 1, 1991. His 58 stolen bases that year paced the AL for the eleventh time in 13 season. He led the major leagues five of those years in base thefts and has 1,117 career stolen bases through the strike-shortened 1994 season.

The Athletics won the AL West again in 1992 but lost the AL Championship Series rematch with the Toronto Blue Jays, four games to two. The Blue Jays acquired Henderson for the 1993 AL pennant race. Rickey batted .289 with an outstanding .432 on-base percentage and 53 stolen bases but performed ineffectively in the post-season. The Blue Jays, nevertheless, repeated as AL and World Series champions. Rickey returned to the Oakland Athletics for the 1994 season.

Henderson's base stealing has overshadowed his other baseball accomplishments, but he can do everything. Rickey's keen batting eye, unorthodox stance, and ability to hit for both average and power make him difficult to face. "He's the type of guy who keeps pitchers awake all night the night before they're going to pitch," says former Texas Rangers manager Bobby Valentine. "They have to make sure they don't walk him because he turns a walk into a double or a triple. Then, when they throw strikes, . . . he can hit the ball out of the ballpark."

Henderson reaches base 40 percent of the time, consistently ranking among AL leaders in bases on balls. Rickey averages more than 90 walks a season and has led the AL in walks three times. He makes nearly 140 hits a season, recording 150 or more safeties six times and leading the league with 135 in

1981. Henderson holds the record for game-opening homers with 66 through 1994. Besides averaging 103 runs scored per season, Rickey has led the AL in that category five times. Through 1994, he has batted .289 with 1,652 runs scored, 2,216 hits, 364 doubles, 226 home runs, 814 RBIs, and 1,478 walks.

Lou Piniella, his former New York manager, calls Henderson "the consummate player." Rickey has performed in 10 All-Star Games and fields superbly. Athletics pitching coach Dave Duncan claims, "He's easily the best defensive left fielder in the game."

Some criticize Henderson's snapping of his glove at fly balls and performing his rituals either at the plate or on the base paths as hotdogging. Others claim Rickey's base stealing does not contribute significantly to his team's wins. Baseball authorities, however, deny the criticisms. Toronto Blue Jays manager Cito Gaston praised Henderson's 1989 AL Championship Series performance; "That isn't hotdogging, it's winning." Rickey ranks fourth behind only Babe Ruth, Ted Williams, and Nap Lajoie in total player rating, which measures players' contributions to their teams' wins.

Others have accused Henderson of malingering. As a base stealer, however, "what he does," affirms former Chicago Cubs outfielder Willie Wilson, "is the equivalent of jumping out of a car that's going 20 miles an hour. And he's done it every day for a dozen years." New York Yankee star Don Mattingly adds, "He needs days off. . . . The pounding he takes astounds me." Rickey's minor league manager Trebelhorn declares, "He is a great competitor. Not once, whether he was playing for or against me, have I seen him give anything but his best effort."

Off the field, Henderson works to stay in shape. "I . . . do extra stretching, sit-ups, push-ups," he says, "and some Nautilus weights for my shoulders just to maintain the strength I've got to have." Rickey eats carefully and sleeps regularly, does not smoke, and seldom drinks alcoholic beverages. He loves children, generously gives autographs and souvenirs, and relaxes to the music of Luther Vandross. Henderson, his wife Pam, and their two daughters reside in Hillsborough, near San Francisco.

BIBLIOGRAPHY: *Current Biography Yearbook* (1990), pp. 293–297; Peter Gammons, "Light Years Ahead of the Field," *Sports Illustrated* 65 (July 28, 1986), pp. 34–40, 50; Peter Gammons, "Man of Steal," *Sports Illustrated* 73 (October 1, 1990), pp. 60–68; Rickey Henderson, *Off Base: Confessions of a Thief* (New York, 1992); Danny Knobler, "Baseball's Best Leadoff Hitters," *Sport* 81 (July 1990), pp. 40–45; Ron Kroichick, "Rickey Henderson: Man of Steal," *Sport* 82 (March 1991), pp. 52–56; John Thorn and Pete Palmer, eds., *Total Baseball*, 3rd ed. (New York, 1993); Denise Tom, "Henderson Not Afraid of Big Apple," *USA Today*, December 18, 1984, pp. C1–C2; Craig Wolff, "Yankee Maverick Sets the Pace," *New York Times Biographical Service* 17 (August 1986), pp. 990–992.

Gaymon L. Bennett

LARRY HOLMES
(November 3, 1949–   ) ——————————————————————— *Boxing*

Larry Holmes ranked among the most dominant boxing champions of the late 1970s and early 1980s. Holmes was born on November 3, 1949, in Cuthbert, Georgia, the seventh of 12 children of John Holmes and Flossie Holmes. His father worked as a sharecropper and construction worker to support his family. By the mid-1950s, the Holmes family had relocated to Easton, Pennsylvania. Larry attended school there until seventh grade and then worked in a car wash to help support his brothers and sisters.

Holmes became known as a street fighter in Easton but was persuaded to channel his aggression toward amateur boxing at St. Anthony's Youth Center. The boxing club became Larry's second home, where his presence kept him out of trouble. As a heavyweight, he won 19 of 22 amateur bouts and several titles. By 1973, Holmes began a professional fighting career. After working as a sparring partner for legendary champion **Muhammad Ali,** Larry burst upon the boxing world by winning the World Boxing Council (WBC) version of the heavyweight championship with a thrilling 15-round decision over Ken Norton in Las Vegas, Nevada, on June 9, 1978. The triumph marked the undefeated Holmes's twenty-eighth consecutive victory. When World Boxing Association (WBA) champion Ali retired in 1979, Larry assumed his place as the sport's most dominant heavyweight.

From 1978 to 1983, Holmes, the self-proclaimed "People's Champion," successfully defended his WBC title 17 times. Many of Larry's title fights were telecast live nationally at a time when boxing was enjoying a resurgence in popularity. Armed with a punishing left jab and a solid defense, he usually dominated matches. Opponents normally struggled to win a round. Holmes did not possess one-punch knockout power but often wore down his adversaries with constant, unrelenting punishment. "I think he's the most underrated heavyweight champion we've ever had," renowned trainer Ray Arcel declared in 1982. "The trouble with Holmes is that he has tried to match the ring personality of Ali. You can't command the acknowledgment of greatness."

Larry's more competitive bouts included his 1979 victory over hard-hitting Earnie Shavers in Las Vegas, a 1981 struggle against Renaldo Snipes in Pittsburgh, Pennsylvania, and an exciting win over Gerry Cooney in Las Vegas in 1982. The 1982 bout unfortunately was promoted with racial overtones. Holmes's victories over Shavers and Snipes saw him dramatically recover from knockdowns to knock out his opponents. Richie Giachetti, his trainer and manager, praised his resilient fighter: "Larry has never been indestructible. But he is as close as any human will ever get, because when he is hurt, he comes back. That's why he is the champion and everybody else is a challenger." Ray Arcel echoed Giachetti's sentiments: "The guy's got perfect coordination. He has sharp reflexes and tremendous mental energy. He knows what he's doing in there at all times." Holmes also easily dispatched of Muhammad Ali in 11 rounds in 1980 at Las Vegas, where the former champion had attempted an ill-advised comeback. Larry was emotionally drained by the fight and wept in the ring after defeating his former idol.

Lingering promotional disputes with Don King caused Holmes to renounce his claim to the WBC title late in 1983. The general public and the fledgling International Boxing Federation (IBF), however, recognized Larry as their champion. Holmes defended the IBF crown three times before losing it in an upset to reigning world light heavyweight champion Michael Spinks in Las Vegas on September 22, 1985. If Larry had won that fight, he would have equaled Rocky Marciano's 49–0 mark as heavyweight champion. At the post-fight press conference, Holmes uttered some disparaging remarks about Marciano in the presence of the late champion's family. This incident greatly hurt Larry's public image. Spinks also defeated him in a rematch seven months later in a hotly disputed decision.

Although announcing his retirement after the second loss to Spinks, Holmes returned to the ring to face powerful youthful champion **Mike Tyson** in 1988. Larry showed his age and suffered three knockdowns before being stopped in the third round of a fight many of his fans wished he had not accepted. Holmes surprised many people by returning to the ring again in the 1990s. Despite heavy criticism by boxing writers who hoped he would remain retired, Larry surprisingly defeated leading contender Ray Mercer to earn a title fight with champion Evander Holyfield. Holmes lost the Holyfield bout on a decision but accorded himself well considering he was 42 years old.

Larry, as of May 1995, continues to box and sports a professional record of 60–4. He married Diane Robinson in 1979 and has three daughters. Holmes has earned in excess of $100 million in his career. Although widely acclaimed as boxing's best heavyweight from 1978 to 1985, Larry seemed to resent not being publicly adored on the same scale as Ali. He, unlike Ali, never defended his championship abroad, which may have reduced his international appeal. The more than financially secure Holmes wisely invested his money in real estate in the Easton area. Larry owns a restaurant, a hotel, and an impressive office complex.

BIBLIOGRAPHY: Herbert G. Goldman, ed., *The Ring 1986–87 Record Book* (New York, 1987); William Nack, "Champ Who Would Be Champ," *Sports Illustrated* 53 (September 22, 1980), pp. 74–78; William Nack, "A Classic Confrontation," *Sports Illustrated* 56 (June 7, 1982), pp. 42–50; Pat Putnam, "Holmes, Sweet Holmes," *Sports Illustrated* 51 (October 8, 1979), pp. 24–27; Pat Putnam, "Doom in the Desert," *Sports Illustrated* 53 (October 13, 1980), pp. 34–40; Pat Putnam, "Night They Called It a Daze," *Sports Illustrated* 55 (November 16, 1981), pp. 32–36.

John Robertson

BO JACKSON
(November 30, 1962–) ————————————— *Football and Baseball*

Bo Jackson starred in both professional football and major league baseball. Vincent Edward "Bo" Jackson, was born in Bessemer, Alabama, on November 30, 1962. Although other athletes have attempted playing professional football and baseball concurrently, few have reached Jackson's heights of stardom. Bo's meteoric athletic career began at McAdory High School in McCalla, Alabama, a suburb of Birmingham, where he was named an All-State football running back in 1981 after gaining 1,173 yards and scoring 17 touchdowns his senior year. Jackson, who hit .450 and .447 as a baseball center fielder his last two seasons, set a national high school record with 20 home runs one season and boasted a career 90 stolen bases. Bo won the State high school decathlon championship twice, setting State track and field records in six events.

Jackson, who has five brothers and four sisters, is the son of A. D. Adams, a steelworker, and Florence Bond, a domestic. Bo was offered a multiyear baseball contract in 1982 by the New York Yankees (AL) but attended Auburn University instead. The six-foot-one-inch, 222-pound Jackson, who majored in family and child development, immediately starred on the gridiron. Bo led the Tigers in 1982 to a 9–3 finish and 33–26 triumph over Boston College in the Tangerine Bowl. The following season, his 1,213 yards (7.7-yard average) rushing and 12 touchdowns helped 11–1 Auburn to the Southeastern Conference (SEC) Championship. Bo sparked the Tigers to a 9–7 Sugar Bowl victory over the University of Michigan, being named the game's Most Valuable Player (MVP) and garnering consensus All-America honors.

Jackson missed six games with a shoulder separation during the 1984 season but led Auburn to a 21–15 Liberty Bowl conquest of the University of Arkansas. Bo ran for 88 yards and scored 2 touchdowns as the game's MVP. Auburn football coach Pat Dye used a triple-option wishbone offense that failed to take full advantage of Bo's running ability. "If Jackson ran from the I-formation," University of Pittsburgh coach Johnny Majors declared, "he'd pose the same sort of problems [as Herschel Walker]. I thought Walker was more dangerous because he carried more, but Bo probably has more ability to make people miss him." Coach Dye switched to the I-formation in 1985, unleashing Jackson for 17 touchdowns and 1,786 yards rushing, the second most yards gained in a single season in SEC history. "My goal is to go through the season injury free," Bo said, "and everything else will take care of itself." Jackson removed himself from the University of Tennessee and University of Florida games, both losses, because of a bruised thigh. Media and fans questioned Bo's motivation for removing himself, but he played against the University of Alabama with two broken ribs.

In 1985, Jackson was named All-SEC running back for the third year, was selected unanimous All-America, and earned the Heisman Memorial Trophy as the nation's outstanding college football player. "The Heisman means a great deal to me," Bo said. "I'm going to do everything in my power to uphold the tradition." Former Auburn All-America quarterback Pat Sullivan, 1971 Heisman Trophy winner, commented, "I think he is most deserving and I think he has handled himself in a classy manner. I am proud to be an alumnus of the same school." Coach Dye observed, "As anyone who knows him can tell you, he's [Jackson] just as impressive a person as he is an athlete." Jackson also captured the 1985 United Press International (UPI), Walter Camp Foundation and *The Sporting News* Player of the Year awards and garnered the Tangueray Award for excellence in amateur sports. Bo earned two additional post-season MVP honors his senior year, producing 129 yards and 2 touchdowns in a losing battle with Texas A&M University in the Cotton Bowl and a whopping 171 yards and 3 scores in the Japan Bowl. He achieved 21 100-yard performances between 1982 and 1985 and established 13 Auburn game, season, or career marks, including a career 4,303 yards rushing (6.6-yard average) and 43 touchdowns.

Jackson played three seasons with the Tigers' baseball squad, amassing a career .335 batting average, 28 home runs, and 70 RBIs in 89 games. Bo's best season came in 1984, when he hit .401 with 17 homers and 43 RBIs in 42 games. He was rated higher than any other player eligible for the June 1985 player draft and was picked by the California Angels (AL) but chose to complete his final year of eligibility at Auburn. "I wanted to have four years of college," Jackson said, "before I got into pro football or pro baseball. But there were times when I wanted to just up and leave." Bo, the first three-sport letterman at Auburn in 30 years, also starred in track and field. He twice made the NCAA indoor 60-yard dash semi-finals, recording a lifetime best time of 6.18 seconds.

Jackson was drafted first overall in 1986 by the National Football League's (NFL) Tampa Bay Buccaneers and the United States Football League's (USFL) Birmingham Stallions. Baseball's Kansas City Royals (AL) drafted Bo in the fourth round of the annual major league amateur free agent draft. He accepted a reported $200,000 from the Royals. Many skeptics wondered why Jackson accepted a much lower contract offer when Tampa Bay had proposed $7 million over four years. Bo said, "I want to play some ball. Baseball, not football; the outfield instead of the backfield." Jackson played 53 games in left field for the Memphis Chicks of the Southern League before the Royals called him up in September 1986. Bo hit .207 in 25 games, belting a 475-foot homer (the longest ever in Royals Stadium) against the Seattle Mariners and a broken bat grand-slam homer over the center-field fence. Jackson, the fastest runner among then active major leaguers, was clocked from home plate to first base in 3.62 seconds. Bo worked for three weeks in the Arizona Instructional League before the start of the 1987 season.

Although exhibiting tremendous speed and power, Jackson lacked consistency. In a game against the New York Yankees, Bo became only the twenty-fifth major league player to strike out 5 times. He struck out 158 times in 116 games in 1987 but still batted .235 with 22 homers and 53 RBIs. Peter Gammons, *Sports Illustrated* writer, noted, "Bo hasn't even played 100 games as a professional, and already he's on his way to joining Reggie [Jackson] and Fernando [Valenzuela] as the only baseball players everyone knows by their first name." Jackson was chosen to play in the 1989 All-Star Game, clubbing 32 homers and driving in 105 runs that season. Bo garnered another MVP award, sparking the AL to a 5–3 triumph over the NL with a leadoff 448-foot homer. He made two hits in four at bats with two RBIs and one stolen base.

In April 1987, Jackson was drafted by the Los Angeles Raiders (NFL) in the seventh round and signed to play with them. Bo set a Raiders' yardage record, dashing 91 yards for a touchdown against the Seattle Seahawks. He played in the 1989 NFL Pro Bowl after amassing 950 yards rushing that year. Nike's athletic shoes TV commercials featured him with "Bo knows . . . [baseball and football and basketball, etc.]" advertisements, touting his outstanding versatility in sports. Peter King, *Sports Illustrated* writer, suggested, "[Bo has] the best combination of speed and power ever to run in an NFL backfield. This is not just me saying this; this is every man in every NFL front office." On January 13, 1991, during a Raiders' NFL playoff game with the Cincinnati Bengals, Jackson severely injured his left hip on a routine tackle. Bo suffered an alarming loss of cartilage in the joint, halting his pro football career. During four NFL seasons, he rushed 515 times for 2,782 yards (5.4-yard avarage) and 16 touchdowns and caught 40 passes for 352 yards (8.8-yard average) and 2 touchdowns. Two months later, the Kansas City Royals placed Jackson on waivers, relieving them of 75 percent of his $2.45 million salary. A Kansas City source explained, "This is a no-brainer. It was the only sound business decision to make based on the facts."

The Chicago White Sox (AL) picked up Jackson's contract. During spring training in March 1992, *Sports Illustrated* writer Steve Wulf lamented the "image of [Bo] in Sarasota, Florida last week, limping into second base on a sure triple. I missed seeing the climb up the wall and the titanic homer off Mike Moore and the rifle throw to nail Harold Reynolds at the plate—the three feats most often mentioned by Bo's former Royal teammates." On April 5, 1992, Jackson underwent successful hip replacement surgery and spent several months in rehabilitation. No one expected Bo to wear a major league uniform again. How wrong! The following April, he served as Chicago's designated hitter and smashed a home run in his first official swing. Jackson made 17 hits in his first 65 at bats, including three doubles and three home runs. By the end of July, the White Sox had won 12 of 16 games in which Bo had driven in a run. In a classic understatement, he declared, "I'm just trying to do my job." The White Sox, however, did not resign Jackson, who slumped to .232 in 85 games. In January 1994, Bo signed with the California Angels (AL). During the strike-shortened 1994 season, he batted .279 with 13 home runs and 43 RBIs as a designated hitter. In April 1994, Jackson retired from professional baseball. In his career, Jackson batted .250 with 144 home runs and 415 RBIs in 694 games. Bo married Linda Garrett on September 5, 1987, and has three children, Garrett, Nicholas, and Morgan.

BIBLIOGRAPHY: *Auburn University Football Media Guide,* Cotton Bowl ed. (Auburn, AL, 1985); *Contemporary Authors,* vol. 141 (1994), pp. 238–239; Cotton Bowl Football Program, Auburn vs. Texas A&M, Dallas, TX, January 1, 1986; Peter Gammons, "Will Bo Be a Hit or a Miss?" *Sports Illustrated* 66 (May 4, 1987), pp. 36–38; Jerry Greene, *Orlando Sentinel,* June 21, 1986; Bo Jackson and Dick Schaap, *Bo Knows Bo* (New York, 1990); David L. Porter, ed., *Biographical Dictionary of American Sports: Football* (Westport, CT, 1987); Steve Wulf, "It Hurts Just to Watch Him," *Sports Illustrated* 76 (March 16, 1992), p. 80.

James D. Whalen

REGGIE JACKSON
(May 18, 1946–) _____ *Baseball*

Reggie Jackson made newspaper headlines for both his home runs and flamboyant playing style. Reginald Martinez Jackson was born on May 18, 1946, in Wyncote, Pennsylvania, the son of Martinez Jackson, a semi-pro baseball player and tailor, and Clara Jackson. Reggie grew up in suburban Philadelphia, graduating from Cheltenham Township High School and excelling in four sports there. Jackson received a football scholarship to Arizona State University but quit after coach Frank Kush moved him from offense to cornerback. Reggie switched to the baseball team, which featured Sal Bando, Rick Monday, and other luminaries. He quickly made his presence known, becoming an All-America outfielder and being the first player to hit a home run out of Phoenix Stadium.

Jackson remained extremely close to his dad. When his mother left, she took all four children except Reggie with her. Reggie recalled, "He was a father during the day and a mother at night." Of his early years, Jackson often said, "Everyone else had more than we did. My father always had something to throw on the table, but we felt poverty." His father inspired him, saying, "I told Reggie that if he didn't make the team, he'd have to work in my shop." In 1984, Reggie gave his five hundredth home run ball to his father out of appreciation. Three years later, he revealed, "I will carry the scars of that breakup with me as long as I live."

In the first round of the 1966 amateur draft, Kansas City A's American League (AL) club owner Charles Finley made Jackson the second player selected and signed him for a reported $90,000. The New York Mets (NL) already had chosen catcher Steve Chilcott. The 6-foot, 195-pound, left-handed Jackson started his professional baseball career with Lewiston, Idaho, of the Northwestern League (NWL) and followed with a stint at Modesto, California, of the California League. Birmingham, Alabama, of the Southern Association marked Reggie's last stop before the A's promoted him to Kansas City in 1968. The same year, he married Hispanic college friend Jeannie Campos. Jackson's only experience with marriage ended in divorce five years later.

Reggie followed the A's to Oakland in 1968 and helped them win three consecutive World Series from 1972 through 1974. In 1969, he threatened Babe Ruth's and Roger Maris's season home run record and eventually finished with 47 round-trippers, a new club record. Jackson was named the AL Most Valuable Player (MVP) in 1973, having led the AL with 32 homers and 117 RBIs. Although Reggie tied for the AL lead in home runs with 36 in 1975, Finley became disenchanted with the slugger's attitude. The star's holdouts remained a constant source of irritation for the irascible owner. The A's traded Jackson to the Baltimore Orioles (AL) in 1976. The following season, Reggie became a free agent and signed with the New York Yankees (AL).

New York and Jackson seemed an ideal match. Reggie immediately won the adulation of the fickle New York fans. His towering home runs and his proud, confident swagger on the field made the New Yorkers cheer unrestrained. He once boasted, "If I played in New York, they'd have to name a candy bar after me!" In just three swings, "Mr. October" slugged 3 home runs in the sixth and final game of the 1977 World Series against the Los Angeles Dodgers. Jackson's record of 5 homers for the 1977 Classic overshadowed the Yankees' second consecutive world's championship. For these years, Reggie definitely was "the straw that stirred the Yankees' drink." In 1980, Jackson again led the AL with 41 home runs. Constant squabbles with New York Yankees owner George Steinbrenner, manager Billy Martin, and brooding catcher Thurman Munson finally brought an abrupt end to Reggie's five-year love-hate relationship with the Big Apple. The Reggie bar also appeared, swiftly relegated to trivia history. After a poor performance in the strike-torn 1981 season, he joined the California Angels (AL).

Jackson continued his hitting magic with the Angels in 1982, pacing the AL in homers with 39 and directing California to an AL West championship. Reggie spent four more seasons wearing the California halo but never surpassed 27 home runs. He played his final season in 1987 with the Oakland Athletics (AL), batting .262 and hitting the last 15 of his 563 lifetime home runs. Jackson ranks sixth on the all-time home run list. During his 21-year major league career featuring his induction into the National Baseball Hall of Fame in 1993, Reggie amassed 2,584 hits, scored 1,551 runs, and produced 1,702 RBIs and 228 stolen bases. He played on 11 divisional titlists, six AL pennant winners, and five World Champions. His lifetime .357 World Series batting average included his .755 slugging mark, the best in major league history. Jackson led the AL three times in slugging average. Reggie's 2,597 strikeouts surpassed all major league players. His towering home run in the 1971 All-Star Game at Tiger Stadium in Detroit remains legendary.

Jackson remains a mystery to most people. National Baseball Hall of Famer **Frank Robinson** said of Reggie in 1969, "He wants to be popular, but he doesn't know how." Jackson is often misunderstood, especially by African Americans, "I'm arrogant when I want people to back off! I have made a special effort to help my own people, but it has backfired."

Reggie was never known for his ability with the glove. His nonchalance in right field led to his celebrated dispute with Yankee manager Billy Martin in 1978. Jackson confessed, "The only way I'm going to get a Gold Glove is to buy some paint!" During the twilight of his career, he said, "In those days I was solely concerned about one thing—Reggie Jackson hitting home runs." In 1974, Jackson remarked, "There are 200 million people in this world and 180 million are white. It is only natural that many of my friends are white!"

Jackson brought a theatrical air to baseball, hitting long dramatic home runs and then following his clouts over the fence with his eyes. Reggie then began his slow gait around the bases with as much style and drama as Babe Ruth. Since his baseball career, he has concentrated on his real estate holdings, Chevrolet dealership, and 120 antique cars.

BIBLIOGRAPHY: Maury Allen, *Mr. October* (New York, 1981); Reggie Jackson, *Reggie*, 2nd ed. (New York, 1984); Gene Karst and Martin Jones, Jr., *Who's Who in Professional Baseball* (New Rochelle, 1973); "One Man Wild Bunch," *Time* 103 (June 3, 1974), p. 5; Michael Shatzkin, ed., *The Ballplayers* (New York, 1990); Art Spander, "A Different Spring for Mr. October," *The Sporting News*, April 11, 1988, p. 40; John Strege, "Reggie: He Earns His Keep," *The Sporting News*, May 2, 1983, p. 2; Robert Ward, "Reggie Jackson in No-Man's Land," *Sport* 64 (June 1977), p. 89–96.

William A. Borst

FERGUSON JENKINS
(December 13, 1943–) ───────────────────────── *Baseball*

Ferguson Arthur Jenkins has seen the mountaintops of joy and the dark valleys of tragedy. Jenkins has gone from the 1971 National League (NL) Cy Young winner, who led the NL in victories (24), innings pitched (325), and complete games (30), to being arrested in Toronto, Canada, in August 1980 for possession of drugs. Ferguson went from being elected to the National Baseball Hall of Fame on January 8, 1991, to his wife Katherine dying four days later of injuries sustained in an automobile accident.

Jenkins, born on December 13, 1943, in Chatham, Ontario, remains the greatest Canadian pitcher to reach the major leagues. His father, Ferguson Holmes Jenkins, played baseball in the 1930s when African Americans were not allowed in the major leagues. "Fergie" inherited his father's athletic skills, lettering in baseball, basketball, and ice hockey at Chatham High School. He developed his poise as a pitcher by appearing as a singer in his childhood. Furthermore, Jenkins acknowledged, "I had good control. That helped a lot. I influenced hitters to swing at pitches." In 1993 a mellower Fergie discussed his pitching philosophy: "Concentrate on the batter. The more time you get them out the easier it was to sit in the dugout and relax." An ice hockey star, he played for the Junior B affiliate of the Montreal Canadiens National Hockey League (NHL) club and then declined pro hockey offers for a baseball career.

The Philadelphia Phillies (NL) signed Jenkins, who spent 4 years in the minors before reaching the major leagues late in the 1965 season. The Phillies traded Ferguson in April 1966 to the Chicago Cubs (NL), where he changed from a relief pitcher into a starter and blossomed as an "iron man" pitcher, usually completing his starting assignments. During his 19-year major league career, he completed 267 of his 594 games started.

Jenkins, who tied a team mark by notching six consecutive 20-game-victory seasons with the Chicago Cubs from 1967 to 1972, lauded his catchers and infielders, stating, "You never do anything alone, especially in a team sport." Ferguson described his pitching approach in 1990: "I used my head. There are so many throwers in baseball today. They outnumber the guys who can pitch. You don't have to throw 95-mph to get hitters out. You can change speeds and move the ball around." His control marked the key ingredient, as he remains the only pitcher in major league history to strike out more than 3,000 batters (3,192) while walking under 1,000 (997) hitters. Fergie, an excellent batter, belted six home runs and knocked in 20 runs during his Cy Young 1971 year.

Following a mediocre 14–16 mark in 1973, Jenkins was traded to the Texas Rangers American League (AL) club. Fergie rebounded nicely the next year, sharing the AL lead with 25 victories and pacing the AL with 29 complete games. After the next season, Jenkins became a baseball vagabond. Ferguson joined the Boston Red Sox (AL) in 1975 but returned to the Rangers in 1977. Although no more 20-game-win seasons transpired, Jenkins still pitched steadily. During his second stint with Texas, Ferguson enjoyed his best performance in 1978 with an 18–8 record.

In regard to his arrest and conviction on the drug charges, Jenkins later said: "There are still so many drugs in sports that I hesitate to even talk about it. A lot has happened in baseball and other sports since I had my trouble. I guess the thing that surprises me is that so many players didn't pay attention. The other thing that boggles my mind is that the biggest drug problem is with alcohol, and it's legal." Despite this tragic episode, Canada showed its appreciation for Jenkins in 1980 by awarding him that nation's highest civilian award, The Order of Canada, for his humanitarian work.

Fergie was signed as a free agent by the Chicago Cubs (NL) after the 1981 season, returning to the team for whom he had starred. He led the Cub staff with a 14–15 record and a 3.15 ERA and recorded his 3,000th strikeout in a game against the San Diego Padres. His illustrious career ended in 1982 an overall record of 284 wins, 226 losses, and 3.34 ERA. Jenkins ranks among the top 25 in all-time major league victories, strikeouts, shutouts, and innings pitched.

Upon being released by the Cubs in March 1984, Jenkins returned to his

Blenheim, Ontario, farm. At age 40 with a tired arm, Ferguson did not look back: "To be honest, I was actually looking forward to retirement. I ended up playing longer than I expected after severing my Achilles tendon in 1976. I thought my career was over then. After that, I was always aware it could end at any moment. I had no regrets. I was just happy that I had the opportunity to come back to Chicago a second time to end my career with the Cubs." He moved to Guthrie, Oklahoma, and found that the life of the rancher kept him fit.

Retirement did not end his baseball career, as Jenkins soon became a pitching coach with the Oklahoma City, Oklahoma, 89ers (American Association). During 1993 and 1994, Ferguson served as a roving pitching instructor with the Cincinnati Reds (NL) organization. In November 1994, the Chicago Cubs signed him as pitching coach. He stated, "I would like to manage in the majors." He adds, "I want to teach some youngsters exactly what I was taught because it's not that hard, but you have to apply yourself."

BIBLIOGRAPHY: *Chicago Cubs Vineline* 2 (March 1987), pp. 24–25; 5 (February 1990), p. 12; 6 (February 1991), p. 11; Eddie Gold and Art Ahrens, *The New Era Cubs* (Chicago, IL, 1985).

Duane A. Smith

JACK JOHNSON
(March 31, 1878–June 10, 1946) ————————————————— *Boxing*

Jack Johnson ranks among the most controversial prizefighters in American history. As the first African-American heavyweight champion, Johnson both inspired his fellow African Americans and frightened white Americans. Jack became an important symbol of racial tension in the early twentieth century.

Arthur John Johnson was born on March 31, 1878, in Galveston, Texas, to Henry Johnson, a porter and school janitor, and Tina Johnson. Although his parents encouraged him to get a good education, Johnson quit school after the fifth grade and began several manual labor jobs. Jack painted wagons, baked bread, exercised racehorses, and loaded and unloaded ships at the Galveston docks.

Upon working as a janitor in a local gymnasium, Johnson saw boxing up close and became entranced with the sport. Jack began training in the gymnasium and fought numerous bouts against local talent, soon being labeled "the best black boxer in Galveston, Texas." He then drifted from one amateur bout to another in Chicago, Illinois, Boston, Massachusetts, New York City, and other cities. In 1897, at age 19, Johnson turned professional. During the next 11 years, Jack fought 77 times. His 1903 victory over "Denver Ed" Martin gave him the "unofficial" African-American heavyweight championship. Leading white fighters, including John L. Sullivan and Jim Jeffries, refused to fight Johnson, however, because of his race. By 1908, Johnson's international reputation grew so powerful and the lack of good heavyweight contenders was so clear that he finally was allowed to fight for the championship outside the United States. On December 26, 1908, in Sydney, Australia, Jack soundly defeated reigning champion Tommy Burns.

White boxing fans spent the next two years trying to find a Caucasian fighter to defeat Johnson. After five prospects lost to the champion, Jeffries came out of retirement as "The Great White Hope" to challenge the champion. "The Fight of the Century" featured Jack demolishing his challenger on July 4, 1910, in Las Vegas, Nevada.

White anger exploded at this point in Johnson's career. Race riots followed Jack's victory over Jeffries. Whites generally initiated the riots, fearing that Johnson's success would encourage other African Americans to challenge the system of racial discrimination that made most African Americans second-class citizens. His personal lifestyle also infuriated most whites. Jack violated one of white America's most sacred racial codes when he married a white woman, Etta Terry Duryea in 1911. Shortly after her suicide in 1912, he married another white, Lucille Cameron. Such disregard for racial etiquette probably led federal authorities to indict and try Johnson for violation of the Mann Act, which forbade transporting women across state lines for immoral purposes. Both Duryea and Cameron had made such journeys in Johnson's company. Jack, convicted in 1913, fled to France to avoid a prison term. For the next two years, he lived in exile and conducted boxing and even wrestling exhibitions to survive. Johnson defended his title in Havana, Cuba, in April 1915 but was knocked out by Jess Willard, the last of several "White Hopes." Although claiming he lost the fight purposely, Jack probably suffered defeat primarily because of his lack of physical conditioning and insufficient practice. After four more years of exile, he returned to the United States in 1920 and was imprisoned for a year. Johnson spent the rest of his life writing, boxing in exhibitions, and "dabbling in various business enterprises." In 1924, after divorcing Lucille Cameron, Jack married another white, Irene Pineau. He died in an automobile accident on June 10, 1946, in Raleigh, North Carolina.

From a purely athletic point of view, Johnson proved a remarkable prizefighter and probably ranked among the greatest of all heavyweight champions. The 6-foot-1½-inch 195- to 205-pounder remained an impressive physical specimen. Although possessing a powerful knockout punch, Jack excelled particularly at defense and counterpunching. Biographer Sal Fradella states that the heavyweight possessed "cat-like precision and skill." His loss of only 8 of 113 professional bouts attests to his boxing skill. Even in the ring, however, his personal style created enemies among whites. Johnson often taunted his white opponents. In the Jeffries fight, for example, Jack mocked "The Great White Hope" during clinches, " 'Come on, Mr. Jeff. Let me see what you got. Do something, man.' " He laughed at his fallen white opponents with his golden front tooth gleaming in the sun, enraging whites.

Johnson's major importance, then, remained symbolic. Since Jack was an African American, most whites disliked his holding the championship. His taunting in the ring and rejection of racial separation outside the ring inflamed white passions even more. Novelist Jack London reflected this hatred when he urged Jeffries to " 'wipe that smile of Jack Johnson's face.' " If most whites despised him, most African Americans probably saw him as a hero striking blows for African-American pride. Ironically, Johnson distanced himself from those African Americans who worshiped him. According to Larry Gerlach, Jack "rejected black women, distrusted successful black men, surrounded himself with white functionaries, and lived increasingly in a white world even to the point of affecting an English accent."

Johnson stands as a particularly ironic symbol and an immensely skilled prizefighter, whose personal attributes and image among both whites and African Americans far overshadowed his athletic prowess. He exhibited bravery, flaunting racist conventions. This sad, tragic figure, however, largely forgot the very people who were his greatest supporters. In 1990, the International Boxing Hall of Fame inducted him.

BIBLIOGRAPHY: Finis Farr, *Black Champion: The Life and Times of Jack Johnson* (London, England 1965); Sal Fradella, *Jack Johnson* (Boston, MA, 1990); Al-Tony Gilmore, *Bad Nigger! The National Impact of Jack Johnson* (Port Washington, NY, 1975); Earl Gutskey, "80 Years Ago, the Truth Hurt," *Los Angeles Times*, July 8, 1990, sec. C, p. 1; Jack Johnson, *Jack Johnson Is a Dandy: An Autobiography* (New York, 1969); John Lardner, *White Hopes and Other Tigers* (New York, 1951); David L. Porter, ed., *Biographical Dictionary of American Sports: Basketball and Other Indoor Sports* (Westport, CT, 1989); Randy Roberts, *Papa Jack: Jack Johnson and the Era of White Hopes* (New York, 1983); Jeffrey T. Sammons, *Beyond the Ring: The Role of Boxing in American Society* (Urbana, IL, 1988).

Anthony O. Edmonds

MAGIC JOHNSON
(August 14, 1959–) ————————————————————— *Basketball*

Magic Johnson ranks among the most popular ambassadors for professional basketball. Earvin Johnson, Jr., was born on August 14, 1959, in Lansing, Michigan, the second son of Earvin Johnson, Sr., and Christine Johnson. Like many Lansing inhabitants, his father relocated there because of the employment opportunities at the huge Oldsmobile automobile factory. Earvin Johnson, Sr., tutored his son in basketball fundamentals. Johnson's penchant for the quick assist and inside move was forged out of necessity. To get maximum playing time at the school and boys' club level, Magic needed to be a better-than-average team player who could move the ball quickly and effectively through "heavy traffic."

At Everett High School in Lansing, George Fox coached Johnson. Magic, helped by several gifted players, guided Everett High School to the Class A State quarterfinals and semifinals. He was named UPI Prep Player of the Year in Michigan and made the All-State team. As a senior, Johnson enjoyed an astonishingly successful season. Everett High School completed a 27–1 record and took the Class A State championship crown. His statistics reveal an athlete of tremendous versatility, who sparkled on offense and defense. Besides averaging 28.8 points per game and 16.8 rebounds per game, Magic made 208 assists and 99 steals.

In 1977, Johnson began attending Michigan State University. Magic possessed unique ability to entertain, cheer, and be adored by those who saw him play. **Michael Jordan, Kareem Abdul-Jabbar,** and **Wilt Chamberlain** exhibited greater dominance but did not enjoy the rapport that Johnson established with his various audiences.

At six foot nine inches and 225 pounds, Johnson combined both height and lightness/quickness that allowed him to play any position on the basketball court. Magic realized that, just as the sky hook marked Abdul-Jabbar's most potent weapon, his signature move would be the explosive pass. The "alley oop" combination was not created by him, but his mastery of it brought crowds to their feet. "Johnson had a real sense of the court and tremendous anticipation for his teammates' moves."

At Michigan State University Johnson built on his high school successes. During the 1977–1978 season, Magic scored 511 points and averaged 17.0 points a game. A year later, he played 1,159 minutes and scored 548 points or 17.1 points a game. Although Johnson proved an exciting player to watch, his appeal rested on a radiant smile and a persona trumpeting a message of a happy player having the time of his life on a basketball court. In 1979, Magic made *The Sporting News* All-America First Team, was named the NCAA Division I Tournament Most Outstanding Player, and played on the NCAA championship team. His final Michigan State game set the stage for a special relationship with Larry Bird that lasted throughout the next decade. In the 1979 NCAA championship game, Johnson's Michigan State recorded a 75–64 victory over Bird's Indiana State University. His nickname, "Magic," came from people enjoying his skills, his sleight of hand, and especially his bubbling and engaging character. The laugh, the roll of the eyes, and the boyish smile epitomized a magical personality.

Johnson's National Basketball Association (NBA) playoff record marked a litany of excellence. From 1979 to 1991 with the Los Angeles Lakers (NBA), Magic played 7,403 minutes, scored 3,640 points, and averaged 19.6 points per game. Besides being NBA finals MVP in 1980, 1982, and 1987, he held the career playoff record for most assists (2,320) and most steals (358), the NBA finals record for most assists per game (14.0, 1985) and the NBA finals single-game record for most points by a rookie (42 on May 7, 1980, against the Philadelphia 76ers). His list of records seems endless. From the outset, Johnson possessed the magic or Midas touch with the Lakers. Although signed originally for a $600,000 contract, Magic eventually agreed to a $25 million multiyear deal. Many, however, wondered whether this extroverted, genial giant would fit in with the Lakers, a team that had thrived under the unspectacular, quiet leadership of Abdul-Jabbar. Johnson's presence actually freed up Abdul-Jabbar, enabling the aging superstar to have an especially successful 1979–1980 season. In the 1980 NBA championship finals, Abdul-Jabbar was injured and the Lakers faced elimination. Magic stepped in and played like a man possessed, leading the Lakers to a 123–107 triumph. Douglas Noverr and Lawrence Ziewacz remarked, "In three years the irrepressible 'Magic Man' with the million dollar smile had won high school, college, and professional basketball titles—a feat unparalleled in the annals of basketball history."

His many regular-season honors included being the NBA MVP in 1987, 1989, and 1990 and an NBA All-Star First Team member from 1983 to 1991. Johnson's presence overshadowed that of Jordan, Bird, and **Charles Barkley** as the major drawing card for the U.S. Dream Team at the 1992 Barcelona, Spain, Summer Olympics. The favored U.S. team won the Gold Medal, as the soccer-mad continent of Europe surprisingly embraced basketball and especially the charismatic Johnson.

Nevertheless, a revelation in late 1991 forever cast Magic in a totally different light. He tested positive for human immunodeficiency virus (HIV), retired, attempted a short-lived return to the professional ranks, and vowed to become a spokesman in the battle against AIDS. Johnson served during 1992 as a presidential adviser on AIDS but then resigned because he felt the government lacked the commitment to battle the scourge of AIDS. At his November 1991 press conference, delivered at the Great Western Forum of the Los Angeles Lakers, Magic remained calm and collected. "I'm going to go on. I'm going to go on a happy man." He urged people to understand the nature of AIDS and that "safe sex is the way to go." Johnson implied that he contracted the disease from heterosexual contact, thus letting a world audience know that even an incredibly gifted, very fit athlete is vulnerable.

Time coverage of the press conference concluded: "While there is no reason to defy the player or accord him any more sympathy than that lent to the roughly 1 million others in the US and millions elsewhere in the world who have been infected, there is ample reason to feel grateful for his courage and his sanity and to hope that somehow, with his dauntless smile, he might even give us something more to cheer about at the saddest moment of his life."

Johnson continues to tour the world and play in tournament basketball games. Magic remains fit and well, having taken part in various AIDS educational ventures. Fans will always remember him for his "running, jumping, slithering—suspension of disbelief." He and his wife Cookie have one son, Earvin III, and one daughter, Elisa. At the 1993 NBA finals, Johnson served as a "color" commentator. In a career of unbelievable ups and downs, Magic in April 1994 briefly coached his beloved Lakers to a 5–11 record. Two months later, he bought a minority interest in the club. In 1994, *Sports Illustrated* ranked Johnson and Larry Bird eighth on its "40 for the Ages List."

BIBLIOGRAPHY: Sally B. Donnelly and Dick Thompson, "It Can Happen to Anybody, Even Magic Johnson," *Time* 138 (November 18, 1991), pp. 26–27; Douglas A. Noverr and Lawrence E. Ziewacz, *The Games They Played: Sports in American History, 1865–1980* (Chicago, IL, 1988); David L. Porter, ed., *Biographical Dictionary of American Sports: Basketball and Other Indoor Sports* (Westport, CT, 1989); Matthew Siegel, biographical material and promotional guides, Naismith Memorial Basketball Hall of Fame, Springfield, MA, 1994.

Scott A.G.M. Crawford

MICHAEL JOHNSON
(September 13, 1967–) ————————————————— *Track and Field*

Michael Johnson ranks among history's finest dashmen in both the 200 meters and 400 meters. In 1992, Johnson became the only runner to break both 20 seconds in the 200 meters and 44 seconds in the 400 meters. Michael Duane Johnson, the youngest of five children of Paul Johnson, a truck driver, and Ruby Johnson, a schoolteacher, was born on September 13, 1967, in Dallas, Texas. Michael grew up in the middle-class Oak Cliff section of Dallas and began running track at age 11 "as something to do" at Atwell Junior High School. Although Michael showed promise early as a runner and finished second in his first 200-meter dash, his family put more "emphasis on education" than sports. He "loved track" but ran it mainly "as a way to get to a better college." Coaches commented that Johnson "looked more like an Oxford scholar" than an athlete because he wore black horn-rimmed glasses in competition. Michael, who had participated in classes for gifted students in elementary and junior high schools, attended Skyline Senior High School, reputedly "the best high school in Dallas."

Johnson concentrated on the 200 meters throughout high school and recorded a personal best time of 21.30 seconds. In 1986, Michael captured the 200 meters in the District championship and finished second in the 200 meters at the State championships. He graduated from Skyline High School in 1986 and earned an athletic scholarship to Baylor University. Baylor track and field coach Clyde Hart "recruited Johnson to run relays" and did not believe the young Dallas dashman would become a world-class sprinter. Michael, however, demonstrated his potential by clocking 200 meters in 20.41 seconds before suffering injuries in 1987. He finished second in the 200 meters in 20.07 seconds at the 1988 Southwest Athletic Conference (SWC) championship but did not complete the 200 meters in the 1988 NCAA championships because of a cracked fibula. Indoors, the Baylor trackman garnered second in the 400 meters at the 1989 Track Athletic Congress (TAC) championship and first in the 200 meters at the NCAA championship, setting an American record of 20.59 seconds. An injury, suffered in the 1989 SWC championship, however, kept Michael out of the 1989 NCAA championship outdoors and gave him "the label of being injury prone."

In 1990, Johnson stayed healthy and realized his world-class sprinting potential. After defending his indoor NCAA 200-meter title, Michael won the indoor TAC 400-meter championship. Outdoors, he anchored Baylor's 4 × 200-meter and 4 × 400-meter relay teams and clocked final relay legs of 18.5 seconds for 200 meters and 43.5 seconds for 400 meters. Johnson captured the 1990 NCAA 200-meter title outdoors and anchored Baylor to victory in the 4 × 400-meter relay with a sprint of 43.7 seconds. Earlier, in the 4 × 400-meter heats, Michael ran fast enough "just to qualify" for the final and recorded 400 meters in 43.5 seconds. If he had not "jogged" the final 30 meters, he would have certainly "turned in history's first sub-43 relay leg." Johnson scored major 200-meter victories in the 1990 TAC championships and Seattle, Washington, Goodwill Games. In 1990 Michael lost only once in the 200 meters and ran undefeated in the 400 meters. Moreover, he recorded personal best times of 19.85 seconds for 200 meters and 44.21 seconds for 400 meters. Raymond Pierre, a former Baylor teammate, summarized Michael's 1990 season, "We were all surprised it took so long for him to get where he should have been."

Track and Field News (TFN) ranked Johnson first in both the 200 and 400 meters and recognized him as its 1990 Athlete of the Year. Experts compared Michael to **Tommie Smith,** the only runner to have held simultaneous world records in the 200 and 400 meters in 1967. Smith used an extraordinary knee lift and "monstrous stride length," but Johnson, wrote Randall Northam of *Athletics Weekly,* "runs with no knee lift to speak of and a stride length which would not inconvenience an elderly jogger." Despite his pedestrian gait, Michael lowered the world record in the 200 meters to 20.55 seconds indoors, raced undefeated at the distance outdoors, and garnered major wins in the 1991 TAC and World Championships. At the latter, he "proved that he was in a class by himself." Johnson set a meet record of 20.01 seconds and defeated the field by .33 second, the largest winning margin since the 1936 Berlin, Germany, Olympic Games. Michael also ran undefeated in the 400 meters, recording a personal best of 44.17 seconds.

Johnson ranked as the world's premier 200- and 400-meter dashman in 1991 and was favored to win the 200 meters in the 1992 Summer Olympic Games at Barcelona, Spain. Michael contracted food poisoning prior to the Olympic Games, however, and failed to qualify for the Olympic 200-meter final. He recovered well enough to garner a Gold Medal in the 4 × 400-meter relay, in which the United States set a world record of 2 minutes 55.74 seconds. Before the Olympic Games, Johnson improved his 400-meter best to 43.98 seconds. No dashman had broken 20 seconds for the 200 meters and 44 seconds for the 400 meters. Afterward, Michael acknowledged that his "whole career has been based on being the best in the world at both" distances. In 1993, he concentrated on the 400 meters and captured the USA Track and Field (USATF) championship in 43.74 seconds. Johnson clocked 43.65 seconds to prevail in the 400 meters in the 1993 World Championship at Stuttgart, Germany. In the World Championship 4 × 400-meter relay, his anchor leg of 42.94 seconds marked history's fastest and secured a world record of 2 minutes 54.29 seconds for the United States. In 1994, the United States Olympic Committee (USOC) named Johnson its Track and Field Athlete of the Year. *TFN* also selected him its Male Athlete of the Year. At the 1994 Goodwill Games in St. Petersburg, Russia, Michael won the 200-meter dash in 20.10 seconds and anchored the winning 4 × 400-meter relay team. He also ran the world's fastest 400-meter race, clocking 44.04 seconds at the International Amateur Athletic Federation's (IAAF) Grand Prix at Berlin, Germany. In February 1995, Johnson set a world indoor record in the 400 meters at the inaugural Reno, Nevada, Air Indoor Track & Field Games. Michael covered the 400-meter distance in 44.97 seconds, running the first lap in an astounding 21.3 seconds. The record lasted only three weeks, as he clocked a sensational 44.63 seconds to win the 400-meter dash on March 5 at the USA/Mobil Indoor Track and Field Championships at Atlanta, Georgia. Johnson finished first in the 400 meters and shared second overall in the 1995 Grand Prix Indoor Final Standings. He swept the 400 meters and 200 meters at the USATF Outdoor Championships at Sacramento, California, in June 1995. His 400-meter time of 43.66 seconds was the fastest in the United States and fourth fastest ever, while his wind-aided 200-meter time of 19.83 seconds was the fastest under any conditions in the world in 1995. No American had won that rare sprint double since Maxey Long in 1899. Michael, a 1990 graduate of Baylor University, lives in Waco, Texas.

BIBLIOGRAPHY: James Dunaway, "Michael Johnson," TAC/TAFWA Bio Data Sheet, 1991; Jon Hendershott, "19.85 & 44.21," *Track and Field News* 43 (November 1990), pp. 40–41; Jon Hendershott, "Johnson: What Happened?" *Track and Field News* 45 (October 1992), p. 16; Garry Hill, "Johnson Plan Perfect," *Track and Field News* 46 (November 1993), p. 11; Dave Johnson, "Johnson Cracks 44," *Track and Field News* 45 (September 1992), pp. 16–17; Dave Johnson, "Another WR for U.S.," *Track and Field News* 45 (October 1992), p. 37; Dave Johnson, "U.S. Stomps WR," *Track and Field News* 46 (November 1993), p. 26; Sieg Lindstrom, "Johnson: No Respect?" *Track and Field News* 43 (August 1990), p. 12; Sieg Lindstrom, "Johnson Makes Euro Impact," *Track and Field News* 43 (September 1990), p. 21; Sieg Lindstrom, "Johnson: 2 + 4 = No. 1," *Track and Field News* 44 (January 1991), pp. 4–5; Merrell Noden, "Making Tracks: Michael Johnson Ranks as the World's Best at 200 and 400 Meters," *Sports Illustrated* 74 (May 20, 1991), pp. 46–50; David L. Porter, ed., *Biographical Dictionary of American Sports: 1992–1995 Supplement for Baseball, Football, Basketball, and Other Sports* (Westport, CT, 1995); Don Potts, "Johnson Up to Snuff," *Track and Field News* 44 (November 1991), p. 10.

Adam R. Hornbuckle

RAFER JOHNSON
(August 18, 1935–) ———————————————— *Track and Field*

Rafer Johnson, one of the first African Americans to excel in the decathlon, a 10-event track and field competition spanning two days, won the Gold Medal in the event at the 1960 Summer Olympic Games at Rome, Italy. Rafer Lewis Johnson, the oldest of five children of Lewis Johnson, a handyman and Elma Johnson, was born on August 18, 1935, in Hillsboro, Texas. In 1937, the Johnsons moved to the ghetto of Dallas, Texas. "I don't care if I never see Texas again," Johnson later remarked. Rafer believed that if his family had stayed in Texas, he would not have attended college or represented the United States in the Olympic Games. Nevertheless, his father described Rafer as a contented child, who kept out of trouble, joked around, and "always wore a smile."

In 1945, the Johnsons moved to Kingsburg, California. They lived in an abandoned boxcar for a year before Edward Fishel, the owner of a nearby animal-feed-processing plant, furnished them a home and hired Lewis as a machinist and Elma as a domestic. In Kingsburg, the Johnsons encountered racial hostility, mainly from the chief of police who ordered Fishel to fire Rafer's parents. When Fishel refused, the police chief personally harassed the Johnsons until resigning and leaving town. With the chief's departure, the Johnsons made Kingsburg their permanent home.

At Kingsburg High School, Rafer displayed great all-around athletic skill and earned varsity letters in baseball, basketball, football, and track and field. He batted .400 in baseball, scored 17 points a game in basketball, and averaged nine yards per carry as a football halfback. In 1954, Johnson won the California State championship in the 120-yard high hurdles and placed second in the 220-yard low hurdles. The same year, the six-foot-three-inch, 190-pound Kingsburg High School senior also placed third in the Amateur Athletic Union (AAU) national decathlon championship. Rafer decided to concentrate on the decathlon in 1953 after watching Bob Mathias, the 1948 and 1952 Olympic decathlon champion, perform in nearby Tulare, California. "I decided to be a decathlon man," he recalled, when "I realized I could have beaten most of those guys in the meet."

After being offered athletic scholarships by dozens of colleges, Johnson accepted one from the University of California at Los Angeles (UCLA) in 1954. Rafer performed in basketball and track and field, served as senior class president, maintained a "B" average, and graduated with a B.S. degree in physical education in 1959. At UCLA, he developed into a champion decathlete and won the event at the Pan-American Games in 1955. In a welcome home meet in Kingsburg, Johnson set a world decathlon record with 7,985 points. The next year saw Rafer win both the NCAA and AAU decathlon titles and qualify for the U.S. Olympic team in the decathlon and long jump. A knee injury and a torn stomach muscle hampered him at the 1956 Melbourne, Australia, Summer Olympic Games. He withdrew from the long jump and finished second in the decathlon to Milton Campbell, who set an Olympic record with 7,937 points.

Johnson did not compete in 1957, undergoing surgery to repair his injured knee. Rafer returned to competition the following year. His chief competition came from Vasiliy Kuznetsov of the Soviet Union, the first decathlete to score over 8,000 points with an 8,014-point performance in May 1958. In the 1958

USA-USSR dual meet, Johnson defeated his Soviet counterpart and established a world record of 8,302 points. Although Kuznetsov raised the world record to 8,357 points in 1959, Rafer eclipsed that total with an 8,683-point performance in the 1960 Olympic Trials. In the 1960 Summer Olympic Games at Rome, Italy, however, his greatest challenge did not come from Kuznetsov. His former UCLA teammate, Chuan-Kwang "C. K." Yang, of Taiwan, who had won the 1959 AAU decathlon championship, provided the most formidable opposition. Close friends, yet fierce rivals, Johnson and Yang had traded wins several times before the 1960 Olympic Games. Rafer led Yang at Rome by only 67 points before the final event of the decathlon, the 1,500-meter run. Yang won the race, but his margin of victory was not enough to surpass Johnson. Rafer won the Gold Medal with an Olympic record 8,392 points. After the Olympic competition, he told reporters, "I'm through."

Johnson won the Sullivan Award in 1960 and retired from athletics that year. Although Rafer declined an offer from the Los Angeles Rams National Football League (NFL) club to play professional football, his brother Jimmy starred at defensive back for the San Francisco 49ers (NFL) from 1961 to 1976. He acted in *The Fiercest Heart, The Pirates of Tortuga, Wild in the Country, Sins of Rachel Cade, A Global Affair, The Games,* and *Soul Soldier.* Johnson participated in the 1968 presidential election campaign of Senator Robert F. Kennedy and was accompanying the senator the night of his assassination, following the candidate's victory in the California Democratic primary. Since then, Rafer has pursued business, public service, and sportscasting. During the opening ceremonies of the 1984 Summer Olympic Games at Los Angeles, Johnson carried the Olympic torch into the Los Angeles Coliseum and ignited the Olympic flame. Presently, he serves as the president of Rafer Johnson Enterprises and resides in Sherman Oaks, California. Johnson was inducted into the National Track and Field Hall of Fame in 1974 and the U.S. Olympic Hall of Fame in 1983.

BIBLIOGRAPHY: *Current Biography Yearbook* (1961), pp. 222–224; Earl Gutsky, "Two Friends, 10 Events: Johnson Outlasted Yang 30 Years Ago in Olympic Decathlon," *Los Angeles Times,* June 6, 1990, pp. C1, C13; Bill Mallon and Ian Buchanan, *Quest for Gold: The Encyclopedia of American Olympians* (New York, 1984); Cordner Nelson, *Track's Greatest Champions* (Los Altos, CA, 1986); Bob Phillips, "Still Carrying the Torch," *Scholastic Coach* 58 (August 1988), pp. 38–40, 82–83; David L. Porter, ed., *Biographical Dictionary of American Sports: Outdoor Sports* (Westport, CT, 1989); Roberto L. Quercetani, *A World History of Track and Field Athletics* (London, England, 1964); University of California, Los Angeles, Sports Information, letter to Adam R. Hornbuckle, August 1993; David Wallechinsky, *The Complete Book of the Olympic Games,* rev. ed. (New York, 1988); *Who's Who Among Black Americans, 1992–1993* (Detroit, MI, 1993).

Adam R. Hornbuckle

DEACON JONES
(December 9, 1938–) ——————————————————— *Football*

During the 1960s, the phrase "Fearsome Foursome" held the same ring of authority in football as "the Four Horsemen" did for the University of Notre Dame backfield in the 1920s. The "Fearsome Foursome" described the outstanding defensive line of the Los Angeles Rams National Football League (NFL) team. The four Rams linemen, tackles Merlin Olsen and Roosevelt Grier and ends Lamar Lundy and Deacon Jones, ranked among the best postwar-era players at their positions, combining speed with enormous strength. Left end Deacon Jones, perhaps the greatest of the four, was rated by both Olsen and Chicago Bears star **Gale Sayers** as the finest defensive football player ever.

Born December 9, 1938, in Eatonville, Florida, David Jones was one of eight children of Ismael Jones, a carpenter, and Mattie Jones. He grew up in a poor family and starred in basketball, track and field, and football at Hungerford High School in Orlando, Florida. At Mississippi Vocational College and South Carolina State College, Jones was nicknamed "Deacon" for leading his football squads in prayers. Deacon was not considered a topnotch professional prospect, being selected by the Los Angeles Rams in only the fourteenth round of the NFL draft. Jones initially substituted at defensive tackle for Lamar Lundy but slowly gained full recognition and began to show his outstanding skills by 1964. Deacon keenly studied films of Gino Marchetti, the great Baltimore Colts defensive end. With deadly quickness, he ran a 9.7-second 100-yard dash and proved an overwhelming pass rusher and clean tackler. Former Rams coach George Allen recalled Jones "was quicker and more agile than the other defensive linemen of his day and led the trend toward quicker, more agile defensive linemen." Allen added, "I never knew a defensive lineman who was as quick off at the snap of the ball as the Deacon. Or as quick at getting to the quarterback." The familiar football term *sack* entered the sports vernacular largely through Jones's prowess. An All-NFL selection from 1965 through 1970 and the NFL's Defensive Player of the Year in 1967 and 1968, he was selected to the AFL-NFL 1960–1984 All-Star Second Team in 1984, and the All-Time NFL Team in 1994. He was elected to the Pro Football Hall of Fame in 1980 after finishing his NFL career with the San Diego Chargers in 1972–1973 and Washington Redskins in 1974. His NFL career accomplishments included the recovery of over a dozen fumbles, a 50-yard return of a pass interception, and two tackles for safeties. Jones, an enthusiastic, inspirational leader, captained the Rams and played his best in crucial games.

At six foot four inches and 250 pounds, Jones enjoys golf, table tennis, and jazz. He married Iretha Oberton in 1962 and is currently associated with Canadian football.

BIBLIOGRAPHY: George Allen with Ben Olan, *Pro Football's 100 Greatest Players* (Indianapolis, IN, 1982); Arnold Hano, "The Awesome Power of Deacon Jones," *Sport* 47 (January 1969), pp. 58–64; David L. Porter, ed., *Biographical Dictionary of American Sports: Football* (Westport, CT, 1987); *The Sporting News Football Register* (1974).

Leonard H. Frey

K. C. JONES
(May 25, 1932–) ————————————————————— *Basketball*

K. C. Jones starred on both college and professional championship basketball teams. K. C. Jones was born on May 25, 1932, in Tyler, Texas. His father, K. C. Jones, worked as a restaurant cook and autoworker, while his mother, Eula Jones, toiled as a maid. He is the eldest of five children and grew up in the segregated, Jim Crow South. His father, an outgoing hard worker, enjoyed using his musical ability in church. Young K. C., usually shy, followed his father's example by expressing himself in gospel singing. His other liberating activity was sports.

K. C.'s inward, quiet mother taught her son the importance of diligence and hard work. K. C. never forgot his African-American origins, although he relished the diversity in his own heritage. He later discovered that two of his great-grandparents were Cherokee and Cheyenne Indians and another was German-Jewish. His family moved around Texas during the Great Depression in the 1930s. Jones later recalled that "the odds against black people seemed as large as a mountain." K. C. learned to cook early to help his parents and eventually enjoyed doing it.

His family's forced mobility restricted K. C.'s education. Jones first entered school at age seven, having grown up with few books or newspapers. He never learned to read well and withdrew even more. When K. C. was only nine years old, the depression caused his father to abandon the family. Eula the next year took her five children on the train to San Francisco, California. The more supportive Bay City area atmosphere encouraged K. C. to try harder in school. Jones discovered an outlet and a means of expression in recreational sports, starting with tennis. He soon abandoned tennis, however, because he thought it was too expensive to participate in. According to K. C., "Tennis couldn't be a black kid's game then. It was too expensive, and who was going to let you use their court?" Jones then played softball, football, and basketball. At Commerce High School, he made the All-Northern California All-Star basketball team on defense and was chosen an All-Star in football.

K. C. did not consider entering college until "something wonderful happened" during his senior year in high school. "Miss Mildred Smith, my history teacher . . . was a white lady who saw something in this black boy that caused her to pick up the telephone and call Phil Woolpert, the basketball coach at the University of San Francisco. . . . She didn't give up, she made more than one call. She kept after him to give me a scholarship to USF. . . . Her caring changed my life."

During that summer, Jones grew four inches to six foot one inch. At the same time, however, he "completely lost [his] shot." K. C. realized that he "would have to accept [his] new limits as a shooter and change [his] game." Consequently, Jones became "the director—the play-maker." "The team would be the talent. From now on the points I would score wouldn't show up on the box score under my name, but my teammates would score more and play better because of my efforts on the floor. Parts of the game that some more talented players paid less attention to—defense and passing—I would master."

K. C.'s Jesuit San Francisco teachers inspired him more than most of his previous instructors, enabling him to derive a sense of self-esteem from both his studies and sports. As a sophomore in the fall of 1952, Jones began to room with six-foot-nine-inch freshman **Bill Russell**. Russell's shyness and life experiences in the South resembled his own. K. C. recounted, "He and I became inseparable. . . . It was like two minds working in the same direction with the same thoughts and the same goals."

A burst appendix sidelined Jones in 1953–1954, giving him an extra year of eligibility on the basketball team. K. C. and Russell led the San Francisco Dons to NCAA titles in 1955 and 1956. The 1956 win over the University of Iowa made the Dons the first undefeated team to win the NCAA championship. In 102 career games, he scored 901 points and averaged 8.8 points per game.

Jones played on the U.S. basketball team, which won a Gold Medal at the 1956 Melbourne, Australia, Summer Olympic Games. The Boston Celtics (NBA) selected K. C. and traded for Russell, but the former performed two years of military service first. K. C. played football in the U.S. Army as a wide receiver and first joined the Los Angeles Rams National Football League (NFL) club after serving his hitch but soon opted for his preferred sport with the Boston Celtics National Basketball Association (NBA) squad.

As a defensive guard, Jones helped the Celtics win eight consecutive NBA championships. In his nine seasons with the Celtics from 1958 to 1967, K. C. led Boston in assists (2,904) and scored 4,999 career points (7.4-point average.) Russell called him "the man with the square eyes" because of his intensity and focus on television.

After retiring as a player, Jones served as assistant basketball coach at Harvard University in 1967 and 1968 and head coach at Brandeis University from 1968 to 1971. K. C. returned to the NBA as assistant basketball coach with the Los Angeles Lakers in 1971 and 1972. The Lakers won their first 33 games that year and garnered the NBA championship, his ninth. As a coach of the weak San Diego Conquistadors of the American Basketball Association (ABA), Jones eked out a 30–54 record and a playoff spot in 1973–1974. K. C. coached the Capitol (Washington) Bullets from 1973–1974 to 1975–1976, gallantly trying to meld strong-willed players and improve the team's weak defense. The Bullets failed to secure the 1975–1976 Central Division championship for the first time in six years and were eliminated from the playoffs, causing Jones to be fired. K. C. deferred too much to his assistant coaches and players.

Jones was "devastated" and "began to fall apart as a man" when he failed to receive any job offers. K. C.'s stint as assistant coach of the Milwaukee Bucks in the 1976–1977 season and subsequent firing did not help. When opportunities looked bleakest, the Celtics hired him as assistant coach in 1977. After several disappointing seasons blamed partly on head coach Bill Fitch, Red Auerbach, new Celtics president, in 1983 named Jones head coach.

K. C. emphasized the Celtics' defense and "made the game fun again," according to center Robert Parish. Boston won the 1984 NBA title over the Los Angeles Lakers but lost the 1985 crown to the same team. The Celtics captured the 1986 title by vanquishing the Houston Rockets, lost to Los Angeles in 1987, and were eliminated by the Detroit Pistons in 1988 in the Eastern Division finals. Jones retired as Celtics coach at the end of the 1987–1988 season. After serving as Celtics' vice president for basketball operations in 1988–1989, K. C. became an assistant coach of the Seattle SuperSonics in 1989–1990 and head coach the next two seasons. As an NBA head coach, Jones compiled a 522–252 career record. In September 1994, the Detroit Pistons (NBA) hired him as assistant coach.

Jones coached in the NBA All-Star Game in 1975 and 1984 through 1987. His style involved relying democratically on the input of his staff and players rather than dictating decisions. Washington, D.C., papers criticized Jones while he was Bullets coach in the 1970s, alleging "his assistants run the team."

Jones has five children by his first marriage to Beverly Cain, the sister of a fellow basketball player on the 1956 U.S. Olympic squad. Their children are Leslie, K. C., Kelley, Brynna, and Holly. After their divorce, K. C. married his current wife, Ellen, and has one son, Kent. He was elected to the San Francisco Bay Area Basketball Hall of Fame in 1986 and Naismith Memorial Basketball Hall of Fame in 1989. His number, 25, was retired by the Boston Celtics and hangs with the championship banners in Boston Garden.

BIBLIOGRAPHY: Almanac of Famous People (Detroit, MI, 1989), p. 1036; Current Biography Yearbook (1987), pp. 286–289; K. C. Jones with Jack Warner, Rebound (Boston, MA, 1986); David L. Porter, ed., Biographical Dictionary of American Sports: Basketball and Other Indoor Sports (Westport, CT, 1989); Mary Mace Spradling, ed., In Black and White (Detroit, MI, 1980); Who's Who Among Black Americans (Detroit, MI, 1984), p. 817; Who's Who in America, 47th ed. (1992–1993), p. 1744.

                                                              Frederick J. Augustyn, Jr.

MICHAEL JORDAN
(February 17, 1963–   ) ———————————————————— *Basketball*

Michael Jordan, an enormously successful and gifted professional basketball player, ranks among the most popular athletes of all time. Jordan also shocked the sports world in October 1993 when he walked away from professional basketball at the height of his success to make an unlikely bid for stardom in baseball. Michael, the son of James Jordan and Delores Jordan, was born on February 17, 1963, in Brooklyn, New York, where his father was stationed in the military. He grew up in the North Carolina port city of Wilmington, where he played various sports. Jordan, not an immediate success in basketball, was even cut from his high school team, Wilmington Laney. Michael later told writer Bob Greene that this disappointment helped him because "I knew that I didn't want to have that feeling ever again." This incident marked one of the few times Jordan ever came up short on a basketball court. By his senior year of 1981, Michael was considered among the nation's best prep players. He made numerous High School All-American teams and accepted a basketball scholarship offer to play for the University of North Carolina under their legendary coach Dean Smith.

Jordan enjoyed a storybook freshman season, which ended when his last-second jump shot gave the Tar Heels a 63–62 victory over Georgetown University in the 1982 NCAA title game. Michael averaged around 20 points per game for the Tar Heels the next two seasons and gained numerous accolades, including All-America First Team in 1983 and 1984 and Atlantic Coast Conference (ACC) Player of the Year in 1984. The consensus 1984 national Player of the Year, he starred for the United States Gold Medal team at the 1984 Los Angeles, California, Summer Olympics.

The Chicago Bulls made Jordan the number-three pick in the 1984 National Basketball Association (NBA) draft, after he decided not to return to North Carolina for his senior season. Michael's quickness, acrobatic moves, and spectacular leaping abilities were tailor-made for the fast-paced NBA game. He averaged 28 points per game as a rookie and won the NBA Rookie of the Year award. Jordan missed most of the next season with a foot injury but scored 63 points in a playoff loss to the storied Boston Celtics. Michael then led the NBA in scoring in the 1986–1987 season with a 37.1 points per game average, the highest ever for anyone except **Wilt Chamberlain.** He won seven consecutive NBA scoring titles, averaging over 30 points per game in each of these seasons. Jordan scored 50 or more points in an NBA game 35 times, including a 69-point outburst against the Cleveland Cavaliers in 1990. Michael, NBA Most Valuable Player (MVP) in 1988, 1991, and 1992, was voted to the All-NBA First Team every season from 1987 through 1993. He demonstrated the versatility of his game, being named to the NBA All-Defensive First Team 1988 through 1993 and being selected Defensive Player of the Year in 1988.

In the early 1990s, Jordan added team success to individual accomplishments. Michael led the Chicago Bulls to the NBA title in 1991, 1992, and 1993 and was named NBA finals MVP each of those years. He also starred for the so-called Dream Team, the U.S. Gold Medal team of NBA stars in the 1992 Barcelona, Spain, Summer Olympics.

Yet Jordan's allure cannot be summed up simply by statistics. By the end of the 1980s, Michael had become perhaps the best known and most popular athlete in the world. Several lucrative commercial endorsements, most notably a long-running association with the Nike Shoe company, made him a household name across the world. Countless children wore "Air Jordan" shoes, ate Jordan's cereal, drank his sport drink, wore his clothes, and vowed to "be like Mike." Some estimates put Jordan's annual income in the $50 million range by the early 1990s. Michael's appearance marked an event in every NBA city. *Sports Illustrated* named Jordan Sportsman of the Year in 1991, calling him "the consummate player and the ultimate showman" and adding that he was "unquestionably the most famous athlete on the planet and one of its most famous citizens of any kind." Michael married Juanita Vanoy in 1989 and has three children, Jeffrey, Marcus, and Jasmine.

Almost inevitably a backlash occurred. Much of it focused on Jordan's fondness for high-stakes gambling, particularly on the golf course. Yet NBA officials exonerated Michael of wrongdoing, and the controversies did little to diminish his popularity. After leading the Bulls to the 1993 NBA title, his career appeared to reach its zenith.

This all changed in July 1993, when the body of James Jordan was found in South Carolina, the victim of an apparent murder days earlier on a rural North Carolina highway. Michael resented unfounded media attempts to link the murder with his gambling activities. On October 6, 1993, he shocked the sports world by announcing his retirement from professional basketball. "I've reached the pinnacle," Jordan declared. "I have nothing more to prove in basketball." Michael denied that his father's death had anything to do with his retirement, but many observers speculated otherwise. He then pulled his second big surprise, announcing his goal of trying to make the major leagues as a baseball player. He had not played baseball since high school. Some fans applauded his vision and courage, while others saw his quest as hopeless. Jordan spent the 1994 season with the Class AA Birmingham Barons (SL), a farm team of the Chicago White Sox American League (AL) club. Michael batted only .202 and remained controversial, blasting the Bulls and several of his teammates in interviews. In the final scheduled basketball game in Chicago Stadium, he scored 52 points to help the White team to a 187–150 victory over Scottie Pippen's Red team in a September 1994 exhibition.

Jordan played in the Arizona Instructional League following the 1994 baseball season. Jordan retired from professional baseball in March 1995 and returned to the Chicago Bulls later that month. Michael quickly regained his previous form, scoring the winning basket against the Atlanta Hawks in his fourth game back and scoring 55 points against the New York Knicks at Madison Square Garden the next game. Through 1994–1995, he has scored 21,998 career points for a 32.3 point average, highest in NBA history, and ranks fifth in steals with 1,845.

BIBLIOGRAPHY: Bob Greene, *Hang Time: Days and Dreams with Michael Jordan* (New York, 1992); David Halberstam, "A Hero for the Wired World," *Sports Illustrated* 75 (December 23, 1991), pp. 76–81; Walter Iooss and Mark Vancil, *Rare Air: Michael on Michael* (San Francisco, CA, 1993); Curry Kirkpatrick, "The Unlikeliest Homeboy," *Sports Illustrated* 75 (December 23, 1991), pp. 70–75; Mitchell Krugel, *Jordan: The Man, His Words, and His Life* (New York, 1994); Jack McCallum, "Alone on the Mountaintop," *Sports Illustrated* 75 (December 23, 1991), pp. 64–69; Gene L. Martin, *Michael Jordan: Gentleman Superstar* (Greensboro, NC, 1987); Jim Naughton, *Taking to the Air: The Rise of Michael Jordan* (New York, 1992); Sam Smith, *The Jordan Rules* (New York, 1992).

Jim L. Sumner

JACKIE JOYNER-KERSEE
(March 3, 1962–) ——————————————————————— *Track and Field*

Since the late 1980s, Jackie Joyner-Kersee has led the world in the heptathlon, a grueling seven-event track and field competition spanning two days. Jackie has won two Olympic titles and two World Championships, setting four world records in the event. Jacqueline Joyner-Kersee, the second of four children of Alfred Joyner and Mary Joyner, was born on March 3, 1962, in East St. Louis, Illinois. Her grandmother, Ollie Mae Johnson, insisted that she be named Jacqueline after the First Lady Jacqueline Kennedy because she believed that someday the child would "be the first lady of something." Jackie's parents, a young, hard-working couple, struggled against great economic hardships. Alfred Joyner, who starred as a football player and track and field athlete at Lincoln High School, abandoned his education and athletic aspirations after the birth of his son, Alfred, Jr., in 1960. Alfred held several odd jobs before gaining permanent employment as a railroad switchman in Springfield, Illinois, in 1962. Mary, who worked as a nurse's assistant, encouraged her children to excel in school because she saw education as the "way out" of the ghetto.

Academic and athletic achievement provided Joyner the "way out" of East St. Louis. At age 9, Jackie joined the East St. Louis Railers Track Club. Nino Fennoy, the Railers' coach, recognized that Jackie possessed the physical talent to succeed in track and field and also the "mental and spiritual attributes to weather the ups and downs" that accompany the sport. In 1976, at age 14, Joyner won the first of four consecutive National Junior Olympic titles in the five-event pentathlon. Jackie led Lincoln High School to three Illinois State Track and Field titles and, as a senior in 1980, set a State high school record of 20 feet 7½ inches in the long jump. She also captured the long jump in the 1980 Track Athletic Congress (TAC) Junior championships and placed eighth in the long jump in the 1980 Olympic Trials. Joyner improved her long jump best by over 2 inches in the Olympic Trials and excelled as a forward on the basketball team, leading Lincoln High School to the State championship in 1980. The same year, Jackie graduated in the top 10 percent of her class and received a basketball scholarship to the University of California at Los Angeles (UCLA). A four-time basketball team starter, she joined the top 10 Lady Bruins in assists, rebounding, and scoring.

In 1981, Joyner's mother died suddenly from meningitis at age 36. The death marked a turning point in Jackie's life, as she gained "a clearer sense of reality" and recognized that her mother's determination had passed on to her. Joyner then became the protégé of Robert Kersee, an assistant track and field coach at UCLA, who persuaded her to specialize in the heptathlon. After totaling Jackie's best performances in the heptathlon events, Kersee showed her that she was only 400 points shy of Jane Frederick's national record. The 100-meter hurdles, an event requiring more technique than "raw speed," proved Joyner's only weakness. In 1982, Jackie won the first of two NCAA and first of five TAC titles in the heptathlon. Two years later, she captured the heptathlon in the Olympic Trials and established an American record of 6,520 points. In the 1984 Summer Olympic Games at Los Angeles, California, Joyner won the Silver Medal and missed the Gold Medal by 5 points. Jackie also placed fifth in the long jump, while her brother Al won the triple jump. Although long jumping 23 feet 9 inches for an American record the following year, she lost her national standard in the heptathlon to a resurgent Frederick with 6,803 points.

Track and Field News ranked Joyner third in the heptathlon in 1985. Her rival Frederick, however, considered Jackie the leader of a "new generation" of heptathletes, who possessed "real" rather than "forced talent" for the event. Jackie, who graduated from UCLA in 1985, married Bob Kersee the following year. The marriage transformed her into a global force in the heptathlon, as she reclaimed the American record with a 6,841-point performance in Gotzis, Austria, and then established a world record of 7,148 points in the Goodwill Games at Moscow, Russia. Upon becoming the first American woman to hold a world record in a multievent, Joyner-Kersee remarked that "I've paid my dues. I knew good things would come my way because I have been humble and patient, waiting for this to happen." At Houston, Texas, 27 days later, Jackie surpassed her world record by 10 points in the National Olympic Festival. For her 1986 accomplishments, she was named Athlete of the Year by *Track and Field News* and Sportswoman of the Year by the U.S. Olympic Committee. Her other awards included the Jesse Owens Memorial Award as the nation's top track and field athlete and Sullivan Award as the nation's premier amateur athlete.

In 1987, Joyner-Kersee soared to new heights in the long jump and heptathlon. After winning both events at the TAC championships, Jackie captured the long jump in the Pan-American Games at Indianapolis, Indiana. Her performance equaled the world record of 24 feet 5½ inches, held by East Germany's Heike Drechsler-Daute. She then became the first woman in 22 years to hold an individual and multievent world record concurrently. In the 1987 World Championships at Rome, Italy, Joyner-Kersee captured both the long jump and heptathlon and became the first woman to capture both an individual and multievent in either an Olympic or World Championship setting. The same feat had been accomplished by Harold Osborn, who won Olympic titles in the high jump and decathlon in 1924. "Those calling her America's greatest athlete since Jim Thorpe," wrote David Woods of *The Sporting News*, "might not be exaggerating."

Since 1988, Jackie has remained the world's leader in the heptathlon. She tallied 7,215 points for a world record at the 1988 U.S. Olympic Trials and exceeded that total with 7,291 points in the Summer Olympic Games at Seoul, South Korea. Joyner-Kersee also earned the Gold Medal in the long jump but lost the world record to Russia's Galina Chistyakova. Although prevailing in the long jump in the 1991 World Championships to Tokyo, Japan, Jackie failed to complete the heptathlon because of an injury sustained in the 200 meters. She successfully defended her heptathlon title in the 1992 Summer Olympic Games at Barcelona, Spain, but finished third in the long jump. In the 1993 World Championships at Stuttgart, Germany, Joyner-Kersee began the 800 meters, the final event of the heptathlon, 7 points behind Germany's Sabine Braun, the defending world champion. Jackie, who described the experience as her "greatest test of strength and character," defeated Braun by three seconds in the 800 meters and won the World Championship with 6,837 total points. She remarked afterward, "I will enjoy this one most of all." In 1994, Joyner-Kersee finished first in both the 100-meter hurdles and the long jump at the USA Track and Field Outdoor Championships in Knoxville, Tennessee. The 1994 St. Petersburg, Russia, Goodwill Games featured Jackie taking the heptathlon with 6,606 points. She also won the long jump at the International Amateur Athletic Federation (IAAF) Mobil Grand Prix final in Paris, France, and placed first in the Grand Prix overall standings, earning $130,000.

In February 1995, Joyner-Kersee set an American record in the 50-meter hurdles at the inaugural Reno, Nevada, Air Indoor Track & Field Games. Jackie covered the 50-meter hurdle distance in just 6.67 seconds and later won the long jump. The following month, she leaped 22 feet ¾ inches to capture the long jump title at the USA/Mobil Indoor Track and Field Championships at Atlanta, Georgia. Joyner-Kersee finished first in both the 60-meter hurdles and long jump and third overall in the 1995 Grand Prix Indoor Final Standings. Jackie overcame asthma and a sore hamstring muscle to capture the heptathlon with 6,375 points and the long jump with a wind-aided leap of 22 feet 7 inches at the USATF Outdoor Championships at Sacramento, California, in June 1995. She looks forward to competing in the 1996 Summer Olympic Games at Atlanta, Georgia, so that she can end her "career on American soil."

BIBLIOGRAPHY: Neil Cohen, *Jackie Joyner-Kersee* (New York, 1992); *Current Biography Yearbook* (1987), pp. 293–296; Michael D. Davis, *Black American Women in Olympic Track and Field: A Complete Illustrated Reference* (Jefferson, NC, 1992); Jon

Hendershott, "Jackie Joyner-Kersee," *Track and Field News* 43 (September 1990), pp. 38–39; Jon Hendershott, "JJK Down, Braun Up," *Track and Field News* 44 (November 1991), p. 59; Ruth Laney, "Jackie in Another League," *Track and Field News* 41 (November 1988), p. 75; Bill Mallon and James Dunaway, "Jackie Joyner-Kersee," *USTAF Bio Data Sheet* (1992); David L. Porter, ed., *Biographical Dictionary of American Sports: Outdoor Sports* (Westport, CT, 1988); Roberto L. Quercetani, *Athletics: A History of Modern Track and Field Athletics (1860–1990)* (Milan, Italy, 1990); David Wallechinsky, *The Complete Book of the Olympics*, rev. ed. (New York, 1988).

Adam R. Hornbuckle

DICK LANE
(April 16, 1928–) ————————————————————————— *Football*

Dick "Night Train" Lane, one of professional football's all-time top corner-backs, played 14 National Football League (NFL) seasons from 1952 to 1965 with the Los Angeles Rams, Chicago Cardinals, and Detroit Lions and was elected to the Pro Football Hall of Fame in 1974. Richard Lane was born on April 16, 1928, in Austin, Texas, the son of Will Lane and Johanie Mae King. His natural mother left him when an infant. He was brought up by a foster mother, Mrs. Ella Lane, whom he called "Mama Ella." His foster mother, a widow, already had four children, meaning that Dick battled poverty. Mama Ella depended entirely on the income she received for doing laundry in her home and faced an intense struggle to make ends meet.

Lane's next battle involved competing in sports because Mama Ella considered his frame too fragile to participate in sports. As Dick put it, "Mama Ella felt that I was too small and that every bone in my body would be crushed." After attending Keating Junior High School in Austin, he arrived at Anderson High School. Although only a light 130 to 135 pounds, Lane lettered two of the three years he played football and basketball under coach W. E. Pigford. The struggle against poverty persisted, forcing Dick to perform odd jobs. He recalled, "At various times, I was a shoe shine boy, a stock boy and an extra waiter in hotels. I did this after football and basketball practice and I came home in the wee hours of the night to do my homework. It was tough, real tough, at the time—but it bolstered me for the obstacles that were to come."

Lane's foster mother suffered serious illness shortly after he finished high school. Dick moved to Scottsbluff, Nebraska, where his natural mother was living. In 1947, he enrolled at Scottsbluff Junior College (now Western Nebraska Community College) and, as a 165-pound freshman, starred as an offensive end–defensive back in football and captained the basketball team. Although Lane received some mention as a Junior College football All-America, difficulties with his mother caused him to quit school and join the U.S. Army in 1948. Corporal Lane, a Special Services assistant, played football the next four years with Fort Ord, California. In 1951 as an offensive end,

Dick caught 18 touchdown passes. Discharged in 1952 and with his wife, Geraldine, pregnant, Dick worked in a California aircraft factory and played basketball for the company team at night.

During his search for another job, the now 175- to 180-pound Lane walked into the nearby Los Angeles Rams (NFL) office with his scrapbook wrapped in brown paper and convinced coach Joe Stydahar and two of his assistants, Hampton Pool and Red Hickey, to sign him to a $4,500 contract. The Rams initially used Dick as offensive end, but the unfamiliar terminology confused him. With future Hall of Famers Tom Fears and "Crazylegs" Hirsch firmly entrenched in starting jobs, his chances did not look good. After switching to defense, he seemed more comfortable. During scrimmages, he made some spectacular plays. Stydahar once ran out on the field and yelled, "Great work, kid. Great work. Keep it up." His brief tenure with the offensive unit, however, spawned his marvelous nickname. Lane consulted Fears frequently in his dormitory room, where the star pass-catcher liked to play Buddy Morrow's rendition of "Night Train" on his phonograph. When teammate Ben Sheets stopped by Fears's room, Dick often was there with "Night Train" playing in the background. "Hey," said Sheets one day, "there's Night Train." The nickname stuck, although some teammates later shortened it to just "Train."

Blessed with outstanding speed, exceptional agility, excellent reflex action, and a fierce determination to win, Lane burst into NFL stardom in his 1952 rookie season. Dick intercepted 14 passes in a 12-game schedule, still the season record. Two of his thefts were returned for touchdowns, an 80 yarder against the Green Bay Packers and a 42 yarder against the Pittsburgh Steelers. His 298 interception return yards that season ranks third best in the all-time NFL list. In 1954, Los Angeles traded him to the Chicago Cardinals (NFL), where he again led the NFL in interceptions with 10.

Lane also quickly proved a violent open-field tackler, particularly well known for his deadly necktie tackles. Dick always strongly denied, however, playing the game dirty. "Listen, it's tough enough playing out there without being told exactly where you have to grab a man and how," he told a reporter. Lane eventually more frequently took chances on the field, even though sometimes his tactics backfired. "Sure, Dick gets burned once in a while," Joe Schmidt, the Detroit Lions great middle linebacker, once admitted. "But he comes up with the big play a lot of times, too. I'd say, percentage-wise, he's way ahead of the game." Hugh Devore, who coached Green Bay and the Philadelphia Eagles, called Lane "one of the best." Los Angeles Rams and Washington Redskins coach George Allen remarked, "He had guts and when he went for the ball he usually got it. He played on instinct and he had a feel for the play. Somehow he always seemed to get good position on the receiver." Vince Lombardi, legendary Green Bay Packers coach, once instructed quarterback Bart Starr, "Don't throw anywhere near him. He's the best there is."

Lane, a sharp dresser and colorful personality, was well liked by his teammates but gained the reputation, deserved or not, of being a troublemaker.

Dick's unhappiness with Hampton Pool in Los Angeles and later with Pop Ivy of the Chicago Cardinals led to trades. The six-foot-two-inch, 210-pound Lane's first four years as a Detroit Lion from 1960 to 1963 marked the pinnacle of his career. Dick had earned All-NFL acclaim only in 1956 while with the Cardinals but was named All-NFL cornerback four straight years from 1960 through 1963. A majority of his six Pro Bowl appearances came with the Lions. Lane's finest moment may have come in the first Playoff Bowl game in Miami, Florida, after the 1960 season. Dick blocked an extra point try near the end of the game, giving the Lions a 17–16 victory over the Cleveland Browns. Players themselves most talked about the Pro Bowl game the following year in Los Angeles. Lane scored the first touchdown of the game with a 42-yard interception after an attack of appendicitis the night before. Two days later, Dick's appendix was removed.

In Detroit, Lane's marital difficulties resulted in a divorce from his wife, Geraldine. Dick married blues singer Dinah Washington on July 2, 1963, but she died six months later. He then married Mary Opal Cowser, a school-teacher, and divorced her on September 4, 1964. Dick has two sons, one each by his first and third marriages.

Injuries reduced Lane to a part-time player in his final 1964 and 1965 NFL campaigns. Dick's 68 career interceptions rank him third in NFL history behind Paul Krause and **Emlen Tunnell,** while his 1,207 career interception return yards remain second on the all-time list. In 1969, he was named the NFL's all-time top cornerback by the Pro Football Hall of Fame. He also was selected to the AFL-NFL 1960–1984 All-Star Team and the All-Time NFL Team in 1994.

The Lions subsequently employed Lane for the next several years as special staff assistant. Dick complained of his lack of opportunity for a position of any real authority and desired to coach. He, therefore, ended his 12-year association with the Lions in 1972 to become an assistant football coach at Southern University in Baton Rouge, Louisiana. Lane accepted a similar post at Central State University in Wilberforce, Ohio, in 1973 and was unanimously elected to the Pro Football Hall of Fame in 1974. Dick, citing his salary cuts in taking the Southern and Central State positions, his failure to secure an NFL coaching post, and his previous business failures in Chicago, Illinois, and Detroit, Michigan, joined the organization of comedian and TV star Redd Foxx in Los Angeles, California. In 1975, he was appointed executive director of Detroit's Police Athletic League and held that position until his retirement in 1993.

BIBLIOGRAPHY: George Allen with Ben Olan, *Pro Football's 100 Greatest Players* (Indianapolis, IN, 1982); Dave Anderson, *Great Defensive Players of the NFL* (New York, 1967); Jerry Green, *Detroit Lions* (New York and London, 1973); Chuck Klonke, Larry Paladino, and Richard L. Shook, *Lions Pride: 60 Years of Detroit Lions Football* (Dallas, TX, 1993); Richard "Night Train" Lane file, Pro Football Hall of Fame Library, Canton, OH; *The Lincoln Library of Sports Champions*, vol. 7 (Columbus, OH, 1974); David S. Neft et al., eds., *The Football Encyclopedia*, 2nd ed. (New York, 1994); David L. Porter, ed., *Biographical Dictionary of American Sports: Football* (Westport, CT,

1987); Don R. Smith, *Pro Football Hall of Fame All-Time Greats* (New York, 1988); George Sullivan, *Pro Football A to Z* (New York, 1975).

Jack C. Braun

BOB LANIER
(September 10, 1948–   ) —————————————————————— *Basketball*

Bob Lanier, famed for his size 19-inch shoes, spent 14 years in the National Basketball Association (NBA) with the Detroit Pistons and Milwaukee Bucks. Robert Jerry Lanier, Jr., was born September 10, 1948, in Buffalo, New York, the son of Robert Lanier and Nannette Lanier. The elder Lanier remained his best friend and mentor while growing up. Bob, Jr., developed insecurity during his teenage years because he grew to six foot eight inches by age 14. He wore men's clothes and believed people always stared at him. "Pops in his way always tried to make things easier for me," Lanier recalled. "He joked about my size and he was the only one who could make me laugh about how big I was." Bob did not make his high school basketball team until his junior year but played well enough to earn a hoop scholarship to St. Bonaventure University in New York.

Since NCAA rules did not allow freshman participation, Lanier's first year with the basketball team came as a sophomore. The 6-foot-11-inch 265-pounder quickly established himself as a team leader, guiding the Bonnies to a 23–2 win-loss record and the school's second NCAA tournament appearance. Bob, a consensus All-America Second Team, tallied 26.2 points and 15.6 rebounds per game. As a junior, he improved his performance to 27.2 points and 15.5 rebounds per game, but St. Bonaventure slipped to a 17–7 record and missed a tournament bid.

During Lanier's junior year at St. Bonaventure, the New Jersey Nets of the American Basketball Association (ABA) offered him $1.2 million to leave school. Bob told his father. After the initial surprise, the elder Lanier advised his son, "Stay in college and get your degree. I know you're going to be a superstar, but I don't want you to be a dumb superstar." Bob heeded his father's advice and earned his bachelor of science degree in business administration.

As a senior, Lanier recorded his best basketball season. The unanimous All-America selection averaged 29 points and 16 rebounds per game. St. Bonaventure enjoyed its best mark in school hoop history, posting a 25–1 record and returning to the NCAA tournament. Bob scored 28 points in the first-round game against Davidson College and paced the Bonnies over North Carolina State University in the second round. St. Bonaventure's only blemish of the regular season had come in a 2-point loss to Villanova University. The Bonnies avenged that loss with a 97–74 win over Villanova in the third round. Lanier scored 18 points against Villanova before suffering a season-ending knee injury. St. Bonaventure lost in the 1970 NCAA semi-finals to the University of Jacksonville, 91–83, and to New Mexico State University, 79–73, in the contest for third place without Bob's services. During his college career, he scored 2,067 points, hauled down 1,180 rebounds, and averaged 27.5 points and 15.7 rebounds per game.

Although Lanier's knee injury required surgery, the Detroit Pistons made Bob the first selection of the 1970 NBA draft. The Pistons struggled to one of the NBA's worst records in 1969–1970 with a lowly 31–51 record and had not boasted a winning record since 1956, as the Fort Wayne Zollner Pistons. With Lanier, Detroit showed instant improvement with a 45–37 record. Bob averaged 15.6 points and 8.1 rebounds per game and played in all 82 games that season. At year's end, he made one of the NBA's greatest All-Rookie squads with Dave Cowens, Pete Maravich, Calvin Murphy, and Geoff Petrie.

As a second-year player, Lanier played an even more important role for the Pistons after the loss of star guard Dave Bing for half the season. Bob's averages skyrocketed to 25.7 points per game, eighth best in the NBA, and 14.2 rebounds per game, which ranked him ninth in the NBA. He also received his first All-Star Game selection. Detroit, however, reverted to its losing ways, compiling a 26–56 record for two coaches. Coach Bill Van Breda Kolff resigned after 12 games and was replaced by Earl Lloyd. Four other Pistons coaches followed, saddling Lanier with a reputation for getting coaches fired.

Detroit had hoped to secure a franchise player when they drafted Lanier. "I was their big hope, and they wanted me to start leading them to a championship," said Bob. Although Lanier led the Pistons in scoring and rebounding and played in the All-Star Game seven of his first nine seasons, Detroit never won an NBA title. The Pistons made the playoffs four of Bob's nine seasons but won only one of five playoff series. Lanier was often criticized for Detroit's failures. "I understand that," Bob countered, "but the game is played with five men."

In February 1980, Detroit traded Lanier to the Milwaukee Bucks for Kurt Benson. The trade finally gave Bob a chance to play with a contender. The Bucks, a mediocre 29–27 when Lanier joined the team, won 20 of their final 26 games with Bob. The Bucks did not capture an NBA title with Lanier but made the playoffs each of his five seasons there and captured two Eastern Conference championships. "He does nothing but good things for the Bucks," Boston Celtics star Larry Bird commented in 1981. "Kareem's the best player in the league, but Lanier is second."

Lanier retired after the 1983–1984 season. During 14 NBA campaigns, Bob played in 959 games, logged over 32,000 minutes, and only fouled out 49 times. He ranks nineteenth on the NBA career scoring list with 19,248 points (20.1 points per game average) and grabbed 9,698 rebounds (10.1 per game average). Lanier made the NBA All-Star team eight times, seven times with Detroit and once with Milwaukee. Bob was named All-Star MVP for his performance in the 1974 game, when he scored 12 of his 24 points in the fourth quarter to lead the Western Conference to a 134–123 triumph over the Eastern Conference.

In 1993, Lanier was named to the Naismith Memorial Basketball Hall of Fame. Bob worked as a color commentator for NBA radio, until joining the Golden State Warriors as an assistant coach in 1994. In February 1995, Bob replaced Don Nelson as head coach of the Golden State Warriors. Golden State finished with a 12–25 mark under Lanier in 1995. He and his wife Shirley have four children.

BIBLIOGRAPHY: Ira Berkow, "The Bucks Start Here," *Sport* 72 (February 1981), pp. 28–33; "Hawkins, Lanier, Head Hall of Fame Inductees," *Jet* 81 (February 24, 1992), p. 48; Barry McDermott, "Big Boosts from Big Bob," *Sports Illustrated* 52 (April 7, 1980), pp. 86ff; Ronald L. Mendell, *Who's Who in Basketball* (New Rochelle, NY, 1973); *New York Times*, April 6, 1981; *Official NCAA Final Four, Record and Fact Book* (Overland Park, KS, 1994).

Brian L. Laughlin

BUCK LEONARD
(September 8, 1907–   ) _____ *Baseball*

Buck Leonard, among the greatest professional baseball players of all time, never played an inning of major league baseball. Leonard played when racial segregation restricted African Americans to the Negro Leagues. Yet Buck persevered, excelled, and eventually became recognized as a standout first baseman fully equal to Lou Gehrig, Jimmie Foxx, George Sisler, and other top major league first basemen of his era. Walter Fenner Leonard was born on September 8, 1907, in the eastern North Carolina city of Rocky Mount, the oldest of six children of John Leonard and Emma Leonard. His father worked for the Atlantic Coast Line Railroad, one of Rocky Mount's largest employers, and died when Buck was only 11 years old. Leonard tried to work odd jobs, such as delivering papers, and continue attending school. Buck could not make enough money this way to help support his family and thus dropped out of school at age 14. He never returned, although obtained his high school degree by correspondence after completion of his playing days. Leonard handled various jobs in Rocky Mount, but mostly repaired air brakes for the railroad.

On the side, Buck played baseball for local African-American teams, the Black Swans and the Elks. In 1933, he lost his job with the railroad, as the Great Depression forced layoffs. Since times were hard, the almost-26-year-old Leonard wanted to see if he could make a living playing baseball full-time. Buck played briefly for the Portsmouth, Virginia, Firefighters before joining the Baltimore Stars, coached by Ben Taylor, one of the best-known Negro National League (NNL) managers. The Stars folded during the 1933 season, and he completed the campaign with the Brooklyn Giants.

Leonard's misfortune changed dramatically in 1934, when he signed with the Homestead Grays of Pittsburgh, one of the best NNL clubs. Hard-hitting

Buck quickly became a star. He combined with standout catcher **Josh Gibson**, another powerful slugger, to lead the best team in Negro Leagues history. Leonard and Gibson, dubbed the "Thunder Twins," favorably compared to the New York Yankees American League (AL) duo of outfielder "Babe" Ruth and first baseman Lou Gehrig. Buck patterned his game after that of the Yankee first baseman, being nicknamed the "black Lou Gehrig." They led Homestead to nine consecutive NNL pennants from 1937 through 1945 and also the 1948 title. During this period, Leonard played in 12 All-Star Games and excelled in numerous off-season unofficial contests played between African-American players and white major leaguers.

The solidly built 5-foot-10-inch 185-pounder hit both for average and power. Trying to pitch a fastball past Leonard resembled trying to sneak a sunrise by a rooster. Although there are gaps in NNL statistics, Buck consistently batted over .300. Some accounts credit him with a lifetime .340 batting average, although recent works list him with a .324 lifetime average. His best batting averages included .383 in 1940, .375 in 1945, .410 in 1947, and .395 in 1948. Leonard, more than just a hitter, worked hard on his fielding. Observers compared Buck favorably to George Sisler, the premier defensive major league first baseman.

Leonard was one of several African-American players interviewed by Washington Senators (AL) owner Clark Griffith in the early 1940s concerning playing in the major leagues. But nothing further transpired. By the time major league baseball reintegrated in 1947, Buck already was too old. He stayed with the Grays until the team folded in 1950. Leonard played in Mexico through 1955 and in several games for the Portsmouth, Virginia, club, of the Piedmont League in 1953. After retiring from baseball, Buck returned to Rocky Mount. He worked there for a funeral home, served as a truant officer in the local school system, and operated a real estate business. In the early 1960s, Leonard was employed as vice president of the Rocky Mount team in the Carolina League. Buck married Sarah Wroten, a schoolteacher, in 1937. She died in 1966. They did not have any children.

Leonard and other Negro Leagues stars began to gain long-deserved recognition in the 1970s. Buck was elected to the National Baseball Hall of Fame in 1972, the same year as former teammate Gibson, and the North Carolina Sports Hall of Fame in 1974. He served as honorary captain of the National League All-Stars in 1994, when that game was held in Pittsburgh, Pennsylvania.

Despite being denied the chance to play major league baseball, Leonard lacks bitterness. Buck knew he possessed enough skills to play for anybody but figured the times just were not right. Besides, he kept too busy playing baseball to protest. Leonard recently told an Associated Press writer, "There was a lot of racism. Sometimes it was frustrating, but I think it made us play better other times. We couldn't play with whites back then. So we just went out and played ball and tried to show everyone that we were just as good as the whites." By all accounts, he was more than successful.

BIBLIOGRAPHY: A. J. Carr, "At Age 40, Leonard Belted 42 HR's," *The Sporting News*, March 4, 1972; A. J. Carr, "Buck Leonard, Lou Gehrig of Black Baseball," *The Sporting News*, March 4, 1972; Dick Clark and Larry Lester, eds., *The Negro Leagues Book* (Cleveland, OH, 1994); Phil Dixon and Patrick Hanigan, *The Negro Baseball Leagues: A Photographic History, 1867–1955* (Mattituck, NY, 1992); John Holway, *Voices from the Great Black Baseball Leagues* (New York, 1975); John Holway, *Josh and Satch: The Life and Times of Josh Gibson and Satchel Paige* (Westport, CT, 1991); Robert W. Peterson, *Only the Ball Was White* (Englewood Cliffs, NJ, 1970); James A. Riley, *The Biographical Encyclopedia of the Negro Baseball Leagues* (New York, 1994); Rob Ruck, *Sandlot Seasons: Black Sport in Pittsburgh* (Urbana, IL, 1987).

Jim L. Sumner

SUGAR RAY LEONARD
(May 17, 1956–) ——————————————————————— *Boxing*

Sugar Ray Leonard, one of the most talented boxers of his generation, won world titles in five different weight divisions and was largely responsible for the resurgence in boxing's popularity in the early 1980s. The fifth of seven children of Gertha Leonard, a nurse, and Cicero Leonard, a supermarket manager, Ray Charles Leonard was born on May 17, 1956, in Wilmington, South Carolina, and spent much of his childhood in Palmer Park, Maryland. Ray did not excel at athletics until his brother Roger goaded him into visiting a local gym. "He was sitting at home reading comic books all day," recalled Roger. Leonard quickly excelled in boxing and used the sport as an escape from the crime and violence that engulfed his neighborhood. "He never did talk too much," his mother recalled. "But I never had any problems with him. I never had to go to school once because of him."

With coaching from Dave Jacobs and Janks Morton, Leonard won the 1973 National Golden Gloves championship in the 132-pound division, the 1974 Amateur Athletic Union (AAU) title, and the 1975 Pan-American Games Gold Medal. Ray, well schooled in ring movement and counterpunching, combined these skills with blazing hand speed to dazzle his overmatched opponents. His amateur career culminated with a Gold Medal performance in the light welterweight division at the Montreal, Canada, Summer Olympic Games in 1976. He announced his retirement after the Olympics but was persuaded by Mike Trainer, a financial adviser, to box professionally to support his wife Juanita and young son, Ray, Jr. In his first professional bout, Leonard, dubbed "Sugar Ray" by the media, won a six-round decision over Luis Vega on February 5, 1977, in Baltimore, Maryland. Ray was paid $40,000 for his initial fight, a remarkable sum for a professional debut.

Leonard's ring savvy, good looks, and buoyant personality endeared him to television sports audiences, as he remained much in demand to box on network television. Ray, guided by Mike Trainer, refused to become attached to a single promoter or network. His free agent status consequently allowed him to quickly move from one lucrative deal to another. He enjoyed continuing success in the professional ranks against Pete Ranzany, Andy Price, Marcus Geraldo, and other worthy foes. These victories propelled him into a title fight versus Wilfred Benitez, who held the World Boxing Council (WBC) version of the world welterweight championship. In a memorable contest at Las Vegas, Nevada, Leonard and Benitez engaged in a classic tactical battle on November 30, 1979. Ray won by a 15-round technical knockout. "Fighting Benitez was like looking in a mirror," he stated after the bout. "Both of us anticipated the other's moves."

After knocking out England's Davey "Boy" Green in his first title defense, Leonard lost his crown to Panamanian Roberto Duran by decision at Montreal, Canada, on June 20, 1980. Ray fought Duran's brawling type of bout instead of relying on his masterful boxing skills. "Duran can't change his style, but I can," he boasted before their highly publicized rematch in New Orleans, Louisiana, on November 25, 1980. In the fight, Leonard totally baffled the undertrained Duran with his ring movement this time. In an abrupt ending, Duran quit in round eight and defaulted the title to Ray.

In June 1981, Leonard added the World Boxing Association (WBA) junior middleweight title by stopping Uganda's Ayub Kalule. On September 16, 1981, Ray knocked out WBA welterweight champion **Thomas Hearns** at Las Vegas in the fourteenth round in one of the best bouts of the 1980s. Now recognized as the undisputed welterweight champion, he easily knocked out unheralded Bruce Finch at Reno, Nevada, on February 15, 1982. During training for a welterweight title defense against Roger Stafford in Buffalo, New York, Leonard complained of vision problems in his left eye. Doctors diagnosed Ray as having a detached retina, forcing him to retire temporarily from the sport in 1982.

Leonard returned to the ring on May 11, 1984 and scored an unimpressive knockout victory over Kevin Howard but then retired once again. Missing the spotlight, Ray reemerged to challenge reigning world middleweight champion **Marvin Hagler** for the latter's title on April 6, 1987. Despite the 35-month layoff, he surprised the boxing world by defeating the fearsome Hagler in a 12-round decision at Las Vegas. Although some journalists thought that Hagler had done enough to retain his title, every major boxing publication supported the judges' decision. This bout marked the final great highlight of Leonard's ring career, although a 1988 victory over Canada's Donny Lalonde in Las Vegas enabled him to capture both the WBC super middleweight and light heavyweight titles. A controversial draw with Hearns in a rematch at Las Vegas, coupled with a defeat in New York City to rising star Terry Norris, prompted Ray to retire permanently.

Leonard, who earned more than $20 million in purses, compiled a sparkling record of 36 wins (25 knockouts), two losses, and one draw. His honors included being voted *The Ring*'s Fighter of the Year three times (1979, 1981, 1987) and *Sports Illustrated*'s Sportsman of the Year in 1981. The U.S. Olympic Hall of Fame elected him in 1985. Ray has remained involved in boxing as a television analyst and manager of light heavyweight prospect Andrew Maynard. In 1994, *Sports Illustrated* ranked him thirty-second on its "40 for the Ages List."

BIBLIOGRAPHY: Robert Cassidy, "Terry Norris Retires Sugar Ray Leonard," *KO Magazine* (June 1991), pp. 28–31; Nigel Collins, "Sugar Ray . . . Still in Style," *The Ring* 66 (August 1987), pp. 28–32; William Nack, "Sugar Sure Is Sweet," *Sports Illustrated* 51 (November 26, 1979), pp. 92–106; William Nack, "On Top of the World," *Sports Illustrated* 51 (December 10, 1979), pp. 26–29; Bert Randolph Sugar, "The Leonard-Duran Fight Explained," *The Ring* 60 (February 1981), pp. 23–27; Bert Randolph Sugar, "The Night Leonard Hearned the Title 'Sugar Ray,'" *The Ring* 60 (November 1981), pp. 18–25.

John Robertson

CARL LEWIS
(July 1, 1961–) _____ *Track and Field*

Carl Lewis, one of track and field's greatest performers, dominated the sprints and the long jump during the 1980s and early 1990s. Frederick Carlton Lewis, the third of four children of William Lewis and Evelyn (Lawler) Lewis, was born on July 1, 1961, in Birmingham, Alabama. His parents starred athletically at Alabama's Tuskegee Institute. His father performed as a football pass receiver and track and field sprinter, while his mother, whom Carl described as the "track star of the couple," finished sixth in the 80-meter hurdles in the 1951 Pan-American Games and planned to represent the United States in 1952 Olympic Summer Games until an injury dashed her hopes. After graduating from Tuskegee, Carl's parents taught in Montgomery, Alabama.

In 1963, the Lewis family moved to Willingboro, New Jersey, near Philadelphia, Pennsylvania, to take advantage of greater social and economic opportunities. Carl's father taught social studies at John F. Kennedy High School, while his mother instructed physical education at Willingboro High School. Evelyn hoped to form a girls' track and field team at Willingboro, but the school's principal did not support her idea. "My mother wanted young girls to have the same opportunities she had in sports," explained Carl, "so she and my father established the Willingboro Track Club." Carl and his sister Carol began competing for their parents' track club at ages seven and six, respectively. Carl acknowledged that Carol, who also became a world-class long jumper, "was amazingly good, bigger than most boys her age and much more talented than most, including me."

Carl, coached by his parents, developed into history's finest prep long jumper. His performances of 23 feet 11¼ inches indoors and 25 feet 10 inches outdoors in 1978 attracted national attention. In 1979, the Willingboro High School senior established a national high school record of 26 feet 6 inches in the long jump at the International Prep Invitational. When asked if he could jump with the world's best after placing second in the 1979 Amateur Athletic Union (AAU) championships, Lewis replied confidently that "when I am my best, and they are at their best, it should be competitive." Carl, proving to be competitive indeed, captured the Bronze Medal in the Pan-American Games, improving the national high school record to 26 feet 8 inches. After being ranked fifth among the world's best long jumpers by *Track and Field News* in 1979, he admitted that "my goal is to be the best of all-time."

Dozens of colleges and universities offered Lewis athletic scholarships. Carl selected the University of Houston, however, because track and field coach Tom Tellez impressed him "more than any other coach with his knowledge" of the sport. Tellez instructed him to use the hitch-kick long jumping technique, in which he would continue to run through the air instead of hanging after takeoff. After mastering the hitch-kick in 1980, Lewis won the first of two consecutive indoor and outdoor NCAA long jump titles and qualified for the U.S. Olympic team in the long jump and the 4 × 100-meter relay. In 1981, Carl garnered the Southwest Conference (SWC) long jump title indoors in a world record of 27 feet 10½ inches. He also captured the 100 meters and the long jump in the 1981 NCAA championships, a feat accomplished only by William DeHart Hubbard in 1925 and **Jesse Owens** in 1935 and 1936. In the 1981 Track Athletic Congress (TAC) championships, Lewis also won the first of five 100-meter crowns and the first of six long jump titles. Neil Amdur of the *New York Times* compared Carl to Owens, stating that each possessed "equal ability and world class credentials" and "seemed blessed with strong characters."

Lewis left the University of Houston and joined the Santa Monica Track Club in 1982. Carl continued to train under Tellez, who also coached the Santa Monica Track Club. At the 1982 U.S. Olympic Committee (USOC) Sports Festival, he exceeded **Bob Beamon**'s venerable long jump world record of 29 feet 2½ inches by 4 inches. Officials ruled the jump illegal, however, because Lewis fouled. In the 1983 TAC championships, Carl won the long jump in a sea-level best of 28 feet 10¼ inches and the 200 meters in the sea-level best of 19.75 seconds. He collected Gold Medals in the 100 meters, long jump, and 4 × 100-meter relay at the 1983 World Championships in Helsinki, Finland. In the 4 × 100-meter relay, he anchored the United States in the world record time of 37.86 seconds. Lewis, who opened the 1984 Olympic year with an indoor long jump world record of 28 feet 10¼ inches at the Millrose Games, earned Gold Medals in the 100 meters, 200 meters, 4 × 100-meter relay, and long jump in the 1984 Summer Olympic Games at Los Angeles, California. By taking Gold Medals in each of these events, Carl duplicated Owens's 1936 Olympic performance. His time of 19.80 seconds in the 200 meters marked an Olympic record, while the clocking of 37.83 seconds in the 4 × 100-meter relay set a world standard.

After the 1984 Summer Olympic Games, Lewis continued to dominate the sprints and long jump. Carl vaulted 28 feet 9½ inches at the 1987 Mt. San Antonio Relays, a competition in which he exceeded 28 feet 3½ inches six times. Later that year, he captured the long jump in the Pan-American Games at Indianapolis, Indiana, and the World Championships at Rome, Italy, setting meet records of 28 feet 8½ inches and 28 feet 5½ inches, respectively. Lewis, however, finished second in the 100 meters, as Canadian Ben Johnson won the World Championship in a world record of 9.83 seconds. "If you asked me before the race, could anybody run that fast, I would have said no," Carl later remarked. "Now that it's over, I can believe it." He attempted to duplicate his 1984 Olympic performance at the 1988 Summer Olympic Games in Seoul, South Korea. Lewis clocked 9.92 seconds in the 100 meters, an American record, but again finished second. Johnson won the Olympic title in a remarkable world record time of 9.79 seconds. Carl later received the Gold Medal after Johnson was disqualified for a positive drug test. In the 200 meters, Lewis finished second to close friend and Santa Monica Track Club teammate Joe Deloach, who established an Olympic record of 19.75 seconds. Carl won the long jump in an Olympic mark of 28 feet 7 inches but did not compete in the 4 × 100-meter relay because the U.S. team was disqualified for passing the baton outside the exchange zone in the qualifying heats. After the Olympics, he remarked that "I did as well as I could; I've got two Golds and a Silver. I'm very proud." In September 1989, Lewis became the world record holder in the 100 meters when the International Amateur Athletic Federation (IAAF) revoked Johnson's 9.83-second clocking.

The early 1990s witnessed the highest and lowest moments of Carl's career. At the 1991 World Championships in Tokyo, Japan, he, at age 30, conquered the 100 meters in a world record of 9.86 seconds. "Coach Tellez told me in 1988 that I could run in the 9.8s," remarked Lewis. "When I heard the time after the race, I was simply numb." In the long jump, however, Carl finished second to **Michael Powell.** Powell claimed the world title in a world record performance of 29 feet 4½ inches. Lewis, who jumped 29 feet 2¾ inches, saw his 10-year winning streak end at 65 meets. Later, Carl anchored the victorious U.S. 4 × 100-meter relay in a world record of 37.50 seconds. Lewis captured an unprecedented third Gold Medal in the long jump during the 1992 Summer Olympic Games at Barcelona, Spain. In defeating Powell, Carl remarked, "It's only the beginning; we're going to have some great duels. Neither of us will win every one." He anchored the 4 × 100-meter relay foursome to a Gold Medal and world record performance of 37.40 seconds. Despite finishing fourth in the 100 meters at the 1993 World Championships in Stuttgart, Germany, Lewis won the Bronze Medal in the 200 meters. In April 1994, Carl anchored the 4 × 200-meter relay team to a world record 1 minute 18.68 clocking at Walnut, California. At the 1994 St. Petersburg, Russia, Goodwill Games, he anchored the winning 4 × 100-meter relay team. Lewis placed second in the long jump with a leap of 27 feet 8¾ inches and a disappointing sixth in the 100 meters at the USATF Outdoor Championships at Sacramento, California, in June 1995.

Despite Carl's accomplishments, America has not embraced him the same way it has other sports superstars. The nation has been concerned more with rumors of homosexuality and the use of performance-enhancing drugs than his track and field accomplishments. At the 1984 Summer Olympic Games, spectators booed Lewis for passing his four final attempts in the long jump rather than trying for the world record. Reflecting on his public persona, Carl observed, "There was always something new to talk about, always something new thrown at me. But that's life. All the way through, I ran, I enjoyed it, and I made a lot of money." His older brother, Mack, explaining America's attitude toward Lewis, acknowledged, "He does not fit the mold of the black athlete in America." Carl, who remains single, did not emerge from the poverty of the urban ghetto; rather, he came from the comfort of the middle-class suburbs. He, however, has enjoyed great celebrity status throughout Europe and Asia, where his exploits have earned millions of dollars in product endorsements. In 1985, the U.S. Olympic Hall of Fame enshrined him. *Sports Illustrated* in 1994 ranked him eleventh on its "40 for the Ages List."

BIBLIOGRAPHY: Lewis H. Carlson and John J. Fogarty, *Tales of Gold* (Chicago, 1987); Roy Conrad, "Carl Lewis Aiming for Very Top," *Track and Field News* 32 (August 1979), p. 53; *Current Biography Yearbook* (1984), pp. 233–236; Michael Janofsky, "Another Attempt at America's Heart," *New York Times Biographical Service* (May 1992), pp. 656–657; Yvonne Lee, "Lewis Still No. 1 American," *Track and Field News* 42 (January 1989), p. 11; Carl Lewis with Jeffrey Marx, *Inside Track: My Professional Life in Amateur Track and Field* (New York, 1992); Cordner Nelson, *Track's Greatest Champions* (Los Altos, CA, 1986); David L. Porter, ed., *Biographical Dictionary of American Sports: Outdoor Sports* (Westport, CT, 1989); David Wallechinsky, *The Complete Book of the Olympic Games*, rev. ed. (New York, 1988).

Adam R. Hornbuckle

POP LLOYD
(April 25, 1884–March 19, 1965) ————————————————— *Baseball*

Pop Lloyd, banned from the major leagues by baseball's unwritten apartheid law, ranked among the outstanding players of his era. In 1977, 12 years after his death, Lloyd was named to the National Baseball Hall of Fame. Honus Wagner and Connie Mack, white contemporaries of Pop, preceded him into the National Baseball Hall of Fame by some 40 years. Authorities generally acclaimed Wagner the best National League (NL) player of his time, while Mack led the Philadelphia Athletics to nine American League (AL) pennants during a record 50-year career as a major league manager. Both praised Lloyd's playing ability and talent.

John Henry Lloyd was born on April 25, 1884, in Palatka, Florida. Little is known of John's early struggling years. Pop's father died while John Henry was an infant. He was denied the chance to attend school, being forced to work as a delivery boy to survive. Despite these disadvantages, Lloyd matured into a generous, friendly, and clean-living adult.

John Henry's professional career began in the freewheeling days of independent African-American teams prior to the establishment of the Negro Leagues. He started out as a catcher for the Macon, Georgia, Acmes. The Acmes, however, lacked the funds to purchase even a catcher's mask. Pop, therefore, wore a wire basket over his head when behind the plate. That winter he worked for a Florida resort hotel, waiting tables and playing for the resort's baseball team.

Lloyd's diamond talents were too abundant to remain confined to his home state. In 1906, John Henry became the second baseman for the powerful all-African-American Cuban X-Giants. Mack first saw him play there. A post-season exhibition with Mack's Philadelphia Athletics featured four hits by the Giants' Lloyd. John Henry played shortstop with Sol White's Philadelphia Giants from 1907 through 1910. Mack, who watched the Giant develop into possibly the game's greatest shortstop, declared, "You could put Wagner and Lloyd in a bag together, and whichever one you pulled out you couldn't go wrong." Wagner, also a shortstop, heard John Henry being referred to as "the Black Wagner." After seeing Pop play, Wagner was honored to have such a great player named after himself.

Lloyd also performed in the superb Cuban Winter League (CWL) from 1908 through 1930, immediately adored by the island's fans. Cubans, impressed by Pop's defensive skills, dubbed John Henry "Cuchura," meaning a scoop or shovel. For the Havana Reds in 1910, he hit .438 in exhibition games with Ty Cobb's Detroit Tigers, third-place AL finishers, and Mack's World Series champion, Philadelphia Athletics. Cobb was so outplayed by African-Americans Lloyd, Grant Johnson, and Bruce Petway that he refused ever again to compete against African Americans.

Lloyd played for six CWL champions in 13 seasons, leading the league in hits (73) while batting .372 during the 1924–1925 campaign. The following season, John Henry hit .373 and paced the CWL in doubles (eight) and home runs (three). Pop, who also posted batting averages of .388 in 1912–1913 and .393 in 1915–1916, enjoyed a .321 career mark in CWL competition.

Lloyd, a six-foot 180-pounder, played and sometimes managed professionally through 1932. A left-handed batter, Pop batted .353 in 27 years at the top level of African-American baseball. John Henry performed when player contracts were nonexistent or ignored, enabling him to sell his services to the highest bidder. Between 1914 and 1917, he moved from **Rube Foster**'s Chicago American Giants to the New York Lincoln Stars and then back to the Giants. Lloyd consequently competed in three unofficial Black World Series during this period, two for Chicago and one against them with the Lincoln Stars. John Henry helped Chicago triumph over the Brooklyn Royal Giants in 1914 and New York Lincoln Stars in 1917 and hit a series-leading .390 for the Lincoln Stars in 1915, as they split 10 games with the American Giants.

Lloyd first managed in 1911 as a skipper for the New York Lincoln Giants. In 1923, John Henry guided the Hilldale Club of Philadelphia to the Eastern Colored League's initial pennant. He also piloted the Lincoln Giants when they staged the first all-African-American game in Yankee Stadium on July 10, 1930, with the Baltimore Black Sox.

Although best remembered as a great shortstop, Lloyd later returned to second base and then played first base in the twilight of his career. Pop retired in 1932 as an Atlantic City, New Jersey, Bacharach Giant but continued to play semi-pro baseball until age 58. Nicknamed "Pop" because of instilling confidence in younger players, he was considered the elder statesman of black baseball even after retiring as an active player.

John Henry and his wife Nan remained popular and participated in Atlantic City civic activities. They had no children but loved youngsters and supported the city's youth programs. Lloyd served as commissioner of Atlantic City's Little Leagues. In 1949, the city dedicated the $150,000 John Henry Lloyd Baseball Park with a ceremony attended by state and local politicians and many friends, fans, and benefactors. The tear-choked, soft-spoken Lloyd displayed his own impeccable character, responding, "I gave my best when I was playing ball, and today I mean to give the best that I have in expressing appreciation of the honor that has been given me this day. . . . And I promise that this day, more than anything else, inspires me to continue to live righteously, so that I may justify the confidence you kind folks have shown me."

Recently, Pop Lloyd Field has suffered from neglect, but restoration efforts are under way through the action of a committee presided over by former Negro League pitcher Max Manning. The committee also has established the John Henry Lloyd Lecture and Humanitarian Award, with tennis pioneer **Arthur Ashe, Jr.,** being the initial recipient.

Lloyd became a janitor in the local school system and died in Atlantic City on March 19, 1965, at age 80. Nan Lloyd lived another decade and planned to attend her husband's admission to the Black Athletes Hall of Fame in Las Vegas, Nevada, when she died on March 1, 1975. Manning, who remembers John Henry as a contented person, recalls, "He just had the right attitude toward sports and people."

BIBLIOGRAPHY: *Atlantic City Press,* March 23, 1964; April 7, 1993; *The Baseball Encyclopedia,* 9th ed. (New York, 1993); John Holway, *Blackball Stars* (Westport, CT, 1988); Merl F. Kleinknecht files, Galion, OH; Robert W. Peterson, *Only the Ball Was White* (New York, 1970); David L. Porter, ed., *Biographical Dictionary of American Sports: Baseball* (Westport, CT, 1987); James A. Riley, *The All-Time All-Stars of Black Baseball* (Cocoa Beach, FL, 1983); James A. Riley, *The Biographical Encyclopedia of the Negro Baseball Leagues* (New York, 1994); Mike Shatzkin, ed., *The Ballplayers* (New York, 1990); Tweed Webb, "Lloyd's Widow Succumbs Before Hall of Fame

Date" *St. Louis American,* March 1975; Charles E. Whitehead, *A Man and His Diamonds* (New York, 1980).

Merl F. Kleinknecht

JAMES LOFTON
(July 5, 1956–   ) ————————————————————— *Football*

James Lofton, a standout veteran 16-year football receiver, was noted for his graceful, acrobatic catches. James David Lofton was born on July 5, 1956, at Ft. Ord, California, the youngest of four children. His father, Emmanuel Michael Lofton, Sr., served in World War II combat and competed in football, basketball, and track and field at Prairie View State College. After retiring from the U.S. Army as a lieutenant colonel, the elder Lofton moved to Los Angeles, California, to become a bank executive. His mother, Violet Lofton, put 7-year-old James on a plane from Philadelphia, Pennsylvania, to join his father on the West Coast. James did not realize for several months that his parents were getting a divorce. He did not see his mother again for 12 years.

Lofton grew up near the Inglewood-Watts line, not far from the Forum. Although a latchkey kid, James did not consider his lot burdensome. He recalled, "I was just a kid who played at the park. I wore pants that were too short for me, but I never felt poor." One special memory that Lofton retained from his childhood came when his father took James to Super Bowl I between Green Bay and Kansas City in 1967.

The slender 5-foot-10-inch, 130-pound Lofton started lifting weights as a sophomore at Washington High School in Los Angeles. By his senior year, James starred as a lanky, speedy quarterback at 6 foot 2 inches, 165 pounds. He also excelled in track and field, becoming the California State long jump champion as a senior. Roy Fowlkes, Lofton's football coach at Washington, recalls how James's father, a smiling, pleasant individual, came to every game. Fowlkes also lauded the younger Lofton: "James had a beautiful personality. Of all the young men I coached, if there's anyone I would want my sons to pattern themselves after in terms of their attitude toward people, toward athletics, towards academics, toward life in general, it would be James Lofton."

Lofton attended prestigious Stanford University on a track and field scholarship, graduating in 1978 with a 3.2 (B+) average in industrial engineering. As a track and field standout, James qualified for the NCAA 1978 championships in the 100-meter, 200-meter, and 400-meter dashes and long jump. His 27-foot effort in the long jump marked the best distance in the world that year. Lofton starred as a football wideout only his senior year, catching 68 passes for 1,216 yards and a nation-leading 16 touchdowns. The 8–3 Cardinal won the Sun Bowl that year, with Lofton being selected as Senior Bowl Most Valuable Player (MVP).

Lofton found the transition to the National Football League (NFL) startingly easy. Although reporting to the Green Bay Packer (NFL) training camp late because of track and field commitments, the 1978 first-round draft pick and sixth overall selection astounded veteran quarterback Lynn Dickey by mastering the offensive playbook in two days. James's mastery of the game surpassed not just the cerebral, as he delighted Green Bay fans on the field by catching 46 passes for 818 yards for a 17.8 yards per catch average and six touchdowns. His performance earned him the National Football Conference (NFC) Rookie of the Year award and All-Pro status, a distinction he repeated seven more times in his career. Lofton excelled at wide receiver for Green Bay through 1986, enjoying five 1,000-yard seasons and leading the NFL in average yards per catch twice with 22.4 in 1983 and 22.0 in 1984. James, much respected by his teammates, served as Green Bay's player representative and played a key role in the 1982 strike, organizing workouts, keeping fellow players informed, and being team spokesman.

Lofton's NFL career almost ended because of two criminal sexual charges brought against him within a 27-month period between 1984 and 1987. In October 1984, James and running back Eddie Lee Ivery were accused of sexual assault on a Milwaukee exotic dancer, a charge later reduced to criminal trespass. In December 1987, Lofton was tried for rape involving a woman he had picked up at the Top Shelf Lounge in Green Bay. The jury quickly acquitted him, judging that the woman consented.

Although Lofton was cleared in court, his days with the Green Bay Packers were finished. Robert Harlan, president of the Packers, acknowledged that "the public backlash was tremendous." James, host of a local television show, member of the board of directors of the Milwaukee Ballet, and active supporter of Special Olympics, United Way, March of Dimes, the Boys' Club of Milwaukee, and other charities, was suspended for the last game of the 1986 season because of the alleged sexual assault charge. In April 1987, the Packers dealt him to the Los Angeles Raiders (NFL) for two midround draft picks.

Lofton, a born-again Christian, welcomed his return to Los Angeles, his boyhood home. James tried to put the Green Bay incidents into perspective: "I made mistakes. I've asked for forgiveness. And I've just got to go on." The 1987 campaign marked an excellent year for James professionally, as he averaged 21.5 yards per catch for the silver and black. The 1988 season proved less productive, however. In 1989, Lofton nearly left pro football, being cut by the Raiders in camp and rejected by the Philadelphia Eagles (NFL) after a tryout. Nick Nicholau, a receivers coach with the Buffalo Bills (NFL), knew James from their days with the Raiders and recommended him to Marv Levy, Bills' head coach. The Bills in 1989 signed Lofton, who enjoyed three excellent seasons with Buffalo and played on three Super Bowl teams. In 1992, James broke Steve Largent's all-time 13,089 reception yardage record when he amassed 13,821 career reception yards. The Bills released Lofton in 1993. After training with the Los Angeles Raiders, James finished the season with the Philadelphia Eagles and caught 13 passes for 167 yards and a 12.8 yards per catch average. Through 1993, his career statistics numbered 764 catches for 14,004 yards and 75 touchdowns. In 1994, he joined Cable News Network (CNN) as an NFL football analyst.

Lofton married Beverly Fanning, runner-up in the 1975 Miss Arkansas contest, in 1980. This cheerful, considerate, and supportive woman stuck with James throughout the dark times in Green Bay. The Loftons have one son, David James.

BIBLIOGRAPHY: Michael Bauman, "James Lofton: Lofty Goals, Lofty Talent," *Football Digest* 13 (January 1984), pp. 32–39; Dave D'Alessandro, "Mountain Climbers," *The Sporting News*, September 7, 1992, p. 58; Mark Heisler, "James Lofton: Ready for a Fresh Start," *Football Digest* 17 (October 1987), pp. 66–75; R. S. Johnson, "Interview: James Lofton," *Sport* 76 (October 1985), pp. 31–38; Malcolm Moran, "NFL Playoffs: The Conference Championships: Lofton Brings Healing Touch," *New York Times*, January 18, 1991, sec. A, p. 26; Malcolm Moran, "The Worst Is Over for Lofton and Bills," *New York Times*, January 22, 1991, sec. B, p. 8; David L. Porter, ed., *Biographical Dictionary of American Sports: Football* (Westport, CT, 1987); Timothy W. Smith, "Pro Football: The Decline and Return of James Lofton," *New York Times*, January 19, 1992, sec. 8, p. 3; Rick Telander, "A Picture Perfect End," *Sports Illustrated* 57 (December 6, 1982), p. 52.

John H. Ziegler

RONNIE LOTT
(May 8, 1959–) ———————————————————— *Football*

Ronnie Lott is destined for the Pro Football Hall of Fame. Widely regarded as the game's premier defensive safety during the 1980s when his San Francisco 49ers National Football League (NFL) club won four Super Bowls, Lott combined skilled defensive coverage with bone-jarring tackles. Veteran quarterback Jim Everett tabbed Ronnie "the best defensive player I've seen."

Ronnie Mandel Lott was born on May 8, 1959, in Albuquerque, New Mexico, to Roy D. Lott, career member of the U.S. Air Force, and Mary (Carroll) Lott. The oldest of three children, Ronnie, his brother Roy, Jr., and sister Suzie moved to Washington, D.C., in 1964 and to Rialto, California, near San Bernardino, in 1969. As a child, Lott enjoyed the velocity of the sport. "I always loved the great hits," Ronnie declared.

At Eisenhower High School in Rialto, Ronnie lettered three years in football, basketball, and baseball and received All-Citrus League honors three years in football and basketball and two years in baseball. In 1977, his honors included being named a *Parade Magazine* High School All-America in football and earning the Ken Hubbs Memorial Award as the San Bernardino area's outstanding athlete.

Lott entered the University of Southern California (USC) in 1977 and received his bachelor's degree in public administration in 1981. Although a reserve guard on the Trojan basketball team during his sophomore and junior years, he attracted fame on the gridiron. As a football defensive back under coach John Robinson, Ronnie achieved All-America and All-Pac-10 honors his junior and senior years. USC won the NCAA football championship in 1978 and ranked number two nationally in 1979, winning Rose Bowl games both seasons. In 1980, Lott intercepted eight passes to rank second nationally and was chosen team Most Valuable Player (MVP) and Most Inspirational Player. His defensive backfield mates, all future pro football players, may have comprised the best-ever college combo. They included Dennis Smith of the Denver Broncos, Jeff Fisher of the Chicago Bears, and Joey Browner of the Minnesota Vikings.

The San Francisco 49ers (NFL) selected the six-foot, 200-pound defensive back as their first-round choice (eighth overall) in the 1981 NFL draft. Ronnie's distinguished 10-year career there paralleled San Francisco's claim as the team of the 1980s. San Francisco won four Super Bowls, defeating the Cincinnati Bengals in 1982, the Miami Dolphins in 1985, the Bengals again in 1989, and the Denver Broncos in 1990. The hard-hitting, intense Lott played cornerback from 1981 through 1984 and free safety from 1985 through 1990. Ronnie was named All-Pro in 1981, 1983, 1986, 1987, and 1989, making the Pro Bowl nine seasons as cornerback or free safety. He holds 49er career records for interceptions (51), interception yardage returns (643), and interception touchdowns (5). In 1983, Ronnie led the 49ers with 108 tackles, usually a linebacker's figure, and was named Defensive Back of the Year by the NFL Alumni Association.

Lott's forte, hitting and intimidation, was featured in the 1989 Super Bowl XXIII, as the 49ers defeated Cincinnati, 20–16. Bengals' running back Ickey Woods ran wild against San Francisco in the first quarter until Ronnie's punishing tackle seemed to unnerve him. Forty-niner coach George Seifert boasted that "Ronnie Lott's [power] had a direct impact on us winning the football game."

Following the 1990 season and San Francisco's loss, 15–13, to the New York Giants in the National Football Conference (NFC) championship game, the 49ers did not protect Lott. The 49ers expected to sign the 10-year veteran at a reduced salary for one year before hiring him for the coaching staff. Ronnie, unwilling to accept the 49er's judgment that his skills had diminished, signed a 2-year contract in March 1991 with the Los Angeles Raiders (NFL) for $800,000 per year. As the Raiders' strong safety, his third defensive backfield position, he played every game of the 1991 season, led the NFL in interceptions with eight, and was voted to his tenth Pro Bowl. In 1992, Lott paced the Raiders in tackles and finished second in passes defended but intercepted just one.

On March 2, 1991, Lott married Karen Collmer. They have a daughter, Hailey, and a son, Isaiah, and live in Cupertino, California. He also has a son, Ryan, born in 1979.

Under the NFL's new policy of free agency in March 1993, Lott signed a 2-year, $3.6 million contract with the New York Jets. Although finishing second on the Jets with 3 interceptions during the 1993 season, Ronnie seemed less dominating than in years past. Yet his leadership skills remain unquestioned. He leads current NFL players with 63 career interceptions, seventh highest all-time. Coach Seifert praised Lott as "one of the most committed players I've been around." To Ronnie, leadership means respect. "When you die, people will come to your funeral [not because of] how much money you made. They'll come because they respect you." Lott's toughness has earned him the respect of his peers and a future spot in the Pro Football Hall of Fame. In 1994, Ronnie was named to the All-Time NFL team. The New York Jets released him in March 1995. The Kansas City Chiefs (NFL) signed him the following month.

BIBLIOGRAPHY: *Current Biography Yearbook* (February 1994), pp. 36–39; *Los Angeles Raiders Media Guide* (1992); Ronnie Lott with Jill Lieber, *Total Impact* (New York, 1991); *New York Times*, March 9, 1993; Michael W. Tuckman and Jeff Schultz, *The San Francisco 49ers: Team of the Decade* (Rocklin, CA, 1989).

David Bernstein

JOE LOUIS
(May 13, 1914–April 12, 1983) ———————————————— *Boxing*

Joe Louis remains one of the most famous and admired prizefighters in American sports history. Louis became the first African-American heavyweight champion after **Jack Johnson,** who most white people thought had brought shame to the sport. Louis symbolized racial harmony to whites and racial progress and pride to African Americans.

Joseph Louis Barrow was born on May 13, 1914, in a sharecropper's cabin near Lafayette, Alabama, the seventh of eight children of Munn Barrow, a farmer, and Lillie Barrow. Joe's first 10 years passed uneventfully, as he mainly worked in the fields and played childhood games unrelated to boxing. He "never squared off or showed any signs of being a boxer."

His life changed significantly in 1924. After Joe's mother had divorced and remarried, the new family moved to Detroit, Michigan. Like many other African Americans, they sought economic advancement by moving north. Joe disliked Bronson Trade School and the violin lessons his mother insisted he take. As a teenager, he became fascinated by prizefighting and spent long hours at a local gymnasium watching young fighters practice.

Louis lost his first bout to Johnny Miler in late 1932 but soon became an accomplished amateur. Under the guidance of Detroit African-American businessman John Roxborough, Joe turned professional in 1934. In the next 15 years, his only loss came to German Max Schmeling in 1936. Louis captured the world heavyweight championship in 1937, when he defeated titleholder James Braddock. During the next 12 years, "The Brown Bomber," as sportswriters nicknamed him, defended his title a record 25 times. His triumphs included a stunning one-round "revenge" knockout of Schmeling in 1938, a miraculous last-round knockout of Billy Conn in 1941, and a controversial decision over Jersey Joe Walcott in 1947. He retired as champion in 1949.

Louis was acclaimed as a crafty boxer and powerful slugger. Many prize-fighting historians ranked Joe the most skillful heavyweight champion, while *The Ring* in 1987 named him the third greatest heavyweight fighter of all time. According to boxing historian Alexander Johnson, Louis "would have made a splendid fight against any ring great that ever lived."

Joe's boxing skill, however, was surpassed by his symbolic role. Since Louis appeared to be docile and deferential to whites outside the ring and respectful of his fallen opponents in the ring, white Americans, especially outside the South, praised him for being a "good, non-threatening" member of his race. Sportswriter Bruce Dudley praised Joe for being "clean, modest, . . . and un-assuming." Louis became especially popular among whites after humiliating Schmeling in 1938. Many Americans saw Schmeling's defeat as a triumph of American values over Nazi racism and totalitarianism. Significantly, Joe was introduced to American soldiers during World War II as "the first American to K.O. a Nazi."

The image of Louis to his fellow African Americans was more complicated. A few appreciated Joe's effort to placate whites, but most proudly hailed his accomplishments because they seemed to open up new areas of American life for African-American participation. These African Americans especially applauded his attempts to integrate facilities at American military bases during World War II. Numerous African-American writers and professors believed that his victories over white boxers gave a special thrill to African Americans, who could not fight openly against white racism.

Joe's personal life remained less happy and positive than his professional one. Louis married four times, wedding Marva Trotter twice (1935 and 1946), Rose Morgan in 1955, and Martha Jackson in 1959. The Trotter marriages produced his two children, Jacquelin and Joe, Jr. Louis also experienced serious financial problems. Due to bad investments and poor judgment in his choice of financial advisers, Joe owed $1,250,000 in back federal taxes when he retired in 1949. These monetary burdens led him to attempt an unsuccessful comeback during 1950–1951, when he lost bouts to new champion Ezzard Charles and Rocky Marciano. According to historian Edward Henderson, when Marciano knocked out Louis, "people who didn't know him wept in Madison Square Garden."

Despite his remarkable professional record of 69 victories (49 by knockout) and only three defeats, Louis spent his ring retirement out of the public limelight. Besides being a professional wrestler and unsuccessful fast-food entrepreneur, he served as a front man for boxing promoter James Norris. In 1970, Joe was committed to a mental hospital for five months. During his last few years, he served as an official greeter at Caesar's Palace Casino in Las Vegas,

Nevada. Louis died there in 1983, a sad ending for an American sports hero. In 1990, Joe was elected to the International Boxing Hall of Fame.

BIBLIOGRAPHY: Gerald Astor, ". . . *And a Credit to His Race": The Life and Hard Times of Joe Louis Barrow, a.k.a. Joe Louis* (New York, 1974); Joe Louis Barrow, Jr., and Barbara Munder, *Joe Louis: 50 Years an American Hero* (New York, 1988); James A. Cox, "The Day Joe Louis Fired Shots Heard 'Round the World," *Smithsonian* 19 (November 1988), p. 70; Anthony O. Edmonds, *Joe Louis* (Grand Rapids, MI, 1973); Robert Horn, "Two Champions and Enemies: Bad Blood Existed Between Jack Johnson and Joe Louis," *Sports Illustrated* 72 (May 14, 1990), p. 109; Chris Mead, *Joe Louis: Black Hero in White America* (New York, 1985); Jeffrey T. Sammons, *Beyond the Ring: The Role of Boxing in American Society* (Urbana, IL, 1988).

Anthony O. Edmonds

WILLIE McCOVEY
(January 10, 1938–) ——————————————————— *Baseball*

Willie Lee McCovey, nicknamed "Stretch" throughout his baseball career, ranked among the game's most feared sluggers, particularly during his years with the San Francisco Giants National League (NL) club. Born on January 10, 1938, in Mobile, Alabama, McCovey was the seventh of 10 children of Frank McCovey, a railroad worker, and Ester (Jones) McCovey. Mobile produced several major league stars, including **Henry Aaron.** As a youth, Willie avoided gangs and befriended those involved in athletics. "I was lucky. The kids who were my friends went into sports. We dominated the playground leagues we were in, all through childhood—baseball, football, softball, basketball," he recalled. Since his family was poor, he at age 12 began working several odd jobs to help his family.

Upon turning age 16, McCovey quit school and traveled to Los Angeles, California, to seek work. By then, however, his reputation as a top baseball player on the Mobile playground circuit had grown. New York Giants (NL) scout Alex Pompez followed the advice of Mobile playground director Jess Thomas and prodded his club to give Willie a tryout. After careful scrutiny, the Giants determined that he offered potential and assigned him to the club's Class D club in Sandersville, Georgia, for $175 a month. Future star and NL president **Bill White,** who also played then in the Giants' minor league chain, worked with McCovey on his batting swing. Taking heed of White's advice, Willie batted .305 with 19 home runs and 119 RBIs that year. His biggest year in the minor leagues, however, came in 1959, when he batted .372 and slugged 29 home runs in less than one-half season for Class Triple A Phoenix of the Pacific Coast League (PCL).

The Giants, located by then in San Francisco, promoted McCovey in mid-season. On July 30, 1959, Willie made his major league debut against the Philadelphia Phillies at Seals Stadium in San Francisco. Facing future National Baseball Hall of Famer Robin Roberts, the big rookie blasted two triples and two singles in four at bats. In the remaining 52 games, he batted .354, hit 13 home runs, and drove in 38 tallies. These achievements earned him the 1959 NL Rookie of the Year award. The Giants returned McCovey to the minor leagues for part of the 1960 season but recalled him at the end of the season. Willie spent the remainder of his career in the major leagues.

During the next few years, the Giants platooned both McCovey and young star Orlando Cepeda at first base. Writer Charles Einstein stated, "There is no question that both Cepeda and McCovey were affected by the dilemma, that neither enjoyed it, and that their lack of enjoyment was visible." "I didn't think I was part of anything," recalled Willie. His statistics, however, remained impressive. During the Giants' NL pennant–winning 1962 season, "Stretch" batted .293, drove in 54 tallies, and belted 20 home runs. Against the New York Yankees, McCovey hit a game-winning home run and nearly won the 1962 World Series for the Giants. Willie hit a memorable World Series–ending line drive to second baseman Bobby Richardson with the tying and winning runs on base. In 1963, he finished the season with an NL-leading 44 home runs.

By 1965, McCovey anchored first base on a daily basis. A Cepeda injury, followed by a trade in May of the ensuing year, made Willie San Francisco's regular first baseman. His prominence with the Giants grew larger. During the next several years, McCovey terrorized NL pitchers. From 1966 to 1968, Willie hit 36, 31, and 36 home runs, respectively, and drove in at least 90 runs each season. His banner year, however, took place in 1969, when he led the NL with 45 home runs and 126 RBIs. He also batted .320 and set an NL record for most walks in a single season with 121. During that year's All-Star Game, McCovey contributed 2 home runs to help lead the NL to a 9–3 victory and won the Arch Ward Memorial Trophy as that game's MVP. For Willie's efforts throughout that year, the Baseball Writers Association of America (BBWAA) bestowed the NL MVP award on the San Francisco first baseman.

Despite his magnificent season, McCovey played mostly in pain. Calcium deposits in his hip contributed to an intense pain and bleeding when he swung a bat. Willie also performed with an arthritic knee that had hampered him previously. His demeanor, however, remained consistent. Arnold Hano of *Sport* magazine described him as "a quiet giant of a man with a long, sad face and a style so nonchalant some people thought he was lazy." McCovey's stardom also coincided with the sociopolitical turbulence outside of baseball. Like many of his peers, Willie often faced scrutiny from those with a political agenda. "I do what I think is right. I have experienced prejudice. I know something's got to be done, but I'm not knowledgeable as to what should be done," he retorted. "No matter what, I am a Negro. I'm not going to put them [militants] down. But I don't condone violence on any side. I do not support anybody who believes in violence. It's not my bag." McCovey eventually, however, participated in charitable organizations, including chairing the Willie McCovey March of Dimes Annual Charity Golf Tournament.

In 1970, McCovey broke his own major league record for walks with 137, but injuries hampered his subsequent years as a player. For the next three seasons, Willie's overall offensive production slipped. In October 1973, the Giants dealt him to the San Diego Padres (NL). McCovey spent three years with the Padres before joining the Oakland Athletics American League (AL) club, where Willie appeared in only 11 games in September 1976. In January 1977, the Giants resigned the veteran, much to his delight. "I'm part of San Francisco; people associate me with San Francisco, I'm known there. San Francisco is my home. Literally everything I've accomplished, I've accomplished in San Francisco. I don't want to play anywhere else," he declared. In his first season back, he hit 28 home runs in 141 games. But his statistics fell dramatically after that, causing McCovey to complete his outstanding career with the Giants in 1980.

By his retirement, the slugger from Mobile had accumulated 521 home runs (tenth on the all-time list); 1,555 RBIs (twenty-fifth best); a .515 slugging average (thirty-third best); and a .270 batting average. Willie also appeared in six All-Star Games, including 1963, 1966, and 1968–1971. Despite impressive lifetime statistics, McCovey remained pessimistic about his chances for induction into the National Baseball Hall of Fame. "The Hall of Fame is politics. I don't feel I've had the publicity I deserve," he claimed. In 1986, nevertheless, 346 members of the BBWAA voted to enshrine the left-handed slugger into the distinguished gallery of the Cooperstown museum.

BIBLIOGRAPHY: *Current Biography Yearbook* (1976), pp. 261–263; Charles Einstein, *Willie's Time* (Berkeley, CA, 1980); Arnold Hano, *Willie Mays* (New York, 1970); *New York Times Biographical Service* (March 12, 1977), p. 417; (June 1980), p. 862; *Who's Who Among Black Americans*, 6th ed. (Detroit, MI, 1990), p. 848.

Samuel O. Regalado

JOHN MACKEY
(September 24, 1941–) ——————————————————— *Football*

John Mackey, a brilliant tight end, starred both on and off the gridiron. He was born on September 24, 1941, in Brooklyn, New York, one of six children of Walter Mackey and Dora Mackey, and grew up in Roosevelt, New York, where his father pastored the Mt. Sinai Baptist Church. The very quiet, humble, competitive, courageous, intelligent, industrious, and muscular youth enjoyed a brilliant athletic career at Hempstead High School, winning the Thorp Award as Nassau County's best football player.

Mackey graduated from Hempstead High School in 1959 and majored in history and political science at Syracuse University, earning a B.A. degree in 1963. John played right halfback for the undefeated football freshmen in 1959 and substituted for the varsity squad. Back **Ernie Davis,** Mackey's roommate, taught him how to handle tacklers and utilize his running speed to make large gains. In 1961, coach Ben Schwartzwalder switched John to a starting end. The Orangemen won 7 of 10 games that year, defeating the University of Miami, 15–14, in the Liberty Bowl. In 1962, Mackey made All-America, almost single-handedly helped Syracuse upset Navy, and scored on 41- and 69-yard passes to help the East triumph, 25–19, over the West in the Shrine game. John married Sylvia Ann Cole, a fashion model, on December 28, 1963. They have three children, Lisa, John, and Linda.

The Baltimore Colts National Football League (NFL) club drafted Mackey in the second round in 1963. John became the first Colt rookie to bring a lawyer with him to help negotiate his contract. Subsequently, nearly every rookie followed suit. Johnny Unitas combined with the six-foot-two-inch 220-pounder the next nine seasons to form one of the best quarterback-end duos in pro football history. "When Mackey came into the league he was the first tight end who had it all," stated defensive back Kermit Alexander. "John had size, hands, and speed." Coach Don Shula called Mackey "the perfect blocker. Then, when we turn him loose as a pass receiver, he has the toughness to get by the linebacker and the speed to outrun the safetyman."

As a rookie in 1963, Mackey caught 35 passes for 736 yards and seven touchdowns and paced the Colts in kickoff returns with nine for 271 yards. No other rookie made the Pro Bowl. A thigh injury limited his performance in 1964, when the Colts lost the NFL title game, 27–0, to the Cleveland Browns. John caught 40 passes for 814 yards and seven touchdowns in 1965, often bowling over defensive backs like a runaway steer for long yardage. "Those people on defense climb all over him," Dick Bielski, Baltimore's end coach, observed. "The lucky ones fall off." Writers awarded Mackey, a five-time Pro Bowl participant, All-Pro honors from 1966 through 1968. Few tight ends have matched John's 1966 season, when he made 50 receptions for 829 yards. During 1966, Mackey caught aerials for touchdown runs of 51, 57, 64, 79, 83, and 89 yards. Despite the presence of ends Raymond Berry, Willie Richardson, Ray Perkins, and Jimmy Orr, John made a career-high 55 receptions for 686 yards in 1967. Orr remarked, "He helps the outside receivers because the defense has to give him a lot of attention or he'll rip them apart." Baltimore won the NFL title in 1968 with a 13–1 mark, as Mackey led the Colts with 45 catches for 644 yards and five touchdowns. Coach Shula also utilized John's fine running ability for 10 end-around plays, netting 103 yards. In Super Bowl III, however, the New York Jets upset the Colts, 16–7.

Doctors removed bone chips from Mackey's right knee before the 1970 season, limiting his mobility. Nevertheless, John caught a 54-yard pass from Unitas in the final four minutes to help the Colts edge the Chicago Bears, 21–20. Baltimore won 11 of 14 contests, defeating the Dallas Cowboys, 16–13, in Super Bowl V. Mackey set a Super Bowl record, scoring on a 75-yard tipped pass from Unitas. John ran his own pattern and noticed the aerial sailing over the head of teammate Eddie Hinton. After Hinton and Cowboy defender Mel Renfro both deflected the football, Mackey grabbed it at the

45-yard line and scampered for the score. John started the first three games in 1971 until an elbow injury sidelined him. Baltimore traded Mackey in 1972 to the San Diego Chargers, where his playing career ended.

During 10 NFL seasons, Mackey caught 331 passes for 5,236 yards and 38 touchdowns. The NFL in 1969 named John, whose 15.8-yard average per reception ranked him highest among all-time tight ends, as the best tight end in pro football history. Coaches previously had used tight ends to block for running backs, but Mackey made the bland position a dangerous game-breaking one. The superb athlete often was released on unsuspecting defensive backs to catch passes and make wild, galloping runs. John, the prototype of the modern pro tight end, possessed ideal size, the speed of a sprinter, sure hands and reach of a wide receiver, powerful drive of a running back, and the superior strength of a blocker.

In January 1970, Mackey was chosen the first African-American president of the NFL Player's Association (NFLPA). John challenged the NFL establishment by organizing a players strike, making fans, owners, and many writers unhappy. The dispute centered around the owners' contribution to the players' pension fund. Mackey's leadership enabled the NFLPA to survive frantic, bitter negotiations with the owners, eventually signing an improved pension and benefits contract. John's 1972 antitrust suit against the NFL overturned the Rozelle rule, a compensation clause restraining the right of a player to bargain with another club. The landmark case helped the foundation for subsequent relations between the NFL management and the NFLPA and eventually triggered free agency. In his final year of eligibility, Mackey in 1992 was elected to the Pro Football Hall of Fame. The Pikesville, Maryland, resident presides over John Mackey Enterprises, a wholesale food distributing business.

BIBLIOGRAPHY: Nathan Aaseng, *Football's Toughest Tight Ends* (Minneapolis, MN, 1981); George Allen with Ben Olan, *Pro Football's 100 Greatest Players* (Indianapolis, IN, 1982); Dave Anderson, "Negotiators Quarterback," *New York Times,* July 22, 1970, p. 46; Gwilym S. Brown, " 'I'm Going to Punish Them for Last Year,' " *Sports Illustrated* 35 (August 30, 1971), pp. 30–32, 34; "4 with Singular Styles Stride into Hall," *New York Times,* August 2, 1992, sec. 8, p. 8; *The Lincoln Library of Sports Champions,* vol. 8 (Columbus, OH, 1974); Marty Ralbovsky, *Super Bowl* (New York, 1972); *The Sporting News Football Register* (1972); Rick Telander, "A Most Suspicious Snub," *Sports Illustrated* 74 (February 11, 1991), p. 210; Robert McG. Thomas, Jr., "A Radical Look for Hall of Fame," *New York Times,* January 26, 1992, sec. 8, p. 7; George Vecsey, "John Mackey's Great Escape," *Sport* 43 (June 1967), pp. 48–49, 85–87; *Who's Who in America,* 37th ed. (1972–1973), p. 1979.

David L. Porter

KARL MALONE
(July 24, 1963–) ————————————————————— *Basketball*

Karl Malone, nicknamed "the Mailman," consistently delivered points on the basketball court. Karl Anthony Malone was born on July 24, 1963, in tiny Summerfield, Louisiana, the youngest of eight children of P. J. Malone and Shirley Ann (Jackson) Malone. His father abandoned the family when Karl was only three. His mother worked in sawmills during the day and poultry houses at night to support the family. She rejected welfare assistance, declaring, "It was my responsibility to take care of my children. I believe every tub should sit on its own bottom." In 1975, Shirley married Ed Turner and jointly operated Turner's Grocery & Washateria.

Malone, highly recruited after averaging 30 points and 20 rebounds per game for three years, led Summerfield High School to three consecutive State basketball titles. Karl attended Louisiana Tech University in nearby Ruston, explaining, "I wanted to stay near home because, deep down, I'm a small-town guy who wants to be near friends and relatives." A poor student in high school, he thought that he "didn't need to do any school work" because "I was special and that things would just come to me." Unable to play for the Bulldogs as a freshman because he did not meet NCAA freshman academic standards, Malone later admitted that sitting out a year "was the best thing that ever happened to me." The layoff made him "hungry" as a student and athlete. During the next three years, Karl posted a 2.6 grade-point average in elementary education and was named First Team All-Southland Conference in basketball each season. Teammates called him "the Mailman" because of his clutch play. In the spring of 1985, Malone decided to forego his final year of college ball and enter the National Basketball Association (NBA) draft.

Many NBA scouts questioned Karl's attitude, specifically his temper and apparent lack of desire, and believed he needed another college year to develop his athletic skills. The Utah Jazz (NBA), however, eagerly selected the six-foot-nine-inch, 256-pound Malone as the thirteenth pick in the first round. Although inconsistent and sometimes immature as a rookie, he still made the 1986 All-Rookie team and quickly developed into one of the NBA's premier power forwards. Malone's rise to superstar status was due partly to the guidance of coach Frank Layden and playmaking skills of point guard John Stockton but primarily to Karl's determination to improve himself as a player and person.

Malone demonstrated his dedication statistically by improving his free throw percentage from .481 his rookie year to .778 by 1993–1994 and physically by lifting weights to increase his strength and endurance. The NBA's strongest player, Karl possesses unusual quickness, speed, and agility for his size. He ranks among the most durable players in NBA history, missing only four games in his first ten seasons and playing more than 3,000 minutes for eight consecutive seasons from 1988 to 1995. When asked how he could average nearly 40 minutes per game with his bruising low-post play, Malone replied, "It's where men are made. In the paint either put up or shut up. I want to play all 48 [minutes]. I don't want nobody coming in for Karl Malone." An opponent observed, "When you play the Mailman, be ready to bang, be ready to run, be ready to go all night long."

Karl epitomizes a complete player, averaging 10.9 boards per game through the 1994–1995 season. The leading rebounder in Jazz history (8,929) has paced the team in rebounding each of his ten seasons and has ranked seven times among the NBA's top 10 rebounders. He remains also a multidimensional offensive force. Best known for powerful low-post moves to the basket and thunderous dunks at the end of fast breaks, Malone ranks as the NBA's best outside-shooting power forward. Karl, a prolific and remarkably consistent scorer, averaged between 24 and 31 points per game from 1988 to 1995. The Jazz's scoring leader each of the last nine seasons from 1987 to 1995, he consistently ranks among the NBA's top scorers. After finishing second among NBA scorers four straight years from 1989 to 1992, Malone placed third in 1993, fifth in 1994, and fourth in 1995. Through the 1994–1995 season, the Jazz's all-time leading scorer with 21,237 points ranked fifth in NBA history with a career season scoring average of 26.0 points per game.

After being All-NBA Second Team in 1988, Malone made the First Team each of the next seven years from 1989 to 1995. Elected to the Western Division All-Star team eight consecutive years from 1988 to 1995, Karl was named the Most Valuable Player (MVP) of the 1989 game and co-MVP in 1993 with Jazz teammate John Stockton. When professionals were allowed to participate in Olympic basketball, he helped the first U.S. Dream Team capture the Gold Medal at the 1992 Summer Olympic Games in Barcelona, Spain.

Malone's outspoken candor occasionally has created controversy. Karl has voiced concerns about playing against AIDS-infected **Magic Johnson,** challenged **Charles Barkley**'s assertion that athletes are not role models for youth, criticized team ownership for not being more aggressive in acquiring players, and repeatedly asked that his contracts be renegotiated to keep pace with spiraling salaries. On the other hand, the unfailing polite, sincere, modest Malone campaigns against substance abuse and tries hard to be one of those athletes "who live their lives by example."

Karl, who as a child dreamed of being either a cowboy or a truck driver, owns several cattle ranches and a long-haul trucking company. He frequently makes summer deliveries in his personal 18-wheel rig, decorated with hand-painted Western murals on both sides of the 64-foot trailer. In 1990, Malone married Kay Ann Kinsey, former beauty queen and Miss Idaho USA for 1987, and has two daughters, Kaydee and Kylee.

BIBLIOGRAPHY: *Current Biography Yearbook* (1993), pp. 360–364; Chuck Daley with Alex Sachare, *America's Dream Team: The Quest for Olympic Gold* (Atlanta, GA, 1992); Jack McCallum, "Big Wheel," *Sports Illustrated* 76 (April 27, 1992), pp. 62–74; Karl

Malone, "One Role Model to Another," *Sports Illustrated* 78 (June 14, 1993), p. 84; Craig Neff, "The Mailman Does Deliver," *Sports Illustrated* 62 (January 14, 1985), pp. 88, 90, 94; *Salt Lake Tribune*, January 31, 1993 February 20, 1993; October 17, 1993; *The Sporting News*, November 8, 1993; *The Sporting News NBA Register* (1994–1995); *Utah Jazz Media Guide* (1994–1995); Ralph Wiley, "Does He Ever Deliver!" *Sports Illustrated* 69 (November 7, 1988), pp. 72–77.

Larry R. Gerlach

MOSES MALONE
(March 23, 1955–) _____ *Basketball*

Moses Malone dominated the National Basketball Association (NBA) as a powerful offensive rebounding center in the early 1980s, winning three Most Valuable Player (MVP) awards. Moses Eugene Malone was born on March 23, 1955, in Petersburg, Virginia, and grew up with his mother, Mary (Hudgins) Malone, a nurse's aide and supermarket meat packer, in a decrepit row house in a poor African-American neighborhood. His father, a heavy drinker, left home when Moses was only two years old.

Moses, nicknamed "Sweet Moses" by his mother, remained shy, awkward, and inarticulate as a youngster. Basketball fascinated him, as he practiced the sport constantly. His mother declared, "He always loves his basketball and that what give that boy his courage." Moses, who stood at six foot three inches by age 12, grew so fast that he always played basketball with older boys.

At Petersburg High School, Malone made 30 rebounds in his first freshman game. Moses set new Virginia high school basketball standards, leading his team to 50 consecutive victories and two State championships. During his high school career, the dominating center averaged 39 points, 26 rebounds, and 10 blocked shots a game. As a senior, he made High School All-America and became the most highly recruited scholastic player in history. Malone barely scraped by academically, graduating in 1974.

Over 300 colleges offered Malone scholarships, with the University of Maryland prevailing. Writer Tom Boswell described Malone as "one of the few players . . . who can dribble behind his back, lead the fast break, shoot from the outside, and generally act like a guard when he isn't blocking shot after shot." Robert Hayes, Petersburg assistant basketball coach, served as a father figure and counselor for the serious-minded, hard-working Moses.

In 1974, the Utah Stars of the American Basketball Association (ABA) drafted Malone as their third-round choice and signed Moses to a $3 million, five-year contract after he enrolled at the University of Maryland. His signing stirred cries of protest because a high school basketball player had never gone directly to the pros. Moses, however, replied that he had "seen the pros on TV" and claimed that he was "quicker" than they. He also denied that "experience meant that much under the rack."

The 6-foot-10-inch Malone immediately silenced the critics, capitalizing on his spring and quickness to make the ABA Western Division All-Star team. During his rookie season, Moses averaged 18.8 points per game and paced the Stars with 14.6 rebounds per game as a defensive center and offensive forward. He led the ABA in offensive rebounds and ranked fourth in total rebounds. After the Utah franchise went bankrupt during the 1975–1976 ABA season, the St. Louis Spirits signed Malone. His initial NBA season in 1976–1977 was divided between the Portland Trail Blazers, Buffalo Braves, and Houston Rockets.

Malone starred with Houston through 1982, establishing scoring and re-bounding standards. With the Rockets, Moses averaged over 20 points a game and emerged as the NBA's leading rebounder. In 1976–1977, he broke the NBA record for offensive rebounds with 437 and sparked the 49–33 Rockets to the Eastern Conference finals. In 1979, Malone was voted NBA MVP and *The Sporting News* Player of the Year. Moses led the NBA in rebounds with 17.6 per game in 1978–1979 and finished fifth in scoring with 24.8 points per game. Two years later, he again paced the NBA in rebounds and the Rockets to the NBA finals against the Boston Celtics. In 1981–1982, Malone added an accurate 15-foot jump shot to his arsenal, raised his points per game average to a career-high 31.1, defended his rebounding crown, and earned MVP hon-ors for a second time. Teammate **Elvin Hayes** declared, "I've never seen a big man who is that active at both ends of the court. I've never seen a big man who can kill you offensively from both inside and outside, who drives to the basket with the quickness that he does, and who is such an outstanding offensive rebounder. He may very well be the best all-around big man ever to play this game." David DuPree described Malone as "the NBA's most dominating complete player." Another sportswriter labeled Moses "the world's richest blue collar worker." Malone admitted, "I have always tried to be the greatest worker."

In September 1982, the Philadelphia 76ers signed Malone to a six-year, $13.2 million contract. Philadelphia, led by **Julius Erving,** had finished second three of the previous five years and hoped Moses would catapult them to an NBA title. The 65–17 76ers boasted the best NBA record in 1982–1983, as Malone averaged 24.5 points a game and led the NBA in rebounding for the third consecutive campaign. Despite tendinitis, Moses averaged 25.8 points and 18 rebounds per game to help Philadelphia defeat the Los Angeles Lakers in the NBA finals. He claimed both NBA MVP regular-season and post-season MVP honors. Malone again paced the NBA in rebounding in 1983–1984 and 1984–1985, sparking Philadelphia to the NBA playoffs both times.

In June 1986, the 76ers traded Malone to the Washington Bullets. Moses's productive scoring and rebounding helped the Bullets reach the NBA playoffs the next two seasons. In August 1988, the Atlanta Hawks signed him to a three-year contract worth around $1.5 million annually. Malone's point pro-duction and rebounding, however, steadily declined during those three seasons. Moses played with the Milwaukee Bucks (NBA) in 1991–1992 and 1992–1993 and the Philadelphia 76ers (NBA) in 1993–1994, before joining the San Antonio Spurs (NBA) in August 1994.

Although not tall for an NBA center, the muscular 250-pounder performed very well with taller opponents. His combined ABA-NBA career featured 29,580 points (20.3 points per game average), 17,834 rebounds, and 1,733 blocked shots in 1,455 games. The three-time NBA MVP made the All-NBA First Team in 1979, 1982, 1983, and 1985 and the All-NBA Second Team in 1980, 1981, 1984, and 1987. Moses was selected to the NBA All-Star Game 12 consecutive seasons from 1978 to 1989 and led the NBA in rebounds six times, including five in a row. Without the benefit of college coaching, he relied more than most players on basic instincts. The consistent, serene Malone paced himself well. Phil Elderkin called Moses "smart, durable, and steady . . . just your average, everyday superstar."

Malone married Alfeda Gill and has two children.

BIBLIOGRAPHY: Ray Buck, "Wholly Moses," Sport 73 (January 1982), pp. 31–32; Anthony Cotton, "I Can Do Many Things," Sports Illustrated 57 (November 1, 1982), pp. 46–49; Current Biography Yearbook (1986), pp. 332–334; Frank Deford, "Bounding into Prominence," Sports Illustrated 50 (February 19, 1979), pp. 60–64; Ronald O. Howell, "Basketball's Million Dollar Baby," Ebony 35 (January 1980), pp. 38–40; Don Kowet, "Moses Malone: Undergraduate in the ABA," Sport 60 (January 1975), pp. 76–77; David L. Porter, ed., Biographical Dictionary of American Sports: Basketball and Other Indoor Sports (Westport, CT, 1989); Pat Putnam, "Don't Send My Boy to Harvard," Sports Illustrated 41 (November 4, 1974), pp. 20–21; The Sporting News Official NBA Register (1994–1995).

David L. Porter

JUAN MARICHAL
(October 24, 1937–   ) —————————————————————————— Baseball

Juan Marichal rivaled Sandy Koufax of the Los Angeles Dodgers as the best major league pitcher of the 1960s. Juan Antonio Sanchez Marichal was born on October 24, 1937, in Laguna Verde, Dominican Republic, and grew up in a palm bark shack. His father, a poor farmer, died of alcoholism when Juan was only 3 years old. His mother, who brought him up, inherited 400 mostly uncultivated acres. Marichal nearly died when he was 12 years old. Juan went swimming after a heavy meal and suffered spasms, remaining unconscious for six days. His brother, Gonzalo, and brother-in-law, Prospero Villona, stimulated his interest in baseball. Marichal, nicknamed "Manito," "The Dominican Dandy," and "Laughing Boy," quit high school after the eleventh grade and played amateur baseball for Monte Christi, the United Fruit Company, and the Dominican Air Force and professionally with the Escogido Leones. Juan married 16-year-old Alma Rosa Carrajal on March 28, 1962, and has three children.

In 1958, San Francisco Giants National League (NL) scouts Horacio Martinez and Alex Pompez signed Marichal for a $500 bonus. Juan pitched brilliantly for Michigan City, Indiana, of the Midwest League in 1958, Springfield, Massachusetts, of the Eastern League in 1959, and Tacoma, Washington, of the Pacific Coast League in 1960 before joining the San Francisco NL club at midseason. In his major league debut on July 19, 1960, he shut out the Philadelphia Phillies, 2–0, and surrendered only an eighth-inning single to Clay Dalrymple. A 6-2 mark and 2.66 ERA highlighted his rookie season. In 1962, Marichal's 18 triumphs helped the Giants capture the NL pennant, but an injured finger restricted his World Series action to four innings against the New York Yankees.

The six-foot, 185-pound right-hander, an easygoing prankster with an impish grin and chubby face, exhibited confidence and fierce determination on the mound. Juan, who drew enthusiastic crowds, used a high leg kick, making it difficult for batters to see the ball. He mastered 13 different pitches, varying his deliveries of the fastball, curve, slider, and screwball. "No man," manager Herman Franks asserted, "has the assortment of pitches Juan has." Slugger **Frank Robinson** observed, "Juan has no set pattern. He's got all that stuff, and he'll throw any of it in any situation." Marichal demonstrated pinpoint control. "He can throw all day within a two-inch space in, out, up or down," slugger **Hank Aaron** acknowledged. "I've never seen anyone as good as that." Speedster **Lou Brock** added, "This guy has more craftsmanship than anybody I've ever seen."

From 1963 to 1969, Marichal compiled six 20-game victory seasons as the period's winningest pitcher. During that span, Juan enjoyed four consecutive 20-game victory seasons (1963–1966) and led the NL twice in victories (1963, 1968), complete games (1964, 1968), innings pitched (1963, 1968), and shutouts (1965, 1969) and once in best pitching percentage (1966) and ERA (1969). His best records included 25–8 in 1963, 21–8 in 1964, 22–13 in 1965, 25–6 in 1966, 26–9 in 1968, and 21–11 in 1969. "When you get a hit off . . . Marichal," infielder **Joe Morgan** remarked, "the umpire should stop the game and present you with the ball." Juan compiled ERAs below 3.00 nine times and struck out over 200 batters six seasons. In 1971, his 18 victories contributed to San Francisco's Western Division title. The Giants, however, lost the NL Championship Series to the Pittsburgh Pirates. Marichal, who did not experience a losing record until 1972, was sold to the Boston Red Sox American League (AL) club following the 1973 campaign. Juan posted a 5–1 mark with Boston in 1974 and pitched briefly for the Los Angeles Dodgers (NL) in 1975 before retiring to his 1,000-acre farm in Santo Domingo.

During his 16-year major league career, the injury-prone Marichal won 243 games, lost 142 decisions, and recorded a 2.89 ERA in 471 contests. Juan struck out 2,303 batters and walked only 709 in over 3,500 innings, hurling 52 shutouts. "Put your club a run ahead in the later innings," manager Alvin Dark commented, "and Marichal is the greatest pitcher I ever saw." "Even when Koufax was around," slugger Dick Allen affirmed, "I thought Marichal was the best." An eight-time NL All-Star, Juan surrendered only two runs in 18 innings. He won the first 1962 and the 1964 All-Star classics and earned MVP honors in the 1965 contest. *The Sporting News* named Marichal on its NL All-Star team in 1963, 1965, 1966, and 1968. Juan hurled a no-hit game on June 15, 1963, against the Houston Colt 45s and one-hit shutout on August 2, 1961, against the Dodgers. In June 1963, he outdueled Warren Spahn of the Milwaukee Braves, 1–0, in 16 innings. Marichal's six season-opening games set an NL record.

Juan participated in a wild, bean-ball affair with Los Angeles at Candlestick Park on August 22, 1965. In the third inning, Koufax pitched Marichal inside. Catcher John Roseboro fired the ball back hard to Koufax just past Juan's ear. In an explosion of rage, fear, or panic, Marichal struck Roseboro three times on the head with his bat. Blood streamed down John's face from a deep wound to the scalp. Juan was ejected from the game, as fans nearly rioted. President Warren Giles suspended him for nine days and fined him an NL record $1,750. Roseboro filed a $110,000 lawsuit against Marichal, who was deluged with hate mail.

Juan believed Latin American players suffered subtle discrimination. "Our skin may be lighter," he stated, "but the breaks we get from baseball and on the outside are much less than the Negro player gets." In 1983, Marichal became the first Latin American player chosen to the National Baseball Hall of Fame through the regular selection process.

BIBLIOGRAPHY: The Baseball Encyclopedia, 9th ed. (New York, 1993); "The Dandy Dominican," *Time* 87 (June 10, 1966), pp. 88–92; Charles Einstein, "The Juan Marichal Mystery," *Sport* 35 (June 1963), pp. 49–51, 72; Charles Einstein, "Juan Marichal at the Crossroads," *Sport* 45 (April 1968), pp. 58, 60, 88; *The Lincoln Library of Sports Champions*, vol. 8 (Columbus, OH, 1974); Lowell Reidenbaugh, *Cooperstown: Where Baseball's Legends Live Forever* (St. Louis, MO, 1983); Al Stump, "Always They Want More, More, More," *Saturday Evening Post* 240 (July 29, 1967), pp. 68–71; *The Sporting News Baseball Register* (1975); Jack Zanger, "A Unique View of Juan Marichal," *Sport* 44 (September 1967), pp. 18–20, 85–86.

David L. Porter

MIKE MARSH
(August 4, 1967–   ) ——————————————————— Track and Field

One of the fastest 100-meter and 200-meter dashmen of all time remains Mike Marsh, who astonished many track and field experts by winning the Gold Medal in the 200 meters at the 1992 Summer Olympic Games in Barcelona, Spain. Michael Lawrence Marsh was born on August 4, 1967, in Los Angeles, California, the son of Jonnie Brown, a certified public accountant. His step-father, Thomas Brown, works as a real estate agent. Mike, an only child who spent his primary school years in south-central Los Angeles, never knew his natural father. His initial participation in sports came "playing baseball in the streets and racing the neighborhood kids on the sidewalks." Marsh, who "joined his first track club in sixth grade," captured the 1985 California State high school championship in the 200 meters. Before graduating from Los Angeles' Hawthorne High School that year, he had clocked 10.6 seconds in the 100 meters and 20.82 seconds in the 200 meters.

Marsh entered the University of California at Los Angeles (UCLA) on a track and field scholarship in 1985. Mike acknowledged that "he had wanted to attend UCLA since the fifth or sixth grade." He entered UCLA, however, when the track and field team boasted talented sprinters, including Danny Everett, Steve Lewis, and Henry Thomas. UCLA coaches employed Marsh in the 100 meters, resulting in a third-place 1987 NCAA championship finish and a first-place 1989 Olympic Festival finish. Mike's sixth-place finish in the 100 meters at the 1988 U.S. Olympic Trials qualified him for the U.S. Olympic team as an alternate in the 4 × 100-meter relay team. He attributes his lack-luster success at UCLA to a persistent hamstring injury and "a host of little problems." In 1989, however, Marsh garnered a Gold Medal in the World University Games at Duisburg, Germany, anchoring the U.S. 4 × 100-meter relay team. Dave Johnson of *Track and Field News* observed that Mike's best times of 10.07 seconds in the 100 meters and 20.35 seconds in the 200 meters marked a "distinguished college" athletic career.

After graduating from UCLA in 1989, Marsh joined the Santa Monica Track Club in Houston, Texas. "I always thought I was talented, but when I first came to Houston I didn't know what I could do. I believed that Houston was going to make me the best sprinter I could possibly be." Under Santa Monica track coach Tom Tellez, the world-renowned mentor of sprinters **Carl Lewis** and Leroy Burrell, Mike began to realize his potential with the world record–breaking U.S. 4 × 100-meter relay teams. At the 1990 European Track and Field Championships, France had established a world record of 37.79 seconds in the 4 × 100-meter relay and had eclipsed the standard of 37.83 seconds held by the United States since 1984. "The 4 × 100 is an American affair," proclaimed Tellez, who insisted the United States "must be world champions and take the world record away from the French." Tellez assigned Marsh to run the first leg of the 4 × 100-meter relay in Monaco, where the United States equaled France's world record. Mike later led off the 4 × 100-meter relay in Zurich, Switzerland, helping the United States establish a new world record of 37.67 seconds. Despite his contributions to these world record relay performances, Marsh was disappointed in his first year with the Santa Monica Track Club. Mike finished just seventh in the 100 meters and fifth in the 200 meters at the 1991 Track Athletic Congress (TAC) championships. "If I continue to just run in the back," he remarked, "I will leave track and field."

In 1992, Marsh finally achieved individual fame in the 100 meters and 200 meters. Mike, wrote Jeff Hollobaugh of *Track and Field News*, "shocked the track world with scintillating sprint clockings" of 9.93 seconds in the 100 meters and 19.94 seconds in the 200 meters. At the 1992 Olympic Trials, Marsh placed second to **Michael Johnson,** the world's premier 200-meter dashman, and improved his time to 19.86 seconds. Mike also finished fourth in the 100 meters and qualified for the 4 × 100-meter relay team. In the semifinals of the 200 meters at the 1992 Barcelona, Spain, Summer Olympic Games, he clocked 19.73 seconds for Olympic and American records and history's fastest sea-level time. "I wanted to relax and just basically get into the final and I ended up running that fast," he remarked. Marsh had just missed the 200-meter world record by .01 of a second! Although capturing the Gold Medal, Mike remembers "relaxing so much that I didn't even drive out of the blocks" in the 200-meter final. He also earned another Gold Medal in the 4 × 100-meter relay, helping the United States set a world record of 37.40 seconds. Marsh once acknowledged that his goal as a track and field performer was "for people to be pleased with the way I handle success, but just as much, with the way I handle defeat." After capturing the 200 meters in the USA Track and Field (USATF) Championships, Mike finished fourth in the World Championships in 1993.

In April 1994, he helped the Santa Monica Track Club 4 × 200-meter relay team set a world record of 1 minute 18.8 seconds at Walnut, California. At the St. Petersburg, Russia, 1994 Goodwill Games, Marsh ran the first leg for the victorious 4 × 100-meter squad. In March 1995, Mike placed third in the 60-meter dash at the USA/Mobil Indoor Track and Field Championships at Atlanta, Georgia. He edged Maurice Greene and Dennis Mitchell to win the 100-meter dash in 10.23 seconds and placed a disappointing sixth in the 200 meters at the USATF Outdoor Championships at Sacramento, California, in June 1995.

BIBLIOGRAPHY: Bob Hersh, "Marsh Sets AR Early," *Track and Field News* 45 (October 1992), pp. 14, 16; Jeff Hollobaugh, "Marsh More Than a Relayer," *Track and Field News* 45 (June 1992), p. 7; Dave Johnson, "Move Was Key for Marsh," *Track and Field News* 45 (October 1992), p. 17; Walt Murphy, "U.S. Runs WR 37.40," *Track and Field News* 45 (October 1992), p. 36; David L. Porter, ed., *Biographical Dictionary of American Sports: 1992–1995 Supplement for Baseball, Football, Basketball, and Other Sports* (Westport, CT, 1995).

Adam R. Hornbuckle

WILLIE MAYS
(May 6, 1931–) ———————————————————————— *Baseball*

Willie Mays became the highest-paid player in major league baseball history on February 11, 1966, when he signed a two-year contract with the San Francisco Giants National League (NL) club for $130,000 a year. Fans have considered him a "million-dollar" ballplayer almost from the day he first donned a major league uniform. Willie Howard Mays was born on May 6, 1931, in Westfield, Alabama, to William Mays and Ann Mays, both excellent athletes.

His father, a steel mill worker, once played for the Birmingham, Alabama, Black Barons of the Negro National League (NNL), while his mother starred in high school track and field. Mays's parents were divorced soon after his birth, and he was brought up by his Aunt Sarah in Fairfield. His mother remarried and gave birth to 10 more children, eight girls and two boys. She died in 1953 giving birth to the tenth child. Willie often has helped his half brothers and half sisters financially.

At age 10, Mays began playing in sandlot games with boys four and five years older. Willie attended Fairfield Industrial High School, where he starred in basketball and football. Since his high school did not have a baseball team, he pitched for his father's steel mill team and also played baseball for a local semi-pro team. With his father's help, Mays tried out with the Birmingham Barons (NNL) in 1948 and was signed by manager Lorenzo "Piper" Davis. In 1950, New York Giants' (NL) scouts Bill Harris and Ed Montague saw Willie play. On their recommendation, the Giants paid the Barons $10,000 for the 5-foot-10½-inch, 170-pound right-handed outfielder and assigned him to Trenton, New Jersey, of the Interstate League (ISL). Mays batted .353 there. Willie spent just 35 games with the Class AAA Minneapolis Millers of the American Association (AA) in 1951. His .477 batting average there earned him a spot on the New York Giants roster. Under manager Leo Durocher, Mays played in his first major league game on May 25, 1951. Durocher, Willie's favorite manager, exerted the greatest influence on his career. Mays affirmed, "There's no doubt in my mind that Leo did more for me in baseball than anyone else. I was a scared, nervous kid, just up from the South, when I came to the Giants and Leo gave me a lot of encouragement. Maybe he did some things wrong, but for me he did so many things right." With Durocher's confidence and patience, Willie became the regular center fielder and helped the Giants win the 1951 NL pennant after being 13½ games behind the Brooklyn Dodgers. His .274 batting average and 20 home runs earned him NL Rookie of the Year.

Mays was drafted into the U.S. Army in May 1952. After military service, 1952 and 1953, Willie returned to the New York Giants in 1954 and captured the NL batting title with a .345 average. *The Sporting News* voted him the NL's Most Valuable Player (MVP). Mays led the Giants to the 1954 NL pennant and World Series championship in four games over the Cleveland Indians, making an unbelievable catch of a towering drive by first baseman Vic Wertz. Sports historian John L. Evers declared, "No player ever made a more publicized catch, which many considered to be the greatest ever made on any baseball diamond. This feat epitomized Mays' career. His defensive play, ranging from his famous basket-catch to nailing a runner at home plate with a perfect throw, was accomplished with a unique flair."

Mays soon emerged as one of major league baseball's all-time "superstars." During 19 seasons with the Giants' organization (5 in New York and 14 in San Francisco), Willie batted above .300 10 times. He led the NL in home runs 4 times and scored over 100 runs in 12 consecutive seasons. In 1972, San Francisco traded Mays to the New York Mets (NL). The Mets signed Willie to a 10-year deal and utilized him after 1973 as a part-time coach and goodwill ambassador. From 1954 to 1973, Mays played in every All-Star Game with a composite batting average over .300. Willie participated in four World Series and 20 World Series games, with a .239 batting average. In 1955, he became the first major league player to steal 20 bases and hit at least 50 home runs in the same season. Twice Mays slugged over 30 home runs and swiped over 30 bases in the same season. Willie slammed 4 home runs in 1 game, twice belted 3 home runs in a contest, and 63 times hit 2 home runs in a game.

Mays ended his 22-year playing career in 1973. During his career, Willie played in 2,992 games, recorded 1,903 RBIs, and scored 2,062 runs. His 3,283 hits included 523 doubles, 140 triples, and 660 home runs. Mays ended his career with a .302 batting average and .981 fielding average. Willie, twice named the NL MVP, was selected Player of the Decade (1960–1969) and inducted into the National Baseball Hall of Fame in 1979.

In October 1979, Mays joined the Bally Manufacturing Corporation, a company owning a hotel gambling casino. Due to rules governing the major leagues, Willie was forced to end all participation in baseball. In 1985, Commissioner Peter Ueberroth lifted the restrictions on his involvement with baseball.

In February 1956, Mays married Marghuerite Wendall Kennedy Chapman. The marriage lasted just five years, but the couple adopted a three-year-old boy, Michael. Willie and Michael remain very close. Mays states, "He has changed my life, my purpose, my outlook." In 1971, Willie married Mae Allen.

In his book *Men at Work,* George Will wrote, "The truth is that Mays was, from the first, a superb craftsman. Mays's 'instincts' were actually the result of meticulous work." Manager Bill Rigney lauded Willie, "He is the best player I ever saw. He is a 'complete' player."

BIBLIOGRAPHY: *Current Biography Yearbook* (1966), pp. 270–273; David L. Porter, ed., *Biographical Dictionary of American Sports: Baseball* (Westport, CT, 1987); *The Sporting News Official Baseball Register* (1974); George F. Will, *Men at Work* (New York, 1990).

James E. Welch

CHERYL MILLER
(January 3, 1964–   ) _____ *Basketball*

"Best ever" women's basketball player accolades described Cheryl Miller as an 18-year-old in 1983, when she became the first female to dunk a basketball in regulation play. An all-around performer, Miller set many basketball records as a high school, university, and international player. Cheryl, the first woman basketball player nominated for the prestigious Sullivan Award in 1985–1986, received the Naismith Player of the Year Award in 1986 for the third consecutive year.

Cheryl was born to Saul Miller and Carrie Miller in Riverside, California, on January 3, 1964, the third of five children. Miller, nicknamed "Silk" because of her smooth, fluid court play, credits her father, who earned All-State honors as a basketball player, for encouraging all his children to be athletes. Two brothers, Saul, Jr., and Reggie, played basketball like their father. Brother Darrell played outfield with the California Angels (AL) baseball team, while sister Tammy competed in high school volleyball.

Cheryl, the pivotal player on the 1984 United States Gold Medal Olympic Women's Basketball team, set seven individual season- and game-high records that year with the University of Southern California (USC) basketball team. During the next two years, Miller broke most of these USC records, including scoring (3,018 points), rebounding (1,534), field goals made (1,159), free throws made (700), and steals (462) in 218 games. USC retired Cheryl's playing uniform in 1986, making her the first Trojan basketball player (male or female) to be accorded that honor.

Cheryl's strength, skill, and unparalleled blend of grace and power enabled her to lead the Riverside Poly High School team to an incredible 132–4 record from 1979 through 1982. As a high school player, Miller deservedly earned many honors. *Parade* selected her to its All-America team four consecutive years, making her the only athlete, female or male, to be so honored. Cheryl's other basketball honors included All-America (1979–1982), Amateur Athletic Union (AAU) All-America (1979–1982), and *Street and Smith* High School Player of the Year (1981, 1982). Her 105 points in a regulation game set a national record in five-player high school girls basketball. Miller enjoyed a multidimensional high school career. Academics remained important to her. Despite all the media attention, Cheryl maintained a "B" grade point, kept active in the Black Student Union, finished runner-up for homecoming queen, and participated on the varsity softball team.

Two hundred fifty colleges recruited the six-foot-two-inch triple-threat player. Miller shot from anywhere, rebounded in the heaviest of traffic under the basket, and played superbly. Coached by Linda Sharp, USC won the recruiting battle for her services. Cheryl joined teammates, twins Paula and Pam McGee, Kathy Doyle, Tracy Longo, Rhonda Windham, and Cynthia Cooper, in defeating Louisiana Tech University, leading the Trojans to their first national championship in 1982–1983. By the next year, Miller had grown to her full stature of six feet three inches and averaged 20 points and 10 rebounds per regular-season games. USC again prevailed over Louisiana Tech that year, 72–61, for their second consecutive NCAA championship. Cheryl brought a style to the women's games, giving her all. "I'm very, very sensitive. . . . I would cut off my right arm for the university." At times people criticized her style, claiming she was out for herself and not for her team or women's basketball. Miller continued, "When people challenged my loyalty, that hurt."

Cheryl was named 1984 NCAA Most Valuable Player (MVP), *NBA Today* Women's Player of the Year, Kodak All-America, and Broderick Basketball Player of the Year and shared the Broderick Cup for the Female Athlete of the Year Award with Olympic Gold Medal swimmer Tracy Caulkins. Her team did not win the national championship the following two years, but she set more records. In 1985, Miller was named Naismith Player of the Year and ESPN Woman Athlete of the Year, again received the Broderick Cup (as she did her senior year), won the Naismith Trophy, was selected to the NCAA Final Four All-Tournament team, and was chosen MVP in the West NCAA Regional, Pac-West, Trans-America Basketball Classic, and Maryland Thanksgiving tournaments.

Cheryl prized those awards, but when asked in 1984 what her biggest basketball thrill was, she responded, "Biggest thrill in basketball? That's easy! Right now it will be hard to beat playing in the Olympics. The only thing would be winning the Gold Medal. If we do that, I don't know if I'll ever come down from Cloud Nine." The national and international media audiences publicized her superior athletic skills. An energetic, emotional player, Miller triggered the transformation of women's basketball into a dynamic spectacle. Cheryl led the Olympic team in scoring at the 1984 Los Angeles, California, Summer Games and helped the squad win the Olympic Gold Medal. Although the USSR team boycotted that Olympics, the USA's first place marked a marvelous accomplishment.

Miller returned to USC and continued her pace-setting play, graduating with a bachelor's degree in sport journalism. Cheryl's education prepared her well for becoming a spokesperson for philanthropic causes, conducting frequent media interviews, and broadcasting women's basketball. In 1985, for example, she proved an effective spokesperson for the Civil Rights Restoration Act in Congress, Los Angeles Literacy Campaign, American Diabetics Association, YWCA Shelter for Battered Women, and Riverside Hospice Program and appeared on "Face the Nation." Los Angeles Mayor Tom Bradley declared a "Cheryl Miller Day" in 1985, while *Sports Illustrated* named her the Best College Player, Male or Female, in 1986. She received awards from the YWCA and the Black Achievement.

In 1986, Miller was drafted in the first-round pick of the National Women's Basketball Association, but insufficient financing caused it to fold that same year. Cheryl in 1986 played on the Gold Medal U.S. team defeating the USSR at the Goodwill Games in Moscow, Russia, in July and at the World Basketball Championship in August.

Basketball had been a central force in Miller's life and created opportunities for her. Cheryl looked beyond basketball to see what else could be accomplished. As an 18-year-old, Miller once philosophized, "You have to keep things in perspective. I read stories in the paper, and I try not to believe them. The writers are always trying to blow things out of proportion." Cheryl also graciously said, "A hundred other women have contributed to basketball. I've been blessed with this talent of being at the right place at the right time. . . . Right now there are a lot of opportunities. . . . I'd like to try them." In 1986, Miller continued to practice for the Pan-American Games and was playing in her normal aggressive style when she heard a "pop." Cheryl tore her anterior cruciate ligament and ripped her lateral meniscus cartilage. Extensive surgery and slow recovery kept her from the 1987 Pan-American Games and the 1988 Seoul, South Korea, Summer Olympics.

Miller, forced to the sidelines, utilized her undergraduate degree in sports journalism. Cheryl worked for ABC-Sports in 1988, handling halftime interviews during men's college basketball games, and conducted interviews at the 1988 Calgary, Canada, Winter Olympic Games. She continued to work as a sports media journalist until joining her alma mater as head basketball coach in 1993. Southern California finished ninth in the *USA Today*/CNN final poll with a 26–4 record, losing to Louisiana Tech University, 75–66, in the Mideast regional final. In 1994, Southern California finished with an 18–9 regular season record, but was eliminated by the University of Memphis in the first round of the NCAA tournament.

As a 21-year-old in 1985, Miller had stated, "No coaching, definitely no coaching. I do not have the patience. I'm a player, I'll always be a player." Cheryl, one of women's basketball's greatest and most visible players, faces a new challenge in trying to build the team to equal the ones she led a decade earlier. In 1991, the International Women's Sports Hall of Fame inducted her. Four years later, she was selected to the Naismith Memorial Basketball Hall of Fame.

BIBLIOGRAPHY: Rick Brown, " '84 Olympics: Miller's Time to Shine," *Des Moines Register*, July 12, 1984, p. S3; Jane Burns, "USC Star Miller Looks Ahead to Life Away from Basketball," *Des Moines Register*, March 16, 1986; Jule Deardorff, "Making Some Headway in Pay," *Des Moines Register*, December 19, 1993, p. D3; Phil Elderkin, "USC's Cheryl Miller Living Up to High School Rave Notices So Far," *Los Angeles Times*, December 7, 1982; Michael Hurd, "Queen of the Court," *USA Weekend*, March 7, 1986; Michael Lecesse, "Her Aim: To Get Well," *USA Weekend*, July 1987; David L. Porter, ed., *Biographical Dictionary of American Sports: Basketball and Other Indoor Sports* (Westport, CT, 1989); E. A. Sherman, " 'Best Ever' Tag Follows Cheryl Miller," *Chicago Tribune*, March 20, 1984; University of Southern California Sports Information Office, Los Angeles, CA, letter to David L. Porter, March 22, 1988; Gordon S. White, Jr., "The Ghost of Lew Alcindor Is a . . . Girl," *Des Moines Register*, February 4, 1982, p. B3.

Janice A. Beran

TOM MOLYNEUX
(1784–August 4, 1818) ——————————————————————— *Boxing*

Tom Molyneux, an African-American bare-knuckle fighter, became most famous for nearly defeating British champion Tom Cribb in 1810. Much of Molyneux's life remains mysterious. Disagreement arises even over how to spell his name, with "Molyneau" and "Molyneaux" given as variants. Tom was born in Maryland, Virginia, or South Carolina in 1784. According to legend, he worked as a slave of Virginia planter Algernon Molyneux. Algernon allegedly freed Tom after the latter had won a fight on which his owner had wagered heavily. Molyneux had won his freedom by the early 1800s and lived in New York City, where he worked as a dock hand. He probably continued his prizefighting informally with fellow workers.

Molyneux moved to England in 1809 possibly because more opportunities existed to box there than in the United States. In London, Tom met Bill Richmond, an African-American boxer from Staten Island who also had moved to England. Richmond became Tom's manager, trainer, and confidant. After Molyneux had won eight bouts, Richmond deemed him ready to challenge British Champion Tom Cribb. Authorities generally touted Cribb as the best prizefighter in the world.

The Molyneux-Cribb bout was held on December 19, 1810, in Sussex. A cold rain made conditions miserable. According to boxing historian Elliott Gorn, the nervous British fans feared that England "might lose the championship, a symbol of national virility." Molyneux dominated the fight until the twenty-third round. Cribb could not return to the ring after a knockdown and probably would have been ruled out had his manager not claimed a foul. The ensuing discussion gave Cribb time to rest. Cribb ultimately wore down the American challenger, who could not continue after the fortieth round. In spite of the defeat, Tom certainly impressed English sports chronicler Pierce Egan. Egan wrote that Molyneux "proved himself as courageous a man as ever an adversary contended with." Egan especially liked Tom's expertise in "the science" of prizefighting.

After one intervening victory, Molyneux again lost to Cribb in just 13 rounds in September 1811. Tom fought sporadically over the next few years, mainly giving exhibitions in Ireland and Scotland. Tuberculosis, combined with a serious case of alcoholism, led to his death on August 4, 1818, in Galway, Ireland.

Many boxing historians consider Molyneux the first important American prizefighter. Ring historian John Durant called Tom "the first American fighter to make a name for himself." His African-American heritage only enhanced his reputation among his fellow African Americans. *The Ring's* Boxing Hall of Fame inducted him in 1958, four years after similarly honoring Cribb.

BIBLIOGRAPHY: Arthur Ashe, Jr., *A Hard Road to Glory: A History of the African-American Athlete, 1619–1918,* vol. 1 (New York, 1988); John Durant, *The Heavyweight Champions,* 6th ed. (New York, 1976); Elliott J. Gorn, *The Manly Art: Bare-Knuckle Prize Fighting in America* (Ithaca, NY, 1986); David L. Porter, ed., *Biographical Dictionary of American Sports: Basketball and Other Indoor Sports* (Westport, CT, 1989); Thomas B. Shepherd, comp., *The Noble Art* (London, England, 1950).

                                                                        Anthony O. Edmonds

Hank Aaron. Courtesy National Baseball Library & Archive, Cooperstown, N.Y.

Kareem Abdul-Jabbar. Courtesy Basketball Hall of Fame

Muhammad Ali. Courtesy *The Sporting News*

Arthur Ashe, Jr. Courtesy *The Sporting News*

Elgin Baylor. Courtesy Basketball Hall of Fame

Cool Papa Bell. Courtesy National Baseball Library & Archive, Cooperstown, N.Y.

Jim Brown. Courtesy *The Sporting News*

Wilt Chamberlain. Courtesy Basketball Hall of Fame

Bob Gibson. Courtesy National Baseball Library & Archive, Cooperstown, N.Y.

Josh Gibson. Courtesy National Baseball Library & Archive, Cooperstown, N.Y.

Elvin Hayes. Courtesy Basketball Hall of Fame

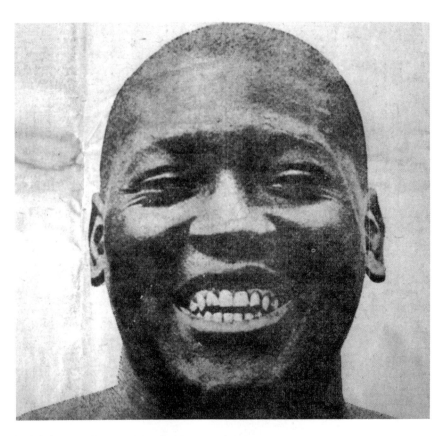

Jack Johnson. Courtesy Nevada Historical Society

Magic Johnson. Courtesy Malcolm Emmons/*The Sporting News*

Michael Jordan. Courtesy Don McAdam/*The Sporting News*

Jackie Joyner-Kersee. Courtesy *The Sporting News*

Joe Louis. Courtesy *The Sporting News*

Willie Mays

Isaac Murphy. Courtesy Keeneland Library, Lexington, Kentucky

Satchel Paige. Courtesy National Baseball Library & Archive, Cooperstown, N.Y.

Walter Payton. Courtesy Malcolm Emmons/*The Sporting News*

Jerry Rice. Courtesy Greg Trott/*The Sporting News*

Oscar Robertson. Courtesy Basketball Hall of Fame

Frank Robinson. Courtesy National Baseball Library & Archive, Cooperstown, N.Y.

Jackie Robinson. Courtesy National Baseball Library & Archive, Cooperstown, N.Y.

Bill Russell. Courtesy Basketball Hall of Fame

Barry Sanders. Courtesy Betsy Rowe/*The Sporting News*

Emmitt Smith. Courtesy Fotosports International/*The Sporting News*

ART MONK
(December 5, 1957–) ————————————————————— *Football*

Art Monk has caught more passes than any other professional football player. The quiet Monk remains among the most respected National Football League (NFL) players, known for his hard work, dedication, and class. James Arthur Monk was born on December 5, 1957, in White Plains, New York, the son of Arthur Monk, a welder, and Lela Monk, a domestic, and is a second cousin of the famous jazz composer and musician Thelonius Monk. Although a talented musician in his youth, Art found his future in athletics, not music. He excelled in football at White Plains High School but was better known for his track and field exploits. Authorities considered him one of the nation's best high school hurdlers.

Monk accepted a football scholarship to Syracuse University and played there from 1976 through 1979. Art performed well there but never achieved the acclaim of earlier Syracuse players **Jimmy Brown, Ernie Davis,** Floyd Little, or Larry Csonka. He finished his college career with 102 pass catches, 1,644 yards receiving, 1,140 rushing yards, and over 1,000 yards in kick returns.

The Washington Redskins picked Monk in the first round of the 1980 NFL draft. Art immediately started at wide receiver for the Redskins and remained in that role for the next 14 seasons there. He possessed good speed, but there were faster NFL receivers. The six-foot-three-inch 210-pounder had good size for a receiver, but there were bigger receivers. But no one worked harder than Monk, no one ran routes better, and absolutely no one caught the tough passes over the middle as well. Art rarely dropped a pass and excelled in the clutch, being nicknamed "Mr. Third Down" and "the King of Third and Nine." Most of all, he impressed observers with his prodigious work ethic. His college coach Frank Maloney remarked, "He fears failure. That's why he works out like a madman. He fears the end of his career. He fears slowing down. That's a wonderful thing to have, that fear." Monk likewise, acknowledges, "I don't know where this came from, but I always felt I've got to do better—it's good, but I've got to do better! I worked hard because I never felt I had the talent."

A model of consistency, Monk caught 58 passes his rookie season and steadily improved. In 1984, Art grabbed 106 aerials, becoming the first NFL player to surpass 100 in a season. This record lasted until 1992, when Sterling Sharpe of the Green Bay Packers broke it. Monk caught 91 passes in 1985, finishing 1 behind NFL leader Roger Craig of the San Francisco 49ers. Art's best game came in 1985, when he caught 13 passes against the Cincinnati Bengals. His biggest moment, however, occurred in 1992, when he snared his 820th pass to surpass Steve Largent as the leading pass receiver in NFL history. Monk played in three Pro Bowls and in Super Bowls XVIII, XXII, and XXVI. A foot injury sidelined Art from Super Bowl XVII. He caught a touchdown pass against the Denver Broncos in Super Bowl XXII and grabbed 7 passes against the Buffalo Bills in Super Bowl XXVI. The Redskins won both contests. During this period, Art became the acknowledged team leader.

Many football authorities noticed that Monk was slowing down after the 1992 season and expected a younger player to replace him in the starting lineup. But the reliable veteran surprised them by catching 41 passes in 1993 at age 36. Due to the new salary cap, Washington could not sign Monk. Art, therefore, signed with the New York Jets (NFL) for the 1994 season and broke Largent's record of 177 games with at least one catch in the fourteenth game that year. He ended the 1994 season with pass receptions in 180 consecutive games before being released by the Jets in March 1995. Through the 1994 season, Monk had caught 934 passes for 12,607 yards and 67 touchdowns.

Monk and his wife Desiree have three children, James Arthur, Jr., Danielle, and Monica. In 1992, Art told *Sports Illustrated,* "I do two important things in my life. I play football and I spend time with my family. Most everything else is a distraction." This dedication has helped make him one of the best receivers to ever play football.

BIBLIOGRAPHY: "Art Monk: A Good Catch for the Redskins," *Football Digest* 14 (July–August 1985), pp. 34–39; "The King of Third and Nine," *Washington Post Magazine,* September 9, 1990; William Nack, "A Monk's Existence," *Sports Illustrated* 77 (September 7, 1992), pp. 32–40; *Washington Redskins Media Guides* (1980–1993).

Jim L. Sumner

WARREN MOON
(November 18, 1956–) _____ *Football*

Warren Moon always considered quarterback his natural position, but coaches and scouts often disagreed. Moon's childhood, however, prepared him for the conflicts that he would face later in his athletic career. Harold Warren Moon was born on November 18, 1956, in Los Angeles, California, the only son among seven children. His father, Harold Moon, a laborer, died when Warren was only seven, leaving his mother, Pat, to care for the entire family. Pat worked double shifts as a nurse and taught Warren to cook, sew, and iron. Warren credits her as being "the most influential person in my life. She did so much with so little and kept everything in line around the house."

Moon's athletic prowess surfaced while playing Pop Warner football at age 10 for the Baldwin Hills Trojans. Warren later starred at quarterback for Hamilton High School in Los Angeles, earning the city's Most Valuable Player (MVP) and Second Team High School All-America. Moon's senior season started the first of his many battles with football recruiters and scouts. No one believed that Warren could be a major college quarterback. He did not sign or move to another position, opting instead to play at West Los Angeles Junior College. After that season, coach Don James of the University of Washington signed Warren to play quarterback.

Moon later regretted his decision due to the small African-American enrollment at Washington and the many racial slurs directed at him. Warren nearly quit, but his mother's advice helped him through this difficult time. He recalls, "My mother told me that I had never quit anything before. So I followed her suggestion to stay there, stick it out, and make the best of it. Those experiences taught me an awful lot about people."

Moon's mother proved right. The boos turned to cheers, when Warren led the University of Washington to the Pacific Eight Conference championship and a 27–20 Rose Bowl victory over the University of Michigan in 1977. The media selected Moon Pac-Eight Player of the Year and Rose Bowl MVP.

Despite his success, Moon again battled scouts over his gridiron position. National Football League (NFL) scouts considered Warren too small and too much of a scrambler to be an effective NFL quarterback. Racial questions also arose concerning the leadership abilities of an African-American quarterback.

Moon avoided the controversy by signing with the Edmonton Eskimos of the Canadian Football League (CFL), where quarterbacks ran and passed. Warren started slowly in the CFL but gradually developed into its premier star. He did not start a single game his first three seasons but played in every game. Edmonton won three Grey Cups, symbolizing the CFL championship. In 1981, he became a starter and helped Edmonton win its fourth consecutive Grey Cup. The 1982 campaign saw Moon start every game. Warren passed for 5,000 yards and 36 touchdowns, as Edmonton won an unbelievable fifth consecutive Grey Cup.

Edmonton's Grey Cup streak stopped in 1983, although Moon experienced his greatest pro season. Warren passed for 5,648 yards and 31 touchdowns. On October 15, 1983, he set a pro football single-game passing record with 555 yards. Moon also led Edmonton in rushing and was selected CFL MVP. His teammates observed, "Warren created a lot of opportunities that other quarterbacks couldn't. When it looked like he'd be sacked, he'd escape, scramble around, and find an open receiver."

After the 1983 CFL season, Moon sought to establish himself as an NFL quarterback. No NFL team had drafted Warren, leaving him free to sign with any team. The Seattle Seahawks (NFL) seemed the natural choice since his off-season home was there, but he eventually signed a five-year contract with the Houston Oilers (NFL) and reunited with his former Edmonton coach, Hugh Campbell. He explained, "It was a tough decision turning down Seattle because friends are very important to me, but Houston gave me a chance to be part of something that is being built."

Moon won the starting quarterback job and made his NFL debut on September 2, 1984, against the Los Angeles Raiders. The Oilers won only three games in 1984, but Warren passed for a team-record 3,338 yards and made several All-Rookie teams. The Oilers improved only slightly in 1985 and 1986 with five victories each season, as Moon continued to play consistently. Despite missing two games in 1985, Warren passed for 2,709 yards. In 1986, he broke his own team record by passing for 3,489 yards.

Despite having arthroscopic knee surgery in 1987, Moon played the entire season and helped the Oilers make the playoffs for the first time in his career there. A shoulder injury suffered in the 1988 season opener sidelined him for five games, but the Oilers overcame this obstacle and made their second consecutive playoff appearance. Warren, meanwhile, was selected for his first Pro Bowl.

Moon's 1989 season marked his most prolific since joining the Oilers. Houston made its third straight playoff appearance, as Warren passed for 3,631 yards to set a new Oilers record and completed 280 passes out of 464 attempts for a 60.3 percentage. A second consecutive Pro Bowl start highlighted his fine season. Late in the 1989 season, however, Moon criticized the Oilers controversial, flamboyant head coach Jerry Glanville for his tactics on the football field. Warren stated, "The media rarely came to talk to us about football. We felt the distractions. This football team was more like a circus."

Glanville was replaced following the 1989 season by Jack Pardee, who brought his run-and-shoot offense to the Oilers. This offense featured four wide receivers, including Haywood Jeffires and Ernest Givins, and fit Moon's talents perfectly. In 1990, Warren led the NFL in completions (362), passing yardage (4,689), and touchdown passes (33). His passing yardage broke his own Oiler record and ranked as the fifth highest in NFL history.

Houston qualified for the American Football Conference (AFC) playoffs for the fourth consecutive year, but a dislocated thumb sidelined Moon. Nevertheless, Warren garnered Associated Press (AP) Offensive Player of the Year, United Press International (UPI) AFC Offensive Player of the Year, and *USA Today* AFC MVP honors. His selection to a starting role in the Pro Bowl spotlighted his outstanding performance.

The 1991 season epitomized the roller-coaster type of experiences marking Moon's career. Warren set new NFL records for passing attempts (655), completions (404), and yardage (4,690). The Oilers won their divisional title, qualifying for a team-record fifth consecutive playoff appearance. Houston missed a Super Bowl appearance, being eliminated in the AFC playoffs by the Denver Broncos.

Moon's daring style of play haunted him in 1992. A broken arm suffered while attempting to scramble for a first down forced Warren to miss five games. Despite the injury, he completed 224 passes for 2,521 yards and 18 touchdowns. These statistics made Moon the all-time leading passer in professional football with 51,428 combined yards in the CFL and NFL. The Houston Oilers, however, missed the Super Bowl, allowing the Buffalo Bills to stage the largest comeback in NFL playoff history and win, 41–38.

The Oilers fired their defensive coordinator and hired the controversial, volatile Buddy Ryan to coach the defense. Houston hoped that this move would finally produce a Super Bowl appearance. The Oilers, however, won only one of their first five games. Moon hit absolute bottom in week six, when head coach Jack Pardee benched him in favor of reserve quarterback Cody Carlson. After Carlson was injured early in the game, Warren returned as starting quarterback. The Oilers defeated the New England Patriots. The offense and defense both began to play well. Houston set a team record with 11 straight regular-season wins and won the AFC Central Division title. Their playoff jinx continued, however, with a first-round loss to the Kansas City Chiefs. Moon finished second in all AFC passing categories with 520 attempts, 303 completions, 3,485 yards, and 21 touchdowns. Warren summarized, "I've never been through a season like this one. It has been a season of definite highs and lows. This is a season you could write a book on, and it'd be a very interesting book."

In April 1994, Houston traded Moon to the Minnesota Vikings (NFL). Warren completed 371 of 601 passes for 4,264 yards and 18 touchdowns for Minnesota in 1994 and made the Pro Bowl for the seventh consecutive time. During his CFL-NFL career, he has completed 4,372 of 7,529 passes for 59,177 yards and 358 touchdowns.

Moon and his wife, Felicia, live in Houston with their two sons and two daughters. They donate considerable time to charities, including the United Negro College Fund, Urban League, and Special Olympics. In 1989, Warren founded the Crescent Moon Foundation to provide scholarships and services to underprivileged students in the Houston area. Houston and Harris County proclaimed February 21, 1988, as "Warren Moon Day." Travelers Insurance Company named him their 1989 NFL Man of the Year, while the Texas Jaycees selected him as one of five Outstanding Young Men of Texas in 1990.

Moon's only remaining goal in his NFL career is to win the Super Bowl. "It's not an obsession, but it's my last obstacle," Warren admits. Above all, however, he wants to be viewed favorably by his fans. "I just want to be looked at as a guy who is trying to help as many people as he can. I definitely want to excel in my sport, and I think I do. But I take it a little bit further in some of the things I do off the field and the way I handle myself off the field. I don't ever want to embarrass this city because I know I represent this city, and that's important to me."

BIBLIOGRAPHY: *Current Biography Yearbook* (1991), pp. 407–411; "Houston's $6 Million Man," *Ebony* 40 (November 1984), pp. 93–97; L. Mpho Mabunde, ed., *Contemporary American Black Biography*, vol. 8 (Detroit, MI, 1995); "Now There's a New Moon in Canada," *Sport* 75 (August 1984), p. 49; Ron Reilly, "How High the Moon?" *Sports Illustrated* 58 (January 11, 1987), pp. 28–31; Randy Riggs, "The Number 1 Star in Texas," *Austin American Statesman*, September 9, 1990, p. C1.

John Hillman

ARCHIE MOORE
(December 13, 1913 [or 1916]–) ————————————————— *Boxing*

Archie Moore, nicknamed the "Magnificent Mongoose" and "Ancient Archie," held the light heavyweight boxing championship. He was born Archibald Lee Wright on December 13, 1913, in Benoit, Mississippi, or 1916, in Collinsville, Illinois. Much like **Satchel Paige,** Moore kept his birthdate secret. "Maybe I was three years old when I was born," Archie explained. His parents were Tommy Wright, a day laborer, and Lorena Wright, who preferred the 1913 birthdate. After his parents separated, he was brought up by an uncle, Cleveland Moore, and aunt, Willie Moore, of St. Louis, Missouri and took his name from them.

Boxing attracted Moore from boyhood, as he preferred the gymnasium to the schoolroom. Archie's career reflected a grim determination to become a champion and truly remarkable ability to learn from defeat, stressing the importance of a positive attitude and continuing to try. His boxing career spanned from 1936 to 1965. Moore fought his first bout as a welterweight against Poco Kid, recording a two-round knockout. In 1939, true boxing artist and former middleweight champion Teddy Yarosz clearly outpointed Archie in "a good ten-round lesson."

His early managers kept him on a crushing schedule, accepting virtually every fighting opportunity. Moore recalled, "I would fight for short money in little towns; then, my body still clammy with sweat because the little arena had no showers and I couldn't afford a hotel room, I would ride a dusty, dirty bus or freight train to the next town still hurting and bruised from my last fight." Archie's world consisted of "two-bit flophouses" and "crummy little restaurants." He also worked for the Civilian Conservation Corps during the depression. But Archie still maintained a deep religious faith, stating, "I couldn't have accomplished what I did without God's help." Moore overcame a serious ulcer ailment from 1940 to 1942, when Charlie Johnston and Jimmy Johnston took over his management. Archie's reputation as a hard hitter and clever boxer was established in his light heavyweight class. The best fighters in his class avoided him as being too good. His managers unfortunately lacked the proper connections. Moore waited some 16 years before fighting on December 17, 1952, against Joey Maxim for the light heavyweight championship. Archie conducted a strenuous publicity campaign, even placing a full-page advertisement in the *St. Louis Post-Dispatch.* He reputedly was age 38, but his trim body resembled someone 12 years his junior, the product of hard work and dedication. Moore decisioned Maxim in a 15-round contest. Archie received only $800, while Joey had a $100,000 guarantee.

Jack Kearns became Moore's manager, helping him seek the heavyweight title and big money. The "dream come true" arrived on September 22, 1955, when Archie fought Rocky Marciano. Moore came close to the title, flooring Rocky in the second round with a vicious right uppercut. The referee, however, stepped in between as the champion regained his feet, giving the latter precious seconds to recover. The rest of the bout, a slugging match, was dominated by Marciano, who knocked out Archie in nine rounds. When asked after the match which punch had hurt him most, a weary Archie replied, "All of them."

Moore remained the top contender because Marciano retired undefeated. The following year, Archie fought young 22-year-old heavyweight prospect Floyd Patterson. Moore, more than twice Patterson's age, succumbed to a fifth-round knockout, ending his ambitions for the heavyweight title.

Yet Archie's determination predominated. Moore's "finest hour" came in his 1958 match with light heavyweight Yvonne Durelle. Durelle, a very tough French-Canadian, floored him three times in the first round and once in the fifth round. The remarkable Archie, however, recovered miraculously, knocking out his opponent in the eleventh round to earn *The Ring*'s Fighter of the Year honors. He retained the light heavyweight title for 10 years until into his midforties. His last big-name fight came in 1962, when he suffered a four-round knockout at the hands of Cassius Clay (later **Muhammad Ali**).

Moore's perseverance and dedication earned the admiration of the boxing world. Archie likewise mastered the business aspect of the sport. His religious dedication to God inspired his maximum effort. He maintained, "I have always done the best I could." Moore passed his lessons in life to young boys of inner-city San Diego, California, his adopted home, stating "Now I want to show Him my gratitude by helping others." Archie established the program ABC ("Any Boy Can"), which taught youth to respect others' rights and make them "feel important" as the main path to accomplishment. Moore stressed the Golden Rule as life's fundamental lesson, successfully persuading many young people to abandon a life of violence and drugs. Archie made many personal appearances at schools, addressing students on the matter of self-respect. His sincere regard for the destiny of young people gained many admirers.

Moore's professional career spanned 228 bouts, including a record 140 knockouts, 53 wins by decision, 17 decision losses, and 7 knockout losses. His consistent ability to rebound from misfortune inspired others. Archie was elected to *The Ring*'s Boxing Hall of Fame in 1966 and the International Boxing Hall of Fame in 1990. Moore's autobiography, *Any Boy Can: The Archie Moore Story*, closes with his philosophy: "You see, faith is in my corner."
BIBLIOGRAPHY: Frank Deford, "The Ageless Warrior," *Sports Illustrated* 70 (May 8, 1989), pp. 103–109; Sid Friedlander, "The Archie Moore Story," *New York Post*, January 26–30, 1959; Herbert G. Goldman, ed., *The Ring 1986–1987 Record Book and Boxing Encyclopedia* (New York, 1987); Irv Goodman, "Archie Moore's Secret of Perpetual Youth," *Sport* 26 (May 1959), pp. 23, 82–85; Archie Moore and Leonard B. Pearl, *Any Boy Can: The Archie Moore Story* (Englewood Cliffs, NJ, 1971); David L.

Porter, ed., *Biographical Dictionary of American Sports: Basketball and Other Indoor Sports* (Westport, CT, 1989); Bert Randolph Sugar, ed., *The Great Fights* (New York, 1981).

William J. Miller

LENNY MOORE
(November 25, 1933–) ————————————————— *Football*

Lenny Moore, one of professional football's all-time great flanker–running backs, played 12 National Football League (NFL) years from 1956 to 1967 with the Baltimore Colts and was elected to the Pro Football Hall of Fame and the Pennsylvania Sports Hall of Fame in 1975. Leonard Edward Moore was born on November 25, 1933, in Reading, Pennsylvania, 1 of 11 children of George C. Moore, a steelworker-laborer, and Virginia E. (Talley) Moore. "I'm not ashamed to admit our family was on welfare, because that's the way it was," recalled Moore. "My father and mother had a tough time giving their family the things they needed." At Reading High School, he lettered in baseball, played on a district championship basketball squad, and won a Silver Medal in the State track championships. Lenny particularly excelled in football as 165-pound senior in 1951, playing 425 minutes out of a possible 540, scoring 23 touchdowns, making All-State, and leading the Red Knights to their best-ever 9–1 season. Coach Andy Stopper remarked, "He was so good that when you told people how good he was they thought you were lying!"

Without his football prowess, college would have been impossible. "I never thought about it," said Moore, "because there would be no way I could ever do it, you know, financially. I became aware after the college scholarship offers started coming in. But even then, I really didn't have the grades." But with Stopper's encouragement and the opportunity to pass an entrance examination, he chose nearby Penn State University. Lenny dazzled the opposition for three years there, getting by on raw ability alone. He reflected, "When I should have been perfecting my fakes or my blocking or learning more of the fine points of holding on to the ball, I didn't." Nevertheless, as a six-foot-one-inch, 175-pound junior in 1954, Moore led a Charles "Rip" Engle–coached Penn State team to a 7–2 record. Lenny established a then single-season rushing mark of 1,082 yards. Engle boasted, "He's the most exciting and productive back I have ever seen, and he's gifted with a sixth sense that is possessed only by great runners." Penn State compiled a lackluster 5–4 record in 1955, but Moore finished his college career with three still-existing school rushing records. Besides averaging 19.8 yards per try against Rutgers University in 1955, Lenny averaged the most yards per carry in one season (8.0 yards in 1954), and the most yards per carry for a career (6.2 yards from 1953 to 1955).

Moore did not make All-America, however. Some professional scouts questioned whether his long, sparse frame could endure the pounding of NFL football. The Baltimore Colts (NFL) pondered making Lenny their first-round draft choice in 1956, but coach Weeb Ewbank wanted an opinion from Penn State. Assistant coach Joe Paterno said, "Go tell Weeb not to miss this guy because if he does, it'll be the greatest mistake he could ever make." Although initially considering the Canadian Football League, Moore finally signed with Baltimore for $10,000. Lenny quickly lived up to his rave notices, rushing for 649 yards, catching 11 passes for 102 yards, scoring nine touchdowns, and winning NFL Rookie of the Year acclaim. He caught passes and ran with the ball better than most NFL stars and, thus, became a perfect running mate for passing ace Johnny Unitas, helping the Colts rule the pro football world. "I used to hand him the ball, get out of the way and admire his work," said Unitas. The Colts initially as a combination flanker and running back, with primary responsibility for catching passes. Baltimore employed Lenny much more often on the outside. He performed well but apparently not up to his full potential. In 1957, Moore's fumble against Detroit enabled the Lions to score a last-second touchdown and defeat the Colts, 31–27. Lenny, who had a hard time living this down, pledged to stop loafing in practice and became a much more dedicated player.

In his third NFL season in 1958, the now 190- to 198-pound Moore played a leading role in Baltimore's march to the NFL championship. Lenny won All-NFL honors for the first time, contributed 1,639 combined net yards, including 938 yards on receptions, and scored 14 touchdowns. In the famous 23–17 overtime victory over New York in the NFL title game, he grabbed six passes for 101 yards. Moore put the Giants in a hole at the start of the game with a 60-yard pass-run play. Late in the game, Lenny caught a vital first down pass when the Colts started their drive to tie the score in regulation time. In the overtime, he made a key block on **Emlen Tunnell** that sprung Alan Ameche loose for the winning touchdown. The 1959 season marked a virtual carbon copy of the preceding year. Baltimore won a second straight NFL championship over the Giants, 31–16, as Moore earned All-NFL acclaim again. In the NFL title game, he converted on a 59-yard pass-run maneuver on the sixth play to give the Colts a quick 7–0 lead.

Lenny continued to make the right moves for the Colts. Colts defensive tackle "Big Daddy" Lipscomb nicknamed him "Sputnik." " 'Sput' has so many moves," declared Colts defensive end Gino Marchetti, "that a tackler can't get a good hold on him. I try to tackle him in training camp, but most of the time he's by me before I know it." Los Angeles Rams and Washington Redskins coach George Allen acknowledged, "With the exception of quarterbacks, Lenny Moore may have beaten my teams more than any other player I ever coached against. He was one of the most explosive players ever and almost impossible to contain for a full game." Moore still averaged around 500 yards rushing and 40 to 50 pass receptions a year, winning All-NFL honors again in 1960 and 1961.

In 1961, the Colts acquired brilliant receiver Jimmy Orr. Since Baltimore lacked speed at the running back position, Ewbank moved fleet-footed Lenny to the inside and put Orr on the flank. Moore's pass receptions yardage and rushing average dropped, as he faced a hard time adjusting to running through the big linemen instead of moving outside in the wide-open pass-catching lanes. For the first time, nagging injuries plagued him. Lenny complained of a head injury and missed his first NFL game ever in 1961. He cracked a kneecap in the final preseason NFL contest in 1962 and underwent an emergency appendectomy and suffered a head injury in 1963.

In 1964, Coach Don Shula relegated Lenny to second team duty behind Tom Matte. The Colts lost their opening game to the Minnesota Vikings and faced the Western Division favorites, the Green Bay Packers, in the second game. In the first quarter, Shula inserted Moore in the lineup. Unitas quickly connected with Lenny on a 58-yard aerial for a go-ahead touchdown. Late in the game, Moore scored the winning touchdown on a 4-yard jaunt to help Baltimore upset the Packers, 21–20. Two weeks later, following a 35–20 victory over the Los Angeles Rams, Lenny was awarded the game ball for his stellar play. When Baltimore met Green Bay for a second time, Moore again provided the game-breaker with 2 touchdowns in a 24–21 victory. The two victories over Green Bay clinched a divisional title for the Colts, ending the Packers' three-year Western reign. The 1964 campaign marked Lenny's finest season. He scored at least 1 touchdown in every game, recording a sensational 20 for the year. From the last game of 1963 into 1965, he tallied at least 1 touchdown in a record 18 straight games and tallied at least 1 touchdown rushing in 11 consecutive contests. Both set NFL records. The Associated Press (AP) named him the NFL's Comeback Player of the Year, while the Newspaper Enterprise Association selected him the NFL's Most Valuable Player (MVP). Once again, he made everyone's All-NFL team.

Moore retired after the 1967 campaign, leaving behind awesome career totals. Lenny had amassed 12,449 combined net yards to rank ninth among the all-time NFL leaders, having rushed for 5,174 yards (a 4.8 average per carry), caught 363 passes for 6,039 yards (a 16.6 average per reception), returned 49 kicks for 1,180 yards (a 24.1 average per return), and gained 56 yards on punt returns. He also had scored 678 points on 113 touchdowns. Lenny, named All-NFL five times (1958–1961 and 1964), played in seven Pro Bowls (1956, 1958–1962, and 1964), starting six of them.

Moore, who had done some local radio announcing in Baltimore while a player, was hired by CBS Network in 1968 as a "color" commentator analyst. Lenny's contract, however, was not renewed the following year. The next few lean years included a failed business, some local radio work, a few speaking engagements, community relations work and personal appearances, and television work selling the "New Army" recruitment program. In February 1975, shortly after his election into the Pro Football Hall of Fame, he became the director of promotions for the Baltimore Colts. Moore remained in this position until the club moved to Indianapolis, Indiana, in 1984. Since 1984, Lenny has been a program specialist with the Maryland Department of Juvenile Services in Baltimore, an agency working with troubled youth.

His wife, Francis Elizabeth (Martin) Moore, an ex-schoolteacher whom he married on December 25, 1956, and the mother of his four children, Leslie, Carol, Toni, and Terri (an older fifth child, Lenny, was born out of wedlock to Lorraine Jenkins), filed for divorce. Although a reconciliation shortly followed, the Moores separated in 1969 and eventually divorced in 1973. Lenny's second wife, Erma (King), whom he married on July 13, 1974, died of cancer in October 1975, shortly after his induction into the Pro Football Hall of Fame. He lives with his third wife, Edith (Randolph), whom he married on July 17, 1976.

BIBLIOGRAPHY: George Allen with Ben Olan, *Pro Football's 100 Greatest Players* (Indianapolis, IN, 1982); J. Douglas Arnold, ed., *15 Berks County Sports Legends* (Reading, PA, 1988); Paul R. Beers, *Profiles in Pennsylvania Sports* (Harrisburg, PA, 1975); Jack C. Braun, telephone interview with Lenny Moore, July 25, 1994; Leonard "Lenny" Moore file, Pro Football Hall of Fame Library, Canton, OH; David S. Neft et al., eds., *The Football Encyclopedia,* 2nd ed. (New York, 1994); Murray Olderman, *The Running Backs* (Englewood Cliffs, NJ, 1969); Tim Panaccio, *Penn State vs Pitt: Beast of the East: A Game-by-Game History of America's Greatest Football Rivalry* (West Point, NY, 1982); David L. Porter, ed., *Biographical Dictionary of American Sports: Football* (Westport, CT, 1987); Ridge Riley, *Road to Number One: A Personal Chronicle of Penn State Football* (Garden City, NY, 1977); Don R. Smith, *Pro Football Hall of Fame All-Time Greats* (New York, 1988); George Sullivan, *Pro Football A to Z* (New York, 1975); Mike Tully, *Where Have They Gone?: Football Stars* (New York, 1979).

Jack C. Braun

JOE MORGAN
(September 19, 1943–   ) ————————————————————————— *Baseball*

Joe Morgan, one of the best all-around players in baseball history and member of the National Baseball Hall of Fame, also succeeded in broadcasting and business. Joseph Leonard Morgan was born on September 19, 1943, in Bonham, Texas. Unlike many African-American athletes, Morgan did not suffer from a deprived childhood. His autobiography noted, "I can't recall ever being without. When I wanted a bike, I got a bike; when I needed shoes and clothes, I got them right away." Joe also recalled, "We were a regular churchgoing family and different family members sang in the choir."

When Morgan was age five, his family moved to Oakland, California. His home was located only a few blocks from the old Emeryville ballpark, where the Oakland Oaks of the Pacific Coast League played. Joe attended almost every home game and played baseball at every opportunity. Although starring in the Babe Ruth League and at Castlemont High School, he received no offers to play professional baseball. After high school graduation, Morgan stood only five feet seven inches and weighed just 155 pounds. Joe enrolled at

Oakland City College (later Merritt College) as a business major. During Morgan's first year of college, however, scout Bill Wright of the Houston Colt 45s National League (NL) club saw Joe's potential and signed him for a $3,000 bonus. Wright recounted, "Morgan was small, and there wasn't much he could do about that. But . . . I liked his aggressiveness. He was self-assured without being cocky."

Morgan started his professional baseball career in 1963 with Modesto, California, of the Class C California League. After 45 games, Joe was promoted to Durham, North Carolina, of the Class B Carolina League. Morgan, the only African American on the team, considered quitting because of the segregation he encountered. But manager Billy Goodman persuaded Joe to stay and developed him rapidly as a player. Morgan's performance led the Houston Colts to promote him for eight games after Durham had finished its season.

Morgan, who spent the fall in the Instructional League in Florida, opened the 1964 season at San Antonio, Texas, in the Class AA Texas League and won the Most Valuable Player (MVP) award there. The Colts again called him up at the end of the season. Joe spent the entire year in Houston and met Nellie Fox, who developed Morgan into a star. Fox, nearing the end of his playing career and competing with Morgan for the second base job, helped the rookie immeasurably. Fox realized Joe had the ability to be a great player. In his autobiography, Morgan relates how Fox persuaded him to choke up on the bat and keep his right arm away from his body in order to hit more and harder line drives. Joe consequently began flapping his left arm as he awaited the pitch. Fox also helped the rookie to make the double play correctly, catch everything possible with two hands, "feel the ball," and use a small glove so that the ball would never stick in the webbing or depth of the pocket. Morgan enjoyed a great year and was named *The Sporting News* NL Rookie of the Year. The left-handed batter made 163 hits, hit 14 homers, and led the NL with 97 walks.

During his seven full years with Houston, Morgan experienced both peaks and valleys. In April 1967, Joe married his first wife, Lisa Stewart, his high school sweetheart, by whom he had two daughters, Lisa and Angela. He was named to the 1966 NL All-Star team but was replaced because he fractured his kneecap. But the second baseman disliked Houston manager Harry Walker, whom he considered a racist and bigot.

Morgan welcomed his trade to the Cincinnati Reds (NL) after the 1971 season and became a main cog in the Big Red Machine, appearing in five NL Championship Series and three World Series. With Cincinnati, Joe won consecutive NL MVP awards in 1975 and 1976. Roy Blount, Jr., in *Sports Illustrated* lauded him as the only ballplayer who could "do the following things extremely well: Field, hit for average, hit the long ball, steal bases, . . . draw walks, . . . avoid strikeouts, maintain a lively, sunny disposition, and think."

After the 1980 season, Morgan returned to the Houston Astros. The next year, Houston traded Joe to the San Francisco Giants (NL). In his second season with the Giants, he earned NL Comeback Player of the Year honors. After having been dealt to Philadelphia (NL), Morgan helped the Phillies win the NL championship in 1983. After Philadelphia released him, Joe joined the Oakland Athletics American League (AL) club. He disliked the AL style of play and retired after the 1984 campaign.

During his 22 major league seasons, Morgan compiled a .271 batting average with 2,518 hits, 449 doubles, 96 triples, and 268 homers. Joe batted in 1,134 runs, stole 689 bases, and walked 1,865 times, setting NL records for most games, seasons, home runs, and putouts by a second baseman. He also holds the major league records for most lifetime home runs (266) and games played by a second sacker, making the NL All-Star team nine times and winning five Gold Glove awards. Morgan's achievements earned him election to the National Baseball Hall of Fame in 1990 and selection to its board of directors in 1993.

Morgan has also achieved success off the field. Joe earned a bachelor's degree from California State University at Hayward, operates several successful businesses, and enjoys a successful broadcasting career. He began as an announcer for the Cincinnati Reds and then handled network color for NBC and ABC. In 1986, Morgan joined the San Francisco Giants to cover baseball broadcasts locally. Four years later, Joe joined John Miller on national broadcasts for ESPN.

Morgan, divorced from his first wife, married his second wife, Theresa, a white woman, in 1990. They have twin daughters, Ashley and Kelly. Initial problems of acceptance by both families have eased. Joe and Theresa have many friends, including wine growers who help them produce and bottle Joe Morgan Cabernet.

The always smiling Morgan, one of the best-liked men in baseball, contributed tremendously both on and off the field. Joe recalled, "I used to tell people that when you get Joe Morgan you're not just getting a ballplayer—you're getting a guy who's going to do whatever he can to help the organization. You help your team by doing more than just playing baseball; you help your team win in the clubhouse." In both baseball and his life off the field, he has been a model ambassador for the sport and has shown that an athlete can have a successful second, postplaying career.

BIBLIOGRAPHY: Nathan Aaseng, *Little Giants of Pro Sports* (New York, 1980); Roy Blount, Jr., "His Time Has Come," *Sports Illustrated* 44 (March 1, 1976), pp. 57–62; Joel H. Cohen, *Joe Morgan—Great Little Big Man* (New York, 1978); *Current Biography Yearbook* (1984), pp. 285–288; Larry Linderman, "Sport Interview," *Sport* 75 (June 1984), pp. 285–288; Joe Morgan and David Morgan, *Joe Morgan: A Life in Baseball* (New York, 1993); David L. Porter, ed., *Biographical Dictionary of American Sports: Baseball* (Westport, CT, 1987); Lawrence Ritter and Donald Honig, *The 100 Greatest Baseball Players of All Time*, rev. ed. (New York, 1986); Robert H. Walker, *Cincinnati and the Big-Red Machine* (Bloomington, IN, 1988).

Ralph S. Graber

EDWIN MOSES

(August 31, 1955–   ) ——————————————————— *Track and Field*

From 1976 to 1988, Edwin Moses led the world in the 400-meter intermediate hurdles. During that span, Moses set four world records and won 122 consecutive races for the longest winning streak in all sports. Edwin Corley Moses was born on August 31, 1955, in Dayton, Ohio, the second of three sons of educators Irving Moses and Gladys Moses. His father worked as an elementary school principal and science teacher, while his mother served as curriculum supervisor for the Dayton school system. As a child, Edwin showed a penchant for science, art, and music. He built model rockets, dissected frogs, drew pictures, sculpted objects, and played the saxophone. Moses's interest in track and field blossomed in the third grade after attending the Dayton Relays. His first sporting love, however, remained swimming, which he enjoyed while visiting an aunt at Daytona Beach, Florida.

In the Moses household, performing well in school marked a priority for Edwin and his brothers Irving, Jr., and Vincent. Edwin, 1 of 20 African-American students at Fairview High School in Dayton, chose to be bused to Fairview, four miles from his neighborhood, to escape the racial tensions that plagued nearby Dunbar High School. In track and field, Moses concentrated on the 120-yard high hurdles and 440-yard dash. His best times were around 15 seconds in the high hurdles and 50 seconds in the quarter mile. Moses described himself "as competitive, but nowhere near national class." After graduating from Fairview High School in 1973, Edwin entered Atlanta, Georgia's distinguished Morehouse College. As the recipient of an academic scholarship, he pursued a double major in physics and mechanical engineering and graduated in 1978 with a 3.57 grade-point average. "I could have had a 4.00 average," Moses remarked in *Track and Field News*, "but I had to make sacrifices" for the 1976 Summer Olympic Games.

Edwin competed as a high hurdler and quarter-miler at Morehouse. As a freshman in 1974, he improved his times to 14.2 seconds in the 120-yard high hurdles and 48 seconds in the quarter mile. In 1975, Lloyd Jackson, the Morehouse track and field coach, encouraged Moses to try the 400-meter intermediate hurdles. Jackson considered this race more appropriate for Edwin's hurdling and quarter-miler running skills. In his only attempt at the longer hurdle race that year, he clocked 52 seconds flat. Moses steadily improved in the 400-meter hurdles throughout 1976, lowering his time from 50.1 seconds at the Florida Relays in March to 48.8 seconds at the King Games in May. "I knew I had the basic talent," Edwin observed of his meteoric rise to world-class heights. He added "It was just a matter of putting everything together." After failing to qualify for the finals at the NCAA Division III Championships and finishing fourth in the Amateur Athletic Union (AAU) Championships, Moses captured the Olympic Trials in an American record of 48.30 seconds.

In the 1976 Summer Olympic Games at Montreal, Canada, Edwin lowered the American standard to 48.29 seconds in the semifinals and won the Gold Medal in a world record of 47.64 seconds.

Over the next 12 years, Moses compiled an unprecedented record in the 400-meter hurdles. In 1977, Edwin lowered the world record to 47.45 seconds. He also captured the first of six AAU/TAC (Track Athletic Congress) championships, the others coming in 1979, 1981, 1983, 1986, and 1987. That year, Moses also captured the first of three World Cup titles, the others coming in 1979 and 1981. Unable to defend his Olympic title in 1980 because of the U.S.-led boycott of the Moscow, Russia, Olympic Games, Edwin made up for his disappointment by lowering the world record to 47.13 seconds in Milan, Italy. In 1980, *Track and Field News* named him Athlete of the Year. The next year witnessed Moses clock 47.14 seconds, then history's second fastest time, and defeat Volker Beck of East Germany, the 1980 Olympic champion, in the World Cup at Rome, Italy. Named Athlete of the Year by *Track and Field News* again in 1981, Edwin did not compete in 1982 because of an injury. Harald Schmid of West Germany assumed the number-one position in the 400-meter hurdles that year. In response to Schmid's time of 47.48 seconds, Moses remarked that now "I have to go into all my races prepared to do even better than before." In 1983, Edwin defeated Schmid in capturing the World Championship at Helsinki, Finland. Later that year, Moses lowered the world record to 47.02 seconds at Koblenz, Germany. In the 1984 Summer Olympic Games at Los Angeles, California, he won a second Gold Medal in the 400-meter hurdles. Edwin, who did not compete in 1985, triumphed in the 1986 Goodwill Games at Moscow, Russia.

Moses's most remarkable achievement as a 400-meter hurdler was winning 122 consecutive races. His victory streak started after finishing second to Schmid on August 26, 1977, in Berlin, West Germany. Edwin ran nearly a decade without a loss until Danny Harris defeated him on June 3, 1987, in Madrid, Spain. "I ran a good race," he said afterwards, "[but] the guy that beat me is 10 years younger and ran the race of his life." In defending his World Championship at Rome, Italy, later that year, Moses narrowly defeated both Harris and Schmid by .02 seconds. In the 1988 Summer Olympic Games at Seoul, South Korea, he suffered a crushing defeat and finished only third in the 400-meter hurdles to fellow American Andre Phillips and Senegal's Amadou Ba. Phillips, who established an Olympic record of 47.19 seconds, said afterward that "it would take me until I'm 45 to do the things Edwin has. I still think he's the man to beat."

Moses, who has not raced since 1988, revolutionized the 400-meter hurdles. Edwin perfected taking only 13 strides between each of the 10 barriers early in his career, whereas his competition used the typical combination of 13, 14, and 15 strides. Moses, who worked briefly for General Dynamics, coached himself and used a computer to analyze his running form and physiological performance. Dr. Leroy Walker, a former U.S. Olympic team coach, described

Edwin's understanding of the race and himself as "so infinite as to make any coach superfluous, possibly an unnecessary confusion." Moses, who won the Sullivan Award in 1983, was named *Sports Illustrated* Sportsman of the Year in 1985. Edwin belongs to the Helms Athletic Foundation Hall of Fame and the U.S. Olympic Committee Hall of Fame. Moses, who lives in Laguna Beach, California, married Myrella Bordt, a German-born artist and fashion designer, in 1982.

BIBLIOGRAPHY: Jed Brickner, "Phillips Rings Moses' Bell," *Track and Field News* 41 (November 1988), p. 28; *Current Biography Yearbook* (1986), pp. 388–391; Jon Hendershott, "T&FN Interview: Edwin Moses," *Track and Field News* 29 (September 1976), pp. 33–34; Jon Hendershott, "An Artist in Solitude," *Track and Field News* 32 (March 1980), pp. 8–13; Dave Johnson, "T&FN Interview: Edwin Moses," *Track and Field News* 36 (December 1983), pp. 66–67; Frank Litsky, "Loss by Moses Brings a Sense of Relief," *New York Times*, June 23, 1987, pp. A25–A28; Bill Mallon and Ian Buchanan, *Quest for Gold: The Encyclopedia of American Olympians* (New York, 1984); Edwin Moses with Jon Hendershott, "Boycott Changed Everything," *Track and Field News* 33 (January 1981), pp. 6–8; "Moses' Streak Is Ended at 122," *New York Times*, June 5, 1987, pp. D19–D22; Cordner Nelson, *Track's Greatest Champions* (Los Altos, CA, 1986); David L. Porter, ed., *Biographical Dictionary of American Sports: Outdoor Sports* (Westport, CT, 1989); Roberto L. Quercetani, *Athletics: A History of Modern Track and Field Athletics, 1860–1990* (Milan, Italy, 1990); David Wallechinsky, *The Complete Book of the Olympic Games* (New York, 1988).

Adam R. Hornbuckle

MARION MOTLEY
(June 5, 1920–   ) ——————————————————————— *Football*

Although Marion Motley grew up just miles from the Pro Football Hall of Fame in Canton, Ohio, he never imagined as a boy that he would someday be enshrined there. Marion Motley, one of four children of Shakeful Motley and Blanche Motley, was born on June 5, 1920, in Leesburg, Georgia. His father moved to Canton, Ohio, to work in a foundry when Marion was only three years old.

Motley grew up in a predominantly African-American neighborhood, where he learned to play baseball and football in pickup games on vacant lots. At Canton McKinley High School, Marion began to develop as an athlete. Motley played baseball, basketball, and football in high school, but football marked his best sport. In three varsity seasons with Marion at fullback, McKinley lost only three games. All three setbacks came from Massillon High School teams, mentored by future Cleveland Brown head coach Paul Brown. Brown later impacted Motley's own career.

After graduating from high school, Marion enrolled at South Carolina State University. In 1940, he rejoined his high school mentor, Jimmy Aiken, who had become head football coach at the University of Nevada—Reno. Motley played football at Nevada—Reno from 1940 to 1942 and produced several long touchdowns, including a 105-yard punt return and 95-yard interception return. *Illustrated Football Annual* placed him on their All-America checklist, calling him "a 22-karat back."

A knee injury forced Marion to leave Nevada—Reno. He enlisted in the U.S. Navy on Christmas Day of 1944. The U.S. Navy assigned him to Great Lakes Naval Base in Illinois, where he played on the base football team under coach Paul Brown. The Great Lakes team attracted national attention in 1945, defeating heavily favored University of Notre Dame, 39–7.

Motley also accomplished a rare feat while serving on Brown's Great Lakes team, knocking his coach down. The incident occurred one day when Marion was nursing a badly sprained toe. After Brown inadvertently stepped on Motley's toe during a demonstration, Marion without thinking clubbed him with his forearm. For years after the incident, Brown warned players, "Don't step on Marion's feet, or he'll hit you."

After completing his naval service, Motley returned to Canton and worked in a steel mill. Marion weighed various alternatives, including returning to Nevada—Reno to complete his collegiate eligibility. The All-America Football Conference (AAFC) had been formed in 1946, with Brown selected as the first coach of the Cleveland Browns. Brown desperately needed a fullback and recruited his former navy player, Motley. Marion and teammate **Bill Willis** became the first African Americans to play professional football in the postwar era.

Motley and Willis slipped quietly into professional football, not reporting to the Browns until after training camp opened. Paul Brown recalled Marion's signing. "He was twenty-seven years old and, with a family to support, had taken a mill job. I called Oscar Barkey, a friend from Canton, and asked him to drive Marion to our training camp and have him ask for a tryout. I felt that was the best way to handle the situation, again in light of the potential publicity, because there was nothing unusual in a player's coming to his former coach and asking him for a chance to play."

Motley's recollections differed slightly. "I wrote Brown after I got out of the service and asked for a job, but he turned me down and wrote back that he had enough backs." Marion suggests the real reason for inviting him to camp was to provide a roommate for Willis. The six-foot-two-inch 235-pounder proved tremendously valuable to the Browns.

Motley possessed total confidence in his ability to play professional football. "I knew this was the one big chance in my life to rise above the steel mill existence and I really wanted to take it. I had no doubt that I could make the team because I had played against some of the best competition around during the war and I measured up pretty well." His sprinter's speed and awesome power provided the Browns the fullback they needed to complement their passing attack.

From 1946 to 1949, Motley led Cleveland in rushing and helped the Browns win all four AAFC championships. The Browns tallied 47 wins, 4 losses, and

3 ties. Marion finished as the leading career AAFC rusher, gaining 3,024 yards on 489 carries, averaging 6.4 yards per carry, and scoring 31 rushing touchdowns. His 964 yards in 1948 led all AAFC rushers. The media selected him as First Team All-AAFC fullback from 1946 to 1948. An accomplished receiver, he caught 45 passes for 644 yards and 4 touchdowns. Motley also played fierce defense at linebacker since AAFC rules did not permit full two-platoon football. Marion's defensive forte remained his goal line play.

The AAFC-NFL merger did not stop Motley's ability to run the football. In 1950, Marion led the NFL in rushing with 810 yards on 140 attempts. The Cleveland Browns won the NFL championship in their first year of merged play. On October 29, 1950, he experienced his finest pro rushing day with 188 yards gained on only 11 carries and averaged 17.1 yards per carry.

Motley's age and damaged knees reduced his effectiveness as runner from 1951 to 1953, while a leg injury suffered in 1954 sidelined him the entire season. The Browns traded Marion to the Pittsburgh Steelers (NFL) for Ed Modzelewski in 1955, when he played his last season primarily at linebacker.

Motley led the Browns in rushing six of his eight years there and finished with 4,712 yards on 826 carries and 31 touchdowns. Cleveland won 40 games and lost only 8 during his NFL career from 1950 to 1953, capturing 4 Eastern Conference titles and 1 NFL championship. Marion claimed that he could have produced even greater statistics had Brown utilized greater variety in his offense. Brown instructed Motley clearly and concisely, "Don't get fancy once you pass the line of scrimmage. Just run right at them and over them." Marion wanted Brown to install a flip play to take advantage of his sprinter's speed, but the latter replied that the play was not designed for him. According to Motley, "There's no telling how much yardage I might have made if I ran as much as some backs do now."

Marion married Eula Coleman in 1943 and has three sons. He subsequently worked in the Cleveland area in several capacities, including the U.S. Postal Service, State of Ohio Lottery, and Ohio Department of Youth Services. Motley also scouted part-time for the Washington Redskins (NFL) under his former quarterback Otto Graham. His outstanding career earned him induction into the Pro Football Hall of Fame in 1968. Motley was selected in 1969 to the All-NFL team of the 1940s and in 1994 to the All-Time NFL Team.

BIBLIOGRAPHY: Jack Clary, Cleveland Browns: Great Teams' Great Years (New York, 1973); Joseph Horrigan, Great Athletes—The Twentieth Century (Pasadena, CA, 1982); Bill Levy, Return to Glory—The Story of the Cleveland Browns (Cleveland, OH, 1967); David L. Porter, ed., Biographical Dictionary of American Sports: Football (Westport, CT, 1987); George Sullivan, Pro Football's All-Time Greats (New York, 1968).

John Hillman

ISAAC MURPHY
(January 1, 1861–February 12, 1896) ———————————— *Horse Racing*

Isaac Murphy, perhaps America's greatest jockey, won an astonishing 44 percent (628) of his 1,412 races and became the first to win three Kentucky Derbies. Murphy was born Isaac Burns on January 1, 1861, in Fayette County, Kentucky. Isaac's father, James Burns, a freeman bricklayer, enlisted in the Union Army during the Civil War and died a Confederate prisoner. His mother, a laundress who died in 1879, immediately moved her family to Lexington, Kentucky, to live with her father, Green Murphy, the town's bell ringer and auctioneer.

James T. Williams convinced young Burns to apprentice as a jockey in 1873, after his partner mentioned that his laundress's son was small for his age. Williams and trainer Eli Jordan taught Isaac horsemanship. The apprentice rode his first race in May 1875 and his first winner, Glentina, at the Lexington Crab Orchard on September 15, 1876. Later that month, Burns changed his surname to his grandfather's last name. In 1877, Murphy won 19 of 43 races in his first full season of racing and recorded 5 second- and 10 third-place finishes.

Two years later, Murphy and his friend Eli Jordan signed with J. W. Hunt Reynolds. Isaac established his national reputation riding Falsetto. He showed courage in the Clark Handicap, squeezing through a narrow space to win by a neck, finished second in the Kentucky Derby, and twice defeated Spendthrift, the outstanding two-year-old of 1878. Pierre Lorillard bought Falsetto for an American record $18,000. Murphy won all 4 races scheduled on July 4, 1879, at Detroit, Michigan, and triumphed in 35 of 75 races that year, placing second 16 times and third 6 times. Isaac's struggle with weight began in 1880, but he continued to prevail with impressive streaks on Checkmate, Boulevard, Leonatus, and Meditator.

Murphy signed with Edward Corrigan in 1884 and captured the Kentucky Derby on Buchanan without spurs or whip, the Clark Handicap, and the Kentucky Oaks. Isaac also took the first running of the rich American Derby on Modesty. A pleased Corrigan changed the name of horse Harry White to Isaac Murphy, on which his jockey later won the Kenwood Stakes. In 1885, Isaac triumphed in the American Derby on Elias Baldwin's Volante and earned an immense $1,000 fee. He rode Freeland against Miss Woodford, the first American thoroughbred to earn $100,000, three times in August 1885. Freeland defeated Miss Woodford in two stakes races but lost by a head in a $2,500 match. These races created great excitement and speculation about a rematch. Richard Carey wrote "Ike Murphy's Ride," describing a mythical $40,000 match race between them. The issue was finally decided in a special sweepstakes, which Murphy's Freeland won by three lengths.

For "Lucky" Baldwin in 1886, Murphy took the Hindoo Stakes and American Derby on Silver Cloud, outdueling jockey "Snapper" Garrison in both races. In the American Derby, Silver Cloud broke away three furlongs from the finish while the favorites were blocked. In 1887, Baldwin paid Isaac $12,000, a record salary for an American jockey. The latter captured eight stakes races on Volante and seven stakes races on the Emperor of Norfolk, considered the greatest he ever rode, and also taught riding at Baldwin's racing school. Murphy won all nine 1888 races, including the American Derby, on the Emperor of Norfolk, and seven races on Michael and Philip Dwyer's Kingston, the winningest American thoroughbred. Isaac also prevailed in the 1888 Jersey Handicap, defeating future National Museum of Racing Hall of Famers James McLaughlin, Garrison, and Fred Taral. Murphy's 58 victories in 1889 included 19 on Kingston, the rich Lorillard Stakes on Salvator, and a narrow triumph over Los Angeles, Badge, and Exile in the Oriental Handicap.

Murphy experienced some of his greatest triumphs and his most tragic defeat in 1890. Isaac won his second Kentucky Derby on Corrigan's Riley and demonstrated great judgment of pace in winning the Suburban Handicap by a neck on James Haggin's Salvator. Haggin's Salvator caught the speedy Cassius a half mile from the finish. Two defeats of Mesach Tenny and Garrison produced a match race, which Murphy's Salvator won by a head. Several clockers claimed that the first mile of this race was run in record time. In describing Isaac's penchant for close races, *The Spirit of the Times* wrote, "No man with a touch of heart disease should ever back his mounts." Murphy won two stakes races on Firenzi but rode erratically in finishing last in the Monmouth Handicap. Authorities suspended him on suspicion of drunkenness. W. S. Vosburgh claimed Isaac's poor ride was caused by excessive dieting. In 1891, Murphy won his third Kentucky Derby aboard Kingman. Isaac, who raced less after 1891, began buying and training horses in 1893. His last race as a jockey came aboard Tupto in 1895.

Murphy married Lucy Osborn in 1882 and died of heart failure at Lexington on February 12, 1896, being buried next to Man o' War in the Kentucky Horse Park. His triumphs included three Kentucky Derbies, five Latonia Derbies (Hindoo Stakes), four Clark Handicaps, and four American Derbies. He was elected to the National Jockeys Hall of Fame at Pimlico and the National Museum of Racing Hall of Fame at Saratoga, New York, and was honored by the Isaac Murphy Memorial Handicap. Corrigan wrote, "He has not a superior, if indeed, an equal, as a rider, and is the very embodiment of honesty and integrity. The latter quality, combined with his great ability, makes him immensely popular, and his appearance in the saddle is always greeted with applause, and that of a deafening kind when one of his great finishes sends his mount to victory." Murphy practiced what he preached, advising, "Just be honest. And you'll have no trouble and plenty of money."

BIBLIOGRAPHY: Betty Earle Borries, *Isaac Murphy: Kentucky's Record Jockey* (Berea, KY, 1988); Frank Borries, "His Record Is His Best Monument," *The Thoroughbred Record* 173 (May 6, 1961), pp. 14, 34; Deba Ginsburg, "Lucky Baldwin's Racing

School," *The Thoroughbred of California* 98 (June 1994), pp. 38–39, 42–43, 46; "Isaac Murphy: Biographical Sketch of the Great Lexington Jockey," *Lexington Leader*, March 20, 1889, p. 3; "Isaac Murphy's Death," *The Thoroughbred Record* 43 (1896), p. 79; *Live Stock Record* 36 (November 12, 1892), p. 327; National Turf Writers Association, *Members of the National Museum of Racing Hall of Fame* (Saratoga Springs, NY, 1976); *The New York Sportsman* 15 (January 20, 1883), pp. 33–34; *New York Times*, September 15, 1885, p. 2; L. P. Tarlton, "Isaac Murphy: A Memorial," *The Thoroughbred Record* 43 (1896), p. 136; "Was Isaac Murphy Poisoned [*sic*]?" *Live Stock Record* 32 (November 22, 1890), p. 329.

Steven P. Savage

EDDIE MURRAY
(February 24, 1956–) ———————————————— *Baseball*

Eddie Murray stood among the most feared hitters of the 1980s. His switch-hitting prowess, durability, and outstanding fielding placed him among the most consistent overall players in major league history. Eddie Clarence Murray was born on February 24, 1956, in Los Angeles, California, the eighth child of Charles Murray and Carrie Murray in a family of 12 members. "It was a close twelve," recalled Murray. "We had a mother and father who loved us. We didn't have everything we wanted as far as material things went, but I wasn't someone who wanted a bunch of things." Self-control ranked among the most important lessons he learned as a child. "If you can't control you, you can't control nothing," his mother taught him. This low-keyed approach later sometimes came under fire from the press and fans, who viewed Eddie as being distant. Teammates close to him, however, knew otherwise. Mike Flanagan, a Baltimore Orioles American League (AL) club teammate, observed that Murray "doesn't feel comfortable in the spotlight. All he needs is the satisfaction that he did his job. He's never been a guy that has been overly infatuated with himself."

From the outset, Eddie was surrounded with baseball talent. Four of his brothers, Charles, Jr., Leon, Venice, and Richard, played professional baseball. Richard even performed with the San Francisco Giants National League (NL) club. When Eddie attended Locke High School in Los Angeles, his varsity baseball teammates included future major league players Gary Alexander, Darrell Jackson, and **Ozzie Smith.** Scout Ray Poitevant advised the Baltimore Orioles to select the future star in the third round of the June 1973 amateur draft. Baltimore signed Murray for a $25,000 bonus. Between 1973 and 1977, the first baseman ascended the Orioles minor league chain and led each of his five teams in home runs. Eddie also earned selection to All-Star teams in each of his leagues.

The Orioles promoted Murray to their starting lineup on opening day in 1977 and saw him enjoy an outstanding rookie season. That year Eddie belted 27 home runs, posted 88 RBIs, and batted .283 to earn AL Rookie of the Year honors from the Baseball Writers Association of America (BBWAA). A consistent all-around player, the Los Angeles native averaged 27 home runs and 101 RBIs between 1977 and 1987. His many outstanding seasons included 1985, when he launched 31 home runs and tallied 124 RBIs. During the 1980s, Murray averaged and collected more RBIs (733) than any other player. The stoic first baseman also won three consecutive Gold Glove awards from 1982 to 1984. The Orioles named Eddie, the team leader in most categories, their MVP six different times. He was selected to the AL All-Star team for six consecutive years from 1981 through 1986.

As his prominence grew, Murray developed into one of the most charitable professional athletes of his time. During his illustrious career, Eddie had donated both time and money to the United Cerebral Palsy Foundation, the United Way, the American Red Cross, Johns Hopkins Children's Center, and New Holiness Refuge Church. Park Heights Academy, one beneficiary, dedicated a classroom in his honor. In 1985, he also donated $500,000 to the city of Baltimore to fund an Outward Bound Camp program in honor of his deceased mother. Murray initiated a program called "Project 33," whereby 50 box seats to each Orioles' game were given to inner-city children. Eddie gave nearly $20,000 a year to this cause.

Despite his contributions to civic organizations, Murray, among baseball's highest paid players, fell out of favor with many Baltimore fans by 1986. Baltimore fans had expected very much of him. A bitter feud developed with Orioles' owner Edward Bennett Williams, who criticized Murray's play. A cleavage with the local media also contributed to Eddie's turbulent 1986 season. He demanded a trade throughout the year. The Orioles finally dealt the sensitive first baseman to the Los Angeles Dodgers (NL) in December 1988.

Murray spent three full seasons with the Los Angeles Dodgers from 1989 to 1991. During that span, the durable first baseman played in no less than 153 games. The always productive Eddie averaged 21 home runs, 93 RBIs, and 160 hits while in Los Angeles and batted a career-high .330 in 1990. The following season, he earned selection as the NL's All-Star first baseman and led the NL with a .992 fielding percentage. The New York Mets (NL) signed him as a free agent in November 1991.

With New York, Murray made an immediate impact and finished the 1992 season as team leader in RBIs (93), hits (144), and most offensive categories. Eddie's accomplishments earned him the Met Life "Met of the Year" award. He also broke Keith Hernandez's major league record for assists by a first baseman (1,682) and extended his new mark to 1,837 career assists. In 1993, Murray again led the Mets in most offensive categories, including batting (.285), games (154), at bats (610), hits (174), doubles (28), and RBIs (100). These efforts earned Eddie a second consecutive "Met of the Year" trophy.

The switch-hitting veteran signed with the Cleveland Indians (AL) in December 1993 and in April 1994 became the first Cleveland player to hit a home run at their new Jacobs Field. During the strike-shortened 1994 season, he broke the major league record for most games played by a first baseman and established a new major league mark for home runs hit from both sides of the plate in a single game with 11. In 18 seasons, Murray has batted .288 and amassed National Baseball Hall of Fame credentials. Besides being eighteenth on the all-time list for games played (2,706), he also ranks thirteenth with 10,167 at bats, twenty-first with 3,000 hits, third with 17 grand slams, nineteenth with 458 home runs, and fourteenth with 1,738 RBIs. Murray became just the second switch hitter and only the twentieth hitter in major league baseball history to reach 3,000 hits when he singled off Mike Trombley of the Minnesota Twins in the sixth inning on June 30, 1995. Eddie broke two ribs in a collision at home plate two days later.

The six-foot-two-inch, 220-pound first baseman married Janice Zenon in 1993. His extensive community work earned him nominations for the prestigious Roberto Clemente Award in 1984 and 1985.

BIBLIOGRAPHY: William Barry Furlong, "Time for Eddie Murray," *Sport* 71 (June 1981), pp. 55–56; Jim Henneman, "Just How Good Is He?" *The Sporting News*, June 26, 1984, p. 30; Frederick C. Klein, "The Richest Oriole," *Wall Street Journal*, April 5, 1982, pp. 15–16; Ken Rosenthal, "The Two Sides of Eddie," *Chicago Evening Sun*, July 23, 1987, pp. 1, 8; Eric Siegal, "Eddie Murray: Soft-Spoken Oriole Does His Talking with Bat and Glove," (Baltimore) *The Sun Magazine* (August 19, 1979), pp. 6–9, 11; Gordon Verrell, "A Lower Profile in La-La Land," *The Sporting News*, March 6, 1989, p. 20; *Who's Who Among Black Americans*, 6th ed. (Detroit, MI, 1990), p. 934.

Samuel O. Regalado

DAN O'BRIEN
(July 18, 1966–) ————————————————— *Track and Field*

In the early 1990s, Dan O'Brien emerged as the world's leading performer in the two-day, 10-event decathlon by winning two consecutive World Championships and setting the world record. Daniel Dion O'Brien, the son of a biracial couple, was born on July 18, 1966, in Portland, Oregon. According to Larry Hunt, track and field coach at Henley High School in Klamath Falls, Oregon, Dan's father was "black, about 6–3 and said to be very athletic. His mother was half-Finnish and both were once college professors." At age two, Jim O'Brien and Virginia O'Brien of Klamath Falls adopted Dan, bringing him up with four other adopted children and two of their own. "I was gifted with some incredible genes," remarked O'Brien. As a Henley High School senior, Dan earned All-State honors in football, basketball, and track and field in 1984. An all-around track and field performer, he won the decathlon in the 1984 Track Athletic Congress (TAC) Junior Championships.

Track and Field News ranked O'Brien as the nation's top high school decathlete in 1984, but no college showed interest in him except the University of Idaho. Academic ineligibility, however, sidelined him from competition from 1985 to 1987. Dan confessed that his "two big interests then were drinking beer and playing golf." In 1987, he lived in a University of Idaho dormitory without paying tuition or attending classes. That year, Dan accumulated $8,000 in debt and was arrested for writing bad checks. O'Brien told *Track and Field News* in 1990 that "I had to screw up totally in order to grow up." In 1987, Mike Keller, track and field coach at the University of Idaho, enrolled Dan in Spokane, Washington, Community College to improve his grades. At Spokane, O'Brien started to train with Rick Sloan, an assistant track and field coach at Washington State University. Dan, who improved his decathlon score to 7,891 points under Sloan, revealed that his renewed success in "track and field got [him] moving in the right direction." At the 1988 Olympic Trials, an injury sustained in the long jump forced him to withdraw from the competition. He watched the remainder of the decathlon from the sidelines, thinking "there was no reason I couldn't be up with those guys. I knew I had the talent."

By the end of 1988, O'Brien's scholastic performance had improved and enabled him to return to the University of Idaho. Although favored to win the 1989 NCAA decathlon title after a 7,987-point performance, Dan sustained an injury in the Big Sky Conference championship and missed the national title meet. O'Brien tallied 8,267 points at the 1990 Washington State University's Cougar Invitational and scored a wind-aided 8,483 points to finish second in the TAC championship. On the first day of competition, Dan long jumped 26 feet 3½ inches to eclipse Daley Thompson's decathlon long jump world record by 1 inch. His first-day performance of 4,656 points marked an American record. "I knew Dan would do well the first day," remarked Dave Johnson, the 1990 TAC decathlon champion, "but I didn't expect over 4,600!" O'Brien scored 8,358 points and finished second to Johnson in the Goodwill Games at Seattle, Washington. Dan led the competition up to the final event, the 1,500 meters, but Johnson defeated him in the "metric mile" by less than 10 seconds. At the 1991 TAC championships, O'Brien captured the national title with a wind-aided total of 8,844 points. Despite the wind, Dan's tally comprised history's second highest score to Thompson's 8,847-point world record. After capturing the 1991 World Championship in an American record of 8,812 points, he remarked that "9,200 in 1992 is totally possible."

Before the 1992 Olympic Trials, decathlon authority Frank Zarknowski lauded O'Brien: "God has never given anyone more talent in the decathlon. There's never been anyone with his combination of great sprinting, great throws, and great vaulting." Dan proved Zarknowski's words true at the 1992 Olympic Trials, finishing the first day of competition in a world record of 4,698 points. On the second day, however, he failed to clear any height in the pole vault and placed eleventh in the Olympic Trials. O'Brien, who made no excuses for his lackluster performance, told the press that he would "go home and regroup for the Talence [France] meet. That should be a perfect opportunity for me to show everyone I'm capable of breaking the world record."

Dan prevailed at Talence with a world record decathlon performance of 8,891 points. His first-day world record show of 4,720 points included a decathlon long jump world record of 26 feet 6¼ inches. "Who is the World's Greatest Athlete?" he rhetorically asked the press. "You're looking at the World's Greatest Athlete. That's what I wanted to prove at this meet." Coach Keller added, "Our goal is to score so many points in the next four years that no one will be able to touch that record in our lifetime." O'Brien captured the heptathlon in the 1993 indoor World Championships at Toronto, Canada, garnering a world record of 6,476 points. Later that year, Dan won the decathlon at both the USA Track and Field (USATF) Outdoor Championships and the World Outdoor Championships at Stuttgart, Germany. In 1994, his decathlon titles included the outdoor USATF championships at Knoxville, Tennessee, and the St. Petersburg, Russia, Goodwill Games. He captured the decathlon at the USATF Outdoor Championships at Sacramento, California, in June 1995.

BIBLIOGRAPHY: Jon Hendershott, "Respectable Once Again," *Track and Field News* 43 (December 1990), pp. 4–6; Jon Hendershott, "O'Brien Fires Up Decathlon," *Track and Field News* 44 (August 1991), p. 19; Jon Hendershott, "Difficult Questions to Ask," *Track and Field News* 45 (August 1991), p. 26; Bob Hersh, "Don't Sell O'Brien Short," *Track and Field News* 44 (November 1991), p. 19; Jeff Hollobaugh, "Forget Barcelona," *Track and Field News* 45 (November 1992), pp. 4–5; Glen McMicken, "Dec: Goodbye Dan, Hi Dave," *Track and Field News* 45 (August 1992), pp. 26–27; Dick Patrick, "O'Brien Sets Course for 'Greatest' Tag," *USA Today*, August 4, 1992, pp. C1–C2.

Adam R. Hornbuckle

SHAQUILLE O'NEAL
(March 6, 1972–) —————————————————— *Basketball*

Seven-foot-one-inch, 301-pound Shaquille O'Neal ranks among the most dominating all-time National Basketball Association (NBA) players, thrilling crowds with his thunderous dunks and monstrous blocked shots. Shaquille Rashaun O'Neal was born on March 6, 1972, in Newark, New Jersey, the son of Philip Harrison, a U.S. Army sergeant, and Lucille O'Neal. O'Neal, whose first name means "little warrior," was born two years before his parents married and grew up with five siblings.

His public schooling came in Jersey City and on military bases in Bayonne and Eatontown, New Jersey, Fort Stewart, Georgia, and Germany. Classmates often teased him about his name. Shaquille had difficulty making friends and was a juvenile delinquent. "I'd beat people up, hit teachers, spit on people, break into cars and take tapes. I was a real jerk, but I thought I was cool." His six-foot-seven-inch father often disciplined him physically. At age 13, O'Neal finally began to listen to his father's advice and became a leader. "Thank goodness," Shaquille acknowledges, "I had two parents who loved me enough to stay on my case."

O'Neal cleaned up his act and started applying his energies to basketball. Shaquille starred at Cole High School in San Antonio, Texas, averaging 30 points, 22 rebounds, and six assists a game as a senior before graduating in 1989. Cole finished 36–1 his junior year and captured the Texas Class AAA High School State championship with a 36–0 mark his senior year. O'Neal tallied 27 points, grabbed 36 rebounds, and blocked 36 shots in one game alone.

Louisiana State University (LSU) won the intense recruiting battle for O'Neal's services. Shaquille's powerful inside game, along with All-America guard Chris Jackson's outside shots, sparked coach Dale Brown's Tigers to a 23–9 mark in 1989–1990. Although just a freshman, O'Neal averaged 13.9 points, 3.6 blocked shots, and 12 rebounds a game. Shaquille ranked sixth nationally in blocked shots and ninth in rebounds. LSU tied for second place in the Southeastern Conference (SEC) and reached the second round of the National Collegiate Athletic Association (NCAA) tournament.

O'Neal enjoyed a banner 1990–1991 season for the 20–10 Tigers, earning Associated Press (AP) and United Press International (UPI) Player of the Year honors. Shaquille's powerful inside game catapulted LSU to a share of the SEC title. He paced the nation with 411 rebounds, ranked third with 140 blocked shots (5 per game), and placed seventh nationally with 774 points, averaging nearly 28 points a game. Lack of an outside game caused LSU's elimination in the first round of the NCAA tournament.

The 1991–1992 season witnessed O'Neal help the 21–10 Tigers finish second in the SEC and reach the second round of the NCAA tournament. Shaquille again earned All-America honors, leading the nation with 157 blocked shots (5.2 per game), placing second with 421 rebounds (14.0 average), and scoring 722 points (24.1 average). Only **David Robinson** of the U.S. Naval Academy blocked more shots in a single NCAA season. O'Neal explained, "My philosophy has been to never, ever, let a man who's lighter or smaller than me dog me out."

In 90 games spanning three LSU seasons, O'Neal tallied 1,941 points for a 21.6 points average, converted 61 percent of his field goals, snared 1,217 rebounds, and blocked 412 shots. Shaquille ranks second to Robinson in NCAA career blocked shots average with 4.6 per game and fifth in career rebound average with 13.5 a game. He skipped his senior season to enter the 1992 NBA draft, becoming the most celebrated big man available since **Kareem Abdul-Jabbar.**

The Orlando Magic won the NBA lottery and made O'Neal the first player chosen overall. It took a herculean feat for Orlando general manager Pat Williams to sign Shaquille to a $40 million, seven-year contract. The salary cap forced the Magic to restructure five contracts, trade a player, and renounce the rights to another player in order to sign O'Neal. The move paid immediate dividends for Orlando, as Shaquille won both NBA Rookie of the Year and All-Rookie First Team honors. During 1992–1993, he ranked second with 1,122 rebounds (13.9 average) and 286 blocked shots (3.53 average), fourth with a 56.2 field goal percentage, and eighth in scoring with 1,893 points (23.4 average). Orlando placed fourth in the Atlantic Division with a 41–41 mark.

In a nationally televised game on February 7 against the Phoenix Suns, O'Neal destroyed the entire hydraulic basket support system. Shaquille dunked a follow shot with such force that the basket collapsed, delaying the game 35 minutes. Nine days later, he tallied a season-high 46 points against the Detroit Pistons. San Antonio Spurs general manager Bob Bass remarked, "The NBA is a big man's game with its open court. One who is highly skilled, like Shaq, has a chance of having a big impact."

In 1993–1994, David Robinson of San Antonio edged O'Neal for the NBA scoring title. Shaquille tallied 2,377 points, averaging 29.3 per game. He ranked first with a 59.9 field goal percentage, second with 1,072 rebounds (13.2 average), and sixth with 231 blocked shots (2.85 average). His 15 blocked shots against the New Jersey Nets on November 20, 1993, and 14 offensive rebounds against the Boston Celtics on February 15, 1994, also paced the NBA. Orlando compiled a 50–32 record, finishing second in the Atlantic Division and making the playoffs for the first time.

In 1994–1995, O'Neal led the NBA in scoring with 2,315 points (29.3 point average), finished second in field goal percentage (58.3 percent), and third in rebounding (11.4 average). Shaquille ranked second in the NBA MVP balloting and made the ALL-NBA record. Orlando reached the NBA finals, losing four straight games to the Houston Rockets.

O'Neal, whose thunderous dunks and monstrous blocks have thrilled crowds, has been the NBA marquee player since the original retirement of **Michael Jordan.** Every Magic home and road game virtually sells out, as Shaquille's dominance over more experienced players has left NBA followers aghast. In just three NBA seasons, he has tallied 6,585 points (7.3 per game), made 58.2 percent of his floor shots, recorded 3,095 rebounds, and blocked 709 shots. He also appeared in the 1993, 1994, and 1995 All-Star Games. O'Neal acknowledged, "I can compensate [for my lack of experience] with my size and natural ability and especially with my will. What I think I have is inner strength—the drive, the will, the determination to succeed." The media has begun comparing Shaquille, who has appeared in NBA All-Star Games three seasons, with great centers **Wilt Chamberlain, Bill Russell,** and Kareem Abdul-Jabbar. "The thing about Shaq," **Magic Johnson** noted, "is he's mean— and nasty. He'll be great, and I mean great. The guy's a monster, a true prime-time player."

O'Neal led the American Dream II squad to a Gold Medal at the World Championship of Basketball in August 1994 at Toronto, earning MVP honors. *USA Basketball* named him 1994 Male Athlete of the Year.

O'Neal, who remains single, has an engaging smile and wears a size 21 shoe. Shaquille's $30 million in endorsements include Pepsi, his own signature ball, his own line of clothing, a Reebok basketball shoe, Scoreboard trading cards, and a Kenner toy action figure. In 1993, he coauthored *Shaq Attack!* with Jack McCallum and released rap video albums, *Shaq Diesel* and *Shaquille O'Neal: Larger than Life.* O'Neal also costarred in a 1994 movie, *Blue Chips,* with Nick Nolte and will appear in a 1996 movie, *Kazaam.*

BIBLIOGRAPHY: David DuPree, "Magic Rookie Has Stuff of NBA Legends," *USA Today*, February 18, 1993, pp. C1–C2; Curry Kirkpatrick, "Shaq Attack," *Sports Illustrated* 74 (January 21, 1991), pp. 38–42; David Moore, "Shaquille's Big Deal," *Sport* 84 (January 1993), pp. 52–57; Shaquille O'Neal, "The Real Shaquille," *USA Weekend*, October 1–3, 1993, pp. 6–8; Shaq O'Neal and Jack McCallum, *Shaq Attack!* (New York, 1993); David L. Porter, ed., *Biographical Dictionary of American Sports: 1992–1995 Supplement for Baseball, Football, Basketball, and Other Sports* (Westport, CT, 1995); *The Sporting News Official Basketball Register* (1994–1995).

David L. Porter

JESSE OWENS
(September 12, 1913–March 31, 1980) ——————— *Track and Field*

Jesse Owens, one of America's most legendary African-American athletes, captured four Gold Medals in track and field at the politically charged 1936 Berlin, Germany, Olympic Games. James Cleveland Owens was born on September 12, 1913, in Oakville, Alabama, the grandson of slaves. His parents, Henry Owens and Emma (Alexander) Owens, were poor cotton sharecroppers who had 10 children. Jesse, a shy stutterer, began picking cotton at age six and attended a one-room school. The Owens moved to a Cleveland, Ohio, slum when he was nine years old. His parents nicknamed him "J. C.," but his first Cleveland teacher misunderstood his Alabama accent and started calling him "Jesse." Owens starred in track and field in junior high and at Cleveland East Technical High School. "We couldn't afford any kind of equipment," he recalled, "so we ran and ran and ran." Under coach Charles Riley, Jesse won three titles at the national interscholastic track and field meet in 1933 in Chicago, Illinois. After tying the world record of 9.4 seconds in the 100-yard dash, he captured the 200-yard dash and broad jump titles.

Owens married Ruth Solomon in 1931 and had three daughters, Gloria, Beverly, and Marlene. He attended Ohio State University in Columbus without earning a degree. Jesse worked seven hours a night in Columbus and perfected his running and jumping skills under coach Larry Snyder. In 1935 at Madison Square Garden in New York, he shattered the world 60-yard dash record. His 6.4-second mark lasted 40 years. On May 25, 1935, at the Western Conference Track and Field meet at Ann Arbor, Michigan, Jesse enjoyed the greatest single-day performance in track and field history. Within a 45-minute span, Owens broke five world records and tied one. He had injured his back falling down a flight of stairs a week earlier. Despite suffering back pain, Jesse equaled the 9.4-second world record in the 100-meter dash. Ten minutes later, he demolished the world broad jump record with a leap of 26 feet 8½ inches. This mark, which Owens cherished the most, remained until 1960. Within the next 25 minutes, he smashed world marks in the 220-yard dash (20.3 seconds) and 220-yard low hurdles (22.6 seconds) in a straightaway. The times were automatically recognized as world records for the slightly shorter 200-meter distances. "All I could remember," Jesse recalled, "was that my back was killing me."

Owens's next great triumph came at the 1936 Olympic Games, where he garnered four Gold Medals. The Berlin, Germany, Games were charged with political, social, and commercial significance, as Adolf Hitler showcased his Nazi dictatorship and Aryan supremacy beliefs. Hitler boasted publicly that his athletes would prevail, while the German press scorned "America's black auxiliaries." Jesse found it "eerie and frightening" to hear the roar of 100,000 spectators shouting "Heil Hitler!" as the Nazi leader entered the Olympic Stadium. Owens quickly demolished Hitler's supremacist propaganda, using his sheer grace and matchless speed to eclipse four Olympic records. He equaled Eddie Tolan's world record of 10.3 seconds in taking the Gold Medal in the 100-meter final, edging future U.S. Congressman Ralph Metcalfe. After helpful advice from German competitor Luz Long, Jesse qualified for the long jump finals and then leaped an Olympic record 26 feet $5\frac{5}{16}$ inches. Owens defeated Mack Robinson, a brother of **Jackie Robinson,** by five yards in the 200-meter dash. His 20.7-second clocking marked the fastest ever done at that distance on a curve. Jesse established a commanding lead for the American 400-meter relay team, which triumphed in Olympic record time of 39.8 seconds. Sportswriters in 1973 called Owens's remarkable feat "the most significant sports story of the century." Jesse not only captured one more Gold Medal than the entire German track and field team, but none of the other 892 track and field athletes representing 52 nations snared more than one Gold Medal. He embodied the Olympic dream that athletes can transcend political and military lines in a noble quest for friendship and glory. American newspapers falsely claimed that Hitler refused to congratulate Owens after his first victory, but the International Olympic Committee president had ordered Hitler after the first day to stop greeting German winners at his box.

Owens received a hero's welcome in the United States, including a ticker-tape parade in New York City. The Amateur Athletic Union (AAU), however, suspended Jesse from all further amateur competition because he refused to complete a barnstorming tour of Sweden with his Olympic teammates.

Owens sought to capitalize on his fame and raced professionally against humans, horses, dogs, and automobiles but endured racial discrimination, job and business investment failures, and bankruptcy. During World War II, he conducted government physical fitness programs for African Americans in Philadelphia, Pennsylvania, and directed African-American workers at Ford Motor Company in Detroit, Michigan. In 1946, Jesse joined the Leo Rose Sporting Goods Company as head of sales. After being transferred to Chicago, Illinois, in 1949, he served as secretary of the Illinois State Athletic Commission from 1952 to 1955 and helped African-American youngsters at the Southside Boys Club. In 1955, the U.S. Department of State sponsored his goodwill tour of India, Malaya, and the Philippines. As an Illinois Youth Commission member, he organized the Junior Sports Jamboree in 1956. Owens later formed a public relations firm in Phoenix, Arizona, and earned substantial income addressing athletic, business, religious, and civic groups. He traveled

200,000 miles a year delivering speeches and tirelessly raising funds for the U.S. Olympic Committee. Jesse, who did not participate in the civil rights movement, opposed an African-American boycott of the Mexico City 1968 Olympic Games. For his citizenship, public service, and patriotism, he received the NCAA Theodore Roosevelt Award in 1974, the Presidential Medal of Freedom in 1976, and the Living Legacy Award in 1979.

Owens died in Tucson, Arizona, on March 31, 1980, of lung cancer, caused by 35 years of heavy cigarette smoking. A 1949 *Ebony* poll named Jesse the greatest African-American athlete of all time. The next year, the Associated Press (AP) voted him the greatest track and field athlete of the first half of the twentieth century. His honors included charter membership in the National Track and Field Hall of Fame (1974) and U.S. Olympic Hall of Fame (1983). Owens had soared far above a world of athletic competition, enlarging the sport's possibilities by setting 11 world records. A role model rather than an inspirational leader or trailblazer, Jesse affirmed, "I just came along at a time when the black American needed an image."

BIBLIOGRAPHY: Associated Press and Grolier, *The Olympic Story: Pursuit of Excellence* (New York, 1979); William J. Baker, *Jesse Owens: An American Life* (New York, 1986); Myron Cope, "The Amazing Jesse Owens," *Sport* 37 (October 1964), pp. 60–63, 98–99; *Current Biography Yearbook* (1956), pp. 475–477; Duff Hart-Davis, *Hitler's Games* (New York, 1986); Norman Katkov, "Jesse Owens—The Ebony Express," *Sport* 16 (April 1954), pp. 28–31, 78–81; Richard D. Mandell, *Nazi Olympics* (New York, 1971); *New York Times*, April 1, 1980; Jesse Owens with Paul Neimark, *Jesse: The Man Who Outran Hitler* (New York, 1978); "The True Olympian," *Newsweek* 95 (April 14, 1980), p. 60; *Who Was Who in America* (1977–1981), p. 440.

David L. Porter

ALAN PAGE
(August 7, 1945–   ) ——————————————————— *Football*

When President Bill Clinton visited Minnesota in 1994, he jogged with his friend Alan Page and the latter's wife, Diane. The trio ran along the colorful river front in the old flour milling section of Minneapolis. At the end of the short jogging run, Diane was acknowledged the winner by her husband and the president. During his professional football career, Page became the first National Football League (NFL) player to complete a marathon race. "One of my two hobbies is jogging," admitted Alan afterward. "The other is collecting toy trucks. I run between 50 and 60 miles a week during good weather and I try to get out every day."

Alan C. Page was born in Canton, Ohio, on August 7, 1945, the son of Howard Page and Georgianna Page. Page graduated from Canton Central High School, where he played prep football three years and made the All-City, All-County, and All-State mythical grid teams. Alan was intensely recruited by numerous colleges and accepted a scholarship to the University of Notre Dame, where he starred as a football defensive end.

Page received All-America honors as a senior football player and graduated in 1967 with a bachelor's degree in political science. Alan attributes his success largely to the guidance he received from his parents. In 1978 he earned a law degree from the University of Minnesota, completing the academic work in three and one-half years. Page then passed the law examinations, making him eligible to practice law. "Thurgood Marshall, Roy Wilkins, and Martin Luther King, Jr., were individuals who helped develop my interest in the law," states Page. "They sparked my interest because of their beliefs and actions in seeking equal justice and equal opportunity."

Page, a first-round choice by the Minnesota Vikings (NFL) in the 1967 draft, anchored the 1967 front four defensive line, the "Purple People Eaters," and was selected Rookie of the Year. Alan proved instrumental in the Vikings' four Super Bowl appearances with lineman Carl Eller, Jim Marshall, and Gary Larson. The Viking defensive line ranked about the quickest of all time in the NFL. Many sports experts regarded Page as the quickest defensive lineman off the ball in NFL history. Since purple was the Viking team color, the players were nicknamed the "Purple Gang." One ingenious sports reporter called the defensive line the "Four Norsemen." "Speed, quickness, agility, size," acknowledges Alan, "there are a lot of people with those things. I had the good fortune to be healthy and be able to play every week. I was fortunate to be part of a great group of guys, extremely talented football players who enjoyed what they did."

Page appeared in the Pro Bowl from 1969 to 1977 and was selected All-Pro from 1970 to 1977. In 1970, Alan was chosen the NFL Defensive Lineman of the Year and Defensive Player of the Year. In 1971, he was selected the NFL's MVP, making him the first defender to win this top honor. Page's leadership qualities were recognized when he was selected as player representative from 1970 to 1974 and again in 1976 and 1977. Alan represented NFL players on the Executive Committee from 1972 to 1975.

In 1978, Minnesota traded Page to the Chicago Bears. Alan performed for the Bears through 1981, completing his 15-year professional football career there. Page's trade came partly because his playing weight had dropped from 245 pounds to 210 pounds and his gridiron union activities alienated management. Coach Bud Grant also disliked Alan missing the pre-season conditioning because of his law school involvement. Many years later, Page remained bitter regarding the trade.

Alan was married twice, first to Addie Johnson on December 17, 1966, and then to his present wife, Diane (Sims) Page, on June 5, 1973. Diane, an outstanding distance runner, is the mother of their four children, Nina, Georgi, Kami, and Justin. Honors have been frequently bestowed on Page, who set NFL records for safeties and blocked punts, was selected on the Viking's Silver Anniversary Team in 1985, and was named to the AFL-NFL All-Star Team for the 1960–1984 era. Alan has declared, "I don't miss football. It was great while it lasted, but for me it was time to move on and use my head for something other than a battering ram and a place to keep my helmet."

Page's civic activities have been extensive. In 1981, the U.S. Junior Chamber of Commerce honored Alan as one of America's Ten Outstanding Young Men. He chaired the 1972 United Negro College Fund and served on its advisory board for several years, co-hosting its Telethon in 1984. Page chaired the Minnesota Council on Physical Fitness in 1972, volunteered for the Chicago Multiple Sclerosis Read-a-Thon in 1979, and served on the board of directors of the Chicago Association of Retarded Citizens. Alan, state chairman for the American Cancer Society, served as a commentator on National Public Radio and as a color commentator for Turner Broadcasting System on the College Football "Game of the Week" in 1982.

From 1979 to 1984, Page joined a prestigious Minneapolis law firm. His partners included Orville Freeman, governor of Minnesota and U.S. Secretary of Agriculture, Don Frazer, multi-term mayor of Minneapolis, and Leonard Lindquist, a state commissioner, among others. This law firm emphasized a team approach. In 1985, Alan was selected special assistant attorney general of Minnesota. Page replaced a retiring justice of the state supreme court, winning the election handily, and still serves in the post.

Alan was inducted into the Pro Football Hall of Fame in Canton, Ohio, on July 30, 1988, and chose as his presenter Willarene Beasley, principal of North High School in Minneapolis, symbolizing his stand for higher education. He was featured on Aetna's 1994 calendar of African-American history. In 1994, Page also became one of the first four recipients of the Aetna Voice of Conscience Award because his foundation helps young people who aspire to broader academic and career horizons.

Alan planned for a career beyond football, achieving success in the workplace. He continues to participate in law activities, education, sports charities, and civic organizations. As for the future, Page said, "At some point I would like to be a teacher. I believe it would be exciting, challenging and interesting to teach at the law school level."

BIBLIOGRAPHY: Steve Aschburner, "Page Is Headed for Hall of Fame," *Minneapolis Star-Tribune*, February 3, 1988, p. C1; Barbara Bigelow, ed., *Contemporary Black Biography*, vol. 7 (Detroit, MI, 1994), pp. 215–218; Stan W. Carlson, letter to Alan Page, September 3, 1993; *Chicago Bears Media Guide*, (1980–1981); Tony Moton, "Page Reflects on His Life and Times in the NFL," *Minneapolis Star-Tribune*, July 29, 1988, p. C1; Misti Snow, "Alan Page Answers Questions-Mindworks," *Minneapolis Star-Tribune*, May 25, 1993, pp. E1–E2; "Vikings Front Four," *Ebony* 25 (January 25, 1970), pp. 83–86.

Stan W. Carlson

SATCHEL PAIGE
(July 7, 1906–June 8, 1982) ———————————— *Baseball*

Robert LeRoy "Satchel" Paige, one of the best-known Negro League players, ranked among the first athletes to successfully blend his baseball talents with showmanship. He was the son of John Paige, Sr., a gardener, and Lula Paige and was born on or about July 7, 1906, in Mobile, Alabama. With 11 brothers and sisters, he quickly learned to depend on himself. Satchel rarely attended school, often becoming the source of much mischief around town. As a youngster, he worked at the train station carrying suitcases. Paige once tried to steal a man's satchel but was captured immediately by the owner. A friend observed the incident and gave him his permanent nickname.

Paige was sent to Mt. Meigs reform school after being caught stealing costume jewelry. At Mt. Meigs, he played baseball and perfected his pitching skills. After leaving the reform school, Satchel pitched for several semi-pro baseball teams including the Mobile Tigers. In 1926, he began his professional baseball career with Chattanooga, Tennessee, of the Negro Southern League. Paige was known as "just a big ol' tall boy," who could throw the ball extremely hard without much control. In 1923, the six-foot-four-inch, 180-pound right-hander joined the Birmingham, Alabama, Black Barons of the Negro National League (NNL) and fashioned an 8–3 record. Satchel posted records of 10–11 in 1929 and 10–4 in 1930, becoming the main gate attraction for the ball club.

In 1931, Paige joined the Nashville Elite Giants when the franchise moved north as the Cleveland Cubs. Before the season ended, however, Satchel signed with the Pittsburgh Crawfords. The Crawfords were a new team put together by Gus Greenlee. That year, Paige pitched the Crawfords to a 6–5 victory over the Homestead Grays. During the early 1930s, he achieved his greatest popularity with marks of 32–7 in 1932, 31–4 in 1933, and 10–1 in 1934. Satchel matched up against the Philadelphia Stars' ace left-hander Slim Jones at Yankee Stadium that year. The game, considered the greatest ever played in the Negro Leagues, was called due to darkness and ended in a 1–1 tie.

The next year, Paige encountered several salary disputes and played periodically for other clubs. For a white semi-pro team in Bismarck, North Dakota, he won 134 of 150 games. Satchel also pitched that year for the Kansas City Monarchs. As a Monarch, Paige defeated a team of well-known major leaguers led by Detroit Tiger pitcher "Schoolboy" Rowe. Upon returning to the Crawfords in 1936, he compiled a 24–3 record.

In 1937, Paige moved to Santo Domingo and pitched the Ciudad Trujillo team to a championship. He led the Dominican League in wins with an 8–2 record. Banned from the NNL for jumping his contract, Satchel toured the United States with a team he assembled. His contract became the property of the Newark Eagles in 1938, but he never played a game there and instead moved to Mexico. He hurt his arm there and was told he would never pitch again.

Paige then joined the Kansas City Monarchs' traveling team as a gate attraction and saw his arm strength and pitching improve. Satchel added the "bee-ball," "jump ball," "trouble ball," "long ball," and his famous "hesitation pitch" to his repertoire. Paige joined the Monarchs regular team late in 1939 and pitched them to four consecutive Negro American League (NAL) pennants from 1939 to 1942, winning three games during a clean sweep of the Homestead Grays in the 1942 World Series. Satchel compiled a 9–5 record that year after finishing with a 6–0 mark in NAL play the previous season. The 1943 Monarchs team posted a losing record after surrendering many key players in the draft. Paige pitched increasing numbers of exhibition games but still played impressive baseball. In 1946, Satchel pitched the Monarchs to a fifth NAL pennant, but Kansas City dropped the World Series to the Newark Eagles. He missed the last three games while making arrangements to play in a Caribbean league.

In 1948, well-known Cleveland Indians owner Bill Veeck brought Paige to the major leagues, where he became the oldest rookie player. Satchel fashioned a 6–1 record as Cleveland won the 1948 American League (AL) pennant and World Series over the Boston Braves. The hurler followed Veeck in 1951 to the St. Louis Browns (AL), where he sat in his rocking chair in the bullpen during games. In 1965, at age 59, he pitched three innings for the Kansas City A's (AL) to become the oldest player to ever pitch in a major league baseball game.

Paige's success led to numerous stories making him a "living legend" of baseball. Frequently, Satchel sat his outfielders behind the mound while striking out the opposing side with the tying run on base. He once deliberately walked Howard Easterling and **Buck Leonard** to pitch to **Josh Gibson,** one of the best hitters of all time. Of course, Paige struck out Gibson. National Baseball Hall of Famer Leonard recalled, "Satchel was a humdinger; he was the best pitcher I ever saw, black or white."

An early predecessor of basketball's Harlem Globetrotters, Paige routinely billed himself as "guaranteed" to strike out the first nine batters during an exhibition game and usually did just that. Satchel was more than just a comedian not taking his baseball lightly. "I ain't no Clown. . . . I'm a baseball pitcher and winning baseball games is a serious business," he once commented.

After perfecting his control, Paige could throw 20 straight pitches over a chewing gum wrapper. Crush Holloway, a fellow Negro League player, remarked that "Paige didn't have nothing but a fastball, but he had such great control . . . when he turned it loose, it was on you." Buck O'Neil, Satchel's teammate on the Monarchs, agreed. "He could hit a gnat's eye and Satchel's fast ball seemed to shrink." Some hitters described Paige's fastball as "like a half-dollar," while others claimed it was like trying to hit a "marble," a "pea," or an "aspirin tablet." Biz Mackey, one of the greatest catchers, joked that Satchel threw the ball so hard that it disappeared before it reached the catcher's mitt.

Paige's skill and penchant for showmanship enabled him to attract a large audience of fans and post impressive statistics. Satchel's pitching prowess became world renowned. New York Yankee slugger Joe DiMaggio regarded Paige as "the best and fastest pitcher I ever faced." St. Louis Cardinals' great

Dizzy Dean agreed. "I know who the best pitcher I ever did see, and it's old Satch Paige."

Paige married Janet Howard of Pittsburgh, Pennsylvania, in October 1934. They had no children before their August 1943 divorce. On October 12, 1947, Satchel married Lahoma Brown of Stillwater, Oklahoma. They had six children, Pamela Jean, Carolyn Lahoma, Linda Sue, Robert LeRoy, Jr., Lula Ouida, and Rita Jean. Lahoma also had a daughter, Shirley, through a previous marriage.

In 1971, Paige was inducted into the National Baseball Hall of Fame, the first old Negro Leaguer to attain such recognition and distinction. Satchel called this honor "the proudest day of my life." His now-famous, oft-quoted admonitions, included "Don't look back; something might be gaining on you." On June 8, 1982, Paige died in Kansas City, Missouri.

BIBLIOGRAPHY: *The Afro-American*, 1930–1948; James Bankes, *The Pittsburgh Crawfords* (Dubuque, IA, 1991); Barbara Bigelow, ed., *Contemporary Black Biography*, vol. 7 (Detroit, MI, 1994), pp. 219–222; Janet Bruce, *The Kansas City Monarchs* (Lawrence, KS, 1985); *The Chicago Defender*, 1927–1948; John Holway, *Josh and Satch* (New York, NY, 1991); Leroy "Satchel" Paige, *Pitchin' Man* (Cleveland, OH, 1948); LeRoy "Satchel" Paige, *Maybe I'll Pitch Forever* (Garden City, NY, 1962); Robert W. Peterson, *Only the Ball Was White* (Englewood Cliffs, NJ, 1970); *The Pittsburgh Courier*, 1931–1946; Mark Ribowsky, *Don't Look Back: Satchel Paige in the Shadows of Baseball* (New York, 1994); James A. Riley, *The All-Time All-Stars of Black Baseball* (Cocoa, FL, 1983); James A. Riley, *The Biographical Encyclopedia of the Negro Baseball Leagues* (New York, 1994); James A. Riley, interviews with former Negro League players, James A. Riley collection, Cocoa, FL; Mike Shatzkin, ed., *The Ballplayers* (New York, 1990); *The Baseball Encyclopedia*, 9th ed. (New York, 1993).

James A. Riley

JIM PARKER
(April 3, 1934–   ) ——————————————————— *Football*

As an offensive and defensive lineman with the Ohio State University (OSU) Buckeyes and as an offensive lineman with the Baltimore Colts National Football League (NFL) club from 1957 to 1967, Jim Parker set the standard for the very large lineman. Nicknamed "Big Jim" and "Jumbo," Parker weighed around 260 pounds in college and dominated his offensive line in the 1960s. Jim's combination of size, speed, and agility allowed him to completely control his side of the line of scrimmage both as a collegiate and NFL player. NFL coaching great George Allen lavishly praised him, "Jim Parker is one of those who rises above even the best. I do not think there is much doubt that he was the outstanding offensive lineman of all time, even though it may be more difficult to judge players at this position than at any other position."

James Thomas Parker was born on April 3, 1934, in Macon, Georgia. The son of Charles Parker, Sr., a track laborer for the Central of Georgia Railroad, spent his early years in Macon with his six brothers and sisters. Due to family poverty and his need for a job, Jim hitchhiked to Toledo, Ohio, after his junior year in high school and lived with an aunt and uncle while working on a construction job during the summer. He stayed in Toledo, attending Scott High School his senior year. An OSU alumnus recommended Parker to Woody Hayes, the legendary football coach there. Hayes convinced Jim to become a Buckeye. As an African-American athlete in the 1950s, Parker could not have attended any major university in the South. Ohio State thus presented an excellent opportunity for him.

Parker's presence made his teammates more outstanding players. Coach Hayes, for example, credited Jim with having much to do with the success of Howard "Hopalong" Cassady, Ohio State's 1955 Heisman Trophy winner. Similarly, coach George Allen described Parker as "the best pass blocker ever." Jim, according to Allen, never lost his poise and ranked among the best run blockers. Allen credits much of Johnny Unitas's success as the premier NFL quarterback of the 1960s to Parker's excellence as the model NFL line-man. These qualities ensured Jim's induction into both the National Football Foundation (NFF) College Football Hall of Fame and the Pro Football Hall of Fame at the earliest moment of eligibility.

Parker's efforts produced championships at both the collegiate and profes-sional levels. Jim made an immediate impact at Ohio State, anchoring the line for the Big Ten Conference (BTC) championship and mythical national title team in 1954. During his next two seasons, he made consensus All-America. Parker won the Outland Trophy as the outstanding college lineman in 1956, the same year he graduated from Ohio State with a B.A. degree in physical education. Jim displayed great pride in his graduation from Ohio State. He had realized that the southern segregated school system, which he had at-tended, had left him behind his fellow students academically at Ohio State.

The Baltimore Colts made Parker their first-round draft choice in 1957. Jim made All-Pro at left tackle from 1958 to 1961 and at guard the next four seasons. He participated in the Pro Bowl from 1959 through 1966 and an-chored a line that helped the Colts win Eastern Conference championships in 1958, 1964, and 1967. Parker's NFL career ended when his knee failed to respond to medical treatment, forcing him to retire graciously. Jim's coach, Don Shula, considered his retirement "one of the most unselfish moves ever made in sport."

Throughout his career, Parker remained a team-oriented person. Jim, an extremely friendly and well-liked player, did not showboat or act as a self-centered individual. He took great pride in the successes of his team and the personal achievements of Cassady and Unitas.

Professional football coaches have described Parker as the best offensive lineman of all time. In both college and professional football, Jim excelled personally and made his teammates better football players. Both remain qual-ities desired in athletes. Parker and his wife, Mae, have four children and live in Columbia, Maryland. Parker works in private business in the Baltimore region.

BIBLIOGRAPHY: George Allen with Ben Olan, *Pro Football's 100 Greatest Players* (Indianapolis, IN, 1982); Jerry Brondfield, *Woody Hayes and the 100 Yard War* (New York, 1974); Woody Hayes, *You Win with People* (Columbus, OH, 1975); Jim Parker files, NFF College Football Hall of Fame, University of Notre Dame, Notre Dame, IN; Jim Parker files, Ohio State University Athletic Department, Columbus, OH; Jim Parker files, Pro Football Hall of Fame, Canton, OH.

Harry A. Jebsen, Jr.

FLOYD PATTERSON
(January 4, 1935–) ———————————————————————— *Boxing*

Floyd Patterson became the first boxer to regain a heavyweight title. Floyd Patterson was born on January 4, 1935, in Waco, North Carolina, the son of Thomas Patterson, a railroad worker, and Anabelle Patterson. Floyd, whose life has been a constant battle against his own reticence, had eight brothers and two sisters. He grew up in the Brooklyn, New York, slums, shunning school to find seclusion in the darkness of his own room or in movie theaters. Patterson also liked to visit the zoo, where he often slept at night or in the nearest subway station. Floyd's lifestyle led to brushes with the law. His despairing mother committed him to the Wiltryck School for emotionally disturbed children in upper New York State. There, Patterson met Vivien Costen, one of the two most influential persons in his life. Floyd had been illiterate at age 11. Costen taught him to read and enjoy the company of others, generally bringing him out of a shell. "She was like a mother to me," Floyd recalled, a totally dedicated teacher to the less fortunate.

Upon returning to New York City, Patterson wandered into Gramercy Gymnasium and Health Center. The facility was operated by Constantine "Cus" D'Amato, a boxing authority. D'Amato had handled "Rocky" Graziano, one-time middleweight champion. "Cus," the second most influential person in Patterson's life, was firmly impressed with Floyd's newly found determination, speed afoot, and fast-moving hands. He also curtailed Patterson's bobbing and jumping excessively in the ring, helping him develop rapidly. "Cus" led him to two Golden Glove championships.

At age 17, Floyd won the middleweight Gold Medal at the 1952 Summer Olympics in Helsinki, Finland. It took him only 18 minutes to dispose of four opponents. Patterson turned professional upon returning to New York City. Under D'Amato's careful guidance, he on September 12, 1952, defeated Eddie Goldbold in a fourth-round knockout. His last bout, a seventh-round knockout by **Muhammad Ali,** occurred on September 20, 1972.

Patterson sought the heavyweight championship. Floyd's only loss along the way came to ring stylist Joey Maxim in a close eight-round decision on June

7, 1954. "It was the fight in which I learned the most," he recalled. "I knew I could lose a fight." He also added, "He's the only fighter that never hurt me once."

Patterson reached his goal on November 30, 1956, when he fought veteran light heavyweight champion **Archie Moore** for the heavyweight crown, vacated by Rocky Marciano. Floyd was only 22 years old, less than half Moore's age. He entered the fight a 3:1 underdog against "Ancient Archie." Youth prevailed, however, when Patterson won the heavyweight crown with a decisive fifth-round knockout over the old warrior. At the time, Floyd was the youngest contender to ever take the heavyweight championship. Ironically, if Moore had won, he would have been the then oldest heavyweight titlist.

The heavyweight championship proved a mixed blessing for Patterson. Sportswriters accused Floyd of lacking that necessary "killer instinct" for a real champion. Once Patterson helped retrieve an opponent's fallen mouthpiece in the ring. After 1956, he defended his crown by defeating easily several "setup" fighters. Newsmen called D'Amato "cautious Cus" and Patterson "the invisible champ." Pete Rademacher, who never had fought a professional match before, embarrassingly floored Floyd on November 22, 1957, in the first round before being knocked out in the sixth.

In June 1959, European heavyweight champion Ingemar Johansson of Sweden fought Patterson. The Swede, the best of a poor crop of "stand up" fighters, was not much respected in the United States and rated a 4:1 underdog. The first two rounds proved a dull sparring match, as the fighters felt each other out. Floyd later recalled, "I was quite confident, because he didn't seem like anything. . . . I thought it was only a matter of time." In the third round, however, Ingemar suddenly nailed him with a vicious straight right to the jaw that knocked him out immediately. Patterson came to seconds later on the floor. Floyd never saw the punch and headed for a neutral corner after rising, thinking he had floored his opponent. The completely dazed Patterson hit the canvas six more times before the referee stopped the bout. Johansson was declared the new champion!

The humiliated Floyd retreated into seclusion again and left New York City in disguise. Although seeking solitude, Patterson observed: "You have to learn to win by learning while you lose." His demeaning experience taught him that "a defeat can make a man more determined," as he trained and planned carefully. Almost exactly a year later, Floyd in June 1960 reversed that defeat by knocking out Johansson in five rounds. The Swede had not trained properly, making Patterson the first heavyweight to regain the crown. A third match saw Floyd repeat his victory with a sixth-round knockout.

Patterson married Sandra Hicks in 1956 and followed her beliefs in converting to Roman Catholicism that year. Floyd lost the heavyweight championship in September 1962 to ex-convict "Sonny" Liston, whose massive strength made anyone apprehensive. Patterson succumbed to Liston in just two minutes of the first round. Floyd fought another decade, recording 64 fights, with 40 knockouts and eight defeats. Subsequently, he was elected to *The Ring*'s Boxing Hall of Fame in 1977, the Olympic Hall of Fame in 1987, and the International Boxing Hall of Fame in 1991. Patterson served for seven years on the New York State Athletic Commission.

His autobiography, *Victory over Myself* (1962), reveals the struggles Floyd had to endure to achieve the world heavyweight championship and stands as a lesson for all of us.

BIBLIOGRAPHY: Ralph Citro, ed., *Computer Boxing Update* (Blackwood, NJ, 1993); Constantine "Cus" D'Amato and Murray Olderman, "Everybody Wants a Piece of Patterson," *True* (October 1956), pp. 34–35, 64; Herbert G. Goldman, ed., *The Ring 1986–1987 Record Book and Boxing Encyclopedia* (New York, 1987); Frank Graham, Jr., "Prizefight Prodigy," *Sport* 16 (April 1954), pp. 20–22, 59; Frank Graham, Jr., "Floyd Patterson in Waiting," *Sport* 21 (October 1956), pp. 45–47, 71–72; Milton Gross, "The Floyd Patterson Story," *New York Post*, September 9–11, 1957; W. C. Heinz, "The Floyd Patterson His Friends Know," *Sport* 29 (November 1960), pp. 20, 82–85; Ed Linn, "The Sorrow of Floyd Patterson," *Sport* 28 (January 1960), pp. 12–15, 80; Paul O'Neil, "Meet the Next Heavyweight Champion," *Sports Illustrated* 4 (January 30, 1956), pp. 19–21, 52–54; Floyd Patterson and Milton Gross, *Victory over Myself* (New York, 1962); Bert Randolph Sugar, ed., *The Great Fights* (New York, 1981).

William J. Miller

WALTER PAYTON
(July 25, 1954–) ———————————————————— *Football*

Walter Payton, who spent his entire National Football League (NFL) career with the Chicago Bears, set records establishing him as one of the very best backfield performers in NFL history. Besides being a great football player, Walter planned well for the years following his gridiron days. During Payton's last season, Bears' quarterback Jim McMahon admitted, "What we'll miss most about Wally—just his being around. What he will miss, and be missed in, is the Bears' locker room—for his humor, his pranks, even the way he fishes playfully through reporters' pockets as they talk with him."

Walter J. Payton was born in Columbia, Mississippi, on July 25, 1954, the son of Peter Payton and Alyne Payton. At Columbia High School, Walter did not play football until his junior year. He possessed all the needed natural instincts, developing quickly. His Jackson State University performances earned him the nickname "Sweetness," which carried over into his great NFL years. "My teammates," he said, "called me 'Sweetness' to describe my style of running."

In 1973, Payton led all NCAA Division II football players in scoring with 160 points. Walter, selected 1974 College Player of the Year by *The Football Roundup*, became the leading career scorer in NCAA history with 464 points. Later, he was elected to the Southwestern Athletic Conference Hall of Fame. During his college career, Payton scored a then-record 66 touchdowns, rushed for 3,563 yards (6.1 yards per carry average), and kicked five field goals and 54 points after touchdowns. Walter caught 27 passes for 474 yards, punted for a 39-yard average, and averaged an incredible 43 yards per kickoff return. He completed 14 of 19 passes for 4 touchdowns, making him truly a triple-threat performer. Payton played in the College All-Star Game 21–14 loss to the Pittsburgh Steelers and also performed in the Shrine All-Star (East-West) Game and Senior Bowl. In describing his football philosophy, Payton explained, "Football was something I had to fulfill in life. Just like some people want to fly to the moon. Some people want to fly to Rome."

The Chicago Bears selected Payton in the first round of the NFL draft. Walter started 172 of 178 games with the Bears, including 156 consecutive contests during 12 seasons, and established many records. Payton holds the single-game rushing record with 275 yards against the Minnesota Vikings in November 1977 and set the all-time NFL rushing record in 1984. Walter, who retired following the 1987 season, rushed for 16,726 career yards on 3,838 carries (a 4.4-yard average) and scored 110 touchdowns. He surpassed **Jim Brown**'s career rushing record by 4,214 yards and netted 21,803 combined yards, bettering Brown's standard by 6,344 yards.

Payton established most Bears' rushing records and owns at least five NFL records, including most career yards rushing, most career combined yards, most 100-yard games, highest single-game rushing yardage, and most rushing attempts. In 1980, Payton earned an unprecedented fifth consecutive rushing title with 1,460 yards. During his playing days, Payton built many valuable business connections. Regarding business, Walter said, "It's my next football field. A lot of times it's like being a coach. You have the ideas. You know what you want to get accomplished."

Payton also won numerous awards. At age 23 in 1977, Walter became the youngest pro football player to win the NFL's Most Valuable Player (MVP) award. In 1976, *The Sporting News* selected Walter as the NFL's Player of the Year, while United Press International (UPI) voted him runner-up for the MVP award. He won the Jim Thorpe Trophy as the NFL's MVP and received several other MVP and Player of the Year awards. For several years, Payton led balloting for All-Pro selections. Walter appeared in nine Pro Bowl games through 1986 and was chosen 1984 Black Athlete of the Year.

During the mid-1980s, Payton still excelled. Quarterback McMahon replied, "I don't think Wally's lost any quickness. I've seen him make some moves that he's been making throughout his career. He never was a breakaway threat, but we don't need him to be a breakaway threat." In 1985, Walter became the first NFL player to accumulate 2,000 yards from scrimmage three consecutive seasons, making him the only player to accomplish this feat four times in a career.

When the Chicago Bears posted a 15–1 season in 1985, he finished third in rushing with 1,551 yards and nine touchdowns (4.8-yard average) and caught 49 passes for 483 yards (9.9-yard average). In 1986, Walter became the first NFL player to surpass 15,000 career rushing yards, scored his 100th rushing touchdown, and recorded his 75th 100-yard rushing game.

Payton owns a diner in Schaumburg, Illinois, and remains prominent in charity and civic activities. Walter has served as honorary chairman of the Illinois Mental Health Association and has assisted Heart Association activities. His other projects include the March of Dimes, Boy Scouts, Piccolo Research Fund, United Way, and Peace Corps.

Payton possesses enormous strength, bench pressing 390 pounds and leg pressing more than 600 pounds. Walter's autobiography, *Sweetness*, was published in 1978. He won the Maxwell Club's Bert Bell Award as the NFL's Player of the Year in 1985 and set an NFL record (since broken) by gaining over 100 yards in nine consecutive games. The Pro Football Hall of Fame, which enshrined Payton in 1993, named him to its AFL-NFL 1960–1984 All-Star Second Team. In 1994, Walter was selected to the All-Time NFL Team.

In 1979, he formed Walter Payton Enterprises, an investment firm. Football ability, both college and professional, gave him an education and the pro career a good financial start. He dedicated his life in part to assist others in getting an opportunity to achieve.

Walter and his wife Connie have a son, Jarrett, and a daughter, Brittany, and reside in suburban Barrington, Illinois. Payton maintains interest in his children's achievements and has become an excellent role model for all young persons.

BIBLIOGRAPHY: AP News Release, November 21, 1983; *Chicago Bears Media Guide* (1989); Chicago Bears Press Releases, Summer 1985; *Minneapolis Star-Tribune*, September 23, 1985; *New York Times*, October 8, 1984; Walter Payton, *Sweetness* (Chicago, Il, 1978); Walter Payton, letter to Stan Carlson, November 14, 1993; *The Sporting News Pro Football Register* (1986).

Stan W. Carlson

CALVIN PEETE
(July 18, 1943–) _____ *Golf*

If Calvin Peete had ever believed "three strikes and you're out," he would never have become a successful professional golfer. Peete already had faced the equivalent of three strikes against him before he ever picked up a golf club. Calvin's first strike came as an African American hoping to make it in the overwhelmingly white, country club world of professional golf. His second strike resulted from an accident at age 12, when he fell out of a tree and broke his left elbow in three places. Peete's permanently crippled left arm could not be straightened. Strike three: Peete only began to play golf at age 23. Calvin's talent and determination, however, enabled him to overcome all these obstacles and eventually earn over $2 million on the Professional Golfers Association (PGA) Tour. He still golfs on the Senior Tour while also pursuing business interests.

Calvin Peete, the youngest of 9 children of Dennis Peete and Irenia (Bridgeford) Peete, was born on July 18, 1943, in Detroit Michigan. When his parents separated in the early 1950s, he lived with his grandmother on a small Missouri farm, for two years. Peete moved to Florida to rejoin his father, who was starting a new family. Eventually Calvin had 10 more brothers and sisters. He attended school through eighth grade and then worked with his father in central Florida as a farm laborer. At age 17, Peete purchased a 1956 Plymouth station wagon. For 10 years, Calvin sold inexpensive clothes and jewelry at farm labor camps along the eastern seaboard. Diamonds, set in his front teeth, helped advertise his wares and earned him the nickname "The Diamond Man." Benjamin Widoff, a Fort Lauderdale businessman, liked Peete and helped him invest in some apartment buildings. By his mid-20s, Calvin was established as a businessman.

Friends introduced Peete to golf in 1966. Taken by the game, Calvin practiced hard and shot an 87 in his first full round of 18 holes. Within two years, he was a scratch golfer. Peete turned professional in 1971 and played on the mini-tour. After twice failing to qualify for the PGA Tour, Calvin earned his card in 1976 and then averaged only about $20,000 in winnings during his first three years. After Peete rededicated himself to "the basics," his game really started to come together. Calvin's first PGA Tour victory came in the 1979 Greater Milwaukee Open, a tournament he won again three years later. In 1982, he also tied Craig Stadler with four tournament wins, ranking among the top 10 finishers in 10 of his 26 tournaments.

Peete, only 5 foot 10 inches tall and 165 pounds, did not rank among the long hitters on the PGA Tour. Calvin's arm injury limited his back swing and forced him to swing compactly. But he compensated for his loss in length with precision. Tom Watson once described Peete as "the most accurate striker of the ball in golf." Despite his looping swing, Calvin still regularly placed at or near the top of PGA statistics for driving accuracy and greens hit in regulation. His balance and precision garnered 12 career PGA Tour wins, including the 1982 Anheuser-Busch Classic, 1983 Atlanta Classic, 1985 Phoenix Open, 1985 and 1986 Tournament Players Championship (TPC), and 1986 U.S.F.&G. Tournament. *Sports Illustrated's* Barry McDermott observed that Calvin's 1985 TPC victory came "against the best field that will tee off all the year on one of the most unrelenting, terrorizing courses the pros play."

Peete's nine victories from 1982 through 1985 led the PGA Tour. Calvin won the 1984 Vardon Trophy for lowest scoring average and played on the 1983 and 1985 Ryder Cup teams. Upon learning that only high school graduates could compete for the Ryder Cup, he got his former wife, Christine, a teacher, to tutor him, took his books on the road, and successfully earned his high school equivalency diploma.

Despite his days as "The Diamond Man," Peete did not exhibit a flamboyant style. "While other pros strut the fairways in rainbow hues," David MacDonald wrote in 1983, "Peete wears muted colors and has a solemn expression. . . . His only affectation is a droopy Fu Manchu mustache. 'I grew it,' he says with a wry smile, 'to look a little *different.*' "

Peete's nongolf activities, most notably his work with the Sickle Cell Anemia Foundation, also set him apart. For his professionalism and community work, Calvin received the 1981 Ben Hogan Award, the 1983 Good Guy Award from Gordon Gin, and the 1986 Jackie Robinson Award from *Ebony* magazine. He remains modest about his own accomplishments, downplaying similarities between himself and Bill Spiller, Ted Rhodes, **Charlie Sifford,** and golf's other African-American pioneers. "To be first at something is a different song," Peete says. Although Calvin may not have faced the same obstacles on the PGA Tour, his personal journey has still been remarkable.

Peete married Christine Sears on October 24, 1974; they had five children, Charlotte, Calvin, Rickie, Dennis, and Kalvanetta, before their divorce. Calvin remarried in January 1994, and he, his wife, and their young daughter live in North Fort Myers, Florida.

BIBLIOGRAPHY: Peter Alliss, *The Who's Who of Golf* (Englewood Cliffs, NJ, 1983); *Golf Digest Almanac* (1987); Barry McDermott, "Long Shot Out of a Trap," *Sports Illustrated* 52 (March 24, 1980), pp. 26–31; Barry McDermott, "Call It a Major Win, for Peete's Sake," *Sports Illustrated* 62 (April 8, 1985), pp. 40–42, 47; Barry McDermott, "Peete . . . But No Repeat," *Sports Illustrated* 64 (January 20, 1986), pp. 36–37; David MacDonald, "Golf's Most Unlikely Star," *Reader's Digest* 123 (October 1983), pp. 169–170, 173–174; Kenny Moore, "His Was a Great Act of Faith," *Sports Illustrated* 58 (April 25, 1983), pp. 36–38, 43–45.

Luther W. Spoehr

JOE PERRY
(January 27, 1927–) ————————————————— *Football*

As a high school and college student, Joe Perry anticipated a career as an electrical engineer. Joe's academic record indicated that he would achieve this goal because he received A's in both calculus and advanced trigonometry. His combination of size, speed, and intelligence, however, led him instead to a 16-year career as a National Football League (NFL) running back.

Fletcher Joe Perry was born in Stevens, Arkansas, on January 27, 1927, the son of Fletcher Perry and Laura Perry. The Perrys moved to Los Angeles, California, when he was just a small boy. The warm southern California environment encouraged outdoor sporting activities, enabling Perry to become an excellent athlete. At David Starr Jordan High School in Los Angeles, Joe played basketball and baseball and ran in track and field with great success. He displayed his remarkable all-around athletic abilities in track by running the 100-yard dash in 9.7 seconds, the 220-yard dash in 21.9 seconds, putting the shot 55 feet, broad jumping 23 feet 6 inches, and high jumping 6 feet 3 inches.

His family refused to sign the release for him to play high school football, but Perry forged his mother's signature. Unfortunately, Joe broke his ankle on the first day of practice. He, nevertheless, begged his mother for permission to play once the injury had healed. She relented, declaring, "If you want to break your fool neck, I guess you may as well go ahead."

Following high school graduation, Perry served in the U.S. Merchant Marine and enrolled in Compton Junior College. In 1944, he scored an incredible 22 touchdowns. After playing one more junior college football season, Joe enlisted in the U.S. Navy and was assigned to Alameda Naval Air Station near San Francisco, California. The Alameda base football team was coached by John Woudenberg, tackle for the San Francisco 49ers of the All-America Football Conference (AAFC). Woudenberg introduced Perry to Tony Morabito, the 49ers' owner. Morabito grudgingly agreed to watch Joe in action. Against San Francisco State University, Morabito saw him score five touchdowns of at least 49 yards.

Shortly afterward, Perry signed a contract with the Bay Area team and made an immediate impact on the 49ers offense. On his very first run from scrimmage, Joe scampered 58 yards for a touchdown. By the end of his rookie 1948 season, he replaced Norm Standlee as starting fullback and rushed for 562 yards on 77 carries. Perry scored 10 touchdowns, with his 7.3 yards per carry, leading all AAFC rushers. In 1949, Joe paced the AAFC in rushing with 783 yards and was selected All-AAFC fullback. The next year, the 49ers joined the NFL in the AAFC-NFL merger. He remained their leading rusher, gaining 647 yards on 124 attempts in 1950 and 677 yards on 136 attempts in 1951.

All-America halfback Hugh McElhenny joined Perry in the backfield in 1952, giving the 49ers one of the most potent inside and outside rushing offenses in professional football. Joe finished third in the NFL in rushing that year with 725 yards. The 1953 and 1954 seasons marked the most productive of his long career. Perry led all NFL running backs in 1953 with 1,018 yards and then surpassed that figure in 1954 with 1,049 yards. These two remarkable seasons made Joe the first NFL runner to record consecutive 1,000-yard campaigns. The sports media selected him All-Pro both seasons, while United Press International (UPI) named him Player of the Year.

Rival NFL coaches envied Perry's abilities. Buddy Parker of the Detroit Lions considered Joe "the fastest, hardest-hitting and most dangerous back in the game." Cleveland Browns head coach Paul Brown claimed that Perry had the fastest start of any professional football back. Brown stated, "He hits the hole before the defensive line can recover from the charge. Besides his speed, he has unbelievable strength."

Perry's teammates also marveled at his speed and strength. Reserve quarterback Frankie Albert nicknamed him "Joe the Jet," stating, "I'm telling you, when that guy comes by to take a handoff, his slipstream darn near knocks

you over. He's strictly jet-propelled." Pro Football Hall of Fame quarterback
Y. A. Tittle, who joined the 49ers in 1951, was warned about Joe's swiftness.
Tittle recalls, "In my first game, I took the ball from center and turned to
hand it off to Perry. Just then something swooshed by me like a motorcycle.
Suddenly Joe was 10 yards down the field, and I still held the ball."

Perry's vicious running style resulted in numerous injuries, including broken ribs, separated shoulders, sprained ankles, torn ligaments, and broken
teeth. Due to his severe facial injuries, Joe became one of the first NFL
players to wear a face mask. In one game against the Los Angeles Rams, he
lost nine teeth. Head coach Buck Shaw recalls, "Joe wouldn't leave the field.
Before he was through, he scored three of our four touchdowns." Perry never
achieved the 1,000-yard plateau again after the 1954 season but still led San
Francisco in rushing in 1955 with 701 yards and in 1958 with 758 yards.

After the 1960 season, head coach Red Hickey traded many of his 49er
veterans. San Francisco dealt Perry to the Baltimore Colts (NFL). Joe surprised many skeptics, becoming the Colts' leading rusher at age 34 with 675
yards on 168 carries. After Perry spent one more season with Baltimore, the
49ers resigned him for the 1963 season, primarily to qualify him for an NFL
pension.

The six-foot, 200-pound runner finished his pro career with 9,723 yards
rushing, 2,021 yards receiving, and 84 touchdowns scored. At the time of his
retirement, Perry ranked first on the list of all-time NFL runners. Due to Joe's
outstanding achievements, the Pro Football Hall of Fame selected him for
membership in 1969 in his first year of eligibility.

Perry during the off-season worked in several capacities, including as a car
salesman and disc jockey. Joe, who married twice and had one daughter,
served as a scout and assistant coach for the 49ers from 1968 to 1976 and also
worked in sales for Gallo Wines.

BIBLIOGRAPHY: Melvin Durslag, "Takes Two to Touchdown," *Collier's* 134 (September 3, 1954), pp. 34–36; *The Lincoln Library of Sports Champions* (Columbus, OH,
1974); David L. Porter, ed., *The Biographical Dictionary of American Sports: Football*
(Westport, CT, 1987).

John Hillman

FRITZ POLLARD
(January 27, 1894–May 11, 1986) ———————————————— *Football*

Fritz Pollard, an all-star halfback in both college and professional football,
served as the first African-American head coach in the National Football
League (NFL). Frederick Douglass Pollard was born on January 27, 1894, in
Chicago, Illinois. His father, John William Pollard, worked as a barber, while
his mother, Catherine Amanda (Hughes) Pollard, toiled as a seamstress. The
sixth of seven children, Pollard grew up in the previously all-white Rogers

Park section of Chicago. He was nicknamed "Fritz" by the many German-speaking residents in the neighborhood. Pollard believed that growing up in an all-white community made him an overachiever, but he also experienced the sting of racial prejudice. When asked many years later about the first time he remembered being the victim of racial discrimination, Fritz simply replied, "The minute you're born."

Following the examples set by his father, a boxing champion in the Union Army, and his older brothers and sisters, superb high school athletes, Pollard starred in football, baseball, and track and field. During his senior year in high school, Fritz made All–Cook County teams in track and field and football. Despite his small stature, the five-foot-seven-inch, 150-pound Pollard used his speed, agility, and know-how to score touchdowns. Fritz concentrated on football, believing he had a better chance to succeed in that sport.

After graduating from high school in 1912, Pollard looked for a college to showcase his football talent. Knowing little about college or how to gain admission, he briefly attended five different colleges between 1912 and 1914. Family friend and former Harvard University football star William Lewis warned Fritz that "he was becoming nothing but a tramp athlete." Pollard consequently attended Springfield High School to remedy a foreign-language deficiency. He married Ada Laing in June 1914 and had four children, Fritz, Jr., Leslie, Gwendolyn, and Eleanor. In 1915 he entered Brown University.

Brown football team members at first harassed and ostracized Pollard before the latter gained acceptance through superior play and perseverance. Fritz later recalled that "back in those days the black, at best, was accepted grudgingly at most colleges." He won national acclaim in Brown's 3–0 upset victory over Yale University in 1915, providing strong defensive play and numerous spectacular long runs. During that Yale Bowl game, authorities escorted Pollard onto the field through a special gate just before the kickoff to avoid an ugly racial incident. When Fritz ran with the ball, Yale fans taunted him by singing verses of "Bye, Bye, Blackbird." In January 1916, Brown played in the Rose Bowl game in Pasadena, California, against Washington State University. Although having a subpar performance on a muddy field in Brown's 14–0 defeat, Fritz became the first African American to compete in the Rose Bowl.

In 1916, Pollard led Brown to its most successful season with eight victories and only one defeat. Fritz enjoyed his best games in wins over Yale and Harvard, considered by many the premier college football teams. After that season, he was selected an All-America halfback on Walter Camp's elite team. Camp remarked that Pollard was "one of the greatest runners I have ever seen." Fritz became only the second African American picked by Camp and the first selected to a backfield position. The following spring, however, he neglected his studies and was declared ineligible for the 1917 season. He later admitted that "I was young and foolish and crazy. I was Fritz Pollard, All-America, and my head was getting a little bit big back then."

When the United States fought in World War I, Pollard accepted a position as physical director in the army's YMCA unit at Camp Meade, Maryland, in early 1918. In the fall of that year, he became head football coach at Lincoln University. The Akron Pros recruited him to play professional football in 1919. Fritz and Jim Thorpe of the Canton Bulldogs achieved stardom in a league that by 1922 was called the NFL. Pollard led the Akron Pros to a championship in 1920 and played professionally until 1926. During the 1921 season, Fritz took over as Akron head coach and became the first African-American head coach in a major team sport and the first in NFL history. He later coached NFL teams in Milwaukee and Hammond, Indiana, but with less success than in Akron. As in college football, Pollard encountered harassment and prejudice in the pro game. Fritz recalled that "the white players were always trying to hurt me, and I had to protect myself if I was going to stay in the game." In some cities, fans threw rocks and bottles at him as he entered the playing field.

After retiring as a player, Pollard coached two all-African-American teams, the Chicago Black Hawks (1928–1932) and the New York Brown Bombers (1935–1937). Both teams produced excellent records, showing that African American could play against whites without racial incidents and that African-American players possessed the ability to play in the NFL. Fritz also pursued a business career, operating an African-American investment firm in Chicago during the 1920s until the stock market crash of 1929 forced him into bankruptcy. After moving to New York, he established the first African-American tabloid newspaper, the *Independent News,* and owned it until 1942. Pollard also made his mark in the entertainment business, serving as casting agent for his former Akron teammate **Paul Robeson** in the film *The Emperor Jones.* During the 1930s, Fritz booked African-American entertainers in nightclubs and integrated many previously all-white clubs. In 1942, he operated a rehearsal studio in Harlem, where he produced Soundies, an early form of music-videos. In 1947, Fritz married Mary Ella Austin; they had no children.

After World War II, Pollard produced a feature motion picture, *Rockin' the Blues,* wrote a nationally syndicated sports column, and became a successful tax consultant. His many honors included being the first African American elected to the National Football Foundation College Football Hall of Fame in 1954 and receiving the Whitney M. Young, Jr. Memorial Award in 1975. Fritz ultimately was deeply disappointed that he had not been elected to the Pro Football Hall of Fame. He died in Silver Spring, Maryland, on May 11, 1986. Fritz Pollard, Jr., a Little All-America football player and a Bronze Medal winner in the 1936 Olympic Games, summed up his father's career by saying, "He was really a pioneer. He was a *real* pioneer."

BIBLIOGRAPHY: Frank Bianco, "For Brown the Wrong Shoe Was on the Foot in the '16 Rose Bowl Game," *Sports Illustrated* 53 (November 24, 1980), pp. 112–114; John M. Carroll, *Fritz Pollard: Pioneer in Racial Advancement* (Urbana, IL, 1992); Ocania Chalk, *Black College Sport* (New York, 1976); Carl Nesfield, "Pride Against Prejudice:

Fritz Pollard Brown's All-American Pre–World War I Vintage," *Black Sports* (November and December 1971); *New York Times Bibliographical Service* (May 1986), p. 705.

John M. Carroll

MIKE POWELL
(November 10, 1963–) ——————————————— *Track and Field*

On August 30, 1991, Mike Powell bounded 29 feet 4½ inches to garner the World Championship and surpass **Bob Beamon** as world record holder in the long jump. Michael Anthony Powell, the youngest of Carolyn (Eaddy) Powell Carroll's three children, was born on November 10, 1963, in Philadelphia, Pennsylvania. His father, Preston Powell, a teacher, died when Mike was a child. His mother, an accountant, then married Arnie Carroll. In 1974, the Carrolls moved to West Covina, California, where Carolyn took a new accounting position. At West Covina's Edgewood High School, Mike excelled in basketball and track and field and described himself then as "six foot one, 150 pounds and springs." Powell, who played point guard and outjumped most centers, captained Edgewood as a senior and led his basketball team to the 1981 State championship tournament. In track and field, Mike long jumped 21 feet 11 inches as a junior and 23 feet 7 inches as a senior. A high jumper as well, he captured second in the 1981 State championship while topping 7 feet. Powell, whose heart remained in the long jump, often stood in the house and imagined himself "flying across the dining room and landing in the living room," making the Olympic team on the last jump of the Trials. Then "I would get up and yell and cheer like crazy."

After graduating from high school in 1981, Powell entered the University of California at Irvine on a basketball scholarship. Mike also long jumped at California—Irvine, improving his personal best to 26 feet 5¼ inches in 1983. The performance marked a turning point, making him realize that he "could make the Olympic team or something." After that jump, Blair Clausen, the California—Irvine track and field coach, believed Powell eventually could "break the world record." Clausen told Mike, "You can do as much as you want to do" in the long jump. In 1984, Powell finished second in the Track Athletic Congress (TAC) championship and sixth in the Olympic Trials. As an unattached competitor in 1985, Mike finished third in the TAC championships, improved his distance to 26 feet 9¾ inches, and earned a 10-place world ranking in the long jump. Powell asked **Carl Lewis** for advice in the long jump at the 1985 TAC championship but does not recall what the star said. Mike admitted that "I was in awe to be sitting there talking to him and to realize that he was talking to me." Powell competed for the University of California at Los Angeles (UCLA) in 1986, but neither performed well in any major meets nor improved his personal best. In 1987, he graduated from UCLA with a Bachelor of Arts degree in sociology.

A tendency to foul out of competition had hampered Powell's success as a long jumper throughout college. Although favored to win the long jump at the 1986 NCAA championship, Mike finished with "no measurement." In the 1987 TAC championship, he fouled in three attempts beyond 28 feet. Willie Banks, triple jump world record holder and his training partner, nicknamed him "Powell the Foul" and "Mike Foul" for his proclivity to step over the takeoff board. In 1987, Powell began working with Randy Huntington, a former assistant track and field coach at the University of Oregon and University of California at Berkeley. "I'd been watching 'Mike Foul' for years," recalled Huntington. Huntington introduced Powell to "controlled maximum velocity" in the long jump approach and takeoff and put Mike on a five-year program of honing every aspect of his long jump technique. "He's got to interpret the dream he has in his mind," Huntington declared. "I'm incapable of doing this for Mike. He's got to do it for himself, but he's got to do it with respect to the model that I have." Huntington's regime prepared Powell for a Silver Medal performance behind Lewis at the 1988 Summer Olympic Games in Seoul, South Korea. Mike's jump measured 27 feet 10¼ inches. In 1990, Powell garnered his first TAC championship and recorded a long jump of 28 feet 5 inches. He ranked first in the world that year and began to "dream of breaking Beamon's world record."

For nearly 23 years, long jumpers had tried to break Beamon's world record of 29 feet 2½ inches. Many track and field authorities claimed Beamon's mark, established during the 1968 Summer Olympic Games at Mexico City, at an elevation of 7,575 feet, would stand well into the twenty-first century. Lewis initially closed the gap on Beamon with a sea-level performance of 28 feet 10¼ inches in 1983, while Armenian Robert Emmiyan bounded 29 feet 1 inch at an elevation of 6,499 feet in 1987. In the fifth round of the long jump final at the World Championships in Tokyo, Japan, however, Powell leaped 29 feet 4½ inches to exceed Beamon's standard by 2 inches. "Breaking the world record was traumatic; I wanted to let it sink in," exclaimed Mike. Powell, who ended Lewis's winning streak of 65 long jump finals, remarked that winning the World Championship was "like a heavyweight fight. You can't beat the champ with a split decision. You have to knock him out." In the 1992 Summer Olympic Games at Barcelona, Spain, he settled for a Silver Medal in the long jump. Lewis captured his third consecutive Gold Medal.

In 1993, Powell won the long jump at the USATF Outdoor Championships at Eugene, Oregon, and defended his World Championship at Stuttgart, Germany. His 28 foot 2¼ inch leap at Stuttgart outdistanced the competition by 17 inches. The following year, Mike captured long jump titles at the USATF Outdoor Championships at Knoxville, Tennessee, and the Goodwill Games at St. Petersburg, Russia. On July 31, 1994, he matched his world record with a wind-aided leap of 29 feet 4½ inches at Sestriere, Italy. Powell split a 44-pound gold jackpot by sweeping the long jump titles at the Golden Four track and field meets in Oslo, Norway, Zurich, Switzerland, Brussels, Belgium, and

Berlin, Germany, and ranked first in the final 1994 Outdoor European Grand Prix Standings. Mike leaped 28 feet ¾ inch to win the long jump at the USATF Outdoor Championships in Sacramento, California, in June 1995.

BIBLIOGRAPHY: Barbara Bigelow, ed., *Contemporary Black Biography,* vol. 7 (Detroit, MI, 1994), pp. 227–230; Jon Hendershott, "Powell Fears No One," *Track and Field News* 44 (September 1991), p. 5; Garry Hill, "Lewis Edges Powell," *Track and Field News* 45 (October 1992), p. 42; Jeff Hollobaugh, "Powell Had Better Jumps," *Track and Field News* 43 (September 1990), p. 15; Ruth Laney, "Powell's Dream Jump," *Track and Field News* 44 (November 1991), p. 31; Sieg Lindstrom, "Things Less Foul for Powell," *Track and Field News* 41 (December 1988), p. 34; Sieg Lindstrom, "Next Stop 10 Yard," *Track and Field News* 45 (March 1992), pp. 52–54; Sieg Lindstrom, "The Coach Behind Powell," *Track and Field News* 45 (March 1992), pp. 56–57; Dick Patrick, "Powell's Long Chase for Gold at Hand," *USA Today,* August 5, 1992, pp. C1–C2.

Adam R. Hornbuckle

KIRBY PUCKETT
(March 14, 1961–   ) ————————————————————————— *Baseball*

Kirby Puckett, considered by some the strongest little man in baseball, has proven a true gentleman of the game. Kirby Puckett was born on March 14, 1961, in Chicago, Illinois, the youngest of nine children. His father, William, a onetime left-handed pitcher in the Negro Leagues, worked two jobs to support the family, while his mother, Catherine, managed the home. Kirby grew up in the Robert Taylor Homes "projects" on the South Side of Chicago. Many saw their hopes die there, but Puckett proves that will not always be the case. Kirby once wrote, "My mom was determined that the baby of the family would stay out of trouble. I was sheltered. I didn't hang out. I didn't even go to movies. At night I was home. It's as simple as that."

Puckett started playing baseball between the buildings of the projects, just one mile south of Comiskey Park. Kirby participated in sandlot baseball until he was 15 years old. At Chicago's Calumet High School, he performed on his first organized team. Under coach James McGhee, Puckett starred as a third baseman and earned All-America honors. Following graduation in 1979, Kirby did not receive any baseball offers at either the college or professional levels. With the help of a friend, he began working at the local Ford plant. The job did not last very long, however, and he knew that he had to get another job or start college. In the summer of 1980, Bradley University coach Dewey Kalmer spotted Puckett at a Kansas City Royals American League (AL) club free agent tryout. Kalmer offered Kirby a baseball scholarship and converted him to center fielder. Following his father's death in 1981, Puckett left the Peoria, Illinois, college to live closer to his mother. Kirby enrolled at Triton Community College in River Grove, Illinois. In his only season at Triton in 1982, he hit .472, belted 16 home runs, stole 42 bases, and was named the

Region IV Junior College Player of the Year. In 1993, Puckett was inducted into the Triton Hall of Fame.

In the January 1982 free agent draft, the Minnesota Twins (AL) made the right-hand-hitting and -throwing five-foot-eight-inch, 178-pound outfielder their first selection and third pick overall and assigned him to Elizabethton, Tennessee, of the Appalachian League (ApL). At Elizabethton, Puckett led the ApL in batting (.382), at bats (275), runs (65), hits (105), total bases (135), and stolen bases (43). Kirby was named to the ApL All-Star team and the ApL's Player of the Year by *Baseball America*. In 1983, he was assigned to Visalia, California, of the California League (CaL). Puckett led the CaL in at bats (548), finished second in doubles (29), fourth in triples (7), and sixth in batting (.314), being named to the CaL All-Star team and CaL Player of the Year. Kirby's 1984 season began with the Toledo, Ohio, Mud Hens of the International League.

On May 8, 1984, he joined the Twins for a game with the California Angels. Puckett became only the ninth player to get four hits in his first major league game. Kirby, named to the Topps' Major League All-Rookie team, finished third in the balloting to Alvin Davis of the Seattle Mariners for the AL Rookie of the Year honors. Since his first full season in 1985, he has been considered the heart and soul of the Twins. During that span, Puckett has compiled a .320 batting average with 184 home runs and 955 RBIs and has averaged 152 games per year.

Kirby has appeared in ten consecutive All-Star Games from 1986 to 1995, being elected a starter in 1986, 1989, 1992, 1993, and 1994. In All-Star competition, he has batted .316. In the 1993 All-Star Game, Puckett was named Most Valuable Player (MVP) while delivering a double and home run, knocking in two runs, and scoring a run in three at bats. Kirby has played in AL Championship Series against the Detroit Tigers in 1987 and Toronto Blue Jays in 1991. The Twins won both Championship Series in five games. In 10 AL Championship Series games, he has batted .311 with three home runs and nine RBIs. Puckett, named the 1991 AL Championship Series MVP, appeared in World Series against the St. Louis Cardinals in 1987 and the Atlanta Braves in 1991. The Twins won both World Series in seven games. Kirby's World Series statistics include a .308 batting average, 16 hits, two home runs, and seven RBIs. In 1991, he became the ninth player to end a World Series game with a home run. His eleventh-inning round-tripper came against Charlie Leibrandt.

From 1984 to 1994, Puckett has batted .318 with 2,135 hits (the most by any major leaguer during that decade), 184 home runs, 988 runs scored, and 986 RBIs. Kirby's best offensive year came in 1988, when he batted .356 with 234 hits, 24 home runs, 109 runs scored, and 121 RBIs. In 1989, Puckett won his only AL batting title with a .339 average. During his career, Kirby has won six Gold Glove (1986–1989, 1991–1992) and five Silver Slugger (1986–1989, 1992) Awards.

Puckett resides in Edina, Minnesota, with his wife, Tonya (Hudson) Puckett, a daughter, Catherine, and a son, Kirby, Jr. With his wife, Kirby has donated $250,000 to the University of Minnesota to start a program that will award scholarships of $3,000 for up to five years to minority students demonstrating their academic potential and having financial need.

With **Dave Winfield,** he serves as a commissioner of a Twin Cities Little League. Through his Puckett 8-Ball Billiards Invitational, Kirby raises funds for the Minneapolis-based Children's Heart Fund. He acknowledges, "I know I'm in a very, very, very, good position. All I want to do is thank God—He gave me the talent, the know-how. And there are a lot of people who helped me along the way." Dave DeLand notes, "Kirby is genuine, the type of person—let alone ballplayer—many parents point to and tell their children, 'Watch him and learn.'"

BIBLIOGRAPHY: Dave DeLand, "Helping Hands," *Beckett Baseball Monthly* 114 (September 1994), pp. 22–23; Henry Hecht, "Cal Can Bring 'em Up Right," *Sports Illustrated* 61 (July 23, 1984), pp. 56–57; *Minnesota Twins Media Guide* (1993), pp. 79–84; Kirby Puckett and Mike Bryan, *I Love This Game: My Life and Baseball* (New York, 1993); Rick Telander, "Minny's Mighty Mite," *Sports Illustrated* 66 (June 15, 1987), pp. 46–49.

James E. Welch

BUTCH REYNOLDS
(June 8, 1964–   ) ———————————————————————— *Track and Field*

On August 17, 1988, Butch Reynolds became history's fastest 400-meter dashman while clocking the distance in 43.29 seconds. His performance eclipsed the world record of 43.86 seconds, held by **Lee Evans** since the 1968 Summer Olympic Games at Mexico City, Mexico. Harry Lee Reynolds, Jr., the second of three children of Harry Lee Reynolds, Sr., and Catherine Reynolds, was born on June 8, 1964, in Akron, Ohio. Reynold's father worked in the Akron rubber industry, while his mother served as a child-care attendant at the Summit County Children's Home in Akron. Harry, Jr., nicknamed "Butch" by his mother, played chess in elementary school and "golfed, bowled, and played basketball and football" at Akron's Archbishop Hoban High School. Reynolds also competed on the track and field team "to stay in shape for the other sports," explained Harry, Sr. What Butch "did in track," however, "was a complete surprise" to his father. Before graduating from Archbishop Hoban High School in 1983, he had run 100 meters in 10.4 seconds, 200 meters in 21.5 seconds, and 400 meters in 48.1 seconds and long jumped 23 feet.

Despite his athletic ability, Reynolds was not highly recruited by college coaches. Clements Caraboolad, his high school football coach, recalled that he "couldn't persuade one college coach to consider Harry for a football career." College coaches "did not like that way he caught the ball," although he made

23 receptions for a 23.1-yard average his senior year. Butch, who also played defense, made 31 tackles and two interceptions that year. Despite his track and field performance that year, he failed to impress major college coaches. Reynolds believed coaches overlooked him because he missed the 1983 Ohio State Track and Field Championship. A knee injury, suffered in the long jump during the regional championships, had sidelined him. Butch's track and field coach consoled him, insisting that his injury happened "for a reason" and that "there is something better out there for you."

West Virginia University, the University of Akron, and Miami University of Ohio offered him scholarships to play basketball and football, but Reynolds competed in track and field at Butler County Community College at El Dorado, Kansas, in 1984. John Francis, track and field coach at Butler Community College, forged Butch into a world-class 400-meter dashman through "six-mile cross-country runs, a weight-training regimen, and repeated long intervals." In 1984, Reynolds captured the 400-meter National Junior College Championship in 45.47 seconds. Later that summer, Butch reached the 400-meter semi-finals at the 1984 Olympic Trials. He competed only one year in track and field at Butler Community College, graduating in 1985 with an associate degree in business and marketing. Reynolds then accepted an athletic scholarship to Ohio State University, an institution better known for football than track and field. Ohio State, led by Larry Snyder from the early 1930s to the 1950s, had set a standard for track and field excellence with **Jesse Owens,** Mal Whitfield, and Glenn Davis. Owens, who won four Gold Medals at the 1936 Berlin, Germany, Summer Olympic Games, drew Butch to Ohio State because the Akron native wanted "to live up to the expectations Owens set for Ohio State athletes."

At Ohio State, Reynolds rapidly emerged as the nation's top collegiate quarter-miler. Former coach Francis told Butch before leaving Butler, "You are going to break Lee Evans's record. You are from Ohio. So go back there and do it." Under Frank Zubovich, track and field coach at Ohio State, Reynolds improved his 400-meter time to 45.36 seconds in 1986 before an injury ended his season. In 1987, Butch clocked 44.10 seconds for 400 meters in the Jesse Owens Classic at Ohio State. The stadium clock, however, incorrectly read 43.78 seconds, prompting him to admit, "I knew I hadn't run that fast." Reynolds captured the 1987 NCAA 400-meter title in 44.13 seconds and the Track Athletic Congress (TAC) title in 44.46 seconds. At the 1987 World Championships, Butch captured a Bronze Medal in the 400 meters and a Gold Medal in the 4 × 400-meter relay. Reynolds recorded 43.93 seconds at the 1988 Olympic Trials and eclipsed Evans's venerable global standard in Zurich, Switzerland, before the 1988 Seoul, South Korea, Summer Olympic Games. "The thing everyone said I had to do has been achieved," declared Butch. He added that "it's a 'clean' record—no altitude, no wind, nothing to tarnish it." Reynolds, however, finished second in the 400 meters at the 1988 Summer Olympic Games, with teammate Steve Lewis capturing the race in a junior

world record of 43.87 seconds. Butch still earned a Gold Medal in the 4 ×
400-meter relay, helping the U.S. foursome equal the world record of 2
minutes 56.16 seconds, held by the United States since the 1968 Summer
Olympic Games.

Track and Field News ranked Reynolds as the world's top 400-meter runner
in 1988 and 1989. Butch lost his premier position in 1990 to **Michael Johnson,**
who defeated him handily in their only 400-meter race that year. That year,
the International Amateur Athletic Federation (IAAF) also suspended Reynolds for supposedly testing positive for nandrolone, a banned steroid. Two
years of decisions by TAC and IAAF officials and rulings by federal judges
and U.S. Supreme Court justices followed before Butch was permitted to
participate in the 1992 U.S. Olympic Trials. Reynolds qualified for the U.S.
Olympic team as an alternate on the 4 × 400-meter relay squad, but the IAAF
clung to its original decision and did not permit him to compete in the Summer Olympic Games at Barcelona, Spain, under any conditions. Butch eventually sued the IAAF for $34 million in lost income and punitive damages and
was awarded $27 million by a federal judge in December 1992. An appeals
Court reversed the federal judge's decision in May 1994. In 1993, Reynolds
returned to competition in the 400 meters, winning the World Indoor Championship at Toronto, Canada. Outdoors, Butch finished second to Johnson at
both the USA Track and Field (USATF) Championships and the World Championships at Stuttgart, Germany. He also performed on the triumphant U.S.
4 × 400-meter relay team at the World Championships, helping establish a
world record of 2 minutes 54.29 seconds. Reynolds covered the 400 meters
in 44.42 seconds to place second behind Johnson at the USATF Outdoor
Championships at Sacramento, California, in June 1995.

BIBLIOGRAPHY: Ed Gordon, "Reynolds Slashes WR to 43.29," *Track and Field News*
41 (October 1988), pp. 24–26; Bob Hersh, "Mexico Mark Matched," *Track and Field
News* 41 (November 1988), p. 35; Kenny Moore, "Preparing a Big Move," *Sports
Illustrated* 67 (September 7, 1987), pp. 36–39; Ohio State University Sports Information, letter to Adam R. Hornbuckle, January 1993; Keith Peters, "Youthful Lewis Pre-
vails," *Track and Field News* 41 (November 1988), p. 14; David L. Porter, ed.,
*Biographical Dictionary of American Sports: 1992–1995 Supplement for Baseball, Foot-
ball, Basketball, and Other Sports* (Westport, CT, 1995).

                                                              Adam R. Hornbuckle

WILLY T. RIBBS
(January 3, 1956–) ——————————————————————— *Auto Racing*

Willy Ribbs in 1991 won acclaim as the first African American to participate
in the prestigious Indianapolis 500 auto race. William Theodore Ribbs, Jr.,
was born on January 3, 1956, in San Jose, California, the son of William T.
Ribbs, Sr., a plumber, and Geraldine (Henderson) Ribbs. Ribbs attended San
Jose public schools and San Jose City College from 1973 to 1975. Willy, whose
father competed as an amateur road racer, learned race car driving in England

in 1977 and performed very well there, winning 6 of 11 races. Ribbs, a Dunlop Tire "Star of Tomorrow," was named International Driver of the Year. His American racing debut came at the 1978 Long Beach Grand Prix, where he finished tenth in a warmup race for young drivers.

Ribbs was scheduled to compete in a 1978 National Association for Stock Car Auto Racing (NASCAR) race at Charlotte, North Carolina, when he evidently offended the local establishment with his boasting and was fined for driving the wrong way on a one-way street. The incidents barred Willy from stock car competition for the next three years. He later acknowledged, "I was, in effect, blacklisted." The self-confident Ribbs, a former skilled boxer, boasted like his friend **Muhammad Ali.** Both had been barred from their respective sports for extensive periods. Willy's outspoken, aggressive personality may have hurt him in securing corporate sponsors. "The way I drive cars," Ribbs boasted, "is so smooth it puts chills on the arms of any person watching. I'm ultra-fast, aggressive, and smooth."

From 1981 to 1984, Ribbs drove for Red Roof Inns in a semi-pro series. Jim Trueman, former owner-president of Red Roof Inns and major auto racing sponsor, recruited Willy at Monterey, California. In 1983, wealthy contractor Neil DeAtley asked Ribbs to join Englishman David Hobbs as second driver for a two-car Camaro racing team for the Trans-Am series. The Budweiser-financed team dominated the 1983 Trans-Am circuit with nine wins. Willy captured five Trans-Am races, earning Rookie of the Year honors. Before the first 1984 race, Ribbs was fired from the DeAtley team because of an incident with competitor Bob Lobenberg during warmups. According to Willy, Lobenberg sought to force him off the track. The Jack Roush team of Livonia, Michigan, signed Ribbs to drive Ford Capris for the 1984 Trans-Am season. Willy's 1984 honors included the Inter-American Western Hemisphere Driving Championship and Motorsports Press Association All-American Drivers Award. With Ribbs's help, Ford snatched the 1984 manufacturer's title from DeAtley's Chevrolet.

Willy won seven 1985 Trans-Am series races, placing second in points and becoming Sports Car Club of America (SCCA) Trans-Am All-Time Money Earner. He aspired to become the first African American to compete in the Indianapolis 500 and secured boxing promoter Don King as his manager. The Miller Brewing Company agreed to sponsor Ribbs, but he lacked a competitive car to drive. Willy ultimately failed to qualify in an Indy car owned by independent Sherman Armstrong, reaching only 170 miles per hour.

In 1986, Ribbs drove for a privately sponsored team on the NASCAR Winston Cup circuit. The following season, Willy joined Dan Gurney's team of four-cylinder turbo-charged Toyota Celicas on the International Motorsports Association (IMSA) circuit and won three out of four races at one point. In the final race, Toyota needed to defeat Chevrolet Corvettes and Camaro V8s to win the manufacturer's crown. Shortly into the race, Ribbs dropped to last place because he needed a new tire. Willy brilliantly drove his car to a third-place finish, dramatically passing the Chevrolets to garner the manufacturing title for Toyota. In 1987 and 1988, Ribbs garnered IMSA GTO Driver of the Year accolades. The *New York Times* lauded Willy as "America's only nationally known black race driver."

Nevertheless, Ribbs encountered problems in securing NASCAR and Indy car sponsors. Black audiences showed little interest in stock car or auto racing because no other African Americans competed. Willy's outspoken, aggressive personality and clashes with other drivers restricted his ability to secure much-needed major corporate sponsorships. In an unprecedented move, the IMSA in 1987 suspended Ribbs 30 days for punching a competitor. Willy countered, "You're going up the ladder, and there are other young lions in the den trying to prove the same thing."

In 1990, Ribbs returned to Indy-style competition, placing tenth at the Molson Indy at Vancouver, Canada, and starting seven other races. Willy in April 1991 joined the Walker Motorsports team, financed by Derrick Walker and actor Bill Cosby. Walker had managed drivers to five Indianapolis 500 triumphs during the 1980s, but his team did not have corporate sponsors or sufficient funding in the weeks preceding the Indianapolis 500 race.

Ribbs on May 19, 1991, became the first African American to qualify for the prestigious Indianapolis 500 race, bumping former champion Tom Sneva with just 45 minutes left in the final practice session. Willy drove the four laps around the 2½-mile oval at an average speed of 217.538 miles per hour, the day's fastest time, to earn $20,000 for his team. The crowd roared as he completed his historic run in the 1990 Lola-Buick V-6. Willy rose partway out of the cockpit, raised his arm high into the air, slapped hands with safety patrolmen, and gave everyone the thumbs-up signal. "We knew we were out of time, and the clock was ticking," Ribbs acknowledged. "We had to Hail Mary our way into the Indy 500." He added, "I am glad everybody was here to witness history because it can only be done once."

Two days before the Indianapolis 500 race, McDonald's consented to sponsor Ribbs for that event alone. Quaker Motor Oil, Coca-Cola, Kleen Coty, and Kodak joined as associate sponsors. Willy looked forward to competing in the seventy-fifth annual Indianapolis 500, but engine problems sidelined him after only five laps. Ribbs placed eleventh in the June 1991 Detroit Grand Prix and competed in the July 1991 Cleveland Grand Prix. Friends and San Jose businessmen raised around $50,000 to help him finish the 1991 Indy car season. The lack of permanent corporate sponsorship, however, kept Willy from 1992 Indy car competition. "If this is what I am going to be subjected to over and over again, if this is what the sport is all about," he lamented, "I don't know if I can endure it."

In May 1993, Ribbs qualified for his second Indianapolis 500 race in a 1992 Lola-Ford Cosworth. This time Willy drove 194 laps, finishing in twenty-first place. "The priority was not to make any mistakes," he indicated. "I haven't raced in a year and a half, so I wanted to get some race miles under my belt."

Ribbs indeed had made his mark as an African-American pioneer on the Indianapolis race car circuit. Willy did not qualify for the 1994 Indianapolis 500 race.

Willy married Suzanne Hamilton on November 22, 1979, and has one child, Sasha.

BIBLIOGRAPHY: Barbara Carlisle Bigelow, ed., *Contemporary Black Biography*, vol. 2 (Detroit, MI, 1992); *Des Moines Register*, May 20, 1991; May 27, 1991; May 31, 1993; *New York Times*, May 20, 1991; May 24, 1991; May 31, 1993; *New York Times Magazine*, October 9, 1988.

David L. Porter

JERRY RICE
(October 13, 1962–) ————————————————————— *Football*

Jerry Rice has scored more touchdowns than any other National Football League (NFL) player. Jerry Lee Rice was born on October 13, 1962, in Starkville, Mississippi, the son of Joe Nathan Rice, a brick mason, and Eddie B. Rice. Rice, the sixth of eight children, has two sisters, Eddie and Lositine, and five brothers, Joe, Tom, James, Jimmy, and Zebedee. Jerry grew up in Crawford, a sleepy town of some 500 souls 38 miles southeast of Starkville. He enjoyed a happy, idyllic childhood, although material things were not always plentiful. Rice recalled, "We had to wait our turn for things like clothes and shoes." As a youngster, Jerry enjoyed basketball and football and idolized Dallas Cowboy wide receiver Drew Pearson. Rice's favorite pastimes included riding his neighbor's horse, which he would chase down and catch in an adjoining pasture. Jerry credits such exercise with building the speed, endurance, and shiftiness so essential to any skilled wideout. At B. L. Moor High School, he ran the five miles to and from Crawford. Rice readily admits, "That's what made me . . . running those dirt roads and country fields."

As a teenager, Jerry worked summers with his father building houses throughout Oktibbeha County. He revealed superb hand-eye coordination in this trade, being able to catch four bricks simultaneously thrown to him by his father or brothers in his big, soft hands. At tiny Moor High School, Rice started participating in football when he was chased down by a vice principal while cutting classes. After six swats with a leather strap, Jerry was directed to football practice. His speed and remarkable receiving ability soon made him a star. During his senior year in 1980, he made 35 touchdown receptions and averaged 30 points a game as a basketball forward.

Surprisingly, colleges did not highly recruit Rice. Scouts considered Jerry inexperienced because he only played football two years at B. L. Moor and lacked speed with 4.8-second clocking in the 40-yard dash. Coach Archie Cooley of Mississippi Valley State University in Itta Bena alone personally scouted him. Cooley liked Rice so much that he eventually shifted his offense from a traditional pro-set to a run-and-gun five wideout system to take advantage of Jerry's talent. Rice's freshman year in 1981 provided lackluster results, but the hard-driving Cooley motivated Jerry to work on his strength and speed in the off-season. The extra work paid off. In 1982, Rice starred for the red and green clad Delta Devils, catching 66 passes for 1,129 yards and 7 touchdowns. Jerry set an NCAA Division I-AA record against Tennessee State University with 279 receiving yards. Coach Cooley remarked that Rice "could catch a BB in the dark," while his teammates nicknamed him "World" because he seemingly could catch anything in the world.

By his junior year in 1983, Rice teamed with quarterback Willie "Satellite" Totten to topple more Division I-AA records. Jerry's marks included most season catches (102) and most season yards (1,450), winning All-America honors. During his senior year in 1984, the fine receiver "Satellite Express" hit full throttle. The 9–2 Delta Devils averaged a national-high 60.9 points and 637 yards per game. Coach Cooley's exciting brand of football proved so popular that Valley State moved their home games to spacious Mississippi Memorial Stadium in Jackson to accommodate the fans. Opposing teams often triple-teamed Rice, who still produced. In 1984, Jerry led Division I-AA in scoring with 162 points and made a record-breaking 103 receptions, 1,682 yards, and 27 touchdowns. Rice set 18 I-AA career records, including most catches (301), most receiving yards (4,693), and most touchdowns (50).

The San Francisco 49ers (NFL) selected Rice as their number-1 draft choice (number 16 overall) in April 1985 and signed him to a $2.1 million, five-year deal. The 49ers veterans did not take kindly to the brash rookie with his BMW and personalized license plate "World." Jerry's fancy poodle haircut won him the nicknames "Fifi" and "Bert" (of Sesame Street). He suffered from the "dropsies" in training camp and was overwhelmed by the complexity and precision of the 49er playbook. Candlestick Park fans expected a great deal from the highly touted Rice and booed him unmercifully when he did not deliver, at one time reducing him to tears at halftime. By the end of 1985, however, Jerry had caught 49 passes for 927 yards and scored four touchdowns, including one rushing, to garner National Football Conference (NFC) Rookie of the Year honors.

In 1986, Rice hit his stride, gathering in an NFC-high 86 passes for 1,570 yards and making 15 touchdown receptions to set a 49er team record. Along the way, Jerry won All-Pro honors and played in his first Pro Bowl. One unpleasant memory from this season came when he fumbled a sure touchdown pass reception in the 49–3 playoff loss to the New York Giants. Personally, he enjoyed some of his new-found wealth, building his parents a home in Starkville and buying a Porsche for himself and a Jaguar for his fiancée, Jackie Mitchell.

A wonderful year followed for Rice, both personally and professionally. After marrying Jackie, Jerry became a father of a daughter, Jaqui, on June 7. An exceptional parent, he regularly got up with his infant daughter at night, even on workdays. On the field, Rice gathered in 65 passes for 1,078 yards and 22 touchdowns to set an NFL record. Jerry caught a touchdown pass in 13 consecutive games, breaking the record shared by Pro Football Hall of Famer Elroy "Crazylegs" Hirsch and Buddy Dial. He also became the first receiver since Hirsch in 1951 to lead the NFL in scoring with 138 points. Rice's superb 1987 performance won him many honors, including the NFC Most Valuable Player (MVP), Bert Bell Award, Len Eshmont Award, Jim Thorpe Memorial Trophy, Associated Press (AP) Offensive Player of the Year Award, All-Pro, Pro Bowl starter, and NFL Player of the Year awards from *Sports Illustrated, Pro Football Weekly, The Sporting News,* and *Football Digest.*

By 1988, defenders concentrated on the dangerous Rice, often disguising their coverage and then triple-teaming Jerry. Nevertheless, he set a record for most touchdowns in post-season play (six) and ran wild in Super Bowl XXIII against the Cincinnati Bengals, catching 11 passes for 215 yards and one touchdown to earn the game's MVP honor. Rice's delight in this achievement turned sour, however, when media stories focused on Joe Montana's skills and Coach Bill Walsh's retirement rather than on Jerry's attainments. In a move he later regretted, Jerry told the press: "It's not that I wanted all the attention. I just wanted respect for what I achieved."

Since 1988, Rice has worked each year at defining the wide receiver position anew. Jerry broke the NFL record for yards received with 1,483 in 1989 and caught 5 touchdown passes in a 1990 game against Atlanta, tying a record shared by Bob Shaw of the 1950 Chicago Cardinals and Kellen Winslow of the 1981 San Diego Chargers. On September 5, 1994, he scored three times against the Los Angeles Raiders to surpass **Jim Brown** as the NFL career touchdown leader with 127. Rice broke the record when he outleaped Albert Lewis on a 38-yard touchdown pass from Steve Young late in the fourth quarter. Jerry's 112 pass receptions in 1994 marked a personal best. He has caught passes in 144 consecutive regular season games through 1994 and holds the NFL record for most seasons (9) with at least 1,000 yards in pass receptions. He has paced the NFL in reception yardage five times (1986, 1989, 1990, 1993, 1994) and in touchdowns six times (1986, 1987, 1989, 1990, 1991, 1994).

Rice continues to excel in post-season competition. Jerry caught 10 passes for 149 yards and three touchdowns, as the 49ers routed the San Diego Chargers, 49–26, in Super Bowl XXIX. His Super Bowl records include most points (42), touchdowns (7), receptions (28), reception yardage (512), touchdown receptions (7), and combined net yardage (527). He twice tied Super Bowl game marks for most points (18), touchdowns (3), and touchdown receptions (3). Rice's NFL post-season records include most catches (100) and reception yardage (1,539).

Through the 1994 season, Rice has caught 820 passes for 13,275 yards and 131 touchdowns and has rushed for 8 touchdowns. In 1994 Jerry was named to the All-Time NFL team and U.S. Sports Academy Professional Male Athlete of the Year. Rice, an All-Pro and Pro Bowl selection for nine consecutive seasons, plans to play until 1998 and is destined to set records of enormous proportions. The lighter, more mature 190-pounder recently reflected, "I'm more at peace with myself. There are things I cannot control that are solely up to coaches and the quarterback. I'm more at peace with all of that."

BIBLIOGRAPHY: Pete Axthelm and Pamela Abramson, "The 49er with Golden Hands," Newsweek 111 (January 11, 1988), p. 62; Howard Balzer, "Rice Grabs MVP Honors," The Sporting News, January 30, 1989, p. 17; Current Biography Yearbook (1990), pp. 45–49; Jaime Diaz, "He's the Catch of the Year," Sports Illustrated 59 (November 14, 1983), p. 68; Glenn Dickey, "Beers with Jerry Rice," Sport 80 (November 1989), pp. 19–20; Tom Fitzgerald, "The San Francisco Threat," The Sporting News, January 4, 1988, pp. 12–13; Tom Fitzgerald, "TSN Tributes—3 Jobs Well Done: NFL Player of the Year," The Sporting News, February 1, 1988, p. 21; Thomas George, "Pro Football: For Rice It's Catch as Catch Can," New York Times, November 1, 1992, sec. 8, p. 3; John Rolfe, Jerry Rice (New York, 1993); Art Spander, "49ers' Rice Won't Let Success Go to His Head," The Sporting News, September 25, 1989, p. 8; Rick Telander, "Picture-Perfect End," Sports Illustrated 57 (December 6, 1982), p. 52; USA Today, December 29, 1994, p. 4C; January 30, 1995, pp. 1C–8C; Ralph Wiley, "Rice Is a Breed Apart," Sports Illustrated 67 (September 28, 1987), pp. 40–43; Ralph Wiley, "A Step Above 'Em All," Sports Illustrated 70 (January 30, 1989), pp. 30–31.

John H. Ziegler

OSCAR ROBERTSON
(November 24, 1938–) ————————————————— *Basketball*

Phog Allen and Red Auerbach, legendary basketball coaches/executives, dealt with some of the most extraordinary talents in the history of the game. Allen coached **Wilt Chamberlain** at the University of Kansas, while Auerbach designed the fabled Boston Celtics teams from the 1950s through 1970s with stars Bob Cousy, Bill Sharman, **K. C. Jones,** and **Bill Russell.** Yet Allen and Auerbach both named Robertson as the best, most versatile player in their basketball experience.

Oscar Palmer Robertson, nicknamed "The Big O," was born on November 24, 1938, in Charlotte, Indiana, the youngest of three sons of Mazel (Bell) Robertson, and grew up in straitened circumstances in Indianapolis, Indiana. With his brother, Bailey, who later performed for the Harlem Globetrotters, Oscar played his first basketball at the local YMCA. He became an all-around athletic star at Indianapolis Crispus Attucks High School, excelling in track and field as a high jumper, in baseball as a pitcher, and in basketball as a guard. Robertson led Crispus Attucks to two State basketball titles and a 45-game winning streak, making All-State teams three times. Besides being chosen for several All-America high school teams, Oscar also graduated sixteenth in a class of 171 students.

Robertson, heavily recruited for basketball nationally, picked the University of Cincinnati because of its nearness to his home. The first African American to play basketball for the Bearcats, Oscar surpassed all expectations by averaging 33.8 points per game for a three-year period. He set 14 NCAA University Division scoring records, tallying 62 points against North Texas State University his senior year. This mark stood until 1988, when Hersey Hawkins of Bradley University scored 63 points against the University of Detroit. An All-America his three varsity seasons, Robertson captained the 1960 U.S. Olympic team that won the Gold Medal at the Rome, Italy, Summer Games. Oscar, unhappy with racial tension, struggled for awhile in his academic work and came close to flunking out. "What difference does it make whether I do or not?" he confided to a friend. "My future is in basketball anyhow." Nevertheless, he eventually earned a bachelor's degree in business administration in 1960.

The Cincinnati Royals National Basketball Association (NBA) club made Robertson a territorial choice. Oscar continued with his consistent, spectacular court play, averaging 30.5 points per game his first season. His scoring average in 14 NBA seasons exceeded 25 points per game, as he led the NBA in assists six times. Oscar's greatest single season came in 1963–1964, when he averaged 31.4 points and 11 assists per game, finished second behind Chamberlain in scoring, and won the NBA's Most Valuable Player (MVP) award. At the close of his NBA career, he ranked as the all-time leader in assists (9,887) with over 9 per game. An All-NBA First Team choice for 10 consecutive seasons, he finished second to Chamberlain in a 1971 nationwide vote for the All-Time NBA team.

An NBA championship eluded Robertson until his trade to the Milwaukee Bucks (NBA) in 1969. Despite Oscar's individual brilliance at the University of Cincinnati, the Bearcats did not win their two consecutive NCAA titles until after his graduation. At Milwaukee, he teamed with youthful Lew Alcindor (**Kareem Abdul-Jabbar**) to help the Hawks win the 1971 NBA title in only the third year for the franchise. Robertson was selected unanimously to the Naismith Memorial Basketball Hall of Fame in 1979 in his first year of eligibility, having scored 26,710 points and a record 7,694 free throws. The six-foot-five-inch 215-pounder possessed the dominating brilliance of a **Michael Jordan,** attracting similarly enthusiastic crowds.

Robertson especially admired **Jackie Robinson,** who integrated organized baseball. "He did something few of us could have done," Oscar told a friend. "He took a horrible beating for the sake of a principle, and all of us gained by it. Every Negro in America owes him a debt of gratitude. I'd give anything if I could be like him." Hoop fans eventually expressed similar admiration for Robertson, who suffered many indignities on the path to becoming a basketball legend.

Robertson married Yvonne Crittenden, a teacher, and has three daughters, Shana, Tia, and Mari. Oscar lives in Indianapolis, where he works as an analyst for ABC-Sports Radio.

BIBLIOGRAPHY: Al Hirshberg, *Basketball's Greatest Stars* (New York, 1963); Zander Hollander and Alex Sachare, eds., *The Official NBA Basketball Encyclopedia* (New York, 1989); *The Lincoln Library of Sports Champions*, vol. 11 (Columbus, OH, 1974); David L. Porter, ed., *Biographical Dictionary of American Sports: Basketball and Other Indoor Sports* (Westport, CT, 1989); Art Rust, *Illustrated History of the Black Athlete* (Garden City, NY, 1985).

Leonard H. Frey

PAUL ROBESON
(April 9, 1898–January 23, 1976) ——————————————— *Football*

Paul Robeson, one of the great African Americans of the twentieth century, fought for racial equality in sport and all of American society. Paul Bustill Robeson was born on April 9, 1898, in Princeton, New Jersey, to Rev. William Drew Robeson, a North Carolina runaway slave and Presbyterian minister, and Maria Louisa (Bustill) Robeson, a teacher who died when Paul was nine. During high school in Somerville, New Jersey, Robeson discovered both his mental and physical talents. Academically, Paul graduated at the top of his class. In extracurricular activities, he debated skillfully, sang solos for the glee club, acted in plays with the drama club, and excelled in baseball, basketball, football, and track and field. Robeson achieved the highest score on a state-wide examination for a Rutgers College scholarship. Paul recalled, "Equality might be denied," because he was an African American, "but I *knew* I was not inferior."

Robeson continued to display his remarkable physical, artistic, and mental abilities when he became the sole African American enrolled at Rutgers College from 1915 to 1919. Paul was elected to the national scholastic fraternity, Phi Beta Kappa, in his junior year and led his class academically. He won every oratorical competition for which he was eligible and delivered the graduation class oration. Besides achieving scholastic honors, he earned 12 varsity letters. Robeson caught for the baseball team, played center in basketball, threw the discus and javelin, shot putted, competed in the pentathlon in track and field, and starred at end in football. Walter Camp, often called the "Father of American football," designated Paul a two-time All-America and called him the then-greatest defensive end of all time. When he first tried out for the football team, a racial incident marred his first football scrimmage. One player smashed and broke Robeson's nose, while another player jumped on Paul when he was down and dislocated his shoulder. Eventually, Robeson's teammates accepted him. A southern team, Washington and Lee from Lexington, Virginia, even refused to play against an African American, keeping Paul out of that game.

The six-foot-three-inch, 215-pound scholar-athlete attracted the interest of professional football teams just prior to the formation of the National Football

League (NFL). Robeson attended Columbia Law School in New York City and played football on weekends with the Akron Pros in Ohio. Paul performed there with African-American ex-collegian **"Fritz" Pollard** from Brown University. In one memorable 1920 Thanksgiving Day game, his Akron squad defeated the Canton Bulldogs to win the pro championship. Great Native-American athlete Jim Thorpe led Canton. Robeson later played with the Milwaukee Badgers of the fledgling NFL while completing his law degree. Paul competed against the Ohio-based Oorang Indians, featuring Jim Thorpe, where he scored both touchdowns in a 13–0 victory. As a law school student, Paul married Eslanda Cardozo Goode on August 17, 1921. Paul Robeson, Jr., their only child, was born on November 2, 1927. Paul, Sr., gave up his athletic career upon completion of a law degree but later was involved in the integration of baseball.

Robeson only briefly practiced law before attaining prominence in the performing arts as a singer and actor. Paul was denied membership in the American Bar Association because of race and suffered other discriminatory practices in his New York City law firm, causing him to leave his law practice and pursue acting and singing. He starred in several Eugene O'Neill plays and gave concerts that featured his rich bass voice with African-American spirituals and folk songs. By the 1930s, Robeson became politically involved in opposing fascist policies of Hitler's Germany, Franco's Spain, and Mussolini's Italy. Paul also strongly protested imperialism, especially European control of the African continent, and racism in America. After spending most of the 1930s in Europe, he returned to the United States at the outset of World War II.

During World War II, Robeson attempted to desegregate pro baseball. Organized baseball had not allowed African Americans to participate since the segregationist "Jim Crow" policies of the 1880s and 1890s. At the annual major league owner's meeting in 1943, Paul and the Negro Publishers Association both addressed the owners and commissioner Kenesaw Mountain Landis. Robeson told them that if he could be the first African-American lead in an otherwise all-white cast of Shakespeare's *Othello* on Broadway in New York City, it would not be incredible to allow African Americans to play baseball. In 1945, **Jackie Robinson** was signed by Branch Rickey of the Brooklyn Dodgers National League (NL) to play professional baseball. Robinson in 1947 became the first African American to enter major league baseball since the nineteenth century. Two years later, however, Jackie was asked to testify against Paul before the House Un-American Activities Committee. Robeson, a vocal political activist, had spoken out against American racial injustice at the World Congress of the Partisans of Peace in Paris, France. "It is unthinkable," Paul stated, "that American Negroes would go to war [against the Soviet Union] on behalf of those who have oppressed us for generations." These comments by an internationally known American threatened U.S. cold war efforts in what many considered a life or death struggle with the Soviet Union.

Robinson was asked by the House Un-American Activities Committee to "give the lie" to Robeson's statement. Jackie's testimony helped remove African-American support for Paul. Later, the U.S. State Department took away Robeson's passport and helped to destroy Paul's career. A victim of political ideology, he died in Philadelphia on January 23, 1976, in near obscurity. In 1995 Robeson belatedly was elected to the National Football Foundation College Football Hall of Fame.

BIBLIOGRAPHY: Lenwood G. Davis, comp., *A Paul Robeson Research Guide: A Selected, Annotated Bibliography* (Westport, CT, 1982); Martin B. Duberman, *Paul Robeson* (New York, 1988); Philip S. Foner, ed., *Paul Robeson Speaks, Writings—Speeches—Interviews, 1918–1974* (New York, 1978); Freedomways Associates, eds., *Paul Robeson: The Great Forerunner* (New York, 1978); Dorothy Butler Gilliam, *Paul Robeson: All-American* (New York, 1981); W. Augustus Low and Virgil A. Clift, eds., *Encyclopedia of Black America* (New York, 1981); Paul Robeson, *Here I Stand* (London, England, 1958); Paul Robeson [Microfilm] Collection (Bethesda, MD, 1991); Paul Robeson Papers, Rutgers University Archives, New Brunswick, NJ; Paul Robeson, Jr., *Paul Robeson, Jr., Speaks to America* (New Brunswick, 1993); Marie Seton, *Paul Robeson* (London, England, 1958); Ronald A. Smith, "The Paul Robeson–Jackie Robinson Saga and a Political Collision," *Journal of Sport History* 6 (Summer 1979), pp. 5–27.

Ronald A. Smith

DAVID ROBINSON
(August 6, 1965–) ——————————————————————— *Basketball*

David Robinson ranks among the most talented centers ever to play in the National Basketball Association (NBA). Born David Maurice Robinson on August 6, 1965, in Key West, Florida, he was the second child of Ambrose Robinson and Freda Robinson. Ambrose, a career U.S. Naval officer, pushed David to excel in school, once grounding him for six weeks because of a C on his report card. Robinson showed great ability in math and science as a child and built a wide-screen television from a kit at age 12, despite never having used many of the tools required before. After his father showed him a few notes on the piano, David taught himself how to play classical music by ear.

Robinson demonstrated little interest in playing sports as a youth. David participated in basketball and track and field as a high school freshman but quit both sports out of boredom and lack of confidence in his ability. His primary interest remained gymnastics. After growing from five foot five inches at age 15 to six foot seven inches as a senior, he soon quit that sport as well.

Robinson's father retired in 1982 from the U.S. Navy before David's senior year. David transferred to Osbourne Park High School in Manassas, Virginia. The high school team welcomed the new tall student, but Robinson did not express interest in trying basketball again. "The game didn't come naturally to me," David admitted. "I had no particular gift for it. I was just a tall kid."

Although not particularly enthusiastic, he reluctantly tried out for the basket-ball team and ironically was named Osbourne Park's Most Valuable Player (MVP) and Second Team All-Conference.

Since being a young child, Robinson had wanted to follow his father's foot-steps and attend the United States Naval Academy. The school's requirements for applicants to be 6 foot 6 inches or shorter were waived for David, who stood 6 foot 8 inches in 1983, when he entered the Naval Academy. "I didn't care if I played basketball at the academy," he stated. "I just wanted to get good grades and fit in." Robinson again agreed to play basketball but hardly starred as a freshman. Navy coach Paul Evans was amazed at David's inex-perience and lack of knowledge about the game. Robinson never started his freshman year in 1983–1984, averaging only 7.6 points and 4 rebounds per game. Nevertheless, David was named Eastern College Athletic Conference Rookie of the Year. Furthermore, the Middies earned the first 20-win season in Navy history and enhanced Robinson's interest in basketball. David re-ported for his sophomore year at 6 foot 11 inches and 215 pounds. His sta-tistics rose dramatically, as he averaged 23.6 points, 11.6 rebounds, and four blocks per game. He started every game and led Navy to its first NCAA tournament trip in 15 years.

As a junior, Robinson began to rethink his basketball future. NBA scouts and coaches called him a future franchise player. Consequently, David worked harder than ever on his game. Robinson's 207 blocked shots set a college record and were surpassed by only one team nationally. David again led his team to the NCAA tournament and triumphs over the University of Tulsa, Syracuse University, and Cleveland State University before being defeated by the Duke University Blue Devils in the 1986 NCAA Final Eight. When the 1985–1986 season ended, Robinson helped the U.S. squad capture the 1986 World Championship over the Soviet Union.

As a senior in 1986–1987, Robinson increased his scoring average to 28.2 points per game and ranked third best nationally. His 11.8 rebounds per game placed him fourth nationally, while his 4.5 blocked shots per game again led the nation. Besides making a third straight NCAA tournament trip, David was selected consensus All-America and won several Player of the Year awards. Due to his obvious basketball talent and the problems of a seven-footer serving on ships, the U.S. Navy cut Robinson's required commitment from five years to two years. The floundering San Antonio Spurs made David the first pick of the 1987 NBA draft and signed him to one of the largest rookie contracts in sports at $26 million over 10 years. In 1988, he played on the Bronze Medal U.S. squad at the Seoul, South Korea, Summer Olympic Games.

After completing his U.S. Navy service, Robinson quickly paid dividends for the Spurs. David was named the NBA Rookie of the Year, winning Rookie of the Month honors every month of the season. His remarkable 24.3 points and 10 rebounds per game also placed him on the All-NBA Third Team and the All-NBA Defensive Second Team. He led San Antonio from a 21–61 win-loss record the previous year to a 55–27 mark his first season, the best single-season improvement in NBA history. Since that first year, Robinson has continued to progress and has averaged nearly 25 points and 12 rebounds per game for his short career. Nevertheless, as with so many star players, David has been criticized for his team's failure to win an NBA championship.

In 1992, Robinson played for the U.S. "Dream Team" at the Barcelona, Spain, Summer Olympics. Unlike 1988, David and his teammates captured the Gold Medal in dominating fashion. David finished the 1993–1994 season in dramatic style, recording the fourth quadruple double in league history with 34 points, 10 rebounds, 10 assists, and 10 blocked shots. He also edged **Shaquille O'Neal** of the Orlando Magic for the NBA scoring title with 29.79 points per game by scoring 71 points in the final game of the season against the Los Angeles Clippers. No center had led the league in scoring since Bob McAdoo in 1975–1976. Hakeem Olajuwon of the Houston Rockets edged him for NBA MVP honors. David won the NBA MVP Award in 1994–1995, averaging 27.6 points, 10.8 rebounds, 3.23 blocked shots, and 1.65 steals per game in leading San Antonio to an NBA best 62–20 record and to the Western Conference finals. Robinson, who has made the All-NBA First Team three times (1991, 1992, 1994) and Third Team (1990, 1993) twice, and All-NBA Second Team once (1994), has played in six consecutive All-Star Games. He also has made the All-NBA Defensive First Team three times (1991, 1992, 1995).

Robinson, an excellent role model for youth, married Valerie Hoggart in December 1991. David, a "born-again Christian," enjoys playing the piano and saxophone. "Some people think my life is boring," he admitted, "but I wouldn't trade places with anyone. I think I'm having the best time in the world."

BIBLIOGRAPHY: Norman Aaseng, *Sports Great: David Robinson* (Hillside, NJ, 1992); *Current Biography Yearbook* (1993), pp. 497–500; "Inside the NBA," *Sports Illustrated* 80 (February 28, 1994), p. 87; *New York Times*, October 28, 1990; "Players Vote Robinson as MVP," *Jet* 86 (May 16, 1994), p. 53; Phil Taylor, "Spur of the Moment," *Sports Illustrated* 80 (March 7, 1994), pp. 58–60.

Brian L. Laughlin

EDDIE ROBINSON
(February 13, 1919–) ————————————————— *Football*

No gridiron mentor in history above the high school level has come close to Eddie Robinson in football victories. Edward Gay Robinson, college football player, coach, and athletic director, has compiled 397 career victories through 55 seasons of coaching at Grambling State University. Robinson surpassed Bear Bryant's 323 career wins in 1985 and left far behind NFL coach George Halas's 326, Amos Alonzo Stagg's 314, and Pop Warner's 313 career marks. No other college or professional coaches have reached the 300-victory plateau. Incredibly, Eddie's 397 wins, 143 losses, and 15 ties (.729 percent) through

1994 came at one university, attesting to his loyalty, steadfastness, and longevity. His Tigers not only posted three undefeated and seven single-loss seasons but set an all-time NCAA Division I-AA record of 27 consecutive winning campaigns between 1960 and 1986.

Born on February 13, 1919, in Jackson, Louisiana, Robinson moved with his family at age six from the rural farming community to Louisiana's capital Baton Rouge. Eddie, an only child, was influenced by his father Frank, a Standard Oil employee, who urged him to study at school and make best use of his spare time. He attended Baton Rouge McKinley High School and showed interest in football at an early age. To gain entry to gridiron contests at nearby Southern University or Louisiana State University, Robinson lined the fields or parked cars there. "My parents gave me a sense of pride and direction in life," Eddie acknowledged. "There's no work too hard if it gets you what you need or where you want to go."

Although somewhat small of stature his first year at McKinley High School, Robinson worked his way up to starting football quarterback. His squad lacked a passer. Eddie, therefore, volunteered for the job even though he had little previous experience. Like a fiction novel with a happy ending, he led McKinley to three straight undefeated seasons. Before graduating in 1937, Robinson also played on the high school baseball team. Eddie enrolled at Leland College, a small Baptist school in Baker, Louisiana, where he quarterbacked the football squad for four seasons. Robinson played under head coach Ruben Turner, helping Leland win 18 of 19 games his last two years while also serving as assistant coach. Eddie helped design the Leland offense and accompanied Turner on a few recruiting trips. He worked as the campus barber and on a coal truck for 20 cents an hour to help pay his tuition. An English major, he graduated from Leland College in 1941 and earned a master's degree in 1954 from the University of Iowa.

In 1941, Dr. Ralph Waldo Emerson Jones, president of Grambling State University, hired Robinson as athletic director, head of the physical education department, and head football coach and (temporarily) head men's and women's basketball coach. "He was determined to succeed," Jones recalled, "and I saw in him a lot of leadership qualities." Michael Hurd, author of *Black College Football 1892–1992*, observed, "Robinson mowed and lined the field, sewed torn uniforms, taped ankles, groomed the cheerleader squad, directed the band, and wrote game accounts for Louisiana newspapers." Some of Eddie's seniors in 1941 were older than him. When a few players exhibited blatant disrespect, he courageously dismissed them from the squad. After posting a 3–5 record the first season, the Tigers finished 8–0 and unscored upon in 1942.

Robinson received permission from Jones to teach and coach football at Grambling High School during the height of World War II in 1943 and 1944, when football was curtailed at Grambling State University due to player shortage. After returning to the Tigers' lair in 1945, Eddie continued his successful career. His club won nine African-American college national championships and 16 Southwestern Athletic Conference (SAC) titles, as he sent more players

(over 200) to the professional football ranks than any other coach. These players included quarterbacks James Harris and Doug Williams, running backs
Tank Younger and Essex Johnson, offensive linemen Woody Peoples, Willie
Young, Ron Singleton, and Lane Howell, receivers Charlie Joiner and Sammy
White, defensive linemen Ernie Ladd, Willie Davis, and Buck Buchanan, linebackers Henry Davis and Garland Boyette, and defensive backs Willie Brown
and Everson Walls. Younger, in 1949 the first player drafted from a predominantly African-American college, paved the way for future African Americans
in professional football like **Jackie Robinson** had done in professional baseball.
In 1963, Buchanan became the initial African-American college player picked
first overall in the American Football League (AFL) draft. Williams, the first
African-American college player to make a major college All-America First
Team, was picked in 1977 by the Associated Press (AP) at quarterback.

Robinson married childhood sweetheart Doris Mott and has three children.
He uses the winged-T offense and remains a workaholic, often toiling until 2
A.M. or 3 A.M. on new plays and problems relating to his athletic director's
duties. Eddie, who loves his job, says, "The American dream is spelled
'W-O-R-K.' It's that simple." Robinson insists upon a strict dress code for his
players, occasionally eliciting favorable comments from airline personnel. The
Tiger players must wear coats and ties on trips and are not permitted long
hair or fancy jewelry. Over 90 percent of his gridders graduate on time. Eddie
gives snap football quizzes, either nabbing a player in the hallway or on the
practice field. Woe to the Tiger who has not studied his playbook! Upon
recruiting James Gregory, his first white player, in 1968, he declared, "When
you put a football helmet on a young man, he loses his color." A sportswriter
at the Houston Astrodome asked of Eddie's players the name of the white
player. He replied, "Man, he ain't no white boy, he's a Tiger!"

The Tigers consistently drew crowds of over 60,000 fans at Yankee Stadium
in New York, Los Angeles Coliseum, Chicago's Soldier Field, Dallas' Cotton
Bowl, and the Houston Astrodome. For two decades, Grambling has met
Southern University in the Bayou Classic at the Louisiana Superdome. The
game draws 70,000 annual attendance and boasts network television exposure.
"Robinson and Grambling are marquee—Las Vegas–size marquee," Hurd em-
phasizes, "but the Tigers are seldom a gamble at the gate." Grambling in 1976
joined Morgan State University as the first American colleges to play a football
game in Japan. The Tigers defeated the Bears, 42–16, before 50,000 curious
spectators.

Robinson, an emotional coach, has shed tears in public. "The first time I
saw Eddie cry was before a game," remembered Willie Davis. "He had that
great emotion. He would get so caught up in the emotion of winning and
participation until he would just become overwhelmed." Robinson annually
received hundreds of requests to speak at alumni, civic, and charity events. A
shoo-in for election to the National Football Foundation College Football Hall
of Fame after he retires, Eddie already has won numerous honors. He re-

ceived the Walter Camp Foundation's Distinguished American Award, Football Writers Association of America (FWAA) Outstanding Contribution to Amateur Football Award, NCAA's Special Recognition Award after his Tigers broke Bryant's career victory record, and 1993 Bobby Dodd Coach of the Year Award. Louisiana Governor Edwin Edwards proclaimed a special Eddie Robinson Day in 1986. Eddie, a National Association of Intercollegiate Athletics (NAIA) Hall of Fame member, has served as president of NAIA and the American Football Coaches Association (AFCA). In 1983, Grambling's new 22,000-seat Robinson Stadium was named in his honor. A street in Baton Rouge also bears his name. The modest Robinson opined, "I could win 1,000 games and never replace the Bear." But Coach Joe Paterno disagreed, saying, "Nobody has done or ever will do what he has done for this game."

BIBLIOGRAPHY: O. K. Davis, *Grambling's Gridiron Glory* (Ruston, LA, 1982); "Grambling College: Where Stars Are Made," *Look* 33 (December 16, 1969), pp. 72–75; Michael Hurd, *Black College Football 1892–1992* (Virginia Beach, VA, 1993); *The NCAA News* (September 23, 1985), p. 4; David L. Porter, ed., *Biographical Dictionary of American Sports: Football* (Westport, CT, 1987); Rick Reilly, "Here's to You Mr. Robinson," *Sports Illustrated* 63 (October 14, 1985), pp. 32–34, 39.

James D. Whalen

FRANK ROBINSON
(August 31, 1935–) ———————————————————————— *Baseball*

Frank Robinson, baseball player, manager, coach, and executive, set many records, led his teams to championships, and was selected to the National Baseball Hall of Fame in 1982. Robinson was born on August 31, 1935, in Beaumont, Texas, the youngest of 10 children of Frank Robinson and Ruth (Shaw) Robinson. After his father deserted the family, his mother moved with the children to Oakland, California. Of his early years in Oakland, Frank reflected, "All I can remember is that I played. I played from a very early age. I always loved baseball, and I knew it was my best sport. So I played it and the other sports to pass the time."

At age 14, the slender, right-handed hitter started at third base for the Doll Drugstore amateur team and displayed impressive power against older boys. Robinson graduated in 1953 from high school, where he had made the All-City high school team three times. The same year, Frank signed a contract with the Cincinnati Reds' National League (NL) Class C Ogden, Utah, farm club in the Pioneer League for a $3,500 bonus and $400 per month salary. Due to fielding problems as a third sacker, he switched to the outfield. The 17-year-old batted .348 and slugged 17 home runs but experienced racial prejudice for the first time. Robinson, one of only two nonwhites on the team, was not accepted as a roomer in private homes and was rejected at movie theaters. After playing a few games the next season with Tulsa, Oklahoma, of the Texas League, he joined Columbia, South Carolina, of the Sally League (SAL). Frank encountered racial segregation far greater than that in Ogden and received racial insults from the fans. In addition, he injured his right shoulder making a long throw and aggravated it while in the Puerto Rican League that winter.

In 1955, Robinson attended the Cincinnati spring training camp and would have made the Reds' team if he had been able to throw. Due to his swollen shoulder, the Reds returned him to Columbia. Frank was determined to have a good year and told himself, "Have a good year and get out of here." Frank enjoyed another good season at Columbia except for an incident when he took a bat and raced into the grandstand after three drunks who had attacked him viciously with racial slurs. His manager, Andy Anderson, stopped him. The discouraged Robinson decided to quit, but Marv Williams, veteran minor leaguer and the only other African-American player on the team, talked him out of it. Frank hit .390 and led Columbia to the SAL pennant.

The next year, Reds manager Birdie Tebbetts, an excellent teacher and confidence builder, aided Robinson in making the major league club. Frank suffered less pain in his shoulder and had added weight to his six-foot-one-inch frame so that his power increased. He tied the major league home run record for a rookie with 38 and set the rookie mark for being hit by pitches with 20. Robinson crowded the plate so much that his head was actually over it. Frank won the NL Rookie of the Year award, the first of many honors.

Robinson remained with Cincinnati for 10 years as an outfielder and first baseman, leading the Reds to the NL championship in 1961 and winning the NL Most Valuable Player (MVP) award. Frank married Barbara Ann Cole that year and has a son, Frank Kevin, and a daughter, Michelle. He also attended Xavier University in Cincinnati.

On the field, Robinson played hard and fearlessly and sometimes faced the hatred and retaliation of opponents. Teammate Gene Freese remarked, "He runs into walls, he stands in to pitches, he runs bases like a maniac. When it comes to guts, I've never seen anybody equal him." Jerry Izenberg wrote, "Nobody who ever played this game has been more professional. Nobody who has ever played this game has been less a company man. Nobody . . . has had greater respect from his teammates and incurred greater hatred from his opponents."

Frank's years in Cincinnati brought salary fights with Reds' president Bill DeWitt, who continually criticized him and minimized his achievements to keep his salary down. On December 9, 1965, Cincinnati traded the stunned outfielder to the Baltimore Orioles American League (AL) club, the worst deal in Reds history. In 1966, Robinson led the Orioles to the AL pennant and a sweep of the Los Angeles Dodgers in the World Series. Frank won the AL Triple Crown and MVP award, making him the first player to win the MVP award in both leagues, and also was named the MVP of the World Series.

Robinson remained with the Orioles through the 1971 season, leading Baltimore to more AL pennants in 1969, 1970, and 1971 and another World Series championship in 1970. To gain experience as a manager, Frank piloted Santurce of the Puerto Rican League for five years. Since good young Oriole prospects were ready to move up, Robinson asked to be traded to a California team. On December 2, 1971, Baltimore sent Frank to the Los Angeles Dodgers (NL). Injuries caused a disappointing 1972 season. The Dodgers dealt him in November 1972 to the California Angels (AL), with whom he spent the worst two years of his career. Near the end of the 1974 season, the Angels released him.

Robinson got a break when the Cleveland Indians (AL) signed him. On October 3, 1974, Cleveland chose Frank as manager, making him major league baseball's first African-American manager. He said, "If I had one wish I was sure would be granted, it would be that **Jackie Robinson** could be here . . . today." Robinson hit a home run on his first at bat on opening day in 1975, but events did not bode well for him in Cleveland. The Indians fielded a weak team, while Frank encountered trouble handling some of his players. In 1976, his final year as an active player, the Indians did not fare much better. Robinson, though, hit his 586th (and last) home run on July 6, placing him fourth in the record books. The Indians started poorly in 1977, causing Frank's dismissal on June 19.

During 21 major league seasons, Robinson compiled remarkable statistics. In 2,808 games, Frank batted 10,006 times, scored 1,829 runs, collected 2,943 hits (among them 528 doubles, 72 triples, and 586 homers), and drove in 1,812 runs. He batted .294 with 5,373 total bases and drew 1,420 walks. Besides hitting at least .300 nine times, Robinson belted 30 or more homers 11 seasons and compiled a .537 slugging percentage. On all-time major league lists, Frank ranks among the top 20 players in most categories.

Robinson returned to the game in 1978 as skipper of the Orioles' farm team at Rochester, New York, in the International League and then served as an Orioles coach in 1979 and 1980. The next year, the San Francisco Giants (NL) gave Frank his second chance to manage in the majors. In 1982, he received two more honors, being elected to the National Baseball Hall of Fame and garnering NL Manager of the Year honors for leading a mediocre team into contention. The Giants slipped badly the next two years and even finished last in 1984, causing him to be fired.

Robinson returned to Baltimore as a coach in 1985 and later became an assistant to the Orioles' president. When the Orioles started the 1988 season poorly, Frank was asked to take over as manager. Baltimore, however, fared no better with him at the helm. In 1989, however, Robinson won the AL Manager of the Year award. The Orioles nearly overtook the Toronto Blue Jays for the Eastern Division title. Since then, he has served as one of the Orioles' assistant general managers.

Robinson has made a great impact on baseball as major league baseball's first African-American manager. Frank also compiled remarkable statistics on the diamond and collaborated in writing three significant books on managing, facing racism, and baseball's importance in his life. His determination, leadership qualities, and hard, aggressive play served as an example to those wanting to succeed in a sport or in life. He disclosed what motivated him to succeed in baseball, stating, "The desire to change your life or get something a little better. . . . That was the part that pushed you. To get out of the ghetto, to get off the farm, and not have to go to work in some tough job." Robinson serves as an excellent role model.

BIBLIOGRAPHY: Arthur Daley, *All the Home Run Kings* (New York, 1972); Norman L. Macht, *Frank Robinson* (New York, 1991); David L. Porter, ed., *Biographical Dictionary of American Sports: Baseball* (Westport, CT, 1987); Lawrence Ritter and Donald Honig, *The Hundred Greatest Baseball Players of All Time*, rev. ed. (New York, 1986); Frank Robinson with Dave Anderson, *Frank: The First Year* (New York, 1976); Frank Robinson with Al Silverman, *My Life in Baseball* (New York, 1968); Frank Robinson and Barry Stainbeck, *Extra Innings* (New York, 1988); Cynthia J. Wilbur, *For the Love of the Game* (New York, 1992).

Ralph S. Graber

JACKIE ROBINSON
(January 31, 1919–October 24, 1972) ——————————— *Baseball*

Babe Ruth changed baseball, but even more important, Jackie Robinson changed America. The youngest child of sharecroppers Jerry Robinson and Mallie Robinson, Jack Roosevelt Robinson was the first African-American athlete to play organized baseball in the twentieth century. Jackie was born on January 31, 1919, in Cairo, Georgia. Mallie moved her five children, including one-year-old Jackie, to Pasadena, California, after her husband left the family. Jackie later showed an amazing athletic versatility that allowed him to escape his poverty-stricken life.

After excelling in several sports at Muir Technical High School, the 5-foot-11½-inch, 195-pound Robinson enrolled at Pasadena Junior College. A period at the University of California at Los Angeles (UCLA) followed, where Jackie starred in football, baseball, basketball, and track and field to become the Bruins' first four-letter man. He was named a football All-America in 1940 and undoubtedly would have participated in the 1940 Summer Olympics in track and field had not World War II forced the cancellation of the games. In basketball, Robinson led the Pacific Coast Conference two consecutive seasons in scoring. Financial pressures forced him to leave college in 1941. After playing professional football with the Honolulu Bears briefly in 1941, Jackie enlisted in the U.S. Army and in 1942 was commissioned a second lieutenant. His opposition to the segregation policies in Texas led to his court martial for subordination and subsequent acquittal.

In 1945, Robinson began his professional baseball career with the Kansas

City Monarchs of the Negro American League. Jackie attracted the attention of Brooklyn Dodger National League (NL) club scout Clyde Sukeforth, who was on a special assignment for president Branch Rickey. Rickey planned to integrate the major leagues and needed a special African-American player who blended the key ingredients of baseball skill, intelligence, and most important, grace under pressure to accomplish his revolutionary goals. Rickey's preliminary interrogation of Robinson caused the future National Baseball Hall of Famer to retort at the Dodger executive, "Do you want a player afraid to fight back?" Rickey challenged Jackie, "I need more than a great ball player. I need a man who can fly the flag of his race, who can turn the other cheek. If I get a firebrand who blows his top and comes up swinging . . . it could set the cause back twenty years."

Robinson signed his historic contract with the Brooklyn Dodgers on October 23, 1945, and played for the Montreal Royals of the International League (IL) for the 1946 season. Jackie promptly led the Royals to the IL pennant and a victory in the Little World Series, leading the league in hitting and being chosen IL Most Valuable Player (MVP). His accomplishments proved no easy task, given the many nasty racial taunts he received most of the season. Although Robinson was listed as a shortstop, the Brooklyn Dodgers placed the 28-year-old rookie at first base in 1947. Jackie endured an ill-fated petition from his own players, the threat of a strike in St. Louis, the constant racial insults of opposing players, knock-down pitches, and resistant managers, such as Ben Chapman of the Philadelphia Phillies, but he lost weight and nearly suffered a nervous breakdown. Robinson persevered to hit .297 and led the NL with 29 stolen bases, being named the NL's first Rookie of the Year. In 1949, Jackie switched to second base and paced the NL in both batting with a .342 mark and stolen bases with 37. The NL named him its MVP.

Several other African-American players had entered the major leagues, meaning Robinson no longer had to restrain his emotions. Jackie, one of the most daring, aggressive, and electrifying runners in baseball, refused to endure any more racial slurs or taunts. He fast became one of the most feared, respected players in organized baseball. Robinson stole home 19 times in his career and in 1955 against the New York Yankees at age 36 became 1 of only 12 players to steal home in a World Series. Pittsburgh Pirates manager Bobby Bragan declared, "He was the best I ever saw at getting called safe after being caught in a rundown." Bojangles Bill Robinson called Jackie "Ty Cobb in Technicolor."

From 1947 through 1956 with Brooklyn, Robinson compiled a .311 batting mark. Jackie helped the Dodgers win NL pennants in 1947, 1949, 1952, 1953, 1955, and 1956 and was selected to play in each All-Star Game from 1949 through 1954. The Dodgers planned to trade him to the New York Giants (NL), an ironic move given his hostile rivalry with Leo Durocher of the Giants, but Robinson retired rather than change uniforms. In 1962, the sportswriters elected him to the National Baseball Hall of Fame. In 1,382 games, Jackie made 1,518 hits, including 273 doubles, 54 triples, and 137 homers, scored 947 runs, knocked in 734 runs, and stole 197 bases.

For the next 16 years, Robinson pursued several business interests and participated as a civil rights leader. As a vice president of Chock Full o' Nuts, he hired many African Americans. Nevertheless, Jackie remained uncertain that he had ever made it in a white man's world. The Dodgers retired his uniform, number 42, a few months before his premature death from hypertension and diabetes at Stamford, Connecticut, on October 24, 1972. Robinson's last public appearance came while celebrating the twenty-fifth anniversary of his breaking the color barrier in baseball prior to the first game of the 1972 World Series. The nearly blind Jackie told a silent Riverfront Stadium crowd in Cincinnati, Ohio, "I will be more pleased the day I can look over at third base and see a black man as manager." In 1987, major league baseball named its Rookie of the Year award after him. He was survived by Rachel Isum, his wife of 27 years, and two of their three children.

BIBLIOGRAPHY: Bill Borst, A Fan's Memoir: The Brooklyn Dodgers, 1953–1957 (St. Louis, MO, 1984); Roger Kahn, The Boys of Summer (New York, 1972); Gene Karst and Martin Jones, Jr., Who's Who in Professional Baseball (New Rochelle, NY, 1973); James A. Riley, The Biographical Encyclopedia of the Negro Baseball Leagues (New York, 1994); Jackie Robinson with Charles Dexter, Baseball Has Done It (Philadelphia, PA, 1964); Jack Robinson with Alfred Duckett, I Never Had It Made: An Autobiography (New York, 1972); Jack Robinson and Carl T. Rowan, Wait Till Next Year: The Story of Jackie Robinson (New York, 1960); Jack Robinson and Wendell Smith, Jackie Robinson: My Own Story (New York, 1948); Mike Shatzkin, ed., The Ballplayers (New York, 1990); Jules Tygiel, Baseball's Great Experiment: Jack Robinson and His Legacy (New York, 1983).

William A. Borst

SUGAR RAY ROBINSON
(May 3, 1921–April 12, 1989) ——————————————————— Boxing

Authorities regard Sugar Ray Robinson, world middleweight champion on five different occasions, as the greatest pound-for-pound fighter ever to grace a boxing ring. Born Walker Smith, Jr., in Detroit, Michigan, on May 3, 1921, he developed an interest in boxing at an early age and idolized his hometown hero, world heavyweight champion **Joe Louis**. "I wanted to be like Joe Louis and I used to carry his bag to the gymnasium," he recalled. In hopes of emulating Louis, young Smith began training as a boxer to participate in local amateur tournaments. "I started fighting when I was fifteen. I wasn't old enough [to legally box competitively], so I had to borrow a name." He persuaded local fighter Ray Robinson to lend him his amateur boxing identification card and adopted his name. With talent that belied his youth, Ray became one of the nation's most feared amateur boxers by winning national

Golden Gloves titles in 1939 and 1940. A Robinson adviser described Ray's ring style as "sweet as sugar," giving him an enduring nickname.

Robinson turned professional on October 4, 1940, stopping Joe Escheverria in 2 rounds in New York City. Ray's graceful ring movement and tremendous punching power quickly made him a fan favorite and feared ring figure. From 1940 through 1942, he won his first 40 professional bouts and scored 29 knockouts before losing to rugged Jake LaMotta in Detroit. Robinson, fighting mostly as a welterweight, thoroughly dominated his division. Ray won the first of his six world titles with a 15-round decision over Tommy Bell for the vacant world welterweight title on December 20, 1946, in New York City. In the next four years, he successfully defended his title five times. One of those defenses ended tragically, as challenger Jimmy Doyle died after being knocked out by Robinson in a 1947 Cleveland, Ohio, bout. Ray had a premonition that Doyle would be seriously injured in the fight and nearly canceled the bout, but his handlers persuaded him to enter the ring.

Robinson had outgrown the 147-pound division by 1947 and moved up a weight class to challenge reigning world middleweight champion Jake LaMotta for his crown. Ray stopped LaMotta in 13 rounds in Chicago, Illinois, on February 14, 1951, in a brutal affair dubbed "the St. Valentine's Day Massacre" by the press. After several nontitle fights, he toured Europe. In a major upset, Englishman Randy Turpin dethroned him as world middleweight titlist in London, England, on July 10, 1951. Two months later, however, Robinson regained the championship by stopping Turpin in 10 bloody, fast-paced rounds in New York City. After two title defenses in 1952, Ray attempted to defeat Joey Maxim, the reigning light heavyweight champion, in one of boxing's most famous contests. Despite easily outboxing the slow-moving Maxim, Robinson was forced to retire in his corner after the thirteenth round because of the sweltering heat at New York's Yankee Stadium. The bout marked the only "knockout" defeat Ray suffered in his illustrious career.

In a stunning move, Robinson retired from boxing at the end of 1952 and began a second career as an entertainer. When this decision proved to be financially unsound, Ray returned to the ring in 1955 and knocked out middleweight champion Carl "Bobo" Olson in Chicago on December 9 in the second round. He lost his title to Gene Fullmer by decision on January 2, 1957, but regained it four months later in Chicago, where his single smashing left hook floored Fullmer for the full count. Boxing historians have lauded this punch "the perfect punch knockout," with Robinson listing it as a career highlight. On September 23, 1957, welterweight champion Carmen Basilio scored a considerable upset in New York City, taking Ray's title by decision. He, however, outpointed Basilio in Chicago on March 25, 1958, winning the middleweight championship for a record fifth time. Robinson retained the championship for nearly two years before losing to Boston's Paul Pender in the challenger's hometown on January 22, 1960. Pender also defeated Ray in a Boston rematch later that year. Robinson twice in the early 1960s failed to defeat Fullmer for his National Boxing Association version of the world middleweight title.

Ray, now over 40 years old, still boxed, much to the dismay of those who remembered him when his skills were unrivaled. Robinson claimed that he fought not merely to make a living. "I have several good, sound investments," Ray told *The Ring* editor Nat Fleischer in 1964. "But I believe a career such as mine should end in a happy climax and I have high hopes I can make it such." A final loss to rising contender Joey Archer in Pittsburgh, Pennsylvania, in 1965 convinced Robinson that a sixth middleweight crown was unlikely and brought his retirement from the sport. Ray's career record included 174 wins (109 by knockout), 19 losses, six draws, and two no-contests.

Subsequently, his stature as the greatest boxer of all time has become widely accepted. Boxing authority Bert Sugar, in *The 100 Greatest Boxers of All Time*, lists Robinson as number one and marveled at Ray's unique ability to knock out an opponent while moving backwards. "Being knocked out by Sugar Ray Robinson was more of an honor than a disgrace," wrote Sugar. Ray was married twice, to Edna M. Holly from 1943 to 1960 and to Millie Wiggins Bruce from 1965 until his death. He established the Sugar Ray Youth Foundation in Los Angeles, California, to aid wayward youngsters. Robinson eventually was stricken with Alzheimer's disease and made only limited public appearances. His wife Millie, fully aware of Ray's greatness, jealously protected his privacy and suffering until his death in Culver City, California, on April 12, 1989, at age 67. Perhaps the ultimate compliment came from **Muhammad Ali** in 1975. Ali asserted, "I believe I am the greatest heavyweight of all time, but Ray Robinson was the greatest fighter of all time." Robinson was elected to *The Ring*'s Boxing Hall of Fame in 1967 and the International Boxing Hall of Fame in 1990.

BIBLIOGRAPHY: Sam Andre and Nat Fleischer, *A Pictorial History of Boxing* (New York, 1975); Nat Fleischer, "Maxim Outclassed but Heat Fells Robinson," *The Ring* 31 (September 1952), pp. 4, 41; Nat Fleischer, "Why Does Robinson, at 44, Go on Fighting?" *The Ring* 43 (December 1964), pp. 24, 47; Peter Heller, *In This Corner: Former World Champions Tell Their Stories* (New York, 1973); Bert R. Sugar, ed., *The Ring 1983 Record Book* (New York, 1983); Bert Randolph Sugar, *The 100 Greatest Boxers of All Time* (New York, 1984).

                                                                    John Robertson

WILMA RUDOLPH
(June 23, 1940–November 12, 1994) ———————————— *Track and Field*

Track and field star Wilma Rudolph won three Gold Medals at the 1960 Rome, Italy, Summer Olympic Games. Wilma Glodean Rudolph was born on June 23, 1940, in Bethlehem, Tennessee, the fifth of 8 children of Edward Rudolph, a railroad porter, and Blanche Rudolph, a domestic. With children from other marriages, Rudolph was 1 of 22 children in the family. At age four, Wilma contracted double pneumonia and scarlet fever and did not have use of her left leg for several years. "We thought she would die," her mother feared. "All I can remember is being ill and bedridden," Wilma recalled. "The only thing I really wanted when I was a child," she stated, "was to be normal . . . to be able to run, jump, play, and do all the things the other kids did in my neighborhood." Rudolph walked with a cumbersome brace until age six and a specially made high-top shoe the next five years. The shoe allowed her to walk, but Wilma could not run, jump, or skip like other youngsters. With perseverance, she became more mobile and athletic.

Rudolph competed at Burt High School in Clarksville, Tennessee, in both basketball and track and field. Wilma made All-State in basketball three years, once scoring a State record 49 points in a single game. She also excelled as a sprinter for the Tennessee State Track Club Tigerbelles while still in high school. During her junior year in high school, Rudolph qualified for the U.S. Olympic team in the 200 meters and 4 × 100-meter relay. At the 1956 Melbourne, Australia, Summer Olympic Games, Wilma helped the 400-meter relay team win a Bronze Medal in her first international appearance. She later attended Tennessee State University, starring for the track and field team.

After the 1956 Olympic Games, the six-foot, 130-pound Rudolph competed only sporadically until 1960. Wilma won the National Junior championship at both 75 yards and 100 yards in 1957 but missed the 1958 campaign due to pregnancy with her daughter, Yolanda. In 1959, she triumphed in the 100 meters at the Amateur Athletic Union (AAU) championships and won a Silver Medal in the 100 meters at the Pan-American Games in Chicago, Illinois.

Outstanding success came to Rudolph in 1960. Early that year, Wilma won the AAU title in both the 100 and 200 meters. Rudolph's 200-meter time of 22.9 seconds marked her first individual world record, making her the first woman to break 23 seconds for the half-lap. One week later, she repeated her double victories in both sprints at the Olympic Trials.

The 1960 Summer Olympic Games at Rome, Italy, featured Rudolph winning Gold Medals in her three events—the 100 meters, the 200 meters, and the 4 × 100-meter relay. In the 100, Wilma equaled the world record in the semi-finals with an 11.3-second clocking. Her 11.0-second final time shattered the previous mark but was not allowed as a world record because of a following wind. A few days later, Rudolph set an Olympic record of 23.2 seconds in her opening 200-meter heat and easily won the final in 24.0 seconds. Wilma's Olympic career ended by anchoring the victorious U.S. 400-meter relay team. The 400-meter relay team set a world record of 44.4 seconds in the semi-finals and won a Gold Medal with a 44.5-seconds clocking. On her triumphant European tour, the European press nicknamed her "*la gazelle noire*" (The Black Gazelle) for her beauty, speed, and grace. No American woman had won three Gold Medals in track and field at the same Olympics since Babe Didrickson in 1932. Coach Ed Temple had dreamt before the Olympics that

Rudolph would win both sprints and anchor the 4 × 100-meter relay team to the Gold Medal.

Rudolph then had to deal with worldwide fame. At her first major press conference, Wilma burst into tears because she was unaccustomed to dealing with the crush of the world press. A U.S. official helped the shaken Rudolph away. One reporter warned Wilma, "Your life will never be the same." She discovered, "How right he was."

Rudolph proved even more dominant in 1961, winning the 100-yard dash in 11.1 seconds at the Drake Relays, equaling her 100-meter world record in a USA-USSR dual meet in Moscow, Russia, and breaking that mark a few days later with an 11.2-second sprint at an invitational in Stuttgart, Germany. Wilma also won the 1961 AAU 100-yard title, her third consecutive victory in that event. For her efforts, she earned the 1961 Sullivan Award as the nation's most outstanding amateur athlete. Rudolph's career culminated in 1962 with her fourth consecutive AAU 100 title. Wilma's last race marked one of her most stunning victories. In the USA-USSR dual meet, she overcame a large lead by the Soviet Union on the anchor leg to give the United States a win.

Rudolph won numerous accolades throughout her career. In 1960 and 1961, the Associated Press (AP) selected her Female Athlete of the Year. Her other honors include the 1961 Babe Didrickson Zaharias Award as the nation's outstanding female athlete, 1961 Christopher Columbus Award by the Italian press as the most outstanding international athlete, 1960 Helms Athletic Foundation World Trophy for the North American continent, and 1960 *Los Angeles Times* Award for Women's Track and Field. Wilma was elected to the National Track and Field Hall of Fame in 1974, the International Women's Sports Hall of Fame in 1980, and the U.S. Olympic Hall of Fame in 1983.

The mother of four children established the Wilma Rudolph Foundation, a nonprofit program benefiting disadvantaged children both academically and athletically. Wilma taught school, became a U.S. goodwill ambassador to French West Africa, cohosted a network radio show, and held several business positions. She served as the women's track and field coach and special consultant on minority affairs at DePauw University in Greencastle, Indiana. The elegant Rudolph lectured as a motivational speaker for American youth. "I stress that having self-determination is very important in life, and that athletes can provide very important lessons in that kind of self-determination. Hand-in-hand with athletics must be a strong emphasis on academic achievement. They complement each other in the attainment and maintenance of self-worth and productivity in life itself. My life is proof of that."

Wilma died on November 12, 1994, at her Brentwood, Tennessee, home after battling several months with brain cancer. Ollan Cassell, executive director of USA Track and Field, eulogized, "She was the greatest. The symbol of Wilma equalled that of **Jesse Owens**. I think she was for women what Jesse Owens was for men."

BIBLIOGRAPHY: Michael D. Davis, *Black American Women in Olympic Track and Field: A Complete Illustrated Reference* (Jefferson, NC, 1992); *Des Moines Sunday Register,* November 13, 1994, p. A3; Jon Hendershott, *Track's Greatest Women* (Los Altos, CA, 1987); Bill Mallon and Ian Buchanan, *Quest for Gold: The Encyclopedia of American Olympians* (New York, 1983); James A. Page, *Black Olympian Medalists* (Englewood, CO, 1991).

Bill Mallon

BILL RUSSELL
(February 12, 1934–) ———————————————— *Basketball*

Bill Russell, one of the greatest basketball players ever, moved from a small Jesuit college to 10 National Basketball Association (NBA) titles with the Boston Celtics. New York Knick great Willis Reed lauded Russell, "He stands above all the rest. There are men with God-given ability and there are men who make the most with the skills they've got. Few fit both categories. Russell did."

William Fenton Russell was born on February 12, 1934, in Monroe, Louisiana, to Charles Russell and Katie Russell. The Russells moved from Monroe to Oakland, California, when Bill was only five to escape the prevalent racism of the Deep South. Despite the locale change, the memory of racism led Bill to fight discrimination throughout his career. Shortly thereafter, his parents separated and his mother died. Russell's father worked full-time, spent little time with his sons, and left the elder brother, Charles, to take care of young Bill.

Russell failed to make the basketball team in junior high and barely made McClymonds High School junior varsity as a freshman. Bill continued to grow taller and stronger, playing well enough to earn a basketball scholarship to the University of San Francisco. The Dons were hardly known for their basketball team, but the addition of Russell and guard **K. C. Jones** transformed them to one of the nation's best. By his junior year, Russell had become a six-foot-nine-inch-tall center and one of the nation's most talked about players. During his final two years, he led San Francisco to 55 straight victories, two consecutive number-one rankings, and two NCAA basketball championships and was chosen the Most Valuable Player (MVP) of the 1955 NCAA tournament. San Francisco defeated La Salle University, 77–63, in the 1955 NCAA finals and the University of Iowa, 83–71, in the 1956 NCAA finals. During his career with San Francisco Russell averaged 20.7 points per game and proved a tenacious rebounder. Before joining the NBA, Russell joined the U.S. Olympic team and captured a Gold Medal at the 1956 Melbourne, Australia, Summer Olympics.

To draft Russell, Boston coach Red Auerbach traded veterans "Easy" Ed Macauley and Cliff Hagan to the St. Louis Hawks. Russell signed an NBA contract with the Boston Celtics right after the Olympics for $24,000 a year. The Celtics, under coach Auerbach, contained outstanding offense with future Naismith Memorial Basketball Hall of Famers Macauley, Bob Cousy, and Bill Sharman but lacked the defense to become a championship club. Russell did not exhibit great offensive skills, but his rebounding and shot blocking skills shut down most Celtic opponents. During his rookie season in 1956–1957, Bill pulled down 19.6 rebounds and scored 14.7 points per game to help the Celtics capture their first NBA title. After Russell injured an ankle his second season, the Celtics lost to the St. Louis Hawks for the 1958 NBA crown. Russell's second title came the next year in his third NBA season. Cousy praised Bill, "He meant everything. We didn't win a championship until we got him in 1957, we lost it when he was injured in 1958, and we won it back when he was sound again in 1959." The Celtics did not relinquish the NBA crown again until the 1966–1967 campaign, when the Philadelphia 76ers compiled an outstanding record.

Russell and **Wilt Chamberlain** of the Philadelphia Warriors, San Franciso Warriors, and Philadelphia 76ers engaged in one of the greatest rivalries in all professional sports. Defensive-minded Bill battled Chamberlain, one of the most offensively gifted players of all time. As for who won the rivalry, Chamberlain recalled, "I've been in seven playoffs with Boston where it came down to the final game and Boston won six." Auerbach described Bill as "the single most devastating force in the history of the game. He's his own man." "The foundation of Russell's play," sportwriter Gilbert Rogin observed, is "his admirable mind and purpose, his intelligence—he knows what to do with the ball—and his pride."

Upon the retirement of Auerbach in 1966, Russell took over as player-coach of the Celtics and became the first African-American head coach of a modern major professional sports franchise. Despite the retirement of Cousy, the Russell-coached team made it to the 1967 NBA playoff semi-finals and lost to Chamberlain's Philadelphia 76ers. The Celtics' incredible string of the eight straight titles had ended. Russell remained player-coach for two more seasons, helping the Los Angeles Lakers both seasons to two final NBA titles. His overall record as Celtic coach included 162 wins and 83 losses.

Russell won NBA MVP honors five times in 1958, 1961, 1962, 1963, and 1965 and was named the All-Star Game MVP in 1963, being selected to the All-NBA First Team three times and All-NBA Second Team seven seasons. In 13 campaigns, Bill played 40,726 minutes spanning 963 games, scoring 14,522 points (15.1-point average), and pulling down 21,620 rebounds (22.5 average). Boston captured an amazing 11 NBA crowns, including seven straight, during that time. Statistics unfortunately were not kept on Russell's forte, blocked shots, leaving fans to wonder how many shots he knocked away.

After retiring from the Celtics, Russell was involved in television and acting. In 1973, the Seattle SuperSonics (NBA) hired Bill as coach and general manager. He coached the SuperSonics four seasons, compiling a 162–166 record, and coached the Sacramento Kings (NBA) to a 17–41 mark in 1987–1988. Russell was named to the NBA's 25th and 35th Anniversary All-Time teams in 1970 and 1980, respectively. Bill married Rose Swisher in 1956 and has three children. Russell worked as a sports announcer for WTBS national cable television in Atlanta, Georgia, and wrote two books, *Go Up for Glory* (1966) and *Second Wind: The Memoirs of an Opinionated Man* (1979).

In 1974 Russell was elected (over his personal objections) to the Naismith Memorial Basketball Hall of Fame. In his memoirs, Bill stated, "my intention was to separate myself from the star's idea about fans and fans' ideas about stars. I have very little faith in cheers, what they mean or how long they will last, compared with the faith I have in my own love for the game. The Basketball Hall of Fame is the biggest cheer of all, and it means testimonials, dinners, souvenirs and memories. As an ex-athlete, I don't think that diet is good for me, or my relationship with others."

BIBLIOGRAPHY: Arthur Ashe, Jr., *A Hard Road to Glory: A History of the African-American Athlete Since 1946*, vol. 3 (New York, 1988); Associated Press, *The Sports Immortals* (Englewood Cliffs, NJ, 1972); *Contemporary Authors*, vol. 108 (1983), pp. 415–417; Bill Russell with Taylor Branch, *Second Wind: The Memoirs of an Opinionated Man* (New York, 1979); Bill Russell and William McSweeny, *Go Up for Glory* (New York, 1966); Edna Rust and Art Rust Jr., *Art Rust's Illustrated History of the Black Athlete* (Garden City, NY, 1985).

Brian L. Laughlin

BARRY SANDERS
(July 16, 1968–) ———————————————————————— *Football*

Barry Sanders won the Heisman Trophy and two National Football League (NFL) rushing titles. Barry David Sanders was born on July 16, 1968, in Wichita, Kansas, the son of William "Willie" Sanders, a self-employed carpenter and roofer, and Shirley Sanders. Sanders was the sixth of 11 children, including two older brothers, Boyd and Byron. William, a strong-minded father, encouraged Barry's interest in sports but also emphasized humility, Christian values, self-discipline, and Bible study. Another positive influence was his oldest brother, Boyd, who overcame a troubled youth to enter the ministry. Sanders got into his share of fights in school, throwing rocks at cars and stealing candy from local groceries. He recalls, "One time I started a fire on the floor of our bathroom at home. One time Byron and I got arrested for trespassing at Wichita State." The deeper training ultimately prevailed, when Barry's adolescent interests turned toward physical conditioning and sports. He and Byron often spent weekend nights running up and down the stairs of Wichita Stadium to build up their wind and endurance.

As a child, Sanders played keep-away and pickup football games on local sandlots. Barry did not play organized football until ninth grade, when he stood 5 feet tall and weighed 105 pounds. At North High School in Wichita, the coaching staff used Sanders as a defensive back and deemed him too small at five foot eight inches and 170 pounds for running back. Barry finally became starting running back his senior year for the last five games of the 1985 season. During that span, he gained over 1,000 rushing yards to set an All-City record with 1,417 yards.

Despite such an attainment, Sanders was not well recruited. Barry wanted to attend the University of Oklahoma like his idol, Billy Sims, but only the University of Tulsa, Iowa State University, and Oklahoma State University made scholarship offers. He chose Oklahoma State because it offered the best business administration program.

As a freshman in 1986, Sanders played sparingly behind future All-Pro **Thurman Thomas** and Mitch Nash, a former Oklahoma High School Player of the Year. Barry remembers biding his time: "I was completely content with what I was doing there. . . . I wasn't expected to play. But I remember my father always saying that the cream rises to the top." Sanders rushed 74 times for 350 yards and two touchdowns. Barry spent much time in the weight room during the off-season, bulking up to 200 pounds and enlarging his already well-developed legs to the size of tree trunks. During his free time, Sanders enjoyed studying and spending much quiet time in his dorm room. The room became a welcome haven after Barry grew up in a house filled with 13 people. The lively bar scene in Stillwater held no interest for him at all.

In 1987 as a sophomore, Sanders began the season with a bang by returning a kickoff 100 yards for a touchdown on opening day against Tulane University. The following week, Barry returned a punt 68 yards for a score against the University of Houston. By the end of the year, he alternated at tailback with Thomas and ultimately carried the ball 111 times for 622 yards and nine touchdowns. Sanders finished the year first in kickoff returns and second in punt returns and was selected as All-America kick returner. Notoriety phased Barry little, as he remained quiet, modest, and self-contained. He dressed simply, avoiding gold chains, jewelry, and even watches. As Sanders once noted, "I feel uncomfortable being valued because of how well I play football. I'm an average person. I really am."

Barry's junior year at Oklahoma State marked his *annus mirabilis*, as he set 32 NCAA records. He rushed 344 times for 2,628 yards, 39 touchdowns, and a glittering 7.6-yard average. His 295.5 all-purpose yards per game broke Whizzer White's 1937 University of Colorado record of 246.3 yards. Likewise, Sanders's total rushing yards exceeded the 2,342 yards run off by **Marcus Allen** at the University of Southern California in 1981. Barry's touchdown total broke the old record of 29, shared by Lydell Mitchell of Penn State University and Mike Rozier of the University of Nebraska. With Sanders at tailback, the 9–2 Cowboys compiled a third-place Big Eight Conference (BEC) finish and destroyed the University of Wyoming, 62–14, in the Holiday Bowl. Ironically, Barry's two best games came in losing efforts against BEC arch-rivals Nebraska and Oklahoma. He rushed for 215 yards and 2 touchdowns against the Sooners and rambled for 189 yards and 4 touchdowns against the Cornhuskers.

Sanders won the Heisman Trophy overwhelmingly, although he personally favored quarterback Rodney Peete of the University of Southern California. Barry, the first junior to win the award since **Herschel Walker** of the University of Georgia in 1982, joined such distinguished company as Doc Blanchard, Doak Walker, Vic Janowicz, Roger Staubach, **Archie Griffin,** and his hero, Billy Sims. Sanders also was named *The Sporting News* Football Player of the Year and recipient of the Walter Camp Player of the Year and Maxwell Awards.

Barry planned to attend his senior year at Oklahoma State, but the Cowboys' placement on probation and family financial pressure made him reconsider. His father, Willie, opposed Barry's playing one more year for Oklahoma State: "Why should he risk those legs of gold for nothing?" Similarly, Barry considered Big Eight football a full-time job involving 50 to 60 hours a week for which he was not paid. He was tired of bagging groceries part-time in Stillwater, Oklahoma, for pocket money. Sanders observed that academic pressures and the Heisman attention took their tolls: "I'm still trying to finish up finals from the first semester. . . . It's been kind of hectic the last few months." Sanders applied for and received a draft exemption from the NFL. Barry was drafted in the first round by the Detroit Lions (NFL) in 1989 as the third overall pick behind Troy Aikman and Tony Mandarich.

Coach Wayne Fontes's "silver stretch" Lion offense seemed tailor-made for the quick, explosive Sanders. As the only back with four wideouts, Barry raced for 1,470 yards (5.3-yard average) and 14 touchdowns in 1990 to break team records set by Sims. He finished second in rushing behind Kansas City's Christian Okoye (1,480 yards) and won NFL Rookie of the Year honors. Sanders, also selected All-Pro, started as running back for the National Football Conference (NFC) in the Pro Bowl. Barry remembered his offensive line, giving each player a Rolex watch and a $10,000 check.

Since his rookie year, Sanders has continued to improve. Chicago Bears defensive end Trace Armstrong summed up his great talent: "He's like a little sports car. He can stop on a dime and go zero to sixty in seconds." Barry won the NFL rushing title in 1991, racking up 1,304 yards on 255 attempts for a 5.1-yard average and 13 touchdowns. In 1991, the Lions captured the Central Division crown but lost to the Washington Redskins in the NFC title game. Sanders again excelled in 1992, totaling 1,548 yards with an NFL-leading 16 rushing touchdowns. Although Detroit fell to 5–11, Barry still ran for 1,352 yards, was selected to the All-NFL Second Team, and started in the Pro Bowl for the fourth straight year. Despite a season-ending injury in 1993, he still gained 1,115 yards in 243 attempts for 3 touchdowns and a 4.6-yard rushing average. In September 1994, Sanders gained nearly 200 yards to help the Lions upset the defending Super Bowl champion Dallas Cowboys, 20–17.

Barry won his second NFL rushing title that year, gaining 1,883 yards on 331 carries for a 5.7-yard average and 7 touchdowns. His honors included making the All-NFL First Team for the fifth time and the Pro Bowl for the sixth time. Through 1994, he rushed 1,763 times for 8,672 yards (4.9-yard average) and 62 touchdowns and caught 210 passes for 1,782 yards and 6 touchdowns.

Although a premier athlete and media personality, Sanders maintains a reserved manner and modest lifestyle. Barry has changed his own car's tire in the Silverdome parking lot and was appalled by $900 suit price tags in the exclusive Barney's menswear shop in New York. The deeply religious Sanders tithes regularly to his Baptist Church in Wichita, conducts a game-day chapel service, and leads a Bible study group every Wednesday night. Upon winning the Heisman Trophy, Barry used the honor to reach young people with an important message: "I have never used drugs. I try to study and stay out of trouble." Perhaps the most important part of his life is the religious part: "There is a notion that being a Christian makes a person soft, passive, and limp. I believe a real man is a man of God." Sanders, still single, practices celibacy.

BIBLIOGRAPHY: Paul Attner, "Small Size, But Big Chunks," *The Sporting News*, December 19, 1988, pp. 12–13; *Current Biography Yearbook* (1993), pp. 504–507; Thomas George, "Pro Football: Carrying Teammates and the Ball," *New York Times*, October 20, 1991, p. 8–1; Bob Hersom, "Mr. Touchdown and Mr. Nice Guy," *The Sporting News*, October 24, 1988, p. 34; Tom Kowalski, "Sanders Left Other Players in Awe," *The Sporting News*, January 15, 1990, pp. 12–14; William Ladson, "Two for the 90's," *Sport* 81 (August 1990), pp. 56–58; Austin Murphy, "A Lamb Among Lions," *Sports Illustrated* 73 (September 10, 1990), pp. 60–66; William Nack, "Barry Breaks Away," *Sports Illustrated* 70 (April 10, 1989), pp. 24–31; David L. Porter, ed., *Biographical Dictionary of American Sports: 1989–1992 Supplement for Baseball, Football, Basketball, and Other Sports* (Westport, CT, 1992); "Sanders Was Unstoppable in Heisman Voting, Too," *The Sporting News*, December 12, 1988, p. 31; Rick Telander, "Big Hand for a Quiet Man," *Sports Illustrated* 69 (December 12, 1988), pp. 46–48; "Walter Camp Prize to Sanders," *The Sporting News*, December 5, 1988, p. 34.

John H. Ziegler

DEION SANDERS
(August 9, 1967–) _____ *Football and Baseball*

Deion Sanders, one of the most versatile athletes in American sports history, starred in college football, baseball, and track and field and plays both professional football and baseball. Basketball, however, proved Deion's favorite sport. He was chosen Second Team All-State at North Fort Myers, Florida, High School, averaging 24 points per game as a senior.

Deion Luwynn Sanders was born on August 9, 1967, at Fort Myers, Florida, to Fred Sanders and Connie Sanders, but his parents soon divorced. Connie, who married Willie Knight about five years later, remained the primary influence in Deion's life. She encouraged him to play sports and to avoid the drug environment, which permeated their neighborhood. Deion claimed that athletics saved him from a life of crime. "It would've been easy for me to sell drugs," he recalled. "But I had to practice. My friends didn't have practice; they went straight to the streets and never left."

Sanders began his sports career with T-ball at age 5. As a Little League baseball player, Deion used his speed to steal home plate regularly. He began to play Pop Warner football at age 10 and helped his team win the 1979 national championship. He played quarterback, running back, and safety and scored an estimated 120 touchdowns in three years, leading his squad to a 38–1 win-loss record. His mother especially wanted Deion to play football, while his stepfather urged him to concentrate on baseball.

At North Fort Myers High School, Sanders was named to Southwest Florida All-Star teams in football, basketball, and baseball and was selected High School Athlete of the Year as a senior. Deion, a quarterback, running back, and safety in football, gained 839 yards passing and 499 yards rushing as a senior. "He was a great safety," his football coach recalled. "The other team didn't throw many passes in the middle of the field with Deion there. He'd pick them off." A basketball teammate nicknamed him "Prime Time" because of his flair for the spectacular.

Sanders entered Florida State University as a freshman in 1985 but did not play quarterback because the Seminoles featured a pro passing attack. Deion started at cornerback for four years, scoring six touchdowns on punts and interception returns and earning consensus All-America honors as a junior and senior. After finishing third in the balloting for the Jim Thorpe Award his junior year, he won that honor his final season as the nation's top defensive back. As a senior, Sanders led the nation in punt returns with a 15.2-yard average. The Seminoles defeated the University of Nebraska, 31–28, in the 1988 Fiesta Bowl and Auburn University, 20–17, in the 1989 Sugar Bowl.

Sanders also performed well in baseball and track and field. An outfielder in baseball, Deion played on the fifth-place team at the 1987 College World Series and was selected a 1988 pre-season All-America. He competed in track and field instead, winning the 100-meter and 200-meter sprints and running the third leg of the 4×100 championship relay team in the Metro Conference meet. Florida State named Sanders its Most Valuable Performer. At the NCAA Track and Field championships, Deion achieved All-America recognition. His 100-meter and 200-meter times qualified him for the 1988 Summer Olympic Trials, but he declined to try out. He skipped spring college sports altogether his senior year to sign a contract with the New York Yankees American League (AL) baseball club.

Sanders spent the 1988 and 1989 seasons in the Yankees minor league organization, batting .234 and stealing 1 base in 14 games for New York in 1989. Deion split the 1990 campaign between Columbus, Ohio, of the International League and New York, hitting only .158 and pilfering 8 bases for the

Yankees. The Atlanta Braves National League (NL) organization acquired him in 1991 and alternated him with Otis Nixon in center field the next three seasons. Sanders hit .304, stole 26 bases, and led the NL in triples in 1992. In the 1992 World Series against the Toronto Blue Jays, Deion batted .533 and stole 5 bases. He became only the third player ever to move directly from a World Series to professional football. Versatile Jim Thorpe and Greasy Neale also accomplished that remarkable feat. Atlanta traded him to the Cincinnati Reds (NL) in May 1994, but his campaign ended prematurely in August with the baseball player strike. Through 1994, Deion has batted .263 with 46 doubles, 28 triples, 27 home runs, 113 runs batted in (RBIs), and 103 stolen bases in 409 games. In July 1995, the Cincinnati Reds traded Sanders to the San Francisco Giants (NL).

The Atlanta Falcons selected Sanders as the fifth player taken in the 1989 National Football League (NFL) draft. Deion earned *The Sporting News* All-Pro honors as a defensive back from 1991 through 1994, was named All-Pro kick returner in 1992, and performed in the Pro Bowl from 1991 through 1994. His NFL career with the Falcons featured 24 interceptions for 520 yards and three touchdowns, 93 punt returns for 789 yards and two touchdowns, and 147 kickoff returns for 3,888 yards and three touchdowns. No other major leaguer has repeated his 1989 feat of clouting a home run and scoring a touchdown the same week. Sanders, who relishes his role as a versatile athlete, maintained, "I've always said I love football and that baseball is my girlfriend."

The San Francisco 49ers (NFL) signed Sanders as a free agent in September 1994. Upon returning to Atlanta to face the Falcons, Deion returned an interception for a touchdown. Sanders earned National Football Conference (NFC) Defensive Player of the Year honors in 1994, intercepting 6 passes for 303 yards (50.5-yard average) and 3 touchdowns. In Super Bowl XXIX, the 49ers routed the San Diego Chargers, 49–26. "Neon Deion" always found the spotlight in any sports event in which he participated. Sanders, whose goals included being famous, wealthy, and admired, especially desired "success. Enormous success." Deion lives in Alpharetta, Georgia, an Atlanta suburb, with Carolyn Chambers, his fiancée. They have one daughter, Deiondra, and one son, Deion, Jr.

BIBLIOGRAPHY: *Atlanta Braves Media Guide* (1993); Barbara Bigelow, ed., *Contemporary Black Biography,* vol. 4 (Detroit, MI, 1993); Florida State University, Sports Information files, Tallahassee, FL; Ed Hinton, "One Thing or . . . the Other," *Sports Illustrated* 76 (April 27, 1992), pp. 38–40, 45; Peter King, "Time for a Game Plan," *Sports Illustrated* 77 (August 24, 1992), pp. 20–23; Curry Kirkpatrick, "They Don't Pay Nobody to Be Humble," *Sports Illustrated* 71 (November 13, 1989), pp. 52–56, 58–60; Dave Scheiber, "Decisions, Decisions," *Sports Illustrated* 71 (July 3, 1989), pp. 30–32, 34; *The Sporting News Official Baseball Register* (1994); *The Sporting News Pro Football Register* (1994); Stew Thornbury, *Deion Sanders, Prime Time Player* (Minneapolis, MN, 1993); Rick Weinberg, "Deion Sanders," *Sport* 85 (July 1994), pp. 68–70, 72–73.

Robert T. Bowen, Jr.

GALE SAYERS

(May 30, 1943–) ——————————————————————— *Football*

Gale Sayers enjoyed one of the most spectacular rookie seasons in professional football history. Sayers, one of America's most legendary African-American athletes, was born in Wichita, Kansas, on May 30, 1943. His father, Roger, worked as an auto mechanic. As a young child, Sayers moved with his parents to Omaha, Nebraska. At Central High School in Omaha, Gale performed sensationally in track and field and football.

Understandably, numerous colleges heavily recruited Sayers. Historian **Arthur Ashe, Jr.,** claimed Gale signed 17 letters of intent! Sayers eventually selected the University of Kansas, where coach Jack Mitchell made much of his extraordinary talents. He not only possessed great acceleration but protected the ball well and possessed the ability to stop, turn, and thread his way through defenses. Gale, an elusive, intelligent running back, was cast in the mold of **Barry Sanders** of the mid-1990s.

In both 1963 and 1964, Sayers was named an All-America halfback at the University of Kansas. As a 20-year-old, Gale gained 1,125 yards on 158 carries. His 7.1-yard rushing average led the nation. He set many Big Eight Conference (BEC) records as a Jayhawk, rushing for 2,675 yards, catching passes for 408 yards, and adding 835 yards on kick returns.

Despite Sayers's stellar achievements at Kansas, reservations remained about Gale's ability to repeat his collegiate successes in the tougher arena of the National Football League (NFL). Otto Graham, the 1965 College All-Stars coach, refused to play him in the summer classic in Chicago. The six-foot, 199-pound Sayers was built along classic lines with the powerful torso of a football player and the long, explosive legs of the track runner.

Gale was selected the number-one draft pick by both the Kansas City Chiefs American Football League (AFL) club and the Chicago Bears (NFL). The mid-1960s saw professional football in turmoil with acrimonious exchanges between the AFL and the NFL. He picked the Bears, believing that he would receive lots of playing time in the NFL.

Bears coach George Halas wanted to bring Sayers slowly along because Gale already had experienced some serious injuries. In the pre-season, however, the rookie demonstrated his rare athleticism. Against the Los Angeles Rams, Sayers thundered to a 77-yard punt return, reeled off a 93-yard kickoff return, and then fired a 25-yard southpaw pass for a touchdown to help the Bears win, 28–14.

In his second regular-season game, Gale faced the Rams again. He ran 80 yards with a screen pass and threw another touchdown pass, highlighting a 31–6 Bears victory. Rosey Grier, the Rams' great tackle, noted, "I hit him so hard. I thought my shoulder must have busted him in two. I heard a roar from the crowd and figured he had fumbled. Then there he was, 15 yards away and going for the score."

On December 12, 1965, Sayers may have turned in the greatest single-game running performance in professional football history. Gale came close to emulating the incredible exploits of Red Grange of the University of Illinois, who carried the ball 21 times for 402 yards and five touchdowns against the University of Michigan Wolverines on October 18, 1924. In the Bears 61–20 thumping of the San Francisco 49ers, Sayers scored six touchdowns on an 80-yard pass reception, four relatively short rushes, and an 85-yard punt return. His extraordinary exhibition of brilliance took place on a slippery, muddy field. George Halas, the grand old man of professional football with nearly one-half century of coaching under his belt, acknowledged, "It was the greatest performance I have ever seen on the football field."

Sayers, NFL Rookie of the Year in 1965, was named a unanimous All-NFL selection from 1965 to 1969 and led the NFL in rushing in 1966 and 1968. During his NFL career, Gale rushed for 4,956 yards on 991 carries and tallied 39 touchdowns. He also caught 112 passes for 1,307 yards (11.7-yard average) and 9 touchdowns. Gale returned 91 kickoffs for 2,781 yards (30.6-yard average) and 6 touchdowns and 27 punts for 391 yards and 2 touchdowns. Altogether, Gale established eight NFL and 15 Chicago Bears records. In 1969, he received the George Halas Award as professional football's most courageous player.

In the ninth game of the 1968 season, Sayers suffered the first of several critical injuries. A crushing tackle on his right knee resulted in massive ligament damage. Although Gale gained 1,032 yards to take his second rushing title a year later, his electrifying surge of speed remained just a memory. The *Chicago Daily News* lamented, "Gone are that instant acceleration from medium to top speed and the incomparable ability to change directions on a dime without hesitation or loss of speed." Sadly, a preseason 1970 injury caused serious ligament damage to his left knee. Although rehabilitation and repeated surgeries seemed promising, Sayers quit during the 1972 preseason. Don Smith wrote, "The old magic had simply vanished." Despite a relatively short 4½-year career, Gale gained 9,435 combined net yards. In three of his four Pro Bowls, he won Offensive Player of the Game honors.

From 1976 to 1981, Sayers served as athletic director at Southern Illinois University in Carbondale. Gale then entered private business and authored or coauthored two books. He and his wife, Ardie Bullard of Omaha, Nebraska, have six children, Gary, Guy, Gaylon, Gale, Lynne, Scott, and Timmy.

In 1977, the Pro Football Hall of Fame enshrined him. At age 34, Sayers became the youngest inductee and may have experienced the shortest playing time of any Hall of Famer. *The Sporting News* named him NFL Rookie of the Year in 1965 and placed him on its NFL Western Conference (WC) All-Star Team from 1965 to 1969. Sayers was selected to the All-Time NFL Team in 1969 and 1994, the All-NFL Team of the 1960s, and the AFL-NFL 1960–

1984 All-Star Second Team. Gale also was enshrined in the National Football Foundation College Football Hall of Fame, the Kansas Sports Hall of Fame, and the Black Athletes Hall of Fame. No journalistic accolade quite captured just how special he was. He was likened to a "twisting tornado on the Kansas plains" and remembered for "fluid, will-of-the-wisp ball-carrying thrusts." The Hall of Fame's Selection Committee commended Sayers, "There never was another to compare with him. What else is there to say!"

Gale declined an athletic scholarship at the University of Nebraska because the Cornhuskers, although having 44 African-American athletes on scholarship, had only two African-American female students. At Kansas his senior year, he participated in a sit-in to protest racial discrimination in campus housing. In 1967, Sayers supported boxer **Muhammad Ali,** who refused to be drafted into the Vietnam War. Despite leaving Kansas degreeless, Gale subsequently completed his undergraduate degree there and also earned a graduate degree at his alma mater. His special hobbies remain jazz and pool.

The depth of Sayers's character is illuminated in the 1970 television movie *Brian's Song.* The story memorializes Brian Piccolo, his Bears' teammate, who died of cancer. The teleplay, based on Gale's autobiography *I Am Third,* was written by William Blinn. Movie critic Leonard Maltin described *Brian's Song* as both "exceptional" and "outstanding," rating the piece as a "milestone of excellence in made-for-TV movies."

BIBLIOGRAPHY: Arthur Ashe, Jr., *A Hard Road to Glory: A History of the African-American Athlete Since 1946,* vol. 3 (New York, 1988); Leonard Maltin, *Movies and TV Guide: 1988* (New York, 1987); David L. Porter, ed., *Biographical Dictionary of American Sports: Football* (Westport, CT, 1987); Don Smith, "Gale Sayers Enshrinee," Release, Pro Football Hall of Fame, Canton, OH, 1977.

Scott A.G.M. Crawford

WENDELL SCOTT
(August 12, 1931–December 23, 1990) —————— *Stock Car Racing*

Wendell Scott pioneered among African-American stock car racers. Wendell was born on August 12, 1931, in Danville, Virginia, and studied at Danville High School, leaving after eleventh grade. He did not perform especially well in athletics or academics but played baseball enthusiastically. Baseball remained his lifelong interest. During World War II, Scott served in the U.S. Army from 1942 to 1945 and saw military service in Cheyenne, Wyoming, and the European sector. An able mechanic, Wendell ended his war service in charge of a convoy of trucks.

Scott joined Grand National racing in 1961 at Spartanburg, South Carolina. Wendell's initial success, however, had come in 1959, when he won the sportsman racing championship at Southside Speedway in Richmond, Virginia. The same year, he captured the Virginia Championship for sportsmen auto drivers.

During his early years, Scott struggled for the financial backing necessary to turn out a competitive racing machine. In one race, Wendell endured the frustration of a broken seat *and* gas pedal.

During the 1961 racing season, Scott ranked thirty-second in national point standings. In 1962, Wendell showed his true racing form. At the wheel of a 1961 Chevrolet, he started 41 races and finished among the top 10 on 17 occasions. In 1963, Scott started 47 races with 15 top-10 finishes. Wendell still drove his faithful 1961 Chevrolet, logging 6,163.4 miles in competitive racing. He recorded his only 1963 National Association for Stock Car Auto Racing (NASCAR) victory at Jacksonville, Florida, race. His next best performance that year came in a fifth place at Spartanburg, South Carolina.

In 1964, Scott began the season in a newer 1962 Chevrolet vehicle. Halfway through the season, Wendell opted for a 1963 Ford and immediately enjoyed greater success. With the Ford, he generated greater acceleration and started being a "charger." The 5-foot-11-inch 165-pounder finished sixth in the Grand National standings in 1966, earning $16,780 in 45 starts, finishing 3 times among the top 5, and ranking 17 times in the top 10. For many years, he occupied the spotlight as the only African-American driver on the circuit.

Scott and his wife Mary lived in Danville, Virginia. They had six children, Wendell, Jr., Frankie, Ann, Deborah, Kay, and Sybil. He held memberships in the American Legion, Veterans of Foreign Wars, and the Baptist Church. Like many auto racers, Wendell possessed superstitious foibles. He never wore green or allowed green coloring on his automobile or allowed peanuts to be consumed in his pits or garage area.

Scott launched his racing career just as NASCAR began to achieve momentum as a sport. The Daytona International Speedway opened in 1959, while speedways opened at Atlanta, Georgia, and Charlotte, North Carolina, in 1960. ABC televised the 1961 Firecracker 400 race at Daytona Beach, Florida, for the "Wide World of Sports" series, signifying national coverage for the sport.

Scott pioneered athletically. An Associated Press (AP) news story dated December 2, 1963, reported, "Wendell Scott, a Negro from Danville, Virginia, yesterday became the first of his race to win a Grand National stock car race and he did it convincingly." In an April 4, 1966, interview, Wendell acknowledged encountering prejudice: "Every now and then somebody would holler something smart alec at me. They still do it once in a while, but nowadays somebody sitting next to them usually shames 'em down."

Scott's best NASCAR season came in 1969, when he finished 11 times in the top 10 and collected $27,542 in prize money. In May 1973, Scott was involved in a 19-vehicle car wreck during the Talladega race. Wendell's 1971 Mercury was demolished, and he suffered the first serious injuries of his racing career. He ended up with three fractured ribs, two fractures in the pelvic girdle, a fractured right knee, two fractures of the left knee, a fractured leg, and an arm laceration that necessitated 60 stitches. Nevertheless, his son Frankie said of his then-51-year-old father, "He's not old, I figure he'll be around five or six more years."

In 1974, Wendell discussed the paucity of African Americans entering auto racing: "Most of them aren't willing to work. They aren't willing to do the hard, greasy labor, sometimes all day and night, that goes into building and maintaining a race day machine so that it'll make the next race."

At his Danville, Virginia, funeral, many NASCAR drivers paid respects to the pioneer starting over 500 Grand National races and finishing among the top five 20 times. Scott died on December 23, 1990, at age 69, having suffered from spinal cancer, bilateral pneumonia, high blood pressure, and kidney ailments. He frequently described himself as an aging pugilist: "I guess I'm like a washed-up prize fighter. He knows it's the last round, and he knows he's beat, but he keeps trying to land that knock-out punch."

The 1977 Warner Brothers movie *Greased Lightning* reviewed Scott's career. Richard Pryor's portrayal of Wendell, both typically frantic and frenetic, has captured the pioneer's feisty nature and delightful sense of humor.

BIBLIOGRAPHY: "Age, Not Race, Hurts Scott," *Charlotte [NC] Observer*, April 4, 1966; Clyde Bolton, "Talladega Crash a Heavy Blow to the Scott Family," *Birmingham [AL] News*, May 11, 1973; Jim Hunter, "Dignity on an Oval Track," courtesy of Bob Mauk, NASCAR, Daytona Beach, FL; Bob Mauk, assorted materials and short biographical sketches, NASCAR, Daytona Beach, FL; "Negro Stock Car Driver Finds Age, Not Race, to Be Handicap," *Greenville [SC] News*, April 4, 1966; "Racers Salute Scott," *Sanford [NC] Herald*, December 27, 1990.

Scott A.G.M. Crawford

ART SHELL
(November 26, 1946–) ——————————————— *Football*

Art Shell made National Football League (NFL) history as only the second NFL African-American head coach. Arthur Shell was born on November 26, 1946, in Charleston, South Carolina, the son of Arthur Shell, Sr, a laborer in a paper mill, and Gertrude Shell. Shell, the oldest of five children, grew up in the Daniel Jenkins Project in Charleston. In this "nice" red-brick project, Art lived in a homey atmosphere where African-American Baptist residents watched out for one another. He very fondly remembered his sickly mother, who died of heart failure at 35: "I was very close to her," he reflected, "closer to her than my father, because I was with her so much. She loved to talk, and I loved to listen." With his mother gone, 15-year-old Art filled the gap by washing dishes, cleaning house, and cooking. His sister, Eartha Smalls, related, "He ran the house as my dad would. He told us life must go on and we had to pull together."

Shell graduated from segregated Bonds-Wilson High School in North Charleston, South Carolina, in 1964, starring in both basketball and football.

Art attended Maryland State College (now Maryland State–Eastern Shore College), earning a B.S. degree in industrial arts education in 1968. At Maryland State, he played center in both basketball and football and later starred at tackle both ways on the gridiron. On the hardwood, his playing style blended finesse and strength reminiscent of **Charles Barkley.** Shell really excelled on the gridiron as an offensive and defensive tackle, winning All-Central Intercollegiate Athletic Association honors from 1965 to 1967, earning All-America status from *Ebony* magazine and the *Pittsburgh Courier* in 1966 and 1967, and being selected Little All-America in 1967 as a senior.

The six-foot-five-inch, 285-pound Shell was drafted in the third round as the eightieth overall selection by the Oakland Raiders American Football League (AFL) club in the 1968 AFL-NFL draft. Art instantly won fame as a hard-driving pass and run blocker, whose combination of speed and bulk made it difficult for defenses to handle. Lyle Alzado, who played with and against Shell, stressed, "I never knew a defensive lineman who got the better of him." Art's most notable game perhaps occurred in Super Bowl XI, a Raiders' 32–14 victory over the Minnesota Vikings. Shell's primary blocking assignment involved containing All-Pro defensive end Jim Marshall, who made no tackles or assists. Raiders' backs rambled for 266 rushing yards, mostly behind Art and close friend, left guard **Gene Upshaw.**

Shell, an iron man even by Raider standards, played 207 career games, ranking third in team appearances behind Upshaw and fearsome Jim Otto. Art enjoyed a superb career, making the Pro Bowl eight times. He was named to *The Sporting News* All-Star team three times and played for two Super Bowl championship teams, the 1976 and 1980 Raiders. Shell's playing career was highlighted by his introduction into the Pro Football Hall of Fame in 1989, an honor only diminished by the death of his father that same year from complications due to diabetes. Art contracted the same disease in 1993.

Since high school, Shell had expressed interest in teaching and coaching. As an NFL player, Art routinely took copious notes in his playbook, asked questions about overall strategy in team meetings, and reviewed film at home. He memorized the assignments of every player on every play to more fully grasp the complexities of the game. John Madden, head coach of the Raiders, therefore, approached Shell during his fifth season in 1972 about someday coaching. Art volunteered as a football coach with the University of California at Berkeley in their 1981–1982 spring practices. When Shell retired as a player in 1982, Al Davis, the Raiders general manager, hired him first as a scout, promoted him to offensive line coach in 1983, and named him head coach in 1989.

On October 3, 1989, Shell became the first NFL African-American coach since **Fritz Pollard** had directed the Hammond, Indiana, Pros from 1923 to 1925. With characteristic diffidence, Art minimized the accomplishment, stating, "The main thing is I know who I am and I'm proud of it. But I'm also a Raider and I don't believe the color of my skin entered into this decision. . . . I was the right person at this time to be the head coach." Others, including his friend Upshaw, viewed the appointment in more historical terms. Upshaw, who believed Shell was fulfilling a **Jackie Robinson** or **Marion Motley** ground-breaking role, observed "He's going to be walking in sand where there's no footprints."

Shell took over a demoralized 1–3 team and immediately made some key changes. Art abolished many of the rules laid down by his predecessor and lectured his players on what it meant to be a Raider, often reviving memories of the glory days of Ken Stabler, Otto, and Daryle Lamonica. The team responded, performing 7–5 the rest of the year. The 12–4 Raiders reached the 1990 American Football Conference (AFC) championship game before being humiliated, 51–3, by the Buffalo Bills.

Art remains shy, soft-spoken, but extremely self-confident. "I have never doubted myself," he asserts. Raiders players find that his bulk can assume a quiet menace, as he drapes his huge arm around an erring athlete to deliver a few fatherly words of advice on a blown assignment or a bonehead mistake. He projects an image of a strict but loving parent who expects the very best from his charges at all times. The kind, understanding Shell gives generous credit to his coaching predecessors. Madden taught Art people skills and motivational techniques, while Tom Flores counseled patience and Mike Shanahan organization. The analytical, patient Shell rarely loses his temper, but team members sit up and take notice when he does. During an October 1994 game, Art benched Jeff Hostetler following a verbal disagreement with the quarterback on the sidelines. Los Angeles finished 9–7 in 1994, but missed the playoffs. In January 1995, Mike White replaced Shell as head coach. Art, who had compiled a 56–41 mark with the Raiders, joined the Kansas City Chiefs (NFL) as offensive line coach in February 1995. Shell and wife Janice have two sons, Arthur III and Christopher.

BIBLIOGRAPHY: Jay Lawrence, "Shell Breaks NFL Barrier," *The Sporting News,* October 16, 1989, p. 54; Jill Lieber, "Dreams Do Come True," *Sports Illustrated* 71 (October 23, 1989), pp. 74–78; Scott Ostler, "No Better Coach," *Los Angeles Magazine* 36 (October 1991), pp. 88–94; Jeannie Parks and Lorenzo Benet, "Wins, Not Race, Are the Issue for New Raiders Coach Art Shell," *People Weekly* 5 (December 4, 1989), pp. 95–96; David L. Porter, ed., *Biographical Dictionary of American Sports: Football* (Westport, CT, 1987); Lou Ransom, "Black Named NFL Coach After 7 Decades," *Jet* 77 (October 23, 1989), pp. 48–50.

John H. Ziegler

CHARLIE SIFFORD
(June 2, 1922–) ——————————————————————— *Golf*

"Don't miss it, Darkie." "Go back to the cotton fields." "Hey, boy, carry my bag." Fourteen years after **Jackie Robinson** broke organized baseball's color line, these were some of the more printable taunts that Charlie Sifford faced as he became the first African-American golfer to play in the 1961 Greater

Greensboro, North Carolina, Open. Incredibly, the harassment continued for much of the first round. But Charlie persevered, shooting a 72 that day and finishing fourth in the tournament.

Unfortunately, Sifford's poise and self-restraint did not mean that he had overcome racism forever. Until November 1961, the constitution of the Professional Golfers Association (PGA) still declared that the PGA was open only to "professional golfers of the Caucasian race." Even after such blatant racism disappeared, Sifford and other African-American golfers, including Lee Elder, Jim Thorpe, and **Calvin Peete,** battled more insidious forms of discrimination. Remarkably, Charlie has continued his fight for nearly half a century.

Charles Luther Sifford was born on June 2, 1922, in Charlotte, North Carolina, the third of six children of Roscoe Sifford, a laborer, and Eliza Sifford. Charlie grew up "in a strict Baptist household where my mother was the boss." Upon starting to caddy at age 10 at the Carolina Country Club (for fifty cents a bag and a dime tip), Sifford also commenced to play golf there. (Within two years, he also began smoking his trademark cigars.) White professionals Clayton Heafner and Sutton Alexander noted Charlie's obsession with the game and encouraged him to develop his skills. But even as a youth, Sifford realized the severe limits on an African-American golfer's career in the South.

In 1940, after an altercation with a white Charlotte shopkeeper, Sifford moved to Philadelphia, Pennsylvania, to live with his uncle. For over three years, Charlie worked as a shipping clerk for the National Biscuit Company. He honed his golf game at Cobbs Creek, a public course where he competed, and then teamed with local legend Howard Wheeler. Sifford was drafted into the U.S. Army in 1943 and then served in the 79th Signal Heavy Construction, taking part in the landing on Okinawa. Following his discharge in 1946, Charlie played in that year's National Negro Open. The United Golf Association held the tournament. Sifford then moved to Detroit, where he so impressed singer/band leader Billy Eckstine that the entertainer made him his personal golf pro. For the next decade, Charlie worked for Eckstine and entered many Negro tour events while waiting for a chance to play in PGA events.

Sifford's first win on the Negro tour came at the 1951 Southern Open in Atlanta, Georgia. Despite the continued competition from Wheeler, Bill Spiller, and Ted Rhodes, among others, Charlie began to dominate. He won the National Negro Open every year from 1952 through 1956. Occasionally, Sifford was allowed to compete with whites and captured non-PGA events, including the 54-hole Rhode Island Open (1956) and the Gardena Valley Open (1959). His first PGA victory occurred in the 1957 Long Beach Open, another 54-hole event.

After California Attorney General Stanley Mosk challenged the PGA constitution's "whites only" clause, Sifford was accepted by the PGA in 1960 and became a full member in 1964. The PGA, however, remained reluctant to challenge local sponsors' control of most tournaments, so Charlie still encountered difficulty getting invitations to play. At last, in 1967, at age 45 and admittedly past his prime, he won the 72-hole PGA Hartford Open tournament. Two years later, Sifford won the Los Angeles Open and began receiving real recognition. *Sports Illustrated* described the five-foot-nine-inch golfer: "Burly, thick-chested, heavy shouldered . . . he lunges down the fairway with the powerful stride of a longshoreman."

Sifford left the PGA Tour in 1974 and became the professional at Sleepy Hollow Country Club in Brecksville, Ohio, near Cleveland, where he stayed for 13 years. But Charlie still enjoyed competitive golf. He won the 1975 PGA Seniors championship and participated in the Seniors Tour from its inception in 1980. Sifford won over $800,000 on the Seniors Tour and the Super Seniors Tour (for golfers over 60 years of age) in far less time than it had taken him to earn $340,000 on the regular tour. Nevertheless, even on the Seniors Tour, Charlie still fought the vestiges of racism, both egregious and subtle, all over again.

Since 1988, Sifford has lived in Kingwood, Texas, a suburb of Houston, with his wife, Rose (Crumbley) Sifford; they have two sons. A nephew, Curtis Sifford, also played on the PGA Tour. Despite the golf careers of his nephew and a few other African Americans, Charlie did not and could not have the impact on the sport that Robinson had on baseball. There have never been legions of African-American golfers, the equivalent of baseball's Negro Leagues, waiting to join the PGA Tour. Indeed, the disappearance of caddies in recent decades has made it difficult for young African Americans even to get the playing time that young Sifford secured at the Carolina Country Club.

As sportswriter William Johnson observed, Sifford is "a survivor, a man of stamina and strong will who simply stayed on his feet while others fell." But the man who played, in sportswriter Jim Murray's words, "under circumstances as adverse as for any athlete who ever lived" still hopes that his career may help inspire others to follow. He will be "an uncle of them all."

BIBLIOGRAPHY: "Blacks on the Greens," *Time* 93 (February 14, 1969), p. 56; Dan Jenkins, "Old Charlie Jolts the New Tour," *Sports Illustrated* 30 (January 20, 1969), pp. 16–17; William Johnson, "Call Back the Years," *Sports Illustrated* 30 (March 31, 1969), pp. 56–69; Jim Murray, "As White as the Ku Klux Klan," *Los Angeles Times*, April 6, 1969; Charlie Sifford with James Gullo, *"Just Let Me Play": The Story of Charlie Sifford, the First Black PGA Golfer* (Latham, NY, 1992).

Luther W. Spoehr

WILLIE SIMMS
(January 16, 1870–February 26, 1927) ———————— *Horse Racing*

Willie Simms, a jockey and trainer, won 1,173 races, including most of his era's major stakes races, as a United States rider and introduced the "American" riding style to England. The son of former slaves, William Simms was born on January 16, 1870, in Augusta, Georgia. Simms, attracted by riding silks, ran away from home and became a jockey. Willie worked for C. H. Pettingill's stable in New York for two years until Con Leighton, Congressman William L. Scott's trainer, discovered him riding in Clifton, New Jersey, in 1887–1888.

Simms rode Banquet, the two-year-old 20–1 underdog, to victory in the 1889 Expectation Stakes over both the favorite, Bellisarius, ridden by Edward "Snapper" Garrison, and Chaos, Banquet's favorite stable mate. At Monmouth Park, New Jersey, Willie rode Chaos, now a 30–1 underdog, to triumph over the favorite, Banquet. The freelancer enjoyed great success at Saratoga, New York, in 1891. In 1892, he signed with Philip J. Dwyer and won the Champion Stakes on Lamplighter. Rancocas Stable hired Simms from 1892 through 1894. Willie rode Dobbins to a dead-heat finish in the famous 1893 match race with Domino, just recently crowned the record money earner.

In 1895, Michael F. Dwyer signed Simms and sent him to England for four months. Willie rode "American" style, with extremely short stirrups, a whip, and spurs, unlike the British jockeys. The English ridiculed his high seat and called him "the monkey on a stick." Nevertheless, Simms won aboard Richard Croker's Eau Gallie, previously raced in the United States as Utica, in the Crawford Plate at Newmarket in April 1895. This victory made him the first American winner of an English race aboard an American-owned and -trained horse. Willie also won easily at Newmarket aboard Banquet. Despite his success, however, British jockeys did not initially copy his more efficient riding style. When Ted Sloan captured 20 races in Great Britain two years later with the same riding style, the English finally adopted the more efficient method.

Simms won many major stakes races, including the Kentucky Derby on Ben Brush in 1896 and Plaudit in 1898, the Preakness on Sly Fox in 1898, and the Belmont Stakes on Comanche in 1893 and Henry of Navarre in 1894. Willie's other stakes victories included the 1901 Annual Champion Stakes on Maid of Harlem, the Brighton Beach Handicap on Ben Brush in 1897 and Ornament in 1898, the 1895 Champagne Stakes and the 1897 Suburban Handicap on Ben Brush, the Dwyer Stakes on Dobbins in 1894 and Octagon in 1897, the 1893 Gazelle and Ladies' Handicaps on Naptha, the 1895 Jerome Handicap on Counter Tenor, the 1896 Latonia Derby on Ben Brush, and the Lawrence Realization on Daily America in 1893 and Dobbins in 1894. Simms earned $20,000 in 1895 and invested it well, becoming one of the wealthiest jockeys. In the United States, he rode 1,173 winners (25 percent) in 4,701 races, placed second 951 times, and finished third 763 times. His $300,000 career earnings even surpassed **Isaac Murphy** by $50,000. Simms won 5 out of 6 races twice, accomplishing the feat on June 23, 1893, and August 24, 1894, at Sheepshead Bay, New York. After retiring as a jockey in 1902, Willie trained horses until 1924.

Simms, who never married, died of pneumonia on February 26, 1927, at age 57 in Asbury Park, New Jersey, and was survived by his mother, Mrs. Ida

Simms Pleasant. In 1895, *The Thoroughbred Record* described Willie as one of the best American jockeys. He possessed "most excellent judgment, especially on horses that require a lot of coaxing and placing. He has beautiful hands and is especially quick and clever in an emergency." The National Museum of Racing Hall of Fame inducted Simms in 1977.

BIBLIOGRAPHY: *The Illustrated Sporting News* (May 23, 1908), p. 7; George Lambton, *Men and Horses I Have Known* (London, England, 1924); *New York Times*, March 1, 1927, p. 24; *The Thoroughbred Record* 41 (1895), pp. 87, 171, 279, 362; Marjorie R. Weber, "Negro Jockeys: Kentucky Derby Winners" (February 1970), unpublished manuscript, Keeneland Library, Lexington, KY; Lyman Horace Weeks, *The American Turf: An Historical Account of Racing in the United States* (New York, 1898); "Willie Simms," *The Blood Horse* 103 (August 8, 1977), p. 3, 548.

Steven P. Savage

O. J. SIMPSON
(July 9, 1947–) ———————————————————————— *Football*

O. J. Simpson, college and professional football player and sportscaster, set numerous National Football League (NFL) rushing records while playing nine seasons as a halfback for the Buffalo Bills. Orenthal James Simpson was born on July 9, 1947, in San Francisco, California, and grew up in the largely African-American Potrero Hill section. His father, Jimmy Simpson, a bank custodian and chef, and his mother, Eunice (Durton) Simpson, a hospital orderly, separated when O. J. was four years old. Eunice brought up her two daughters and two sons largely on her own. As a teenager, Simpson organized a neighborhood gang called the Persian Warriors and spent much of his time in the streets. O. J. also started playing Little League baseball and worshipped outfielder **Willie Mays,** who came to San Francisco with the Giants in 1958. In 1961, he and four of his fellow gang members were taken to the San Francisco Juvenile Hall and held there for the weekend after being caught stealing alcohol from a local liquor store. His uncle, Hollis Simpson, concerned about his nephew's future, arranged to have Mays visit O. J.'s home in the projects and take him for a day. According to Simpson, the day with his baseball idol made him aware that his dream of escaping the projects and making good was possible and that he had a chance. O. J. also began participating in playground sports at the Booker T. Washington Community Center, where Lefty Gordon, a youth counselor, encouraged him in track and field. At Galileo High School in Los Angeles, he first played at tackle in football because of his size, but his coach soon recognized his speed and quickness and moved him to the fullback position.

Although making the All-City football team choice in his senior year and having potential for a college athletic scholarship, Simpson did not exhibit interest in academics or college. When the opportunity came to attend the

City College of San Francisco, a junior college, however, O. J. took it. He was selected a Junior College Football All-America for two years at City College and was named an All-America at the University of Southern California (USC) in 1967 and 1968. In his senior year at USC, Simpson won the Walter Camp Memorial Trophy, the Maxwell Memorial Trophy, and the Heisman Trophy and was chosen the United Press International (UPI) and Associated Press (AP) College Athlete of the Year. For the Trojans, O. J. gained 3,124 yards on 621 carries and scored 34 touchdowns in two seasons. USC won the Pac-10 Conference championship in 1967 and 1968, losing only one conference game. The 1967 Trojans garnered the national championship. At USC, Simpson also ran for the track and field team. The school's 440-yard relay team captured the NCAA championship in 1968 with a 39.5-seconds clocking. In 1967, the relay team set a world record of 38.6 seconds in the 4 × 100 meters. O. J. graduated from USC in 1969 with a bachelor's degree in sociology.

In 1969, the Buffalo Bills (NFL) drafted Simpson. As the NFL's first draft choice, O. J. asked for a then-record-setting sum of $650,000 for a multiyear contract with the Buffalo Bills and eventually signed in 1969 for $350,000 over four years. His first three NFL seasons proved unspectacular. He was not used as the team's primary offensive weapon but rather mainly as a decoy for a passing offense. Under coach Lou Saban, however, Simpson developed into the premier NFL running back. O. J.'s speed, zigzag agility, power, and stutter step style of finding holes combined in an offense built around him. At six foot two inches and over 200 pounds with 9.3-second speed in the 100 yards, Simpson began an assault on NFL records. In 1973, O. J. became the first player to rush for over 2,000 yards in a season. He ran for 2,003 yards in a record 332 attempts and enjoyed 11 games with 100 yards or more rushing. At Buffalo, Simpson was nicknamed "The Juice," and the powerful blocking offensive line he ran behind was dubbed "The Electric Company." In 1973, O. J. was named AP Athlete of the Year, *The Sporting News* Man of the Year, and the NFL's Most Valuable Player (MVP).

Before the 1976 season, he wanted to be traded to a West Coast team. Simpson seriously considered retirement when the Bills refused to trade him. O. J. signed a $2.5 million deal with Buffalo covering three years. In 1976, he rushed for 273 yards against the Detroit Lions. During his 11 NFL years, Simpson gained 11,236 yards on 2,404 carries for a 4.7 yards per carry average. O. J. made 2,142 yards in pass receptions and had 990 yards in return yardage for a career total 14,368 yards. Although Simpson never played in a Super Bowl and the Buffalo Bills made the playoffs only once in 1974 as a wild card team during his tenure with the team, O. J. ranked among the best-known, most admired, and most productive running backs of the 1970s. He was selected to the Pro Bowl in 1972, 1974, 1975, and 1976 and was named NFL Player of the Decade in 1979. In 1972, Simpson had been chosen Collegiate Athlete of the 1960s. During the 1977 season, O. J.'s knee was injured and required an operation. On March 24, 1978, the Buffalo Bills traded him to the San Francisco 49ers (NFL) for five draft choices. He played two seasons with severely diminished abilities and underwent surgery two more times on his injured left knee.

At the height of his success with the Buffalo Bills, Simpson began his career as a feature film actor and played supporting roles in several popular action-adventure and comedy films. O. J. took his acting career seriously and hoped to become a leading role actor. In 1976, he declared, "I want to be an actor. I feel about acting what I used to feel about football. There's an element of the unknown." The major serious roles, however, never came Simpson's way. His most recognizable film role has been that of a bumbling policeman in *The Naked Gun* series. O. J. also performed in the *Roots* miniseries on ABC-TV in 1977. During off-seasons, he worked as a commentator for ABC-Sports from 1969 through 1978 and then NBC-Sports from 1979 through 1983. Simpson's NBC-TV contract also included producing and starring in made-for-television movies. In 1978, O. J. became the spokesman for Hertz Rent-a-Car in several popular commercials and established his own television production company, Orenthal Productions. Three years earlier, he almost had retired from professional football and recognized the stress and cost of stardom. Simpson told *Ebony* magazine, "Unfortunately, I'm the type of person who has to have things to do. I've got to be busy. As a result, I think the people closest to me, my mother, my wife, my kids, have paid more of a price than I have. They don't get enough of me and they don't have me around as much as they'd like." The public perceived O. J. as a man who could easily handle all the pressures and whose winning laugh, charm, and likeability were inexhaustible assets.

In 1983, Simpson returned to ABC-Sports and replaced former NFL quarterback Fran Tarkenton on "Monday Night Football" telecasts. O. J. was paid $600,000 annually for his work, but his association with the famous broadcast team ended after just three seasons. Simpson's extensive television credits have included a role in an HBO comedy series called "First and Ten" from 1986 through 1988, numerous acting roles in made-for-television films on ABC and NBC, several network specials, color analysis for the 1976 and 1984 Summer Olympics, numerous guest appearances, and executive producing. His public image has been that of a likeable individual with a winning personality, charm, class, and superstar presence. As ABC-TV's producer Don Ohlmeyer stated, "O. J. has an image. To a great extent, it's more than an image; it's the way he is. Juice is a black personality; he's a personality period. It transcends color." Simpson successfully parlayed his sports fame into film and the media during his playing career and has been seen as an American success story, rising from urban poverty to national fame.

Besides winning many performance awards during his college and professional football careers, Simpson was elected to the National Football Foundation College Football Hall of Fame in 1983 and Pro Football Hall of Fame in 1985. O. J. was named to the AFL-NFL 1960–1984 All-Star Team and in

1994 to the All-Time NFL Team. Many widely read biographies of O. J. have been written for young readers. In 1970, he published his biography, *O. J.: The Education of a Rich Rookie*, co-authored with veteran sportswriter Pete Axthelm.

Unfortunately, Simpson's private life has not matched his successful public life. O. J. married his high school sweetheart, Marguerite Whitley, on June 24, 1976, and had two daughters, Arnelle and Aaren, and a son, Jason. After Aaren died in an accidental drowning at the family swimming pool, the marriage ended in a 1979 divorce. Simpson married Nicole Brown in 1985 and had two children, Sydney Brooke and Justin. In 1989, O. J. pleaded no contest to charges of physically assaulting and threatening Nicole and was fined, ordered to undergo therapy, given community service, and put on two years' probation. The marriage ended in divorce in 1992. On June 12, 1994, Nicole was murdered outside her West Los Angeles condominium. O. J. was arrested on June 17 after an extensive manhunt and jailed on charges of murdering both Nicole and her friend Ronald Goldman. Three days later, Simpson pleaded innocent to the charges. The most widely watched murder trial in American history began in January 1995 with opening arguments by the prosecution. Simpson authored a best-selling book, *I Want to Tell You* (1995), responding to letters he has received.

BIBLIOGRAPHY: Iris Cloyd, ed., *Who's Who Among Black Americans, 1990/91*, 6th ed. (Detroit, MI, 1992) p. 1153; *Current Biography Yearbook* (1969), pp. 400–402; Frank Deford, "What Price Heroes?" *Sports Illustrated* 30 (June 9, 1969), pp. 33–34, 37, 40; Marc Gunther and Bill Carter, *Monday Night Mayhem: The Inside Story of ABC's "Monday Night Football"* (New York, 1988); Linda S. Hubbard and Owen O'Donnel, eds., *Contemporary Theatre, Film, and Television*, vol. 7 (Detroit, MI, 1989); Dick Kleiner, "Giant Surprise for O. J.: A Day with Willie Mays Set Orenthal Simpson Straight," *Sports Illustrated* 66 (May 11, 1987), pp. 110–111; Dave Newhouse, *Heismen, After the Glory* (St. Louis, MO, 1985); Dave Payne, "An Exclusive Interview with O. J. Simpson," *Football Digest* 8 (November 1978), pp. 42–53; Dave Payne, "A Conversation with O. J. Simpson," *Football Digest* 9 (March 1980), pp. 58–65; Bill Rhoden, "O. J. Simpson," *Ebony* 31 (January 1976), pp. 50–52, 56, 58; O. J. Simpson, *I Want to Tell You* (New York, 1995); Orenthal "O. J." Simpson with Pete Axthelm, *O. J.: The Education of a Rich Rookie* (New York, 1970); Jack Slater, "O. J. Simpson: The Problems of a Superstar," *Ebony* 32 (November 1976), pp. 162–167; Ralph C. Wilson, "O. J. Simpson: Interview," *Playboy* 23 (December 1976), pp. 77–102; Paul Zimmerman, "All Dressed Up, Nowhere to Go," *Sports Illustrated* 51 (November 26, 1979), pp. 38–40, 45.

                                                                    Douglas A. Noverr

MIKE SINGLETARY
(October 9, 1958–) ———————————————————— *Football*

Mike Singletary, the 1990 National Football League (NFL) Man of the Year and holder of a record 10 consecutive Pro Bowl selections, appears destined for the Pro Football Hall of Fame. Singletary's early life, however, gave no indication that Mike would succeed at anything, much less become an NFL superstar.

Michael Singletary was born on October 9, 1958, in Houston, Texas, the youngest of 10 children of Charles Singletary and Rudell Singletary. His father worked as a concrete contractor and an assistant minister at the Church of God and Christ. A sickly child, Mike recalled, "I had pneumonia three or four times. I remember going to the hospital every other day until I was seven or eight years old. In junior high school, I was five feet four and 120 pounds." Two events at age 12 changed Singletary's life dramatically. His parents divorced, and his favorite brother, Grady, died in an automobile accident. Consequently, Mike dedicated his life to excellence and achievement and remembered Grady's last words of advice, "If you're going to do something, be the best you can be."

Singletary stopped eating junk food and began eating vegetables and drinking milk. The illnesses stopped, and Mike grew to 5 foot 10 inches and 180 pounds. He joined the Worthing High School football team and tried out for the only position that he ever wanted to play, linebacker. Singletary's football coach at Worthing High School, Oliver Brown, pushed him relentlessly because he had a tendency to be lazy. Coach Brown's persistence and Mike's hard work paid huge dividends. After his senior year, the latter ranked third among all Texas linebackers on college recruiters' lists.

Singletary's lack of size alone prevented him from being on every team's want list. Since Mike stood just under six feet, many schools considered him too small to play college linebacker. The University of Texas and Baylor University, however, saw his potential. Head coach Grant Teaff of Baylor, a motivator, ultimately persuaded Mike to attend Baylor. At Baylor, Singletary soon became acquainted with another coach who drove him to excel. Head defensive coach Corky Nelson possessed a style much like Oliver Brown's. Mike learned quickly that collegiate football was much different than high school. Nelson shouted at him after practice, "Singletary, you stink! Until you start doing things my way, you're not going to play." Mike became frustrated and extremely hurt. Nelson then softened his tone and told Singletary, "You'll do what I say, when I say it, and how I say it. Mike, I see something special in you that I think is really special. But you're not going to do it by taking shortcuts or trying your own way all the time. You've got to do it our way." Singletary's determined work ethic and coach Nelson's constant supervision enabled him to begin making an impact at Baylor.

During Mike's freshman 1977 season, Baylor switched its defense from the 5–2 formation to the pro style 4–3. Singletary, who anchored the middle line-backer spot, made his first start against the University of Arkansas and responded with 28 unassisted tackles. By the end of the 1977 season, he made All-Southwest Athletic Conference (SWC) Honorable Mention and Newcomer of the Year. As a sophomore, Mike continued to improve, set a Baylor record for tackles in a season with 232, and was named SWC Defensive Player of the Year.

His junior and senior years brought equal success, as the sports media selected Singletary a consensus All-America both years. Baylor played in the 1979 Peach Bowl, defeating Clemson University, 24–18, and the 1981 Cotton Bowl, losing to the University of Alabama, 30–2. Coach Teaff summed up Mike's collegiate career, "There may have been players who hit harder, who tackled better, who ran faster, who were smarter, stronger, or read coverage better. But collectively, nobody did it better than Mike Singletary. And I don't think anyone in the Southwest Conference ever has."

Singletary naturally thought his collegiate success would bring a number-one selection in the 1981 NFL draft. Some NFL scouts hinted that this assumption was true. Mike's lack of size, however, provided a stumbling block. On NFL draft day in 1981, Singletary anxiously waited for his name to be called. Names both familiar and unfamiliar to him surfaced, but never his. During the entire first round, Mike had not been selected and he reacted in an extremely depressed manner. Finally, the Chicago Bears (NFL) drafted him in the second round as the thirty-eighth player selected overall.

Although excited about playing for the Bears, Singletary still hurt about not being a number-one pick. After a short holdout over his contract, Mike reported several days late to the Bears' training camp. He met assistant coach Buddy Ryan, who motivated and challenged him in the same manner as his old high school and college coaches. Ryan made little impression on Singletary when they first met, looking more like a farmer than a football coach. The initial impression soon changed, however, when Buddy began to test Mike to his limits. Ryan required Singletary to run to determine his aerobic conditioning and saw Mike out of breath in about five minutes. Buddy mercilessly shouted, "You little fat rascal, you're out of shape. You're nothing, 50, nothing; just a short little fat guy." This incident aroused Mike's determination. Singletary ran and drilled every day in training camp, studying film and his playbook every night. His constant attention to detail finally paid off when Ryan started him about halfway through his rookie season. Mike did not relax at all after gaining his starting position. He worked even harder and begged Ryan to keep him in the lineup on passing downs. After his third season, Singletary was granted his request.

The Bears under coach Mike Ditka slowly established themselves as one of the better NFL teams. Led by captain Singletary and supported by strong draft picks Dan Hampton, Wilber Marshall, Otis Wilson, Richard Dent, and

William Perry, Buddy Ryan's "46" defense developed into one of the most respected in the entire NFL. The 1984 Bears won their first division title since 1963 but lost the National Football Conference (NFC) championship game to the San Francisco 49ers. The 1985 season, however, marked the finest campaign for any Chicago Bears team in history. After finishing the regular season with a 15–1 record, the Bears marched through the playoffs and eventually demolished the New England Patriots, 46–10, in Super Bowl XX.

The Bears never achieved the high level of the 1985 season again during Singletary's tenure. Although Chicago consistently made the playoffs, the Washington Redskins, New York Giants, or San Francisco 49ers stopped them in their Super Bowl quest. Singletary's play remained the one constant during this period, as Mike finished first or second in tackles each year for the Bears. He made the Pro Bowl a record 10 straight years from 1983 to 1992 and was selected NFL Defensive Player of the Year in both 1985 and 1988. His off-the-field activities, coupled with his superior play, won him the NFL Man of the Year Award in 1990.

Singletary ended his NFL playing career after the 1992 season. Mike Ditka, his coach for 11 of his 12 NFL seasons, summed up the linebacker's value to the Bears, "His intensity, his zeal to do everything perfectly, makes him a leader by example. He's like [Dick] Butkus and Bill George and Joe Schmidt and guys like that. Except he has some qualities they didn't have. He has skill, but his skill is not as good as his work ethic. That's what makes him go." Singletary leads a quiet life today outside Chicago with his wife Kim and four children, Kristen, Matthew, Jill, and Jaclyn. His future endeavors may include coaching, broadcasting, or business, but he currently enjoys retirement and spends time with his family. Mike acknowledged, "I don't know what I'll be doing with my life a few years from now. But I know I will continue to seek God's will and try to do what He wants. I'll be striving to share His good news with people."

BIBLIOGRAPHY: *Current Biography Yearbook* (1993), pp. 539–543; "Last of Breed," *The Sporting News*, December 14, 1992, p. 9; Mike Singletary with Jerry Jenkins, *Singletary on Singletary* (Nashville, TN, 1991); Mike Singletary with Armen Keteyian, *Calling the Shots* (Chicago, IL, 1986); Rick Telander, "Just a Bear of a Bear," *Sports Illustrated* 64 (January 27, 1986), pp. 38–40.

John Hillman

EMMITT SMITH
(May 15, 1969–) ———————————————————— *Football*

At the age of 26, Emmitt Smith has established himself as the best running back in professional football. His family, however, shares his success. Emmitt James Smith III was born on May 15, 1969, in Pensacola, Florida, as the second of six children and has two sisters and three brothers. His father,

Emmitt, Jr., worked for the Pensacola Municipal Bus Depot, while his mother, Mary, served as a document clerk at a bank. His grandparents lived next door, making family the most important element of his early life. According to Smith, "There is nothing that I am today that I would be without family. I could get hurt tomorrow, and football would be over. Family will always be there."

His mother knew that Emmitt would be special even when she was pregnant. Church parishioners marveled at the way he moved about inside her. All agreed that Smith would be a fine athlete like his father. She nicknamed Emmitt "Scoey" after her favorite entertainer, Scoey Mitchell. Smith began playing football at age 7 in the Pensacola youth leagues. His mother began carrying his birth certificate at all times because the opposition found it impossible to believe that a youngster so large could be so young. Due to Emmitt's size, he played with 10-year-olds at age 8, 14-year-olds at age 11, and 16-year-olds at age 12.

When Smith started attending Escambia High School, head coach Dwight Thomas could hardly wait to give the ball to his five-foot-eight-inch, 175-pound running back. In his first varsity game as a freshman, Emmitt ran for 115 yards. During the next four seasons, he gained 8,804 yards in 49 games and scored 101 touchdowns. Smith surpassed 100 yards in 45 games and 200 yards in 18 games, once gaining 301 yards on 28 carries. Emmitt ranks as the second leading all-time high school rusher behind Ken Hall of Sugarland, Texas.

Smith's impressive high school achievements caused college recruiters to flock to Pensacola. Jimmy Johnson, his future professional coach, wanted him to play at the University of Miami but realized it was hopeless. "He wanted to go an I-formation team that ran the ball, and we used a multiple offense, with split backs," admits Johnson. Emmitt's mother, Mary, took charge of his college recruitment. She set down strict rules, including no contact except on Sunday. Smith wanted to attend the University of Florida from the outset. "I didn't want my family to have to go all over the country to see me play," he remarked. "I wanted to stay close to home."

As a college freshman, the five-foot-nine-inch, 190-pound Smith continued his remarkable success with running the football. In his first game against the University of Alabama, he ran for 224 yards. Emmitt reached the 1,000-yard plateau in the seventh game of his freshman season, making him the only player in college football history to achieve this feat. **Tony Dorsett** of the University of Pittsburgh and **Herschel Walker** of the University of Georgia, both former Dallas Cowboys, held the previous record of eight games.

During his junior season, Smith broke the University of Florida career rushing record. Neal Anderson had held the previous record with 3,234 yards. Altogether, Emmitt had rushed for 4,232 yards in 34 games and broke the 100-yard mark in 25 games. Two factors, however, influenced his decision to leave collegiate football after his junior season. The University of Florida lingered in the midst of an NCAA investigation, while the National Football League (NFL) allowed college juniors to declare early for the NFL draft. Smith considered it best for him and his family to opt for the NFL, but he made one promise to his parents. "I told them that I would not build a house until I completed my college education," Emmitt declared. "Nothing can ever happen to change that."

Not all NFL scouts and draft experts considered Smith a top draft choice, many discounting his NFL potential because of his speed. Emmitt ran a 4.55-second 40-yard dash on synthetic turf at Florida, but some scouts had timed him at 4.7 seconds. The missing element in all the evaluations remained his work ethic. Smith never misses practices, plays in pain, and never complains. Emmitt only wants to be given the football and told to run with it.

The Dallas Cowboys (NFL), along with Jimmy Johnson, regarded Smith highly but feared that he would be unavailable at their number-21 draft position. Halfway through the 1990 NFL draft, however, only one running back, Blair Thomas, had been selected. Dallas orchestrated a trade with the Pittsburgh Steelers, moving them to number 17 and enabling them to take Emmitt as their first-round pick. Jerry Jones, Cowboys owner, made the mistake of stating publicly that they had rated Smith as the fourth best player in the entire draft. That remark prolonged contract negotiations through all of training camp. Smith became the Cowboys' starting running back in only his second professional game and finished a fine rookie season with 937 yards on 241 carries. Emmitt, selected to several All-Rookie teams, received several Offensive Rookie of the Year awards.

The 1991 season brought more success for the young running back. Smith had expressed a desire at the end of his first season to be given the ball 25 to 30 times a game. The Dallas coaches complied, allowing Emmitt 365 carries for 1,563 yards and earning him his first NFL rushing title. His success played a large role in the Cowboys' 11–5 record, helping Dallas reach the playoffs for the first time since the Tom Landry era.

Smith firmly solidified his stardom in the 1992 season, rushing for 1,713 yards on 373 attempts, scoring 18 touchdowns, and winning his second consecutive NFL rushing title. With a healthy Troy Aikman for the entire season and a superb passing game featuring Michael Irvin, the Cowboys improved to a 13–3 record, won the National Football Conference (NFC) Eastern Division, and defeated the San Francisco 49ers for the NFC championship. Dallas capped its fine season, demolishing the Buffalo Bills, 52–17, in Super Bowl XXVII. Consequently, Emmitt became the first NFL rushing leader to play on a winning Super Bowl team.

Smith believed that the Cowboys should share their renewed success with him. His original three-year contract had expired. Emmitt thought that he deserved to be one of the highest paid running backs in the NFL. Cowboy owner Jerry Jones demonstrated stubbornness, asserting Dallas could win without him. An 0–2 opening record, however, aroused much discussion and dissension. Jones, realizing that no 0–2 team had ever won a Super Bowl, quickly signed Smith to a new four-year contract for $13.6 million. At Emmitt's signing ceremony, Jones admitted, "Some might wonder who the winners and losers are. When he signs his contract for four years, then the Cowboys are big winners. And when I sign his bonus check then he's a winner."

Smith quickly proved his worth, as the Cowboys began winning and finished the season with a 12–4 record. Despite the loss of almost four games because of the holdout and injuries, Emmitt won his third consecutive rushing championship. Only three other players in NFL history had accomplished this feat. He gained 1,486 yards on 283 carries, averaging 5.3 yards per carry.

The Cowboys won their second consecutive NFL Eastern Division title and once again defeated the San Francisco 49ers, 38–21, for the NFL championship. The Dallas triumph set up a rematch with the Buffalo Bills in Super Bowl XXVIII. Smith performed his finest in the Super Bowl, rushing for 132 yards and two touchdowns in leading the Cowboys to a 30–13 win over Buffalo. Emmitt capped his outstanding season by being named both the Super Bowl MVP and NFL MVP. No other player has won both awards in the same season.

Smith led the NFL with 22 touchdowns in 1994, again earning All-Pro and Pro Bowl honors. Emmitt gained 1,484 yards rushing for 21 touchdowns, but injuries slowed down his quest for a fourth consecutive rushing title. Dallas finished with a 12–4 regular season record, but lost the NFC championship game to the San Francisco 49ers, 38–28.

The future looks bright for this 26-year-old running back, who has already rushed for 7,183 NFL yards (4.4-yard average) and 71 touchdowns. He also has caught 239 passes for 1,576 yards and 4 touchdowns. The hunger for greatness still motivates and drives Smith. Emmitt admits, "I think of being the greatest. I think about it all the time. I'm chasing after legends, after **Walter Payton** and **Tony Dorsett** and **Jim Brown** and **Eric Dickerson,** after guys who made history. When my career's over, I want to have the new kids, the new backs, say, 'Boy, we have to chase a legend to be the best.' And they'll mean Emmitt Smith." If Smith stays healthy, both he and the Cowboys will rewrite the NFL record books in the 1990s. In Emmitt's words, "I'm playing for something else now. I'm playing for Canton, Ohio."

BIBLIOGRAPHY: Barbara Bigelow, ed., *Contemporary Black Biography,* vol. 7 (Detroit, MI, 1994), pp. 248–252; Barry Horn, "Family, Not Football, Ranks Highest with Emmitt Smith," *Dallas Morning News,* January 15, 1993, p. H14; Peter King, "Dare to Be Great," *Sports Illustrated* 80 (January 31, 1994), pp. 22–23; Ed Werder, "Stretching Himself," *Dallas Morning News,* February 6, 1994, pp. S14–S15; Paul Zimmerman, "The 100-Yard Dasher," *Sports Illustrated* 75 (October 21, 1991), pp. 72–75.

                                                            John Hillman

OZZIE SMITH
(December 26, 1954–) _____ *Baseball*

St. Louis teams have fielded some of the finest major league shortstops, including Bobby Wallace, Rabbit Maranville, Leo Durocher, Marty Marion, and Dal Maxvill. Osborne Earl Smith, however, tops that list of outstanding shortstops. Smith was born on December 26, 1954, in the Watts section of Los Angeles, California, and grew up with five brothers and sisters. His father worked as a sandblaster and truckdriver, while his mother was employed as a nurse's aide. Ozzie played baseball with **Eddie Murray** at Locke High School in Watts. He attended California Polytechnic University in San Luis Obispo on an academic scholarship and played shortstop on their baseball team.

The San Diego Padres National League (NL) club drafted Smith in June 1977. Ozzie played his only minor league baseball season at Walla Walla, Washington, where he led the Northwest League in games played, runs scored, and fielding average at shortstop while batting .303. The highly impressed San Diego Padres moved shortstop Bill Almon to third base and installed Smith as their regular shortstop in 1978. Ozzie's maiden campaign included sparkling defense, a .258 batting average, and 40 stolen bases. From 1979 to 1981, he continued dazzling infield play. Smith established a major league record 621 assists at shortstop in 1980 but batted only .221 over the three-year stretch. The Padres, at or near the bottom in most offensive categories, traded him to the St. Louis Cardinals (NL) for hard-hitting shortstop Garry Templeton in February 1982.

Redbird manager Whitey Herzog built teams around defense and speed and found Smith the final piece of the Cardinal puzzle. In 1982, St. Louis won the NL East. Ozzie batted .556 in the three-game sweep of the Atlanta Braves in the NL Championship Series and batted only .208 in the World Series against the Milwaukee Brewers. Nevertheless, the Cardinals won the World Championship in seven games. Sportswriters, announcers, and players lauded Smith's defensive skills, calling him "poetry in motion," "an acrobat on astroturf," and "a combination of baseball and ballet." Ozzie dove to either side, popped up, and threw, as if in one motion. Impossible plays for most shortstops became routine for "the Wizard." He led NL shortstops in fielding average 7 times and in assists 8 times. Smith won the NL Gold Glove 13 times from 1980 to 1992. Through 1994, Ozzie had compiled the third highest career fielding average in history and ranked second in games played at shortstop and career double plays, first in career assists, and fifth in career total chances.

Smith's fielding excellence alone kept him in the major leagues for many years, but that was not enough to satisfy him. At St. Louis, Ozzie worked hard on developing his batting and base-running skills. He developed into an excellent second hitter, a fine bunter, and among the most difficult batters to strike out. In 1994, Smith reached the 100-hits plateau for the seventeenth consecutive season. In the ninth inning of the fifth game during the 1985 NL Championship Series, the 5-foot-10-inch, 162-pound switch-hitter belted his first-ever left-handed home run to defeat the Los Angeles Dodgers, 3–2. St. Louis won the NL pennant in 6 games, only to lose the 7-game World Series to the Kansas City Royals. In 1987, Ozzie reached career highs with 182 hits, 40 doubles, 104 runs scored, 75 RBIs, and a .303 batting average, while winning the Silver Slugger Award at shortstop and helping the Cardinals take another Eastern Division title. The Redbirds conquered the San Francisco Giants in 7 games to capture the NL pennant. The Cardinals fell to the Minnesota Twins, however, in the 7-game World Series, dropping all 4 games played at the Twins' Metrodome. Through the strike-shortened 1994 season, Smith had batted .262 in 2,447 games and made 2,365 hits, 1,205 runs, 26 home runs, 764 RBIs, and 569 stolen bases. Ozzie played in every All-Star Game from 1981 to 1992 and, at age 39 in 1994, was elected to the NL All-Star squad by the fans, gaining the largest NL vote total. He also played in the 1995 All-Star Game.

Smith, who married Denise Jackson on November 1, 1980, has three children, Osborne, Jr., Dustin, and Taryn. Ozzie, a dedicated family man, remains deeply involved in civic and charitable activities, including the American Red Cross, Multiple Sclerosis Society, Annie Malone Children's Home, and March of Dimes. The NAACP, National Conference of Christians and Jews, and National Father's Day Committee have honored him. In 1987, an autobiographical film, *Ozzie: The Movie*, was released. He wrote an autobiography, *Wizard*, in 1988. St. Louis sportswriters named Smith St. Louis Top Sports Figure for 1987. He operates Ozzie Smith's Sports Academy, an indoor facility for baseball and softball instruction, Ozzie's Restaurant and Sports Bar, and two Ozzie's Discovery Zones for children. Smith remains one of the most popular sports figures in St. Louis.

BIBLIOGRAPHY: David Falkner, *Nine Sides of the Diamond: Baseball's Great Glovemen on the Fine Art of Defense* (New York, 1990); *St. Louis Cardinals Media Guide*, 1992; Ozzie Smith with Rob Rains, *Wizard* (Chicago, IL, 1988); Rick Sorci, "Baseball Profile: Ozzie Smith," *Baseball Digest* 50 (January 1991), p. 49.

Frank J. Olmsted

TOMMIE SMITH
(June 6, 1944–) —————————————————————— *Track and Field*

In the late 1960s, Tommie Smith led the world in the 200 meters and ranked among the leading 400-meter specialists, setting world records at both distances. Americans, however, remember Smith less for his record-setting performances than for his African-American power demonstration during the 1968 Summer Olympic Games at Mexico City, Mexico. Tommie, the seventh of 12 children of James Richard Smith and Dora Smith, was born on June 6, 1944, in Clarksville, Texas. When Smith was six years old, his father, a sharecropper, moved his family to Lemoore, California, a community south of Fresno in the fertile San Joaquin Valley. Lemoore was "very rich and very poor," according to Tommie, who remembers riding the bus to school, while "the Caucasian kids would drive their GTO's." Smith's father continued to labor as a share-cropper and also worked as a utility man at the local high school. His mother brought up her children and worked as a domestic. Tommie, who labored on the farms, remembers "picking cotton and giving the 90¢-an-hour wages to my father when I was 9 or 10."

Sharecropping did not become Smith's fate, as he possessed exceptional athletic talents and especially excellent running ability. At Lemoore High School, Tommie exercised his distinctive high-knee-lift running style as a foot-ball halfback and a track and field sprinter. In 1963, he earned an athletic scholarship to San Jose State College, where track and field coach Bud Winter taught the six-foot-three-inch, 180-pound speedster to combine a long-stride with the high-knee lift.

Smith entered the record books in 1965 with a world record–equaling per-formance of 20.0 seconds for 200 meters. The following year saw the San Jose State dashman shatter world records by clocking 19.5 seconds for 220 yards on a straightaway and 20.0 seconds around a curve. Frank Deford of *Sports Illustrated* declared Tommie "the fastest moving human the world has ever known." Later that summer, Smith led the U.S. 4 × 400-meter relay team to a world record of 2 minutes 59.6 seconds for history's first sub-3-minute per-formance. His relay leg of 43.8 seconds marked the then fastest 400-meter circuit ever run. After setting an indoor world record of 46.2 seconds for 440 yards in 1967, Tommie regretted not having "pushed at the end" to break 46 seconds. He demonstrated his capacity for the distance later that summer outdoors, however, by clocking world records of 44.5 seconds for 400 meters and 44.8 seconds for 440 yards. "He's even more amazing that I thought," commented Winters, who added, "I wouldn't be surprised if he runs a 42-plus or 43 for the quarter-mile." Smith also captured the NCAA and the first of two consecutive Amateur Athletic Union (AAU) titles in the 220-yard/200-meter dash in 1967.

In 1968, Tommie joined several African-American athletes involved in a movement to boycott the 1968 Summer Olympic Games in Mexico City, Mex-ico. Harry Edwards, a young African-American sociology professor at San Jose State and leader of the movement, hoped that the boycott would "dramatize to the world the inequities faced by American Negroes in everyday life." Edwards had organized a successful boycott of the annual New York Athletic Club indoor track and field meet that year, but support for his Olympic boycott waned by the U.S. Olympic Trials. Consequently, Edwards encouraged ath-letes who decided to compete in the Olympic Games to "protest in their own fashion." Smith, who decided against boycotting the Olympics, competed in the 200 meters and captured the Gold Medal in a world record of 19.83

seconds. Teammate John Carlos, the Olympic Trials champion at 200 meters, garnered the Bronze Medal. After accepting their medals, Tommie and John lowered their heads and raised black-gloved fists during the flag raising and playing of the national anthem. "We are black, and we're proud to be black," remarked Smith, who later maintained that the black-gloved fists represented the unity of Black America. As a consequence of their black power display, the U.S. Olympic Committee suspended Tommie and Carlos from the U.S. Olympic team and ordered them to return home.

Smith, who majored in the social sciences, graduated from San Jose State College in 1969 and played professional football with the Cincinnati Bengals National Football League (NFL) club for three years as a pass receiver. Tommie became the track and field coach at Oberlin College in 1972 and later its athletic director. He then served as track and field and cross country coach at Santa Monica College and was named to the National Track and Field Hall of Fame in 1978. Although his victory-stand gesture has overshadowed his remarkable sprinting performances of the late 1960s, Smith does not regret his actions. Tommie has maintained that he acted on his own, "not because someone told me to do it. I felt it was my contribution, not only to all people but especially to athletes, to let them know they do have a place in life."

BIBLIOGRAPHY: Neil Amdur, "Tommie Smith at 34: His Struggle Goes On," *New York Times*, December 24, 1978, pp. D1, D4; Arthur Ashe, Jr., *A Hard Road to Glory: A History of the African-American Athlete Since 1946*, vol. 3 (New York, 1988); Pete Axthelm, "Boycott Now—Boycott Later," *Sports Illustrated* 28 (February 26, 1968), pp. 24–26; Frank Deford, "He Is Built for Chasing Beyondness," *Sports Illustrated* 26 (May 22, 1967), pp. 34–43; Harry Edwards, *The Revolt of the Black Athlete* (New York, 1969); David L. Porter, ed., *Biographical Dictionary of American Sports: Outdoor Sports* (Westport, CT, 1989); Roberto L. Quercetani, *Athletics: A History of Modern Track and Field Athletics, 1860–1990* (Milan, Italy, 1990); Benjamin G. Rader, *American Sports: From the Age of Folk Games to the Age of Spectators* (New York, 1983); Gary Ronberg, "Tommie in a Breeze," *Sports Illustrated* 26 (May 29, 1967), pp. 22–25; David Wallechinsky, *The Complete Book of the Olympic Games* (New York, 1988).

Adam R. Hornbuckle

WILLIE STARGELL
(March 7, 1941–) —————————————————————————— *Baseball*

Willie Stargell played more seasons, hit more home runs, and drove in more runs than any other player in Pittsburgh Pirate National League (NL) baseball club history. Wilver Dornell Stargell was born on March 7, 1941, in Earlsboro, Oklahoma. His parents, William Stargell and Gladys Stargell, had separated before his birth. Willie's mother relocated to Oakland, California, where she worked in a cannery and married Percy Russell, a truck driver.

Stargell attended Encinal High School, playing baseball with future major leaguers Tommy Harper and Curt Motton. In 1959, the Pittsburgh Pirates signed Willie for a $1,500 bonus and sent him to Roswell, New Mexico, in the Sophomore League. There, he got his first taste of overt racism. Stargell, a skinny six-foot-three-inch, 160-pound, left-handed first baseman, could not eat or room with his teammates. At Plainview, Texas, Willie was threatened with death if he took the field. Nevertheless, he performed well. Stargell switched from first base to the outfield and spent 1960 at Grand Forks, North Dakota, in the Northern League, 1961 at Asheville, North Carolina, in the Sally League, and 1962 at Columbus, Ohio, in the International League. Each year, Willie's home run production increased. In 1962, he joined the Pittsburgh Pirates.

Stargell holds several all-time Pirate batting records, including most home runs (475), RBIs (1,540), and extra base hits (953). During his 21 seasons with the Pirates, Willie appeared in 2,360 games and made 2,232 hits for a .282 lifetime batting average. He hit 423 doubles, scored 1,195 runs, and struck out 1,936 times, second only to **Reggie Jackson** on the major league all-time list. Stargell's batting productivity would have been even more impressive had he not played the first half of his major league career at cavernous Forbes Field in Pittsburgh.

Stargell clubbed many prodigious home runs, including the only two balls ever hit out of Dodger Stadium in Los Angeles. During his career, Willie enjoyed six seasons with at least 30 home runs and 13 consecutive campaigns from 1964 to 1976 with 20 or more home runs. His seven All-Star selections included 1964–1966, 1971–1973, and 1978.

In 1971, Stargell led the NL with 48 round-trippers and drove in a career-high 125 runs. Two years later, Willie hit 44 home runs to lead the NL once again. He also led the NL in RBIs in (119), doubles (43), and slugging percentage (.646). Although Stargell's banner seasons twice brought him second place in the balloting for the NL's Most Valuable Player (MVP) Award, some observers contended that lingering racism prevented him from capturing the award.

Stargell, an outstanding left fielder with a rifle arm, moved permanently to first base in 1975. Willie remains perhaps best known for his leadership with the 1979 world champion Pirates. Nicknamed "Pops," the 38-year-old stressed the theme "We are a family" and kept the Pirate clubhouse loose but focused all season. He also led by example. After suffering several off-seasons due to recurring injuries, Stargell had rebounded in 1978 with a .295 batting average, 28 home runs, and 97 RBIs. Willie's performance earned him NL Comeback Player of the Year honors from *The Sporting News*. In 1979, he belted 32 four-baggers with 82 RBIs to lead the Pirates to their sixth NL East championship in 10 years. For his leadership qualities and play, Stargell was selected NL MVP. *The Sporting News* named Willie both its Major League Player of the Year and its Man of the Year. *Sports Illustrated* selected him Co-Man of the Year with Terry Bradshaw, quarterback of the Super Bowl champion Pittsburgh Steelers National Football League (NFL) club.

Stargell excelled during the 1979 NL Championship Series and the World Series. Prior to 1979, Willie had played in 19 NL Championship Series games with little success. In 68 at bats, he had hit .221 with only two home runs and six RBIs. In 1979, however, Stargell batted .455 with two home runs and six RBIs and was named the NL Championship Series MVP.

When the Pirates defeated the Baltimore Orioles in seven games during the 1971 World Series, Stargell batted a feeble .208 with no home runs and only one RBI. Willie's 1979 World Series against the same Baltimore Orioles produced different results. Pittsburgh once again won in seven games, but this time he hit .400 with three home runs, including a game-winning two-run clout in the seventh game, with seven RBIs and 25 total bases. Stargell was named the World Series' MVP.

After the 1979 season, age and infirmities caught up with Stargell. Willie retired after the 1982 season to become a minor league batting instructor with the Pirates. In 1986, he joined the Atlanta Braves (NL) as a coach. Eight years later, the Braves promoted him to Special Assistant of Player Personnel.

In 1988, Stargell was elected to the National Baseball Hall of Fame as 1 of only 17 players chosen in the first year of eligibility. During the enshrinement ceremonies, Willie acknowledged, "I am living proof that hard work earns just rewards. . . . There are no short cuts. There are no substitutions."

Stargell has been married three times and has five children, Wendy, Precious, Dawn, Wilver, Jr., and Kelli. Wendy's affliction with sickle-cell anemia prompted Willie to devote considerable time and effort to charities that seek a cure for the disease. Stargell enjoys dancing, bowling, and cooking. He and his third wife reside in Wilmington, North Carolina.

BIBLIOGRAPHY: Bob Adelman and Susan Hall, *Out of Left Field: Willie Stargell and the Pittsburgh Pirates* (New York, 1976); Eliot Asinof, "Where I Came From, Where I Am Going," *Sport* 70 (April 1980), pp. 29–36; *The Baseball Encyclopedia*, 9th ed. (New York, 1993); Ron Fimrite, "Two Champs from the City of Champions," *Sports Illustrated* 51 (December 14, 1979), pp. 36–42; Hank Newer, "Willie Stargell: The Pride of Pittsburgh," *Saturday Evening Post* 252 (May–June 1980), pp. 26–32; *Pittsburgh Pirates Media Guide* (1988); Bob Smizik, *The Pittsburgh Pirates: An Illustrated History* (New York, 1990); Willie Stargell and Tom Bird, *Willie Stargell: An Autobiography* (New York, 1984).

                                                                Frank W. Thackeray

LUSIA HARRIS STEWART
(February 10, 1955–) _____ *Basketball*

Lusia Harris ranks among the greatest players in women's basketball history. She was born on February 10, 1955, in Minter City, Mississippi, to the Willie Harrises, both vegetable farmers. As the seventh of 11 children, Harris competed with her siblings on their makeshift farmyard basketball court. Lusia, who eventually grew to six foot four inches and developed strength to match, dominated high school basketball at Amanda Elsey High School. Harris captained the quintet, being selected team Most Valuable Player (MVP) from 1971 to 1973 and to the State All-Star team. Another player remarked, "She's incredibly strong. The strength in her arms and hands is exceptional for a girl."

Following high school graduation, Harris enrolled at Delta State University in Cleveland, Mississippi, to help reinstitute its women's basketball team. Coach Margaret Wade invited "Lucy" to join the team. In 1973–1974, the Lady Statesmen compiled a 16–2 winning season and won the State championship. The next year, Delta State won all its games for a 28–0 mark and defeated defending champion Immaculata College to win the National Association of Intercollegiate Athletics for Women (AIAW) tournament. Delta State successfully defended the national title again in 1975–1976 with a 33–1 record and in 1976–1977 with a 32–3 record.

Harris earned All-America status in 1975, 1976, and 1977 as a great all-around player, who excelled under the basket and possessed a surefire eight-foot jump shot. In the 1976 AIAW championship game against Immaculata at Madison Square Garden in New York, Lusia scored 47 points. Another time, she tallied 58 points. During her junior year, Harris averaged an impressive 31 points for the entire season and enjoyed a 62 percent field goal average. Lusia dominated play under the boards, where she averaged 15 rebounds per game. She twice was named MVP of the national tournament and first recipient of the Broderick Cup in 1976–1977. Her play followed her advice, "You have to get rough with the sport. You have to be tough."

Harris, a campus leader, maintained a B+ academic grade average. Delta State University, located in the heart of the Mississippi Delta, maintained a student body ratio of nine white students for each African-American student, yet Lusia was elected Homecoming queen during her junior year.

Coach Wade and the Lady Statesmen, sparked by superstar Harris, drew huge crowds to their games. Around 600 loyal fans from the small school and town followed their team to away games and showed their loyalty by wearing glittery T-shirts emblazoned "Lady Statesmen Are Dyn-o-mite." During the 1975–1976 season, supporters stuck little gummed cotton bolls on themselves and anyone else who would wear them. Students and fans from that southern cotton growing belt loved their team and celebrated when their National Championship team returned home to Cleveland. A caravan consisting of 50 to 60 cars joined them in towns along the way, and the team was escorted into town by a police car with flashing lights.

Harris's play and Delta State's tremendous team record garnered national attention. As a sophomore, Lusia played for the 1975 U.S. team in the Mexico City, Mexico, Pan-American Games. The same year, she also performed for the U.S. World University team at Bogota, Colombia. In 1976, Harris led the Silver Medal U.S. Olympic women's basketball team in both scoring and rebounding. Women's basketball was first included in the 1976 Montreal, Canada, Olympics. Lusia tallied the first field goal and led the United States in scoring. Following the Olympics, she returned to Delta State for her senior year. Playing for and traveling with the select teams to distant international competitions and meeting people from all over the world provided an exciting, educational experience for Lusia.

Harris considered winning the National Championship three consecutive years and performing in the Olympics as her career highlights. Lusia humbly stated, "I really thank God for giving me the talent and the ability to think. . . . One must be willing to understand and to appreciate those things for which she is capable. We, then, too, must be understanding toward our peers and others and work extra hard for the goals we desire and try hard to overcome various obstacles."

Harris graduated in 1977 with a bachelor's degree in health, physical education, and recreation and became the second woman (Denise Long of Iowa was the first) drafted by a men's pro basketball team. The New Orleans Jazz National Basketball Association (NBA) club drafted her in the seventh round. Lusia did not attend the tryouts or regular training camp because she considered it a public relations stunt.

Following graduation, Harris remained with Delta State as an admissions counselor. Lusia traveled to various areas of Mississippi encouraging students to enroll at Delta State. The school meant so much to her that she naturally recruited well. Harris's stature and visibility as a student-athlete made her an effective recruiter.

Lusia married George Stewart in 1977. In 1980, she was invited to join the Houston Angels of the Women's Professional Basketball League (WPBL). By that time, her son was five months old. She agreed to join the team for a few games at the end of the season and played three playoff games before the team was eliminated. Stewart admitted, "That didn't really work out. . . . I was out of shape as you can imagine after having had a baby just five months earlier and not having played basketball in a long while." Lusia did not intend to pursue a basketball career, a fortunate move because the WPBL soon folded for lack of public interest and support.

In 1992, Stewart joined Nera White as the first two women basketball players inducted into the Naismith Memorial Basketball Hall of Fame. Margaret Wade, Lusia's former coach and first women's basketball coach inducted into the same Hall of Fame, declared, "I'm thrilled for Lusia. It's her turn." At the 1993 Hall of Fame induction of the 1976 USSR (Latvian) Olympic Gold Medalist Uljana Semjonova, Stewart escorted her former rival at the festivities. Lusia recalled, "The first time I played against her was in the 1976 Olympics. I thought then and still do today, that it was a great day for the two countries to come together in international competition. . . . I look forward to seeing Uljana again. It will bring back great memories."

In 1980, Stewart was appointed Delta State's assistant women's basketball coach. Lusia declared, "I've always wanted to get into coaching and never wanted to get away from basketball completely. This seemed like a great opportunity." She still held 21 Lady Statesmen records, among them 58 points in one game, 1,160 points in a single season, and 2,981 points in her career. Stewart was selected a Women's Basketball Coaches Association Kodak All-America player, an honor extended to only the elite. In 1991, Lusia was elected to the Mississippi Sports Hall of Fame, one of few females so honored.

After her short coaching stint, Stewart taught physical education and currently teaches special education at Ruleville, Mississippi, Central High School near Cleveland, Mississippi. Now the mother of two children, Lusia hopes to return to coaching once her children are grown. As a coach, she will certainly show her players all the right moves.

BIBLIOGRAPHY: Arthur Ashe, Jr., *A Hard Road to Glory: A History of the African-American Athlete Since 1946*, vol. 3 (New York, 1988); Delta State University Alumni Association, Cleveland, MS, letter to Janice A. Beran, January 28, 1994; *Ebony* 32 (February 1977), p. 92; "Harris-Stewart Elected to Basketball Hall of Fame," *Des Moines Register*, February 1, 1992; Joan Hult and Marianna Trekell, *From Frailty to Final Four, A Century of Women's Basketball* (Reston, VA, 1992); David L. Porter, ed., *Biographical Dictionary of American Sports: Basketball and Other Indoor Sports* (Westport, CT, 1989); Twenty-ninth Annual Mississippi Sports Hall of Fame and Awards Banquet Program, Jackson, MS, April 2, 1991.

Janice A. Beran

DARRYL STRAWBERRY
(March 12, 1962–   ) —————————————————————— *Baseball*

Darryl Strawberry's baseball career has seen both peaks and valleys. Darryl Eugene Strawberry, "The Straw Man," was born on March 12, 1962, in Los Angeles, California, to Henry Strawberry, a postal worker, and Ruby Strawberry. Ruby made a good salary at Pacific Bell, but her husband's compulsive gambling nearly impoverished the family. Darryl lamented the situation, "When one of your parents is an addict, you don't get the complete parent package." At Crenshaw High School, he played with baseball star Eric Davis. After having graduated in 1980, Strawberry signed with the New York Mets National League (NL) club for a $200,000 bonus. His first professional season was spent with the Kingsport, Tennessee, Mets in 1980. Darryl performed for Lynchburg, Virginia, of the Carolina League in 1981 and then starred with Jackson of the Texas League (TL) in 1982. His 34 home runs, 97 RBIs, 100 walks, and .604 slugging average earned him the TL's Most Valuable Player (MVP) Award in 1982. Strawberry started the 1983 season in the International League with Tidewater, the Mets' top farm club, but was promoted for 122 games to the Mets. His .257 batting mark and 26 home runs won him the NL's Rookie of the Year Award. Jim Frey, his early mentor, noticed Strawberry's raw potential in 1983. "He's capable of hitting 50. Got a chance to be a George Brett or a Mike Schmidt, dominant year after year. . . . But a guy like Darryl, he needs attention."

On May 16, 1983, Strawberry belted his first major league home run off Lee Tunnell in an 11–4 win over the Pittsburgh Pirates. In 1984, Darryl led the Mets with 26 home runs, sharing fourth best in the NL, and started for the NL in the All-Star Game, the first of eight straight selections to the classic game. In 1986, his 26 homers tied for sixth best in the NL. He led the All-Star team balloting with 1,619,511 votes. Known for his powerful swing and towering home runs, Strawberry experienced a disappointing World Series against the Boston Red Sox. Darryl hit just .208 with 1 homer in his only fall classic.

In 1987, Strawberry established the Mets' record for home runs with 39, ranking third in the NL in slugging average with .583 and runs scored with 108. Darryl's 36 stolen bases earned him membership in the coveted 30/30 Club. He joined teammate Howard Johnson as the first members of the same team to make the important 30/30 Club, signifying both players hit at least 30 home runs and stole at least 30 bases. The following year, Strawberry led the NL with 39 home runs and a .545 slugging average and placed second in RBIs with 101. Darryl also finished second in the NL MVP balloting and started in right field for the NL All-Stars for the fifth consecutive year.

In 1989, the six-foot-six-inch, 215-pound left-handed slugger dropped to 29 homers and yet finished sixth in the NL. Strawberry's 200th major league home run came off Doug Drabek of the Pittsburgh Pirates on June 9, 1989. Darryl was selected for his sixth straight All-Star Game, but a broken toe sidelined him. Although having trouble with left-handed pitchers, he demonstrates exceptional power to all fields. His big, looping swing has terrorized pitchers during his 12 major league seasons. Strawberry remains a streaky hot hitter, frequently experiencing deep slumps and often carrying his entire team for months at a time. One of Darryl's mammoth home runs jammed the mechanism of the apple rising out of the hat in center field at Shea Stadium in New York. Another broke the clock in the right-field scoreboard at Busch Stadium in St. Louis, Missouri.

Strawberry's career has suffered from frequent moodiness, arguments, contract disputes, marital troubles, alcohol abuse, and general unhappiness. Darryl's petty dispute with teammate Keith Hernandez during a spring training photo session in 1989 eventually led to his unpleasant departure from the team as a free agent in 1991. He finished the 1989 season with 29 home runs, sixth best in the NL, but batted only .225. In 1990, Strawberry played his last season in New York, enjoying his finest campaign. Darryl finished fifth in the NL with 108 RBIs and second in homers with 37, becoming the Mets' career leader with 252 home runs and 733 RBIs.

In 1991, the Los Angeles Dodgers (NL) signed Strawberry as a free agent and reunited him with former Cincinnati Reds slugger Eric Davis. Darryl, his wife Lisa, and their two children, Darryl, Jr., and Diamond, initially adapted to their new climate very well. After arriving in Los Angeles, he acknowledged, "I was stressed out. There was so much built up inside of me. It's painful to go through what I went through, the alcohol rehab, the other things. But it's over now, and I am able to enjoy people and let people enjoy me." Strawberry became a born-again Christian and temporarily improved his whole outlook on life. "Peace of mind is what you really want," Darryl once affirmed. "You have to believe that if you just keeping plugging away that everything will turn out well."

Strawberry regained his stroke in 1991 by belting 28 home runs and recording 99 RBIs. Darryl became only the sixth player in major league history to hit at least 25 home runs in nine straight seasons, ranking behind only National Baseball Hall of Famers Babe Ruth (15), **Willie Mays** (13), Jimmie Foxx (12), Lou Gehrig (12), Eddie Mathews (11), and **Reggie Jackson** (10). A serious back injury required surgery and severely limited his playing time during the 1992 and 1993 seasons with the Dodgers. After the Dodgers released him in April 1994 due to drug problems, Strawberry in June 1994 signed with the San Francisco Giants (NL) and saw action in 29 games. His batting statistics through the 1994 season include a .259 batting mark in 1,352 games, with 294 home runs, 886 RBIs, 793 runs scored, and 205 stolen bases.

Strawberry faced more problems following the 1994 season. In December 1994, Darryl was indicted for not reporting over $500,000 in income from sports autograph shows. He pleaded guilty in February 1995 to charges of income tax evasion in exchange for a recommended three-month term in prison. The same month, Strawberry was suspended 60 days for violating major-league baseball's drug policy and terms of his after-care program. The Giants subsequently released Darryl. In June 1995, the New York Yankees (AL) signed him.

BIBLIOGRAPHY: Duncan Bock and John Jordan, *The Complete Year-by-Year New York Mets Fan's Almanac* (New York, 1992); Gary Carter and John Hough, Jr., *A Dream Season* (Orlando, FL, 1987); Keith Hernandez and Mike Bryan, *If At First . . .* (New York, 1986); Bob Hertzel, "McDowell: Strawberry's Woes Are Just Starting," *The Sporting News,* February 19, 1990, p. 33; *The Los Angeles Dodger Media Guide* (1994); Mike Shatzkin, ed., *The Ballplayers* (New York, 1990); Art Spander, "Mets' Strawberry Is No Longer 'Stressed Out,' " *The Sporting News,* May 28, 1990, p. 12; Darryl Strawberry with Art Rust, Jr., *Darryl* (New York, 1992).

William A. Borst

C. VIVIAN STRINGER
(March 16, 1945–) ———————————————————— *Basketball*

C. Vivian Stoner Stringer remains the only mentor in NCAA women's basketball to coach two different teams to the NCAA Final Four. She was born on March 16, 1945, in Ederborn, Pennsylvania, the daughter of Charles Stoner, a coal miner and musician, and graduated from German Township Senior High School in 1966. Since her high school had no athletic program for girls, Vivian played basketball, baseball, and football with the boys.

Stringer, the third woman coach in the United States to have won at least 500 college victories, reached that milestone at the University of Iowa on January 28, 1994. Vivian's impact on basketball surpasses her remarkable win-loss record. In 1994, she stated, "It's been a passion of mine to develop women's basketball, every aspect of women's basketball. I believed all along that women's basketball could be exciting, that we could draw crowds and there would be great enthusiasm." Anne Griffiths, her Slippery Rock State College basketball coach, remarked, "I never doubted she wouldn't do well." Tom Davis, University of Iowa's men basketball coach, in 1987 prophetically concurred, "Coach Stringer has a brilliant reputation of bringing women's basketball to new heights. . . . Today she's one of the best in the country. Tomorrow?"

Vivian was voted National Coach of the Year in 1982, 1988, and 1993 and named *Sports Illustrated's* National Women's Coach of the Year in 1993. In 1993, she also received the Carol Eckman Award, given annually to the women's basketball coach who demonstrates spirit, courage, commitment, leadership, and service to women's basketball. Stringer demonstrated those qualities in coaching the University of Iowa Hawkeyes to the NCAA Final Four in 1993. She overcame personal tragedy that year as William D. Stringer, her husband, colleague, friend, and fan, suddenly died in November 1992. She is now bringing up her teenage son, David, daughter, Janine, and youngest son, Justin, with the assistance of her close-knit and supportive family.

Stringer's coaching philosophy extends beyond the gymnasium. "We recruit warm, sincere, people to become part of the Hawkeye family . . . that believes, respects and cares for one another. . . . We have a responsibility to study hard, practice hard and play hard. The Iowa experience is about setting . . . reachable goals, attacking the books with the same vigor with which we attack the backboard . . . learning qualities of hard work, perseverance, honesty, and teamwork that will carry us way beyond our days on the court. . . . Success is the total fulfillment of the person on the court, in the classroom, and as an integral member of the community." The commitment to excellence on and off the court is demonstrated by Vivian's careful analysis of opponents' game plans, meticulously planned practices, brilliant game plans, devotion to many charitable organizations, and love for her three children.

Stringer prepared for her coaching and teaching career by earning a Bachelor of Science degree in health and physical education in 1970 from Slippery Rock State College. As a student there, Vivian performed for nationally ranked tennis, field hockey, and softball teams. She earned a Master of Science degree in organization and administration in physical education from Slippery Rock in 1974. In 1971, she joined Cheyney State College in Pennsylvania as an assistant professor of recreation, health, and physical education and head women's basketball coach. Cheyney State posted an impressive 251–51 win-loss record in her 12 seasons there. In the first-ever NCAA Women's Basketball Championship in 1982, Cheyney State finished second behind Louisiana Tech. Her honors at Cheyney State included Division I Stayfree Coach of the Year in 1982, Philadelphia Sports Writers' Association Coach of the Year twice, and Pennsylvania

Association for Intercollegiate Athletics for Women Coach of the Year in 1982. *Ebony* named her one of the Outstanding Black Women in Sports in 1980.

Stringer's 24-year coaching career through 1995 has produced 520 wins and only 135 losses. Stringer, in her twenty-fourth coaching season in 1994–1995, ranked ninth in career winning percentage (.794) and third nationally for most wins by an active coach. Her record at Iowa includes 269 wins and 84 losses through 1994–1995. The Hawkeyes made nine consecutive NCAA tournament appearances until Stringer suffered her worst coaching season with an 11–17 mark in 1994–1995. Vivian's leadership has established the University of Iowa among the premier women's basketball teams. Attendance at Hawkeye women's basketball games skyrocketed under Stringer. In 1988, 22,157 fans attended the Iowa-Ohio State University game to shatter national single-game records. The tickets for that annual showdown were sold out 30 hours prior to the opening tip, marking the first pregame sellout in women's basketball history. In July 1995, Rutgers University named Stringer its new women's basketball coach.

Her international coaching assignments remain extensive. In 1981, Stringer coached the U.S. Select team to China. Vivian also mentored the World University Games team in 1985 and the U.S. World Championship zone qualification team in 1989. In 1991, she led the U.S. to a Bronze Medal at the Pan-American Games in Havana, Cuba.

Stringer's leadership extends beyond the court into advocacy and administration. Vivian helped develop the Women's Basketball Coaches Association, belongs to the Kodak All-America Selection Committee, and was elected to the Women's Sports Foundation Advisory Board. For three years, she served as the Big Ten Conference representative to the NCAA Division I Mideast Basketball Committee. Stringer also participates as a voting board member of the Amateur Basketball Association of the USA and the Nike Shoe Company Advisory Board.

BIBLIOGRAPHY: Arthur Ashe, Jr., *A Hard Road to Glory: A History of the African-American Athlete Since 1946*, vol. 3 (New York, 1988); Jane Burns, "Stringer Puts 500 Victories in Perspective," *Des Moines Register*, January 21, 1994, p. S1; Jane Burns, "Makeshift Lineup Reaps Milestone," *Des Moines Register*, January 29, 1994, p. S1; C. Vivian Stringer Biography, Cheyney State College, Cheyney, PA, January 1983; University of Iowa Women's Sport Relations, Iowa City, IA, letters to Janice A. Beran, January 6, 1994; February 6, 1994.

Janice A. Beran

LAWRENCE TAYLOR
(February 4, 1959–   ) ——————————————————— *Football*

Lawrence Taylor may have been the most dominating defensive player in National Football League (NFL) history. At the very least, Lawrence transformed professional football during the 1980s by making the pass-rusher a highly visible defensive star. No one who saw Taylor early in his career would even have predicted a professional football career for him. Lawrence, the proverbial late bloomer, was born in Williamsburg, Virginia, on February 4, 1959, and grew up in that historic city. His father, Clarence, worked as a dispatcher at Norfolk News shipyards, while his mother, Iris, taught school. Taylor mostly played baseball while growing up and did not begin playing football until age 15. Lawrence excelled at Lafayette High School only after having a late growth spurt and attracted only regional recruiting attention, accepting a football scholarship to the University of North Carolina.

Taylor started slowly at the Atlantic Coast Conference (ACC) school. Lawrence had developed more of a reputation for partying and brawling than for football. In his junior year, he met Linda Cooley, who later became his wife and the mother of his three children, Lawrence, Jr., Tenitia, and Paula. She helped Taylor calm down and focus on football. A position switch from noseguard to linebacker also helped. Lawrence reached his stride as a senior in 1980, when he led North Carolina to an 11–1 mark and sacked opposing quarterbacks 16 times. He was named ACC Player of the Year for 1980 and a consensus All-America.

The New York Giants made Taylor the second pick of the 1981 NFL draft, following only Heisman Trophy winner George Rogers. Lawrence quickly re-paid New York's faith in him, leading the Giants to the playoffs after a 4–12 season the previous year. The 240-pounder's speed, aggressiveness, and fierce will to win astonished onlookers. No linebacker had ever pursued runners with such relentless ferocity. Taylor disclosed, "I played all out every minute, every day—not only in games but in practice, too." His specialty involved tackling the passer behind the line of scrimmage. Lawrence glamorized the so-called sack so much that in 1982 the NFL started keeping official sack statistics. Taylor disrupted offenses to an unprecedented extent. NFL coaches changed their offensive alignments to allow for an extra blocker to contain Lawrence, while defensive coaches began intensive searches for his clones.

The high point of Taylor's career came in 1986. Lawrence compiled 20.5 sacks that season, the best single-season mark of his career, and led the Giants to their first Super Bowl victory. In Super Bowl XXI, New York defeated the Denver Broncos, 39–20. Keyed by Taylor, New York's defense allowed only two touchdowns in three post-season victories. Lawrence was named the NFL's Most Valuable Player (MVP), an unprecedented accomplishment for a defensive player. Taylor accomplished all this only two years after developing an addiction to cocaine. Lawrence spent a short time in a rehabilitation center following the 1984 season but claimed to have overcome his substance abuse problems by playing golf.

Taylor continued to perform in stellar fashion throughout the 1980s, despite facing some adversity. In 1987, Lawrence crossed the NFL Players Association picket line during a strike. He also missed time that season because of a hamstring injury. The following campaign, Taylor tested positive for drugs and was suspended for four games. Lawrence recovered to lead the Giants to their second Super Bowl triumph following the 1990 season. New York edged the Buffalo Bills, 20–19, in Super Bowl XXV.

Taylor's skills began to slip in the early 1990s. Lawrence was not selected to the Pro Bowl squad following the 1991 season, after having been named every campaign from 1981 through 1990. He missed much of the second half of the 1992 season with a ruptured Achilles tendon but returned in 1993 to lead the Giants to a playoff spot. The linebacker announced his retirement after the season, finishing his NFL career with 132.5 official sacks and nine interceptions. In 1994, the Giants retired Taylor's uniform number, 56. The World Wrestling Federation signed Lawrence in February 1995 to battle 390-pound Bam Bam Bigelow in a feature match at Wrestlemania XI.

Taylor, clearly the most influential defensive player of his era, possessed sufficient speed to run 97 yards for a touchdown after intercepting a pass against the Detroit Lions in 1982. Lawrence hit hard enough to end a player's career, sacking Washington Redskins quarterback Joe Theisman in a nationally televised Monday night game in 1985.

Writer Paul Zimmerman in 1994 noted, "Taylor created havoc. He turned games around with his patented strip sack, slapping the ball free. The stampede was on. Everyone had to have a player like Taylor, honing in on the passer from the right side." Lawrence stated simply: "I'm a wild man in a wild game."

BIBLIOGRAPHY: J. E. Bradley, "L. T. and the Home Team," *Esquire* 104 (December 1985), pp. 306–308; *Current Biography Yearbook* (1990), pp. 578–581; John Delcos, "Lawrence Taylor Is Winning the Battle with Time," *Football Digest* 20 (April 1991), pp. 44–47; Jill Lieber, "Invincible?: No, Just Real Mean," *Sports Illustrated* 66 (January 26, 1987), pp. 36–38; Milton Shapiro, "Search and Destroy," *New York Times Magazine* (August 26, 1984), pp. 18–23; Barry Stanton, "Interview: Lawrence Taylor," *Sport* 76 (November 1985), pp. 17–21; Lawrence Taylor and David Falkner, *LT: Living on the Edge* (New York, 1987); Paul Zimmerman, "Terrific Tayloring," *Sports Illustrated* 73 (September 17, 1990), pp. 30–37; Paul Zimmerman, "Don't Cross This Line," *Sports Illustrated* 81 (September 5, 1994), p. 50.

Jim L. Sumner

MARSHALL TAYLOR
(November 26, 1878–June 21, 1932) ———————————————— *Bicycling*

Marshall Walter Taylor, among the first internationally recognized African-American athletes, won national and world sprint bicycling championships in the era of the sport's greatest popularity. One of eight children of Gilbert Taylor, an impoverished coachman, and Saphonia Taylor, he was born on November 26, 1878, in Indianapolis, Indiana, and quit school after eighth grade. Taylor worked as a janitor for the local Hay & Willits bicycle firm, performing trick riding exhibitions in front of the store to attract customers. Marshall's fancy mounts, dismounts, and riding stunts on a safety bicycle attracted sizable crowds. Nicknamed "Major," he wore a military-style uniform with large brass buttons. In 1892, Taylor won his first local bicycle race. Marshall joined the See-Saw Circle, the local African-American bicycling club, and in 1894 broke the mile track record on the Capitol City Velodrome. White track officials resented Major's bicycling success and barred him from Velodrome competitions.

George Munger, bicycle racer and manufacturer, hired Taylor as his personal valet and company messenger. Munger, realizing Marshall's world bicycling championship potential, gave him training and racing tips. Munger's bicycle firm moved in 1895 to Worcester, Massachusetts, where Major joined the African-American Albion Cycle Club and could enter any race. Taylor, who grew to five foot seven inches and 155 pounds, won several large regional amateur competitions before turning professional. Marshall placed eighth in the December 1896 grueling six-day 1,732-mile race from New York City to Houston, Texas. "The wonder of the race," the *New York Times* wrote, "is 'Major' Taylor, the little colored boy who serves as the professional mascot for the South Brooklyn Wheelmen." Promoter Billy Brady managed Major with great success in numerous sprint meets at the Manhattan Beach track. Taylor competed in best-of-three-match sprints, often earning $500 a race. Marshall endured constant discrimination, including being choked by one competitor, often being awarded second place when he had actually finished first, being banned from southern competitions, and being forced to stay in segregated hotels or with African-American families. The devout Baptist toted the Bible with him constantly and refused to race on Sundays.

Taylor, who bought a fashionable, seven-bedroom Victorian house in Worcester, overcame unethical tactics that fellow racers used against him to break bicycling records in the mile and every other short-distance event within two years. In 1899, Marshall won the world one-mile sprint championship before 18,000 people at Montreal, Canada, overtaking Tom Butler 10 feet from the finish. Taylor, who also captured the two-mile sprint title, wrote, "I never felt so proud to be an American." The League of American Wheelmen recognized Marshall as national champion, but the new National Cycling Association (NCA) did not follow suit until the next year. Taylor did not defend his world title at Paris, France, in 1900 but won the NCA sprint championship before 10,000 spectators at Newark, New Jersey. Marshall edged 19-year-old Frank Kramer of Indiana for the crown, utilizing tactical cunning, expert bike-handling skills, and a sharp finishing sprint. Iver Johnson Arms & Cycle Works of Fitchburg, Massachusetts, signed Major to a $1,000 contract to ride their bikes the next two seasons.

International bicycling competitions increasingly attracted Taylor's attention. In 1901, Marshall won 42 races at various distances in 16 European cities, defeating world champion Edmund Jacquelin in Paris, France. After winning the first heat with Jacquelin, the confident Major said, "I was so positive that I could defeat him again." Taylor married African-American socialite Daisy Morris in March 1902 and triumphed in 40 European races that spring. Marshall ranked among the nation's best-paid athletes, earning $35,000 in 1902, and held seven world records. Major kept an exhausting racing itinerary, sandwiching a third European excursion between two Australian tours. Taylor's wife gave birth in Australia to their only child, a daughter, Sydney, named after her birthplace. Taylor, although accorded celebrity status abroad, was refused service at a San Francisco restaurant upon his return to the United States. Marshall collapsed and suffered a nervous breakdown, forcing cancellation of his 1904 European tour. French promoters Victor Breyer and Robert Coquelle sued Major for $10,000 for breach of contract, causing the NCA to suspend him. The French promoters dropped their suit in 1907, when Taylor agreed to return to the European circuit and race on Sundays. Marshall defeated the best European riders except Jacquelin on the 1907 tour.

Major retired from sprint racing in 1910 after suffering several defeats on the European circuit, having netted $75,000 in savings in a 16-year career. Taylor, who already had designed an extension for bicycle handlebars, wanted to learn the mechanical trade at Worcester Technical School. His application was rejected, however, because he lacked a high school diploma. Marshall pursued several unsuccessful business enterprises, including the Taylor Manufacturing Company, a home heating firm, and an apartment complex, forcing his family to move into a smaller home by 1925. His wife soon left him to live in New York City. Taylor wrote an autobiography, *The Fastest Bicycle Rider in the World,* recounting his travels and racing achievements, but could not find a publisher. Marshall paid to have the autobiography published in 1928 and peddled copies around Worcester. Alderman James Bowler, a former competitor, found Major a job in Chicago. On June 21, 1932, Taylor died of a heart attack at a Cook County Hospital charity ward in Chicago. The honest, courageous, God-fearing, clean-living, gentlemanly athlete had overcome racial prejudice and other obstacles to become the world sprint champion.

BIBLIOGRAPHY: Judy Keene, "Marshall Taylor—Bike Champ from Indianapolis," *Indianapolis Magazine* (May 1977), pp. 41–54; Robert Lucas, "The World's Fastest Bicycle Rider," *Negro Digest* (May 1948), pp. 10–13; Peter Nye, *Hearts of Lions: The History of American Bicycle Racing* (New York, 1988); Andrew Ritchie, *Major Taylor: The Extraordinary Career of a Champion Bicycle Racer* (Mill Valley, CA, 1988); Andrew Ritchie, "Marshall 'Major' Taylor," *Competitive Cycling* (November 1978), pp. 12–13; (December 1978), p. 7; Robert A. Smith, *A Social History of the Bicycle* (New York, 1972); Marshall W. Taylor, *The Fastest Bicycle Rider in the World* (Brattleboro, VT, 1928).

David L. Porter

FRANK THOMAS
(May 27, 1968–) ————————————————————— *Baseball*

Frank Thomas has played only seven seasons of major league baseball, but the Chicago White Sox have never fielded a slugger of comparable caliber in their 95-year history. Frank Edward Thomas, Jr., was born in Columbus, Georgia, the youngest of five children born to Frank Thomas, Sr., and Charlie

Mae Thomas. His father was employed as a bail bondsman and textile worker. Frank starred in baseball, football, and basketball at Columbus High School. Bobby Howard, his high school baseball coach, observed Frank hit some 400-foot home runs at Columbus. Thomas considered Howard a tough disciplinarian, who pushed him to develop all of his skills. Frank said, "I would've signed to play baseball, but nobody wanted me." He, therefore, accepted a football scholarship to Auburn University and played tight end as a freshman but continued to focus on baseball. For Auburn, Thomas clouted 21 home runs in 1987, batted .385 in 1988, and drove in 83 runs with a .403 batting average in 1989. In 1987, 19-year-old Frank, the youngest member of the U.S. Pan-American team, batted .338 on their exhibition tour. *The Sporting News* selected Thomas for their 1989 All-America College baseball team.

The Chicago White Sox American League (AL) baseball club scouted Thomas for three years before drafting him in June 1989 as the seventh player selected overall. After batting .365 in 17 games with the Sarasoto, Florida, Gulf Coast League White Sox, Frank finished the 1989 season with Sarasota of the Florida State League. In 1990, he batted .323 in 109 games for Birmingham, Alabama, in the Southern League before joining the Chicago White Sox. The six-foot-five-inch, 270-pound right-handed slugger hit .330 in 60 games for the White Sox.

Although incredibly strong, Frank remains extremely disciplined at the plate. White Sox outfielder Tim Raines reports, "I've been in the majors 13 years and I've never seen a hitter with such a keen eye at the plate." From 1991 to 1994, Thomas averaged 34 home runs, 113 RBIs, 106 runs, and 121 bases on balls per season. These numbers prompt many authorities to compare him with Babe Ruth. In 1993, Frank set a White Sox record with 41 home runs and earned the AL Most Valuable Player (MVP) award. He won *The Sporting News* Silver Slugger Award as designated hitter in 1991 and at first base in 1993 and 1994. The damage Thomas has inflicted on AL pitchers certainly justifies his nickname "the Big Hurt."

Frank's defense remains suspect. Thomas noted, "I also got a little tired of hearing 'Yeah, but he can't field.'" So in the off-season, he began a weight training program and worked on defense. In 1991, Chicago manager Jeff Torborg worked endlessly on Thomas's throwing mechanics. Shoulder pain finally forced Frank into the designated hitter role for 101 games. Off-season surgery helped eliminate the pain, while hard work on fielding and throwing improved his defense. He still made 15 errors at first base in 1993, the second highest AL total. Thomas hit .353 and received 10 walks in the 1993 AL Championship Series, which the White Sox dropped to the Toronto Blue Jays in 6 games. Frank played on the AL All-Star team in 1993, 1994, and 1995.

Thomas enjoyed a banner season in 1994, leading the AL in runs scored (106), walks (109), slugging percentage (.729), and on-base percentage (.487) and ranking second in home runs (38), third in batting average (.353), total bases (1,291), and doubles (34), and fourth in RBIs (101) and hits (141). Thomas, close to a Triple Crown when the 1994 strike started, became the first AL player to win Most Valuable Player (MVP) honors consecutive seasons since Roger Maris in 1960 and 1961. Jimmie Foxx, Hal Newhouser, Yogi Berra, and Mickey Mantle remain the only other AL players to accomplish the feat.

During his remarkable career through the strike-shortened 1994 season, Frank has played 643 games, batted .326, made 741 hits, received 525 bases on balls, recorded 142 home runs and 484 RBIs, and scored 463 runs. The White Sox have amply rewarded Thomas with a contract extension worth $29 million from 1995 to 1998 and two option years totaling an additional $14 million. Frank also made several commercial endorsements, including Reebok shoes for $8 million. Frank vows, "I want to get a hit every time up, and I see myself with the Sox for my whole career."

Despite the fame and wealth that Thomas has earned in such a short time, his top priority remains his family. Frank married Elise Silver, whom he met at spring training in 1991. Although Elise's father works as an attorney and her mother serves as Associate Dean of the Graduate School of Business at Columbia University, her family is deeply rooted in baseball. Silver Stadium, the home of the Rochester, New York, Red Wings of the International League, is named for her great uncle, Maury Silver. Frank has a son, Sterling, and a daughter, Sloan. He has enabled his mother and father to retire, financially helps his siblings and their families, and maintains close contact with them. He generously assists his old Boys Club and other charities.

BIBLIOGRAPHY: Steve Aschburner, "Frank Thomas of White Sox Puts Big Hurt on Opposing Pitchers," *Baseball Digest* 52 (December 1993), pp. 34–37; John Dewan, ed., *The Scouting Report: 1994* (New York, 1994); Zander Hollander, ed., *1994 Complete Handbook of Baseball* (New York, 1994); Skip Myslenski, "Perfectly Frank," *Chicago Tribune*, Sunday Special, August 7, 1994, sec. 3, pp. 1, 8–9; Steve Wulf, "The Big Hurt," *Sports Illustrated* 79 (September 13, 1993), pp. 41–43.

                                                                        Frank J. Olmsted

ISIAH THOMAS

(April 30, 1961–   ) ——————————————————————————— *Basketball*

Isiah Thomas, one of the finest pure point guards and flashiest ball handlers in basketball history, starred on one NCAA and two National Basketball Association (NBA) championship teams. Isiah Lord Thomas III was born on April 30, 1961, in Chicago, Illinois, the ninth child of Isiah Thomas II, an International Harvester plant foreman, and Mary Thomas. Thomas grew up in a west side neighborhood known for gangs and drugs. Isiah's father, prone to near-violent bursts of anger after losing his job, left home in 1964. Mary, a strong-willed woman, worked for Chicago's Department of Human Services and brought up seven boys and two daughters.

Sportswriter Ira Berkow lauded Thomas as a "prodigy in basketball the way

Mozart was in music." Isiah provided sparkling dribbling and shooting displays at halftime of Catholic Youth League games when only three years old. Thomas led St. Joseph Prep School of Westchester, Illinois, to second place in the State High School basketball tournament as a junior and earned All-America accolades as a senior. In the 1979 Pan-American Games, Isiah scored 21 points in the championship game over Puerto Rico.

Thomas selected Indiana University over more than 100 other colleges and led the 21–8 Hoosiers in scoring, assists, and steals and to a 1980 Big Ten Conference (BTC) title. No freshman had made the Associated Press (AP) All-Big Ten squad before. Isiah directed Indiana to the 1981 NCAA championship at Philadelphia, Pennsylvania. His two second-half steals sparked coach Bobby Knight's team to a 63–50 rout of favored University of North Carolina in the NCAA final. The consensus All-America scored a game-high 23 points, earning Most Valuable Player (MVP) honors.

The six-foot-one-inch, 182-pound 20-year-old left Indiana after his sophomore year, having scored 968 points (15.4-point average) in 63 games. Although admiring Knight's basketball leadership, Thomas disliked his coaches' occasional dehumanizing treatment of players. The Detroit Pistons selected Isiah second in the first round of the 1981 NBA draft and signed him to a four-year, $1.6 million contract. He bought his mother a ranch house in Clarendon Hills outside Chicago.

The boyish, smiling Thomas influenced NBA playing styles more than any small point guard since Bob Cousy. Isiah dazzled spectators with his accurate long-range shooting, adept ball stealing, brilliant ball handling, creative passing, and penetrating drives. Cousy acknowledged, "He has done things on the basketball floor that no one else has done before." The Pistons surged from 21 wins to 39 victories in Thomas's rookie season. Isiah, the fourth rookie to start an All-Star Game, was named *The Sporting News* NBA Rookie of the Year. In 1982–1983, Thomas led the NBA in minutes played (3,093), averaged a career-best 22.9 points a game, and ranked second in 3-point field goal percentage. The 1983–1984 Pistons enjoyed their first winning season in seven years with a 49–33 record, as Isiah averaged 21.3 points, 11.1 assists (second best), and 2.5 steals (second) per game. Although just in his third season, he passed Dave Bing as the all-time club leader in assists. In 1984–1985, Thomas broke Kevin Porter's NBA season record for assists with 1,123 (13.9 average).

Thomas averaged 20.6 points and 10 assists a game in 1986–1987, leading the Pistons to the Eastern Conference finals. The Boston Celtics defeated Detroit in the seven-game series, best remembered for Isiah's errant pass in the waning moments of Game 5. Piston coach Chuck Daly observed, "We can beat any team in the league when he's running the team . . . and his concentration's there." In June 1987, Thomas protested that sports broadcasters perpetuated stereotypes about African-American athletes. "When [Larry] Bird makes a great play," Isiah contended, "it's due to his thinking, and his work habits. It's all planned out by him. It's not the case for blacks. All we do is run and jump. We never practice or give a thought to how we play. It's like I came dribbling out of my mother's womb."

Detroit became a bruising, intimidating, defense-oriented team under coach Daly. After winning the 1987–1988 Central Division title with a 54–28 mark, the Pistons upset Boston in the six-game Eastern Conference finals and reached the NBA finals for the first time against the Los Angeles Lakers. In the third quarter of Game 6 at the Great Western Forum, Thomas set NBA playoff records by scoring 25 points and making 11 field goals in one quarter and tied NBA finals marks by making 14 field goals in one half and six steals. Despite a badly sprained ankle, Isiah tallied 43 points and eight assists in the 103–102 loss. According to Roland Lazenby of *The Sporting News,* Thomas gained "enough respect to last a lifetime." The Lakers, nevertheless, repeated as NBA champions.

Detroit won its first two NBA crowns the next two seasons. The Pistons boasted the NBA's best regular-season record in 1988–1989 with a 65–17 mark, as Thomas contributed 18.2 points and 8.3 assists per game. With center Bill Laimbeer, forwards Rick Mahorn and Dennis Rodman, and guards Thomas, Joe Dumars, and Vinnie Johnson, Detroit defeated the Chicago Bulls for the Eastern Conference title and swept the Los Angeles Lakers for the NBA championship. Isiah's *Bad Boys!,* coauthored with Matt Dobek, recounted Detroit's title quest. In 1989–1990, Thomas averaged 18.4 points and 9.4 assists a game to pace the 59–23 Pistons to another Central Division crown. Detroit defeated the Chicago Bulls again in the Eastern Conference finals and the Portland Trail Blazers in five games for the NBA championship, with Isiah earning MVP honors.

Thomas retired in April 1994 after tearing his left Achilles tendon, having scored 18,822 points (19.2-point average), made 9,061 assists (fourth best), and 1,861 steals (sixth best) in 979 games. Isiah, selected to 12 consecutive All-Star Games from 1982 through 1993, was named MVP in 1984 with 21 points and 15 assists and 1986 with 30 points and 10 assists. In 111 playoff games, Thomas scored 2,261 points (20.4-point average), dished out 987 assists, and posted 234 steals. Isiah made the All-NBA Rookie Team in 1982, the All-NBA First Team from 1984 through 1986, and the All-NBA Second Team in 1983 and 1987.

In June 1994, the Toronto Raptors expansion franchise named Thomas vice president for Basketball Operations. Isiah, who married Lynn Kendall in 1985 and has one son, Joshua, and one daughter, Lauren, resides in Bloomfield Hills, Michigan. He fulfilled a promise to his mother by earning a bachelor's degree in criminal justice from Indiana in 1987. The NBA has voted Thomas, who has worked with inner-city Detroit children and campaigned against drug use, the Walter Kennedy Award for civic responsibility. "Athletes are role models," Isiah stressed. "We ought to take advantage of that opportunity and make other people's lives better."

BIBLIOGRAPHY: Barbara Bigelow, ed., *Contemporary Black Biography,* vol. 7 (Detroit, MI, 1994), pp. 257–261; David Bradley, "The Importance of Being Isiah," *Sport* 79 (May 1988), pp. 24–27, 29; Jeff Coplon, "How I Do What I Do," *Sport* 77 (February 1986), pp. 59–62, 64; *Current Biography Yearbook* (1989), pp. 571–576; Loren Feldman, "Isiah's Prophecy," *Gentleman's Quarterly* 58 (February 1988), pp. 190–195; Jack McCallum, "There's Just No Doubting Thomas," *Sports Illustrated* 66 (May 18, 1987), pp. 30–32, 37; William Nack, "I Have Got to Do Right," *Sports Illustrated* 66 (January 19, 1987), pp. 60–64, 66–68, 70, 72–73; William F. Reed, "There's No Doubting Thomas," *Sports Illustrated* 54 (April 6, 1981), pp. 15–16; Isiah Thomas with Matt Dobek, *Bad Boys! An Inside Look at the Detroit Pistons 1988–89 Championship Season* (Indianapolis, IN, 1989).

Brian L. Laughlin and David L. Porter

THURMAN THOMAS
(May 16, 1966–   ) ———————————————————————— *Football*

Thurman Thomas has starred in football since playing at Willowridge High School in Missouri City, Texas, where he was selected an All-State performer and the Player of the Year by the Houston Touchdown Club. Thomas fully appreciates having received an education while starring on the gridiron and believes, "Give back to society something to help others achieve."

The son of the Gilbert Cockrells, Thomas was born in Houston, Texas, on May 16, 1966, and performed well enough as a prepster in football that many colleges recruited him. In 1992, Thurman was inducted into the Texas High School Hall of Fame. At Oklahoma State University, he developed into one of the nation's very best running backs. During his college career, Thomas carried the ball 897 times for 4,595 yards and 43 touchdowns. Thurman's career yardage marked the second best in Big Eight Conference (BEC) history. He undoubtedly would have ranked as the top BEC rusher but was hampered much of his junior year. His left knee was injured badly in a pickup basketball game the summer before the football season. After this injury, he underwent arthroscopic surgery.

Thomas enjoyed an outstanding college sophomore year, gaining 1,650 yards on 327 carries. Thurman holds the Oklahoma State University record for most yards rushing in a game, garnering 293 yards against Iowa State University in 1987. He earned First Team Associated Press (AP) and United Press International (UPI) honors on their All-BEC elevens for three successive years.

From high school to college and pro football, Thomas performed as an unselfish team player and always credited his success to the assistance given him by his teammates and opponents. **Emmitt Smith** of the Dallas Cowboys confided, after the 1994 Super Bowl, "I told him [Thomas] that I loved him. He's a great player and I told him I probably wouldn't see him in Hawaii because of my shoulder injury."

As a college senior, Thomas finished seventh in the Heisman Trophy balloting. Thurman's college career ended in a Sun Bowl game against West Virginia University, as he ran for 157 yards and set a record with 4 touchdowns. When including his yardage in the Sun Bowl and two Gator Bowl appearances, he amassed 5,004 yards in his college career and scored 48 touchdowns.

As a college sophomore, Thomas made the *Football News* and *The Sporting News* All-America Second Teams and AP Third Team. Thurman two years later garnered First Team AP All-America Team and Second Team UPI honors. During his college career, he attained 21 100-yard games. He received a bachelor's degree in hotel and restaurant management.

In the 1988 National Football League (NFL) draft, Thomas was selected by the Buffalo Bills in the second round as the fortieth player chosen. In his seven NFL seasons, Thurman has made his name synonymous with the phrase "the world's best all-purpose running back." Thomas led the NFL in total yards from scrimmage four consecutive years, eclipsing by one year the record set by the great **Jim Brown.** Thurman totaled 1,913 yards in 1989, 1,829 yards in 1990, 2,038 yards in 1991, and 2,113 yards in 1992, being selected the NFL's Most Valuable Player (MVP) in 1991. He earned five consecutive trips to the Pro Bowl, from 1989 to 1993, but did not play in the 1992 game.

During the 1993 season, Thomas rushed for 1,315 yards on 356 carries for a 3.7 yard per carry average and scored six touchdowns. Thurman also caught 48 passes for 387 yards (an 8.1-yard average). In the Super Bowl, he unfortunately fumbled twice in the Bills' loss to the Dallas Cowboys. Thomas, nevertheless, stayed after the game to answer questions by the press, taking responsibility for his mistakes. The Buffalo Bills lost four consecutive times in Super Bowl competition. After the 1994 Super Bowl, Thurman acknowledged, "There was no doubt those fumbles were the key to the ball game. After the second one, in the second half, it seemed like the momentum switched." Bills' linebacker Cornelius Bennett stressed, "Thurman is my teammate and my best friend. If people pick on him, then we'll just have to deal with it."

Thomas, often asked about his fumbles in two Super Bowls, responds, "It wasn't a matter of me being careless with the ball. It was just that as I got the football at certain times, there was someone around me and I couldn't tuck it away." Coach Marv Levy lauds Thurman, "I sure don't castigate him because he fumbled. He was very conscious not to fumble. You take chances when you go out on the field."

Thomas's offensive production declined in 1994, when Buffalo struggled to a 9–7 record and missed the playoffs. In 1994, Thurman gained 1,093 yards (3.8-yard average) for 7 touchdowns and caught 50 passes for 394 yards and 2 touchdowns. Through the 1994 season, he has rushed 2,018 times for 8,724 yards (4.3-yard average) and 48 touchdowns and caught 345 passes for 3,402 yards (9.9-yard average) and 43 touchdowns.

In 1991, Thomas repaid his college partly for his education. On June 18,

1991, Thurman announced a major financial contribution to the Oklahoma State University Athletic Department. The contribution, a combination of cash and deferred gifts, totaled $1 million. The amount included a cash gift of $125,000 and a $750,000 life insurance policy purchased by Thomas, naming Oklahoma State University Athletics as the beneficiary. A $125,000 insurance policy on Thurman also was purchased by head coach Pat Jones to benefit Oklahoma State University Athletics. Additional benefits involved the use of Thomas's name and his making personal appearances, including being pictured in the Oklahoma State University trading card set issued by Collegiate Collections in mid-September 1991. Thurman autographed 500 of those cards.

Thomas, an excellent role model, contributes to the Buffalo Bills Foundation, established in 1986. Over the past five years, the foundation has distributed over $200,000 to more than 85 different charities. With other Buffalo Bills players, Thurman has given his time and efforts to help raise the funds distributed during the NFL season.

His activities also are directed toward health services, educational facilities, religious charities, and youth/family athletic programs. Grants have been given to worthy groups in all eight countries in the Buffalo area and national organizations with local affiliation. Thomas has raised funds for the American Heart Association, Arthritis Foundation, Camp Good Days, Children's Hospital of Buffalo, Cystic Fibrosis, Diabetes Foundation, Easter Seals, State Troopers Helping Hands, Kids Escaping Drugs Telethon, Leukemia Society, Roswell Park Cancer Institute, Sickle Cell Anemia, United Way, YMCA, and Variety Club Telethon. Thurman and quarterback Jim Kelly "went the extra mile to support community activities." "My part," affirmed Thomas, "was establishing the Thurman Thomas Scholarship Fund. More than $23,000 was raised and awarded in six scholarships to Erie Community College."

BIBLIOGRAPHY: *Buffalo Bills Media Guide* (1994); *Minneapolis Star-Tribune*, January 30–31, 1994; Sports Information Releases, Oklahoma State University, Stillwater, OK, December 19, 1987; June 18, 1991; Thurman Thomas, letter to Stan W. Carlson, January 30, 1994.

Stan W. Carlson

JOHN THOMPSON, JR.
(September 2, 1941–) ————————————————— *Basketball*

John Thompson, Jr., became the first African American to coach an NCAA championship team. John Robert Thompson, Jr., was born on September 2, 1941, in Washington, D.C., the son of John Robert Thompson, Sr., and Anna Thompson. John, a physically imposing man at 6 foot 10 inches, 280 pounds, and his wife Gwendolyn have two sons. John III played guard on the Princeton University varsity basketball squad, while Ronny performed at guard for his father at Georgetown University. They also have one daughter, Tiffany.

Thompson, the youngest of four children and only son, grew up in the housing projects of Anacostia. His father, a hard-working tile factory employee and mechanic, was illiterate but firmly believed in education. His mother, unable to get a teaching job with her certificate from a two-year college, worked instead as a maid and a practical nurse. John attended a parochial school until poor eyesight led officials to incorrectly diagnose him as a slow learner. He performed better after transferring to a public elementary school in the still-segregated Washington, D.C., system.

Thompson, recruited to play basketball as a center for Washington's Archbishop Carroll High School and an All-America, led his team to two City championships and 55 consecutive victories. These successes remain Washington-area records. John attended Providence College, where he graduated in 1964 with a bachelor's degree in economics. He played varsity basketball his sophomore, junior, and senior years, leading the Friars his sophomore year to the 1962 National Invitational Tournament (NIT). In his junior year, Thompson paced Providence to the NIT championship. As a senior, John helped Providence make the 1964 NCAA tourney and was designated New England College Player of the Year.

Thompson strove to become a well-rounded person at Providence, not just a star on the basketball court. Former teammate Jim Benedict, a sophomore starting guard when John was a senior center, reminisced that "being black was just one part of John's life. . . . Being academically prepared, someone you'd view as a real good student, was another side of John. . . . John drove himself to be a total person."

The Boston Celtics National Basketball Association (NBA) drafted Thompson, who backed up **Bill Russell** for two years. In 74 games, John scored 262 points and averaged 3.5 points per game. In 1966, he rejected NBA offers from the Chicago Bulls and New Orleans Buccaneers to become a social worker and teacher at Federal City College. Thompson earned a master's degree in guidance and counseling in 1971 at Federal City College, now the University of the District of Columbia. John also coached basketball at the Roman Catholic St. Anthony's High School from 1966 to 1972, compiling an impressive 128 wins and 22 losses. At St. Anthony's, Thompson developed his coaching techniques. John's style involved passing the ball to the big players, not underscoring finesse.

In 1972, Thompson became head basketball coach at the academically elite Georgetown University and immediately improved their dismal 3–23 record. John also emphasized the need for his athletes to demonstrate academic achievement. Scholarship players were required to attend classes regularly, not just maintain passing grades.

Thompson faced racism, reminiscent of his earlier life when segregation was the law. His players performed well enough the 1974–1975 season for Georgetown to receive its first invitation in 32 years to the NCAA post-season tournament. The Hoyas also competed in the NCAA tourney in the 1975–1976 season, although again did not win.

In the 1976 Summer Olympic Games in Montreal, Canada, assistant basketball coach Thompson helped his U.S. team recapture the Gold Medal. Georgetown advanced to the NCAA tournament in 1979–1980 and 1980–1981, being eliminated in the first round.

The "Ewing era," named after the seven-foot center **Patrick Ewing,** lasted from 1981 through 1985. Georgetown appeared in the NCAA Final Four for the first time in 1981–1982 but lost a 63–62 heartbreaker to the University of North Carolina Tar Heels. In Ewing's junior year, the Hoyas captured their first NCAA championship, defeating the University of Houston, 84–75, in the 1984 title game. During Ewing's senior year, Villanova University defeated Georgetown in the 1985 NCAA finals.

The 1981–1982 season saw Georgetown make its first Final Four appearance, as Thompson became the first African-American coach in that tournament. John responded in typical, straightforward fashion: "There have been several people who were more qualified than I am to be here, but they were denied the opportunity. I don't take any honor and dignity in being the first black anything, anywhere."

Thompson's team's intimidating playing style wears down opponents and forces turnovers. John, whom his players addressed respectfully as "Mr. Thompson" or "Coach," admitted that he is "not Mr. Nice Guy." Indeed, he remains one of the most controversial, successful coaches in college basketball today.

Thompson's coaching trademark is a towel that he uses on the court to wipe away the perspiration from his brow. John shields his players from the press. The media criticized Georgetown's frequent free-for-alls with other teams. John admitted that the Hoyas' "style of play lends itself to aggressiveness. We cover the full court for forty minutes, and that brings about and creates frustrations in ourselves and in other people at times."

The media has accused Thompson of deliberately recruiting all-African-American teams for an overwhelmingly white university located in a 70 percent African-American city. Many of Thompson's teams were all African American. John responded, "Black kids play basketball like Canadian kids play hockey. They start playing early, and they care about it a lot, generally more than suburban or rural white kids do. That's why they're so good at it." John remains assertively authoritative over his players, admitting, "I'm the director. I'm going to pick the script and I'm going to give them their roles. They're the actors. . . . I don't want anybody making up new lines, putting on their own act."

Thompson coached the 1988 U.S. Olympic basketball team at the Seoul, South Korea, Summer Olympics. The Soviets ironically won the Gold Medal, while the favored U.S. team took the Bronze.

Alonzo Mourning, a center who succeeded Ewing as star material in 1988–

1989, was rescued by Thompson from the bad influence of a drug dealer. John supervises his athletes' outside friendships. In early 1989, Thompson objected to the NCAA's decision to tighten admission standards for student athletes. Proposition 48 eventually required freshman scholar-athletes to have at least a high school 2.0 grade-point average in a college prep curriculum and achieve a minimum 700 SAT score. John emphasized the racial bias of some tests and the substandard curricula of some potentially gifted inner-city high school students. His sense of justice was hurt: "I feel that had this been in existence when I started into school, I would not have been provided with an opportunity to get a college education." After walking off the court and boycotting a game against Boston College in January 1989, Thompson convinced the NCAA to delay implementation of the new rule until 1991.

Thompson sees money, not race, dividing American society. Born in straightened economic circumstances, John resolved to demonstrate his achievement in recognized American standards of success. His $300,000 annual Georgetown salary makes him the highest paid person on campus. Thompson's honors include election to the Providence College Hall of Fame in 1974, earning the Patrick Healy Award from Georgetown in 1982, and being named U.S. Basketball Writers Association Coach of the Year in 1982, National Association of Basketball Coaches (NABC) Coach of the Year in 1984–1985, and United Press International (UPI) Coach of the Year in 1987. Through the 1994–1995 regular season, John has garnered a .724 winning percentage with a 523–199 record, 18 post-season tourney bids, and perhaps most important, a 97 percent graduation rate for his players.

BIBLIOGRAPHY: *Current Biography Yearbook* (1989), pp. 576–580; *The Hoya*, May 28, 1993; David L. Porter, ed., *Biographical Dictionary of American Sports: Basketball and Other Indoor Sports* (Westport, CT, 1989); Leonard Shapiro, *Big Man on Campus: John Thompson and the Georgetown Hoyas* (New York, 1991); Mary Mace Spradling, ed., *In Black and White* (Detroit, MI, 1985 supp.), p. 371; *Who's Who Among Black Americans* (Detroit, MI, 1994), p. 1451; *Who's Who in America*, 47th ed. (1992–1993), p. 3342.

Frederick J. Augustyn, Jr.

EMLEN TUNNELL
(March 25, 1925–July 24, 1975) ───────────────────── *Football*

In 1942, doctors told Emlen Tunnell that he would never play football again. Twenty-five years later, Tunnell became the first African American named to the Pro Football Hall of Fame. Emlen was born on March 25, 1925, in Bryn Mawr, Pennsylvania. After his graduation from Radnor High School, he entered the University of Toledo in 1942. Tunnell soon suffered the broken neck that seemed to end his football career. Although able to play basketball and help Toledo reach the finals of the National Invitational Tournament (NIT),

Tunnell wore a neck brace for a year and was turned down in his attempts to enlist in the U.S. Army and U.S. Navy. Undaunted, Emlen joined the U.S. Coast Guard and served there until early 1946. Upon his return to civilian life, Tunnell enrolled at the University of Iowa and tried out for football with 300 other candidates. Emlen began as the twenty-first halfback but soon became one of the Hawkeyes' most important players and excelled on defense. In 1947, Emlen asked coach Eddie Anderson for more time on offense but surprisingly was demoted to the third team. Anderson claimed his skills would best be used in spot situations. Tunnell fumed and considered not returning for his senior year. Then an eye operation forced him to drop out of school.

In the summer of 1948, Tunnell hitchhiked 150 miles to the offices of the New York Giants National Football League (NFL) club and asked for a tryout. The Giants had never employed an African-American player. None of the coaches had ever heard of Emlen, but team owner Tim Mara told him, "Since you had enough guts to come over and ask for a tryout, we'll give you one." Tunnell so impressed the Giants coaches that he earned a $5,000 contract along with a $1,000 bonus. Few African Americans played in the NFL at the time. The Giants' roster was heavily laden with players from southern schools, but Tunnell always insisted that he had no racial problems with his new teammates. Emlen's own personality enabled him quickly to become one of the most popular players on the team. His teammates also accepted him because he could help them win. In his first appearance with the Giants in an exhibition game against the Green Bay Packers, he intercepted four passes.

Although Tunnell continued to lobby for time on offense, New York coach Steve Owen quickly decided Emlen was too valuable on defense to waste. The six-foot-one-inch, nearly 200-pound Tunnell, bigger than most defensive backs of the time, also combined speed with devastating tackling. Emlen's greatest attribute proved his ability to "read" his opponents and put himself in the right place to make a tackle or interception. He spent long hours each week studying film until he knew exactly what to expect from each opponent. Teammate Frank Gifford, who noticed Tunnell's knack for being in the right spot, said, "At first I thought he was just lucky. Then I realized he was just great."

Tunnell played a key role in Coach Owen's "umbrella defense," a strategy that revolutionized NFL defenses in the early 1950s. Owen's scheme called for the defensive ends to drop off the traditional six-man line and become linebackers while four defensive backs formed a near-impregnable umbrella against passes. In its 1950 unveiling, the umbrella defense shut out the high-powered Cleveland Browns for the first time in their history. Tunnell also became the NFL's top kick returner, combining exceptional hands, good speed, remarkable toughness, and marvelous elusiveness. Kick returners live on the edge in the NFL, and injuries are common, but Emlen ignored the bruises and a few broken bones to play in 158 consecutive games. Nicknamed the Giants' "offense on defense," he scored three touchdowns on punt returns

and a fourth touchdown on a kickoff return in 1951. His runbacks of interceptions and kicks in 1952 netted 924 yards, 30 more than the NFL rushing
leader. The next season, only two offensive backs topped Emlen's 819 return
yards.

Tunnell starred on the Giants' 1956 NFL championship team and on the
1958 Eastern Division titlists. Emlen in 1959 joined Green Bay, where he
helped former Giants assistant coach Vince Lombardi win a Western Division
title in 1960 and an NFL championship in 1961. At his retirement following
the 1961 season, Tunnell held NFL career records for most interceptions with
79, yards gained on interceptions with 1,282, total punt returns with 258, and
yards gained on punt returns with 2,209. Emlen played in nine different Pro
Bowls and, although All-NFL selections did not include defensive backs until
1951, he was subsequently chosen at safety four times. After retiring as a
player, Tunnell served as a Giants assistant coach and scout from 1962 through
1973. No African American had coached in the NFL since the early 1920s.
In 1974, New York appointed Emlen assistant director of pro personnel. On
July 24, 1975, however, he suffered a fatal heart attack at the Pleasantville,
New York, training camp. He was survived by his wife Patricia, whom he had
married in 1962.

In 1969, Tunnell was named safety on the All-Time NFL Team covering
the league's first 50 years. Two years earlier, Emlen was elected to the Pro
Football Hall of Fame. He became not only the first African American so
honored but also the first player to be elected for purely defensive contributions. When informed of his election to the Hall of Fame by then-curator Dick
McCann, the modest Tunnell asked, "Who should I thank?" "Thank yourself,"
McCann told him.

BIBLIOGRAPHY: Gerald Eskenazi, *They Were Giants in Those Days* (New York,
1976); *New York Times*, July 24, 1975, p. 32; Don R. Smith, *Pro Football Hall of Fame
All-Time Greats* (New York, 1988); *The Sporting News Football Register* (1966); Emlen
Tunnell file, Pro Football Hall of Fame, Canton, OH.

Robert N. "Bob" Carroll

MIKE TYSON
(June 30, 1966–) ——————————————————————————— *Boxing*

Boxer Mike Tyson became the youngest fighter to win a portion of the world
heavyweight championship. Michael Gerald Tyson, the youngest of three children of John Kilpatrick and Lorna Tyson, was born on June 30, 1966, in
Brooklyn, New York, and grew up with his mother in the tough Bedford-
Stuyvesant section of Brooklyn. Bullies frequently targeted Tyson as a youth.
"They [the bullies] used to take my sneakers, my clothes, my money," Mike
recalled. "My mother didn't believe in violence. She detested it. Being that
way, I was very shy, almost effeminately shy." Tyson eventually struck back

at his tormentors. "I don't know what possessed me to fight, but when I started hitting [one of them], I was loving it. I let so much frustration out." Mike fought often and frequently found himself in trouble with the law. Officials sent him at age 13 to the Tryon School for Boys in upstate New York, where he began to box under the tutelage of Bobby Stewart, former Golden Gloves champion. Stewart saw potential in him and contacted Cus D'Amato, who had guided **Floyd Patterson** to the world heavyweight title. D'Amato took custody of Tyson and enrolled him in his Catskill, New York, boxing school.

Mike posted a fine amateur record, winning the 1984 National Golden Gloves heavyweight title. He failed to qualify for the U.S. Olympic team, however, because Henry Tillman eliminated him. He turned professional on March 6, 1985, stopping Hector Mercedes in one round in Albany, New York. Eighteen straight knockouts, many inside the first round, followed, making Tyson's punching power evident. Sterling Benjamin, who lasted only 58 seconds with Mike, lamented, "He has a sledgehammer." Eddie Richardson, who was knocked out by Tyson in 77 seconds, was asked if he had ever been hit that hard before. Richardson replied, "Yeah, about a year ago I was hit by a truck!" His most noteworthy early victory came in a 30-second demolition of former contender Marvis Frazier on national television. Tyson, at age 20, captured the World Boxing Council (WBC) version of the heavyweight crown on November 22, 1986, knocking out Trevor Berbick in two rounds in Las Vegas, Nevada. Mike won the remaining two titles recognized by boxing's sanctioning bodies, recording decisions over World Boxing Association (WBA) titlist James Smith and International Boxing Federation (IBF) champion Tony Tucker in 1987. Full acclaim as world heavyweight champion came in his June 1988 knockout of "linear" champion Michael Spinks, who had twice defeated **Larry Holmes.**

Following his victory over Spinks, Tyson scored easy triumphs over Frank Bruno and Carl Williams in 1989. Mike created headlines outside the ring with a surprise marriage to actress Robin Givens in February 1988. The marriage ended in a stormy divorce one year later. Several negative incidents, including street scuffles and driving offenses, generated more unfavorable publicity for the young champion. Many observers blamed his troubles on the deaths of D'Amato and comanager Jim Jacobs, who had acted as his father figures.

Tyson's reign as heavyweight champion came to a sudden, shocking end in Tokyo, Japan, on February 10, 1990, when unheralded James "Buster" Douglas, a 42–1 underdog, rose from an eighth-round knockdown to stop Tyson in round 10. Promoter Don King protested that Douglas had benefited from a long count, but the WBA, WBC, and IBF all recognized Douglas as the new champion. Mike began a comeback attempt four months later, knocking out Henry Tillman in one round. An equally impressive victory over fringe contender Alex Stewart in December 1990 and two solid victories over Canada's Donovan "Razor" Ruddock in 1991 seemingly gave Tyson a chance to regain the championship. Mike was scheduled to face new champion Evander Holyfield in November 1991 but suffered a rib injury, causing a postponement of the fight.

Tyson's comeback abruptly ended in February 1992, when an Indianapolis, Indiana, jury found him guilty of raping a contestant in the Miss Black America Pageant seven months earlier. Mike was sentenced to a six-year jail term in the Indianapolis Youth Center. He steadfastly maintained his innocence, claiming to be the victim of a scheming woman intent on seeking publicity and winning a large financial settlement. During his time in prison, Tyson developed an interest in the Muslim religion. He was released from prison in March 1995 and bought a mansion in Las Vegas. Tyson, who retained Don King as promoter, agreed to a six-fight deal with MGM Grand in Las Vegas and a three-year deal with Showtime Event Television. The first bout was scheduled with Peter McNeeley for August 1995.

To date, Tyson's professional record stands at 41–1 with 36 knockouts. During "Iron Mike's" absence from the ring, he remained a force in the sport. A 1993 poll of boxing experts by *The Ring* disclosed that 98 percent predicted Tyson would return to the sport and 47 percent believed he would regain the world championship.

BIBLIOGRAPHY: Robert Cassidy, "Mike Tyson Gores Alex Stewart," *KO Magazine* (April 1991), pp. 32–55; Nigel Collins, "Welcome to the Tyson Era," *The Ring* 66 (March 1987), pp. 30–39; Steve Farhood, "Boxing Insiders Have Their Say," *The Ring* 72 (May 1993), pp. 24–31; Herbert G. Goldman, ed., *The Ring 1986–87 Record Book* (New York, 1987); Richard Hoffer, "The Fight," *Sports Illustrated* 72 (February 19, 1990), pp. 12–29; J. David Miller, "The Comeback of Mike Tyson," *KO Magazine* (November 1990), pp. 32–59; William Nack, "Ready to Soar to the Very Top," *Sports Illustrated* 64 (January 6, 1986), pp. 23–27; Pat Putnam, "Smash Dance," *Sports Illustrated* 75 (July 8, 1991), pp. 14–19; Jeff Ryan, "The Troubled Times of Mike Tyson," *KO Magazine* (January 1989), pp. 32–59.

John Robertson

WYOMIA TYUS-TILLMAN
(August 29, 1945–) ————————————————— *Track and Field*

Wyomia Tyus-Tillman, the first Olympian to successfully defend a sprint title, won the 100-meter dash in the 1968 Mexico City, Mexico, Summer Olympics, after having won the event four years earlier in the Tokyo, Japan, Summer Olympics. Tyus also anchored the winning, world record–setting 4 × 100-meter relay at the Mexico City Games after earning a Silver in the same event at the Tokyo Games. Her four medals then comprised the most ever garnered by an American woman in Olympic track and field.

Tyus set her first world record at the 1964 Tokyo Games, attaining 11.2 seconds in the 100 meters. Four years later, Wyomia lowered her record to 11.0 seconds. Her mark was not bettered in Olympic competition until the 1984 Los Angeles, California, Games. Tyus also tied the world standard in the

100-yard dash in 1965, achieving a 10.3-second clocking. Wyomia won three Amateur Athletic Union (AAU) titles in the 100 meters/100 yards, two in the 200 meters/200 yards, and three in the indoor 60-yard dash and also prevailed in the 200-meter dash at the 1967 Pan-American Games.

Tyus was born on August 29, 1945, in Griffin, Georgia. Her father, Willie, dairy farmed and constantly encouraged her to compete in sports even against boys. Her mother, Maria, a laundress, did not want her daughter to participate because she thought sports unfeminine. Wyomia entered sports both to keep up with and away from her three older brothers. "There were lots of times when my brothers didn't want me tagging along. I had to be extra good just to get the chance to play with them. When other kids would complain they didn't want a girl on their team, my brothers would always say, 'Well, okay, we'll take her,' but they knew I could play just as well as anyone else, if not better."

In high school, Tyus realized that a young woman could both compete in sports and remain popular and accepted by her peers. "I felt that sports and social life could go hand in hand. And what better place to meet the boys than on the athletic field? Some of the guys did not want their girl friends competing and developing muscles. But I enjoyed sports too much to worry about those kinds of boys. I always felt that whomever I was dating just didn't have the choice of telling me I couldn't do something."

Tyus excelled in both basketball and track and field in high school. In 1962, Wyomia won the 100-yard dash at the Girls' AAU championship in Los Angeles, California. She set an American age-group record of 11 seconds and lowered it to 10.9 seconds the following year.

The recipient of a work-aid scholarship, Tyus enrolled in fall 1963 at Tennessee State University and joined the most successful women's program in the annals of American track and field. Under legendary Ed Temple, the Tigerbelles produced more than 30 AAU and Track Athletic Congress (TAC) national championships. Forty of Temple's athletes competed in the Olympic Games, with 38, including Wyomia, earning their college degrees. Tyus insists the Tigerbelles accomplished more than just run track: "We got our degrees and became teachers, doctors, lawyers, and many other things. Coach Temple, who was an advisor as well as a coach, told us we were not going to be athletes all our lives, so we had to take advantage of this opportunity to get a college education."

Authorities did not expect Tyus to win a medal in the 100 meters at the 1964 Tokyo, Japan, Olympic Games. Wyomia barely made the team at age 19, finishing third in Olympic Trials behind Marilyn White and Edith McGuire, two of her Tigerbelle teammates. Tyus, who had never defeated McGuire in either high school or college, started fast at Tokyo, however, and won easily. As a confident graduating senior in 1968, she encountered little trouble at Mexico City in defending her Olympic title.

Tyus retired from amateur athletics after her final Olympic victory, marrying

Duane Tillman and having her first child. In 1973, Wyomia joined the newly established Professional International Track Association (PITA) circuit. She competed for three years, never being defeated in the 60-yard dash. The venture collapsed, however, because sports fans were not ready for professional track and field. Wyomia recalls receiving only $600 per victory.

Tillman, who was elected to the National Track and Field Hall of Fame in 1980, the Women's International Sports Hall of Fame in 1981, and the U.S. Olympic Hall of Fame in 1985, has two children, Simone and Tyus. Wyomia works in public relations in the Los Angeles area and frequently conducts sports clinics for young athletes. She continues to emphasize academics and the well-rounded individual, although wanting young people to enjoy sports. "We want everyone to feel like winners," she wrote, "which they are if their primary goal is a healthy desire to participate in their favorite sport, without having to be so competitive."

BIBLIOGRAPHY: Lewis H. Carlson and John J. Fogarty, *Tales of Gold: An Oral History of the Summer Olympic Games Told by America's Gold Medal Winners* (Chicago, IL, 1987); Michael D. Davis, *Black American Women in Olympic Track and Field: A Complete Illustrated Reference* (Jefferson, NC, 1992); Bill Mallon and Ian Buchanan, *Quest for Gold: The Encyclopedia of American Olympians* (New York, 1984); David L. Porter, ed., *Biographical Dictionary of American Sports: Outdoor Sports* (Westport, CT, 1988).

Lewis H. Carlson

GENE UPSHAW, JR.
(August 15, 1945–) _____ *Football*

From small college All-America to the Pro Football Hall of Fame to national labor union leader marks the personal odyssey of Gene Upshaw. Few football peers are surprised by Upshaw's success, either on the gridiron or in the political arena. Gene commanded respect in the locker room but knew he had to earn whatever he accomplished. "Gene is a born politician," stated former Oakland Raider teammate **Art Shell.** "We used to call him 'Governor.'"

Eugene Upshaw, Jr., was born on August 15, 1945, in Robstown, Texas, 20 miles west of Corpus Christi, to Eugene Upshaw, an oil field worker, and Cora (Riley) Upshaw, a domestic worker. The oldest of three sons and the brother of Marvin, who also joined the pro football ranks, Gene excelled in track and field, baseball, and football at Robstown High School while earning extra money picking cotton for $1.25 per hundred pounds. In 1963, Upshaw enrolled at Texas A&I University, 25 miles south of Robstown. "I never liked football—the contact, the hitting, the violence," Gene confided, "but I played the game because I knew I was good at it. I didn't get a scholarship from high school. I walked onto the football field at Texas A&I and just sort of looked around. Coach Gil Steinke said, 'Get a uniform on him.' I had a scholarship three days later." By his senior year, the six-foot, 200-pound freshman offensive center and tackle had grown to six foot five inches and 265 pounds. As a senior, Upshaw was selected for the All–Lone Star Conference First Team and the National Association of Intercollegiate Athletics (NAIA) and Coaches All-America teams and received Associated Press (AP) Little All-America honorable mention. Although Gene originally was projected as a third-round pro draft choice, his stellar play in the Senior Bowl and Coaches All-American Bowl raised his value among pro scouts. Upshaw received his bachelor's degree in secondary education from Texas A&I University in 1968.

The Oakland Raiders American Football League (AFL) club selected Upshaw as their first-round choice and seventeenth overall in the 1967 AFL-NFL (National Football League) draft. His Raider career from 1967 to 1982 included 14 years in Oakland and 1 year in Los Angeles on injured reserve and paralleled the club's rise to the winning elite among professional football programs. During Gene's tenure, the Raiders made 11 playoff appearances (1967–1970, 1972–1977, 1980) and won three AFL and American Football Conference (AFC) championships. The Raiders participated in three Super Bowls, succumbing to the Green Bay Packers, 33–14, in 1968 and scoring victories of 32–14 over the Minnesota Vikings in 1977 and 27–10 over the Philadelphia Eagles in 1981.

Upshaw, the prototype of the big, mobile offensive guard, demonstrated adeptness at leading the run or protecting the passer in the Raiders' long-threat aerial game. Art Shell recalls, "[Gene] ran like a deer. He used to tell the tailbacks, 'Run the sweep my way and see if you can catch me.'" Upshaw's durability enabled him to participate in 207 consecutive games during his 217-game career. The Raider captain for 10 years, he was named AFC Lineman of the Year in 1973, 1974, and 1977, NFL Lineman of the Year in 1977, and Pro Bowl participant six times. His visibility extended beyond the football field. Gene participated in 1970 on the Democratic Party Central Committee of Alameda County, California, and later served on the Alameda County Planning Commission, California Board of Governors for Community Colleges, and California Governor's Council on Wellness and Physical Fitness. Charitable work involved Upshaw with the March of Dimes, Easter Seals, Salvation Army, Sickle Cell Anemia, and Cystic Fibrosis. In 1980, Gene received the Byron "Whizzer" White Humanitarian Award from the NFL Players Association (NFLPA) for outstanding contributions to team, community, and nation. Two years later, the A. Philip Randolph Award was bestowed upon him by the AFL-CIO as one of the outstanding African-American leaders in the United States. In 1987, he became the fourth Oakland Raider to be inducted into the Pro Football Hall of Fame. Gene was selected to the AFL-NFL 1960–1984 All-Star Second Team and in 1994 to the All-Time NFL team.

Upshaw, meanwhile, moved to the top of the player's union, having progressed from Raider player's representative (1970–1976), to the NFLPA Executive Committee in 1976, to union president in 1980 under executive director Ed Garvey. After an eight-week player's strike during the 1982 season, Gene succeeded Garvey as executive director in 1983. Two years later, he became president of the Federation of Professional Athletes, American Federation of Labor and Congress of Industrial Organizations (AFL-CIO), a member of the AFL-CIO executive board, and the highest-ranking African American in organized labor.

Upshaw's union leadership proved less fiery than the confrontational Garvey, but some considered Gene militant. This perception, he insisted, followed him because he was African American. Upshaw noted that "when a white leader takes a strong position on some issue, they are not called militant; they are viewed as 'taking a strong position.' But if you're black and you take a strong position, you're viewed as militant." Chicago Bears' linebacker **Mike Singletary** was not fazed. "Gene is like a coach who used to play the game— he understands our needs." Following the fractious effects of the 1982 strike, his agenda involved restoring the players' faith in their union, enhancing both the union's public image and communication with management.

Upshaw's greatest union challenge arose after an ill-fated 1987, 24-day players' strike over free agency, fought by the club owners with substitute teams. Subsequently, a court ruled that although a 1982 collective bargaining agreement had lapsed in 1987, the players were still bound by its provisions. Gene responded simply, but provocatively, to his union's setback, decertifying the union and making the players free agents in the eyes of the court. Such a standing removed the owners' antitrust protection, invoked when faced by a collective union opposition. Upshaw's risky strategy, deemed brilliant by his AFL-CIO brethren, totally upset the bargaining equation. Former NFL commissioner Pete Rozelle observed that the owners "had never considered a situation where the union would cease to exist. . . . Decertification changed everything." Five more years of legal maneuvers and negotiation finally ended in January 1993. The owners and players, under federal court supervision, agreed to a seven-year contract incorporating significant elements of player free agency while awarding the owners a salary cap for each team. For Gene, a compromise had been forged. He acknowledged, "We've got people on my side that don't like the deal, and [the owners] have got people on [their] side that don't like the deal. So it must be the right kind of deal."

Upshaw lives in Great Falls, Virginia, with his second wife, Teresa Buich. They have two sons, Justin and Daniel. A third son, Eugene III, is from Gene's first marriage in 1967 to Jimmye Hill, which ended in divorce. Upshaw makes a special effort to treat everyone the same. "My earliest memory is picking cotton in the Texas heat. . . . You don't feel like pushing people around when you remember the years you spent tearing up your hands picking cotton." Gene has enjoyed very successful careers as a football player and labor leader. His significant efforts have changed the way the game is played and the manner in which its business is conducted.

BIBLIOGRAPHY: Peter M. Gareffa, ed., *Newsmakers: The People Behind Today's Headlines* (Detroit, MI, 1988), pp. 432–435; *Los Angeles Times,* June 12, 1993; *New York Times,* January 7, 1993; David L. Porter, ed., *Biographical Dictionary of American Sports: Football* (Westport, CT, 1987); *The Sporting News Football Register* (1983); *Who's Who Among Black Americans* (Detroit, MI, 1992), p. 427.

David Bernstein

DEBI THOMAS VANDEN HOGEN
(March 25, 1967–   ) ————————————————————————— *Figure Skating*

Debi Thomas Vanden Hogen won fame as the first African-American national and international figure skating champion. Debra Janine Thomas was born on March 25, 1967, in Poughkeepsie, New York, the daughter of McKinley Thomas, a computer industry worker, and Janice Thomas. Debi's parents moved to San Jose, California, in 1969 and divorced when she was 11 years old.

Ice show comic Werner Groebli, the Mr. Frick of the Ice Follies, impressed Thomas. Debi began skating at age five, wearing secondhand boots so tight that her feet ached. In 1974, she began taking figure skating lessons for six hours a day and loved it. "You can walk without moving," Thomas explained. Most figure skating competitors came from wealthy white families, but Debi grew up in a working-class African-American family. Janice sometimes skipped mortgage payments to enable her daughter to train and travel. Judges in the subjective sport sometimes discriminated against Thomas, deliberately giving higher scores to less talented white competitors. Debi's first victory did not come until age nine in the novice division of the Central California Interclub Association.

Her mother, a programmer-analyst in Silicon Valley, provided a very strong role model. Janice personally sewed Debi's costumes, beaded her dresses, choreographed her routines, repaired her broken skates, and took her to ice shows and ballets. Debi recalled, "It was my mom who put it all on the line for me."

By the mid-1980s, Thomas had become a premier figure skater. In 1985, Debi finished second to Tiffany Chin at the U.S. Senior Ladies Nationals and captured first place at the National Sports Festival in Baton Rouge, Louisiana. The U.S. Olympic Committee named her 1985 Amateur Athlete of the Year in figure skating.

The 1986 season marked the pinnacle of her career. The five-foot-six-inch, 116-pound Thomas won both the U.S. Senior Ladies National and World Championships at Geneva, Switzerland, making her the first African American to take either title. At the 1986 World Championships, Debi captured the short program and performed four triple jumps and a beautiful double axle in the long program to defeat six-time European champion Katarina Witt of East Germany. An Achilles tendon injury caused her to finish second to Jill Trenary in the 1987 U.S. Senior Ladies Nationals. Witt bested her in the 1987 World Championships at Cincinnati, Ohio.

Thomas trained with British coach Alexander McGowan and for several days with ballet stars Mikhail Baryshnikov and George de la Pena for the 1988 U.S. Senior Ladies Nationals at Denver, Colorado, and the 1988 Calgary, Canada, Winter Olympic Games. Baryshnikov taught Debi "to think like a tiger," while de la Pena instructed her to use her arms more and develop greater confidence. "She's a spitfire," de la Pena recalled. "She's lusty, she's fun and she has a great sense of humor." Debi boldly started her U.S. Senior Ladies long program with two triple jumps and became the first figure skater in 54 years to regain the National title, outpointing Trenary. At the 1988 Olympics, Debi's disappointing freestyle program performance led to a Bronze Medal. Thomas, seemingly wanting to flaunt her athleticism, was determined to jump higher and more often with very difficult manuevers. Debi paid for her flights of daring with some awkward and costly landings, ultimately finishing third behind Witt and Elizabeth Manley of Canada. "Well, back to school," she commented afterward. "I gave it away." At the 1988 World Championships in Budapest, Hungary, Thomas again placed third behind Witt and Manley in her final amateur skating performance.

The muscular Thomas proved natural for figure skating. Elegance, intelligence, and athleticism marked Debi's skating. Her physical style of skating did not become widely accepted by judges until the 1980s. American audiences loved her triple jumps, daring, determination, and seemingly outgoing personality. Thomas competed in a predominantly white sport and acknowledged that more African-American skaters had not developed because of their lack of exposure to figure skating.

Thomas excelled in the classroom at San Mateo, California, High School, Stanford University, and the University of Colorado. Debi became only the second figure skater to win a U.S. Senior Ladies National title while attending college and even took calculus, chemistry, and German while preparing for the Olympics. "Combining my schoolwork with my skating program is very difficult, but there's no way I could give one of them up," she reflected. "Things like the importance of an education and being whatever you can be," she added, "give me an inner strength to pull things off on the ice." In March 1988, Thomas married Brian Vanden Hogen, whom she had met while studying at the University of Colorado. Debi returned to her premedical studies at Stanford University and hopes to practice orthopedic surgery.

Vanden Hogen did not regard herself as a role model. Debi had decided, "I want to be a doctor, and I want to be a star, and I'm going to. I didn't think I had to see a black woman do this to believe it's possible." Nevertheless, she has been an inspiration to young African-American women and a symbol both nationally and internationally. One figure skating coach summed up, "She has such a sense of the fullness of life."

BIBLIOGRAPHY: Pete Axthelm, "Cool as Ice, Witt Hits Gold," *Newsweek* 111 (March 7, 1988), pp. 62–64; Tom Callahan, "The Word She Uses Is 'Invincible,'" *Time* 131 (February 15, 1988), pp. 44–46, 48, 57; Lynn Norment, "Debi Thomas . . . ," *Ebony* 41 (May 1986), pp. 147–148, 150; Ed Perez, "A Degree and U.S. Medal Figure in Her Hopes," *USA Weekend* (January 31–February 2, 1986), p. 11; David L. Porter, ed., *Biographical Dictionary of American Sports: 1989–1992 Supplement for Baseball, Football, Basketball, and Other Sports* (Westport, CT, 1992); E. M. Swift, "Books or Blades, There's No Doubting Thomas," *Sports Illustrated* 64 (February 17, 1986), pp. 22–24, 29; E. M. Swift, "Another Miracle on Ice?" *Sports Illustrated* 64 (March 17, 1986), pp. 54–56, 61, 68; E. M. Swift, "Cashing in on the Collywobbles," *Sports Illustrated* 64 (March 31, 1986), pp. 28–30, 35.

David L. Porter

HERSCHEL WALKER
(March 3, 1962–   ) ————————————— *Football and Track and Field*

Herschel Walker, among the most versatile athletes in recent history, participated in football, international track and field, and the Olympic Games as a member of the American bobsled team. Herschel Junior Walker was born on March 3, 1962, in Wrightsville, Georgia, to Willis Walker, Sr., and Christine (Taylor) Walker, the fifth of seven children. His father gave up farming to work in a kaolin (clay) plant, while his mother was employed in a pants factory. At birth, a nurse suggested that *junior* be added to his name since he looked "like a junior." His mother made *Junior* his middle name because there was already a Willis, Jr. As a boy, Herschel sang in the youth choir at the Baptist Church.

Walker began football in the fifth grade following in the footsteps of his older brothers, Willis, Jr., and Renneth, who played for the Johnson County High School team. Until a teenager, Herschel could not outrun his older sister, Veronica. His father said, "There was always an argument at night about who could run the fastest. . . . there would be . . . all this bragging, and the next day they would all be outside running." Veronica preceded Herschel at the University of Georgia, being one of the first females awarded a full scholarship in track and field.

Track and field comprised Walker's favorite sport in high school, as he ran a 9.9-second 100-yard dash while a junior. Herschel's coach introduced him to a conditioning program of sit-ups, push-ups, and wind sprints. Walker followed this throughout his career, exhibiting little interest in weight training. Herschel led his team to a State Class A track and field championship in 1979, winning the 100- and 220-yard dashes and the shot put. He started as a forward on the basketball team.

Walker began his high school football career as a five-foot-nine-inch, 185-pound fullback in the ninth grade. By his senior year, Herschel had grown to six foot one inch and 210 pounds and had moved to tailback. The Johnson

County team finished undefeated as 1979 Class A State champions. He rushed for 3,167 yards, scored 45 touchdowns, and was named a consensus prep All-America. *Parade Magazine* selected him High School Back of the Year. With Walker the most sought-after recruit, over 100 colleges contacted him. Herschel also earned honors as valedictorian of his class, president of the Beta Club, a scholastic honor society, and an "A" student for his high school career. His high school coach said of Herschel, "He worked at it just like he worked at everything else."

In fall 1980, Walker followed sister Veronica to the University of Georgia on a football–track and field scholarship. In his first football game against the University of Tennessee, Herschel entered the game as the third tailback and brought Georgia back from a two-touchdown deficit with two scores in a 16–15 win. He led Georgia to an undefeated season and the national championship, defeating the University of Notre Dame in the 1981 Sugar Bowl, 17–10. Walker scored two touchdowns despite suffering a shoulder dislocation on the second offensive series, being named Most Valuable Player (MVP) for the game. Always looking to share the glory, Herschel summarized his 1980 season by saying, "The older players looked after me this year. I was able to play well because I got a lot of help."

In his freshman year, Walker set an NCAA rushing record with 1,616 yards to break **Tony Dorsett**'s mark. Herschel ranked third in the Heisman Trophy balloting, the highest finish ever by a freshman. He was named All-America in six polls, being the first freshman ever selected by the Football Writers Association of America and by Kodak.

In 1981, Walker rushed for 1,891 yards to set a sophomore record and placed second in the Heisman Trophy voting. Herschel's junior year saw him gain 1,752 yards, score 17 touchdowns, win the Heisman and Maxwell Trophies, and be named a consensus All-America. Following the Florida game, Charlie Pell, Gator head coach, said, "Walker is the best back I've ever seen where I was involved as a player or a coach." An assistant called him "another dimension in football." In February 1983, Herschel surrendered his senior year eligibility to sign a very lucrative contract with Donald Trump's New Jersey Generals of the newly formed United States Football League (USFL).

During his collegiate football career, Walker established 11 NCAA records, 16 Southeastern Conference (SEC) marks, and 41 University of Georgia records. Herschel carried the ball 994 times, gaining 5,259 yards. When asked if he was tired after carrying the ball 47 times against the University of Florida in 1981, he replied, "No, the ball isn't heavy."

In his college-track career, Walker was twice selected NCAA All-America. Herschel joined Olympian Mel Latany on the 1981 400-meter relay team, which finished second in the NCAA. He was twice chosen All-SEC in track and field and participated for the 1982 U.S. National team. In the summers of 1981 and 1982, he competed in international competition in Europe.

During three years with the New Jersey Generals, Walker carried the ball

1,143 times, gained 5,562 yards, and scored 54 touchdowns. Herschel became an outstanding pass receiver, as his three-year record included 139 receptions for 1,484 yards and 7 touchdowns. He was named a USFL All-Star in 1983 and 1985, earning Player of the Year honors in 1985.

The Dallas Cowboys National Football League (NFL) club drafted Walker in 1985 and, when the USFL failed, signed him in August 1986. Herschel spent just over three years there before being traded to the Minnesota Vikings (NFL) for five players, a first draft choice, and six additional conditional draft choices. He played 3½ years for the Vikings before signing as a free agent with the Philadelphia Eagles (NFL) in 1993. Walker led the Eagles in rushing in 1993 and 1994, pass receiving in 1993, and touchdowns in 1994. His NFL career record through 1994 included 1,907 rushes for 7,996 yards and 60 touchdowns and 460 pass receptions for 4,387 yards and 18 touchdowns. He played in the Pro Bowl in 1987 and 1988. The Eagles released Walker in March 1995 after signing Ricky Watters. In April 1995, Herschel joined the New York Giants (NFL).

Walker's professional football career ended his dream to participate in the Olympics in track and field. In 1991, Herschel tried for the Winter Olympic Games as a bobsledder. With less than a year's training, he made the team and participated in the 1992 Albertville, France, Games. His athletic versatility was displayed when he performed as a featured dancer with the Dallas Ballet during his career with the Cowboys.

Walker in 1983 married Cynthia De Angelis, who participated on the women's track and field team at Georgia. They have no children.

BIBLIOGRAPHY: Robert. T. Bowen, telephone conversation with Philadelphia Eagles Sports Information Department, July 5, 1994; Dale Conley, *War Between the States* (Atlanta, GA, 1992); Loran Smith with Lewis Grizzard, *Glory! Glory!* (Atlanta, GA, 1981); *The Sporting News Pro Football Register* (1994); Sports Information Department files, University of Georgia, Athens, GA.

Robert T. Bowen, Jr.

GWEN TORRENCE WALLER
(June 12, 1965–) _____ *Track and Field*

Gwen Torrence Waller, one of history's most versatile female sprinters, ranked among the world's top performers in the 100 meters, 200 meters, and 400 meters during the late 1980s and early 1990s. Gwendolyn Lena Torrence was born on June 12, 1965, in Atlanta, Georgia. Her father died of a stroke when she was eight years old. Her mother, Dorothy, worked as a nanny and housekeeper to support Gwen and her older siblings. Torrence grew up in an Atlanta housing project under the supervision of her older brother Willie. Dorothy recalled that "if there was something Gwen didn't want to do in school, she would run home, and Willie would take her back. When she'd get into fights with other girls, Willie would come rescue her."

Before her high school years, the Torrences moved from the Atlanta housing project to suburban Decatur, Georgia. At Columbia High School in Decatur, Gwen discovered her penchant for running as a tenth-grader. "The first time I saw Gwen run," recounts Ray Bonner, a Columbia physical education teacher and football and track and field coach, "a football player by the name of Fred Lane lit out after her on the track. Fred couldn't catch her. And he was fast." Bonner persuaded a reluctant Torrence to join the track and field team, stressing "that God gave her a gift, and if she didn't use it, he was going to be very upset." Gwen joined the track and field squad provided that she could practice by herself "in the evening . . . after everyone else had left." She captured the 100 meters and 200 meters in the Georgia State championships and the Track Athletic Congress (TAC) Junior championships as a senior and graduated from Columbia High School in 1983.

The University of Georgia offered Torrence an athletic scholarship, but she preferred "to be a hair stylist, or work at Rich's or Macy's department store." Bonner intervened, however, telling Gwen, "You're a black female. You need that diploma." She entered the University of Georgia as a student in the Developmental Studies Program. The program held a national reputation for "coddling jocks" as a result of a 1983 lawsuit against the university by English instructor Jan Kemp, who was fired for failing student athletes. Torrence spent four quarters in the program before joining the university mainstream. Gwen acknowledged that she "had never written a paper" before entering the University of Georgia but successfully completed the Developmental Studies Program in 1985 and made the dean's list the next year. In 1987, she became the first University of Georgia athlete, male or female, to win both the 100 meters and 200 meters in the NCAA championships. The Atlanta native captured the 100 meters and 200 meters and anchored the triumphant U.S. 4 × 100-meter relay in the World University Games at Zagreb, Yugoslavia, triumphed in the 200 meters in the Pan-American Games at Indianapolis, Indiana, and placed fifth in the 200 meters in the World Championships at Rome, Italy.

The turning point in Torrence's athletic career came in 1986, when she defeated **Evelyn Ashford Washington,** the 1984 Olympic 100-meter Gold Medalist, in the 55-meter dash indoors at the Millrose Games in New York. "Before that I was running good times, but nobody noticed because I hadn't beat Evelyn," recounted Gwen. Her 6.57-second clocking set a Millrose Games record. A powerful indoor sprinter, Torrence won 25 consecutive indoor finals at 55 and 60 meters from 1986 to 1989. In February 1989, Gwen lost the 60 meters at the *Los Angeles Times* meet in a photofinish to Dawn Sowell of Louisiana State University. She, however, garnered the 1989 TAC 60-meter title and placed second in the 60 meters at the indoor World Championships in Budapest, Hungary. Her 7.07-second time marked an American record for 60 meters. Torrence, who earlier had placed fifth in the 100 meters and sixth in the 200 meters at the 1988 Seoul, South Korea, Summer Olympic Games, was pregnant most of 1989 and did not compete outdoors. On November 25, 1989, she gave birth to Manley Waller III. Gwen's husband, Manley Waller II, a former University of Georgia sprinter, works as a computer specialist for a Decatur sporting goods company.

Under Lewis Gainey, track and field coach at the University of Georgia, Waller resumed her training in January 1990. After finishing seventh in the 200 meters at the TAC championships that year, Gwen commented that "everybody says they get stronger after they have a child. That really is a myth. You just get that much more determined." Upon returning to racing form in 1991, she captured the 200 meters and placed second in the 100 meters at the TAC Championships. At the 1991 World Championships in Tokyo, Japan, Waller finished second to Germany's Katrin Krabbe in both the 100 and 200 meters. Gwen won both the 100 and 200 meters at the 1992 Olympic Trials. She finished fourth in the 100 meters and won Gold Medals in the 200 meters and the 4 × 100-meter relay at the 1992 Barcelona, Spain, Summer Olympic Games. Although recording a personal best of 10.86 seconds in the 100 meters, Waller protested the result. Gwen claimed that "two of the three medalists" were using performance-enhancing drugs. "I think Gwen's a sore loser," responded Jamaican Juliet Cuthbert, the Silver Medalist. Gwen "had a bad day," added Cuthbert. "She's very upset." Waller, whose 21.72-second clocking in the 200-meter semifinal marked a personal record, later apologized for her remarks that might "have brought harm to anyone, especially my teammates."

The 1992 *Track and Field News* world rankings listed Gwen second in the 100 meters, first in the 200 meters, and third in the 400 meters. At the USA Track and Field (USATF) Championships, Waller took second in the 100 meters and first in the 200 meters. Gwen garnered a Gold Medal in the 4 × 400-meter relay, two Silver Medals in the 200 meters and the 4 × 100-meter relay, and a Bronze Medal in the 100 meters at the 1993 World Championships in Stuttgart, Germany. In 1993, *Track and Field News* ranked her third in the 100 meters, second in the 200 meters, and fourth in the 400 meters. She won the 60 meters and the 200 meters in the 1994 USATF Indoor Championships at Atlanta, the latter performance establishing an American record of 22.74 seconds. Waller, who competed despite a sore hamstring, remarked "that this was the first time her family had had a chance to see her run in person since her high school days."

At the 1994 St. Petersburg, Russia, Goodwill Games, Gwen won both the 100 meters and 200 meters and anchored the triumphant 4 × 100-meter relay squad. The 1994 International Amateur Athletic Federation (IAAF) Grand Prix Final Standings listed her fifth overall for the 16 top outdoor invitational meets. In March 1995, Waller captured the 60-meter dash in 7.04 seconds at the USA/Mobil Indoor Track and Field Championships in Atlanta, Georgia. Gwen earned $40,000 for finishing first overall in the 1995 Grand Prix Indoor

Final Standings, ranking first in the 60-meter dash and third in the 200-meter dash. She won the 100 meters in 11.04 seconds and the 200 meters in 22.03 seconds at the USATF Outdoor Championships at Sacramento, California, in June 1995, giving her the first women's sprint double since 1992.

BIBLIOGRAPHY: Sarah Boxer, "Taking Her Sweet Time," Sports Illustrated 68 (May 23, 1988), pp. 60–64; David Davidson, "Sprinting Is No Sweat for Georgia's Torrence," Atlanta [GA] Constitution, May 22, 1985, p. D7; Games of the XXV Olympiad, Barcelona, Spain, NBC Sports Research Information, vol. 8 (1992), pp. 698–699; Garry Hill, "If You Build It . . . ," Track and Field News 47 (May 1994), p. 8; Jon Hendershott, "Sowell Stops Torrence," Track and Field News 42 (March 1989), p. 24; Jeff Hollobaugh, "Gwen's Feet Talk Too," Track and Field News 45 (October 1992), p. 54; Jeff Hollobaugh, "Torrence Raises a Ruckus," Track and Field News 45 (October 1992), p. 55; Ruth Laney, "Fuel for Torrence's Fire," Track and Field News 42 (April 1989), p. 15; Karen Rosen, "Determined Torrence Was Born to Run, Win," Atlanta [GA] Constitution, December 25, 1991, p. F2; Karen Rosen, "Running: A Family Business," Atlanta [GA] Constitution, June 19, 1992, p. A1.

Adam R. Hornbuckle

EVELYN ASHFORD WASHINGTON
(April 15, 1957–) ————————————————— *Track and Field*

Evelyn Ashford Washington forged a track and field career sprinting record second to none among American women. **Wyomia Tyus-Tillman** won two Olympic Gold Medals, **Wilma Rudolph** captured the American imagination in 1960, and **Florence Griffith Joyner** stunned the world at Seoul, South Korea, in 1988, but Washington sustained unsurpassed sprinting excellence over 15 years. During much of that time, Evelyn ranked as both the top American sprinter and premier world sprinter.

Evelyn Ashford was born on April 15, 1957, in Shreveport, Louisiana, the daughter of Samuel Ashford, U.S. Air Force sergeant, and Vietta Ashford. Ashford moved frequently as a military child but grew up mostly in Roseville, California, near the McClellan Air Force Base. The University of California at Los Angeles (UCLA) awarded Evelyn one of the first athletic scholarships given to a woman. The five-foot-five-inch, 120-pound speedster first gained prominence as a UCLA freshman in 1976. After finishing second in the 1976 Association of Intercollegiate Athletics for Women (AIAW) 100-meter dash, she made the U.S. Olympic team and finished fifth at the Montreal, Canada, Summer Olympic Games. In the Olympic final, Ashford defeated eighth-place finisher Marlies Oelsner (later Göhr) of East Germany. Evelyn did not improve much for several years but won the AIAW and Track Athletic Congress (TAC) 100 and 200 meters in 1977 and repeated the 200-meter double in 1978. The 1979 World Cup meet catapulted her to the forefront of world-class sprinters, as she captured both the 100 and 200 sprints over Göhr. "I gained a lot of confidence in 1979," Ashford acknowledged. "At that first

World Cup [1977 when she finished fourth and fifth in the sprints], I was humiliated. I told myself I would never let that happen to me again. I decided I had to find out if I had what it took to become a true world-class sprinter. I had to answer that question for myself."

The careers of Göhr and Ashford became intertwined, as they battled for the title of the world's fastest woman. The two did not meet in 1980 because the United States boycotted the Moscow, Russia, Summer Olympics. In 1981, Evelyn repeated with a sprint double at the World Cup, defeating Göhr in the 100 meters and Marita Koch of East Germany in the 200 meters. The desire for Olympic Gold kept her competing. In 1983, Evelyn admitted, "I don't have a world record, I don't have any Gold Medals. Those are the two major things standing out in my mind, and until I achieve them, I won't be happy with myself, and I won't feel I have achieved my goals or my potential." At the 1983 National Sports Festival, Evelyn ran the 100 meters in 10.79 seconds in the high altitude of Colorado Springs, Colorado, to break Göhr's world mark. In 1984, Ashford reached her pinnacle when she won two Gold Medals at the Los Angeles Summer Olympic Games. Ashford's triumphs included the 100 meters and anchoring the 400-meter relay team.

But Ashford's greatest race probably occurred in Zurich, Switzerland, shortly after the 1984 Summer Olympic Games. Evelyn faced Göhr, who sought revenge for being denied an opportunity at the Gold Medal when East Germany boycotted the 1984 Summer Olympics. Ashford defeated Göhr to win the Zurich race and broke her own 100 meter world record with a 10.76-second clocking, silencing critics downplaying her earlier 10.79 performance because of the altitude assistance. Evelyn exultantly confided, "I usually never felt this way about such a big race, but the time could have been 11.9 for all I cared. I just wanted to beat Göhr."

Ashford took off 1985 so that she and her husband, Ray Washington, a former collegiate college basketball coach, could start their family. On May 30, 1985, Evelyn delivered their first child, Raina Ashley. "Motherhood made me a better runner," she claimed. "My endurance was better."

In 1986, Washington faced both Marlies Göhr and the German Democratic Republic's new sprint and long jump sensation, Heike Drechsler-Daute. Evelyn struggled early in the year, losing the TAC to Pam Marshall. She rebounded to defeat Drechsler-Daute narrowly at the Goodwill Games, as both clocked 10.91 seconds for the 100 meters. In their only 1986 meeting, Washington triumphed over Göhr at Rieti, Italy, while recording the year's fastest time of 10.88 seconds. For her efforts, authorities ranked Evelyn first in the world. This marked her fourth such honor, the most ever by a woman. During her career, she was ranked best among American women in the 100 meters seven times and the 200 meters six times.

After rarely competing in 1987, Washington returned in 1988 to show her old skill. Florence Griffith Joyner, however, redefined women's sprinting in 1988. Evelyn finished second in the 100 meters to Florence at both the Olympic Trials and the Seoul, Korea, Summer Olympic Games. She won a Gold Medal in the 400 relay, however, and prevailed at multiple invitationals that year.

After 1988, Washington competed less frequently. Nevertheless, Evelyn participated in 1992 in her fourth Olympic Games. She did not qualify for the individual 100-meter event at the Barcelona, Spain, Summer Olympic Games but made the sprint relay team. Washington led off for the U.S. relay squad, helping them win the Gold Medal. Her illustrious Olympic career, which featured four Gold Medals and one Silver Medal, ended in 1993.

BIBLIOGRAPHY: Michael D. Davis, *Black American Women in Olympic Track and Field: A Complete Illustrated Reference* (Jefferson, NC, 1992); Jon Hendershott, *Track's Greatest Women* (Los Altos, CA, 1987); Bill Mallon and Ian Buchanan, *Quest for Gold: The Encyclopedia of American Olympians* (New York, 1983); James A. Page, *Black Olympian Medalists* (Englewood, CO, 1991).

Bill Mallon

QUINCY WATTS
(June 19, 1970–) ————————————————— *Track and Field*

Quincy Watts, who won the Gold Medal in the 400 meters in the 1992 Summer Olympic Games at Barcelona, Spain, ranks among history's fastest 400-meter runners. Quincy Dushawn Watts, the son of Rufus Watts, a retired post office employee, and Allitah Hunt, was born on June 19, 1970, in Detroit, Michigan. Watts lived with his mother in Detroit until age 14, when she "decided that he was getting into too much trouble and sent him to Los Angeles to live with his father." Quincy acknowledged that while he "never did drugs or anything," he "was hanging out with the wrong type of crowd, getting into fights, and had to leave Catholic school because the things I did added up." In Los Angeles, California, he began competing in age-group track events. His father quickly recognized Watts's potential as a runner and introduced him to John Smith, the sprint coach at the University of California at Los Angeles. Smith, a former world-class 400-meter dashman, offered Quincy "some pointers."

Watts blossomed into a national-class sprinter at Taft High School in Woodland Hills, California, garnering the first of two consecutive California State championships in the 200 meters in 1986 and the State title in the 100 meters in 1987. In 1987, Quincy also placed second in the 200 meters in the Track Athletic Congress (TAC) Junior championships. The same year, he clocked 10.30 seconds for 100 meters and 20.50 seconds for 200 meters for his best time at both distances. Although persistent hamstring injuries befell Watts throughout 1988, he still placed third in both the 100 and 200 meters in the TAC Junior championships and sixth in the quarter-finals of the 200 meters in the Olympic Trials. Nagging injuries discouraged Quincy, who received much support from Smith. Smith told the young dashman to "keep your head up, because you're going to be great one day. You've got the tools. Just hang in there; everything will work out."

Watts graduated from Taft High School in 1988 and received an athletic scholarship to the University of Southern California (USC), but injuries persisted throughout his freshman and sophomore years. USC track and field coach Jim Bush encouraged Quincy to concentrate solely on the 400 meters. Although having tried the 400 meters in high school, he remembers his first collegiate experience with the race as "a nightmare" and "wondered why I ever thought about trying the race." Upon gaining experience in the 400 meters, Watts demonstrated his potential by taking second place in the NCAA championships and Olympic Festival, third in the TAC Championships, and fourth in the Pan-American Games in 1991. Quincy recorded his best time of 44.98 seconds in the TAC Championships that year. During the Silver Medal performance of the U.S. 4 × 400-meter relay team in the 1991 World Championships at Tokyo, Japan, Watts clocked 43.4 seconds for one of history's fastest 400-meter relay legs. Of his rapid rise to world-class status in the 400 meters, Quincy observed that "I've always had the physical tools to run well in the 400. It was just a mental thing toward the race, of going out fast and not being afraid of tying up and hurting."

Watts graduated from USC with a bachelor's degree in communications in 1992, the same year he won the 400 meters in the Pac-10 and NCAA Championships and finished third in the Olympic Trials. Quincy lowered his personal best time to 43.97 seconds in the semi-finals of the Olympic Trials. During the 1992 Summer Olympic Games at Barcelona, Spain, he captured his semi-final heat in 43.71 seconds. His time surpassed the Olympic and collegiate records of 43.86 seconds, set by **Lee Evans** in 1968. Watts admitted that he "eased off at the end" of the race and "was pretty surprised to see the time was so fast." Quincy soon won the Gold Medal in 43.50 seconds, history's second fastest 400 meters and new Olympic and collegiate records. Although missing the world mark by a mere .21 second, Watts described winning the Gold Medal as "better than anything in my wildest dreams." Quincy garnered a second Gold Medal as a member of the U.S. 4 × 400-meter relay team. The quartet established a world record of 2 minutes 55.74 seconds, surpassing the standard of 2 minutes 56.16 seconds set by the United States in the 1968 Summer Olympic Games. Watts clocked 43.1 seconds for his 400-meter contribution, then the fastest relay leg of all time. In 1993, Quincy finished third in the 400 meters at the USA Track and Field (USATF) Championships and fourth in the World Championships at Stuttgart, Germany. At the latter, however, he earned a Gold Medal in the 4 × 400-meter relay and helped the United States establish a world record of 2 minutes 54.29 seconds. In 1994, Watts won the 700 meters in 45.21 seconds at the St. Petersburg, Russia, Goodwill Games. Quincy did not qualify for the 400-meter finals at the USATF Championships at Sacramento, California, in June 1995.

BIBLIOGRAPHY: Jon Hendershott, "Britain Stuns US," *Track and Field News* 44 (November 1991), p. 25; Jon Hendershott, "The Man Called 'Q,'" *Track and Field*

News 46 (March–April 1992), pp. 52–54; Jeff Hollobaugh, "Watts Breaks OR Twice," *Track and Field News* 45 (October 1992), p. 18; Dave Johnson, "Another WR for US," *Track and Field News* 45 (October 1992), p. 37; Ruth Laney, "Watts Nabs a Pair of Golds," *Track and Field News* 45 (October 1992), p. 19; Sieg Lindstrom, "Watts Steps Up—and Out," *Track and Field News* 45 (July 1992), p. 20; David L. Porter, ed., *Biographical Dictionary of American Sports: 1992–1995 Supplement for Baseball, Football, Basketball, and Other Sports* (Westport, CT, 1995); Track Athletic Congress Press Information, letter to Adam R. Hornbuckle, November 1992; University of Southern California Sports Information, letter to Adam R. Hornbuckle, November 1992.

Adam R. Hornbuckle

BILL WHITE
(January 28, 1934–) ——————————————————————— *Baseball*

Bill White, baseball player, announcer, and executive and the first African American to ever head any major professional sports league, became National League (NL) president in April 1989. William DeKova White was born in Lakewood, Florida, on January 28, 1934. His parents, both sharecroppers, moved north to Ohio for better economic opportunities. Bill grew up in a public housing project in Warren, Ohio. His father, a steelworker, and his mother, Edna Mae White Young, a government secretary, were separated and divorced when Bill was young. He never really knew or developed a relationship with his father. White's mother worked on various military air bases, leaving her son in the care of her mother and sister. Bill, brought up by his maternal grandmother and aunt, learned values of strong family ties, religion, mutual support, and hard work. As a young man, White set his sights on becoming a doctor. After graduating second in his high school class, Bill attended Hiram College in Ohio on an academic scholarship. He complemented his pre-med studies by playing first base for Hiram's baseball team. A New York Giants (NL) scout saw him play and offered him a $2,500 bonus to sign a professional contract. Upon giving up his ambition to become a doctor, White explained, "I needed the money. I promised my mother I'd go back, which I never did. I just needed to add a little bit to help my people send me to college and did better at baseball than I thought."

In 1953 the New York Giants assigned White to play in the minor leagues at Danville, Virginia, making him one of the first African Americans in the Carolina League. At age 19, Bill faced racist taunts and abuse and dealt with segregation in housing and eating. He concentrated on his hitting, compiling a .298 batting average with 20 home runs and 84 RBIs. White played first base with occasional games in the outfield. Bill then played two more full minor leagues campaigns, enjoying excellent seasons at Sioux City, Iowa, and Dallas, Texas. He began 1956 with the Minneapolis Millers in the American Association and then joined the New York Giants, hitting 22 home runs and driving in 59 runs in 138 games. After his solid rookie year, White spent 1957 and 1958 in the military service. Bill played 26 games for the relocated Giants in San Francisco at the end of the 1958 season.

On March 25, 1959, San Francisco traded White to the St. Louis Cardinals (NL). Bill enjoyed seven excellent seasons there. From 1959 through 1965, he hit over .300 four times, batted a career-high .324 in 1962, and drove in over 100 runs each season from 1962 to 1964. The first baseman was named to the NL All-Star team six times and won seven Gold Gloves for his excellent, consistent fielding. In 1964, White helped lead the Cardinals to an NL pennant and World Series championship. In October 1965, St. Louis traded Bill to the Philadelphia Phillies (NL). After spending three seasons with Philadelphia, he was sent back to the St. Louis Cardinals. White finished his playing career mainly as a pinch hitter in 1969. His .286 lifetime batting average included 1,700 hits in 1,673 games.

As a Cardinal in the early 1960s, White protested against spring training segregation. Bill's efforts brought about changes in the St. Louis organization, which provided integrated living and recreational facilities for their players and families in St. Petersburg, Florida. Like many African Americans, he had seen too much unfair and unjust segregation and discrimination. White, however, risked losing his job or being punished by speaking up. Bill asked the press, "When will we be made to feel like humans?"

During his stint with the Philadelphia Phillies, White began his sportscasting career in 1967–1968 for WPVI-TV in Philadelphia. In 1969, Bill worked for radio station KMOX in St. Louis. Two years later, he became sports director at WPVI-TV. From 1971 through 1988, he worked as a broadcaster and baseball analyst for WPIX-TV in New York City and handled the New York Yankees American League (AL) games with broadcast partner Phil Rizzuto. White worked steadily to improve his broadcasting style, being known for his candid observations and independent viewpoints. The St. Louis Cardinals organization had asked Bill in 1969 to manage their minor league team in Tulsa, Oklahoma, which would have made him America's first African-American manager. In 1975, New York Yankees owner George Steinbrenner offered White the general club manager job. However, Bill declined both of these offers. In regard to the Cardinals' minor league managing position, he "had no interest. I didn't want to do anything that depended on 24 other guys doing their jobs." Of the Yankees' management job, he said, "I wasn't ready then." White liked the stability and income from broadcasting. Although divorced, Bill was committed to seeing that his three sons and two daughters all received college educations.

In 1989, White was unanimously chosen by the 12 NL owners to succeed A. Bartlett Giamatti as NL president. Bill saw the position as an opportunity to improve relations between umpires and players and between management and players. He also hoped to promote affirmative action for minorities and women in baseball management positions. White worked quietly behind the scenes to promote affirmative action but was frustrated at the relatively slow pace of progress. A quiet, self-contained person, Bill learned to deal with criticism from all sides in his role as NL president and resisted the urgings of others to become more public, vocal, and issue oriented. He was caught between administering the day-to-day operations of a game he loved and respected and pushing for a program of minority hiring that was resisted, downplayed, or ignored as a priority by the club owners. White preferred to do his job and carry out his responsibilities the way that best suited him and would be the most effective. Bill told one reporter, "But you do the job no matter what your color is." By September 1990, White considered resigning as NL president. As his frustrations grew, he announced his resignation in January 1994. Bill remained until successor Leonard Coleman took over two months later. In his five years as NL president, White held a highly visible position. Many, however, expected Bill to be more outspoken and militant as a prominent barrier-breaker. White's commitment to minority gains and affirmative action in the front offices of baseball stayed consistent. His executive style and leadership illustrated his desire to keep his own personality and private needs and do his job the way he believed effective.

An avid outdoorsman and lover of the rural countryside, White lives in Upper Black Eddy, Pennsylvania, a small rural community in Bucks County, and enjoys fishing in Chesapeake Bay. Bill recalled, "I was raised in public housing, and I said whenever I can afford it, I am going to go out and live in the country."

BIBLIOGRAPHY: "Bill White: The National League's New Boss," *Ebony* 44 (May 1989), pp. 44, 46; Tom Callahan, "Baseball Picks a Pioneer," *Time* 133 (February 13, 1989), p. 76; Murray Chass, "A Pressured Bill White Delays His Resignation," *New York Times*, January 22, 1994; Tim Kurkjian, "Whitewash? National League President Bill White Considering Resignation," *Sports Illustrated* 73 (September 17, 1990), p. 81; Glenn Macnow, "Bill White: Baseball Executive," *Newsmakers 1989 Cumulation* (Detroit, MI 1989); Laura B. Randolph, "Bill White: National League President," *Ebony* 47 (August 1992), pp. 52–53; Jackie Robinson, *Baseball Has Done It* (Philadelphia, PA, 1964); Bill Shannon, ed., *All-Time Greatest Who's Who in Baseball 1872–1990* (New York, 1990); Claire Smith, "Baseball's Angry Man," *New York Times Magazine* (October 13, 1991), pp. 28–31, 53, 56; "White Cites Racism in His Job," *New York Times*, May 29, 1992.

                                                                    Douglas A. Noverr

REGGIE WHITE
(December 19, 1961–) ———————————————————— *Football*

Reggie White strikes fear and terror into the hearts of National Football League (NFL) quarterbacks with his quickness and strength, which have made him the all-time NFL sack leader. Off the gridiron, however, White exhibits a gentle demeanor and spends much of his time doing humanitarian work and preaching the Christian gospel.

Reginald Howard White was born on December 19, 1961, in Chattanooga, Tennessee, the son of Charles White and Thelma (Dodds) White Collier. Reggie, brought up by his mother and grandparents, regularly attended the local Baptist Church, where he received inspiration from his ministers and teachers. His idol while growing up was a white minister, Reverend Ferguson. White recalls, "Reverend Ferguson was the greatest man of God I ever saw. He had a way with kids and teaching. I always wanted to be a Christian, but I never knew how. He said that understanding was the first thing I had to know."

White's goals as a youngster included more than just being a Christian. At age 12, Reggie told his mother that he aspired to be a minister and a professional football player. Reggie achieved his first goal at age 17, receiving his ordination as a Baptist minister.

White began to work on his second goal while a student at Howard High School in Chattanooga. Reggie participated both football and basketball, receiving All-America honors in football and All-State recognition in basketball. Spurning numerous scholarship offers, he played football in his home state for the University of Tennessee.

Although the six-foot-five-inch, 290-pound White lacked finesse during his collegiate career, his strength and explosive power earned him numerous Southeastern Conference (SEC) Player of the Year awards and consensus All-America honors in 1983. The Houston Touchdown Club designated Reggie as one of four finalists for the annual Lombardi Award. He still holds records at Tennessee for most sacks in a single game (4), season (15), and career (32). His combination of playing defense on Saturday for the Volunteers and preaching on Sunday created his nickname, "the Minister of Defense."

After White graduated from the University of Tennessee with a bachelor's degree in human services in 1983, the Memphis Showboats of the newly formed United States Football League (USFL) selected him in their 1984 territorial draft and signed him to a five-year, $4 million contract. Reggie played in 16 games in 1984 for the Showboats, recording 12 sacks. The Philadelphia Eagles NFL club also secured the rights to White by making him their first draft pick in the 1984 supplemental draft.

White also played for Memphis in 1985, registering 11.5 sacks in 18 games. The financial instability of the floundering USFL and a desire to play against the best players caused Reggie to secure a release from the Showboats and sign a four-year, $1.85 million deal with the Philadelphia Eagles on September 21, 1985. He soon entered the starting lineup and tallied 13 sacks in 13 games. His exciting style and big play capability earned him recognition as National Football Conference (NFC) Defensive Rookie of the Year.

White flourished as a pass rusher with the arrival of Buddy Ryan as Eagles' head coach in 1986. Ryan organized the Philadelphia defense around Reggie, who responded with 18 sacks in 16 games. White, selected to the first of eight consecutive Pro Bowls, was named Most Valuable Player (MVP) by the media after recording 4 quarterback sacks.

The 1987 NFL players' strike provided White with the opportunity to exhibit his leadership but drove a wedge between him and Eagles management. Reggie, the union representative, strove to keep his teammates united. The *Philadelphia Daily News* reported, "One of the more memorable images of that season was White wearing a picket sign and blocking a bus loaded with replacement players as it attempted to pull into a South Jersey hotel. Other teams broke ranks: the Eagles never did." Although the strike limited him to only 12 games, White remarkably tied the NFL season record for sacks with 21. Reggie would have broken the NFL mark if he had played the entire season.

White led the NFL in sacks for the second consecutive year in 1988 with 18. Reggie's sack production declined to 11 in 1989, when teammates Clyde Simmons, Seth Joyner, and Jerome Brown joined him to make the Eagles one of the NFL's finest defensive fronts. *Sports Illustrated* polled NFL players that year, asking them to choose the best NFL defensive player. Reggie received 38 percent of the vote, more than three times any other performer.

In 1989, White signed a $6.1 million, four-year contract, making him the highest paid NFL defensive player. His relationship with Eagles management, however, continued to sour. Reggie disagreed with team owner Norman Braman on many issues, including training facilities, the 1987 players' strike, the firing of Buddy Ryan, and most important, the Eagles' commitment to pursuing a championship team. Nevertheless, he continued to perform exceptionally well for new Eagles coach Rick Kotite, recording 15 sacks in 1991 and 14 sacks in 1992.

White became a plaintiff in a 1992 lawsuit against the NFL to enlarge the powers of free agency. A Minneapolis, Minnesota, jury ruled that the NFL had improperly denied players the right to seek employment in the free market. This decision hastened a labor settlement that made Reggie and many other NFL players free agents on March 1, 1993.

Many NFL teams courted White for his services, including the Atlanta Falcons, Cleveland Browns, Detroit Lions, Green Bay Packers, New York Giants, and Washington Redskins. Reggie ultimately signed a $17 million, four-year contract with the Green Bay Packers. He keenly desired to join a franchise committed to winning because he had never been on a championship team in 16 seasons. The Packers and White both played at championship levels in 1993 and 1994. Reggie recorded 13 sacks in 1993 and 8 sacks in 1994, while the Packers advanced to the second round of the playoffs before being eliminated by the Dallas Cowboys.

White's football contract extends only through the 1996 season, but his covenant with God will last forever. Reggie and his wife, Sara Copeland, have built Hope Place, a shelter for unwed mothers, near their home in Tennessee. They have two children, Jeremy and Jecolia, and founded the Alpha and Omega Ministry, which will sponsor a community development bank in Knoxville, Tennessee. White explains, "I'm trying to build up black people's morale, self-confidence and self-reliance to show them that the Jesus I'm talking about is real." Reggie's generosity extends to several Baptist Churches, where he tithes a large portion of his NFL income. As he notes, "The Bible says, 'Faith without works is dead.' That is just another way of saying: 'Put your money where your mouth is.'"

BIBLIOGRAPHY: Barbara Carlisle Bigelow, ed., *Contemporary Black Biography*, vol. 7 (Detroit, MI, 1994); Peter King, "Trip to Bountiful," *Sports Illustrated* 78 (March 15, 1993), pp. 20–23; *The Sporting News Pro Football Register* (1994); *University of Tennessee Football Media Guide* (1994); Paul Zimmerman, "White Heat," *Sports Illustrated* 71 (November 27, 1989), pp. 64–69.

John Hillman

LENNY WILKENS
(October 28, 1937–   ) _____ *Basketball*

Lenny Wilkens, the winningest coach in National Basketball Association (NBA) history, has participated in more NBA games as a player and/or head coach than anyone else in NBA history. Leonard Randolph Wilkens was born on October 28, 1937, in the Bedford-Stuyvesant section of Brooklyn, New York. Many ghetto residents find it terribly difficult to escape an environment of neighborhood violence and urban decay, but Wilkens succeeded. "Bedford-Stuyvesant wasn't as bad as people make it out to be," Wilkens explained. "It wasn't a ghetto to me. It was where I lived. You adjust." Lenny began playing basketball in the early 1950s in the Catholic Youth Organization (CYO). Father Thomas Mannion, his CYO basketball coach at Holy Rosary Church, lauded him, "He was able to attract kids, to lead. He had an impact on the entire neighborhood."

Tommy Davis, his best friend and future major league baseball star, urged Wilkens to try out for the Boys High School basketball team. Not until the middle of his senior year, however, did Lenny finally join the team. In his last half season at Boys High, he averaged 11 points a game. Few colleges outside of New York City had heard of Wilkens, but Father Mannion wrote coach Joe Mullaney of Providence College about Lenny. Mullaney scouted Wilkens in a CYO tournament and offered him a full athletic scholarship.

At Providence, Wilkens developed into one of the greatest players in Friar history. The six-foot-one-inch, 185-pound Lenny lacked size by basketball standards, but his quickness and leadership abilities made him an outstanding point guard. He enjoyed a brilliant senior season, making most All-America teams, and still ranks among the all-time Providence leaders in points and rebounds.

In 1960, the St. Louis Hawks selected Wilkens in the first round of the NBA draft. Despite winning three consecutive Western Division titles, the Hawks fielded a weak backcourt. Veterans Johnny McCarthy and Si Green started at guard, while coach Paul Seymour seldom substituted. "I don't know why you keep me on the bench and let Johnny and Si play all the time," the confident Lenny told Seymour. "I don't make as many mistakes as they do." Midway through his rookie season, Seymour gave Wilkens his chance to play the entire 48 minutes. From that point on, Lenny started at guard and finished the 1960–1961 season with an 11.9 point scoring average.

Wilkens led the Hawks yearly in assists, always ranking among the NBA best, and soon became the team floor general. "Lenny's our superstar. Lenny's our leader," acknowledged Hawks center Zelmo Beatty. Wilkens's name began being mentioned in the same breath as **Oscar Robertson,** Jerry West, and **Hal Greer.** During his eight years with the Hawks, Lenny averaged 15.9 points a game and dished out 3,048 assists. The 1967–1968 season, however, saw Wilkens engage in a bitter public contract dispute with Hawks owner Ben Kerner. After that season, St. Louis traded him to the Seattle SuperSonics (NBA) for Walt Hazzard. Lenny played phenomenally in his first year with the Sonics, recording a career-high 22.4-point scoring average. Seattle, however, won only 30 games, causing coach Al Bianchi's resignation.

Seattle selected Wilkens as player-coach, making him just the NBA's second African-American head coach. Under Lenny, the young Sonics improved annually with 36, 38, and 47 victories. His stellar guard play continued as he finished second in the NBA in assists and scored 18.0 points per game in 1971–1972.

The burden of being a player-coach, however, became increasingly difficult, forcing Wilkens to step down as head coach. In a surprise move, Seattle owner Sam Schulman traded Lenny to the Cleveland Cavaliers (NBA) for Butch Beard. The deal upset Wilkens, who threatened to retire rather than move his wife, Marilyn, and his three young children to Cleveland, Ohio. But the Cavaliers, a youthful expansion team like Seattle, needed Lenny's leadership. The challenge finally put him in a Cleveland uniform.

Wilkens played 2 years in Cleveland, averaging 20.5 points and 16.4 points a game. Lenny finished his 15-year NBA playing career as the player-coach for the Portland Trail Blazers. He retired as a player following the 1974–1975 season, finishing his career with a 16.5 point scoring average. Wilkens played in nine NBA All-Star games and earned Most Valuable Player (MVP) honors in the 1971 game, scoring a game-high 21 points. Lenny scored 17,772 points and dished out 7,211 assists during his NBA career.

His first year solely as an NBA head coach proved disappointing. Portland won only 37 games and replaced him after the 1975–1976 season with Jack Ramsey. The Seattle SuperSonics started the 1977–1978 season with a 5–17 record and hired Wilkens to replace Bob Hopkins as head coach. Under Lenny, the young Sonics compiled a 42–18 record for the remainder of the regular season. Seattle reached the NBA finals before losing to the Washington Bullets in 7 games.

The SuperSonics won their only NBA title the next season under Wilkens, boasting a 52–30 record. Lenny coached Seattle six more years, leading the SuperSonics to six playoff appearances altogether. Before the 1986–1987 season, he returned to Cleveland to coach the Cavaliers. Cleveland appeared in five playoffs during his seven-year tenure there but inevitably lost to **Michael Jordan** and the Chicago Bulls.

The Atlanta Hawks (NBA) named Wilkens as their head coach before the 1993–1994 season. In his first season with Atlanta, Lenny coached the Hawks to a Central Division title and the best Eastern Conference record. He has compiled a 968–814 career NBA coaching record through 1994 and surpassed Red Auerbach in career victories on January 6, 1995, when the Hawks defeated the Washington Bullets. Wilkens will coach the U.S. men's basketball team at the 1996 Atlanta, Georgia, Summer Olympic Games.

Wilkens has shown his leadership abilities at every level from the CYO League in Brooklyn to the NBA both as a player and as a coach. Lenny remains one of the most respected men in the NBA. In 1988, he was elected to the Naismith Memorial Basketball Hall of Fame as a player. Wilkens has contributed to various charitable causes, including the Boys and Girls Club in Seattle, Washington, and the Children's Hospital and the Kidney Foundation in Cleveland.

BIBLIOGRAPHY: *Atlanta Hawks Media Guide* (1993–1994); Raymond Hill, *Unsung Heroes of Pro Basketball* (New York, 1973); Zander Hollander and Alex Sachare, eds., *The Official NBA Basketball Encyclopedia* (New York, 1989); *The Lincoln Library of Sports Champions*, vol. 13 (Columbus, OH, 1974); *The Sporting News Official NBA Guide* (1993–1994); *The Sporting News Official NBA Register* (1993–1994).

Curtice R. Mang

DOMINIQUE WILKINS
(January 12, 1960–   ) ─────────────────────────────── *Basketball*

Dominique Wilkins, nicknamed the "Human Highlight Film," thrilled basketball crowds by driving down the lane and making acrobatic, powerful dunks, reminiscent of **Julius Erving**. Jacques Dominique Wilkins was born on January 12, 1960, in Sorbonnes, France, the second oldest of eight children. Dominique's father, John, was stationed in Paris, France, with the U.S. Army for three years. His parents divorced shortly after settling in a Baltimore, Maryland, housing project. Upon seeing his mother, Gertrude, struggle to feed the children, Dominique vowed, "One day I was going to make her rich." Wilkins then lived with his grandparents in Washington, North Carolina, where he graduated from high school in 1979. Dominique sparked the Washington High School basketball team to a 56-game winning streak and two State championships. As a senior, he averaged 29 points and 16 rebounds a game and made the *Parade* All-America team.

Over 300 colleges, especially North Carolina State University, recruited the shy Wilkins. Dominique startled hometown residents by choosing the University of Georgia, which had not recorded a winning season in seven years and guaranteed him a starting role his freshman year. He recalled, "I wanted to go to a place where I could play right away, to a school where they weren't winning that much and where I could make my name." At North Carolina State, Wilkins continually would have been compared to star David Thompson. Unhappy Washington residents sent threatening letters, spilled paint on the family car, and broke windows at their house. Dominique's family moved in June 1979 to Atlanta, Georgia, where Gertrude worked as a motel maid.

As a freshman, Wilkins tallied 18.6 points per contest for coach Hugh Durham's Bulldogs and thrilled fans by dunking the ball with his back to the basket against the University of Alabama. Dominique averaged 23.6 points per game the following season in leading 19–12 Georgia to its best basketball mark in 50 years and its first National Invitation Tournament (NIT) bid. As a junior, Dominique averaged 21.3 points a game, led 19–12 Georgia in blocked shots, and developed a potent outside shot. His weight increased from 180 to 205 pounds, making the six-foot-eight-inch Wilkins a more effective offensive rebounder. Durham called Dominique "probably the best swing forward in the country. He's a scorer. He's got great speed. He has tremendous shooting ability" and "the ability to score inside and outside." Alabama coach C. M. Newton concurred, "He's got great athletic ability—his leaping, quickness and reaction." Wilkins, the all-time leading Georgia scorer with 1,688 points (21.6-point average) in 78 games, a three-time All-Southeastern-Conference (SEC) selection, and First Team All-America in 1982, skipped his senior year to enter the 1982 National Basketball Association (NBA) draft.

The Utah Jazz drafted Wilkins as the third choice overall and traded him in September 1982 to the Atlanta Hawks for All-Star forward John Drew, Freeman Williams, Jr., and $1 million. His spectacular 1982–1983 season brought him Rookie of the Year honors and a 17.5 points per game scoring average. The muscular dunk specialist possessed a 48-inch vertical leap and 9.8-second speed in the 100-yard dash. Dominique, called "a showman" by Hawks president Stan Kasten, won the NBA Slam Dunk contest in 1985 and 1990 and finished runner-up in 1986 and 1988. Critics, however, claimed that the slam-dunk specialist relished personal statistics more than team performance, exhibited very poor shot selection, and did not bring out the best in his teammates. The Hawks had struggled during his first three seasons.

Wilkins became a more complete player by the 1985–1986 season, improving his shot selection, passing, and defense. Dominique tallied 27 percent of the Hawks' points, leading the NBA in scoring with 30.3 points per game and making the Eastern Conference All-Star team for the first time. Dominique's prolific scoring, 618 rebounds, 138 steals, and 49 blocked shots helped coach Mike Fratello's Hawks win 50 regular-season games. Teammate Cliff Levingston stressed, "Dominique accepted the responsibility of being our leader, the man who has to get us going." He scored 50 points on various jump shots in a first-round playoff game against the Detroit Pistons and led the youthful

Hawks to the second round for the first time in seven seasons. Wilkins remarked, "This season I wanted to prove I was a total player. I wanted to change people's opinion of me. It bothered me that I had never made the All-Star team, that people thought all I could do was dunk."

The Hawks won the 1987 Central Division crown and continued to compile at least 50 wins through the 1988–1989 season. In the 1988 Eastern Conference semi-finals, Wilkins and Larry Bird of the Boston Celtics staged one of the most dramatic shooting displays in NBA history. Dominique scored 16 points in the fourth period and 47 altogether, while Bird tallied 20 in the fourth stanza and 34 for the game. The game marked the crowning achievement of Wilkins's career, but the Celtics prevailed, 118–116. The Hawks struggled after 1989, but Dominique continued prolific scoring while taking fewer shots, recorded career highs in rebounding and assists in 1990–1991, and played better defense, making his teammates better. Star Alex English noted, "He's better than before. Less flashy, but better."

In January 1992, Wilkins tore a right Achilles tendon against the Philadelphia 76ers. Dominique worked very hard to rehabilitate the tendon and, according to his brother Gerald of the Cleveland Cavaliers, became "mentally tougher." He in September 1992 married Nicole Berry, a model turned Georgia State University student. Nicole gave him much needed stability and more maturity. Wilkins the next season scored 29.9 points per game, his best average since 1987–1988. In February 1994, the Hawks traded Dominique and a conditional first-round draft choice to the Los Angeles Clippers for Danny Manning. He helped the American Dream Team II squad to a Gold Medal at the World Championship of Basketball in August 1994 at Toronto, Canada. The Boston Celtics signed Wilkins as a free agent in July 1994.

During his first 13 NBA campaigns, Wilkins has scored 25,389 points, 6,691 rebounds, and 1,377 steals. Dominique's career 25.8-point scoring average ranks fifth in NBA history. The seven-time All-Star Game participant twice scored 57 points in games and holds the Hawks all-time records for scoring, field goals, free throws made, and scoring average. Besides making the All-NBA First Team in 1986, Dominique attained All-NBA Second Team four times and All-NBA Third Team once. The warm, gentle, smiling, even-tempered Wilkins lives in a sprawling 14,000 square foot, four-story suburban Atlanta house with seven bedrooms, a movie room, weight room, maid's room, and elevator. He has generously supported financially his mother, five siblings, and daughter, Aisha, who resides in Los Angeles, California, with her mother, Elizabeth Webster.

BIBLIOGRAPHY: Hank Hersch, "Dan's the Man," Sports Illustrated 80 (March 14, 1994), pp. 24–25; Jack McCallum, "Top Dog of Dunk," Sports Illustrated 55 (November 30, 1981), pp. 44–46; Jack McCallum, "Dominique Had Himself a Picnique," Sports Illustrated 64 (April 28, 1986), pp. 30–32, 37; Jack McCallum, "The Newlywed Game," Sports Illustrated 77 (December 7, 1992), pp. 48–51; David L. Porter, ed., Biographical Dictionary of American Sports: 1989–1992 Supplement for Baseball, Football, Basket-

ball, and Other Sports (Westport, CT, 1992); Stephen Steiner, "The Dominique Wilkins Show," *Sport* 73 (February 1982), pp. 44–48, 66; Rick Telander, "A Hawk Soars Higher," *Sports Illustrated* 74 (March 4, 1991), pp. 34–36; Jack White, "American Scene: In North Carolina: The Strange Case of 'Dr. Dunk,'" *Time* 114 (December 24, 1979), pp. 4–5.

David L. Porter

BILLY WILLIAMS
(June 15, 1938–) ———————————————————— *Baseball*

In 1992, Billy Williams reflected over his 2,488 game major league baseball career, which started with the Chicago Cubs National League (NL) club in 1959 and ended with the Oakland A's American League (AL) club in 1976. "My high point in baseball came after I retired. I got the joy of playing it. I played the game for eighteen years and enjoyed most all of it. In 1987 when I got the call to tell me I had been inducted into the Hall of Fame, that was the high point. Of course, to any player who had played Little League baseball, who has played minor league baseball, who has played major league base-ball—to get that call to invite him to come to Cooperstown, it is the great thrill." For Billy Leo Williams from Whistler, Alabama, a small village near Mobile, baseball had been the key to unlocking the "American Dream."

Williams had traveled a long way from Whistler, where his dad, Frank, "spent most of his waking hours unloading banana boats to put food on the family table." There was not a "lot of time for my Dad and me to play much ball together." Although working as a busboy and laborer for bricklayers, Billy had made other plans. "In all those jobs," he recalled, "I knew there was a better way."

Williams, who was born on June 15, 1938, in Whistler, Alabama, possessed natural baseball skills. His father had played first base for a semi-pro team, while Billy and his three brothers all performed for the Mobile Black Bears. After graduating from Whistler High School, Billy signed with the Chicago Cubs (NL). Chicago sent him to Ponca City, Oklahoma, in the Class D Sooner State League, marking the first time the skinny 18-year-old had been away from home. An African American in a 1956 white world, he found hotels and restaurants closed to him. With the help of friends and a determination to stay in baseball, Williams withstood the pressure and racial comments. Billy overcame discrimination and moved up the Cubs' minor league system to San Antonio Texas, of the Texas League in 1959.

The Chicago Cubs thought highly of their young, sweet-swinging, left-handed outfielder. National Baseball Hall of Famer Rogers Hornsby, who toured the Cubs farm system, telegraphed, "Suggest you bring up Williams. Best hitter on team." When Chicago asked, "He's better than anyone down there?" Hornsby replied, "He's better than anyone up there." Rogers assessed correctly, but the road was not to be easy for Billy.

A stomach disorder and the Texas heat, however, made Williams yearn for home. Consequently, Billy left the team, took a train, and returned to Whistler. He spent a week relaxing and swimming at his favorite spot at Eight Mile Creek. The Cubs, not ready to let Williams get away, visited him. "I was discouraged—I don't know why," recalled Billy. "I was young. I just felt like quitting, that's all. But Buck O'Neill, a famous baseball scout, and my Dad told me baseball was good for me, and I listened." A doctor diagnosed his stomach problem as an ulcer, curable with a proper diet.

Williams returned to baseball reaching the major league in August. Billy played in only 18 games, batting just .152. He found, like rookies usually do, that major league pitchers possessed more skill than hurlers he had faced in the minors. After spending much of 1960 back in the minors, Williams returned to the Cubs to stay, displaying more poise and confidence this time. Billy also got married in 1960 to Shirley Ann Williams and eventually had four daughters. After starting slowly, he became a regular and won NL Rookie of the Year honors. The road to the National Baseball Hall of Fame had begun.

In the 1960s, Williams blossomed into a star. Modest, unassuming Billy joined **Ernie Banks** and Ron Santo in providing the Cubs with power throughout the decade. A longtime favorite of Cub fans, he enjoyed them. "Fans in Chicago are some of the greatest fans in the world. In a small ball park you get to know the fans and to talk to them." The six-time NL All-Star was named *The Sporting News* Major League Player of the Year in 1972. Williams led the NL in hitting that year with a .333 average, the third year in a row he had batted over .300. After being traded to the Oakland A's (AL) in 1975, Billy retired the next season.

His .290 career batting average included 426 home runs among his 2,711 hits and 1,475 RBIs. Williams also played in 1,177 consecutive games for a then NL record but never appeared in a World Series. Billy observed, "Baseball gave me the opportunity to travel, visit many cities, to meet many people, and gather a lot of friends over the years. I think overall it gave me the opportunity to grow up as a young man."

Williams coached at the end of his career, helping both major and minor leaguers for Chicago and Oakland. In 1994, Billy joined the Cubs as the hitting coach and taught the young players the skills he performed so well as a player. As **Lou Brock,** the St. Louis Cardinals great, commented, "Billy is probably the best hitter I saw in baseball."

BIBLIOGRAPHY: Eddie Gold and Art Ahrens, *The New Era Cubs 1941–1985* (Chicago, IL, 1985); David L. Porter, ed., *Biographical Dictionary of American Sports: Baseball* (Westport, CT, 1987); Duane A. Smith, interview with Billy Williams, March 5, 1992; "Williams Enters Hall of Fame," *Cubs Vineline* 2 (February 1987), pp. 6–7.

Duane A. Smith

JOE WILLIAMS
(April 1, 1886–March 12, 1946) _____ *Baseball*

"Smokey" Joe Williams, fireballing baseball pitcher, was named the best "blackball" hurler in a 1952 *Pittsburgh Courier* poll. Joe Williams was born on April 1, 1886, on Baptist Hill in Seguin, Texas, east of San Antonio, to an unknown African-American father and Lettie Williams, a Comanche Indian. "Someone gave me a baseball at an early age," Joe recalled, "and it was my companion for a long time. I carried it in my pocket and slept with it under my pillow. I always wanted to pitch." His baseball career began in 1905 as a pitcher for the San Antonio Broncos, as he reportedly won 28 games while losing 4. Following a 15–9 record the next season with Austin, Williams returned to San Antonio from 1907 to 1909 and amassed 72 wins and 18 losses. In 1909, Joe defeated the touring Chicago Leland Giants, considered one of the premier African-American teams and managed by blackball notable entrepreneur **Rube Foster.** His victory and obvious potential persuaded Foster to have him accompany the Lelands north and pitch for his Chicago American Giants.

At six foot four inches and 200 pounds, Williams used his imposing size to explode his fastball toward the batter. One contemporary pitcher stated, "If I was going to pick a man to throw hard, I'd have to pick Joe Williams. I'd pick him over all of them. . . . It used to take two catchers to hold him. By the time the fifth inning was over, that catcher's hand would be all swollen. . . . He could throw hard." Joe eventually developed intimidating sidearm and crossfire deliveries and various off-speed pitches.

Williams's lengthy career from 1905 to 1932 encompassed Cuban League baseball, blackball leagues, and barnstorming exhibitions against African-American teams, major league squads, and traveling All-Star teams. Blackball players, lured by better money offers, often changed teams. Player contracts were poorly written or ignored completely, while league alignments and squad lists were very fluid. With the exception of exhibitions against white teams, blackball activity rarely appeared in the general press. Barnstorming and exhibitions offered greater economic benefit to African-American team owners. For a 15-member team, pitching proved crucial. Durability and strength marked Williams and other successful hurlers. The powerful Joe often pitched both games of a doubleheader.

From 1912 to 1916, Williams reportedly compiled 31 wins and 22 losses in the Cuban League against integrated teams of white, Latin-American and African-American players. Foster's Chicago American Giants toured the West Coast in the spring of 1912, with Joe posting a 9–1–1 record against Pacific Coast teams. The same summer, he hurled for the New York Lincoln Giants and earned $105 a month. His teammates received only $40 to $75 a month.

In New York, Williams teamed with "Cannonball" Dick Redding to provide one of baseball's most formidable pitching duos. On October 24, 1912, Joe made his first appearance against a major league team and produced a 6–0, four-hit shutout of the National League (NL) champion New York Giants. Two weeks later, he spun another shutout over the American League (AL) New York Highlanders. The success of most blackball players often was measured by their performances versus major league opposition.

In 1913, the touring New York Lincoln Giants reportedly won 101 of 107 games against other African-American teams and white semi-pros squads. Williams captured four of five decisions against major league All-Stars, including victories over National Baseball Hall of Fame hurlers Chief Bender and Grover Cleveland Alexander. Bender lost, 2–1, on a three-hitter. Besides hitting a home run against Alexander, Joe struck out nine and surrendered eight hits in a 9–2 victory.

Williams apparently divided the 1914 season between the Lincolns and the Chicago American Giants, posting a 12–2 record in New York and finishing the year with a 41–3 mark. Misfortune struck Joe in 1915, as he broke his arm and then a wrist. Upon his return in the fall, Williams split decisions with two major league squads. After losing to the New York Giants (NL) Joe bested the NL champion Philadelphia Phillies by a 1–0 margin and struck out 10 batters. From 1917 through 1919, the blackball fireballer faced major league All-Star squads 11 times and emerged with eight victories, four shutouts, and two defeats. His victims included Bender, New York Giant Hall of Famer Rube Marquard twice, and Washington Senator immortal Walter Johnson. Williams hurled a heartbreaking 10-inning, no-hit, 20 strikeout effort against the New York Giants, losing on an error. At the game's end, Giants Hall of Fame outfielder Ross Youngs told Joe, "That was a hell of a game, Smokey!" "Smokey" became the most enduring of his nicknames, which also included "Cyclone" and "Strikeout."

Williams began managing the Lincoln Giants in 1922 but left after two years to join Nat Strong's Brooklyn Royal Giants. In 1924, "Smokey Joe" struck out 25 batters in a 4–3, 12-inning loss to the Brooklyn Bushwicks, Strong's top-flight white semi-pro team. At age 39, he moved the next year to the Homestead Grays of Pittsburgh. Williams supposedly lost only 5 games during the first five years of his eight-year stint there. Joe's four 1927 victories over major league All-Star squads included two shutouts. In 1930, the Grays barnstormed part of the season with the Kansas City Monarchs. The Monarchs transported their own lights, providing barely enough illumination for night games. One evening in the dim light, Williams fanned 27 Monarchs and gave up only one single in a 1–0, 12-inning contest. The Grays also toured in 1930 with the New York Lincoln Giants, staging a 10-game series to determine the East's best blackball team. Homestead prevailed in 6 of the 10 contests. Joe, at age 44, lost two of three starts. He and his wife Beatrice, a showgirl in Harlem and Broadway revues, married in 1922 and had one daughter.

Williams retired after the 1932 season and tended bar in Harlem, being hired mostly to draw patrons and talk baseball. "Smokey" died on March 12, 1946, in New York City. Joe's 22–7–1 career record versus major league squads included an 8–2–1 against Hall of Famers. Two of those losses came at age 45, while two others were 1–0 setbacks. In 1952, he was named best blackball pitcher in a *Pittsburgh Courier* poll of African-American veterans and sportswriters, edging **Satchel Paige** by one vote.

BIBLIOGRAPHY: John B. Holway, *Smokey Joe and the Cannonball* (Washington, DC, 1983); John B. Holway, *Blackball Stars: Negro League Pioneers* (Westport, CT, 1988); Robert W. Peterson, *Only the Ball Was White* (Englewood Cliffs, NJ, 1970); David L. Porter, ed., *Biographical Dictionary of American Sports: Baseball* (Westport, CT, 1987); James A. Riley, *The Biographical Encyclopedia of the Negro Baseball Leagues* (New York, 1994).

David Bernstein

BILL WILLIS
(October 5, 1921–) ———————————————————— *Football*

Bill Willis, one of the most dominant defensive linemen to play pro football after World War II, helped open the doors of the pro game for other African Americans. William K. Willis was born on October 5, 1921, in Columbus, Ohio, the son of Clement Willis and Willana Willis. Willis, whose father died when Bill was only four, was brought up by his grandfather and mother. He attended Columbus East High School and at first was more interested in track and field than football. "I had a brother, Claude, who was about six years older than me," Willis said. "He was an outstanding football player, a fullback in high school, and I was afraid I would be compared with him." Upon finally trying out for football, Bill chose to play in the line despite the great speed that seemingly destined him for the backfield. He started three years at Columbus East High School, winning Honorable Mention All-State honors in his senior year.

After working a year, Willis entered Ohio State University in 1941 and quickly caught the attention of coach Paul Brown. The six-foot-two-inch 202-pounder lacked size for a tackle on a major college team, but his quickness made him a regular as a sophomore. The 9–1 Buckeyes won the 1942 Western (Big Ten) Conference (WC) championship and were voted the number-one college team in the nation by the Associated Press. Wartime call-ups hurt the squad in Bill's final two years. Most of Ohio State's experienced players and coach Brown entered military service, but his own reputation continued to grow. Willis twice was chosen All-WC and in 1944 was named to the United Press (UP) and *Look* All-America teams. Bill, also a standout sprinter on the track and field team, excelled in the 60-yard and 100-yard dash events.

Willis played in the 1944 College All-Star Game at Soldier Field in Chicago against the National Football League (NFL) champion Chicago Bears and was chosen for the honor again in 1945 after his graduation from Ohio State. Yet the door to the NFL remained closed to Bill. No African American had played in the NFL since 1933 when a gentleman's agreement restricted rosters to whites only. Willis accepted a job at Kentucky State College, an African-American school, as head football coach and athletic director. Kentucky State lost only 2 of 10 games, but Bill wanted to play professionally.

Willis read that a new professional league, the All-America Football Conference (AAFC), was being formed and that Paul Brown coached the Cleveland team, called the Browns in his honor. Bill wrote to Brown, asking for a tryout, but did not receive an answer and decided to accept an offer to play for Montreal of the Canadian Football League. Actually Paul was very interested in Willis but, for public relations purposes, did not want to appear to the rest of the AAFC to be inviting an African American to join his team. Brown asked a newspaper friend to telephone Willis and strongly urge Bill to stop by Cleveland's training camp at Bowling Green, Ohio, as an apparent "walk-on." Bill possessed doubts, partly caused by continuing pain in a knee that had been operated on for cartilage repair only a few months before.

When Willis arrived in camp, he immediately played in a scrimmage. Brown inserted Bill at defensive guard in front of center Mike Scarry, an NFL veteran who had jumped to the new AAFC. On the first four plays, Willis exploded into Scarry, flattened or eluded him, and dropped quarterback Otto Graham before a play could begin. Mike insisted Bill must be offsides. "What I had been doing was concentrating on the ball," Willis recalled. "The split second the ball moved, or the center's hands tightened, I charged." After three more plays with the same result, Willis had won a regular assignment. A week later, a second African American, fullback **Marion Motley,** joined the team. Ironically, the Los Angeles Rams of the NFL had signed two African Americans, Kenny Washington and Woody Strode, only weeks before Bill joined the Browns. But Washington and Strode, both past their primes, played only sparingly over the next few years. Willis and Motley both became All-AAFC performers in their first season, and their success convinced other pro teams to hire African Americans.

Although Willis began with the Browns playing both offense and defense, changes in substitution rules soon allowed him to concentrate on the defensive middle guard position. Bill weighed only 210 to 215 pounds, tiny for a pro lineman. Detroit Lions (NFL) middle guard Les Bingaman, for example, tipped the scales at well over 300 pounds. But anything Willis lacked in heft was more than made up by his strength and speed. Coach George Allen recalled, "He was one of the first great pass rushers and equally effective against the run." Bill's sudden explosive charge disrupted enemy plays and elicited comparisons with panthers and other large cats. According to Allen, "He was like a cat, pouncing on people." When defenses double- and triple-teamed him, they left other Browns defenders free to do their damage.

For four seasons, the Browns won consecutive AAFC championships and Willis was named All-AAFC. In 1950, Cleveland moved to the NFL and won that league's title. The Browns named Bill their Most Valuable Player. During the 1950 playoff for the Eastern Division championship, Willis made his most celebrated play. Bill made a game-saving tackle by outrunning a speedy New York Giants halfback who had broken into the clear.

Besides winning All-NFL honors in three of his four NFL seasons, Willis was named to the first three Pro Bowls. Bill then retired to become assistant commissioner of recreation for the city of Cleveland and a much-sought-after speaker at various functions. Ten years later, Ohio governor James Rhodes appointed him deputy director of correctional services. In 1975, Willis was promoted to director of the Department of Youth Services. Bill retired in 1983.

Willis, who married Odessa Porter in 1947, has three sons, William, Jr., Clement, and Dan. Bill was inducted into the National Football Foundation (NFF) College Football Hall of Fame in 1971 and the Pro Football Hall of Fame in 1977.

BIBLIOGRAPHY: George Allen with Ben Olan, *Pro Football's 100 Greatest Players* (Indianapolis, IN, 1982); Bill Barron et al., *The Official NFL Encyclopedia of Football* (New York, 1992); Paul Brown with Jack Clary, *PB: The Paul Brown Story* (New York, 1979); Harold Claassen and Steve Boda, eds., *The Ronald Encyclopedia of Football* (New York, 1960); David S. Neft et al., *Pro Football: The Early Years, An Encyclopedic History, 1895–1959* (Ridgefield, CT, 1987); David L. Porter, ed., *Biographical Dictionary of American Sports: Football* (Westport, CT, 1987); Bill Willis file, Pro Football Hall of Fame, Canton, OH.

Robert N. "Bob" Carroll

DAVE WINFIELD
(October 3, 1951–   ) _____ *Baseball*

Dave Winfield, the only professional athlete drafted by five teams in three different sports, did not spend a day in the minor leagues before his successful major league baseball career. Winfield was first drafted out of high school by the Baltimore Orioles American League (AL) club in 1969 but attended the University of Minnesota. Four years later, Dave was chosen by the San Diego Padres National League (NL) club in baseball and both the Utah Stars American Basketball Association (ABA) and Atlanta Hawks National Basketball Association (NBA) teams in basketball. The Minnesota Vikings of the National Football League (NFL) even drafted him in football, although he had not played a down of high school or college football.

David Mark Winfield was born on October 3, 1951, in St. Paul, Minnesota, the second son of Frank Winfield and Arline (Allison) Winfield. His parents divorced when he was three years old, after which he seldom saw his father. Dave and his brother, Steve, grew up happily with their mother, a St. Paul schools employee, and near many relatives. At St. Paul Central High School, Winfield did not play baseball until his junior year and yet made the All-City and All-State teams as a senior. His success garnered him a partial baseball scholarship at Minnesota.

Winfield made the Minnesota varsity baseball team as a right-handed pitcher his sophomore year, compiling an 8–3 record in 1970–1971. The following year, Dave started the final 11 games of the basketball season. He averaged 11 points and six rebounds per game, helping the Golden Gophers snare the Big Ten Conference championship. An arm injury during the spring baseball season forced him to alternate between the outfield and first base. He spent the summer with the semi-pro Fairbanks Gold Panners in the Alaskan Summer League, improving his hitting.

As a pitcher-outfielder his senior year in 1973, Winfield won 13 games, struck out 109 batters, and hit .385 with nine home runs. Dave led Minnesota to the NCAA College World Series, where he pitched the final game against the University of Southern California (USC) on just three days' rest and shut out the Trojans for eight innings. Minnesota lost the game in the ninth inning, but he was voted tournament Most Valuable Player (MVP) and named to the college All-America baseball team.

The six-foot-six-inch 220-pounder signed with the San Diego Padres for a $50,000 bonus and debuted June 19, 1973. The Padres preferred to use Winfield as an everyday player rather than as a pitcher and inserted him in their outfield immediately. Peter Bavasi, Padres general manager, explained, "He has more physical tools than any free agent we ever signed. He can do the five things you look for in a player with superior potential: run, throw, field, hit for average, and hit with power."

Although overwhelmed in an outfield "the size of an airport," Winfield hit safely in his first six games and ended 1973 with a respectable .277 batting average. After belting 20 home runs in 1974, Dave led the NL with 15 assists in 1976 and won the first of his seven Gold Glove Awards in 1979 for defensive excellence. In 1979, he also batted .308, slugged 34 home runs, and led the NL with 118 RBIs.

Winfield, frustrated by playing on a losing team, signed as a free agent with the New York Yankees (AL) after the 1980 season. His 10-year contract, then the most lucrative in professional sports, exceeded $20 million. Dave led the Yankees in almost every offensive category in 1981 and carried New York to the AL pennant but batted only .045 against the Los Angeles Dodgers in the World Series. Yankee owner George Steinbrenner sarcastically compared him to teammate **Reggie Jackson,** who was nicknamed "Mr. October" for his World Series heroics. Steinbrenner dubbed Winfield "Mr. May."

Despite Steinbrenner's exaggerated expectations and continual belittling of Winfield, Dave played his best baseball in New York. In eight seasons, he averaged 89 runs scored on 161 hits compared to 74 runs and 141 hits at San Diego. His seasonal home run output rose from 19 to 25, while his RBIs increased from 78 to 101. In 1984, Winfield battled teammate Don Mattingly for the AL batting title until the last day of the season, finishing second with a .340 mark. Dave led the AL with 17 assists in 1982 and made only two errors in 1984 for a .994 fielding average, earning his third Gold Glove. He performed well amid controversy and continual conflicts with Steinbrenner both on and off the field and in and out of court. After his departure from New York, he said, "Only I know how much better I could have been without all the distractions."

Back surgery sidelined Winfield for the entire 1989 season. In May 1990, Dave accepted a trade to the California Angels (AL) and regained his enjoyment of the game. In his first 162 games with the Angels, he batted .277 with 114 RBIs and 92 runs scored on 31 doubles, four triples, and 31 home runs. At age 39, Winfield became the oldest player to hit for the cycle in a game. Best of all, Dave's big gap-toothed grin and joking around the batting cage returned.

The Toronto Blue Jays (AL) acquired Winfield in December 1991. At age 40, Dave batted clean-up for the AL pennant winners. He hit .290 and slugged 33 doubles, three triples, and 26 homers, finishing fifth in the AL in runs produced with 174. When asked about his longevity, Winfield responded, "For the last few years people have seen me and acted surprised that I'm still playing. Still playing? I'm kicking butt."

The Blue Jays' post-season success helped erase Dave's painful 1981 experience. Toronto defeated the Oakland Athletics, four games to two, in the AL Championship Series, as he hit a double and two home runs, received five free passes, and scored seven times. Winfield's bat cooled in the World Series, but he hit a double in the eleventh inning of the final game to break a 2–2 tie with the Atlanta Braves. His game winner gave Toronto its first World Series title, as the Blue Jays defeated Atlanta four games to two.

Winfield joined the Minnesota Twins (AL) for the 1993 season. Although his team suffered through a tough 1993 season, Dave enjoyed several personal achievements. On September 13, 1993, his twenty-first home run of the season moved him past Carl Yastrzemski into eighteenth place on the career home run list with 453. Three days later, he recorded his 3,000th hit. Winfield's ninth-inning single off Oakland Athletics reliever Dennis Eckersley made him the 19th player to record 3,000 hits and sparked the Twins to a 13-inning comeback victory. Dave later admitted, "I feel the weight of the world is off me." Minnesota traded him in August 1994 to the Cleveland Indians (AL) after the strike began. He became a free agent four months later without playing a game for Cleveland. Winfield re-signed with the Cleveland Indians in April 1995.

The 12-time All-Star boasts a .281 career batting average with 1,658 runs scored, 3,088 hits, and 1,202 walks. Winfield has slugged 535 doubles and 463 home runs. His 1,829 RBIs lead all active players and rank fifth since 1960. Dave's 2,927 games played places him eighth among all-time leaders, while his 10,888 at bats rank seventh. Although filling the designated hitter's role the last few seasons, the Gold Glove fielder often prevented runners from taking extra bases or scoring with his bulletlike throws from right field.

Baseball does not occupy all of Winfield's time. Dave, a Renaissance Man, reads and travels widely, takes photographs, and collects art. He owns several Burger King franchises and enjoys other business interests. His primary interest off the field, the Winfield Foundation, was established at the beginning of his major league career and is operated with his brother, Steve. The foundation provides antidrug education, free medical exams for underprivileged youth, free admission to ball games, other entertainment, and academic scholarships for deserving scholar-athletes. David Wells of the Detroit Tigers saw his only major league baseball games as a San Diego youngster, thanks to the foundation.

Winfield and his wife, Tonya, maintain homes in California, New Jersey, and Minnesota. Dave has a daughter, Shanel, who lives with her mother in Texas. After Dave's mother died of cancer in 1988, he reconciled with his long-absent father.

BIBLIOGRAPHY: *Current Biography Yearbook* (1984), pp. 457–460; William Ladson, "The Sport Q and A: Dave Winfield," *Sport* 82 (August 1991), pp. 84–86; Michael Martinez, "Winfield an Angel? Yes. No. Maybe," *New York Times Biographical Service* 24 (May 1990), p. 444; Rick Reilly, "I Feel a Whole Lot Better Now," *Sports Illustrated* 76 (June 29, 1992), pp. 56–66; Claire Smith, "Life with Angels a 'Positive Shock' for Hot Winfield," *The Sporting News,* June 24, 1991, pp. 14–15; John Thorn and Pete Palmer, eds., *Total Baseball,* 3rd ed. (New York, 1993); George Vecsey, "Winfield: Triple Threat," *New York Times Biographical Service* 16 (September 1985), pp. 1027–1029; Dave Winfield with Tom Parker, *Winfield: A Player's Life* (New York, 1988).

Gaymon L. Bennett

KEVIN YOUNG
(September 16, 1966–) ———————————————— *Track and Field*

Kevin Young won a Gold Medal in the 400-meter intermediate hurdles at the 1992 Summer Olympic Games in Barcelona, Spain, breaking the world record held by **Edwin Moses** since 1983. Kevin Curtis Young, the last of six children of William Young and Betty Champion, was born on September 16, 1966, in Los Angeles, California. His father works as a counselor with the Plain Truth Outreach Program, while his mother serves as an administrator at the Los Angeles Martin Luther King Hospital. His stepfather, Arthur Champion, preaches.

Young joined the track and field team at Jordan High School in Los Angeles "because they gave you nice sweats to wear" and developed into one of the State's top prep hurdlers. Before graduating from Jordan High School in 1984, Kevin had clocked 14.23 seconds for the 110-meter high hurdles and 37.54 seconds for the 300-meter intermediate hurdles and placed third in the 1984

State championships in the latter. He declined an opportunity to work as a hurdle steward at the 1984 Summer Olympic Games in Los Angeles, working instead as an inventory specialist at the Pasadena Jet Propulsion Laboratory. During the three-hour commute to Pasadena, conversation often turned to the 1984 Olympic Games. Kevin told his carpool companions about his own track and field exploits and that he "was going to make the team in '88."

Although accepted for admission to the University of California at Los Angeles (UCLA) for the fall semester of 1984, Young did not have the financial means to support his studies. Before the start of the fall semester, however, Kevin received a Future Olympian Scholarship to finance his first three years there. He earned an athletic scholarship to finance his final year at UCLA. Success in college meant much for Young because teachers had told him that "there's nothing in the community" for him after graduating from high school. "Once you get the opportunity to go to college," observed Kevin, "you're really going to change mentally. I think that's what I saw happening to me after my freshman year." He disclosed that although he "was 'not adequately prepared' for the UCLA curriculum, I tackled it, making the Dean's List some quarters." The hurdler graduated from UCLA in 1988 with a bachelor's degree in sociology.

Under John Smith, UCLA assistant track and field coach and a premier 400-meter runner in the 1970s, Young quickly adapted to the 400-meter intermediate hurdles. After lowering his time to 48.77 seconds in 1986, Kevin garnered second place in the NCAA Championships and third place in both the Track Athletic Congress (TAC) Championship and Olympic Festival. He captured the NCAA title in 1987 and retained it in 1988. The 1988 Olympic Trials witnessed the UCLA hurdler establish a personal best time of 47.72 seconds, as he edged David Patrick and Danny Harris. Young, Patrick, and Harris finished within .04 of a second of each other for the final position on the Olympic team. Although finishing fourth in 1988 Olympic Games at Seoul, South Korea, Kevin was ranked third globally in the 400-meter intermediate hurdles that year. After publication of the world rankings, John Smith told him, "I believe it is your turn now" to be number one.

The 1988 Summer Olympic Games marked the end of the Moses era in the 400-meter intermediate hurdles. The two-time Olympic champion and world record holder finished third in the Olympic final and retired from competition. In 1989, track and field meet directors throughout Europe removed the 400-meter hurdles from their programs because the race seemingly lost its luster without Moses. "It's all your fault," Smith told Young. "The reason they cancelled the race is because you haven't assumed the responsibility yet of taking over the hurdles and being the one who's going to run more consistent 47s and eventually run sub-47." Kevin posted 1989's fastest time of 47.86 seconds and earned the number-one ranking in the 400-meter hurdles in 1989, but his dominance in the 400-meter intermediate hurdles remained short-lived. Harris and then Zambia's Samuel Matete ranked first globally the next two seasons. Young placed second in the 1990 and 1991 TAC Championship, finished third in the 1990 Goodwill Games, and ended fourth in the 1991 World Championships at Tokyo, Japan. Kevin reaffirmed his premier global standing in 1992, compiling an undefeated season. He claimed the Summer Olympic title at Barcelona, Spain, while setting a shocking world record of 46.78 seconds, eclipsing Moses's 1983 standard of 47.02 seconds. Young's 1993 triumphs in the 400-meter hurdles in both the USA Track and Field (USATF) Championships and World Championships at Stuttgart, Germany, truly made him *Track and Field News'* "Hurdler for the '90s."

BIBLIOGRAPHY: Games of the XXV Olympiad, Barcelona, Spain, NBC Sports Research Information, vol. 8 (1992), pp. 573–574; Ed Gordon, "Young Gets First Sub-48," *Track and Field News* 42 (October 1989), p. 24; Jon Hendershott, "400H: Young in New Wave," *Track and Field News* 45 (August 1992), p. 20; Jon Hendershott, "T&FN Interview: Kevin Young," *Track and Field News* 45 (September 1992), pp. 14–15; Jon Hendershott, "Young Beats Prediction," *Track and Field News* 45 (October 1992), p. 33; Jon Hendershott, "The Man Who Passed Moses," *Track and Field News* 46 (January 1993), p. 5; Sieg Lindstrom, "Kevin Young: A Hurdler for the '90s?" *Track and Field News* 42 (December 1989), pp. 14–15; David L. Porter, ed., *Biographical Dictionary of American Sports: 1992–1995 Supplement for Baseball, Football, Basketball, and Other Sports* (Westport, CT, 1995).

Adam R. Hornbuckle

Appendix 1: Alphabetical Listing of Entries with Sport _____

Hank Aaron—baseball
Kareem Abdul-Jabbar—basketball
Herb Adderley—football
Muhammad Ali—boxing
Marcus Allen—football
Henry Armstrong—boxing
Arthur Ashe, Jr.—tennis
Emmett Ashford—baseball
Ernie Banks—baseball
Charles Barkley—basketball
Elgin Baylor—basketball
Bob Beamon—track and field
Cool Papa Bell—baseball
Barry Bonds—baseball
Ralph Boston—track and field
Valerie Brisco—track and field
Lou Brock—baseball
Jim Brown—football
Lee Calhoun—track and field
Roy Campanella—baseball
Earl Campbell—football
Rod Carew—baseball

Wilt Chamberlain—basketball
Oscar Charleston—baseball
Roberto Clemente—baseball
Ray Dandridge, Sr.—baseball
Ernie Davis—football
Andre Dawson—baseball
Gail Devers—track and field
Eric Dickerson—football
Harrison Dillard—track and field
Tony Dorsett—football
Bob Douglas—basketball
Clyde Drexler—basketball
Charley Dumas—track and field
Julius Erving—basketball
Lee Evans—track and field
Patrick Ewing—basketball
Curt Flood—baseball
George Foreman—boxing
Rube Foster—baseball
Joe Frazier—boxing
Walt Frazier—basketball
Clarence Gaines—basketball

*Competed in more than one professional sport.

Jake Gaither—football

Joe Gans—boxing

George Gervin—basketball

Althea Gibson—tennis

Bob Gibson—baseball

Josh Gibson—baseball

Joe Greene—football

Hal Greer—basketball

Ken Griffey, Jr.—baseball

Archie Griffin—football

Florence Griffith Joyner—track and field

Tony Gwynn—baseball

Marvin Hagler—boxing

Franco Harris—football

*Bob Hayes—track and field

Elvin Hayes—basketball

Thomas Hearns—boxing

Rickey Henderson—baseball

Larry Holmes—boxing

*Bo Jackson—football

Reggie Jackson—baseball

Ferguson Jenkins—baseball

Jack Johnson—boxing

Magic Johnson—basketball

Michael Johnson—track and field

Rafer Johnson—track and field

Deacon Jones—football

K. C. Jones—basketball

Michael Jordan—basketball

Jackie Joyner-Kersee—track and field

Dick Lane—football

Bob Lanier—basketball

Buck Leonard—baseball

Sugar Ray Leonard—boxing

Carl Lewis—track and field

Pop Lloyd—baseball

James Lofton—football

Ronnie Lott—football

Joe Louis—boxing

Willie McCovey—baseball

John Mackey—football

Karl Malone—basketball

Moses Malone—basketball

Juan Marichal—baseball

Mike Marsh—track and field

Willie Mays—baseball

Cheryl Miller—basketball

Tom Molyneux—boxing

Art Monk—football

Warren Moon—football

Archie Moore—boxing

Lenny Moore—football

Joe Morgan—baseball

Edwin Moses—track and field

Marion Motley—football

Isaac Murphy—horse racing

Eddie Murray—baseball

Dan O'Brien—track and field

Shaquille O'Neal—basketball

Jesse Owens—track and field

Alan Page—football

Satchel Paige—baseball

Jim Parker—football

Floyd Patterson—boxing

Walter Payton—football

Calvin Peete—golf

Joe Perry—football

Fritz Pollard—football

Mike Powell—track and field

Kirby Puckett—baseball

Butch Reynolds—track and field

Willy T. Ribbs—auto racing

Jerry Rice—football

Oscar Robertson—basketball

Paul Robeson—football

David Robinson—basketball

Eddie Robinson—football

Frank Robinson—baseball

Jackie Robinson—baseball

Sugar Ray Robinson—boxing

Wilma Rudolph—track and field

Bill Russell—basketball

Barry Sanders—football

*Deion Sanders—football

Gale Sayers—football

Wendell Scott—stock car racing

Art Shell—football

Charlie Sifford—golf

Willie Simms—horse racing

O. J. Simpson—football

Mike Singletary—football

Emmitt Smith—football

Ozzie Smith—baseball

Tommie Smith—track and field

Willie Stargell—baseball

Lusia Harris Stewart—basketball

Darryl Strawberry—baseball

C. Vivian Stringer—basketball

Lawrence Taylor—football

Marshall Taylor—bicycling

Frank Thomas—baseball

Isiah Thomas—basketball

Thurman Thomas—football

John Thompson, Jr.—basketball

Emlen Tunnell—football

Mike Tyson—boxing

Wyomia Tyus-Tillman—track and field

Gene Upshaw, Jr.—football

Debi Thomas Vanden Hogen—figure skating

*Herschel Walker—football

Gwen Torrence Waller—track and field

Evelyn Ashford Washington—track and field

Quincy Watts—track and field

Bill White—baseball

Reggie White—football

Lenny Wilkens—basketball

Dominique Wilkins—basketball

Billy Williams—baseball

Joe Williams—baseball

Bill Willis—football

Dave Winfield—baseball

Kevin Young—track and field

Appendix 2: Entries by Major Sport

AUTO AND STOCK CAR RACING (2)

Willy T. Ribbs

Wendell Scott

BASEBALL (40)

Hank Aaron

Emmett Ashford

Ernie Banks

Cool Papa Bell

Barry Bonds

Lou Brock

Roy Campanella

Rod Carew

Oscar Charleston

Roberto Clemente

Ray Dandridge, Sr.

Andre Dawson

Curt Flood

Rube Foster

Bob Gibson

Josh Gibson

Ken Griffey, Jr.

Tony Gwynn

Rickey Henderson

Reggie Jackson

Ferguson Jenkins

Buck Leonard

Pop Lloyd

Willie McCovey

Juan Marichal

Willie Mays

Joe Morgan

Eddie Murray

Satchel Paige

Kirby Puckett

Frank Robinson

Jackie Robinson

Ozzie Smith

Willie Stargell

Darryl Strawberry

Frank Thomas

Bill White

Billy Williams

Joe Williams
Dave Winfield

BASKETBALL (30)
Kareem Abdul-Jabbar
Charles Barkley
Elgin Baylor
Wilt Chamberlain
Bob Douglas
Clyde Drexler
Julius Erving
Patrick Ewing
Walt Frazier
Clarence Gaines
George Gervin
Hal Greer
Elvin Hayes
Magic Johnson
K. C. Jones
Michael Jordan
Bob Lanier
Karl Malone
Moses Malone
Cheryl Miller
Shaquille O'Neal
Oscar Robertson
David Robinson
Bill Russell
Lusia Harris Stewart
C. Vivian Stringer
Isiah Thomas
John Thompson, Jr.
Lenny Wilkens
Dominique Wilkins

BICYCLING (1)
Marshall Taylor

BOXING (16)
Muhammad Ali
Henry Armstrong
George Foreman
Joe Frazier
Joe Gans
Marvin Hagler
Thomas Hearns
Larry Holmes
Jack Johnson
Sugar Ray Leonard
Joe Louis
Tom Molyneux
Archie Moore
Floyd Patterson
Sugar Ray Robinson
Mike Tyson

FIGURE SKATING (1)
Debi Thomas Vanden Hogen

FOOTBALL (43)
Herb Adderley
Marcus Allen
Jim Brown
Earl Campbell
Ernie Davis
Eric Dickerson
Tony Dorsett
Jake Gaither
Joe Greene
Archie Griffin
Franco Harris
Bo Jackson

Deacon Jones
Dick Lane
James Lofton
Ronnie Lott
John Mackey
Art Monk
Warren Moon
Lenny Moore
Marion Motley
Alan Page
Jim Parker
Walter Payton
Joe Perry
Fritz Pollard
Jerry Rice
Paul Robeson
Eddie Robinson
Barry Sanders
Deion Sanders
Gale Sayers
Art Shell
O. J. Simpson
Mike Singletary
Emmitt Smith
Lawrence Taylor
Thurman Thomas
Emlen Tunnell
Gene Upshaw, Jr.
Herschel Walker
Reggie White
Bill Willis

GOLF (2)
Calvin Peete
Charlie Sifford

HORSE RACING (2)
Isaac Murphy
Willie Simms

TENNIS (2)
Arthur Ashe, Jr.
Althea Gibson

TRACK AND FIELD (27)
Bob Beamon
Ralph Boston
Valerie Brisco
Lee Calhoun
Gail Devers
Harrison Dillard
Charley Dumas
Lee Evans
Florence Griffith Joyner
Bob Hayes
Michael Johnson
Rafer Johnson
Jackie Joyner-Kersee
Carl Lewis
Mike Marsh
Edwin Moses
Dan O'Brien
Jesse Owens
Mike Powell
Butch Reynolds
Wilma Rudolph
Tommie Smith
Wyomia Tyus-Tillman
Gwen Torrence Waller
Evelyn Ashford Washington
Quincy Watts
Kevin Young

Appendix 3: Cross-References for Married Women Athletes ⸺

The following lists the maiden and married names of women athletes.

MAIDEN NAME	MARRIED NAME
Evelyn Ashford	Evelyn Ashford Washington
Valerie Brisco	Valerie Brisco-Hooks
Gail Devers	Gail Devers Roberts
Althea Gibson	Althea Gibson Darben
Florence Griffith	Florence Griffith Joyner
Luisa Harris	Luisa Harris Stewart
Jacqueline Joyner	Jacqueline Joyner-Kersee
C. Vivian Stoner	C. Vivian Stoner Stringer
Debra Thomas	Debra Thomas Vanden Hogen
Gwen Torrence	Gwen Torrence Waller
Wyomia Tyus	Wyomia Tyus-Tillman

Index _____

Note: The locations of main entries in the dictionary are indicated in the index by *italic* page numbers.

About the Editor and Contributors

Frederick J. Augustyn, Jr., subject cataloger of economics and political science, Library of Congress, Washington, DC.

Gaymon L. Bennett, Professor and Chairman, Department of English, Northwest Nazarene College, Nampa, ID.

Janice A. Beran, freelance writer and retired Associate Professor of Leisure Studies, Iowa State University, lives in Ames, IA.

David Bernstein, Professor of History, California State University, Long Beach, CA.

William A. Borst, freelance writer, radio host, and Adjunct Professor, Webster University, resides in St. Louis, MO.

Robert T. Bowen, Jr., Professor Emeritus of Physical Education, University of Georgia, lives in Athens, GA.

Jack C. Braun, Associate Professor of History, Edinboro University, Edinboro, PA.

Lewis H. Carlson, Professor, Department of History, Western Michigan University, Kalamazoo, MI.

Stan W. Carlson, freelance writer, editor, and publisher, lives in Minneapolis, MN.

John M. Carroll, Professor of History, Lamar University, Beaumont, TX.

Robert N. "Bob" Carroll, freelance writer and editor, *Coffin Corner*, resides in North Huntingdon, PA.

Scott A.G.M. Crawford, Associate Professor of Physical Education, Eastern Illinois University, Charleston, IL.

Anthony O. Edmonds, Professor of History, Ball State University, Muncie, IN.

Leonard H. Frey, freelance writer and former Professor of Linguistics, San Diego State University, lives in San Diego, CA.

Larry R. Gerlach, Professor of History, University of Utah, Salt Lake City, UT, Associate Editor, *American National Biography,* and freelance writer.

Daniel R. Gilbert, Professor Emeritus of History, archivist, Moravian College, Bethlehem, PA.

Ralph S. Graber, retired Professor of English, Muhlenberg College, Allentown, PA.

John Hillman, Certified Public Accountant and Lecturer, Department of Accounting, Southwest Texas State University, resides in Waco, TX.

Adam R. Hornbuckle, researcher, History Associates Incorporated, The Historical Montrose School, Rockville, MD, and freelance writer, lives in Alexandria, VA.

Harry A. Jebsen, Jr., Provost, Capital University, Columbus, OH.

Merl F. Kleinknecht, U.S. Postal Service employee, resides in Galion, OH.

Brian L. Laughlin, student, Creighton University Law School, lives in Omaha, NE.

Bill Mallon, physician, Secretary General, International Society of Olympic Historians, and freelance writer, resides in Durham, NC.

Curtice R. Mang, insurance underwriter, lives in Phoenix, AZ.

William J. Miller, retired Associate Professor of History, St. Louis University, St. Louis, MO.

Douglas A. Noverr, Professor of American Thought and Language, Michigan State University, East Lansing, MI.

Frank J. Olmsted, theology teacher, De Smet Jesuit High School, St. Louis, MO.

David L. Porter, Shangle Professor of History, William Penn College, Oskaloosa, IA, Associate Editor, *American National Biography,* and freelance writer.

Susan J. Rayl, Instructor of Physical Education, Iowa State University, Ames, IA.

Samuel O. Regalado, Associate Professor of History, California State University, Stanislaus, Turlock, CA.

James A. Riley, freelance writer, resides in Rockledge, FL.

John Robertson, freelance writer and member, International Boxing Research Organization, lives in Cambridge, Ontario, Canada.

Steven P. Savage, Professor, Department of Anthropology, Sociology, and Social Work, Eastern Kentucky University, Richmond, KY.

Miriam F. Shelden, Professor of Physical Education, University of South Carolina at Spartanburg, Spartanburg, SC.

Duane A. Smith, Professor of History, Fort Lewis College, Durango, CO, and freelance writer.

Ronald A. Smith, Professor of Physical Education, Pennsylvania State University, University Park, PA, and Secretary-Treasurer, North American Society for Sport History.

Luther W. Spoehr, history teacher, Lincoln School, and freelance writer, resides in Barrington, RI.

Jim L. Sumner, Curator of Sports, Recreation, and Leisure, North Carolina Museum of History, Raleigh, NC.

Frank W. Thackeray, Professor of History, Indiana University Southeast, New Albany, IN.

James E. Welch, Associate Professor of Business Administration, Human Resource Management, and Industrial Relations, Kentucky Wesleyan College, Owensboro, KY.

James D. Whalen, freelance writer, lives in Dayton, OH.

John H. Ziegler, Professor, English, Film, and Humanities, Cochise College, Sierra Vista, AZ, and freelance writer, resides in Tombstone, AZ.